Lecture Notes in Computer Science 5802

Commenced Publication in 1973
Founding and Former Series Editors:
Gerhard Goos, Juris Hartmanis, and Jan van Leeuwen

Gottfried Vossen   Darrell D.E. Long
Jeffrey Xu Yu (Eds.)

Web Information Systems Engineering – WISE 2009

10th International Conference
Poznań, Poland, October 5-7, 2009
Proceedings

 Springer

Volume Editors

Gottfried Vossen
University of Münster
European Research Center for Information Systems
Leonardo Campus 3
48149 Münster, Germany
E-mail: vossen@uni-muenster.de

Darrell D.E. Long
University of California
Dept. of Computer Science
School of Engineering
Santa Cruz, CA 95064, USA
E-mail: darrell@cs.ucsc.edu

Jeffrey Xu Yu
The Chinese University of Hong Kong
Dept. of Systems Engineering and Engineering Management
William M. W. Mong Engineering Building
Shatin, N. T., Hong Kong, China
E-mail: yu@se.cuhk.edu.hk

Library of Congress Control Number: 2009934439

CR Subject Classification (1998): H.3.5, H.4, H.5.1, K.3.2, J.3, K.6, C.2, E.5

LNCS Sublibrary: SL 3 – Information Systems and Application, incl. Internet/Web
and HCI

ISSN   0302-9743
ISBN-10   3-642-04408-5 Springer Berlin Heidelberg New York
ISBN-13   978-3-642-04408-3 Springer Berlin Heidelberg New York

springer.com

© Springer-Verlag Berlin Heidelberg 2009
Printed in Germany

Typesetting: Camera-ready by author, data conversion by Scientific Publishing Services, Chennai, India
Printed on acid-free paper   SPIN: 12756445   06/3180   5 4 3 2 1 0

Preface

Welcome to the tenth anniversary of the International Conference on Web Information Systems Engineering, WISE 2009. This year the WISE conference continued the tradition that has evolved from the inaugural conference held in 2000 in Hong Kong and since then has made its journey around the world: 2001 Kyoto (Japan), 2002 Singapore, 2003 Rome (Italy), 2004 Brisbane (Australia), 2005 New York (USA), 2006 Wuhan (China), 2007 Nancy (France), and 2008 Auckland (New Zealand).

This year we were happy to hold the event in Poznan, a city of 600,000 inhabitants in western Poland. Poznan is the capital of the most affluent province of the country – Wielkopolska – which means "Greater Poland". For more than 1,000 years, Poznan's geographical location has predestined the city to be a significant scientific, cultural and economic center with more than just regional influence. The city is situated on the strategic cross-roads from Paris and Berlin in the west, to Warsaw and Moscow in the east, and from Scandinavia through the Baltic Sea in the north to the Balkans in the south. Poznan is a great research and university center with a dynamic potential. In all, 140,000 students are enrolled in 26 state-run and private institutions of higher education here, among which the Poznan University of Economics with its 12,000 students is one of the biggest.

The WISE 2009 Conference provided a forum for engineers and scientists to present their latest findings in Web-related technologies and solutions. The submitted contributions address challenging issues of Web semantics, services, search, visualization, and recommendation, as well as Web computing, tagging, querying, mining and understanding.

The 144 papers submitted for consideration for publication originated from 30 countries from all over the world: Australia, Austria, Belgium, Brazil, Canada, China, Croatia, France, Germany, Greece, Iran, Ireland, Italy, Japan, Latvia, The Netherlands, Norway, Poland, the Russian Federation, Saudi Arabia, Singapore, South Korea, Spain, Sweden, Switzerland, Taiwan, Tunisia, Turkey, UK, and the USA.

After a thorough reviewing process, 33 papers were selected for presentation as full papers – the acceptance rate was 23%. In addition, 17 papers were selected for presentation as short papers, yielding an overall acceptance rate of 35%. The papers published in these proceedings are included in the Springer *Lecture Notes in Computer Science* series provide relevant and up-to-date solutions to problems of the next-generation Web.

This conference was made possible through the efforts of many people. We wish to thank everyone involved, including those who worked diligently behind the scenes and without formal recognition. First, we would like to thank the WISE Steering Committee, in particular Marek Rusinkiewicz (Telcordia Technologies, Inc., USA) and Yanchun Zhang (Victoria University, Australia), for selecting the Poznan University of Economics to hold WISE 2009 conference. Great thanks to the Program Chairs, Darrell Long (University of California, Santa Cruz, USA), Gottfried Vossen (University of Münster, Germany) and Jeffrey Xu Yu (Chinese University of Hong Kong), for putting together an excellent technical program. We thank the Industrial

Program Chairs, Witold Staniszkis (Rodan Systems, Poland) and Henry Tirri (Nokia Research, Finland), who composed two sessions with very interesting presentations from the industrial perspective. Special thanks to the Tutorial Chairs, Tiziana Catarci (Università di Roma "La Sapienza", Italy) and Susan Urban (Texas Tech University, USA), who organized three tutorials on very up-to-date topics, as well as to the Panel Chairs, Ahmed Elmagarmid (Purdue University, USA) and Masaru Kitsuregawa (University of Tokyo, Japan), for the organization of an interesting discussion panel. We like to thank the Workshops Chairs, Bruno Defude (Telecom & Management SudParis), France) and Bernhard Thalheim (University of Kiel, Germany), for their efforts to organize workshops in association with WISE. The following five workshops were announced: (1) *Challenges of SOA Implementation and Applications*, Workshop Organizers: Jerzy Brzezinski (Poznan University of Technology, Poland) and Krzysztof Zielinski (AGH University of Science and Technology, Poland); (2) *Confidentiality and Trust Management in the Social Web*, Talel Abdessalem, (Telecom ParisTech, France) and Bogdan Cautis (Telecom ParisTech, France); (3) *Exploiting Structured Information on the Web*, Dominik Flejter, (Poznan University of Economics, Poland), Tomasz Kaczmarek, (Poznan University of Economics, Poland), and Marek Kowalkiewicz, (SAP Research Brisbane, Australia); (4) *WEB-Based Applications and Technologies for Vehicular Networks and Telematics,* Jarogniew Rykowski (Poznan University of Economics, Poland) and T. Russell Hsing (Telcordia Technologies, Inc., USA) and (5) *Third International Workshop on Web Usability and Accessibility*, Silvia Abrahao (Universidad Politecnica de Valencia, Spain), Cristina Cachero (Universidad de Alicante, Spain) and Maristella Matera (Politecnico di Milano, Italy). The number of submissions to the workshops was insufficient to publish a separate workshop proceedings. Nevertheless, we would like to thank very much all the workshop organizers and Workshop Program Committee members for their big effort.

We thank the Publication Chair Markus Kirchberg (Institute for Infocomm Research, A*STAR, Singapore) and the Publicity Chair Jacek Chmielewski (Poznan University of Economics, Poland), as well the Local Organization Chairs, Willy Picard, and Jarogniew Rykowski (Poznan University of Economics, Poland), who were greatly supported by Rafal Wojciechowski and Elzbieta Masztalerz.

We would like to thank the Program Committee members and reviewers for a very rigorous and outstanding reviewing process. Special thanks go to the City Hall of Poznan for financial support of WISE 2009 tutorials.

We wish to thank Richard DeMillo (Georgia Institute of Technology USA), George Wang (Institute for Information Industry, Taiwan), and Alexander Löser (Technische Universität Berlin, Germany) for graciously accepting our invitations to serve as keynote speakers.

October 2009   Wojciech Cellary
                                                               Chia-Hsiang Chang

Organization

General Chairs

Wojciech Cellary   Poznan University of Economics, Poland
Chia-Hsiang Chang   Institute for Information Industry, Taiwan

Program Chairs

Darrell Long   University of California, Santa Cruz, USA
Gottfried Vossen   University of Münster, Germany
Jeffrey Xu Yu   Chinese University of Hong Kong, China

Program Committee

Witold Abramowicz   Poznan University of Economics, Poznan, Poland
Divyakant Agrawal   University of California, Santa Barbara, USA
Ram Akella   University of California, Santa Cruz, USA
Luca de Alfaro   University of California, Baskin School of Engineering, USA
Michael Altenhofen   SAP Research, Karlsruhe, Germany
Ahmed Amer   University of Pittsburgh, USA
Valeria de Antonellis   Brescia University, Italy
Ismail Ari   HP Labs, USA
James Bailey   The University of Melbourne, Australia
Wolf-Tilo Balke   University of Augsburg, Germany
Lichun Bao   University of California, Irvine, USA
Luciano Baresi   Politecnico di Milano, Italy
Gerald Barnett   University of Washington, USA
Boualem Benatallah   University of New South Wales, Sydney, Australia
Leopoldo Bertossi   Carleton University, Ottawa, Canada
Bharat Bhargava   Purdue University, USA
Lubomir Bic   University of California, Irvine, USA
Nicole Bidoit   University of Paris-South, France
Athman Bouguettaya   CSIRO ICT Centre, Canberra, Australia
Francois Bry   Ludwig Maximilian University, Munich, Germany
Jerzy Brzezinski   Poznan University of Technology, Poland
Susanne Busse   Berlin University of Technology, Germany
Laura Challman Anderson   IBM Almaden Research Center, USA

Qing Liu	CSIRO Tasmania ICT Centre, Hobart, Australia
Jiaheng Lu	Renmin University of China, China
Jianguo Lu	University of Windsor, Canada
Hui Ma	Victoria University of Wellington, New Zealand
Wim Martens	Technical University of Dortmund, Germany
John McInerney	KJAYA LLC, USA
Claudia Medeiros	Institute of Computing, UNICAMP, Brazil
Brahim Medjahed	The University of Michigan, Dearborn, USA
Carlo Meghini	CNR ISTI Pisa, Italy
Emilia Mendes	University of Auckland, New Zealand
Paolo Merialdo	Roma Tre University, Rome, Italy
Jose Palazzo Moreira de Olivera	Federal University of Rio Grande doSul, Brazil
Wilfred Ng	Hong Kong University of Science and Technology, China
Rene Noack	Christian Albrechts University Kiel, Germany
Moira Norrie	ETH Zurich, Switzerland
Jehan-Francois Paris	University of Houston, USA
Cesare Pautasso	University of Lugano, Switzerland
Jaroslav Pokorny	Charles University, Prague, Czech Republic
Alexandra Poulovassilis	University of London, UK
Tore Risch	Uppsala University, Sweden
Mark Roantree	Dublin City University, Ireland
Colette Rolland	Université Paris 1 - Panthon Sorbonne, France
Kevin Ross	University of California, Santa Cruz, USA
Gustavo Rossi	Universidad Nacional de La Plata, Argentina
André Santanch	DCEC – UNIFACS, Brazil
Shin-ya Sato	NTT Network Innovation Laboratories, Tokyo, Japan
Purvi Shah	IBM Corporation, Silicon Valley Lab, USA
Heng Tao Shen	University of Queensland, Brisbane, Australia
Bill Shui	National ICT Australia, Sydney, Australia
Nicolas Spyratos	University of Paris-South, France
Robert Steele	University of Sydney, Australia
Aixin Sun	Nanyang Technological University, Singapore
Katsumi Tanaka	Kyoto University, Japan
Jie Tang	Tsinghua University, China
David Taniar	Monash University, Melbourne, Australia
Dimitri Theodoratos	New Jersey's Science and Technology University, Newark, USA
Riccardo Torlone	Roma Tre University, Rome, Italy
Olga de Troyer	Vrije Universiteit Brussel, Belgium
Stijn Vansummeren	Hasselt University, Belgium

Junhu Wang   Griffith University, Brisbane, Australia
X. Sean Wang   University of Vermont, Burlington, USA
Michal Wodczak   Telcordia Technologies, Poland
Raymond Chi-Wing Wong   Hong Kong University of Science and
                              Technology, China
Raymond K. Wong   University of New South Wales, Sydney,
                              Australia
Tao Xie   San Diego State University, USA
Frank Tsozen Yeh   Fu Jen University, Taiwan
Ben Y. Zhao   University of California, USA
Xiaofang Zhou   University of Queensland, Brisbane, Australia

Local Organization Chairs

Willy Picard   Poznan University of Economics, Poland
Jarogniew Rykowski   Poznan University of Economics, Poland

Industrial Program Chairs

Witold Staniszkis   Rodan Systems, Poland
Henry Tirri   Nokia Research, Finland

Workshops Chairs

Bruno Defude   Telecom and Management SudParis, France
Bernhard Thalheim   University of Kiel, Germany

Tutorial Chairs

Tiziana Catarci   Universitá di Roma "La Sapienza", Italy
Susan Urban   Texas Tech University, USA

Panel Chairs

Ahmed Elmagarmid   Purdue University, USA
Masaru Kitsuregawa   University of Tokyo, Japan

Publicity Chair

Jacek Chmielewski   Poznan University of Economics, Poland

Publication Chair

Markus Kirchberg   Institute for Infocomm Research, A*STAR,
                           Singapore

Wise Society Representatives

Marek Rusinkiewicz   Telcordia, USA
Yanchun Zhang   Victoria University, Australia

Table of Contents

Tagging

Semantics

Search I

Visualization

Search II

Web Services

Trust and Uncertainty

Recommendation and Quality of Service

User Interfaces

Web Understanding

Industrial Session II

Exploiting Structured Information on the Web

Systems

Data Mining and Querying

Querying and Workflow

Architecture

Blighted Virtual Neighborhoods and Other Threats to Online Social Experiences

Richard A. DeMillo

Georgia Institute of Technology
USA

Abstract. The rapid expansion of web presence into many new kinds of social networks has by far outpaced our ability to manage (or even understand) the community, economic, demographic and moral forces that shape user experiences. Online ticket queues, communities of online gamers, online retail malls and checkout sites, Facebook or MySpace communities, web-based town hall discussions, and Second Life destinations are just a few examples of places that users have come to regard as neighborhoods. They are virtual neighborhoods. They begin as attractive destinations and attract both visitors and inhabitants. Some users spend money, and some put down roots in the community. But like many real neighborhoods, virtual neighborhoods all too often turn into frightening, crime-ridden, disease- (or malware-)infested eyesores. Most users are driven away, real commerce is replaced by questionable transactions and billions of dollars of value is destroyed in the process. In blighted inner city neighborhoods you can find a familiar array of bad actors: loan sharks, vagrants, drug dealers, vandals and scam artists. Online neighborhoods fall prey to virtual blight: (1) Bot Blight, where the bad actors use bots and other non-human agents to overwhelm systems that are designed for human beings, (2) Human Blight, where individuals ranging from hackers to sociopaths and organized groups deliberately degrade a virtual neighborhood, (3) Entropy Blight, where abandoned property accumulates dead-end traffic of various kinds. The simple first-generation tools that were deployed to protect online properties have failed -- the collapse of Geocities and the recent apparent defeat of Captcha, a technology to let only humans enter the neighborhood, are evidence of that failure. There is a growing realization of how easily bad actors can create the virtual version of urban blight and how ineffective existing approaches to identity, trust and security will be in battling it.

Speaker

Richard A. DeMillo is an American computer scientist, educator and executive. He is currently Distinguished Professor of Computing and Professor of Management at the Georgia Institute of Technology. In June 2008, he announced his intention to step down as the John P. Imlay Dean of Computing at Georgia Tech after serving in that role for six years. He joined Georgia Tech in 2002 from The Hewlett-Packard Company, where he had served as the company's first Chief Technology Officer. He also held executive positions with Telcordia Technologies (formerly known as Bell

G. Vossen, D.D.E. Long, and J.X. Yu (Eds.): WISE 2009, LNCS 5802, pp. 1–2, 2009.

Communications Research) and the National Science Foundation. He is a well-known researcher and author of over 100 articles, books and patents in the areas of computer security, software engineering, and mathematics.

From 1981 to 1987 DeMillo was the Director of the Software Test and Evaluation Project for the US Department of Defense (DoD). He is widely credited with developing the DoD's policy for test and evaluation of software-intensive systems. In 1987, he moved to Purdue University where he was named Professor of Computer Science and Director of The Software Engineering Research Center. In 1989, he became Director of the National Science Foundation Computer and Computation Research Division and presided over the growth of high performance computing and computational science programs. He also held a visiting professorship at the University of Padua in Padua, Italy where he led the formation of a successful post-graduate program in software engineering.

In 1995 he became Vice President and General Manager of Information and Computer Science Research at Bellcore (which later became Telcordia Technologies), leading the invention of new technologies for e-commerce, networking and communications. In 1997, he collaborated with Richard Lipton and Daniel Boneh to create the "Differential Fault Analysis" method of cryptanalysis, leading to a strengthening of existing standards for internet security.

In 2000, DeMillo joined Hewlett-Packard (HP) as vice president and Chief Technology Officer (CTO). While working at HP, he led the company's introduction of a new processor architecture, a corporate trust and security strategy, and the company's entry into open source software. He was the public spokesman for HP's technology and one of the most visible figures in IT. In 2002, RSA Security appointed DeMillo to its Board of Directors, a position he held until 2007 when RSA was acquired by EMC. He remained at HP through the company's 2002 merger with Compaq computer and was named Vice President for Technology Strategy. He returned to Tech that August to serve as the new dean of the College of Computing.

Cloud Computing

George Wang

Institute for Information Industry
Taiwan

Abstract. Cloud computing is an emerging computing and business model where users can gain access to their applications from anywhere through their connected devices. The proliferation of intelligent mobile devices, high speed wireless connectivity, and rich browser-based Web 2.0 interfaces have made this shared network-based cloud computing model possible. Cloud Computing is very much driven by the increasingly unmanageable IT complexity. We will describe the main technology developments that have made this IT simplification possible: namely Virtualization, SOA, and Service/Systems Management. We believe that the Cloud will grow rapidly at the top SaaS layer (including Application services, Business services and People services). The Cloud model of services can improve the way we manage health care, finance, mobile information, and more; and will help us realize the vision of Intelligent Living. The speaker will also share his view on Cloud Computing opportunities for Taiwan.

Speaker

Dr. George Wang serves as the Executive Vice President, Institute for Information Industry, since June 2007. He is currently responsible for III's R&D in Communications, Telematics, Embedded Software, and Information Security.

Dr. Wang worked at IBM for 29 years. He joined IBM Watson Research Center in 1978. He led Research team in a multi-division effort to carry out research that led to the shipping of transformed IBM mainframes in 1995. He was named to the founding Director of IBM China Research Laboratory in Beijing 7/1995. In 1999, Dr. Wang conceived and established IBM China Development Laboratory and became the head of IBM R&D operations in China. Under his leadership, IBM China Laboratories grew to a 1,600-people organization upon his returning to US 6/2004. He was Vice President, IBM Systems and Technology Group between 7/2004 and 4/2007. Dr. Wang earned various IBM awards including a Corporate Award. In 2005, he earned the Asian American Engineer of the Year Award; and the Outstanding-50 Asian American Business Award, in recognition of his outstanding contributions in the establishment of IBM China R&D Laboratories.

Dr. Wang earned his PhD in physics in 1977 and his MS in computer sciences in 1978, both from Columbia University; and his BS in physics from National Taiwan University in 1970.

G. Vossen, D.D.E. Long, and J.X. Yu (Eds.): WISE 2009, LNCS 5802, p. 3, 2009.
© Springer-Verlag Berlin Heidelberg 2009

Beyond Search: Web-Scale Business Analytics

Alexander Löser

Technische Universität Berlin
DIMA, Einsteinufer 17
10587 Berlin, Germany
aloeser@cs.tu-berlin.de

Abstract. We discuss the novel problem of supporting analytical business intelligence queries over web-based textual content, e.g., BI-style reports based on 100.000's of documents from an ad-hoc web search result. Neither conventional search engines nor conventional Business Intelligence and ETL tools address this problem, which lies at the intersection of their capabilities. This application is an exciting challenge that should appeal to and benefit from several research communities, most notably, the database, text analytics and distributed system worlds. E.g., to provide fast answers for such queries, cloud computing techniques need to be incorporated with text analytics, data cleansing, query processing and query refinement methods. However, the envisioned path for OLAP-style query processing over textual web data may take a long time to mature. Two recent developments have the potential to become key components of such an ad-hoc analysis platform: significant improvements in cloud computing query languages and advances in self-supervised information extraction techniques. In this talk, I will give an informative and practical look at the underlying research challenges in supporting "Web-Scale Business Analytics" applications with a focus on its key components and will highlight recent projects.

1 Speaker

Dr. Alexander Löser is Research Scientist with Technische Universität Berlin. Before, as a Post-doc at the IBM Almaden Research Center and member of the AVATAR project, Alexander investigated and developed search engines for email search and for searching the IBM intranet. Later he joined SAP Research as Research Scientist. He initiated the work on text analytics for SAP's primer community platform 'SDN', that later became a major research focus for the lab. Alexander's current research focuses on planning, optimizing and executing OLAP queries over web-based text data in elastic and distributed execution platforms, such as Hadoop. Alexander published on international conferences and journals including WWW, ISWC, JSAC or JWS and has served on program committees of these and many other conferences. His work on the Avatar Semantic Search System with IBM Research was acknowledged in the Computer World Horizon Awards 2006. Alexander has technically led, managed and successfully delivered on numerous projects funded by European Commission.

G. Vossen, D.D.E. Long, and J.X. Yu (Eds.): WISE 2009, LNCS 5802, p. 5, 2009.
© Springer-Verlag Berlin Heidelberg 2009

Storyboarding – High-Level Engineering of Web Information Systems

Hui Ma[1], Klaus-Dieter Schewe[2], and Bernhard Thalheim[3]

[1] Victoria University of Wellington, New Zealand
[2] Information Science Research Centre, New Zealand
[3] Christian Albrechts University Kiel, Germany

Abstract. A web Information System (WIS) is an information system that can be accessed via the world-wide-web. We will describe the various aspects of web information systems (WISs) such as purpose, usage, content, functionality, context, presentation. Further we will present three major blocks dealing with strategic modelling of WISs, usage modelling of WISs by means of storyboarding, and semantics and pragmatics of storyboarding. Strategic modelling lays out the plan for the whole WIS without drifting into technical details. It specifies the purpose(s) of the system, and what are criteria for the WIS being successful. Usage modelling emphasises storyboarding, which consists of three interconnected parts: the modelling of the story space, the modelling of the actors, i.e. classes of users, and the modelling of tasks. We will first present the modelling language of storyboarding. Then, we will briefly discuss semantic aspects of storyboarding focusing on an algebraic approach to reason about storyboards emphasising the personalisation with respect to preference rules, and the satisfiability of deontic constraints. Finally we will address pragmatics of storyboarding, the necessary complement devoted to what the storyboard means for its users. The part of pragmatics is concerned with usage analysis by means of life cases, user models and contexts that permit a deeper understand of what users actually understand the system to be used for.

1 Speakers

Bernhard Thalheim studied mathematics and computer science at the Technical University Dresden and then at Moscow State University Lomonossov, from which he received a Ph.D. degree in 1979. Back in Germany he completed his Habilitation (= D.Sc.) in Theoretical Computer Science at the Technical University Dresden in 1986. After that he held full professor positions at Rostock University and the Brandenburgian Technical University at Cottbus. Since 2003 he is Chair for Databases and Information Systems at Christian Albrechts University Kiel. His major research interests are Database Theory, Logic in Computer Science, Design Methodologies for Integrated Information Systems, in particular Web Information Systems, and Database Component Ware.

Klaus-Dieter Schewe studied mathematics and computer science at Bonn University (Germany). In 1985 he received his Ph.D. in Mathematics from Bonn University. During 1985 and 1990 be worked with large industrial companies in the

G. Vossen, D.D.E. Long, and J.X. Yu (Eds.): WISE 2009, LNCS 5802, pp. 7–8, 2009.
© Springer-Verlag Berlin Heidelberg 2009

fields of Artificial Intelligence, Software Engineering and Office Information Systems. Returning to Hamburg University in 1990 he worked on Formal specifications and semantics and Database Theory. In 1995 he received the Habilitation (= D.Sc.) in Theoretical Computer Science from the Brandenburgian Technical University at Cottbus (Germany). From 1994 to 1999 he worked at the Computer Science Department of the Technical University Clauthal. From 2000 to 2008 he was Chair of Information Systems at Massey University in New Zealand. Since 2003 he is also the Director of the Information Science Research Centre. Since his habilitation his major fields of interest are Formal specifications and semantics, Logic in Computer Science, Database Theory, Distributed Object Bases and Design of Integrated Information Systems, in particular Web Information Systems.

Hui Ma received a BE in Civil Engineering from Tongji University, China in 1989, a BInfSci (Honours) and a MInfSci in Information Systems from Massey University, New Zealand in 2002 and 2003, respectively, and a Ph.D. in Information Systems from Massey University in 2007. Since 2008 she is Lecturer in Software Engineering at the School of Engineering and Computer Science at Victoria University of Wellington, New Zealand. Her major research interests are distributed databases, web engineering, service-oriented systems and cloud computing, and geographical Information Systems.

Web Queries: From a Web of Data to a Semantic Web

François Bry, Tim Furche, and Klara Weiand

University of Munich
Germany

Abstract. One significant effort towards combining the virtues of Web search, viz. being accessible to untrained users and able to cope with vastly heterogeneous data, with those of database-style Web queries is the development of keyword-based Web query languages. These languages operate essentially in the same setting as XQuery or SPARQL but with an interface for untrained users.

Keyword-based query languages trade some of the precision that languages like XQuery enable by allowing to formulate exactly what data to select and how to process it, for an easier interface accessible to untrained users. The yardstick for these languages becomes an easily accessible interface that does not sacrifice the essential premise of database-style Web queries, that selection and construction are precise enough to fully automate data processing tasks. To ground the discussion of keyword-based query languages, we give a summary of what we perceive as the main contributions of research and development on Web query languages in the past decade. This summary focuses specifically on what sets Web query languages apart from their predecessors for databases.

Further, this tutorial (1) gives an overview over keyword-based query languages for XML and RDF (2) discusses where the existing approaches succeed and what, in our opinion, are the most glaring open issues, and (3) where, beyond keyword-based query languages, we see the need, the challenge, and the opportunities for combining the ease of use of Web search with the virtues of Web queries.

References

1. Bailey, J., Bry, F., Furche, T., Schaffert, S.: Web and Semantic Web query languages: A survey. In: Eisinger, N., Małuszyński, J. (eds.) Reasoning Web. LNCS, vol. 3564, pp. 35–133. Springer, Heidelberg (2005)
2. Berglund, A., Boag, S., Chamberlin, D., Fernandez, M., Kay, M., Robie, J., Simeon, J.: XML Path Language (XPath) 2.0. Recommendation, W3C (2005)
3. Bry, F., Furche, T., Linse, B., Pohl, A.: Xcerpt^{RDF}: A pattern-based answer to the versatile web challenge. In: Workshop on (Constraint) Logic Programming (2008)

G. Vossen, D. D. E. Long, and J. X. Yu (Eds.): WISE 2009, LNCS 5802, pp. 9–10, 2009.
© Springer-Verlag Berlin Heidelberg 2009

Speakers

Prof. Dr. François Bry is a full professor at the Institute for Informatics of the Ludwig-Maximilian University of Munich, Germany, heading the research group for programming and modeling languages. He is currently investigating methods and applications related to querying answering and reasoning on the Web and social semantic Software and Media. In particular his research focuses on query and rule languages for Web data formats such as XML and RDF, complex events and social media. François Bry has a research record of over 140 peer-reviewed scientific publications, some cited over 300 times. He has supervised over 15 doctoral projects. Among his former doctoral students are Slim Abdennadher, dean of Computer Science at the German University in Cairo, Egypt, Sebastian Schaffert, project leader with Salzburg Research, Dan Olteanu, lecturer at Oxford University, and Tim Furche, postdoc at the University of Munich. François Bry regularly contributes to scientific conferences and journals, especially in the areas Web and Semantic Web as an author, reviewer or program committee member. Before joining University of Munich in 1994, he worked in industry in France and Germany, in particular with the research center ECRC. From 2004-2008 he was co-coordinating REWERSE, a network of excellence in the 6th Framework Programme of the European Commission.

Dr. Tim Furche is a postdoctoral researcher at the Institute for Informatics of the Ludwig-Maximilian University of Munich, Germany, in the research group for programming and modeling languages. His research interests are XML and semi-structured data, in particular query evaluation and optimization, and advanced Web systems. His main contributions are on XPath optimization (especially with the article "XPath: Looking Forward") and evaluation and on linear time and space querying of large graphs. He has authored over 40 peer-reviewed scientific publications, some of them cited over 150 times. Tim Furche regularly contributes to scientific conferences and journals, especially in the areas Web and Semantic Web as an author, reviewer or program committee member. From 2004-2008 he was co-coordinating the REWERSE working group on Reasoning-aware Querying.

Klara Weiand is a doctoral student in the KiWi – Knowledge in a Wiki project, working on the development of KWQL, a versatile and powerful but at the same time user-friendly keyword-based query language. She graduated with a Bachelor's degree in Cognitive Science from the University of Osnabrück in 2005. She went on to pursue a Master's degree in Artificial Intelligence at the University of Amsterdam. During this time, she focused on speech and language processing and machine learning while working as a research assistant in computational phonetics and authoring publications in formal semantics, phonetics and forensic artificial intelligence.

Toward a Unified View of Data and Services

Sonia Bergamaschi[1] and Andrea Maurino[2]

[1] University of Modena and Reggio Emilia Italy
[2] University of Milano Bicocca, Italy
sonia.bergamaschi@unimore.it, maurino@disco.unimib.it

Abstract. The research on data integration and service discovering has involved from the beginning different (not always overlapping) communities. Therefore, data and services are described with different models and different techniques to retrieve data and services have been developed. Nevertheless, from a user perspective, the border between data and services is often not so definite, since data and services provide a complementary vision about the available resources.

In NeP4B (Networked Peers for Business), a project funded by the Italian Ministry of University and Research, we developed a semantic approach for providing a uniform representation of data and services, thus allowing users to obtain sets of data and lists of web-services as query results. The NeP4B idea relies on the creation of a Peer Virtual View (PVV) representing sets of data sources and web services, i.e. an ontological representation of data sources which is mapped to an ontological representation of web services. The PVV is exploited for solving user queries: 1) data results are selected by adopting a GAV approach; 2) services are retrieved by an information retrieval approach applied on service descriptions and by exploiting the mappings on the PVV.

In the tutorial, we introduce: 1) the state of the art of semantic-based data integration and web service discovering systems; 2) the NeP4B architecture.

Speakers

Sonia Bergamaschi was born in Modena (Italy) and received her Laurea degree in Mathematics from the Università di Modena on 1977. She is currently full professor of Computer Engineering in the Modena Engineering Faculty at the Università di Modena e Reggio Emilia, where she teaches "Databases", "Database technologies", "Knowledge Representation" and leads the "DBGROUP", i.e. the database research group, at the Dipartimento di Ingegneria dell'informazione (www.dbgroup.unimo.it).

Her research activity has been mainly devoted to knowledge representation and management in the context of very large databases facing both theorical and implementation aspects.

She is author of more than one hundred of articles in international journals and conferences, and her researches have been founded by the Italian MUR, CNR, ASI institutions and by European Community. She has served in the program committees of international and national database and AI conferences. She is a member of the IEEE Computer Society and of the ACM.

For a detailed description of the research activity and of the developed systems see: www.dbgroup.unimo.it.

G. Vossen, D.D.E. Long, and J.X. Yu (Eds.): WISE 2009, LNCS 5802, pp. 11–12, 2009.
© Springer-Verlag Berlin Heidelberg 2009

Andrea Maurino performed researches in several fields of computer science. He started with the definition of models and methods for the design of data intensive web applications, definition of models for the Web services composition and e-government. In all this activities a common feature was the analysis of quality. In fact in the field of web applications he developed techniques for conceptual log based analysis of them. In the area of SOA Andrea Maurino participated to the development of models and techniques for the (semantic) web services selection based on Quality of services/non functional properties. Moreover he participated in the development of new quality oriented egovernment methodologies. Current research interests of Andrea Maurino are the assessment of quality of database preserving the privacy of data and record linkage techniques in coopetitive domains. Recently Andrea Maurino started a research activity to integrate these two complementary worlds for the definition of systems able to find at the same time data and services related to data.

Maximizing Utility for Content Delivery Clouds

Mukaddim Pathan, James Broberg, and Rajkumar Buyya

Cloud Computing and Distributed Systems (CLOUDS) Laboratory
Department of Computer Science and Software Engineering
The University of Melbourne, Australia
{apathan,brobergj,raj}@csse.unimelb.edu.au

Abstract. A content delivery cloud, such as MetaCDN[1], is an integrated overlay that utilizes cloud computing to provide content delivery services to Internet end-users. While it ensures satisfactory user perceived performance, it also aims to improve the traffic activities in its world-wide distributed network and uplift the usefulness of its replicas. To realize this objective, in this paper, we measure the utility of content delivery via MetaCDN, capturing the system-specific perceived benefits. We use this utility measure to devise a request-redirection policy that ensures high performance content delivery. We also quantify a content provider's benefits from using MetaCDN based on its user perceived performance. We conduct a *proof-of-concept* testbed experiment for MetaCDN to demonstrate the performance of our approach and reveal our observations on the MetaCDN utility and content provider's benefits from using MetaCDN.

1 Introduction

Content Delivery Networks (CDNs) provide improved Web access performance to Internet end-users through multiple, geographically distributed replica servers [18]. A commercial CDN lock-in a customer, i.e. content provider, for a particular period of time under specific Service Level Agreements (SLAs) with a high monthly/yearly fees and excess data charges [14]. Thus, far from democratizing content delivery, most CDN services are often priced out of reach for all but large enterprise customers [21]. On the other hand, a commercial CDN realizes high operational cost and even monetary penalization if it fails to meet the SLA-bound commitments to provide high quality service to end-users. Moreover, the main value proposition for CDNs has shifted over time. Initial focus was on improving the user performance by decreasing response time, especially when there is an unexpectedly high load on content provider's Web sites. Nowadays, content providers view CDN services as a way to use a shared network infrastructure with improved *utility* to handle their peak capacity requirements, thus allowing reduced investments in their own Web site infrastructure [13]. Utility refers to the quantification of a CDN's traffic activities and represents the usefulness of its replicas in terms of data circulation in its distributed network. It is vital as system wellness greatly affects the content delivery performance to end-users.

One approach to address these issues is to build a *content delivery cloud* [9], on top of existing *cloud services*, e.g. Amazon Simple Storage Service (S3), Nirvanix

---

[1] It extends traditional Content Delivery Networks (CDNs) model. Available at: http://www.metacdn.org

G. Vossen, D.D.E. Long, and J.X. Yu (Eds.): WISE 2009, LNCS 5802, pp. 13–28, 2009.

Storage Delivery Network (SDN), and Mosso Cloud Files. The use of clouds for content delivery is highly appealing as they charge customers for their utilization of storage and transfer of content, typically in order of cents per gigabyte. They offer SLA-backed performance and uptime guarantees for their services. Moreover, they can rapidly and cheaply scale-out during flash crowds [2] and anticipated increases in demand. However, unlike a fully-featured CDN, they do not provide capabilities for automatic replication, fail-over, geographical load redirection and load balancing.

MetaCDN [6] realizes a content delivery cloud, providing the required features for high performance content delivery. It is an integrated overlay service, which leverages existing *storage clouds*. It allows content providers to revel advanced content delivery services without having to build a dedicated infrastructure. When a user requests content, MetaCDN chooses an optimal replica for content delivery, thereby ensuring satisfactory user perceived experience. The ultimate goal is to improve the quantitative measure of *utility* for MetaCDN's content delivery services. While the notion of utility is enticing in relation to content delivery, only a few previous work [13][17][23][24] have considered it. Our work is in line with them, focusing on maximizing the utility of MetaCDN. We present a request-redirection policy based on the measured utility to ensure high content delivery performance. We also quantify a content provider's benefits from using MetaCDN. We perform a *proof-of-concept* empirical study on a global testbed to evaluate the performance of our approach and provide insights on the MetaCDN utility. The main contributions of this paper are:

- A utility-based request-redirection policy to improve MetaCDN's utility.
- An approach to quantify a content provider's benefits from using MetaCDN.
- An experimental study on a world-wide testbed for performance evaluation.

The rest of the paper is structured as follows. Section 2 provides an overview of related work. It is followed by a brief description of MetaCDN in Section 3. The formulation of utility metric and the devised request-redirection policy is presented in Section 4. Section 5 presents a description of the testbed experiments. Next, in Section 6, empirical results are discussed. Finally, the paper is concluded in Section 7.

2   Related Work

There has been a growing interest in interconnecting provider capabilities in CDNs, such as Content Distribution Internetworking (CDI) [10], multi-provider peering [1], and peering CDNs [19]. These research efforts explore the benefits of internetworking of CDNs, with main focus on offering increased capacity, intelligent server selection, reduced cost, and better fault tolerance. In contrast, our work with the MetaCDN overlay system assumes no cooperation or peering. Rather it follows a brokering approach as in CDN brokering [5]. Our work is a logical fit in existing storage cloud deployments coupled with content delivery capabilities, such as Amazon CloudFront; VoxCAST CDN; Mosso Cloud Files, which leverages content delivery services from Limelight Networks; Nirvanix SDN, which partners with CDNetworks for content delivery; and Edge Content Network (ECN) from Microsoft, which is reported to partner with Limelight Networks for content delivery [16].

Along with the trend-shift in the content delivery space, CDN utility and pricing have gained notable attention. There has been prior work reflecting the utility computing notion for content delivery [7][13][24]. They mostly provide description of architecture, system features and challenges related to the design and development of a utility computing platform for CDNs. On the contrary, we not only provide an overview of the utility model for MetaCDN, but also quantify the perceived utility and devise a utility-based request-redirection policy. Our work is complimentary to the simulation-based evaluation of utility as described in previous work [17][23]. We differ by providing a proof-of-concept implementation for evaluating utility, devising a request-redirection algorithm, and revealing the system performance through a global testbed experiment. In addition, we determine a content provider's perceived utility using an approach complimentary to traditional CDN pricing [14].

Recent innovations such as P4P [25] enables P2P to communicate with network providers through a portal for cooperative content delivery. Our work endorses them in that the MetaCDN overlay system assists toward a systematic understanding and practical realization of the interactions between storage clouds, who provide an operational storage network and content delivery resources, and content providers, who generate and distribute content. Alike collaborative content delivery systems, e.g. Coral [12] and PRSync [22], we develop a request-redirection policy. Our uniqueness lies in quantifying traffic activities while redirecting end-user requests. The literature on request-redirection is too vast to cite here (see [3][8][15] and the references therein for initial pointers to request-redirection in content delivery context).

3   The MetaCDN Overlay

Figure 1 provides an illustration of MetaCDN. It is coupled with each storage clouds via *connectors* that provide an abstraction to hide the complexity associated with different access methodologies of heterogeneous providers. End-users can access the MetaCDN overlay either through a Web portal or via RESTful Web services. In the first case, the Web portal acts as an entry point to the system and performs application level load balancing for end-users who intend to download content that has been deployed through MetaCDN. Content providers can sign up for an account on the MetaCDN system and enter credentials for any storage cloud providers that have an account with. Upon authentication, they can utilize MetaCDN functionalities to deploy content over geographically spanned replicas from multiple storage clouds, according to their performance requirements and budget limitations.

MetaCDN provides the logic and management required to encapsulate the functionality of upstream storage cloud providers with a number of core components. The *MetaCDN allocator* performs optimal provider selection and physical content deployment using four options, namely, *maximize-coverage*, *geolocation-based*, *cost*, and *QoS-optimized* deployment. The *MetaCDN QoS monitor* tracks the current and historical performance of participating storage providers. The *MetaCDN Manager* has authority on each user's current deployment and performs various housekeeping tasks. The *MetaCDN Database* stores information, such as user accounts and deployments, and the capabilities, pricing and historical performance of providers. Finally, the *MetaCDN Load Redirector* is charged with different redirection policies and is responsible for directing end-users to the most appropriate replica according to performance requirements. Further details can be found in a previous work [6].

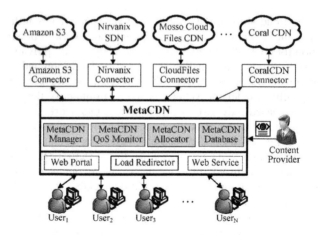

Fig. 1. An abstract view of MetaCDN.

4   MetaCDN Utility

End-users experience little of the complex technologies associated with the content delivery services of MetaCDN. Content providers interact with the service in a limited number of ways, such as enabling their content to be served, viewing traffic reports, and receiving usage-based billing. Since the responsibility to ensure high performance content delivery is largely on the MetaCDN system itself, we aim at improving its content-serving utility. In this section, we formulate the utility maximization problem with quantitative expressions, and devise a utility-based request-redirection policy.

We use $R = \{r_i\}$, $i \in \{1, 2, ..., M\}$ to denote the set of user requests, with r_i being the i-th arriving request to the MetaCDN overlay system, comprising a set of N replicas. Utility maximization in MetaCDN can be achieved from two perspectives. The first aspect is the profit maximization of MetaCDN, which is formulated as:

$$\text{maximize} \quad \sum_{r_i \in R,\, j \in N} U_{mcdn} x_{ij} \quad (Profit) \tag{1}$$

where U_{mcdn} is content-serving utility of the MetaCDN overlay system.

The second aspect examines the general welfare of the content provider for using the MetaCDN infrastructure to maximize its own benefit. Each content provider obtains a perceived utility U_{CP} (benefits) for QoS-constrained content delivery to its end-users via MetaCDN. The measured utility is expressed as the fraction of processed requests (throughput) or the total valuation (weighted throughput). It can be formulated either by maximizing the following one or two measurements:

$$\text{maximize} \quad \sum_{r_i \in R,\, j \in N} x_{ij} \quad (Throughput) \tag{2}$$

$$\text{maximize} \quad \sum_{r_i \in R,\, j \in N} U_{CP} x_{ij} \quad (Weighted\ throughput) \tag{3}$$

where U_{CP} is the content provider's perceived utility; indicator variable $x_{ij}=1$ if MetaCDN replica j serves request r_i within service requirements; and $x_{ij}=0$ otherwise.

4.1 Content-Serving Utility

We now derive the quantitative measure for MetaCDN utility U_{mcdn} and content providers perceived utility U_{CP}. Ideally for the MetaCDN overlay system, the most useful replicas are those exhibiting the highest utility. We quantify utility with a value that expresses the relation between the number of bytes of the served content against the number of bytes of the replicated content. It ranges in [0, 1] and provides an indication of the traffic activities. Formally, utility of a MetaCDN replica i is:

$$u_i = (2/\pi) \times \arctan(\xi) \qquad (4)$$

The main idea behind this metric is that a replica is considered to be useful (high utility) if it serves content more than it replicates, and vice versa. The parameter ξ is the ratio of the serviced bytes to the replicated bytes, i.e.

$$\xi = No\ of\ bytes\ serviced\ /\ No\ of\ bytes\ replicated \qquad (5)$$

The resulting utility from (4) ranges in [0, 1]. The value $u_i=1$ is achieved if the replica only serves content, without replicating (ξ=infinity). It results when a replica already has the content, and does not replicate a new copy of the content for serving successive requests. On the contrary, the value $u_i=0$ is achieved if the replica has the content, however fails to serve (ξ=0) due to service over-provisioning and/or network perturbations under heavy traffic surges. The content-serving utility U_{mcdn} of MetaCDN can be expressed as a mean value of the individual replica utilities, i.e.

$$U_{mcdn} = \sum_{n=1}^{N} u_i \Big/ N \qquad (6)$$

MetaCDN outsources customer's (content provider) content to the replicas and it is charged by the cloud providers based on usage. Since the utility measure captures the usage of storage cloud resources, the measured value can be easily translated into a price of the offered services. The resulting price could be used to derive a content provider's benefits or perceived utility. We draw inspiration from Hosanagar et al. [14], which show that the benefits of a content provider depends on its revenue, benefit from content delivery to its end-users through a CDN, replication cost, and usage-based charges. We adopt this approach by using performance measures of end-users that belong to a content provider. We gauge the throughput for serving requests and the response time improvement by using MetaCDN over direct replica access. We also measure the replication cost and interpret the pricing of storage clouds according to the MetaCDN utility. We express a content provider's perceived utility as:

$$U_{CP} = T(X) + (R - R_d) \times X - \psi b - P(u) \qquad (7)$$

where $T()$ is the weighted throughput for X requests; R and R_d respectively are the perceived response times from direct replica access and via MetaCDN; ψ is the unit replication cost; b is the content size; and $P(u)$ is the utility-based pricing function.

4.2 Utility-Based Request-Redirection

To choose the optimal replica for an end-user request, the MetaCDN Load Redirector module evaluates the utility metric reflecting the state of its replicas and the network conditions between users and replica sites. The measured utility is used for a utility-based request-redirection policy (Figure 2) for MetaCDN to serve data-rich content, thus improving the content delivery performance by relieving network congestions.

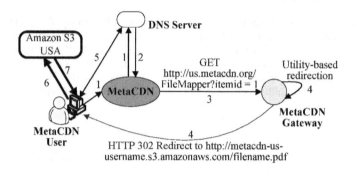

Fig. 2. Utility-based request-redirection in MetaCDN

The sequence of steps for an end-user in the East Coast of the USA to retrieve content through MetaCDN is as follows:

1. The end-user requests for a MetaCDN URL such as *http://www.metacdn.org/ FileMapper?itemid=1*, and the browser attempts to resolve the base hostname *www.metacdn.org*.
2. The user DNS eventually contacts the authoritative DNS (ADNS) for that domain to resolve this request to the IP address of the closest MetaCDN gateway, e.g. *http://us.metacdn.org*.
3. The user (or browser) then makes an HTTP GET request for the desired content on the MetaCDN gateway.
4. In the case of utility-based request-redirection, the MetaCDN Load Redirector is triggered to select the highest-utility optimal replica that conforms to the specified service requirements. At this point, the MetaCDN gateway returns an HTTP redirect request with the URL of the selected replica. The following tests are performed to determine the best replica for serving user requests:
   - Is there a content replica available within required response time threshold?
   - Is the throughput of the target replica within tolerance?
   - Is the end-user located in the same geographical region as the target replica?
   - Is one of the target replicas preferred, according to user requirements or any administrative settings?
   - Is the replica utility the highest among all target sites?
   - If there is more than one replica with same highest utility, which replica site provides the fastest response time?
5. Upon receiving the URL of the selected replica, the DNS resolves its domain name and returns the associated IP address to the end-user.
6. The user sends the request for the content to the selected replica.
7. The selected replica satisfies the end-user request by serving the desired content.

If it is assumed that all candidate target replicas are available and have capacity, i.e. response time and throughput thresholds are met, the MetaCDN system checks for the continent/geographic location and administrative preference (an indicative flag used by MetaCDN manager to manually prefer or avoid a replica). While end-users are directed to the highest utility replica by the MetaCDN Load Redirector, if there is more than one candidate target replica exhibiting the highest utility, the one with the fastest response time is chosen to redirect user requests. In addition, a secondary level of internal redirection enabled by an individual cloud provider ensures that the utility-based request-redirection policy does not overload any particular replica.

While the above request-redirection policy directs users to the best responding replica, an extra feature is realized through its ability to automatically avoid failed replicas or replicas without the desired content. Bypassing occurs in the following two ways. Firstly, if a replica has the desired content, but shows limited serving capacity due to network congestions, it is reflected in its measured utility and exhibits a low value. As a consequence, the replica is not considered as a candidate for redirection. Secondly, if the replica does not have the desired content, it can not serve user requests and thus leads to a content-serving utility of 0. Hence, it is automatically discarded to be considered as a candidate replica.

5 Methodology

We conduct a *proof-of-concept* testbed experiment to determine the content delivery utility of MetaCDN, evaluate the performance of the utility-based redirection policy and measure the user perceived response time and throughput. Figure 3 provides a schematic representation of the experimental testbed and Table 1 provides a summary of the conducted experiment. The global testbed spans six continents with distributed clients, replicas and MetaCDN gateways. All client locations, except Africa, South America and South Asia, have high speed connectivity to major Internet backbones to minimize the client being the bottleneck during experiments. We used test files of size 1KB and 5MB, deployed by the *MetaCDN Allocator* module, which was instructed to maximize coverage and performance, and consequently the test files were deployed in all available replica locations of the storage cloud providers integrated to MetaCDN. While these file sizes are appropriate for our experiments, a few constraints restrict us to use varied and/or even larger sized files. Firstly, the experiments generate heavy network traffic consuming significant network bandwidth, thus larger file trafficking would impose more strain and network congestions on the voluntary clients, which some clients may not be able to handle. Moreover, at some client locations, e.g. India and South Africa, Internet is at a premium and there are checks regarding Internet traffic so that other users in the client domain accessing Internet are not affected.

Fig. 3. Experiment testbed

The experiment was run simultaneously at each client location over a period of 48 hours, during the middle of the week in May, 2009. As it spans two days, localized peak times (*time-of-day*) is experienced in each geographical region. The workload to drive the experiment incorporates recent results on Web characterization [2][3][11]. The high variability and self-similar nature of Web access load is modeled through heavy-tailed distributions. The experiment time comprises epochs of 2 hours, with each epoch consisting of a set of user sessions. Each session opens a persistent HTTP connection to MetaCDN and each client generates requests to it to download each test files, with a timeout of 30 seconds. Between two requests, a user waits for a *think time* before the next request is generated. The mean think time, together with number of users defines the mean request arrival rate to MetaCDN. For statistical significance, each client is bounded to generate a maximum number of 30 requests in each epoch. The files are downloaded using the UNIX utility, *wget*, with the *--no-cache* and *--no-dns-cache* options to ensure that a fresh copy of the content is downloaded each time (not from any intermediary cache) and that the DNS lookup is not cached either.

5.1   Schemes and Metrics for Comparison

The primary objectives are to measure MetaCDN utility, evaluate performance of the proposed utility-based request-redirection policy, and provide observations on how MetaCDN's content-serving ability is varied during the experiment. For performance comparison, we experiment with two other request-redirection policies, namely, *random* and *geo-redirection*. The first policy directs an end-user to a randomly picked replica, whereas the second policy takes into account user preferences and directs him/her to the closest physical replica in the specified region(s).

Table 1. Summary of the experiment

Experiment Testbed	Category	Value	Provider	Locations
	Number of MetaCDN gateways	3	Amazon EC2 and own cluster	Asia/Australia, Europe, and North America
	Number of replicas	40	Amazon, Mosso and Nirvanix	Asia, Australia, Europe, and North America
	Number of clients (end-user nodes)	26	Voluntary	Asia, Australia, Europe, North and South America, and Africa

Experiment Details	Category	Description		
	Total experiment time	48 hours		
	Duration of an epoch	2 hours		
	Maximum user requests/epoch	30 requests from each client		
	Service timeout for each request	30 seconds		
	Test file size	1KB and 5MB		
	Content Deployment	Maximize-coverage deployment		
	Request-redirection policies	Random, Geo, and Utility		

End-user Request Modeling	Category	Distribution	PMF	Parameters
	Session inter-arrival time [11]	Exponential	$\lambda e^{-\lambda x}$	$\lambda = 0.05$
	Content requests per session [2]	Inverse Gaussian	$\sqrt{\dfrac{\lambda}{2\pi x^3}}\, e^{\frac{-\lambda(x-\mu)^2}{2\mu^2 x}}$	$\mu = 3.86, \lambda = 9.46$
	User think time [3]	Pareto	$\alpha k^{\alpha} x^{-\alpha-1}$	$\alpha = 1.4, k = 1$

We measure the *response time* and *throughput* obtained from each client location. The first captures the end-to-end performance for users when downloading a 1KB test file from MetaCDN. Due to the negligible file size, the response time is dominated by DNS lookup and HTTP connection establishment time. Lower value of response time indicates fast serviced content. The latter shows the transfer speed obtained when the 5MB test file is downloaded by the users from the MetaCDN replica infrastructure. It provides an indication of consistency and variability of throughput over time.

The *utility* of MetaCDN is measured according to the model in Section 4.1. A high utility value shows the content-serving ability of the system, and signifies its durability under highly variable traffic activities. To emphasize the impact of request-redirection on the measured utility, we use the *probability* that MetaCDN achieves a given level of utility as the performance metric. Finally, based on the measured observations, we determine the benefits of a content provider from using MetaCDN. Table 2 summarizes the performance indices used in the experimental evaluation.

Table 2. List of performance indices

Performance Index	Description
Response time	The time experienced by a end-user to get serviced
Throughput	Transfer speed to download a test file by a end-user
Utility	Content-serving ability, ranges in [0, 1]
Prob (Utility achieved)	The probability or the fraction of time that the system achieves the given utility
Content provider's benefit	Surplus from using MetaCDN, expressed as a percentage

6   Empirical Results

Due to space constraints, we present results from the following eight representative clients in five continents: Paris (France), Innsbruck (Austria), and Poznan (Poland) in Europe; Beijing (China) and Melbourne (Australia) in Asia/Australia; Atlanta, GA, Irvine, CA (USA) in North America, and Rio de Janeiro (Brazil) in South America.

6.1   Response Time Observations

Figure 4 shows the end-to-end response time experienced by end-users when downloading the 1 KB test file over a period of 48 hours. The measure of the response time depends on the network proximity, congestions in network path and traffic load on the target replica server. It provides an indication of the responsiveness of the replica infrastructure and the network conditions in the path between the client and the target replica which serves the end-user. We observe a general trend that the clients experience mostly consistent end-to-end response time. For all the request-redirection policies, the average response time in all the client locations except Beijing is just over 1 second, with a few exceptions. Notably the users in Beijing experience close to 4 seconds average response time from the MetaCDN replica infrastructure. This exception originates as a consequence of firewall policies applied by the Chinese government, which is also reported in another work [20].

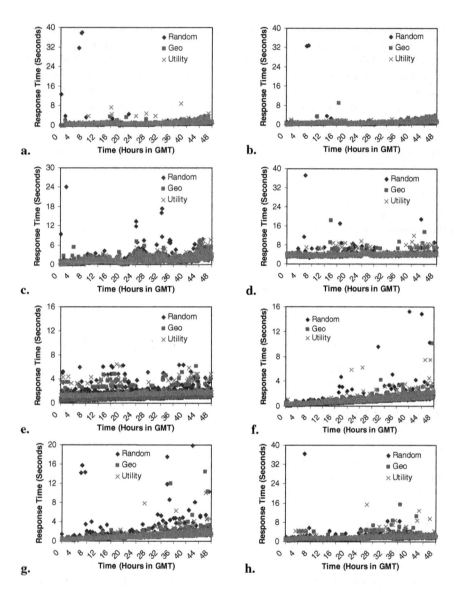

Fig. 4. Response time obtained in each client locations—(a) Paris; (b) Innsbruck; (c) Poznan; (d) Beijing; (e) Melbourne; (f) Atlanta; (g) Irvine; and (h) Rio de Janeiro

At several time instances during the experiment, end-users experience increased response time. The resulting spikes are due to the sudden increases in request traffic, imposing strain on the MetaCDN replica infrastructure. Under traffic surges, the MetaCDN load redirector module activates to handle peak loads. As a consequence, user requests are often redirected to a target replica outside its authoritative domain and/or are served from an optimal distant proximity server(s), thereby, contributing to the increased response time. However, MetaCDN handles peak loads well to provide satisfactory responsiveness to end-users. This phenomenon of increased response time is more visible for the random-redirection policy. As it makes a random choice, often the target replica selection is not optimized, thus leading to highly variable response time. Especially, at several occasions, users observe more than 30 seconds response time, thus leading to service timeout. The geo-redirection policy directs request to the closest proximity server, understandably producing low response time. On the contrary, utility-redirection chooses the highest utility replica, which may not be in close proximity to an individual client location. Nevertheless, we do not find a clear winner between them in terms of response time, as they exhibit changeable performance in different client locations. The utility-redirection performs as well as geo-redirection in that we observe similar performance in all clients except Paris and Melbourne. End-users in Paris enjoy better average response time (0.77 seconds) with geo-redirection, due to their close proximity to the Amazon, Mosso and Nirvanix nodes in Frankfurt (Germany), Dublin (Ireland), and London (UK). For Melbourne, the reason behind better performance of geo-redirection is the existence of the Mosso node in Sydney. For both of these two clients, utility-redirection directs requests to a distant replica than the closest one and results in increased response time.

6.2 Throughput Observations

Figure 5 shows the average throughput obtained per two hours, when downloading content from the MetaCDN replica infrastructure. As expected, we observe that in almost all the client locations, geo-redirection results in highest throughput as the users get serviced from the closest proximity replica. However, it performs worse than random-redirection for the Irvine client. The reason is that random-redirection decision in this location most of the time selects closer proximity Amazon replica(s) with better network path than that of geo-redirection, which chooses Mosso replica. Moreover, the service capability from these two replicas and the network path between the replica and client also contribute to the observed throughput variations.

For most of the clients, except Rio de Janeiro, utility redirection performs much worse than geo-redirection. The reason is understandable, as utility-redirection emphasizes maximizing MetaCDN's utility rather than serving an individual user, thus sacrificing end-user perceived performance. For Rio de Janeiro, geo-redirection leads to closest Mosso node in the USA, whereas utility-redirection results in more utility-aware replica, which is Amazon node(s) in the USA. It could be presumed that Amazon node supersedes the Mosso node in terms of its service capability, better network path, internal overlay routing, and less request traffic strain.

It is observed that users in Poznan enjoy the best average throughput, which is 9MB/s for geo-redirection. The reason is that the client machine is in a MAN network, which is connected to the country-wide Polish optical network PIONEER with high capacity channels dedicated to content delivery traffic. Another client location with high throughput is Atlanta, which achieves speeds of approximately 6.2 MB/s for geo-redirection and 3.3 MB/s for utility-redirection, due to the existence of better network path between the client and the MetaCDN replica infrastructure. This reasoning is deemed valid, since there are Mosso nodes in the same location.

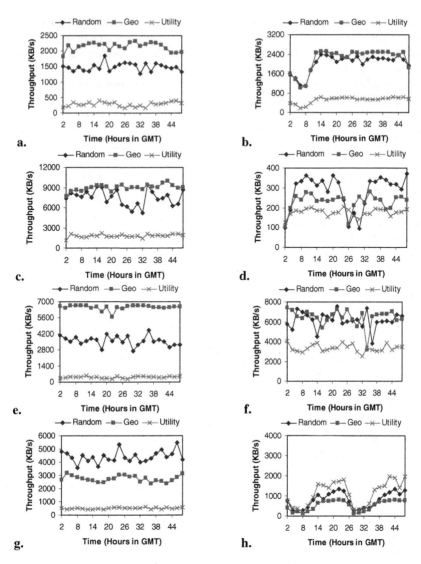

Fig. 5. Average throughput obtained in client locations—(a) Paris; (b) Innsbruck; (c) Poznan; (d) Beijing; (e) Melbourne; (f) Atlanta; (g) Irvine; and (h) Rio de Janeiro

Alike the perceived response time, end-users in China achieves the lowest throughput among all the client locations. The underlying reason is again checks on the request traffic due to firewall policies. We put more emphasis on the results from Melbourne, which is of interest as Australia is not as highly connected as Europe or North America, depending on a small number of expensive international links to major data centers in Europe and the USA. Specifically, we observe that due to the existence of a nearby Mosso node in Sydney, the users in Melbourne experience 6.5 MB/s of throughput with geo-redirection and 3.6 MB/s for random-redirection.

However, for utility-redirection the replica selections result in Amazon node(s) in the USA, thus leading to a lower but consistent average throughput of 410 KB/s.

From these observations, we come to the following decisive conclusions. Although utility-redirection outcomes sensible replica selection in terms of response time, it may not provide a high throughput performance to end-users. Nevertheless, being it is focused on maximizing the utility of the MetaCDN system; it results in high utility for content delivery. We provide sufficient results to support this claim in the next section.

6.3 MetaCDN Utility

Figure 6 shows how MetaCDN utility is varied during the testbed experiment upon replica selection for incoming content requests. Here we have used utility values averaged over three deployed MetaCDN gateways in Asia/Australia, Europe and North America. We observe that utility-redirection produces the highest utility in the system by selecting most active replicas to serve users. It also improves the traffic activities and contributes to uplifting MetaCDN's content-serving ability. It should be noted that there is a warm-up phase at the beginning of the 48 hours experiment during which the replicas are populated with content requests, resulting in low utility values. This is visible during the initial hours for utility and geo-redirection.

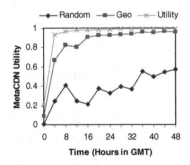
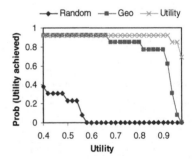

Fig. 6. MetaCDN utility over time   **Fig. 7.** Probability of achieving specified utility

In order to emphasize the content-serving ability of MetaCDN, we now present the probability that the system can achieve required minimum utility. The intention is to show to what extent the system can maximize its own profit. Figure 7 presents the probability (or the fraction of time) that the system observes a utility above a certain utility level during the experiment. The higher the probability, the more likely it is that the specified utility level could be achieved. From the figure, it is noticeable that utility-redirection outperforms other alternatives, as it often produces over 0.95 utility for MetaCDN with a 0.85 probability. Geo-redirection performs well as it has a 0.77 probability that it can achieve 0.9 utility. Finally, random-redirection performs the worst and it can only achieve close to 0.56 utility for MetaCDN with a probability of 0.23. Therefore, a MetaCDN administrator may utilize a redirection policy apart from random, in order to maximize the system's content-serving ability.

6.4 Content Provider's Perceived Utility

We now shed light on the content provider's perceived utility or benefits (Section 4.1) from using MetaCDN, as reported in Table 3. For this purpose, we consider a scenario with 8 client locations belonging to 8 content providers. We use weighted throughput and normalized values of perceived response times from the client locations of respective content providers, using utility-redirection. We also measure the direct replica access time from each of the client locations. Finally, we make use of pricing information of Amazon S3, as reported earlier [6]. The perceived utilities reported in Table 3 are to be considered representative, as they could be varied depending on the heterogeneous pricing structure of different storage cloud providers. In addition, different redirection policy leads to different perceived utility for a content provider.

We observe that a content provider's utility is heavily dependent on the throughput that its end-users receive. Therefore, content providers whose end-users benefit from high throughput also realize high quantitative benefit from using MetaCDN. As Poznan and Atlanta experience highest throughputs, the content provider's surplus for this locations are also highest. The average throughput experienced in Paris is the lowest, thus leading to the least content provider's surplus. It is important to note that the utility-redirection policy, being antagonistic to content provider's utility, can still assists in resulting reasonable perceived utility for the content providers. Thus, the above results show that the MetaCDN system is helpful for content providers, even at times when it uses redirection techniques to maximize its own utility.

Table 3. Content providers' benefits based on user perceived performance

Content Provider	End-user Location	Average Response Time	Average Direct Replica Access Time	Throughput	Perceived Utility (%)
1	Paris	0.99 seconds	0.747 seconds	475.39 KB/s	13.31
2	Innsbruck	1.03 seconds	0.955 seconds	518.67 KB/s	29.29
3	Poznan	1.52 seconds	0.667 seconds	1.80 MB/s	68.99
4	Beijing	4.17 seconds	1.337 seconds	176.54 KB/s	58.14
5	Melbourne	1.72 seconds	0.75 seconds	413.15 KB/s	25.32
6	Atlanta	1.09 seconds	0.605 seconds	3.35 MB/s	66.47
7	Irvine	1.06 seconds	0.391 seconds	504.74 KB/s	25.38
8	Rio de Janeiro	1.81 seconds	1.17 seconds	1.14 MB/s	34.02

7 Conclusion and Future Work

MetaCDN provides sensible performance and availability benefits without requiring the content providers to build or manage complex content delivery infrastructure themselves. In this paper, we have presented an approach to maximize the utility for content delivery via MetaCDN. The utility metric reflects the traffic activities in the system and exhibit the usefulness of its replica infrastructure. We have used the measured utility to devise a redirection policy and quantify the benefit of a content provider for using MetaCDN. We conducted experiments in a global testbed to evaluate the performance of our approach. From the results obtained, we conclude that the utility of MetaCDN is maximized with utility-redirection with sensible replica selection and consistent average response time, however, with the cost of lower throughput in comparison to other policies. In contrast, a content provider's benefit is improved with improvement of the perceived throughput through MetaCDN. Therefore, a MetaCDN administrator should use a redirection policy based on the objective of either maximizing system utility or a content provider's utility. The results are quite encouraging to conduct a set of future work, which includes development of advanced redirection and pricing policies to benefit both MetaCDN and content providers; on-demand autonomic management (expansion/contraction) of replica and gateway deployment; and addition of shared/private host support. Thus, we aim to further enhance the scalability of MetaCDN and fill cloud black holes with seamless integration of non-cloud storage resources.

Acknowledgments. We thank all participants[2] of the testbed experiments for their assistance with providing client nodes to run the experiments from. This work is supported by the ARC and DIISR research grants.

References

[1] Amini, L., Shaikh, A., Schulzrinne, H.: Effective peering for multi-provider content delivery services. In: Proc. of INFOCOM 2004. IEEE CS Press, Los Alamitos (2004)

[2] Arlitt, M., Jin, T.: Workload characterization of the 1998 world cup Web site. IEEE Network 14(3), 30–37 (2000)

[3] Barbir, A., Cain, B., Nair, R., Spatscheck, O.: Known content network (CN) request-routing mechanisms. RFC 3568 (July 2003)

[4] Barford, P., Crovella, M.E.: A performance evaluation of Hyper Text Transfer Protocols. In: Proc. of ACM Sigmetrics, pp. 188–197. ACM Press, New York (1999)

[5] Biliris, A., Cranor, C., Douglis, F., Rabinovich, M., Sibal, S., Spatscheck, O., Sturm, W.: CDN brokering. Computer Communications 25(4), 393–402 (2002)

[6] Broberg, J., Buyya, R., Tari, Z.: MetaCDN: Harnessing 'Storage Clouds' for high performance content delivery. Journal of Network and Computer Applications, JNCA (to appear, 2009)

[7] Canali, C., Rabinovich, M., Xiao, Z.: Utility computing for Internet applications. In: Tang, X., Xu, J., Chanson, S.T. (eds.) Web Content Delivey, vol. II, pp. 131–151. Springer, Heidelberg (2006)

[8] Cardellini, V., Colajanni, M., Yu, P.S.: Request redirection algorithms for distributed Web systems. IEEE Transactions on Parallel and Distributed Systems 14(4), 355–368 (2003)

[9] Cohen, R.: Content delivery cloud (CDC). ElasticVapor: Life in the Cloud (October 2008), http://www.elasticvapor.com/2008/10/cloud-content-delivery-cd.html

[10] Day, M., Cain, B., Tomlinson, G., Rzewski, P.: A model for content internetworking. IETF RFC 3466 (February 2003)

[11] Floyd, S., Paxson, V.: Difficulties in simulating the Internet. IEEE/ACM Transactions on Networking 9(4), 392–403 (2001)

[12] Freedman, M.J., Freudenthal, E., Mazières, D.: Democratizing content publication with Coral. In: Proc. of NSDI 2004, San Francisco, CA, pp. 239–252 (2004)

[13] Gayek, P., Nesbitt, R., Pearthree, H., Shaikh, A., Snitzer, B.: A Web Content Serving Utility. IBM Systems Journal 43(1), 43–63 (2004)

---

[2] Full details of all the participants are listed at http://www.gridbus.org/cdn/

[14] Hosanagar, K., Chuang, J., Krishnan, R., Smith, M.D.: Service adoption and pricing of content delivery network (CDN) services. Management Science 54(9), 1579–1593 (2008)

[15] Kangasharju, J., Ross, K.W., Roberts, J.W.: Performance evaluation of redirection schemes in content distribution networks. Computer Communications 24(2), 207–214 (2001)

[16] Miller, R.: Microsoft building own CDN network. In Data Center Knowledge (January 2008)

[17] Mortazavi, B., Kesidis, G.: Model and simulation study of a peer-to-peer game with a reputation-based incentive mechanism. In: Proc. of ITA 2006, UC San Diego (February 2006)

[18] Pallis, G., Vakali, A.: Insight and perspectives for content delivery networks. Communications of the ACM 49(1), 101–106 (2006)

[19] Pathan, M., Broberg, J., Bubendorfer, K., Kim, K.H., Buyya, R.: An architecture for virtual organization (VO)-based effective peering of content delivery networks. In: Proc. of the 2nd UPGRADE-CN. ACM Press, New York (2007)

[20] Rahul, H., Kasbekar, M., Sitaraman, R., Berger, A.: Towards realizing the performance and availability benefits of a global overlay network. In: Proc. of PAM 2006, Australia (2006)

[21] Rayburn, D.: CDN pricing: Costs for outsourced video delivery. In: Streaming Media West: The Business and Technology of Online Video (September 2008)

[22] Shah, P., Pâris, J.-F., Morgan, J., Schettino, J., Venkatraman, C.: A P2P-based architecture for secure software delivery using volunteer assistance. In: Proc. of P2P 2008. IEEE CS Press, Los Alamitos (2008)

[23] Stamos, K., Pallis, G., Vakali, A., Dikaiakos, M.D.: Evaluating the utility of content delivery networks. In: Proc. of the 4th UPGRADE-CN. ACM Press, New York (2009)

[24] Subramanya, S.R., Yi, B.K.: Utility model for on-demand digital content. IEEE Computer 38(6), 95–98 (2005)

[25] Xie, H., Yang, Y.R., Krishnamurthy, A., Liu, Y., Silberschatz, A.: P4P: Provider portal for (P2P) applications. In: Proc. of ACM SIGCOMM. ACM Press, New York (2008)

Aggregation of Document Frequencies in Unstructured P2P Networks

Robert Neumayer, Christos Doulkeridis*, and Kjetil Nørvåg

Norwegian University of Science and Technology
Sem sælands vei 7-9, 7491, Trondheim, Norway
{neumayer, cdoulk, noervaag}@idi.ntnu.no

Abstract. Peer-to-peer (P2P) systems have been recently proposed for providing search and information retrieval facilities over distributed data sources, including web data. Terms and their document frequencies are the main building blocks of retrieval and as such need to be computed, aggregated, and distributed throughout the system. This is a tedious task, as the local view of each peer may not reflect the global document collection, due to skewed document distributions. Moreover, central assembly of the total information is not feasible, due to the prohibitive cost of storage and maintenance, and also because of issues related to digital rights management. In this paper, we propose an efficient approach for aggregating the document frequencies of carefully selected terms based on a hierarchical overlay network. To this end, we examine unsupervised feature selection techniques at the individual peer level, in order to identify only a limited set of the most important terms for aggregation. We provide a theoretical analysis to compute the cost of our approach, and we conduct experiments on two document collections, in order to measure the quality of the aggregated document frequencies.

1 Introduction

Modern applications are often deployed over widely distributed data sources and each of them stores vast amounts of data, a development partly driven by the growth of the web itself. Web information retrieval settings are a good example for such architectures, as they contain large document collections stored at disparate locations. Central assembly of the total information is neither feasible, as digital rights do not allow replication of documents, nor effective, since the cost of storing and maintaining this information is excessive. In order to achieve interoperability and intercommunication, there exists a need for loosely-coupled architectures that facilitate searching over the complete information available. Peer-to-peer (P2P) networks constitute a scalable solution for managing highly distributed document collections and such systems have often been used in web information retrieval and web search settings [3,6,7,18,15].

---

* This work was carried out during the tenure of an ERCIM "Alain Bensoussan" Fellowship Programme.

G. Vossen, D.D.E. Long, and J.X. Yu (Eds.): WISE 2009, LNCS 5802, pp. 29–42, 2009.

One of the main problems in distributed retrieval lies in the difficulty of providing a qualitative ranking of documents, having as reference the centralised case. At the same time, performance and scalability considerations play a vital role in the development and applicability of such a widely distributed system. Thus, the important problem in the context of unstructured P2P networks is to provide a comprehensive ranking of terms (and documents). Clearly, exchanging all terms and their respective document frequencies would be a solution, however the cost is prohibitive, even for modest network sizes and medium-sized document collections. Therefore, we need a pre-selection of terms at peer level to evaluate the usefulness of terms locally, in order to decide which ones shall be aggregated. The usage of only a sub-part of all terms of a peer is further motivated by the possibility of holding back information, i.e. the more flexible an approach handles such terms, the more stable it is with respect to these types of inaccuracies. This process must work well without consuming excessive bandwidth, regardless of the size of the network topology. Also, the process should not be too specific with respect to the single collections, as both the distribution and the size of the local collections may vary significantly. These are the main issues to be investigated in this paper.

In our approach, peers first form a hierarchical overlay in a self-organising manner, which enables efficient aggregation of information. Then, carefully selected terms and their corresponding frequencies from each peer are pushed upwards in the hierarchy. At the intermediate levels, common terms from different peers are aggregated, thus reducing the total amount of information transferred. At the top levels of the hierarchy, a hash-based mechanism is employed to compute the global frequency values of terms, without requiring a single peer to perform this task. Finally, the information is disseminated to all peers and can be used for ranking documents.

Towards this goal, we investigate the impact of unsupervised feature selection techniques for term selection, i.e. techniques of selecting only the most useful terms of an often prohibitively large overall set of terms. Unsupervised refers to techniques which do not use available class information for term ranking as is often used in the machine learning context, if available. Such techniques can be applied on each peer autonomously, without explicit common assumptions, such as the availability of common labels, as in the case of supervised feature selection. Moreover, as the number both of documents and topics for each peer may vary, feature selection is an important tool, in order to identify terms that a peer is an expert on and can contribute to compute the correct document frequency value for.

The contributions of this work are: 1) we propose a hierarchical term aggregation method, which estimates global document frequencies of terms without assembling all information at a central location, suitable for unstructured P2P networks, 2) we investigate how unsupervised feature selection techniques applied at peer level affect the accuracy of the aggregated information, 3) we provide a cost model to assess the requirements of our approach in terms of transferred data, and 4) we conduct an experimental evaluation on two document collections, one of moderate size to show the applicability of our ideas, and one large collection of over 450.000 documents to demonstrate the scalability and application to web-based data.

The remainder of this paper is structured as follows: in Sect. 2, we provide an overview of the related work. We describe the aggregation process, starting from a description of the architecture, an overview of unsupervised feature selection methods employed at peer level, and eventually by presenting a cost model for assessing the communication cost, in Sect. 3. The experimental evaluation is presented in Sect. 4. Finally, in Sect. 5, we conclude the paper and give an outlook on future work.

2   Related Work

Distributed information retrieval (IR) has advanced to a mature research area dealing with querying multiple, geographically distributed information repositories. Both term weighting and normalisation are identified as major problems in dynamic scenarios [21], for both require global document frequency information. Viles and French study the impact of document allocation and collection-wide information in distributed archives [20]. They observe that even for a modest number of sites, dissemination of collection-wide information is necessary to maintain retrieval effectiveness, but that the amount of disseminated information can be relatively low. In a smaller scale distributed system, it is possible to use a dedicated server for collecting accurate term-level global statistics [10]. However, this approach is clearly not appropriate for large-scale systems.

In [22], the authors examine the estimation of global term weights (such as IDF) in information retrieval scenarios where a global view of the collection is not available. Two alternatives are studied: either sampling documents or using a reference corpus independent of the target retrieval collection. In addition, the possibility of pruning term lists based on frequency is evaluated. The results show that very good retrieval performance can be reached when just the most frequent terms of a collection (an extended stop word list) are known, and all terms which are not in that list are treated equally. The paper does not consider how to actually determine (collect) and distribute this information.

Moreover, we implicitly want to study the effects of pre-selection methods on overlay network generation. Also, our experiments are specifically designed to show the effects of unequally distributed partition sizes.

Content-based search in P2P networks [16] is usually related to full-text search [9,19,24], with most approaches relying on the use of structured P2P networks. Some research focuses on providing P2P web search functionalities, like in [11], where MINERVA is presented, a P2P web search engine that aims at scalability and efficiency. In MINERVA, each peer decides what fraction of the Web it will crawl and subsequently index. In further work, the authors also presented an information filtering approach relaxing the common hypothesis of subscribing to all information resources and allowing users to subscribe to the most relevant sources only [25]. Previous approaches regarding P2P web search have focused on building global inverted indices, as for example Odissea [18] and PlanetP [6]. In PlanetP, summaries of the peers' inverted indices are used to approximate TF-IDF. Inverse peer frequency (the number of peers containing the term) is used instead of IDF. It is questionable how this would scale in large P2P networks with dynamic contents, as also noted in [2]. In [4] superpeers are used to maintain DF for the connected peers. A similar approach is also used in [12]. Bender et al. [5] study global document frequency estimation in the context of P2P web search. The focus is on overlapping document collections, where the problem of counting duplicates is immense. Their system relies on the use of an underlying structured P2P network. A similar approach is described in [13], which is quite different from our setup that assumes an unstructured P2P architecture.

A major shortcoming of all these approaches is that their efficiency degrades with increasing query length and thus they are inappropriate for similarity search. Recently, approaches have been proposed that reduce the global indexing load by indexing carefully selected term combinations [17].

Furthermore, several papers propose using P2P networks in a digital library context [2,7,8,14,15]. In [3], a distributed indexing technique is presented for document retrieval in digital libraries. Podnar et al. [14] use highly discriminative keys for indexing important terms and their frequencies. In [15], the authors present *iClusterDL*, for digital libraries supported by P2P technology, where peers become members of semantic overlay networks (SONs).

3   Hierarchical Aggregation Based on Term Selection

In this section, we describe our approach for aggregating terms and their document frequencies, without central assembly of all data. We employ an unstructured P2P architecture and the overall aim is to provide estimates of frequency values that are as similar as possible to the centralised case, where all documents are available at a single location. We first provide an overview of the DESENT architecture. We then describe how aggregation is realised within our framework along with the feature selection methods we employ on a local level.

3.1   Architecture

DESENT. In order to create a hierarchical overlay network over a purely unstructured (Gnutella-like) P2P network, no matter its network distance, we employ a variant of DESENT [8]. The reasons for this choice are the completely *distributed* and *decentralised* creation of the hierarchy, its low creation cost and robustness. The most important details of the basic algorithm are described in the following; for more in-depth explanations we refer to [8]. The DESENT hierarchy can be used for building overlays for searching, but also for other purposes like aggregation of data or statistics about contents from participating peers – which is the way that DESENT is utilised in this paper.

For an illustrative example of the DESENT hierarchy, see Fig. 1. The bottom level consists of the individual peers ($P_{A_1} \ldots P_{A_n}$ and $P_{B_1} \ldots P_{B_n}$). Then

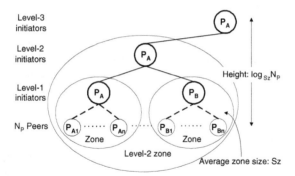

Fig. 1. Example of a P2P hierarchy of height $h=3$ with peers and zones

neighbouring peers (network-wise) create *zones* of approximate size S_Z peers (i.e. groups of peers) around an *initiator* peer (P_A and P_B), which acts as a zone controller. Notice that the height (h) of the hierarchy equals to: $log_{S_Z} N_P$. These level-1 initiators (P_A and P_B) are mostly uniformly distributed over the network, and are selected independently of each other in a pseudo-random way. The initiators form the next level of the hierarchy, they are responsible for the peers in their zones, and they aggregate the summary information of their peers into more abstract summaries.

In the subsequent phases, super-zones are created, which consist of a number of neighbouring zones from the previous level. Each super-zone is represented by a super-zone initiator that is responsible for the initiators in its zone and aggregates the information of these initiators. The zone initiators essentially form a P2P network similar to the original P2P network, and the aforementioned process is repeated recursively, using the zone initiators as peers. In the example of Fig. 1, P_A is initiator both at level-2 and level-3. In this way, a hierarchy of initiators is created, with each initiator creating summaries of information that refer to the contents of all peers in the tree rooted at that initiator. Finally, at the top-level initiator, summary information that spans the contents of the entire network is available.

Aggregation Process. The process of estimating the *frequency of selected terms* can be summarised as follows:

1. A tree-based P2P structure is created using the DESENT protocol [7,8].
2. All peers select up to T terms from their local document collection using one of the techniques described in Sect. 3.2, and send these terms together with the total number of documents to the parent peer in the tree.
3. Each parent peer receives up to $S_Z T$ terms with respective document frequencies, where S_Z denotes the average number of peers in a zone. The parent peer selects up to T terms, these terms are propagated upwards together with the aggregated document frequencies and the total number of documents in the subtree rooted at the peer.

4. The process continues up to the level of the children of the root (i.e., peers at level $h - 1$), where h denotes the height of the tree. Level 0 is the bottom level and level h is the level of the root peer. Instead of performing the last aggregation at the root peer, it is performed by the children of the root. This is achieved by first distributing their aggregated values by hashing to the other root-children peers, and after processing these, the peers send all their aggregated results to all the other level $h - 1$ peers.
5. The estimated document frequency values and the total number of documents are disseminated to the participating peers.
6. The whole process is repeated at regular intervals, in order to capture changes in document contents, as well as improving the estimated values. An alternative to fixed-time intervals would be to employ heuristics to assess the fluctuation in the network, i.e. initiate the process once a given number of peers joins or leaves the network.

Local Feature Selection and Document Frequency Calculation. Each peer P_i selects up to T terms from the $N_{l,i}$ locally stored documents, using one of the unsupervised feature selection techniques described in Sect. 3.2. Feature selection at a peer is based on the peer's local knowledge only. Thus, the result of the feature selection is a *term vector* TV_i, which is the number $N_{l,i}$ and vector of term tuples. Each term tuple in TV_i contains a term t_j and the local document frequency d_j: $TV_i = [N_{l,i}, [(t_1, d_1), ..., (t_T, d_T)]]$.

Level-wise Aggregation. After the $S_Z T$ selected terms from the previous phase have been received, a new term vector is created of the received terms and their frequencies, i.e., $TV_j = [N_s, [(t_1, d_1), ..., (t_{S_Z T}, d_{S_Z T})]]$. N_s is the sum of the received local frequencies, i.e., $N_s = \sum_{i=1}^{S_Z} N_{l,i}$. Furthermore, duplicate terms and their frequencies (i.e., the same term originating from several peers) are aggregated into one tuple, so that in general, in the end the number of terms in the new term vector is less than $S_Z T$. Finally, the term vector is reduced to only contain T terms. Term selection is performed based on the frequency of appearance, therefore terms that have high frequency are favoured. The intuition, which is also conformed by related work in [22], is that it is important to identify terms that are globally frequent and forward such terms to the top of the hierarchy. The generated term vector after aggregation and term selection, again consisting of T terms, is sent to the next level in the tree and this process continues iteratively up to level $h - 1$, i.e., the children of the root.

Hash-based Distribution and Aggregation. Performing the final aggregation at the root peer is a straightforward process, however it makes the system vulnerable, as it induces a single point of failure. Instead, the final aggregation is performed by the children of the root, at level $h - 1$. Notice that in this phase, our approach trades efficiency for robustness. We employ a more costly way to aggregate information, however the overall system becomes fault-tolerant. The actual aggregation is achieved by having the level $h - 1$ peers first distributing their aggregated values, by hashing, to the other level $h - 1$ peers. A recipient peer becomes responsible for a different subset of terms and aggregates their frequencies, thus performing (part of) the task that the root peer would perform. After the aggregation of the received term vectors, the peers send all their aggregated results to the other level $h - 1$ peers. In the end, all level $h - 1$ peers have the complete aggregated values locally available.

The reason for hashing is two-fold. First, it is important that all statistics for one particular term end up at the same node, in order to provide aggregated values per term. Second, the workload of the final aggregation is distributed and shared among the level $h - 1$ peers, thus achieving load-balancing.

Dissemination of Information. In the final phase, the aggregated term vectors are distributed to all participating peers. This is performed by using the hierarchy as a broadcast tree. The term vectors are sent using the tree, until they reach the level-0 peers. The size of the disseminated information is equal to the number of term vectors $(S_Z T)$ multiplied by the number of level $h - 1$ peers. The aggregated terms and document frequencies are now available at all peers locally. As a consequence, any peer can use this information, in order to provide rankings of terms and documents taking into account the global document collection. In the experimental section, we study the accuracy of relevant ranking between pairs of terms to demonstrate the effectiveness of our approach.

3.2   Local Term Selection Approaches

Feature selection algorithms can generally be categorised as either supervised or non-supervised. Supervised methods use provided labels or class assignments for documents. The best features are then selected according to their class labels and the distribution of the feature across classes. In many cases, however, class labels are not available. In the context of distributed collections, such labels are particularly rarely available due to reasons of missing common document types or the general ad-hoc character of the collections themselves. To perform feature selection nevertheless, unsupervised techniques – even though they are fewer than supervised ones – can be used. These methods mainly rely on frequency information of a feature or term within a collection and judge its usefulness.

Following the vector space model of information retrieval we use N as the number of documents in a collection (which can be either global, i.e. the whole collection, or local when only a subset of the collection is considered). Further we use $df(t)$ for the number of documents a term occurs in, also called the document frequency of term t. The number of occurrences of term t in document d is denoted to as the term frequency $tf(t,d)$. In this context, we propose the usage of the following unsupervised methods as possible local feature selection methods in the DESENT system.

Document Frequency (DF). One of the most prevalent techniques is denoted as document frequency thresholding. The main assumptions underlying document frequency thresholding are that terms occurring in very many documents carry less discriminative information and that terms occurring only in very few documents will provide a strong reduction in dimensionality (even though they might be discriminative in some cases). In combination with an upper and lower threshold, feature selection can be applied. This leads to results comparable to supervised techniques.

Collection Frequency (CF). The collection frequency of a term is given by the sum of all term frequencies for a given term (the total number of occurrences of a term in a collection):

$$cf(t) = \sum_{i=0}^{N} tf(t, d_i) \tag{1}$$

The collection frequency therefore ranks terms differently which occur only in few documents but with a higher term frequency.

Collection Frequency Inverse Document Frequency (CFIDF). The collection frequency inverse document frequency is represented by weighting the collection frequency values by the inverse document frequency for a term:

$$cfidf(t) = cf(t)log2(N/df(t)) \tag{2}$$

This measure can possibly cover both aspects the local document frequency and total number of occurrences for a term.

Term Frequency Document Frequency (TFDF). Another, quite recent technique to exploit both the *tf* and *df* factors is presented in [23]:

$$TFDF(t) = (n_1 n_2 + c(n_1 n_2 + n_2 n_3)) \tag{3}$$

n_1 denotes the number of documents in which t occurs, n_2 the number of documents t occurs only once, and $t3$ the number of documents containing t at least twice. An increasing weight c gives more weight for multiple occurrences.

Weirdness Factor (WF). The weirdness factor [1] was initially used to better distinguish special language text from rather common language use. The underlying idea is to identify terms which are very specific to a given collection. Terms have a high weirdness, i.e. are very specific to a given collection, if the ratio between relative local frequency and relative frequency in the reference collection is high:

$$weirdness(t) = \frac{\frac{cf_l(t)}{N_l}}{\frac{cf_r(t)}{N_r}} \tag{4}$$

Here, cf_l denotes the frequency of a term in the local collection, N_l the number of documents in the local collection; cf_r and N_r are the respective values for the reference corpus collection. In our case, we use the British national corpus as reference collection[1] which is a 100 million word corpus representing everyday English. This is feasible since all our collections are in English, otherwise reference corpora in other languages would be necessary.

3.3 Cost Analysis

We employ a simple cost analysis to assess the bandwidth consumption of the proposed approach. The basic parameters that influence the total communication cost (C_{total}) are: the number of peers (N_P) in the network, the average zone size (S_Z), the number of terms (T) in the term vectors propagated by each peer to its parent, and the size of the tuple representing each term (t_{size}). Each tuple of a term vector contains a term (we use as average size 16 characters for representation) and a frequency value (4 bytes). Hence, each tuple needs $t_{size}=20$ bytes. Moreover, each term vector is accompanied by a number (integer) that represents the number of documents associated with the term vector, however this cost is negligible compared to the size of the term vector. Notice that the height of the hierarchy (h) is derived as $h=log_{S_Z}N_P$.

The total number of terms (T_{up}) propagated upwards at each level is calculated by multiplying the number of peers (or initiators) at that level with the number of terms (T) per peer. Thus, the number of terms propagated up until the children of the root are given by:

$$T_{up} = \sum_{i=0}^{h-2}(\frac{N_P}{(S_Z)^i}T) = N_PT + \frac{N_P}{S_Z}T + \ldots + \frac{N_P}{(S_Z)^{h-2}}T \qquad (5)$$

Thus, the cost for propagating term vectors upwards can be derived as:

$$C_{up} = T_{up}t_{size} = N_PTt_{size}\sum_{i=0}^{h-2}\frac{1}{(S_Z)^i} \qquad (6)$$

There exists also a communication cost (C_h) related to hashing the information at the children of the root. Each child hashes its S_ZT term vectors to the other children, and the number of children is $\frac{N_P}{(S_Z)^{h-1}}$, leading to cost

$$C_{out} = S_ZTt_{size}\frac{N_P}{(S_Z)^{h-1}} = Tt_{size}\frac{N_P}{(S_Z)^{h-2}}$$

Then all children need to recollect the aggregated term vectors, leading to a cost $C_{in} = N_P(Tt_{size}\frac{N_P}{(S_Z)^{h-2}})$. Consequently, the total cost is equal to:

$$C_{total} = C_h + C_{up} = (C_{in} + C_{out}) + C_{up} = N_PTt_{size}(\frac{N_P+1}{(S_Z)^{h-2}} + \sum_{i=0}^{h-2}\frac{1}{(S_Z)^i}) \quad (7)$$

---

[1] http://www.natcorp.ox.ac.uk/

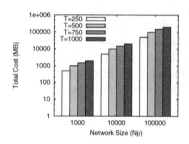

Fig. 2. Total cost (C_{total}) for hierarchical term aggregation

Obviously, compression techniques can further reduce the total cost, however this is out of the scope of this paper. Moreover, the cost for the creation of the DESENT hierarchy is described in [8] and it is not included in this analysis.

In Fig. 2, we graphically depict the total cost in MB for various networks sizes (N_P) ranging from 1K to 100K peers. We use varying values for T ranging from 250 to 1000 terms. Notice that the y-axis is in logarithmic scale. Notice that the total cost corresponds to approximately 1MB per peer, even for large network sizes. Moreover, the total cost is controlled by decreasing the T value.

4   Experiments

We conducted experiments using two document collections. The 20 newsgroups data set[2] consists 18,828 newsgroup documents labelled by and (nearly) evenly distributed across 20 different classes (the groups the articles were posted to). The DMOZ collection is a collection of 483,000 English web pages, which are classified by the DMOZ taxonomy[3]. The collection has been created by retrieving the web pages that are linked from the leaf-classes of the DMOZ taxonomy. The taxonomy path to a page is considered to be the class/category of the page. Both test collections were preprocessed in terms of tokenizing, stop word removal and stemming for the English language.

We identify the following basic parameters for our experiments and study their effect. First, the *number of partitions* or peers, as it affects the scalability of our approach. Then, *the distribution factor*, defined as the size distribution of the local partitions. A high distribution factor denotes equal amounts of documents per partition. Last, the *document similarity*, defined as the degree to which documents in one partition are similar to each other. This simulates cases such as topically homogeneous collections (with a high degree of similarity) or cases of randomly distributed collections. To this end, we use class labels of documents and distribute documents to partitions already containing similar documents, with a higher or lower probability according to the setting. In the case where no labels are available, document clustering could be used instead to determine a measure of similarity.

---

[2] http://people.csail.mit.edu/jrennie/20Newsgroups/
[3] http://www.dmoz.org

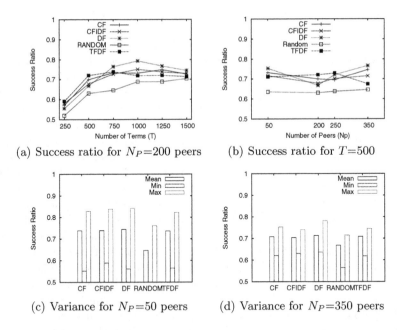

(a) Success ratio for $N_P=200$ peers   (b) Success ratio for $T=500$

(c) Variance for $N_P=50$ peers   (d) Variance for $N_P=350$ peers

Fig. 3. Experimental results for the 20 newsgroups collection

In our experimental evaluation we use varying settings, in order to simulate different use cases. We vary the number of peers to study the scalability of our approach. For each given number of peers, we apply four settings: 1) low similarity, high distribution, 2) low similarity, low distribution, 3) high similarity, high distribution, and 4) high similarity, low distribution. To be able to show the impact of all extreme values of both parameters, we also included mixed setups and also the case of documents which are distributed in equal sized partitions and have no similarity relation to each other at the other end of the spectrum. We apply the aforementioned feature selection methods at the local peer level and further added a random selection experiment to see the actual impact of the techniques with respect to no feature selection performed and to show the overall feasibility of the aggregation method.

4.1 Results for the 20 Newsgroups Collection

In Fig. 3, we study the quality of the aggregated document frequencies in terms of ranking. For this purpose, we define as *success ratio* the percentage of pairs of terms that have the same relative ranking in our approach and in the centralised case. In other words, for any two terms t_i and t_j the success ratio is the fraction of the number of such pairs with the same ranking with respect to the centralised ranking, over all possible combinations of pairs of terms. We chose this performance measure for existing approaches such as the Spearman or Kendall tau rank order correlation coefficients lack the support for rankings of

different lengths, our approach, however, is closely related and basically extends
these methods in its ability to handle different lengths of involved rankings.

Fig. 3(a) shows the results for a network of N_P=200 peers for varying values of T. All feature selection methods achieve high values of success ratio, and
the results improve with increasing T up to 1000 terms, since more information
is propagated upwards and aggregated. For larger values of T, most methods
exhibit a decrease in success ratio, due to more unimportant terms being aggregated thus causing noise, and this effect is stronger in small-size collections,
such as 20 newsgroups. Notice that even the random selection achieves good
performance, which is an argument in favour of the aggregation we employ –
the propagated results are similar to the central case. Naturally, the intentional
feature selection methods perform better by 10-15% except for the values obtained by the weirdness method which are omitted. In Fig. 3(b), we study the
scalability with number of peers. We fix T=500 and the chart shows that the
increased number of peers does not result in decreasing values of success ratio,
an important finding for the scalability of our approach. Especially for small
values of T the document frequency method is not the most stable one and
the collection frequency methods provide better results. However, the document
frequency performance increases with higher numbers of terms being aggregated.

In the following, we measure the mean values for the success ratio, along
with minima and maxima. The values in Fig. 3(c) show the values for a total
number of peers of N_P=50, while Fig. 3(d) shows the values for a total number
of N_P=350. The standard deviation of results obtained by document frequency
values for the smaller number of peers (Fig. 3(c)) is amongst the highest in
this setup. When looking at both plots it is apparent that the $CFIDF$ is the
more stable choice across different numbers of peers (and subsequently for higher
numbers of documents per peer).

4.2   Results on DMOZ Collection

Fig. 4 shows experimental results using the DMOZ collection, in a network of
N_P=784 peers. We provide the success ratio for a different number of terms

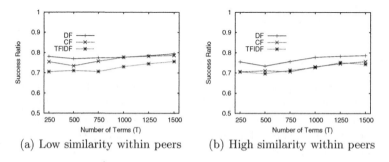

(a) Low similarity within peers   (b) High similarity within peers

Fig. 4. Experimental results for the DMOZ collection. Results are for two experimental
settings, low similarity within peers in 4(a), and high similarity in 4(b).

analogously to Fig. 3. However, in this case the number of terms to be aggregated has a smaller impact on performance. This confirms our finding that the number of documents per peer strongly influences the overall result. We show results for high similarity within peers in Fig. 4(a) and low similarity in Fig. 4(b). The document frequency selection method performs best and the results across different numbers of terms to be aggregated are more stable than with the other collection. Again, this is due to the higher number of average documents per peer for this collection.

5   Conclusions and Future Work

In this paper, we proposed an efficient approach for aggregating the document frequencies of carefully selected terms in a loosely-coupled P2P network of digital libraries. We provided a cost model to assess the requirements of our approach in terms of communication, and we performed experiments on two document collections to demonstrate the impact of local feature selection on and the quality of the aggregated values. In our future work, we intend to study the results of ranking obtained by our approach, for document retrieval using keyword-based queries. Further, we plan on investigating techniques to handle different numbers of documents per peer as this proved to be the most difficult setting in our experiments. Also, we want to perform a more thorough evaluation on very large test collections.

References

1. Ahmad, K., Gillam, L., Tostevin, L.: Weirdness indexing for logical document extrapolation and retrieval WILDER. In: TREC (1999)
2. Balke, W.-T.: Supporting information retrieval in peer-to-peer systems. In: Steinmetz, R., Wehrle, K. (eds.) Peer-to-Peer Systems and Applications. LNCS, vol. 3485, pp. 337–352. Springer, Heidelberg (2005)
3. Balke, W.-T., Nejdl, W., Siberski, W., Thaden, U.: DL Meets P2P – Distributed Document Retrieval Based on Classification and Content. In: Rauber, A., Christodoulakis, S., Tjoa, A.M. (eds.) ECDL 2005. LNCS, vol. 3652, pp. 379–390. Springer, Heidelberg (2005)
4. Balke, W.-T., Nejdl, W., Siberski, W., Thaden, U.: Progressive distributed top-k retrieval in peer-to-peer networks. In: Proc. of ICDE (2005)
5. Bender, M., Michel, S., Triantafillou, P., Weikum, G.: Global document frequency estimation in peer-to-peer web search. In: Proc. of the 9th Int. Workshop on the web and databases (2006)
6. Cuenca-Acuna, F., Peery, C., Martin, R., Nguyen, T.: PlanetP: Using gossiping to build content addressable peer-to-peer information sharing communities. In: Proc. of HPDC (2003)
7. Doulkeridis, C., Nørvåg, K., Vazirgiannis, M.: Scalable semantic overlay generation for P2P-based digital libraries. In: Gonzalo, J., Thanos, C., Verdejo, M.F., Carrasco, R.C. (eds.) ECDL 2006. LNCS, vol. 4172, pp. 26–38. Springer, Heidelberg (2006)

8. Doulkeridis, C., Nørvåg, K., Vazirgiannis, M.: DESENT: Decentralized and distributed semantic overlay generation in P2P networks. Journal on Selected Areas in Communications 25(1) (2007)
9. Lu, J., Callan, J.: Full-text federated search of text-based digital libraries in peer-to-peer networks. Information Retrieval 9(4) (2006)
10. Melink, S., Raghavan, S., Yang, B., Garcia-Molina, H.: Building a distributed full-text index for the web. ACM Transactions on Information Systems 19(3) (2001)
11. Michel, S., Triantafillou, P., Weikum, G.: MINERVA infinity: A scalable efficient peer-to-peer search engine. In: Alonso, G. (ed.) Middleware 2005. LNCS, vol. 3790, pp. 60–81. Springer, Heidelberg (2005)
12. Nottelmann, H., Fuhr, N.: Comparing different architectures for query routing in peer-to-peer networks. In: Lalmas, M., MacFarlane, A., Rüger, S.M., Tombros, A., Tsikrika, T., Yavlinsky, A. (eds.) ECIR 2006. LNCS, vol. 3936, pp. 253–264. Springer, Heidelberg (2006)
13. Papapetrou, O., Michel, S., Bender, M., Weikum, G.: On the usage of global document occurrences in peer-to-peer information systems. In: Proc. of COOPIS (2005)
14. Podnar, I., Luu, T., Rajman, M., Klemm, F., Aberer, K.: A P2P architecture for information retrieval across digital library collections. In: Gonzalo, J., Thanos, C., Verdejo, M.F., Carrasco, R.C. (eds.) ECDL 2006. LNCS, vol. 4172, pp. 14–25. Springer, Heidelberg (2006)
15. Raftopoulou, P., Petrakis, E.G.M., Tryfonopoulos, C., Weikum, G.: Information retrieval and filtering over self-organising digital libraries. In: Christensen-Dalsgaard, B., Castelli, D., Ammitzbøll Jurik, B., Lippincott, J. (eds.) ECDL 2008. LNCS, vol. 5173, pp. 320–333. Springer, Heidelberg (2008)
16. Sahin, O.D., Emekçi, F., Agrawal, D., Abbadi, A.E.: Content-based similarity search over peer-to-peer systems. In: Ng, W.S., Ooi, B.-C., Ouksel, A.M., Sartori, C. (eds.) DBISP2P 2004. LNCS, vol. 3367, pp. 61–78. Springer, Heidelberg (2005)
17. Skobeltsyn, G., Luu, T., Zarko, I.P., Rajman, M., Aberer, K.: Query-driven indexing for scalable peer-to-peer text retrieval. In: Proc. of Infoscale (2007)
18. Suel, T., Mathur, C., wen Wu, J., Zhang, J., Delis, A., Mehdi, Kharrazi, X.L., Shanmugasundaram, K.: Odissea: A peer-to-peer architecture for scalable web search and information retrieval. In: Proc. of WebDB (2003)
19. Tang, C., Dwarkadas, S.: Hybrid global-local indexing for efficient peer-to-peer information retrieval. In: Proc. of NSDI (2004)
20. Viles, C.L., French, J.C.: Dissemination of collection wide information in a distributed information retrieval system. In: Proc. of SIGIR (1995)
21. Viles, C.L., French, J.C.: On the update of term weights in dynamic information retrieval systems. In: Proc. of CIKM (1995)
22. Witschel, H.F.: Global term weights in distributed environments. Information Processing and Management 44(3) (2008)
23. Xu, Y., Wang, B., Li, J., Jing, H.: An extended document frequency metric for feature selection in text categorization. In: Li, H., Liu, T., Ma, W.-Y., Sakai, T., Wong, K.-F., Zhou, G. (eds.) AIRS 2008. LNCS, vol. 4993, pp. 71–82. Springer, Heidelberg (2008)
24. Zhang, J., Suel, T.: Efficient query evaluation on large textual collections in a peer-to-peer environment. In: Proc. of IEEE P2P (2005)
25. Zimmer, C., Tryfonopoulos, C., Berberich, K., Koubarakis, M., Weikum, G.: Approximate information filtering in peer-to-peer networks. In: Bailey, J., Maier, D., Schewe, K.-D., Thalheim, B., Wang, X.S. (eds.) WISE 2008. LNCS, vol. 5175, pp. 6–19. Springer, Heidelberg (2008)

Processes Are Data: A Programming Model for Distributed Applications

Alexander Böhm and Carl-Christian Kanne

University of Mannheim
Mannheim, Germany
{alex,cc}@db.informatik.uni-mannheim.de

Abstract. Many modern distributed applications employ protocols based on XML messages. Typical architectures for these applications follow an approach where messages are organized in queues, state is stored in DBMS, and application code is written in imperative languages. As a result, much developer productivity and system performance is wasted on handling conversions between the various data models (XML messages, objects, relations), and reliably managing persistent state for application instances. This overhead turns application servers into data management servers instead of process servers. We show how this model can be greatly improved by changing two aspects. Firstly, by using a declarative rule language to describe the processing logic. Secondly, by providing a single, unified data model based on XML messages that covers all kinds of data encountered, including process state. We discuss the resulting design choices for compile-time and run-time systems, and show and experimentally evaluate the performance improvements made possible.

1 Introduction

Many modern distributed applications employ protocols based on XML messages (e.g. Web Services [2]). Typical architectures for these applications follow an approach where messages are organized in queues, state is stored in DBMS, and application code is written in imperative languages. As a result, much developer productivity and system performance is wasted on handling conversions between the various data models (XML messages, objects, relations), and reliably managing persistent state for application instances. This overhead turns application servers into data management servers instead of process servers.

The goal of the Demaq project is to investigate a novel way of developing distributed applications. We believe that the state of the art can be greatly improved by changing two aspects. Firstly, by using a declarative rule language to describe the processing logic. Secondly, by providing a single, unified data model based on XML messages that covers all kinds of data encountered, including process state. This novel programming model leverages database technology for managing persistent application state and message processing. Our approach is motivated by the observation that the behavior of a node in a message-driven application is determined by all the messages it has seen so far. The externally

G. Vossen, D.D.E. Long, and J.X. Yu (Eds.): WISE 2009, LNCS 5802, pp. 43–56, 2009.

visible behavior of the node is represented by messages it sends to other nodes. Hence, the node's processing logic can be specified as a declarative query against the message history, and the result is a set of new messages to send. This way, we turn application processing into a declarative query processing problem. In an initial sketch of our vision of Demaq [8], we focused on the general concepts and language syntax, motivated by simple and elegant application specification and developer productivity.

In this paper, we turn towards the performance improvements made possible by our simple message-focused model. We look under the hood of our execution system, reviewing the involved design choices, and introduce techniques that allow to tune the language semantics and execution model to achieve highly concurrent execution and scalability.

Our main contributions include:

- We present the design of a solid transactional execution model for declarative messaging applications.
- We introduce a method to decouple garbage collection of irrelevant messages by allowing for the declarative specification of the relevant suffix of the message history in application programs.
- We introduce a variant of snapshot isolation optimized for message queues to improve concurrency of our run-time system.
- We present experimental results, comparing our implementation to a commercial application server.

The remainder of the paper is organized as follows. We present the elements of our programming model in Sec. 2. We elaborate on our declarative message processing language in Sec. 3, and discuss the corresponding execution model in Sec. 4. Sec. 5 gives a brief overview of our system implementation. Sec. 6 presents experimental results that show significant improvements in performance and scalability compared to a commercial application server. After briefly reviewing related work in Sec. 7, we conclude in Sec. 8.

2   Programming Model

Our programming model describes the application logic of a node in a distributed XML messaging application using two fundamental components.

XML message queues provide asynchronous communication facilities and allow for reliable and persistent message storage. *Declarative rules* operate on these message queues and are used to implement the application logic. Every rule specifies how to react to a message that arrives at a particular queue by creating another message (Figure 1).

XML Message Queues. Distributed messaging applications are based on *asynchronous* data exchange. Queue data structures are ideally suited for message management as they offer efficient message storage and retrieval operations while preserving the order of incoming data.

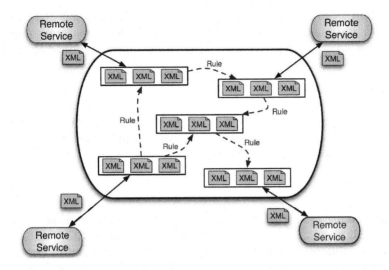

Fig. 1. Programming model

Apart from their typical functionality as intermediate message buffers, our model also uses persistent queues as internal representation of the application state. This approach is based on the observation that the state of every application instance in an individual node results from the messages sent to and received from its communication partners. Instead of *materializing* this state using a separate data model, it can alternatively be retrieved by *querying* the message flow. Hence, instead of a traditional queue semantics where messages are deleted after processing, messages have to be retained as long as they are necessary to compute the state of an instance. We discuss garbage collection in Sec. 3.2.

As logical data model, our message queues use the XQuery Data Model (XDM) [13]. Building on XDM allows us to incorporate existing XML processing systems such as stores and query processors without type system mismatches. For our purposes, XDM is particularly suited, as its fundamental type is the ordered sequence, which nicely captures message queue structure.

Declarative Rules. In our model, the processing logic of an application is specified as a set of declarative rules that operate on messages and queues. Each rule describes how to react to a single kind of event - the insertion of a new message into a queue. Depending on the structure and content of this message, rule execution results in the creation of new messages. These result messages can either become the input for other rules, or be sent to a remote system using queue-based communication facilities.

Our rule language is built on the foundation of XQuery [7]. It allows developers to directly access and interact with the XML messages stored in the queues. Thus, there is no mismatch between the type system of the application programs and the underlying communication format. Additionally, the content of messages and queues can be directly accessed within application programs without crossing system boundaries or requiring complex, intermediate APIs.

3 Language

Every Demaq application consists of three key components which we discuss in the following sections. These are message queues, application rules and user-defined message groups, called *slicings*.

3.1 Queues

Our programming model incorporates two different kinds of queues. *Gateway queues* provide communication facilities for the interaction with remote systems. There are two different kinds of gateway queues, *incoming* and *outgoing* ones. Messages that are placed into outgoing gateway queues are sent, while incoming gateway queues contain messages that have been received from remote nodes.

Queues are also used as persistent storage containers. These *basic queues* allow applications to store messages (e.g. reflecting intermediate results) without sending them to external systems. As a result, messages received from remote communication endpoints and internal state representation are handled in a uniform manner, simplifying application development.

3.2 Slicing the Message History

In Demaq, all application state is encoded in the message history. Rules access the state by posing queries against the history. Of course, processing queries against all existing messages for every processing step is inefficient, and the need to filter the relevant messages for every rule may lead to repetitive code. In addition, keeping the complete message history forever requires unbounded storage capacity. For these reasons, the Demaq language provides mechanisms to declare portions of the message history that are relevant in particular contexts, called *slicings*.

A slicing defines a family of *slices*, where each slice consists of all the messages with the same value for a particular part of the message (*slice key*). To identify the part of a message that should be used as the slice key - and thus as the basis for the partitioning - we rely on a subset of our XQuery-based rule language. Particularly, XPath [6] expressions are used to identify the part of a message that should be used as the slice key.

A slicing is created by specifying a unique name and the *slicing property*. The property definition lists a number of queues on which the slicing is defined. Messages from these queues are partitioned into *slices* according to their property value. All messages that share the same value of the slicing property become part of the same slice. Apart from providing convenient access to the relevant parts of the message history, slicings are also used to specify message retention policies.

Relevant Slice Suffix. Slicings declare which parts of the message history are relevant to the application and thus allow to identify obsolete messages which could be safely removed from the system to reclaim storage space. A simple, value-based partitioning is not enough, however, as it would still require to retain the complete, unbounded message history. Instead, we need a mechanism to specify which messages reflect the relevant application state, and which messages have become irrelevant and may thus be dropped.

To avoid unbounded buffering of message streams, *windows* have been proposed to specify relevant sub-streams [1] based on their position in a stream. The boundaries of such windows are based on the window size or relative to some landmark object in the stream, and the application developer must translate the message retention needs into window specifications.

In Demaq, we allow application developers to directly specify a condition that must be met by the messages that are sufficient to represent the current application state. Access to the slice then yields the smallest suffix which contains such a set of relevant messages. This very powerful semantics allows for a very intuitive, direct expression of relevance conditions on the message history.

To express message retention conditions, our language incorporates an additional construct. This `require` expression is an arbitrary XQuery expression of type boolean. Among all the contiguous sets of candidate messages in the slice that fulfill this condition, the most recent set is considered the currently relevant state of the slice. This set, and any messages more recent than that, are visible to the application. The `require` expression may refer to the candidate set of relevant messages using a special function (`qs:history()`). However, it may not refer to any other messages in the system. The reasons for this latter constraint are simple, efficient evaluation and garbage collection.

Since the `require` expression may not refer to other parts of the system state, and it always includes a complete suffix of the message history, and the fact that we chose the most recent qualifying set, we can guarantee a monotonous behavior of our relevant slice state: We can divide the slice into two parts, a relevant suffix (marked gray in Figure 2) and an irrelevant prefix. Our semantics guarantees that once a message belongs to the irrelevant prefix of a slice, it will never become relevant again. In other words, the boundary between relevant and irrelevant messages only moves toward more recent messages. Thus, it can be represented and tested using a simple message identifier or timestamp comparisons. This allows a simple, decoupled garbage collection strategy: If a message is no longer visible to any application rule because it is not part of any relevant suffix, it can be safely pruned from the message history. Consequentially, storage capacity can be reclaimed in a separate garbage collection process that never conflicts with rule evaluation.

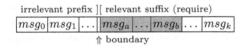

Fig. 2. Message history in a slice of size k+1

3.3 Application Rules

For our application rules, there is a significant overlap with the capabilities of existing, declarative XML query languages, in particular with XQuery [7]. XQuery allows for querying (sequences of) XML documents and document construction, supports XML data types, schema validation, etc.

Building on an existing language, such as XQuery, provides significant advantages. Developers can benefit from previous experience and reuse programming tools and development infrastructure. Additionally, existing query processing techniques can be potentially adapted to our application language. In the following sections, we discuss how the features required for building message-driven applications can be integrated into XQuery.

Assigning Application Rules. Every application rule is assigned to a single queue or slicing. Whenever a message gets inserted into this queue or slicing, the rule is evaluated with this message as the context item. In order to allow application developers to perform this association of rules to queues and slicings, we extend XQuery by incorporating an additional rule definition expression. Rule definition expressions can be used to give a unique name to an XQuery expression and assign it to a particular queue or slicing.

Optionally, an *error queue* can be defined for an application rule. Whenever a runtime error is encountered during the execution of this rule, a corresponding notification message is sent to this queue. Thus, this error handling mechanism allows other rules to handle this error. If no error queue is defined, error notifications are inserted into a system-provided, default error queue.

Enqueuing Messages. Every application rule describes how to react to a message by creating new messages and enqueuing them into local or gateway queues. While XQuery allows for the creation of arbitrary XML fragments, it does not incorporate any primitives for performing side effects. In our model, this is a severe restriction, as there is no possibility to modify the content of the queues underlying our application rules.

We adopt the extensions proposed by the XQuery Update Facility [10] to perform side effects on the message store. Every application rule is an updating expression that produces a (possibly empty) list of messages that have to be incorporated into the message store by enqueuing them to corresponding queues. In order to allow application programs to both specify the XML fragment to be enqueued as well as their target queue, we extend the XQuery Update Facility with an additional **enqueue message** update primitive.

Message Access. While XQuery incorporates powerful features to query (sequences of) XML documents, it does not provide operations for accessing the content of structures such as queues and slices. These read-only access operations can be easily provided by the runtime system in the form of external functions, particularly without requiring changes to the syntax or semantics of XQuery. In application rules, they are used to access the sequence of XML messages stored in a queue or slice.

Example. The example below illustrates the key building blocks of our declarative application language. First, we define two slicings that can be used to retrieve the master data and shopping cart items for a particular customer or transaction. These slicings are defined on the `customers` and `shoppingCart` queues and use XPath expressions to locate the customer/transaction ID in the respective messages. The `require` expressions are used to restrict the part of the message history that is returned by these slicings. For the customer master data, preserving the most recent item of the message history is sufficient, while the `require` expression `fn:false` for the cart items indicates that these items should never be removed from the message history.

In line 7, a new rule `handleCheckout` is defined for the `incomingMessages` queue. The corresponding rule body (lines 8 to 21) is evaluated every time a message is inserted into this queue. It mainly consists of XQuery expressions that are used to analyze the content of the incoming message and derive a result message. In lines 13 and 15, the slice access function `qs:slice` is used to access all relevant state information from the message history. Finally, after the result message has been created, the `enqueue message` expression is used to enqueue it to the `outgoingMessages` queue (line 20).

In this example, we omit the queue definitions expressions for the queues involved (e.g. `incomingMessages`) for reasons of brevity.

```
1  create slicing property masterDataForCustomer
2    queue customers value //customer/customerID require fn:count(qs:history()) eq 1;
3
4  create slicing property cartItemsForTransaction
5    queue shoppingCart value /cartItem/transaction/ID require fn:false();
6
7  create rule handleCheckout for incomingMessages let $request :=
8  //checkout return
9    if($request) then
10     let $transactionID := $request/transactionID/text()
11     let $customerID := $request/customerID/text()
12     let $customerData := qs:slice($customerID, "masterDataForCustomer")[last()]
13     let $customerOrders := qs:slice($transactionID, "cartItemsForTransaction")
14     let $result :=
15       <result>
16         <orderedItems>{$customerOrders//item}</orderedItems>
17         <delivery>{$customerData//address}</delivery>
18       </result>
19     return enqueue message $result into outgoingMessages
20    else();
```

4 Execution Model

The Demaq language provides simple, yet expressive primitives to describe desired reactions to messages in terms of the message history. The use of a declarative language for rule bodies allows data independence and efficient execution using a query optimizer.

Our objective is to create an elegant way to completely specify stateful messaging applications, and not only to monitor or analyze message streams - we not only want to read state, but to modify it. Hence, a crucial aspect of the Demaq design is to define how state can be managed in a reliable way and - at the same time - allow for an efficient and scalable application execution.

The design issues in this context revolve around the transactional coupling of rule execution to the message store. It turns out that modeling both requests and state information as messages yields novel opportunities to improve execution performance. A major reason for this is the append-only strategy for the message history: We never perform in-place updates. As a consequence, there is much less need to synchronize concurrent execution threads, and there are fewer ways how a concurrent modification of the system state can cause conflicts.

The Demaq execution model captures the typical behavior of message-driven applications in a few simple rules and guarantees which are observed by the runtime system. It precisely determines Demaq rule semantics, and at the same time leaves enough freedom for an actual implementation to optimize runtime performance, as we will see in Sec. 5.

Core Processing Loop. The fundamental behavior of messaging applications can be described as a simple loop that (1) decides which message(s) to process next, (2) determines the reaction to that message based on the message contents and application state, and (3) effects the reaction by creating new messages. Actual implementations of the Demaq model may use any form of processing loop(s) that obeys the following constraints:

1. Each message is processed exactly once. This means that the evaluation of all rules defined for the message's queue and slicings are triggered once for every message.
2. Rules are evaluated by determining the result of the rule body as defined by XQuery (update) semantics, extended by the built-in function definitions described in Sec. 3.3. The result is a sequence of pending update operations in the form of messages to enqueue.
3. The overall result of rule evaluation for a message is the concatenation of the pending actions of the individual rules in some non-deterministic order.
4. Processing the pending actions for a message is atomic, i.e. after a successful rule evaluation all result messages are added to the message history in one atomic transaction, which also marks the trigger message as processed.
5. All rule evaluations for the same trigger message see the same snapshot of the message history, which contains all messages enqueued prior to the trigger message, but none of the messages enqueued later. This is motivated by the interpretation of each rule as an isolated statement of fact about the system behavior – if a certain situation arises, a certain action will eventually happen, no matter what other rules are defined for the same situation.

The above list includes strong transactional guarantees necessary to implement reliable state-dependent applications, but still allows many alternative strategies to couple message processing to a transactional message store.

Note that the above model does not allow for message store transactions that span rules. However, application developers do have some control over the amount of decoupled, asynchronous execution: The expressive power of XQuery allows the bundling of complex processing steps into single rules, which are executed in a single transaction and hence allow to constrain the visibility of intermediate results to concurrent transactions. Further, application developers can isolate intermediate messages in local queues that are not accessed by conflicting control paths.

Enqueue-Time Snapshot Isolation. To achieve a maximum of concurrency, our message store uses a variant of snapshot isolation [5] that is made possible by our unified message-based view of state and requests. In general, snapshot isolation freezes the system state visible to a transaction by creating a private version of the state. This avoids locking and improves concurrency, but requires the retention of old state versions and conflict resolution policies.

In our programming model, guaranteeing snapshot isolation is very cheap, because the management of old state versions is trivial. As there are no in-place updates, we can access old versions of the system state by just ignoring newer messages. We simplify this by using the enqueue-time of the trigger message as begin-of-transaction (snapshot) time for our rule evaluation . Hence, rule evaluation can see only all messages enqueued prior to the trigger message. Concurrent rule evaluation transactions do not need to lock parts of the history because updates by definition do not affect their visible part of the message history. We only need to synchronize the message writing transactions to guarantee atomic insertion of result messages. Note that deadlock handling is simple, as the complete set of updates is known before the first update needs to be performed. This strategy tremendously improves the concurrency and scalability of our application engine because very few short-term locks are required for synchronization.

5   System

In this section, we outline the architecture and implementation of the Demaq system that implements our programming model.

When deploying a Demaq application, a rule compiler is used to transform the application specification into execution plans for the runtime system. The runtime system consists of three major components. A transactional XML queue store provides an efficient and reliable message storage. Remote messaging and transport protocol aspects are handled by the communication system. The rule execution engine executes the plans generated by the rule compiler.

Rule Compiler. The purpose of the rule compiler is to transform applications into optimized execution plans for the runtime system. For this compiler, optimization opportunities exist on several levels of an application.

Rule-set rewriting. We can change the overall structure of an application by modifying its set of rules. For example, the compiler merges all rules defined on the same queue into a single, combined rule. This simplifies factorizing common subexpressions across rules and saves the runtime system from invoking the rule execution component multiple times for a single message.

Rule-body rewriting. A significant part of our programming language consists of the XQuery Update Facility, and many optimization techniques developed for XQuery can also be applied to our application rules. To profit from these techniques without reimplementing all of them, the compiler can split rule bodies into two parts, one processed by the Demaq rule execution engine, and one processed by the message store. In case of XQuery-enabled message stores (as is the case in our current implementation), the store-processed part is simply rewritten into an XQuery expression without Demaq-specific constructs, which can then be optimized by the store's XQuery compiler.

Physical optimization. Platform-specific rewrites may be performed to speed up application processing. For example, our runtime system incorporates a special operation which works similar to a link in Unix file systems. This operation avoids a full copy of the message when messages are forwarded unchanged from one queue to another. Another example for a runtime-specific optimization is template folding [19].

Rule Execution Engine. The rule execution engine implements our execution model described in Sec. 4. It decides when and in which order messages from the queue store should be processed, how to incorporate updates, and when to send or receive messages from the communication system. The main challenge in the design of a rule execution engine is to exploit the degrees of freedom of the execution model to provide high processing performance and message throughput. For this purpose, our system relies on multiple concurrent execution threads. Another issue is to find suitable garbage collection strategies to achieve an optimal balance between reclaiming storage capacity and runtime overhead.

Transactional XML Queue Store. Our message store is built on the foundation of a native XML base management system. Our current implementation alternatively uses Natix [14], a research prototype of a native XML data store, or IBM DB/2 Version 9. While XML-enabled database systems provide efficient and reliable XML document processing facilities, they usually manage XML repositories as collections, which are unordered sets of XML documents. As our programming model requires queue-based message storage, a main challenge was to replace the existing, collection-based data handling and recovery facilities to support a queue-based management model. We incorporated these changes into the Natix system. They allow us to use the efficient XML storage facilities as well as the sophisticated recovery and schema management features of Natix for our message queues. For DB/2, we simulate queue-based storage using auxiliary tables. Another challenge is to provide efficient access to the message history.

For this purpose, we rely on the persistent B-Tree indexes provided by the Natix system which we use to implement slicings. Additionally, Natix incorporates our specialized version of Snapshot Isolation (see Sec. 4).

Communication System. The communication system provides all remote communication facilities. It implements both asynchronous and synchronous transfer protocols (such as HTTP and SMTP), and thus allows applications to interact with various types of external communication endpoints.

6   Experiments

In this chapter, we provide a brief experimental evaluation of our programming model. For this purpose, we use the Demaq runtime system introduced in the last section to execute an exemplary online shopping application. The complete source code of this application and additional application examples - such as a Demaq implementation of the TPC-App Application Server benchmark - are available at our project website http://www.demaq.net/.

We also implemented the application as a BPEL process and executed it on a commercial, enterprise-class application server with a relational database back-end. Unfortunately, licensing restrictions do not allow to disclose details about the system, let alone vendor name and software version. However, we believe that the results help to evaluate the performance of our implementation in the light of one of the most advanced application servers available today.

Setup. All measurements were performed on a server equipped with an AMD Athlon 64 X2 Processor 4600, 2 GB of main memory, running Opensuse Linux 10.3. This system was used to run the BPEL application server and our native runtime system with Natix as the underlying message store. An additional client computer was used to send messages via HTTP.

In order to get an impression of the runtime to expect during the following measurements, we first performed an exemplary run of our online shopping application, consisting of 24 messaging operations: The client connects to the server, adds both 10 books and music items (each reflected by a message of 2.5 KB) to the shopping carts, requests the total value of both music and book items, and finally performs a checkout operation. This run was repeated 100 times to reduce the effects of statistical outliers.

The application server required an average of 6.25 seconds in order to run the scenario. Using our native implementation, the same run took 2.18 seconds, which confirms that native XML data handling and avoiding a multi-tiered architecture can help to improve application runtime.

Performance Impact of Context Size. In order to investigate the impact of context size on the runtime performance, we subsequently add 10000 books (each 2.5 KB in size) to the shopping cart of a single application instance. While a single customer buying thousands of books is rather unlikely for our online shopping example, handling thousands of messages in a single application context is no uncommon scenario in other application domains [4].

Figure 3 visualizes the round-trip-time (in seconds) for each request. With growing instance size, the response times of the application server deteriorate. This effect might be caused by performing an in-place update on the corresponding data structure of the runtime context and writing it back to the database back-end. In our runtime system, every additional book can be appended to a queue of the system, thus leaving the response time virtually unaffected.

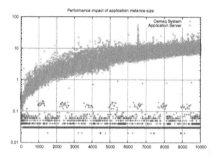

Fig. 3. Effect of context size

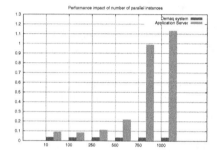

Fig. 4. Effect of active instances

Parallel Application Instances. In this experiment, we investigate the impact of multiple concurrent, active instances, each of them storing 100 book orders (250 KB) and 10 music orders (25 KB). We analyze how the response time of the systems change with an increasing number of parallel instances. For this purpose, our client sequentially requests the server to calculate the overall price of the music order items for each instance.

Figure 4 depicts the average response time (in seconds) for answering a client request. An increasing number of active instances has a considerable impact on the response times of the application server performing expensive instance management operations. For our runtime system, there are no instances that need to be managed. Instead, all messages that belong to a particular context are retrieved by querying the message store. Thus, an increasing number of parallel instances does not interfere with the response time.

7   Related Work

Application Servers Today, distributed applications are usually executed by multi-tier application servers [2]. For XML messaging applications, these tiers typically consist of queue-based communication facilities (e.g. [16,18]), a runtime component executing the application logic, and a database management system that provides persistent state storage. An additional transaction processing monitor ensures that transactional semantics are preserved across tiers.

Application servers allow for the convenient deployment of applications in distributed and heterogeneous environments. However, their use entails several problems which are discussed in literature. These problems include significant functional overlap and redundancy between the different tiers [17,20], and complex and brittle configuration and customization caused by multi-layer, multivendor environments [2]. Further, frequent representation changes between data formats (XML, format of the runtime component, relational database management system) decrease the overall performance [15].

Data Stream Management Systems Data stream management systems (DSMS) and languages (e.g. [1,12]) are targeted at analyzing, filtering and aggregating items from a stream of input events, again producing a stream of result items. Several stream management systems rely on declarative programming languages to describe patterns of interest in an event or message stream. In most cases, these languages extend SQL with primitives such as window specification, pattern matching, or stream-to-relation transformation [3].

In contrast to application servers that provide reliable and transactional data processing, stream management systems aim at low latency and high data throughput. To achieve these goals, data processing is mainly performed in main memory (e.g. based on automata [12] or operators [1]). Thus, in case of application failures or system crashes, no state recovery may be performed, and data can be lost.

XML Query and Programming Languages For an XML message processing system, choosing a native XML query language such as XPath [6] or XQuery [7] as a foundation for a programming language seems to be a natural choice. However, these query languages lack the capability to express application logic that is based on the process state - they are functional query languages with (nearly) no side effects. There are various approaches [9,11,15] to evolve XQuery into a general-purpose programming language that can be used without an additional host programming language.

8   Conclusion

We investigate a new programming model for distributed applications based on XML messaging. In our system, a declarative language that directly operates on messages and queues describes the processing logic in terms of message-driven rules. Application state is modeled exclusively using the message history. By treating application instance management as a data management problem best addressed by a data management server, we get a fresh perspective on how to optimize the architecture of application servers. A result is improved scalability of our execution engine to large numbers of concurrent application instances: In particular, we can avoid loading and saving the complete application state from a database for every processing step, which tends to take up a large fraction of conventional application servers' processing resources. A brief performance evaluation of our runtime system confirms the potential of the proposed approach. It also illustrates the practical benefits of treating process instances as data in terms of scalability and performance.

References

1. Abadi, D.J., Carney, D., Çetintemel, U., et al.: Aurora: a new model and architecture for data stream management. VLDB J. 12(2), 120–139 (2003)
2. Alonso, G., Casati, F., Kuno, H., Machiraju, V.: Web Services: Concepts, Architectures and Applictions. Springer, Heidelberg (2004)
3. Arasu, A., Babu, S., Widom, J.: The CQL continuous query language: semantic foundations and query execution. VLDB J. 15(2), 121–142 (2006)
4. Arasu, A., Cherniack, M., Galvez, E.F., et al.: Linear Road: A stream data management benchmark. In: VLDB, pp. 480–491 (2004)
5. Berenson, H., Bernstein, P.A., Gray, J., et al.: A critique of ANSI SQL isolation levels. In: SIGMOD Conference, pp. 1–10 (1995)
6. Berglund, A., Boag, S., Chamberlin, D., et al.: XML path language (XPath) 2.0. Technical report, W3C (January 2007)
7. Boag, S., Chamberlin, D., Fernández, M.F., et al.: XQuery 1.0: An XML query language. Technical report, W3C (January 2007)
8. Böhm, A., Kanne, C.-C., Moerkotte, G.: Demaq: A foundation for declarative XML message processing. In: CIDR, pp. 33–43 (2007)
9. Bonifati, A., Ceri, S., Paraboschi, S.: Pushing reactive services to XML repositories using active rules. Computer Networks 39(5), 645–660 (2002)
10. Chamberlin, D., Florescu, D., Melton, J., et al.: XQuery Update Facility 1.0. Technical report, W3C (August 2007)
11. Chamberlin, D.D., Carey, M.J., Florescu, D., et al.: Programming with XQuery. In: XIME-P (2006)
12. Demers, A.J., Gehrke, J., Panda, B., et al.: Cayuga: A general purpose event monitoring system. In: CIDR, pp. 412–422 (2007)
13. Fernández, M.F., Malhotra, A., Marsh, J., et al.: XQuery 1.0 and XPath 2.0 data model (XDM). Technical report, W3C (January 2007)
14. Fiebig, T., Helmer, S., Kanne, C.-C., et al.: Anatomy of a Native XML base management system. VLDB Journal 11(4), 292–314 (2003)
15. Florescu, D., Grünhagen, A., Kossmann, D.: XL: a platform for Web Services. In: CIDR (2003)
16. Foch, C.B.: Oracle streams advanced queuing user's guide and reference, 10g release 2 (10.2) (2005)
17. Gray, J.: Thesis: Queues are databases. In: Proceedings 7th High Performance Transaction Processing Workshop, Asilomar CA (1995)
18. IBM. WebSphere MQ (2009), http://www.ibm.com/software/integration/wmq/
19. Kanne, C.-C., Moerkotte, G.: Template folding for XPath. In: Third International Workshop on XQuery Implementation, Experience and Perspectives (2006)
20. Stonebraker, M.: Too much middleware. SIGMOD Record 31(1), 97–106 (2002)

OfficeObjects Service Broker – An Intelligent Service Integration Platform*

Michał Gajewski, Witold Staniszkis, and Jakub Strychowski

Rodan Systems S.A.
Poland

Abstract. We present a brief description of a service integration platform developed by Rodan Systems as the result of the eGov-Bus project with the use of the proprietary OfficeObjects® information management tool set.

1 Introduction

Service engineering has become a rapidly expanding field in all IT application domains. We are presenting a J2EE service development platform implemented in a JSR 286 compliant portal environment. Research and development work, effected with the use of the OfficeObjects® software tools [1], has partially been funded by the eGov-Bus project.. The subsequent product engineering and deployment has been fuelled by its commercial success. The principal research results underlying the development work have been presented in [2,3].

The principal design goal has been development of a complex service development and deployment platform featuring dynamic workflow management facility and advanced knowledge management tools. Generic service specifications may be developed to support solutions within arbitrary IT application domains. Indeed up to date OfficeObjects® Service Broker has been deployed as the eGovernment service environment as well as the B2B integration platform.

2 OfficeObjects Service Broker Features

OfficeObjects® Service Broker may be installed within any JSR 286 portal environment and its portlet-based GUI may be customized according to the application domain requirements. Product software components may be deployed within a distributed architecture of physical or virtual server clusters, thus supporting scalable and fault-tolerate service solutions. The principal system components comprise the dynamic workflow management platform (OfficeObjects® WorkFlow), the knowledge management subsystem (OfficeObjects® Ontology Manager), the electronic form subsystem (OfficeObjects® eForms) and the service information object repository (OfficeObjects® Intelligent Document Manager).

---

* This work has been supported by the European Commission Project eGov-Bus FP
IST-.-2004-26727.

The product run-time features are represented among others by such portlets as the service categorisation tree, the workflow task list, the service information object repository management functions, and the knowledge representation search and manipulation functions. The service development environment integrated within the system ontology model comprise the BPMN process graphic modelling tool, the electronic form modelling and specification tool, and the service ontology modelling tool.

The adaptable workflow management features support specification and deployment of generic complex service processes orchestrating the underlying web services, legacy applications, and human workflow participants. The adaptable workflow process specification includes the BPMN topology model, the process rules defined with the use of the OfficeObject® WorkFlow BPQL (Business Process Query Language), such as among others the routing rules, the workflow participant assignment rules, and the pre- and post-conditions, the process ontology model and the process meta-model application dependent extensions. The principal human participant interface is constituted by the process electronic documents represented by intelligent electronic forms featuring rule-base presentation and access control.

The dynamic workflow adaptability has been implemented by the unique dynamic process modification technique featuring abstract BPQL rules bound at run-time with the use of decision trees and concrete BPQL rules defines within the process ontology.

The OfficeObjects® Ontology Model is based on the Topic Map notation [4] extended by a scripting language TMSL (Topic Maps Scripting Language) comprising such features as topic manipulation, TM model integrity constraint specification, and forward-chaining reasoning. The extensible Topic Map model featuring a generative GUI provides the service ontology specification tools as well as a generic knowledge modelling environment.

The service design methodology presented in [3] comprises all necessary steps and techniques required for the complete service specification and deployment within the target portal environment. The current application portfolio includes solutions accessible via open Internet as well as the SOA integration solutions deployed within restricted access Intranets.

References

1. OfficeObjects® Products, Rodan Systems S.A (2009), http://www.rodan.pl
2. The Administrative Process Generator, eGov-Bus Deliverable Report D 7.1 (2006), http://www.egov-bus.org
3. Draft Detailed Specification of the eGov-Bus Prototype, eGov-Bus Deliverable D 8.1 (2008), http://www.egov-bus.org
4. ISO/IEC 13250, Topic Maps, Information Technology Document Description and Processing Languages (December 1999)

PSILOC World Traveler: Overcoming the Challenges of Adopting Wide–Scale Mobile Solutions

Michał Sieczko

Psiloc sp. z o.o.
Poland

Abstract. The mobile software marketplace today faces several challenges, and companies that aspire to global success in this market must face them holistically or not at all. While many companies are able to market products that prove to be successful in one or two isolated areas, their failure to adopt wide scale solutions means that however innovative their products might be, they are limited in their success by their lack of integration within a simple user experience. PSILOC has shown how innovatively created services may be integrated within an open–platform architecture so that mobile software companies can address all the needs of their increasingly demanding mobile phone customers within a sleek, easy–to–use interface.

World Traveler Platform Case Study

For software companies operating in the rapidly changing mobile software marketplace, keeping ahead of the competition is essential to survival. PSILOC has wagered that a single product, World Traveler, is the next logical step in mobile services integration. Beyond the scope of traditional mobile applications, World Traveler solves many of the problems associated with offering services to mobile phone customers by providing an integrated business platform within which any number of services may be accessed and purchased by customers. Publically released in June 2009 on the Symbian platform, World Traveler improves business travel efficiency by providing an intuitive experience to access the information and resources customers need to simplify their travel experience. With thousands of users downloading World Traveler every day and already more than 100,000 users in the first 30 days of availability. World Traveler offers a broad customer base for companies interested in offering their services to travelers.

Usability Challenge. Mobile devices put major constraints on software interaction with users. Many mobile devices offer only a relatively small screen which limits the amount of information that can be displayed at once. Additionally, limited keyboard selection capabilities further complicate this challenge. PSILOC has taken its leading expertise with mobile applications and scrutinized competing software offerings to find many areas where its strength of experience on the Symbian platform could be leveraged to deliver a superior customer experience both in terms of intuitiveness and reliability. World Traveler's graphic user interface design and user experience has already been applauded by trend–setting bloggers and most notably, by Nokia Corporation.

G. Vossen, D.D.E. Long, and J.X. Yu (Eds.): WISE 2009, LNCS 5802, pp. 59–60, 2009.

Software Distribution Challenge. Distribution (hence, ease of access to services) is the key to success. Most customers still find it tiresome to install applications on their devices. As a member of the Nokia Forum PRO, PSILOC has access to the latest devices and prototypes. PSILOC builds software for models prior to general release and early adopters and opinion leaders appreciate that PSILOC is ready with hardware–tested solutions for them out–of–the–box. Later, this advantage significantly drives widespread adoption because while competitors products remain in their infancy, PSILOC offers a mature, sleek interface so customers can get on with working with our services rather than struggling to get them to work.

Software Engineering Challenge. When designing and building its application architecture, PSILOC not only had to technically address all these challenges but do so under strictly enforced development deadlines set by Nokia's devices release dates. The solution was to deliver fully functional software with upgrades freely available as new services were added. The main architectural concepts include: A) extensibility via plug–ins available for download directly from within the application. B) automatic application upgrades C) a content–driven client–server application with automatically updated information.

Challenge of Scale. Because of the number of devices on which World Traveler was to be used, PSILOC addressed performance and availability issues with special care taken on all aspects of the service backend. This backend is comprised of a geographically dispersed server network that informs the client application of which server to use. Such a strategy allows for not only a number of local fall–back servers but also provides easy load–balancing of traffic all across the globe.

Business Model Challenge. The mobile application marketplace remains limited in its methods of generating revenue streams and monetizing services. There is a comparatively limited span of payment options with a long value chain and competition within the chain contributes to the current limited range of options for paid services. Taking this under consideration, PSILOC realizes that a single company may only offer travel services within its scope of expertise and for this reason, has invited recognized market players to participate by becoming members of the World Traveler platform and developing their own plug–ins for services. Third parties with compelling products can now benefit from a mass distribution scale without the delay and hassle of developing proprietary narrow–channel distribution systems. Third parties benefit from a sleek, integrated business platform for delivering services, PSILOC benefits from a growing customer base thanks to more services becoming available sooner which benefits everyone by making the utility of World Traveler continue to grow at a rapid pace impossible to any one service provider.

Challenge of being an Alternative to the Internet as a Gateway to Services. Traditional services offer mobile applications as an alternative interface to the web front–end. PSILOC has focused on the mobile handset as a prime alternative to the internet because it is the natural context for travelers. Over time, it is estimated that for certain computing applications, mobile handsets will become the primary gateway to services while web front–end services will become secondary as customers increasingly turn to their phones —especially when on the move.

ETSI Industry Specification Group on Autonomic Network Engineering for the Self-managing Future Internet (ETSI ISG AFI)

Ranganai Chaparadza[1], Laurent Ciavaglia[2], Michał Wódczak[3],
Chin-Chou Chen[4], Brian A. Lee[5], Athanassios Liakopoulos[6],
Anastasios Zafeiropoulos[6], Estelle Mancini[7], Ultan Mulligan[7], Alan Davy[8],
Kevin Quinn[8], Benoit Radier[9], Nancy Alonistioti[10], Apostolos Kousaridas[10],
Panagiotis Demestichas[11], Kostas Tsagkaris[11], Martin Vigoureux[3],
Laurent Vreck[7], Mick Wilson[12], and Latif Ladid[13]

[1]Fraunhofer FOKUS, [2]Alcatel-Lucent, [3]Telcordia Technologies, [4]Chunghwa Telecom
Labs, [5]Telefon AB LM Ericsson, [6]GRNET, [7]ETSI, [8]Waterford Institute of
Technology, [9]France Telecom, [10]University of Athens, [11]University of Piraeus
Research Center, [12]FUJITSU Laboratories of Europe, [13]IPv6 Forum

A Call for Contributions to the Specifications for Self-managing Future Network Devices

The area of Autonomic/Self-Managing Networks is still faced with problems of the lack of harmonized steps and efforts towards the establishment of common Specifications of the architectures and functionalities for Self-Management within Future Networks such as the envisaged Future Internet. Ideally, the harmonization can now be achieved through a newly established and well-focused Special Working Group in ETSI – a world renowned Telecommunications Standardization body. The Special Working Group is an Industry Specification Group (ISG) called "Autonomic network engineering for the self-managing Future Internet (AFI) [4]. The AFI aims to serve as a focal point for the development of common Specifications and engineering frameworks that guarantee interoperability of nodes/devices for Self-managing Future Networks.

In [1], [2], the authors ague that, whether an evolutionary approach or revolutionary approach could be taken towards designing the Future Internet, there is a requirement for a Generic Autonomic Network Architecture (GANA) – an architectural Reference Model that allows for the production of "Standardizable" Specifications of Autonomic Behaviors, i.e. Self-* functions of context-aware, policy-driven autonomic Decision-Making-Elements (DMEs) that potentially exhibit cognitive properties, designed for the self-management of diverse networking environments and nodes thereof. We believe that, from such a common, unified architectural Reference Model, either clean-slate based architectural requirements and implementations (which could be similar to the ones addressed in [3]) or incremental evolutionary architectural requirements and implementations

G. Vossen, D.D.E. Long, and J.X. Yu (Eds.): WISE 2009, LNCS 5802, pp. 61–62, 2009.

should then be derived, such that the experiences gained during the implementations can then be used for the evolution and further development of the GANA Reference Model. In [2], authors present how a viable Evolution Path for today's network models, paradigms and protocols like IPv6, can be created as guided by the GANA Reference Model.

In [2], the authors present the rationale behind the call for contributions to the development of a Standardizable Reference Model for autonomic network engineering that should be used as a guide for creating an Evolution Path towards the Self-Managing Future Internet. In [2], different instantiations of the GANA approach (though the GANA is still evolving and is calling for contributions from diverse stakeholders), are presented, which demonstrate its use for the management of a wide range of functions and services, including both, basic network services such as Autonomic Routing and Autonomic Monitoring, as well as enhanced ones such as Autonomic Mobility and Quality of Service (QoS) Management. In order to further develop the GANA Specifications, Requirements Specifications for the desired properties of the Self-Managing Future Internet must be specified by the AFI, and should then be used as input to the development of the GANA. Therefore, contributions to Requirements Specifications must come from end-users, operators, content-providers, etc. We argue that the contributions to GANA must come from the Services/Applications development community as well as the networking community, in order to ensure that the GANA Specifications take into account the behavior of the Services/Applications Layer and its need to inter-work with the adaptive mechanisms of the underlying Network Layer. Therefore, the main motivation of this paper is to bring about awareness to wider communities that potentially can provide input to the activities of the AFI by contributing to the Group Specifications to be produced by AFI in 2010, which are meant to guarantee interoperability for nodes/devices of Self-managing Future Networks such as Future Internet.

References

1. Chaparadza, R.: Requirements for a Generic Autonomic Network Architecture (GANA), suitable for Standardizable Autonomic Behaviour Specifications of Decision-Making-Elements (DMEs) for Diverse Networking Environments. International Engineering Consortium (IEC) in the Annual Review of Com. 61 (December 2008)
2. Chaparadza, R., Papavassiliou, S., Kastrinogiannis, T., Vigoureux, M., Dotaro, E., Davy, A., Quinn, K., Wódczak, M., Toth, A., Liakopoulos, A., Wilson, M.: Creating a viable Evolution Path towards Self-Managing Future Internet via a Standardizable Reference Model for Autonomic Network Engineering. In: FIA Prague 2009 Conference (2009); published in the Future Internet Book produced by FIA
3. Greenberg, A., et al.: A clean slate 4D approach to network control and management. ACM SIGCOMM Computer Comm. Review 35(5), 41–54 (2005)
4. AFI_ISG: Autonomic network engineering for the self-managing Future Internet (AFI), http://portal.etsi.org/afi

Facing Tagging Data Scattering

Oscar Díaz, Jon Iturrioz, and Cristóbal Arellano

ONEKIN Research Group, University of the Basque Country,
San Sebastián, Spain
{oscar.diaz,jon.iturrioz,cristobal-arellano}@ehu.es
http://www.onekin.org/

Abstract. Web2.0 has brought tagging at the forefront of user practises for organizing and locating resources. Unfortunately, these tagging efforts suffer from a main drawback: lack of interoperability. Such situation hinders tag sharing (e.g. tags introduced at *del.icio.us* to be available at *Flickr*) and, in practice, leads to tagging data to be locked to tagging sites. This work argues that for tagging to reach its full potential, *tag management systems* should be provided that accounts for a common way to handle tags no matter the tagging site (e.g. *del.icio.us, Flickr*) that frontended the tagging. This paper introduces *TAGMAS* (TAG MAnagement System) that offers a global view of *your* tagging data no matter where it is located. By capitalizing on *TAGMAS*, tagging applications can be built in a quicker and robust way. Using measurements and one use case, we demonstrate the practicality and performance of *TAGMAS*.

Keywords: Tagging sites, Web2.0, Datasets.

1 Introduction

Tagging, i.e. the activity of associating keywords with resources, has proved to be an effective mechanism for locating and organizing user resources [11]. Places where tagging is conducted, i.e. tagging sites, can be numerous. Indeed, it is very common for users to keep an account in distinct tagging sites depending on a broad range of issues: the resource type (e.g. if bookmarks then, *del.icio.us*; if video then, *Youtube*), the utilities offered by the site (e.g. if LaTeX references need to be obtained, *CiteULike* might be a better option that *del.icio.us*), the supporting community (e.g. if music-related resources such as mp3, videos, lyrics are the resources to tag, *lastfm.com* could be an appropriate site), confidentiality (e.g. if restrict sharing is an issue, you might favour to use *www.bookmarks2.com* rather than *del.icio.us* where private bookmarks are cumbersome to handle), etc. Therefore, tageable resources will most likely be scattered throughout the Web.

Unfortunately, these tagging efforts suffer from a main drawback: lack of interoperability (i.e. *"the ability of two or more systems or components to exchange information and to use the information that has been exchanged"* [4]). Both the tagging process and tagging description differ across tagging sites. Communication protocols, tagging schemas, APIs or graphical-user interfaces, all exhibit considerable variations. This causes tagging sites to become silos with at best a proprietary API. Such situation

G. Vossen, D.D.E. Long, and J.X. Yu (Eds.): WISE 2009, LNCS 5802, pp. 63–74, 2009.

jeopardizes both sharing (e.g. tags introduced at *del.icio.us* to be available at *Flickr*) and holistic viewing (e.g. posing global queries such as resources being tagged as *"Poznan"* no matter which tagging site keeps them). Indeed, a tag set stands for a user's conceptual model about how to describe the content (e.g. tag *"Ajax"*), purpose (e.g. tag *"forProject1"*) or quality (tag *"interesting"*) of resources [8,9]. Such conceptual model is site independent. Unfortunately, there is not currently support for such a holistic view.

This paper describes a **"tag management component"**, *TAGMAS*, that allows for a common way to handle tags no matter the tagging site (e.g. *delicious, Flickr*) that frontended the tags. *TAGMAS* is proposed as an application for *WindowsOS* that offers a global view of *your* tagging data. W3C-backed *SPARQL* [5] and *SPARUL* [6] serve to query and update tagging data, respectively, and in doing so, blackboxes the heterogeneity of the underlying tagging sites. No more need to learn either proprietary APIs or protocol messaging.

The aim is to support tagging interoperability whereby tagging data produced in one site can be seamlessly used in another. Even more important, global queries can now be posed that expand all along the tagsphere. Last but not least, *TAGMAS'* API streamlines application development by abstracting the application from the location of tagging data. As a proof of concept, one application has been implemented, *tagfolio*, that provides a frontend to *SPARQL* query specification on top of *TAGMAS*.

The rest of the paper is organized as follows. Section 2 motivates this work through an example. Section 3 describes query specification in *TAGMAS* by offering a global view over tagging sites. Sections 4 and 5 go down to design and implementation details by describing how *TAGMAS* query expressions are mapped to the proprietary APIs. We evaluate the performance of *TAGMAS* in Section 6. Related work and some conclusions end the paper.

2   Motivation

Consider you have to collect information about *Poznan*, no matter the format this information is: a podcast, a picture or a website. Tagging sites help you by putting the "wisdom of the crowds" into your hands: type the *"Poznan"* tag into your favourite tagging sites, and you will recover a handful collection of resources. Although this implies moving along distinct sites (e.g. *del.icio.us, Youtube* and *Flickr*), the effort could be worth enough.

However, the difficulty frequently rests on finding the right tags to ask for. It is not always easy to find a sensible collection of tags, more to the point if you are a novice. But, after all, the "wisdom of the crowds" is there for novices, not for experts which already have the background to find the right resources by themselves. Rather than explicitly providing the tags themselves, novices can tap on someone else's tags. But tags do not exist independently but attached to a resource. Hence, we tap on a given resource (e.g. the *Wikipedia* entry for *Poznan*), recover how it has been tagged in *del.icio.us* (e.g. *"OstrowTumski"*, *"OldBrewery"*) and use these tags to query *Youtube* or *Flickr*.

This approach certainly facilitates tag location for novices but it severely complicates the procedure for resource retrieval: *for each tag which characterises the resource*

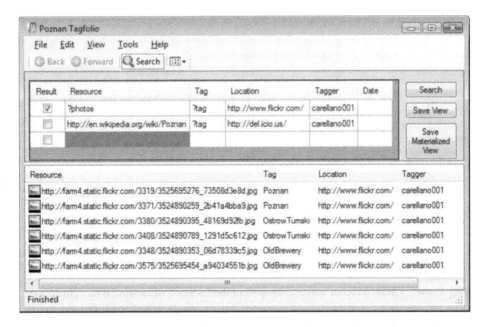

Fig. 1. The *Poznan tagfolio*

http://en.wikipedia.org/wiki/Poznan at del.icio.us, do recover those pictures at Flickr that have such tag. The tricky thing about the previous example is that not only does it access two different sites (i.e. *del.icio.us* and *Flickr*) but these accesses are intertwined. In terms of the relational algebra, the query is not just a union but a join.

If manually conducted this query is very tiresome to support. Going back and forth between *del.icio.us* and *Flickr* is really not an option. What is needed is a declarative query language that hides much of the distribution and diversity of the tagsphere. This is the purpose of *TAGMAS*. On top of such query language, applications such as *tagfolio* can be constructed.

Broadly, a *tagfolio* is a desktop folder that is defined through a query over the tagsphere. When a *tagfolio* is opened, the query is executed, and the outcome populates the folder. Figure 1 illustrates a *tagfolio* that "keeps" photos related with *Poznan* at *Flickr*. The lower panel shows the content of the folder (initially empty). The upper panel serves to specify a query *à la Query-By-Example (QBE)* [13], i.e. each row denotes a selection on a single site, and join variables are denoted by using the same variable name in two different rows (identified through a question mark).

Back to Figure 1, the first row states that photos from *Flickr* should be retrieved (notice the tick in the first column). The condition to be fulfilled is provided by the second row: the photo should at least share a tag (through the *?tag* variable) with the resource *http://en.wikipedia.org/wiki/Poznan* kept at *del.icio.us*. The outcome is then a set of photo references together with the tags fulfilling the condition.

This use case illustrates tag interoperability at work. Instead of each application having to face tag interoperability, this work advocates for a "tag management

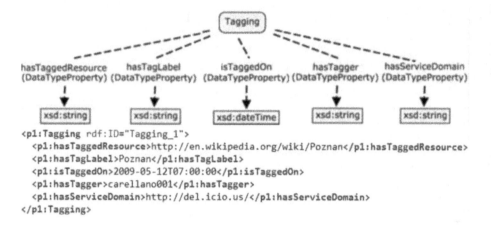

```
<p1:Tagging rdf:ID="Tagging_1">
    <p1:hasTaggedResource>http://en.wikipedia.org/wiki/Poznan</p1:hasTaggedResource>
    <p1:hasTagLabel>Poznan</p1:hasTagLabel>
    <p1:isTaggedOn>2009-05-12T07:00:00</p1:isTaggedOn>
    <p1:hasTagger>carellano001</p1:hasTagger>
    <p1:hasServiceDomain>http://del.icio.us/</p1:hasServiceDomain>
</p1:Tagging>
```

Fig. 2. *TagOnt* ontology and a sample individual

component", *TAGMAS*, that makes transparent the location of tagging data. This paper focus on the query capability: query specification, query transformation and query execution of disperse and heterogeneous tagging sites.

3   TAGMAS Query Specification

TAGMAS offers a global view over heterogeneous tagging sites. As known from the database community, a key point to integrate different data sources is a formal description of each data source that permits its automatic integration by machines, and offers a common model for the user to express queries. This work uses *RDF* as the data model, and introduces *TagOnt* as an ontology to integrate the distinct tagging conventions [10].

TagOnt rests on the observation that in current tagging sites there is not semantic formal agreement on the representation of the notion of tagging, "this means that every system uses a different format to publish its tagging data, which prevents interoperability and does not allow for machine-processability" [10].

Figure 2 depicts the main constructs of *TagOnt* together with an individual. The central *Element* of the ontology is a *Tagging*, i.e. a tuple *(resource, tag, time, tagger, domain)*. The following properties are introduced: *hasTaggedResource* (which holds the resource URL); *hasTagLabel* (i.e. the resource tags); *isTaggedOn* (i.e. date and time of the tagging); *hasTagger* (i.e. person who did the tagging); and *hasServiceDomain* that specifies the tagging site. The latter allows converting tagging data from existing applications without losing its original context. In doing so, *TagOnt* allows for cross-application tagging which is a must in our scenario.

Once the ontology is defined, operations should be available to query and populate the knowledge base. To this end, *SPARQL* and *SPARQL/Update Language (SPARUL)* are used. Figure 3 shows distinct examples based on *TagOnt*, namely:

```
SELECT ?photos        ＼
WHERE {                                                                    A
  ?post1 tagont:hasTaggedResource ?photos.
  ?post1 tagont:hasTagLabel ?tag.
  ?post1 tagont:hasTagger 'carellano001'.
  ?post1 tagont:hasServiceDomain 'http://www.flickr.com/'.
  ?post2 tagont:hasTaggedResource 'http://en.wikipedia.org/wiki/Poznan'.
  ?post2 tagont:hasTagLabel ?tag.
  ?post2 tagont:hasTagger 'carellano001'.
  ?post2 tagont:hasServiceDomain 'http://del.icio.us/'.
}
```

```
INSERT DATA {                                                              B
  [] tagont:hasTaggedResource 'http://farm4.static.flickr.com/3299/3663279424_d73d853ceb.jpg'.
  [] tagont:hasTagLabel 'Poznan'.
  [] tagont:hasTagger 'carellano001'.
  [] tagont:hasServiceDomain 'http://www.flickr.com/'.
}
```

```
DELETE {                                                                   C
  ?post tagont:hasTagLabel ?tag.
} WHERE {
    ?post tagont:hasTaggedResource 'http://farm4.static.flickr.com/3299/3663279424_d73d853ceb.jpg'.
    ?post tagont:hasTagger 'carellano001'.
    ?post tagont:hasServiceDomain 'http://www.flickr.com/'.
  }
```

```
MODIFY                                                                     D
DELETE {
  ?post tagont:hasTagLabel 'Poznan'.
}
INSERT {
  ?post tagont:hasTagLabel 'WISEVenue'.
} WHERE {
    ?post tagont:hasTagLabel 'Poznan'.
    ?post tagont:hasTagger 'carellano001'.
  }
```

Fig. 3. *SPARQL/SPARUL* Query examples

- (A) obtain pictures at *Flickr* with *carellano001* as the tagger, where at least one of their tags has been used to tag also the bookmark *"http://en.wikipedia.org/wiki/Poznan"* at *del.icio.us,*
- (B) attach tag *"Poznan"* to picture *"http://farm4.static.flickr.com/3299/3663279424_d73d853ceb.jpg"* located at *Flickr* with *carellano001* as the tagger,
- (C) delete tags associated with picture *"http://farm4.static.flickr.com/3299/3663279424_d73d853ceb.jpg"* which is kept at *Flickr* with *carellano001* as the tagger. Variables are denoted with an starting question mark, e.g. *"?tag"*,
- (D) rename tag *"Poznan"* to *"WISEVenue"* with *carellano001* as the tagger, so that all resources are re-tagged (no matter the tagging site).

4   TAGMAS Query Transformation

Once the query has been created in *SPARQL/SPARUL*, using the *TagOnt* model, it is then *TAGMAS'* responsibility to transform *SPARQL/SPARUL* requests down to *Calls* to proprietary APIs. Next paragraphs outline the distinct steps (some of them are executed in parallel) that *TAGMAS* follows to realize this process. The example query is used to illustrate the details.

Group Triples in Datasets. First, the *SPARQL* query is re-arranged into *Datasets* (see figure 4(1) and (2)). *Datasets* are a proposal for a query to expand along distinct *RDF* graphs, where each graph consists of triples with subject, predicate and object. When querying a collection of graphs, the *GRAPH* keyword is used to match patterns against named graphs (i.e. a *Dataset*). Conceptually, the vision is like if each tagging site was a *RDF*-graph provider. Unfortunately, this is not yet the case. However, we would like to provide such an illusion since it accounts for aggregating *SPARQL* triples based on its tagging site. Therefore, objects on the *hasServiceDomain* property become *GRAPH* clauses. This *GRAPH*-based query is now the input to the next step.

```
SELECT ?photos                                                    1
WHERE {
  ?post1 tagont:hasTaggedResource ?photos.
  ?post1 tagont:hasTagLabel ?tag.
  ?post1 tagont:hasTagger 'carellano001'.
  ?post1 tagont:hasServiceDomain 'http://www.flickr.com/'.
  ?post2 tagont:hasTaggedResource 'http://en.wikipedia.org/wiki/Poznan'.
  ?post2 tagont:hasTagLabel ?tag.
  ?post2 tagont:hasTagger 'carellano001'.
  ?post2 tagont:hasServiceDomain 'http://del.icio.us/'.
}
-------------------------------------------------------------------
SELECT ?photos                                                    2
FROM NAMED <http://www.flickr.com/>
FROM NAMED <http://del.icio.us/>
WHERE {
  GRAPH <http://www.flickr.com/>{
    ?post1 tagont:hasTaggedResource ?photos.
    ?post1 tagont:hasTagLabel ?tag.
    ?post1 tagont:hasTagger 'carellano001'.
  }.
  GRAPH <http://del.icio.us/>{
    ?post2 tagont:hasTaggedResource 'http://en.wikipedia.org/wiki/Poznan'.
    ?post2 tagont:hasTagLabel ?tag.
    ?post2 tagont:hasTagger 'carellano001'.
  }.
}
-------------------------------------------------------------------
<Query select="?photos">                                          3
  <Where>
    <Call name="?photos=getResources(?tag,null)"
          site="http://www.flickr.com/" account="carellano001"/>
    <Call name="?tag=getTags('http://en.wikipedia.org/wiki/Poznan',null)"
          site="http://del.icio.us/" account="carellano001"/>
  </Where>
</Query>
-------------------------------------------------------------------
<Execution_Plan>                                                  4
  <Project variables="?photos">
    <Join variables="?tag">
      <Call name="?tag=getTags('http://en.wikipedia.org/wiki/Poznan',null)"
            site="http://del.icio.us/" account="carellano001"/>
      <Call name="?photos=getResources(?tag,null)"
            site="http://www.flickr.com/" account="carellano001"/>
    </Join>
  </Project>
</Execution_Plan>
```

Fig. 4. Example case of transformation: (1) *SPARQL* query; (2) *Datasets*; (3) *Calls*; (4) *Execution plan*

Table 1. From *SPARQL* triples to proprietary API operations (highlights are for our running example)

QUERY TRIPLES (A)	CALLS (B)	DELICIOUS REST CALLS (C)	FLICKR XML-RPC CALLS (D)
?post isTaggedOn　　　　?date	?date=getDates(null, null)	?date=posts.Dates()	?date=photos.search() + photos.getInfo()
?post hasTaggedResource "URL" ?post isTaggedOn　　　　?date	?date=getDates("URL", null)	?date=posts.Get ("URL")	?date=photos.getInfo ("URL")
?post hasTagLabel　　　　"TAG" ?post isTaggedOn　　　　?date	?date=getDates(null, "TAG")	?date=posts.All ("TAG")	?date=photos.search ("TAG") + photos.getInfo()
?post hasTaggedResource URL" ?post hasTagLabel　　　　"TAG" ?post isTaggedOn　　　　?date	?date=getDates("URL", "TAG")	?date=posts.Get ("URL", "TAG")	?date= photos.search("URL", "TAG") + photos.getInfo()
?post hasTagLabel　　　　?tag	?tag=getTags(null, null)	?tag=tags.Get()	?tag=tags.getListUser()
?post hasTaggedResource "URL" ?post hasTagLabel　　　　?tag	?tag=getTags("URL", null)	?tag=posts.Get ("URL")	?tag=tags.getListPhoto("URL")
?post hasTagLabel　　　　?tag ?post isTaggedOn　　　　"DATE"	?tag=getTags(null, "DATE")	?tag=posts.Get ("DATE")	?tag=photos.search("DATE") + photos.getInfo()
?post hasTaggedResource "URL" ?post hasTagLabel　　　　?tag ?post isTaggedOn　　　　"DATE"	?tag=getTags("URL", "DATE")	?tag=posts.Get ("URL", "DATE")	?tag=photos.search("URL", "DATE") + photos.getInfo()
?post hasTaggedResource ?url	?url=getResources(null, null)	?url=posts.All()	?url=photos.search()
?post hasTaggedResource ?url ?post isTaggedOn　　　　"DATE"	?url=getResources(null, "DATE")	?url=posts.Get ("DATE")	?url=photos.search("DATE")
?post hasTaggedResource ?url ?post hasTagLabel　　　　"TAG"	?url=getResources("TAG", null)	?url=posts.All ("TAG")	?url=photos.search("TAG")
?post hasTaggedResource ?url ?post hasTagLabel　　　　"TAG" ?post isTaggedOn　　　　"DATE"	?url=getResources("TAG", "DATE")	?url=posts.Get ("TAG", "DATE")	?url=photos.search("TAG", "DATE")

Transform Datasets in Calls. In this step *SPARQL* triples belonging to the same *GRAPH (Dataset)* are transformed to a single *Call*. Each tagging site offers a different way to access the site resources. To isolate from this heterogeneity, a homogeneous syntactic API has been defined. Figure 5 shows the methods of this interface, where it can be observed that the interface is tightly coupled with *TagOnt* ontology, and basically one method has been defined for each property of the *TagOnt* ontology. This interface provides a site-independent way to handle resources (e.g. *getTags* specifies the recovering of the resource's tags regardless of how this operation is finally realised by the site at hand). The transformation of these methods to the concrete API site method has been delayed until execution step.

Table 1 summarises all possible combinations of triples that can appear in a *Dataset* based on *TagOnt* properties. Column (a) holds predicate combinations of the *TagOnt* ontology. Column (b) shows its *Calls* counterpart, where *"?"* elements stand for variables, and upper case elements represent constants (e.g. *"URL"*). Therefore, this table describes how to obtain *Calls* out of *Datasets*. An example is given in figure 4(2) and (3): the *del.icio.us Dataset* becomes the *Call ?tag=getTags("http://en.wikipedia.org/wiki/Poznan", null)* in accordance with *row6* rule (highlighted in table 1). Analogously, *Flickr Dataset* produces the *Call ?photos=getResources(?tag, null)* akin to the *row11* rule, where the variable *?tag* is instantiated with tags obtained from the previous *del.icio.us* operation.

Method Summary	
java.util.Date[]	getDates(java.lang.String url, java.lang.String tag) Return a list of dates, when "url" was tagged or when "tag" was used.
java.lang.String[]	getResources(java.lang.String tag, java.util.Date date) Return a list of resource identifiers tagged with "tag" or tagged in "date".
java.lang.String[]	getTags(java.lang.String url, java.util.Date date) Return a list of tags used to tag "url" or used in "date".

Fig. 5. Site independant *Call* interface

Create the Execution plan. Now, it is the turn to consider dependencies among *Calls*, i.e. whether output parameters of a *Call* become input parameters of another. Two situations can arise:

- if no dependency exists then, a UNION expression is constructed. This means the tagging sites are invoked concurrently and results are merged independently,
- if the output variable of a *Call* C1 is used as an input variable of the other *Call* C2 then, a JOIN expression is created with C1 and C2 as part of the outer and inner loops, respectively.

The latter case arises in our running example: tags recovered after executing *?tag=getTags("http://en.wikipedia.org/wiki/Poznan", null)* at *del.icio.us*, are used as the input parameter for invoking *?photos=getResources(?tag, null)* at *Flickr* (see Figure 4(4)).

The JOIN expression implies that for each tag recovered from *del.icio.us*, a request is issued to *Flickr*. The JOIN outputs the union of the set of *Flickr* pictures obtained in each iteration. The *Execution plan* ends with the projection of the *?photos* variable.

5   TAGMAS Query Execution

At this point, an *Execution plan* is available, but it can not yet be enacted since it is described in terms of *Calls* which is not understood by tagging servers. *"Tagging drivers"* are needed to map *Calls* into the specificities of each server. Each *"tagging driver"* encapsulates the peculiarities of the tagging site at hand (e.g. protocol, data format, etc). Since tagging sites do not provide such drivers, *TAGMAS* provides native support for *del.icio.us* and *Flickr*.

The management of the *"tagging driver"* is realized by the *TaggingDriverManager* component. This component hosts the drivers, and supports the interaction with the distinct tagging sites using *JTBC* (Java TaggingSite Base Connectivity). *JTBC* mimics *JDBC* specification where *"tagging drivers"* are used to encapsulate the specificities of each tagging site.

This approach allows for new sites (e.g. *CiteULike*) to be introduced through interface realization. If queries should now be expanded to *CiteULike*, interfaces *TaggingDriver*, *TaggingConnection* and *TaggingStatement* should be implemented that encapsulate the specificities of *CiteULike* (see Figure 6). The latter is

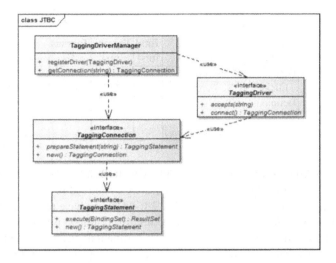

Fig. 6. The structure of the Java TaggingSite Base Connectivity (*JTBC*)

just an implementation that realises each operation for the tagging site (e.g. *DeliciousGetTagsTaggingStatement*, *DeliciousGetDatesTaggingStatement*). The *DeliciousGetTagsTaggingStatement* class encapsulates the protocol, envelop strategy and parameter details specific to *del.icio.us getTags* invocation. The figure 7 describes how *TAGMAS* process previous *del.icio.us Call*
?tag=getTags("http://en.wikipedia.org/wiki/Poznan", null).

```
1  TaggingConnection conn;
2  TaggingStatement statement;
3  Class.forName("driver.delicious.DeliciousDriver");
4  conn=TaggingDriverManager.getConnection("http://del.icio.us/",_
5  "carellano001","tagmas");
6  statement=conn.prepareStatement("getTags");
7  BindingSetImpl params=new BindingSetImpl();
8  params.add("hasTaggedResource",_
9  "http://en.wikipedia.org/wiki/Poznan");
10 ResultSet result=statement.execute(params);
```

Fig. 7. Example snippet of a *del.icio.us Call* at execution stage

First, the driver is loaded (3) and the site's name is used to obtain the specific connection object that links to it (4, 5). This connection acts as a factory (software pattern) and permits to obtain the concrete object statement related to an abstract *getTags* operation (6). Finally the statement is executed (10) with the parameters specified in sentences (7) and (8, 9).

6   Evaluation

This section evaluates *TAGMAS,* measuring what additional latency *TAGMAS* adds compared to direct access without *TAGMAS.* For our measurements *TAGMAS* has been

Table 2. *TAGMAS* overhead

Tagging site	Query	Total (ms)	Tagmas (ms)	Tagmas %
Delicious	getResources(tag)	2331	405	17.4
Flickr	getResources(tag)	1032	427	41.4
Delicious + Flickr	getTags(resource) JOIN getResources(tag)	3818	474	12.4

deployed in an AMD Turion 64 X2 2 GHz CPU with 4GB of memory. The experiments have been realized with a domestic 6Mbps WIFI LAN bandwidth.

We have not spent much effort to optimize *TAGMAS*; we have reused some general purpose modules (i.e. *Jena* parser) that can be improved in next prototypes. Our main goal was to demonstrate the viability of our experimental system. Nonetheless, our results demonstrate that performance of our current prototype is competitive with other remote access Web technologies and is fast enough to be usable in practice.

We measured the latency for two query types: simple selections and joins. Table 2 shows the outcome. The first two rows correspond to a selection query (i.e. *getResources(tag)*) for two remote sites, *del.icio.us* and *Flickr*. The last row amounts for a join involving *Flickr* and *del.icio.us* (it is actually our running query). For each query, we collected the total elapsed time in milliseconds (ms) (third column) and *TAGMAS* latency removing net-time (fourth column). The last column holds the percentage involved by *TAGMAS*.

The first insight is that *TAGMAS* latency keeps almost constant around 420ms, no matter the query. Although the join expression takes around 50ms more to work out, we do not think this is especially significant. Even in the presence of very efficient servers such as *Flickr*, *TAGMAS* accounts for 41% of the total time. Not surprisingly, network latency dominates the query time. This is specially so for joins where sites are invoked several times. For our running example, network latency accounts for as much as 87.6%. Even so, getting the results back for our example query is below 4 seconds, a reasonable time assumed by any user in a prototyped tool.

7   Related Work

Starting with desktops striving to integrate resources disseminated across tagging sites, *Menagerie* introduces *"a framework that supports uniform naming, protection, and access for personal objects stored by Web services"* (e.g. tagging sites) [7]. It perceives a tagging site as a file system: resources (e.g. *Flickr* photos) are files, and folders are obtained after the local structures of the server (e.g. albums for *Flickr*, bundles for *del.icio.us*). The rationales are similar to *TAGMAS*. The main differences stem from how tagging sites are perceived. Somehow *Menagerie* replicates the tagging server structure in the desktop filesystem. By contrast, *TAGMAS* perceives tagging sites as sources of resources, and folders as views, i.e. queries over these tagging sites. This has two important implications. First, the very same resource, e.g. a picture, can be virtually located at different *tagfolios*. You are not longer confined to locate a picture in an album. And second, *tagfolios* are based on tags: if photos are recovered through tags when directly accessing *Flickr*, the user will likely also use tags when accessing *Flickr* from the desktop rather than forcing him to remember the album where photos are kept. These two important advantages rest on the existence of a global schema for tagging data.

Moving to the Web, *ActiveRDF* [12] is an object-oriented API for managing *RDF* data that offers full manipulation and querying of *RDF* data. The aim is to embed Semantic Web data into object-oriented languages. Here, resources and their description are conceived as an *RDF* graph that, with the help of *ActiveRDF*, can be integrated into OO languages. The integration is programmatic (i.e. through an API to manipulate *RDF* structures). Unfortunately, tagging sites do not offer their data as *RDF* graphs but through their own proprietary APIs. This is precisely one of the endeavours of *TAGMAS*, i.e. to abstract away from this heterogeneity, and to provide an *RDF* integrated view of the tagging data, no matter where it is located. *ActiveRDF* applications can then capitalize on *TAGMAS* as a supplier of *RDF* graphs for tagging data. Therefore, the role of *ActiveRDF* in our architecture would be at the application layer.

Keotag [1] is a tag-based metasearch web site that permits to search resources annotated with tags in fourteen different tagging sites (*del.icio.us*, *Technorati*, *Youtube*, *Digg* etc.). The user introduces a tag, clicks on the corresponding tagging-site icon, and related resources are displayed. Queries are then single-site and multi-tag. By contrast *Xoocle* [3] permits to search in some predefined tagging sites (*del.icio.us*, *Flickr*, *Technorati*) based on the tags you kept at you *Stumbleupon* account. The user enters his *Stumbleupon* username, and *Xoocle* displays a list of all his *Stumbleupon* tags [2]. Next the user selects one tag, and *Xoocle* obtains all *del.icio.us'*, *Flickr's* and *Technorati's* resources annotated with this tag. *Xoocle* is limited to single-tag queries that always expand along the same tagging sites. *TAGMAS* expands *Xoocle*'s efforts by providing an integrated and extensible architecture that allows for multi-tag, multi-site queries... and updates.

8   Conclusions

This paper describes *TAGMAS*, an application for *WindowsOS* that encapsulates heterogeneity of tagging site through *SPARQL* and *SPARUL*. The final aim is to streamline the development of tagging-aware desktop applications that now do not have to face such diversity. This will hopefully promote a new crop of tagging tooling that capitalize on tags as the main conduit for localizing and organizing user resources in a holistic way. As a proof of concept, an application, *tagfolio*, has been developed on top of *TAGMAS* (i.e. using *TAGMAS'* API).

Design decisions were taken to facilitate incorporation of additional tagging sites into *TAGMAS*. Finally, our measurements demonstrate the practicality of our approach for medium-scale environments.

Future work includes building drivers for other popular tagging sites (e.g. *Youtube*, *CiteULike*), and providing cache strategies to speed up *TAGMAS* query processing. For instance, the set of user tags tends to consolidate as time goes by. This makes this set a good candidate for caching. Depending on the query patterns, some caching strategies can be envisaged for materializing fractions of the tagging data in a similar way to those available for datawarehousing.

Acknowledgements

This work is co-supported by the Spanish Ministry of Science and Innovation, and the European Social Fund under contract TIN2008-06507-C02-01/TIN (MODELINE), and the Avanza I+D initiative of the Ministry of Industry, Tourism and Commerce under contract TSI-020100-2008-415. Arellano has a doctoral grant from the Spanish Ministry of Science & Innovation.

References

1. Keotag, http://www.keotag.com/
2. Stumbleupon, http://www.stumbleupon.com/
3. Xoocle, http://www.xoocle.com/
4. IEEE Standard Glossary of Computer Networking Terminology (May 1995)
5. SPARQL Query Language for RDF (2007),
   http://www.w3.org/TR/rdf-sparql-query/
6. SPARQL Update (2008), http://www.w3.org/Submission/2008/
   SUBM-SPARQL-Update-20080715/
7. Geambasu, R., Cheung, C., Moshchuk, A., Gribble, S.D., Levy, H.M.: Organizing and Sharing Distributed Personal Web-Service Data. In: World Wide Web Conference, WWW 2008 (2008)
8. Golder, S.A., Hubermann, B.A.: The Structure of Collaborative Tagging System. Technical report, HP Labs (2006),
   http://www.hpl.hp.com/research/idl/papers/tags/tags.pdf
9. Kipp, M.E.I.: @toread and Cool: Subjective, Affective and Associative Factors in Tagging. In: Canadian Association for Information Science (CAIS 2008) (2008)
10. Knerr, T.: Tagging Ontology - Towards a Common Ontology for Folksonomies (2007),
    http://tagont.googlecode.com/files/TagOntPaper.pdf
11. Lund, B., Hammond, T., Flack, M., Hannay, T.: Social Bookmarking Tools (II). D-Lib Magazine (2005), http://www.dlib.org/dlib/april05/lund/04lund.html
12. Oren, E., Haller, A., Hauswirth, M., Heitmann, B., Decker, S., Mesnage, C.: A Flexible Integration Framework for Semantic Web 2.0 Applications. IEEE Software, 64–71 (2007)
13. Ramakrishnan, R., Gehrke, J.: Database Management Systems, ch. 6, pp. 177–192. McGraw-Hill, New York (2003), http://pages.cs.wisc.edu/ dbbook/openAccess/
    thirdEdition/qbe.pdf

Clustering of Social Tagging System Users: A Topic and Time Based Approach

Vassiliki Koutsonikola[1], Athena Vakali[1],
Eirini Giannakidou[1,2], and Ioannis Kompatsiaris[2]

[1] Department of Informatics
Aristotle University
54124 Thessaloniki, Greece
[2] Informatics and Telematics Institute
CERTH
Thermi-Thessaloniki, Greece

Abstract. Under Social Tagging Systems, a typical Web 2.0 application, users label digital data sources by using freely chosen textual descriptions (tags). Mining tag information reveals the topic-domain of users interests and significantly contributes in a profile construction process. In this paper we propose a clustering framework which groups users according to their preferred topics and the time locality of their tagging activity. Experimental results demonstrate the efficiency of the proposed approach which results in more enriched time-aware users profiles.

Keywords: Social Tagging Systems, user clustering, time, topic.

1 Introduction

Social Tagging Systems (STSs) constitute a Web 2.0 application and an emerging trend where web users are allowed to manage and share online resources through annotations. This user-driven approach of information creation and organization is called folksonomy [1] and its strength lies in the fact that its structure and dynamics are similar to those of a complex system, yielding in stable and knowledge rich patterns after a specific usage period. In an STS, users are allowed to use tags in the form of freely chosen keywords to describe publicly available Web resources. They are not restricted by any pre-defined navigational or conceptual hierarchies contributing, thus, in a knowledge space that is built incrementally (by many users) in an evolutionary and decentralized manner.

In an STS, the resources that users share and the people they connect to reveal their preferences. Moreover, the keywords they use to describe resources reveal their viewpoint for the specific topic-domain that these resources refer to [3]. However, despite the abundant user-provided data that has been aggregated by STS and offer valuable information about their interests, only a few studies in the literature take advantage of tagging systems for the purpose of user profile extraction. A current research trend to extract patterns of users' tagging behavior is to employ clustering [7,2,9] for the analysis of the information

G. Vossen, D.D.E. Long, and J.X. Yu (Eds.): WISE 2009, LNCS 5802, pp. 75–86, 2009.

contained in personomies [4]. Personomies refer to the set of tags and resources that are associated with a particular user and contribute to the identification of their multiple interests and to the extraction of more enriched and accurate user profiles. Existing approaches are based on related tags included in different personomies to identify users with similar interests [5,8]. Thus, users profiles are modeled according to their relation with the different tag clusters [2,6]. However, as tagging communities grow the added content and metadata become harder to manage due to the increased content diversity, hence tags become less effective in characterizing users preferences.

In this paper we propose a framework that groups STS users according to two criteria: i) the topic-domain and ii) the time locality of users tagging activity. Our work was inspired by [10] where the authors show that a time-aware clustering approach results in a particularly enriched user clustering process. To this context, the consideration of time aspect along with the topic of tags used by STS users can characterize better and more accurately users interests. Moreover, studying the time aspect of users activity can result in important conclusions about the occasional and more regular users and could help in the evaluation of users credibility. In STS, users rating process is significant because it can contribute to more efficient tag recommendation mechanisms. Furthermore, analyzing users activity over time is crucial in prediction applications which in turn can affect load balancing application and improve the STS's performance. In the proposed approach time is considered by measuring users' similarity in terms of their tagging activity over a specific time period. The main contributions of our work can be summarized as follows:

- We propose a framework to measure similarity between users of an STS, in terms of both the topic and time aspect of their tagging activity.
- We apply a time-aware clustering algorithm that tunes the former criteria according to a weight factor α
- We carry out experiments to evaluate the proposed framework's performance.

The rest of the paper is organized as follows: Section 2 presents the basic notation and problem formulation. Section 3 describes the way we capture similarities between users and the proposed time-aware clustering algorithm. Section 4 presents the experimentation while conclusions are discussed in Section 5.

2   Problem Formulation

As is has been described in Section 1, a Social Tagging System is a web-based application, where users assign tags (i.e. arbitrary textual descriptions) to digital resources. The digital resources are either uploaded by users or, are, already, available in the web. The users are either "isolated" or, more commonly, members of web communities (i.e. social networks) and their main motivation (for tagging) is information organization and sharing. Let U denote the set of users, R the set of resources, T a set of tags and A the set of user annotations (i.e. tag

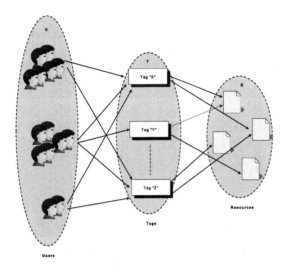

Fig. 1. A web-based social tagging system

assignments). Figure 1 depicts the basic structure of a web-based social tagging system while Table 1 summarizes the basic symbols notation used in this paper.

Table 1. Basic Symbols Notation

Symbol	Definition
m, n, l, p, d	Number of users, resources, tags, user's annotations and timeframes (respectively)
U	Users' set $\{u_1, \ldots, u_m\}$
R	Resources' set $\{r_1, \ldots, r_n\}$
T	Tags' set $\{t_1, \ldots, t_l\}$
A	User's annotation set $\{a_1, \ldots, a_p\}$
UT_i	The set of tags $\{t_x, \ldots, t_y\}$ which have been assigned by user u_i

Definition 1 (FOLKSONOMY OF AN STS). *Given a Social Tagging System (STS), its derived folksonomy F is defined as the tuple $F = (U, R, T, A)$, where $A \subseteq U \times R \times T$ i.e. the users' annotation set A is modeled as a triadic relation between the other sets.*

The above definition was initially introduced in [4] and is also adopted in our approach.

We consider a particular time period $P = \{1, \ldots, d\}$ of d timeframes (i.e. time intervals), during which we record users tagging activity. Two vectors U_p and T_p are used to capture the temporal activity of users and tags, respectively. Specifically, for each user $u_i \in U$, we define the vector $U_p(i, :)$ to track his activity:

$$U_p(i, :) = (U_p(i, 1), \ldots, U_p(i, d))$$

where $U_p(i, j)$, $j = 1, \ldots, d$ indicates the number of tags user u_i has assigned during the timeframe j. All the $U_p(i, :)$ vectors are organized in the $m \times d$ table U_p. For the set of tags T, we similarly define the T_p two dimensional $l \times d$ table which consists of l T_p multidimensional vectors that describe each $t_i \in T$, $i = 1, \ldots, l$.

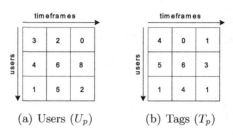

(a) Users (U_p)   (b) Tags (T_p)

Fig. 2. Temporal activity structures

Example 1. In Figure 2(a), which depicts the table U_p, the fact that $U_p(2, 1) = 4$ means that the user identified as 2 has assigned 4 tags during the first timeframe. Similarly, in case of Figure 2(b), which describes T_p the fact that $T_p(2, 2) = 6$ indicates that the tag identified as 2 has been assigned 6 times during the second timeframe.

Moreover, for each user u_i we define a set $UT_i = \{t_x, \ldots, t_y\}$ which includes the tags that user u_i has used in his annotations during a specific time period. For example if the third user has assigned the tags "cat", "dog" and "animal", then his annotation set will be $UT_3 = \{cat, dog, animal\}$.

2.1   Capturing Similarities

The proposed framework performs users clustering considering their similarity in terms of how related the topics of their interest are and whether their tagging activity coincides in time. We consider that two users have common interests if they share common annotations at the same time periods. Users' annotations reveal the topic of their interest. For example a user who tagged a set of photos depicting sports, is considered to be interested in sports. However, if his tagging activity took place during the Olympic games it means that the users' interests mainly focus on the Olympic games and that he is not a regular fan of sports. Another user presenting similar tagging activity is considered to have common interest and should therefore be assigned, by the clustering algorithm, to the same cluster with the first one.

   To measure distance between users with respect to the topic of their interests we estimate their relation with the various tags. Specifically, we define that the relation between a user u_i and a tag t_j corresponds to the maximum similarity between the tags that have been assigned by user u_i and the tag t_j.

Definition 2 (USERS-TAGS SIMILARITY). *The similarity $SS(u_i, t_j)$ between a user u_i and a tag t_j is defined as follows:*

$$SS(u_i, t_j) = max(SemSim(t_f, t_j)), 1 \leq f \leq l, t_f \in UT_i \tag{1}$$

For the estimation of the *Semantic Similarity* between two tags, we need to use external resources (i.e. web ontologies, thesauri, etc) and a mapping technique between tags and the resource's concepts. In our work, we adopted the approach described in [11], due to its straightforward application to our data, according to which the semantic distance between two concepts is proportional to the path distance between them. For example, let t_x and t_y be two tags for which we want to find the semantic similarity and $\overrightarrow{t_x}$, $\overrightarrow{t_y}$ be their corresponding mapping concepts via an ontology. Then, their *Semantic Similarity SemSim* is calculated as:

$$SemSim(t_x, t_y) = \frac{2 \times depth(LCS)}{[depth(\overrightarrow{t_x}) + depth(\overrightarrow{t_y})]} \tag{2}$$

where $depth(\overrightarrow{t_x})$ is the maximum path length from the root to $\overrightarrow{t_x}$ and LCS is the least common subsumer of $\overrightarrow{t_x}$ and $\overrightarrow{t_y}$. Thus, from equations 1 and 2 we capture the topic of interest of user u_i expressed on the basis of the various tags. It should be noted, that our approach is more advantageous compared to the one that would consider a user to be related with a tag in case he has used it in his annotation. According to the proposed approach a user is related to a tag in case he has assigned one or more tags which are semantically close to the specific tag, providing, thus, a more global perspective.

A common measure to capture similarity between two (same dimension) vectors is the *Cosine Coefficient* which calculates the cosine of the angle between them. In the proposed approach we use cosine similarity to compute time similarity between a user u_i and a tag t_j. The calculated similarity is higher in case that tags and users present activity at the same timeframes. Moreover, users that present high similarity with the same set of tags are expected to have a similar tagging activity over time.

Definition 3. *The time similarity $TS(u_i, t_j)$ between a user u_i and a tag t_j is defined as follows:*

$$TS(u_i, t_j) = \frac{U_p(i,:) \cdot T_p(j,:)}{|U_p(i,:)| \cdot |T_p(j,:)|} = \frac{\sum_{r=1}^{d} U_p(i,r) \cdot T_p(j,r)}{\sqrt{\sum_{r=1}^{d} U_p(i,r)^2 \cdot \sum_{r=1}^{d} T_p(j,r)^2}} \tag{3}$$

Values of both SS and TS similarities fluctuate in the interval $[0,1]$, i.e. they are of the same scale. Since vectors U_p and T_p capture users preferences in terms of topic domain and time, we can employ the squared Euclidean distance to compute their between distances. Then, the evaluation of dissimilarity between two users may be expressed by their distance that can be based either on the topic or the time locality of their preferences.

When only the topic of their interests is taken into account, the distance between two users is calculated considering their relation to each of the involved tags. Their distance is then defined as:

$$d_{topic}(u_x, u_y) = ||SS(u_x, :) - SS(u_y, :)||^2$$

When only the time locality of their activity is considered, the distance between two users is calculated over each of the d timeframes. In this case, the distance between two users u_x and u_y is defined as follows:

$$d_{time}(u_x, u_y) = ||TS(u_x, :) - TS(u_y, :)||^2$$

Let U_j denote one of the k user clusters obtained from the clustering process. Membership of a user u_i, where $i = 1, \ldots, n$ to a cluster U_j, where $j = 1, \ldots, k$ is defined by the function f as follows:

$$f(u_i, U_j) = \begin{cases} 1 \ if \ u_i \in U_j \\ 0 \ otherwise \end{cases}$$

Considering the cluster U_j, we can define its center in the topic and time feature spaces as follows:

$$C_{topic}(j, :) = \frac{\sum_{i=1}^{n} f(u_i, U_j) \cdot SS(u_i, :)}{|U_j|}$$

$$C_{time}(j, :) = \frac{\sum_{i=1}^{n} f(u_i, U_j) \cdot TS(u_i, :)}{|U_j|}$$

Then, the respective topic and time objective functions are calculated according to the following equations:

$$E_{topic} = \sum_{j=1}^{k} \sum_{u_i \in U_j} d_{topic}(u_i, c_{topic}(j, :))$$

$$E_{time} = \sum_{j=1}^{k} \sum_{u_i \in U_j} d_{time}(u_i, c_{time}(j, :))$$

The coupling of the two objective functions can be treated as a multi-objective optimization problem where the objective function is formulated as a weighted sum of the E_{topic} and E_{time} objective functions. We define the objective function E to capture the properties of the desired clustering solution:

$$E = \alpha * E_{topic} + (1 - \alpha) * E_{time} \tag{4}$$

The weight factor α fluctuates in the interval $[0, \ldots, 1]$. Then, at the one end, when $\alpha = 1$, $E = E_{topic}$, i.e. our solution proposes an assignment based only on users' topic of interest and completely discards the time aspect. At the other end, when $\alpha = 0$, $E = E_{time}$ and the solution is based only on time locality of users' preferences. For any other value of α the clustering solution considers both criteria at balanced weights.

Based on the above, we define the TOPIC & TIME AWARE CLUSTERING problem as follows:

Problem 1 (TOPIC & TIME AWARE CLUSTERING). Given a set U of m users, a set T of l tags, a set P of d timeframes, an integer value k, and the objective function E, find a CL clustering of U into k clusters such that the E is minimized.

3   The Clustering Algorithm

The proposed clustering framework is a two-step process. In the preprocessing step from the U, T and A datasets the SS and TS similarities are computed which constitute the input to the main clustering process. The clustering process, which is also completed in two steps, assigns users to clusters giving initially priority to the topic of their interests and then refines clusters according to time information. The overall process is depicted in Figure 3.

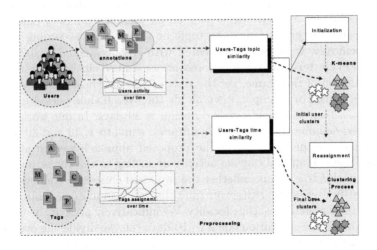

Fig. 3. The clustering framework

In the initialization step, the K-means clustering is employed to produce the k users' clusters based on their preferences about the resources topic-domain. Next, the reassignment step begins with the former k clusters and proceeds iteratively. During each iteration, the algorithm computes the fluctuation of the objective function E caused by moving each user u_i to one of the rest $k - 1$ clusters. If there exist some moves that lead to an improvement in the overall value of the objective function, then u_i is moved to the cluster that leads to the highest improvement. If no such cluster exists, u_i remains in his original cluster. The reassignment phase follows K-means idea for its convergence, ending either after a number of iterations or when the objective function improvement between two consecutive iterations is less than a minimum amount of improvement specified.

4   Experimentation

To carry out the experimentation phase and the evaluation of the proposed clustering framework, a dataset from Flickr[1] was used which consists of about 1200 users who assigned about 2500 tags to describe a set of 6764 images that referred to four topic domains (ancient Greece, Olympics, earthquake and weddings). The time period that the tagging activity was recorded is one year (September 2007-August 2008). As a source of semantic information for tag concepts, we employed the lexicon WordNet [12], which stores english words organized in hierarchies, depending on their cognitive meaning. During the preprocessing phase, we have removed tags that were not included in the wordnet database and were considered as noise. Moreover, users with very little tagging activity have been removed because there were not sufficient evidence about their interests. Thus, we have resulted in a time period of 210 days, that the remaing users have annotated images.

In the first section of our experimentation our purpose is to evaluate how effective the proposed clustering framework is in terms of obtaining more time-aware users clusters. We have experimented for different values of parameter α which indicates the gravity given to topic or time aspect according to Equation 4. Specifically, we have experimented with α values equal to 0.2, 0.5, 0.8 and number of clusters $k = 4, 8, 12$. Moreover, we studied clustering results altering the definition of timeframe, i.e. the time period on whose basis we examine the users' actions. For example, if we divide the overall time period (210 days) in 7 intervals, then the timeframe's duration is 30 days. In our work we have experimented defining the timeframe's duration equal to 1, 10 and 30 days.

To evaluate the performance of the proposed approach we initially depict graphically users' temporal tagging activity according to the clustering assignement. Our goal is to examine whether the proposed clustering framework manages to identify users similarities over time and result in more accurate clusters, in terms of their preferences' time locality. We indicatively present the results for $k = 4$ and timeframe's duration equal to 10 days (i.e. we divide the overall time period into 21 intervals). In Figure 4 we can see the tagging activity over time of the members of each of the four obtained clusters at the end of the initialization step of the clustering algorithm, where only the topic domain has been considered. As it is expected, there is no convention regarding the timeframe that the users of each cluster assign the tags. This holds regardless of the α parameter value since in the initialization step only the topic aspect is considered.

In Figures 5, 6 and 7 we present clusters after the reassignment step for $\alpha = 0.8, 0.5$ and 0.2. For $\alpha = 0.8$ where more gravity is given to the topic aspects, the reassignment step does not include that many users moves since during the initialization step users are assigned in a way that the criterion of topic domain is optimized. Setting the value of α equal to 0.5 the time and topic aspects are equally considered. Thus, we expect that since the algorithm takes time parameter into account, there will not be as much diversity, in terms of time,

---

[1] http://www.flickr.com/

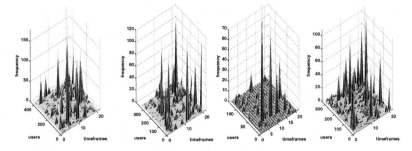

Fig. 4. Users clusters at the end of the initialization step ($\alpha = 0.5$)

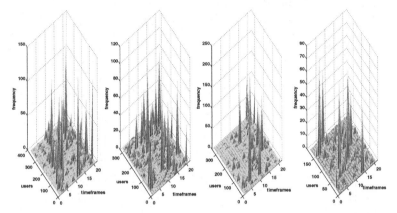

Fig. 5. Users clusters at the end of the reassignment step ($\alpha = 0.8$)

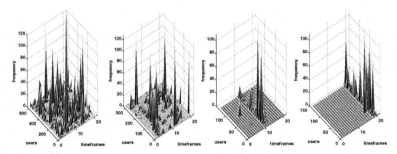

Fig. 6. Users clusters at the end of the reassignment step ($\alpha = 0.5$)

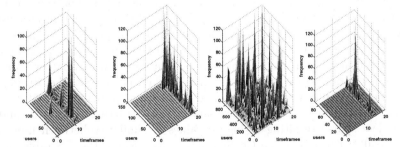

Fig. 7. Users clusters at the end of the reassignment step ($\alpha = 0.2$)

as there was in clusters obtained at the initialization step. Indeed, as depicted in Figure 6 in two of the four obtained clusters we observe that users activity takes place at the same timeframes ($10 - 12$ for the third cluster and $18 - 21$ for the fourth). For $\alpha = 0.2$ where more gravity is given to the time aspect, we can see that, as depicted in Figure 7, the algorithm results in three clusters that contain users with identical temporal preferences. Users with different preferences in time have been assigned to the third cluster. Experimenting with a higher number of clusters we have concluded that users of the third cluster can be furthermore divided and assigned to clusters where no such diversity in their behavior exists.

Table 2. Objective function improvements

$\alpha = 0.2$	Number of clusters		
Timeframe duration	4	8	12
1	9.25%	30.57%	47.37%
10	41.6%	62.82%	74.56%
30	53.68%	91.6%	92.27%
$\alpha = 0.5$			
1	0.06%	3.31%	25.02%
10	25.68%	42.06%	50.77%
30	38.1%	72.92%	75.42%
$\alpha = 0.5$			
1	0.06%	3.31%	25.02%
10	25.68%	42.06%	50.77%
30	38.1%	72.92%	75.42%

Next, we proceed in a quantitative analysis of the clustering results. Since we do not apriory know how users of our dataset should be clustered, we do not have any ground truth values of the dataset and therefore, we cannot use quantities such as precision, recall and F-measure to evaluate the clustering results. Thus, we use objective function values to evaluate clustering results for the different α values and different timeframe definitions. In general, the objective function expresses the sum of distances of each user belonging to a cluster from the cluster's centre and thus lower values of it indicate a better clustering scheme. Table 2 presents the improvements percentages (due to the decrease of objective function) for different values of α and timeframe's duration. According to the results, we can see that in all cases, lower values of α result in higher improvements since in that case more gravity is given to the time aspect. Thus, the initial clusters that were created according to the topic domain of users preferences will be considerably refined to achieve optimization in terms of time criterion. Moreover, we observe that an increase in timeframe's duration results in higher improvements. This is due to the sparseness that our dataset presents, i.e. during the time period of 210 days, both users and tags do not present frequent tagging activity. Thus when we create more compact time structures, tables U_p and T_p become less sparse resulting in higher values of similarity between users and tags (calculated using Cosine Coefficient). Consequently, the TS table carries information that diversify users more, causing more reassignments and higher improvements in objective function values. The appropriate definition of time-frame differentiates according to the dataset nature and significantly affects the clustering results.

5 Conclusions and Future Work

This paper proposes a framework to incorporate time aspect while clustering users of a Social Tagging System. According to the presented approach an initial set of users clusters is created where users are assigned to clusters according to the topic-domain of their interests as indicated by the tags they have assigned to describe resources. Then, users clusters are refined according to the time locality of their tagging activity resulting in more enriched and time-aware clustering results. The degree that the topic and time aspects are considered varies according to the value of a parameter α. Taking both topic and time aspects into account results in more enriched users' clusters whose members present resemblance on the topics of their interest and the time locality of their tagging activity. The results of the proposed approach can be beneficial for the identification of regular and non regular users, tagging recommendation systems (e.g. identifying a user's summer interests), prediction mechanisms and load balancing applications e.t.c.

In the future, we plan to extend our work so as to provide a framework that will incrementally check clusters validity at later time points and it will be able to reassign users membership to clusters. This is important since users interests as well as their tendency to use a social tagging system may change over time. For example users that used to be non regular users of an STS may be very interested in a topic and thus present significant tagging activity and become regular users for a specific period. Thus, our work can be extended so as to operate in a more incremental way. Moreover, we plan to address the issue of leveraging the tuning parameters (i.e. parameter α and timeframe's duration) by studying their affect on the obtained clusters and providing mechanisms that will automatically detect their values that result in more knowledge enriched clusters.

References

1. Wal, V.: Explaining and showing broad and narrow folksonomies. Blog post 2005-02-01, http://www.vanderwal.net/random/category.php?cat=153
2. Gemmell, J., Shepitsen, A., Mobasher, M., Burke, R.: Personalization in Folksonomies Based on Tag Clustering. In: 6th Workshop on Intelligent Techniques for Web Personalization and Recommender Systems, pp. 259–266. ACM, Chicago (2008)
3. Diederich, J., Iofciu, T.: Finding communities of practice from user profiles based on folksonomies. In: 1st International Workshop on Building Technology Enhanced Learning Solutions for Communities of Practice, Crete, Greece (2006)

4. Hotho, A., Jaschke, R., Schmitz, C., Stumme, G.: Information Retrieval in Folk-sonomies: Search and Ranking. In: Sure, Y., Domingue, J. (eds.) ESWC 2006. LNCS, vol. 4011, pp. 411–426. Springer, Heidelberg (2006)
5. Au Yeung, C.M., Gibbins, N., Shadbolt, N.: Discovering and Modelling Multiple Interests of Users in Collaborative Tagging Systems. In: 2008 IEEE/WIC/ACM International Conferences on Web Intelligence and Intelligent Agent Technology Workshops, Sydney, Australia (2008)
6. Dichev, C., Xu, J., Dicheva, D., Zhang, J.: A Study on Community Formation in Collaborative Tagging Systems. In: IEEE/WIC/ACM International Conference on Web Intelligence and Intelligent Agent Technology, pp. 13–16. IEEE Computer Society, Sydney (2008)
7. Shepitsen, A., Gemmell, J., Mobasher, B., Burke, R.: Personalized recommendation in social tagging systems using hierarchical clustering. In: 2008 ACM conference on Recommender systems, pp. 259–266. ACM, New York (2008)
8. Michlmayr, E., Cayzer, S.: Learning User Profiles from Tagging Data and Leveraging them for Personal(ized) Information Access. In: 16th International World Wide Web Conference (WWW 2007) Workshop on Tagging and Metadata for Social Information Organization (2007)
9. Au Yeung, C.M., Gibbins, N., Shadbolt, N.: A Study of User Profile Generation from Folksonomies. In: Social Web and Knowledge Management, Social Web 2008 Workshop at WWW 2008, Beijing, China. (2008)
10. Petridou, S., Koutsonikola, V., Vakali, A., Papadimitriou, G.: Time Aware Web Users Clustering. IEEE Transactions on Knowledge and Data Engineering 20(5), 653–667 (2008)
11. Wu, Z., Palmer, M.: Verm semantics and lexical selection. In: 32nd annual meeting of the association for computational linguistics, Las Cruces, New Mexico, pp. 133–138 (1994)
12. Fellbaum: WordNet, an electronic lexical database. MIT Press, Cambridge (1990)

Spectral Clustering in Social-Tagging Systems[*]

Alexandros Nanopoulos[1], Hans-Henning Gabriel[2], and Myra Spiliopoulou[2]

[1] Institute of Informatics, Hildesheim University, Germany
`nanopoulos@ismll.de`
[2] Faculty of Computer Science, Otto-von-Guericke-University Magdeburg, Germany
{`hgabriel,myra`}`@iti.cs.uni-magdeburg.de`

Abstract. Social tagging is an increasingly popular phenomenon with substantial impact on the way we perceive and understand the Web. For the many Web resources that are not self-descriptive, such as images, tagging is the sole way of associating them with concepts explicitly expressed in text. Consequently, users are encouraged to assign tags to Web resources, and tag recommenders are being developed to stimulate the re-use of existing tags in a consistent way. However, a tag still and inevitably expresses the personal perspective of each user upon the tagged resource. This personal perspective should be taken into account when assessing the similarity of resources with help of tags. In this paper, we focus on similarity-based clustering of tagged items, which can support several applications in social-tagging systems, like information retrieval, providing recommendations, or the establishment of user profiles and the discovery of topics. We show that it is necessary to capture and exploit the *multiple values of similarity* reflected in the tags assigned to the same item by different users. We model the items, the tags on them and the users who assigned the tags in a multigraph structure. To discover clusters of similar items, we extend spectral clustering, an approach successfully used for the clustering of complex data, into a method that captures multiple values of similarity between any two items. Our experiments with two real social-tagging data sets show that our new method is superior to conventional spectral clustering that ignores the existence of multiple values of similarity among the items.

1 Introduction

Social tagging is the process of saving bookmarks to a public Web site and tagging them with free-text keywords. With social tagging, a user expresses the own perspective on *items*, i.e. Web resources like images, videos, scientific papers, thus allowing other like-minded users to find the same information. The success of social tagging resulted to the proliferation of sites like Delicious, Citeulike, Digg, or Flickr. Such sites contain large amounts of tagged data that can be clustered on similarity and then used in information retrieval in social-tagging systems, for the formulation of recommendations in them [8,11], or for the establishment

---

[*] The first author gratefully acknowledges the partial co-funding of his work through the European Commission FP7 project MyMedia (www.mymediaproject.org) under the grant agreement no. 215006.

G. Vossen, D.D.E. Long, and J.X. Yu (Eds.): WISE 2009, LNCS 5802, pp. 87–100, 2009.

of user profiles and the discovery of topics, among other applications. However, similarity-based clustering of socially tagged items calls for methods that take account of the personalized perspectives posed by the users upon the items they tag. In this study, we deal with this challenge by proposing an innovative model for socially tagged items, in which we allow for multiple similarities per item. For this model, we use spectral clustering with tensor factorization. The clusters consist of items that are deemed similar by multiple users, even if each one considers them similar for different reasons!

The need for a new model emerges from the very nature of social tagging: data in a social-tagging system have three dimensions - the items, the users annotating them and the tags used for annotations. There is a 3-way relationship among these three dimensions; in classic database terminology, this means that the data cannot be brought into third normal form. Since conventional clustering algorithms model data in two-dimensional arrays (the rows are the items, the columns stand for the features), the 3-way relationship is solved by projecting away the third dimension: clustering is performed over items-users or items-tags arrays. Obviously, this incurs the loss of valuable information contained in the 3-way relationships.

Nevertheless, even when projecting one dimension away, the clustering of socially tagged items is challenging. The main reasons are the size of the feature space (large number of users or tags) and the complex cluster shapes. Spectral clustering algorithms lend themselves for such data. They capture similarity by spanning a graph structure, in which each item is connected to the k items most similar to it. By concentrating on the k nearest neighbors of each item, spectral clustering methods effectively project the data into a smaller, transformed feature space, in which they can detect complex clusters and suppress noise [13]. We exploit these properties by extending, however, spectral clustering to deal with all three dimensions of socially-tagged data without projecting any dimension.

In particular, we propose the computation of *multiple similarity values* for each pair of items to account for the fact that when all three dimensions are considered, the similarity between two items depends both on the users who tagged them and on the tags they used. To perform spectral clustering with multiple similarity values, we generalize the idea of a similarity graph into a similarity *multigraph* that has multiple edges between any two nodes. Similarity values on a graph would have been recorded on a conventional similarity matrix; for a multigraph, we must use a *tensor*, i.e. a multi-dimensional matrix. Spectral clustering on a matrix corresponds to matrix factorization with Singular Value Decomposition (SVD); accordingly, we perform tensor factorization.

The rest of the paper is organized as follows. Section 2 reviews related work. In Section 3 we give an overview of the proposed approach. Then, in Section 4 we describe our data model in detail and in Section 5 we present our clustering algorithm. In Section 6 we report on our comparison against a conventional spectral clustering method that only captures two-way relationships between items and users and between items and tags. We conclude in Section 7.

2   Related Work

The problem of clustering social data has recently started to attract attention. Giannakidou et al. [3] propose a co-clustering scheme that exploits joint groups of related tags and social data sources, in which both social and semantic aspects of tags are considered simultaneously. Their objective is to improve the retrieval of resources by exploiting their relation to tags. We also exploit the relation of items to tags, but not only: we capture also the relation of tags to users. Instead of co-clustering items with tags, we build solely clusters of items. For building these clusters, both the relation of items to tags and of tags to users are exploited to *induce* multiple similarities between items.

The need to cluster data with multiple similarity measures has been recognized only recently, as applications with very complex data structures started to proliferate. Seele et al have studied the problem of clustering bibliographic data with multiple similarity values [9]. They examined six different similarities on a collection of journal articles by considering, among others, similarities between words in abstracts, between names of authors co-citations etc. These similarities are predefined. In contrast, we *induce* multiple similarities from the tags, i.e. make no a priori assumptions as to their nature and number.

Shashua et al. [10] proposed the use of tensor factorization to cluster data that exhibit n-wise similarities, i.e. the definition of similarity involves more than two objects. Our problem specification is different: we consider *pairwise* similarity between objects, i.e. $n = 2$, but we take account of many pairwise similarities between any two objects.

Banerjee et al. [1] propose a method for multi-way clustering on tensors, thus extending co-clustering from matrices to tensors. However, their objective is to cluster different types of entities that are connected with relation graphs, rather than clustering items with multiple similarities.

3   Overview of Proposed Approach

Existing spectral clustering algorithms [13] first compute the k-NN similarity graph, which connects every item with its k-NN. Next, the Laplacian graph of the k-NN similarity graph is used instead, because of the benefits it offers, i.e., it is always positive-semidefinite (allowing its eigenvector decomposition) and the number of times 0 appears as its eigenvalue is the number of connected components in the k-NN similarity graph. Due to these convenient properties, if c clusters are required to be found, spectral clustering algorithms proceed by computing the c eigenvectors that correspond to the c smallest eigenvalues, and represent each original item with as a c-dimensional vector whose coordinates are the corresponding values within the c eigenvectors. With this representation, they can finally cluster the c-dimensional vectors using simple algorithms, like k-means or hierarchical agglomerative.

As described in Introduction, differently from conventional spectral clustering algorithms, our proposed approach considers multiple similarity values between each pair of items. In particular, let U be the set of all users. For a given tag t, let $U_1 \subseteq U$ be the set of users that tagged an item i_1 with t, whereas $U_2 \subseteq U$ be the set of users that tagged an item i_2 with t too. We can define a similarity value between i_1 and i_2 as follows. We form two vectors v_1 and v_2, both with $|U|$ elements that are set to 1 at positions that correspond to the users contained U_1 and U_2, respectively, whereas all rest positions are set to 0. Therefore, the similarity between i_1 and i_2 is given by the cosine measure between the two vectors v_1 and v_2. Since the above process can be repeated for all tags, the result is several similarity values between each pair of items i_1 and i_2. The set of all multiple similarity values are tag-aware and reflect the personalized aspect of similarity perceived by the users (e.g., two users may tag the same item but using entirely different tags).

To account for the various similarity values between each pair of items, we extend (Section 4) the k-NN similarity graph to a k-NN multidigraph that is the union of multiple simple k-NN graphs, one for each distinct tag. The adjacency matrix of a k-NN multidigraph forms a tensor, i.e., a multidimensional array. In order to attain the aforementioned advantages of the Laplacian, we propose a method (Section 5.1) to extend towards the construction of the Laplacian multidigraph, whose adjacency matrix is again represented as a tensor. To map each item to a feature space comprised from spectral information extracted from the Laplacian tensor, we describe (Section 5.2) how to use tensor factorization that extends SVD to multidimensional arrays. Finally, based on the computed features, we describe (Section 5.3) how the clustering is performed. To help comprehension, throughout the rest of the article we use a running example with the following data.

Example 1 (Data representation). We assume 3 users, U_1, U_2, and U_3, who assign tags to 4 items (henceforth 'items' for simplicity), $I_1, \ldots, I_4$, from a tag-set with 3 tags, $T_1, \ldots, T_3$. Each assignment comprises a triple of the form (user, item, tag). The 9 triples of the example are given in Figure 1a, whereas we additionally denote (in the first column) the ID of the triple. The corresponding view of the data as tripartite graph is depicted in Figure 1b. In this figure, the numbered labels on the edges correspond to the triple IDs in Figure 1a. For instance, the first triple (ID = 1) is: U_1 tagged I_1 with T_1. In Figure 1b this corresponds to the path consisting of all edges labelled as 1. To avoid cluttering the figure, parallel edges (i.e., edges between the same two nodes) with different labels are depicted as one with different labels separated by comma. In this example, we assume that items I_1 and I_2 form one cluster, whereas items I_3 and I_4 form a second cluster. This follows by observing in Figure 1b that, although users tag items from both clusters, they assign different tags to the first cluster than the second. Therefore, the relationships between items-users alone are not able to determine a clustering structure among the items. In contrast, when considering the 3-way relationships between items-users-tags, we are able to better detect the clustering of items.[1]   □

---

[1] Although this example focuses on the comparison between items-users-tags and items-tags relationships, we have to note that we have also verified experimentally that the former are preferable against items-tags relationships, as well.

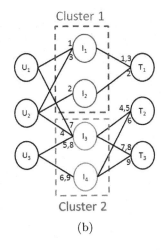

ID	User	Item	Tag
1	U_1	I_1	T_1
2	U_2	I_2	T_1
3	U_2	I_1	T_1
4	U_2	I_3	T_2
5	U_3	I_3	T_2
6	U_3	I_4	T_2
7	U_1	I_3	T_3
8	U_3	I_3	T_3
9	U_3	I_4	T_3

(a)

(b)

Fig. 1. Running example: (a)Input data. (b) Illustration of the tripartite graph.

4   Modelling the Multiple Similarity Values

In this section, we describe the modelling of multiple similarity values with a
k-nearest-neighbor multidigraph. A multidigraph is a directed graph permitted
to have multiple directed edges (henceforth, simply called edges), i.e., edges with
the same source and target nodes.

The input tripartite graph (like in the example of Figure 1b) can be partitioned according to the tags. For each tag t, we get the corresponding underlying
subgraph B_t, by keeping users and items that participate in triples with this
tag.

Example 2 (Partitioning of tripartite graph). For the example of Figure 1, the
partitioning results to 3 (due to the existence of 3 tags) bipartite subgraphs,
which are depicted in Figure 2: Figures 2a, b, and c correspond to the subgraphs
$B_{T_1}, B_{T_2}, B_{T_3}$, for the tags T_1, T_2, and T_3, respectively.   □

Each bipartite subgraph is represented with its adjacency matrix B_t ($1 \le t \le$
$|T|$), whose size is $|I| \times |U|$; that is, its rows correspond to items and its columns
to users. (Henceforth, wherever there is no ambiguity, we use interchangeably
the same symbol for a graph and its adjacency matrix.) Each element $B_t(i, u)$
is equal to 1, if there is an edge between the item i and user u, or 0 otherwise. Therefore, from each adjacency matrix B_t we can compute between every
pair of items i, j ($1 \le i, j \le |I|$), a similarity measure according to the values
in their corresponding rows $B_t(i, :)$ and $B_t(j, :)$. Following the widely used approach for 2 dimensional matrices (like document-term in information retrieval
or user-item in CF), we consider the cosine similarity measure between every pair
of items.

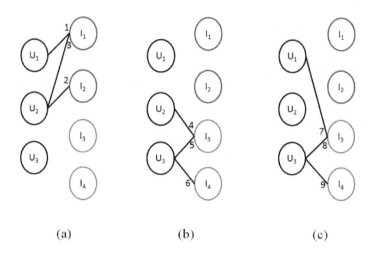

(a)   (b)   (c)

Fig. 2. Partitioning of the tripartite graph of the running example

Having defined a similarity measure, from each subgraph B_t $(1 \leq t \leq |T|)$, we can compute the corresponding k-nearest neighbor (k-NN) graph, N_t, which is a labelled and directed graph (digraph). The node set of each N_t corresponds to the set of items (i.e., each item has a corresponding node). The edge set consists of ordered pair of nodes. There is an edge between items i and j $(1 \leq i, j \leq |I|)$, if j is among the k nearest neighbors of i. Each edge is labelled with the corresponding similarity value.

By considering all k-NN digraphs together, we form the k-NN labelled multidigraph, $\mathcal{N}$. The node set of $\mathcal{N}$ corresponds to the set of items (i.e., each item has a corresponding node). The labelled edges of $\mathcal{N}$ is a multiset resulting from the union of the labelled edges of all N_t for $1 \leq t \leq |T|$. $\mathcal{N}$ summarizes the information about multiple similarities, according to the different tags between all items.

Example 3 (k-NN multidigraph). For the 3 subgraphs in Figure 2, the resulting k-NN multidigraph $\mathcal{N}$, for $k = 1$, is depicted in Figure 3a. The multiple edges between the nodes of $\mathcal{N}$ denote the different similarities between the items, according to the different tags. In Figure 3a, the edges representing similarities according to tag T_i $(1 \leq i \leq 3)$ are annotated with T_i and then follows the corresponding similarity value.[2] Notice that $\mathcal{N}$ correctly captures the clustering structure: edges exist only between items of the same cluster, i.e., between I_1, I_2 for the first cluster and between I_3, I_4 for the second. Conversely, in Figure 3b, which depicts the k-NN digraph (not a multidigraph) when only user-item relationships are considered, the separation of clusters is not clear. □

---

[2] In this small example, to avoid numerical problems, we assign similarity equal to 0 when at least one item has no edge at all in the corresponding bipartite graphs. Moreover, to avoid cluttering the graph, only the non-zero similarities are depicted.

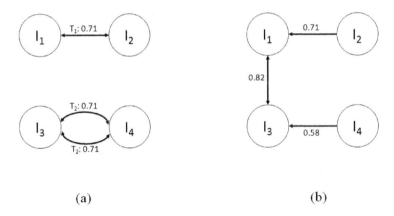

(a)   (b)

Fig. 3. The k-NN multidigraph for the running example

5   The Proposed Clustering Algorithm

5.1   Constructing the Laplacian Tensor

For each k-NN digraph N_t $(1 \leq t \leq |T|)$ of $\mathcal{N}$, compute D_t as a diagonal matrix whose diagonal elements are defined as follows:

$$D_t(i, i) = \sum_{j=1}^{|I|} N_t(i, j) \tag{1}$$

The Laplacian matrix, L_t, of each N_t is computed as follows [7]:

$$L_t = \mathbb{I} - D_t^{-1/2} N_t D_t^{-1/2} \tag{2}$$

where $\mathbb{I}$ is the identity matrix.

The Laplacian tensor of $\mathcal{N}$ is, therefore defined as $\mathcal{L} \in \mathbb{R}^{|I| \times |I| \times |T|}$, whose elements are given as follows:

$$\mathcal{L}(i, j, t) = L_t(i, j) \tag{3}$$

Thus, each matrix L_t, for $1 \leq t \leq |T|$, comprises a frontal slice in $\mathcal{L}$.

Example 4 (Laplacian tensor). For the k-NN multidigraph of Figure 3, the resulting 3-mode Laplacian tensor is depicted in Figure 4, having as frontal slices the 3 L_t matrices $(1 \leq t \leq 3)$.   □

The Laplacian tensor $\mathcal{L}$ has 3 *modes* (illustrated with red arrows in Figure 4): the first mode corresponds to the items, the second mode to the neighboring items, and the third mode to the tags. To perform spectral clustering, we are interested in extracting the spectrum of $\mathcal{L}$ for the first mode. This procecure is explained in the following.

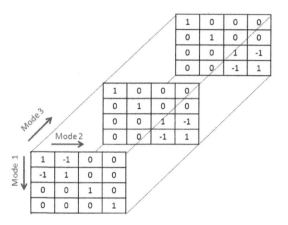

Fig. 4. The Laplacian tensor of the running example

5.2   Factorizing the Laplacian Tensor

In this subsection, we summarize the factorization of the Laplacian tensor using Tucker decomposition [5], which is the high-order analogue of the Singular Value Decomposition (SVD) for tensors. The factorization of the Laplacian tensor will produce the required spectrum of its first (corresponding to items) mode.

First, we have to define the n-mode product $\mathcal{T} \times_n M$ between a general N-order tensor $\mathcal{T} \in \mathbb{R}^{I_1 \times \dots \times I_N}$ and a matrix $M \in \mathbb{R}^{J_n \times I_n}$. The result is an $(I_1 \times I_2 \times \dots \times I_{n-1} \times J_n \times I_{n+1} \times \dots \times I_N)$-tensor, whose entries are defined as follows (elements are denoted through their subscript indexes):

$$(\mathcal{T} \times_n M)_{i_1 i_2 \dots i_{n-1} j_n i_{n+1} \dots i_N} = \sum_{i_n} T_{i_1 i_2 \dots i_{n-1} i_n i_{n+1} \dots i_N} M_{j_n i_n} \qquad (4)$$

Since $\mathcal{L}$ is a 3-order tensor, we henceforth focus only on 1-mode, 2-mode, and 3-mode products.

The Tucker decomposition of the 3-order tensor $\mathcal{L}$ can be written as follows [6]:

$$\mathcal{L} \approx \mathcal{C} \times_1 P_1 \times_2 P_2 \times_3 P_3 \qquad (5)$$

The $P_1 \in \mathbb{R}^{|I| \times |I|}, P_2 \in \mathbb{R}^{|I| \times |I|}, P_3 \in \mathbb{R}^{|T| \times |T|}$ are called the mode-1 (items), mode-2 (neighboring items), and mode-3 (tags) projection matrices, respectively. The 3 projection matrices contain the orthonormal vectors for each mode, called the mode-1, mode-2 and mode-3 singular vectors, respectively. $\mathcal{C}$ is called the core tensor and has the property of all orthogonality. Nevertheless, unlike SVD for matrices, $\mathcal{C}$ is not diagonal. Recently, several algorithms have been proposed to efficiently compute the components of the Tucker decomposition. Due to lack of space, more details about the algorithms and their complexity can be found in a recent survey on tensor factorization [5].

Having performed the Tucker decomposition of the Laplacian tensor $\mathcal{L}$, we are interested in the mode-1 singular vectors that are stored in P_1. A frequently followed approach in spectral clustering, when c clusters are required, is to select the c eigenvectors associated to the c smallest eigenvalues [13]. Similarly, we select the c mode-1 singular vectors in P_1 associated to the smallest singular values in the core tensor $\mathcal{C}$.

Example 5 (Selection of the mode-1 singular vectors). By performing the Tucker decomposition of the Laplacian tensor of the running example (Figure 4), the two selected mode-1 singular vectors from P_1 (recall that in the running example we have two clusters of items) are the following:

$$[0, 0, 0.71, 0.71]^T \text{ and } [0.71, 0.71, 0, 0]^T \qquad \square$$

5.3   Performing the Spectral Clustering

To find c clusters of items using the c mode-1 singular vectors that where computed and selected during the factorization of the Laplacian tensor, we apply the following steps: (1) Normalize the c selected mode-1 singular vectors to have norm equal to 1. (2) Form a matrix $X \in \mathbb{R}^{|I| \times k}$, whose columns are the normalized c selected mode-1 singular vectors. (3) Associate each item i to a point x_i whose coordinates are the contents of the i-th row of X. (4) Choose a distance metric for the $(x_i)_{i=1,...,|I|}$ points. (5) Cluster the points $(x_i)_{i=1,...,|I|}$ into c clusters using a clustering algorithm, according to the chosen distance metric. (6) Assign each item to the cluster of its associated point.

Due to the properties of the Laplacian tensor, in practice (and similarly to conventional spectral clustering on Laplacian graphs), the points in X can be easily clustered (Step 5) using simple and well known algorithms. In the sequel we consider hierarchical agglomerative algorithms for this purpose based on Euclidean distance (Step 4).

Example 6 (Clustering of items). After normalizing the vectors selected in Example 5, we get the X matrix depicted in Figure 5a. A simple hierarchical clustering algorithm, based on Euclidean distance, can easily detect two clusters, the first consisting of the first two points, whereas the second of the latter two points. This result is in accordance to the clusters assumed in the running example, i.e., the first one with the items I_1, I_2 and the second with the items I_3, I_4. To exemplify the effectiveness of the proposed representation, we can contrast the aforementioned result with the one obtained when performing spectral clustering without taking into account the information of tags. In this case, the corresponding X matrix is computed by taking the Laplacian matrix based only on items-users relationships, that is, originally we have a matrix where a user-item combination is set to 1 when the user tagged at least once the item. In this case, the resulting X matrix is depicted in Figure 5b. Evidently, in the latter case a clustering algorithm is not able to correctly detect the two clusters,

$$X = \begin{pmatrix} 0 & 1 \\ 0 & 1 \\ 1 & 0 \\ 1 & 0 \end{pmatrix} \qquad\qquad X = \begin{pmatrix} 0 & 0 \\ 1 & 0 \\ 0 & 0 \\ 0 & 1 \end{pmatrix}$$

(a)   (b)

Fig. 5. The mapping when considering (a) items-users-tags (b) items-users

because items I_1 and I_4 will be incorrectly assigned to the same cluster (due to their identical coordinates), whereas either I_2 or I_3 will join the cluster of I_1, I_4, as their distance from each other is higher than their distance from I_1, I_4.   □

Therefore, the proposed approach can better detect the clustering, because it fully exploits all items-users-tags relationships. This is verified with the experimental results in the following section.

6 Experimental Evaluation

6.1 Experimental Configuration

We experimentally tested the proposed method, denoted as Tensor-based Spectral Clustering (TSC). The baseline method is the Spectral Clustering (denoted as SC), which applies spectral clustering on the item-user 2 dimensional matrix with elements set to 1 when the corresponding item has been tagged at least once (no matter the tag) by the corresponding user.[3] Both TSC and SC have been implemented in Matlab using the same components. Tensor factorization was computed using the Tensor toolbox[4].

We consider two real social-tagging data sets. The first one is Movielens (downloaded from www.grouplens.org/node/73), which contains tags provided by users on movies. Associated information is available for movies. In our experiments we selected the genre (e.g., comedy, drama, etc.), where notice that each movie can belong to more than 1 out of 18 total genres. The second data set is Bibsonomy (provided by the authors of the paper [4]), which contains tags provided by users on Web resources (we excluded the tags of this data set that were given to scientific articles).

Social-tagging data present problems like tag polysemy and sparsity. To address them, we applied the widely used technique of Latent Semantic Indexing (LSI) [2] and reduced the number of dimensions in the modes of users and tags, by maintaining a percentage of them. This reduction was performed by modelling the original triples as a 3-mode tensor and applying Tucker decomposition [5].

---

[3] We have to note that we performed the same comparison against spectral clustering on a item-tag 2 dimensional matrix and found that it is outperformed by TSC as well. We omit the presentation of these results due to lack of space.

[4] http://csmr.ca.sandia.gov/~tgkolda/TensorToolbox/

The item mode is left unchanged, whereas the number of maintained users and tags after this process is expressed as a percentage (default value 30%) of the original number of users and tags (for simplicity we use the same percentage for both). SC also utilize this technique by maintaining the same percentage for users or tags.

For the fifth step of the spectral clustering algorithm, we examined the Unweighted Pair Group Method with Arithmetic mean (UPGMA) hierarchical algorithm that defines the distance between two clusters as the average of the distances of all object pairs, selecting one object per cluster. We considered further hierarchical algorithms, but found that UPGMA performed best.

To measure the quality of the clustering results, we have used the measures of *entropy* (the lower the better) and *Jaccard coefficient* (the higher the better) to evaluate a clustering against the explicit class labels of Movielens. To measure the quality of one clustering (both Movielens and Bibsonomy) we used the *silhouette coefficient* (the higher the better). These measures are defined as follows [12].

Let ζ be a clustering and ξ be the set of classes. $JaccardCoeff(\zeta, \xi) = \frac{f11}{f11+f01+f10}$, where $f11$ is the number of records of the same class that were put in the same cluster of ζ, $f10$ is the number of records that were put in the same cluster of ζ but belong to distinct classes, and $f01$ is the number of records that belong to the same class but appear in different clusters. The entropy measures the degree to which a cluster contains tuples belonging to a single class: $entropy(\zeta, \xi) = \frac{\sum_{C_u \in \zeta} |C_u| e(C_u)}{|\bigcup_{C_v \in \zeta} C_v|}$, where the probability that a tuple in C belongs to L_v is $p_{uv} = \frac{|C_u \cap L_v|}{|C_u|}$ and The entropy of C_u is $e(C_u, \xi) = \sum_{L_v \in \xi} p_{uv} log_2 p_{uv}$.

To compute the silhouette coefficient of a tuple x in cluster $C \in \zeta$, we calculate its average distance a_x from all other tuples in C and from the t uples in the clusters of $\zeta \setminus \{C\}$, say b_x. Then $s(x) = \frac{(b_x - a_x)}{\max(a_x, b_x)}$. The silhouette of C is the average silhouette of its members. The silhouette for the clustering $silhouette(\zeta)$ is the average over the cluster silhouettes, weighted with cluster cardinalities.

6.2   Experimental Results

We experimentally compare TSC and SC and examine sensitivity against the following parameters: the number of neighbors, k (default value 10) and the percentage of maintained users/items (default value 10%). We examine a varying number of clusters c that, following the approach of conventional spectral clustering algorithms [13], we considered it as a user-defined parameter. Therefore, the number of clusters vary up to 18 for Movielens (which is the number of distinct genres) and up to 20 for Bibsonomy.

Figures 6a–c present the results for the Movielens data set against varying number of clusters. The measures are Jaccard coefficient, Entropy, and Silhouette coefficient. In all cases, TSC performs favorably against SC. Analogous conclusion is drawn for the Bibsonomy data set, the results for which (only Silhouette coefficient is applicable) are presented in Figures 6d.

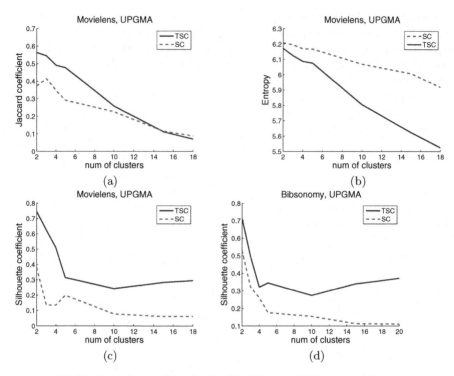

Fig. 6. Experimental results for Movielens and Bibsonomy data set

We tested the sensitivity against the number of nearest neighbors, k, that is used during the creation of the k-NN multidigraph. Figures 7a and b present the results for Movielens and Bibsonomy, respectively. In both cases we require the maximum number of clusters that were examined in the previous experiments (for brevity, for Movielens we present only Silhouette coefficient). When k is very low, the performance of TSC can be negatively affected, because not enough similarity information is captured. For k values in the range between 10 and 20, best performance is attained. Then, as k increases, performance deteriorates, because noise incurs (TSC considers items that are not truly neighbors). Analogous results hold for SC, although deterioration is less pronounced. Nevertheless, in all cases TSC is superior to SC.

Next, we measured the impact of the percentage of maintained users/tags. Figures 8 a and b present the results for Movielens and Bibsonomy, respectively. Again, we required the maximum number of clusters, whereas k is set to 10. As expected, for both TSC and SC, as the percentage of maintained users/tags increases, performance is reduced due to the problems described in Section 6.1. However, TSC is able to attain much better performance than SC even for higher percentage of maintained users/tags, which means that TSC can better cope with these problems.

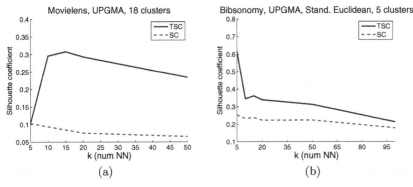

Fig. 7. Experimental results on sensitivity to the number of nearest neighbors, k

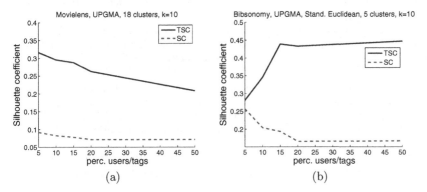

Fig. 8. Experimental results on sensitivity to the percentage of maintained users/tags

7   Conclusions

We have considered the data mining task of clustering items (e.g., Web resources, images, scientific papers, etc.) stored in social-tagging systems. To overcome the problems of existing approaches and avoid breaking the original 3-way relationships that are present in social-tagged data, we proposed the extension of the popular spectral clustering algorithms to directly handle all dimensions without suppressing them with 2-way relationships. The proposed approach consists of the following contributions: (i) We provided the insight that it is necessary to capture and exploit the *multiple* similarity values reflected in the tags assigned to the same item by different users. (ii) To support multiple similarity values, we extended the modeling based on k-NN similarity graphs by using k-NN similarity multigraphs, which allow the existence of multiple edges between two nodes. (iii) We modeled the multigraph structures as *tensors* (i.e., multidimensional arrays) and extended the popular spectral-clustering algorithms by developing a method to construct their corresponding Laplacian tensors. (iv) We described the use of tensor factorization, which extends the Singular Value Decomposition (SVD) to multi-dimensional arrays, to extract spectral features from the Laplacian tensors. (v) Our experimental results with real data indicate the clear advantage, in terms of quality of the final clustering, of the proposed method against conventional spectral clustering that suppresses the original data by considering only 2-way relationships.

As future work, we will extend the proposed clustering method in other kind of data, like documents. Also, we plan to develop model-based CF algorithms that will exploit the proposed clustering method.

References

1. Banerjee, A., Basu, S., Merugu, S.: Multi-way clustering on relation graphs. In: Proceedings of the 7th SIAM International Conference on Data Mining, SDM 2007 (2007)
2. Deerwester, S., Dumais, S.T., Furnas, G.W., Landauer, T.K., Harshman, R.: Indexing by latent semantic analysis. Journal of the American Society for Information Science 41, 391–407 (1990)
3. Giannakidou, E., Koutsonikola, V., Vakali, A., Kompatsiaris, Y.: Co-clustering tags and social data sources. In: Proceedings of the 9th International Conference on Web-Age Information Management (WAIM 2008), pp. 317–324 (2008)
4. Jäschke, R., Marinho, L.B., Hotho, A., Schmidt-Thieme, L., Stumme, G.: Tag recommendations in folksonomies. In: Kok, J.N., Koronacki, J., Lopez de Mantaras, R., Matwin, S., Mladenič, D., Skowron, A. (eds.) PKDD 2007. LNCS (LNAI), vol. 4702, pp. 506–514. Springer, Heidelberg (2007)
5. Kolda, T.G., Bader, B.W.: Tensor decompositions and applications. SIAM Review 51(3) (to appear, 2009)
6. de Lathauwer, L., de Moor, B., Vandewalle, J.: A multilinear singular value decomposition. SIAM Journal of Matrix Analysis and Applications 21(4), 1253–1278 (2000)
7. Ng, A.Y., Jordan, M.I., Weiss, Y.: On spectral clustering: Analysis and an algorithm. In: Proceedings of the Advances in Neural Information Processing Systems (NIPS 2001), pp. 849–856 (2001)
8. Rendle, S., Marinho, L., Nanopoulos, A., Schmidt-Thieme, L.: Learning optimal ranking with tensor factorization for tag recommendation. In: Proceedings of the ACM Conf. on Knowledge Discovery and Data Mining, KDD 2009 (to appear, 2009)
9. Selee, T.M., Kolda, T.G., Kegelmeyer, W.P., Griffin, J.D.: Extracting clusters from large datasets with multiple similarity measures using IMSCAND. In: Parks, M.L., Collis, S.S. (eds.) CSRI Summer Proceedings 2007, Technical Report SAND2007-7977, Sandia National Laboratories, Albuquerque, NM and Livermore, CA, pp. 87–103 (2007)
10. Shashua, A., Zass, R., Hazan, T.: Multi-way clustering using super-symmetric non-negative tensor factorization. In: Leonardis, A., Bischof, H., Pinz, A. (eds.) ECCV 2006. LNCS, vol. 3954, pp. 595–608. Springer, Heidelberg (2006)
11. Symeonidis, P., Nanopoulos, A., Manolopoulos, Y.: A unified framework for providing recommendations in social tagging systems based on ternary semantic analysis. IEEE Transactions on Knowledge and Data Engineering (accepted, 2009)
12. Tan, P.-N., Steinbach, M., Kumar, V.: Introduction to Data Mining. Wiley, Chichester (2004)
13. von Luxburg, U.: A tutorial on spectral clustering. Technical report (No. TR-149) Max Planck Institute for Biological Cybernetics (2006)

Semantic Weaving for Context-Aware Web Service Composition

Li Li, Dongxi Liu, and Athman Bouguettaya

CSIRO ICT Centre, Australia
{lily.li,dongxi.liu,athman.bouguettaya}@csiro.au

Abstract. An Aspect-oriented Programming (AOP) based approach is proposed to perform context-aware service composition on the fly. It realises context-aware composition by semantically weaving context into static Web service composition. A context *weaver* is implemented based on the proposed approach. The proposed semantic weaving allows services to be composed in a systematic way with changing context.

1 Introduction

In recent years, Web service composition has attracted increasing attention in the research community. However, it is far from trivial [1,2]. In addition to functional and nonfunctional requirements, a fully workable context-aware service composition requires the context to be taken into account.

Context is any information (e.g., location and time information), which can be used to characterise the situation to which the Web service is being applied. Information such as location and time may change over time. Context is recognised as important and has been widely studied in the field of Mobile and Pervasive Computing [3,4]. It needs to be explicitly described and managed in Web service composition so that different participating Web services can be connected correctly. Several papers [4,5,6] have identified different context dimensions for different types of Web services, and various attempts have been made to cope with the utilisation of the context. However, they provide little guideline on how to use dynamically changing context in service composition.

Achieving context-aware service composition is challenging [7]. Some methods include hard-coding context and the use of Aspect-oriented programming. Hard-coding context approaches assume that context remains unchanged throughout the service life cycle. In fact, the context of a Web service changes as the state of a predefined environment evolves. Take the popular travel package for example. Assuming a user sends a request to the *composer* to book a travel package to the Gold Coast in Australia. The user also requires tickets to the Gold Coast Theme Parks (e.g., the Dreamworld, Movie World, and Sea World). This example involves Web services that manage booking the flight, hotel, car rental and ticket (e.g., *flightBooking*, *hotelBooking*, *carRental*, and *ticketBooking*). Consider now the user is based in a non-English speaking country. The challenge is to take this contextual information into service composition efficiently without reconstructing the entire composition from scratch.

G. Vossen, D.D.E. Long, and J.X. Yu (Eds.): WISE 2009, LNCS 5802, pp. 101–114, 2009.

Aspect-oriented programming (AOP) [8] is an effective module mechanism used in software engineering for separating *crosscutting* concerns from primary concerns. For example, logging the execution results of some Java methods for debugging is a crosscutting concern since the logging operation may need to appear in multiple classes and methods. In AOP, the logging operation is encapsulated by an *aspect* as a separate module, so the logging operation can be easily removed after debugging is over. This feature of AOP is very desirable for context-aware service composition. The context services as *crosscutting* concerns can be represented by *aspects* to be woven into the primary services determined by the business logic. We can thus separate context services from main services clearly and context services can be updated independently into new contexts without changing the main services. AOP is well suited to context-aware service composition because it provides support for runtime contexts updating.

Charfi et al. [9] present an aspect-oriented extension to BPEL (AO4BEPL) to deal with *crosscuts* in Web service composition. Our work shares similarities with AO4BPEL. Both approaches use AOP technology. However, the discussion in this paper is aimed at introducing semantic weaving instead of syntactic weaving as used in AO4BPEL. We treat context as an *aspect*. Thus the context can be semantically woven into composition at runtime.

There are several properties commonly regarded as context attributes, but there exists no universal context model that applies to all applications [10]. In this paper, the term context relates to the collection of assumptions that are required to perform correct composition of Web services.

Several issues pointed out by Satyanarayanan in Pervasive Computing [3] are applicable to Web services. Typical issues include how context is structured, activated and woven into Web service composition, and how context-aware service composition is achieved. They are the driving force of this paper. Unlike most of the current work, this paper takes a different view that focuses on AOP-based context-aware service composition.

Our main contributions in this paper are summarised as follows:

- We propose to use AOP technology to cope with context-aware Web service composition. We show that AOP can treat context composition in a more systematic way.
- We propose a method of describing context as an *aspect* to reflect the nature of context. The proposed method is generic to be able to cope with different contexts of Web services.
- We define context configuration based on semantic weaving and implement the context weaver. The novelty of our semantic weaving algorithm is that it enables quick and dynamic adaptation by the *composer* in a systematic way.

The proposed approach can work independently or together with existing composition strategies.

The rest of the paper is organised as follows. Section 2 presents how to use *aspect* to describe context. Section 3 discusses semantic context weaving algorithm in service composition. Section 4 provides an overview of related work. Finally, Section 5 is the conclusion.

2   Context as Aspect

Current Web service composition techniques can hardly cope with dynamic changes. Usually, whenever a new context is available, most current composition techniques have to reconsider the whole composition. This is because they are essentially static. Aspect-oriented programming (AOP) [8] is a programming paradigm that allows the composition system to adopt new characteristics as contexts change. In what follows we first briefly introduce AOP. We then discuss how the context is structured to allow context-aware composition with the AOP technology.

2.1   Aspect-Oriented Programming

We expect relevant context services to be invoked automatically whenever a change takes place. Usually, a context service may be applied to a class of service composition scenarios in differen parts. For example, *language translation* context may be needed by services *hotelBooking* and *ticketBooking* separately. This is also referred to as *crosscutting concern* in AOP terminology. Below is a brief introduction to AOP terminology with a focus on Web service composition scenarios [8,11].

- *join points*: *Join points* are well-defined points in the execution of a program. These are points in an automaton, used to depict a Web service.
- *pointcut*: A *pointcut* is a way of detecting a *join point* by a means of configuration. A dedicated *context* service will be applied whenever a *pointcut* is reached.

  The *pointcut* can be checked in different ways. *Type* checking is a popular one. Essentially, *type* checking considers syntactics such as the type of parameters and matching patterns in the names. With the presence of context, semantic checking is necessary to complement *type* checking. More detail is given in Section 3.
- *advice*: An *advice* is a *context* service which deals with context. It can be executed *before*, *after*, or *around* the *joint point* at hand. Figure 1 demonstrates three *advices* in the travel example. The original composition *schema* is on the left hand side (Figure 1) with an *advice* "cut" at *hotelBooking*. On the right hand side (Figure 1) are three *schemata* in accordance with three different actions.
- *aspect*: An *aspect* is the combination of the *pointcut* and *advice*. In the travel example, we add a *context* service to service composition as recommended by *pointcut*.

2.2   Context Structure

As previously stated, AOP allows the changing context to be handled by weaving it into the main services for a new requirement. The context structure is

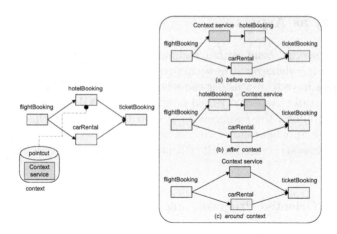

Fig. 1. Before, after, and around advice

important to realise it. The following are two considerations in defining context structure for context weaving in AOP.

The first one is about the syntax of context structure. The following definitions are in BNF with "::=" standing for "is defined as", and "|" for "or".

ctx::= $pos\ des\ serv$
pos::= before |after |around
des::= isMsg (C) |C op val |$des \wedge des$ |$des \vee des$
C::= concept of an ontology
val:= numbers|alphanumeric strings
op ::= $<$ |$=$ |$>$
$serv$::= $automaton$

We use a dotted style notation to address context structure in semantic weaving. The representation $ctx.pos$ is used to refer to one of the positions (e.g., *before*, *after*, and *around*). Similarly, $ctx.serv$ stands for an automaton, whilst $ctx.des$ for a descriptor.

The second one is about the semantic definition of context. We describe context as a concept of an ontology. Generally, an ontology [12] can be described as a tuple in a form $(C, Rel, Axiom)$ with C denoting *Concepts*, Rel is an n-ary predicate $Rel(x_1, x_2, ..., x_n)$, where $x_1, x_2, ..., x_n \in Concepts$, and *Axiom* is a set of axioms specifying the intended interpretation of concepts in some domains. As our focus is on context-aware composition, only standard semantic relations (i.e., equivalent and containment semantic relations) will be considered in this paper. A consideration of other semantic relations will be deferred to a later study. The ontology formalism definition is as follows: $(C, Rel, \emptyset)$, or simply (C, Rel) when $Rel \in \{=, \sqsubset, \sqsupset\}$. For example, if $C = \{C_1, C_2, C_3\}$ with C_1 is the superclass of C_2 and C_3, then the ontology would be: $(\{C_1, C_2, C_3\}, \{C_2 \sqsupset C_1, C_3 \sqsupset C_1, C_1 = C_2 \sqcap C_3\})$. Uppercase characters such as C_1, C_2, and C_3 are used to represent contexts in the following discussion.

3   Context Weaving for Composition

In this section, we explain context weaving that is implemented as a context weaver.With context weaving, a service is instrumented with the context services to generate a new service that is thus context-aware. The syntactic weaving method adopted by aspect-oriented programming [11,8] is not suitable for context weaving. Our approach implements weaving based on the semantics of *join points* (i.e., service messages in this work). Our semantic weaving method is expected to contribute to AOP in the future.

3.1   Automata-Based Service Model

For our context weaving purpose, services are modeled by automata. An automaton is a tuple (Q, s, F, δ), where Q is a set of states, $s \in Q$ the start state, $F \subseteq Q$ a set of final states, and δ contains the transition rules. A transition rule has the forms either $(q, c, ?m, q')$ or $(q, c, !m, q')$, meaning that the state can change from q to q' after reading or transmitting message m if the condition c holds (lowercase letter c standing for the condition). In the future, transitions concerning messages are represented by prefixing the message with ? (reading/receiving) or ! (transmitting/sending), respectively. A message has the structure $mn(v_1 : ty_1, ..., v_n : ty_n)$, where mn is the message name, v_i a message variable and ty_i its type. We assume that all variables are different in a message. The types can be described in XML Schema. The details of types are not required here. There is a special message called `null`, which means there is no message to receive or send for an (internal) transition of service automata. A condition c in transition rules is defined on message variables. For example, if there is a message ?`getPrice`$(p : double)$ before the message !`order`(), then we define the condition $p < 10$ to guard the second message so as to determine whether an order message should be sent or not. For a service automaton S, we use $S.Q$ to represent its states set, and similarly $S.s$ for the start state, $S.F$ final states, and $S.\delta$ transition rules. For service automata with context services, we require that the automata have only one final state.

A service automaton for the example in Section 1 is depicted in Figure 2. For brevity, all transition conditions are `true`. The state set Q is $\{q_1, q_2, q_3, q_4, q_f\}$, in which q_1 is the start state, and q_f is the final state. There are six transition rules in total. For example, the state transition from q_1 to q_2 when receiving the message `flightRes`, which contains the user's name `Name`, the departure airport `Airport`$_1$, the departure data `Date`$_1$, the destination airport `Airport`$_2$ and the return date `Date`$_2$.

3.2   Context Configuration

Messages defined in the service model are syntactic. Syntactic messages do not explicitly express what context these messages involve. Different services may use different message names, variables and types even if they are related to the same contexts. For example, the message b(n : string, p : double) does not tell

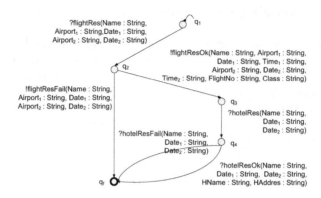

Fig. 2. Services in an automaton

anything about the context applicable to this message. As done in semantic web services [13,14,15], we address this problem by configuring messages with semantic context information.

A context configuration is a mapping from messages to its relevant context. Given a message $mn(v_1 : ty_1, ..., v_n : ty_n)$, its context is described by a configuration in the following form:

$$mn(v_1 : ty_1, ..., v_n : ty_n) \mapsto (C_0, \{(v_1, C_1), ..., (v_n, C_n)\})$$

It means that the message mn is supposed to be run in the context C_0 with each message v_i related to the context C_i. In this context description, the context C_0 is the major context for the whole message, and the contexts C_i are specific ones for each message variable. Specific contexts can be interpreted more accurately when combined with their major contexts. For example, a time context may be concerned when combined with the major context for flight reservation, while not when combined with the major context for ordering books.

Specific contexts have values at run time, which are the values of the corresponding message variables. For example, if a variable v_i is associated with the context Location and it has the value Australia at runtime, then this Location context also has the value Australia. For a message, its configured contexts on variables are required to be not overlapped. That is, if a variable v_i is configured with a context C_i, then any other variable v_j must not be configured with a context C_j where $C_i = C_j$, $C_i \sqsubset C_j$ or $C_j \sqsubset C_i$. Otherwise, we cannot determine the value of context C_i since its value is not unique in one message.

We do not annotate services with context information directly. Thus, a service can be deployed to other contexts by using different context configurations. And we also can configure only those messages concerned in a specific context.

3.3   Semantic Weaving

To implement context weaving, we need to define the *join points* in the service model, which are the possible points where context services can be brought in. As

$$\begin{aligned}
\texttt{next}(q, \emptyset) &= \emptyset \\
\texttt{next}(q, \{(q_1, c, ?m, q_2)\} \cup \delta) &= \{(m, q_2)\} \cup \texttt{next}(q, \delta), \text{ if } q = q_1 \\
\texttt{next}(q, \{(q_1, c, !m, q_2)\} \cup \delta) &= \{(m, q_2)\} \cup \texttt{next}(q, \delta), \text{ if } q = q_1 \\
\texttt{next}(q, \{(q_1, c, ?m, q_2)\} \cup \delta) &= \texttt{next}(q, \delta), \text{ if } q \neq q_1 \\
\texttt{next}(q, \{(q_1, c, !m, q_2)\} \cup \delta) &= \texttt{next}(q, \delta), \text{ if } q \neq q_1
\end{aligned}$$

Fig. 3. The `next` Operator

the method calls in AspectJ [11], service invocations in BPEL has been chosen as the main joint points in AO4BPEL [9]. In our service model, service invocations are embodied by message transmission $!m$ or message reception $?m$. Thus, we use messages as the *join points* in our work. With the context configuration, context services can thus be woven into main services based on the semantics of service messages. For the example in Figure 2, there are six messages and for each message we will determine whether there is possibility to invoke context services either *before*, *after* or *around* this message.

$$\begin{aligned}
\texttt{select}(smsg, \emptyset) &= \emptyset \\
\texttt{select}(smsg, \{ctx\} \cup Ctx) &= \{(ctx, cond)\} \cup \texttt{select}(smsg, \text{if } smsg \vdash ctx.des \Rightarrow cond) \\
\texttt{select}(smsg, \{ctx\} \cup Ctx) &= \texttt{select}(smsg, Ctx), \text{if } smsg \nvdash ctx.des
\end{aligned}$$

Fig. 4. The `select` Operator

3.3.1 Two Operators: `next` and `select`

The operators `next` and `select` are two auxiliary operators used by the semantic weaving algorithm in the next section.

The operator `next` is defined in Figure 3. This operator takes as inputs a state q and a set δ of transition rules in a service automaton, and returns a set of pairs (m, q') with either $(q, c, ?m, q') \in \delta$ or $(q, c, !m, q') \in \delta$ for a certain condition c. By using this operator, we can know what the join-point messages and successor states are at the state q. For example, given the state q_2 and the transition relation δ in Figure 3, the operation $\texttt{next}(q, \delta)$ returns the following set.

$$\{(!\text{flightResFail(Name:String, ...),}q_3),$$
$$(!\text{flightResOk(Name:String, ...), } q_f) \}$$

The operator `select` is defined in Figure 4. Given a message configuration $smsg$, defined as $(C_0, \{(v_1, C_1), ..., (v_n, C_n)\})$, and a set of contexts Ctx, the operation $\texttt{select}(smsg, Ctx)$ returns a set of pairs $(ctx, cond)$, which means that if the condition $cond$ holds, then the context service described in ctx can be applied. This operator depends on the validity check of a context descriptor against the configuration of a message. The validity check is defined in Figure 5. A descriptor $\texttt{isMsg}(C)$ holds on a message if the major context of this message is subsumed under C. This descriptor can be checked statically, so the condition to guard this context is trivially `true`. For the descriptor C `op` val, if there is a context C_i ($1 \leq i \leq n$) in the message configuration $(C_0, \{(v_1, C_1), ..., (v_n, C_n)\})$, then this descriptor is valid together the condition v_i op val, which will be checked at runtime, where op $\in \{<, =, >\}$. Recall that v_i is the value of C_i at runtime. The descriptors $des \wedge des'$ and $des \vee des'$ are checked based on the validity of their sub-descriptors des and des'.

let $smsg = (C_0, \{(v_1, C_1), ..., (v_n, C_n)\})$
R1 : $smsg \vdash \texttt{isMsg}(C) \Rightarrow \texttt{true}$, if $C_0 \sqsubseteq C$
R2 : $smsg \vdash C$ op $val \Rightarrow v_i$ op val,
   if $\exists i : 1 \leq i \leq n. C_i$ op C, where op $\in \{<, =, >\}$
R3 : $smsg \vdash des \wedge des' \Rightarrow cond \wedge cond'$,
   if $smsg \vdash des \Rightarrow cond$ and $smsg \vdash des' \Rightarrow cond'$
R4 : $smsg \vdash des \vee des' \Rightarrow cond \vee cond'$,
   if $smsg \vdash des \Rightarrow cond$ or $smsg \vdash des' \Rightarrow cond'$

Fig. 5. The Validity of context descriptors

3.3.2   Semantic Weaving Algorithm

The semantic weaving algorithm is defined in Figure 6. The inputs of this algorithm include a service automaton S, a set of contexts Ctx and a context configuration $Conf$. The algorithm returns a new service automaton S' that is obtained by weaving applicable contexts from Ctx into the input service automaton S.

This algorithm consists of two parts. The first part includes the code from line (08) to line (26). This part generates for each transition rule a set of pairs of context and applicable condition. Concretely, a tuple of the form $(q, m, q', pCtx)$ is generated from the transition rule $(q, c, !m, q')$ or $(q, c, ?m, q')$, where $pCtx$ is a set of pairs of context and applicable condition computed by using $\texttt{select}$. The code in this part traverses the automaton states following the transitions rules, and after a state is processed, it is recorded in O and it will not be processed again even if there are transition loops. Hence, the first part must terminate after processing all reachable states.

The code from line (27) to line (48) is the second part of the weaving algorithm. This part will insert context services into the service automaton. For a tuple $(q, m, q', pCtx)$, there must be a transition either $(q, c, !m, q')$ or $(q, c, ?m, q')$ in the service automaton according to the first part algorithm. After weaving, the transition $(q, c, !m, q')$ or $(q, c, ?m, q')$ is removed at line (47) and new transitions are created by calling the function $\texttt{createtran}$ and the code at lines (35), (39) and (46). The function $\texttt{createtran}$ is shown in Figure 7. The new transitions connect the context service automata with the original service automaton. Below, we demonstrate the newly generated transitions following the algorithm shown in Figure 6.

Example 1: suppose $pCtx$ includes two applicable contexts $(ctx_1, cond_1)$ and $(ctx_2, cond_2)$ for $(q, c, !m, q')$. The ctx_1 and ctx_2 has the following forms (see Section 2.2 for detail):

   $ctx_1 = \texttt{before } des_1 \ serv_1$, where $serv_1 = (Q_1, s_1, \{q_1\}, \delta_1)$
   $ctx_2 = \texttt{after } des_2 \ serv_2$, where $serv_2 = (Q_2, s_2, \{q_2\}, \delta_2)$

```
(01)  Input:
(02)    S: a service automaton
(03)    Ctx: a set of contexts
(04)    Conf: a context configuration
(05)  Output:
(06)    S': a service automaton that is context-aware
(07)  Code:
(08)    W = {S.s}; //the set of states to be processed
(09)    O = ∅; //the set of processed states
(10)    cserv = ∅;
(11)    while(W is not empty)
(12)    assume q ∈ W and W' = W \ {q};
(13)      O = O ∪ {q};
(14)      N = next(q, S.δ);
(15)      for each (m, q') ∈ N do
(16)       smsg = Conf(m); //get the semantic of of m
(17)       pCtx = select(smsg, Ctx);
(18)            //select applicable contexts for m from Ctx
(19)       cserv = cserv ∪ {(q, m, q', pCtx)};
(20)            //applicable contexts recorded in cserv
(21)       if q' ∉ O then //q' not processed yet
(22)        W' = W' ∪ {q'};
(23)       endif
(24)      endfor
(25)      W = W';
(26)    endwhile
(27)    for each (q, m, q', pCtx) ∈ cserv do
(28)       //weave for each rule that has applicable contexts
(29)      (q'', S'') = createtran(q, pCtx, S, before);
(30)      (q''', S''') = createtran(q'', pCtx, S'', around);
(31)      if q''' = q'' then // no around contexts
(32)      let q₁ be a fresh state;
(33)        S''.Q = S''.Q ∪ {q₁};
(34)        if (q, c, !m, q') ∈ S''.δ then
(35)        S''.δ = S''.δ ∪ {(q'', c, !m, q₁)};
(36)        q''' = q₁;
(37)        S''' = S'';
(38)      else
(39)        S''.δ = S''.δ ∪ {(q'', c, ?m, q₁)};
(40)        q''' = q₁;
(41)        S''' = S'';
(42)      endif
(43)      endif
(44)      (q'', S'') = createtran(q''', pCtx, S''', after);
(45)      S = S'';
(46)      S.δ = S.δ ∪ {q'', true, null, q'};
(47)      S.δ = S.δ \ {(q, c, !m, q'), (q, c, ?m, q')};
(48)    endfor
(49)    S' = S;
(50)    return S';
```

Fig. 6. Semantic weaving algorithm

```
(01) Input:
(02)   q: an entry state for creating transitions
(03)   pCtx: a set of contexts
(04)   S: a service automaton
(05)   pos: the concerned position of contexts
(06) Output:
(07)   q′: an exit state after creating transitions
(08)   S′: a set of states
(09) Code:
(10)   q′ = q;
(11)   S′ = S;
(12)   for each (ctx, cond) ∈ pCtx do
(13)     if ctx.pos = pos then
(14)     let q₁ be a fresh state;
(15)     S′.Q = S′.Q ∪ ctx.serv.Q ∪ {q₁};
(16)     let ctx.serv.F = {q″};
(17)     S′.δ = S′.δ ∪ ctx.serv.δ;
(18)     S′.δ = S′.δ ∪ {(q′, cond, null, ctx.serv.s)};
(19)     S′.δ = S′δ ∪ {(q′, ¬cond, null, q₁)};
(20)     S′.δ = S′.δ ∪ {(q″, true, null, q₁)};
(21)     q′ = q₁;
(22)     endif
(23)   endfor
(24)   return (q′, S′);
```

Fig. 7. The `createtran` algorithm

After weaving, the new transitions include those in δ_1 and δ_2, and also the following *connecting* transitions:

$(q, cond_1, \texttt{null}, s_1)$, $(q, \neg cond_1, \texttt{null}, q'')$, $(q_1, \texttt{true}, \texttt{null}, q'')$,
$(q'', c, !m, q''')$, $(q''', cond_2, \texttt{null}, s_2)$, $(q''', \neg cond_2, \texttt{null}, q'''')$,
$(q_2, \texttt{true}, \texttt{null}, q'''')$, $(q'''', \texttt{true}, \texttt{null}, q')$, where q'', q''' and q'''' are all new states.

Example 2: Consider $pCtx$ including one more applicable context service (ctx_3, $cond_3$), which has the form:

$ctx_3 = \texttt{around}\ des_3\ serv_3$, where $serv_3 = (Q_3, s_3, \{q_3\}, \delta_3)$

For this example, the new transitions also include those in δ_1, δ_2 and δ_2, and the *connecting* transitions become:

$(q, cond_1, \texttt{null}, s_1)$, $(q, \neg cond_1, \texttt{null}, q'')$, $(q_1, \texttt{true}, \texttt{null}, q'')$,
$(q'', cond_3, \texttt{null}, s_3)$, $(q'', \neg cond_3, \texttt{null}, q''')$, $(q_3, \texttt{true}, \texttt{null}, q''')$,
$(q''', cond_2, \texttt{null}, s_2)$, $(q''', \neg cond_2, \texttt{null}, q'''')$, $(q_2, \texttt{true}, \texttt{null}, q'''')$,
$(q'''', \texttt{true}, \texttt{null}, q')$, where q'', q''' and q'''' are all fresh states.

For demonstration purpose, the above examples include only one context service at the positions *before*, *around* and *after*, respectively. Our algorithm allows any number of context services at any positions. Moreover, there is no limit to the number of final states. Our algorithm can be applied easily in both situations.

4   Related Work

A significant amount of research has been done in the areas of Web services composition [16,17,18,19]. A good survey on context-aware frameworks and middleware can be found in [20]. Various attempts have been made to cope with Web service contexts since then. The following is an overview of some recent work in two categories.

4.1   Semantic Context Model

Medjahed et al. [21] introduced a generic definition of Web service context through an ontology-based categorisation of contextual information. The rule-based service matchmaking was proposed to consider the relevant context. Similarly, we construct an ontology (context ontology) to facilitate the detection of *join point* semantically. However, we are more concerned about the support of changing context as we treat the context as *aspect* in AOP. In our view, their work is more on context categorisation.

Gu et al. [22] proposed a Service-Oriented Context-Aware Middleware (SO-CAM) architecture for the building and rapid prototyping of context-aware services, but with focus on infrastructure support to context-aware systems. We are interested in providing a systematical approach to cope with context-aware composition on the fly.

Mrissa et al. [23] proposed a context-based approach for semantic Web services composition. The approach enables developers to annotate WSDL descriptions to describe contextual details; to deploy a context-based mediation architecture to allow explicit assumptions on data flow; to automatically generate and invoke Web service mediator to handle data heterogeneities during Web service composition. The *context ontology* was defined to make context explicit for each concept of a domain ontology. Unlike ours, the approach presented in [23] restricts to data interpretation in Web service composition. It has little support to other heterogeneities such as heterogeneities at the process-level. As such, the proposed approach works at instance level, and are thus not very suitable for coping with some context changes which required substitutions taking place at not only the nonfunctional-level but also the functional-level.

Maamar et al. [24] proposed an approach for context-oriented Web service composition by using agents. The context model presented in [7,24] comprises four types of context: W-context deals with Web services' definitions and capabilities; C-context addresses how Web services are discovered and combined; S-context handles the semantic heterogeneity that arise between Web services; and R-context focuses on the performance of Web services. After identified these different types of context in Web service composition, the authors presented a policy-based approach for developing context-oriented Web services. Three types of policies were introduced to support transitions between the four context levels. They are *engagement, mediation* and *deployment*. While the proposed context model is advantageous in terms of context categorisation, it is less generic than the one defined in [21].

4.2   AOP in Web Service and Web Service Composition

The aspect-oriented programming (AOP) paradigm [8] has been mostly applied to object-oriented programming to date. AOP introduces a new concept called *aspect* aiming at *concerns* in complex systems by using *join points, crosscuts,* and *advices.*

Dynamic AOP [25,26] is widely recognised as a powerful technique for dynamic programming adaptation. Using AOP to increase the flexibility of workflows are discussed in [27,28]. Baumeister et al. [29] examined the use of aspect-oriented modelling techniques in the design of adaptive Web applications to achieve systematic separation of general system functionality and context adaptation. Perhaps Courbis and Finkelstein [30] are the first few authors who used dynamic AOP to adapt Web service composition. However, their work did not address the issues of crosscutting concerns, and of course, no semantic context weaving mechanism is discussed.

Few work discussed the applications of AOP in Web service or Web service composition. WSML [31] realises dynamic service selection and integration of Web services through WSML, with a management layer placed in between the application and the Web services. The main motivation of WSML is to provide management support to achieve high modularity, whereas our main motivation is to deal with context by semantic context weaver to achieve context-aware Web service composition. Ortiz et al. [32] use AspectJ [11] to modularise and add nonfunctional properties to Java Web services. Unfortunately, this approach provides very limited support to Web service composition as it mainly works for Java. The AOP for process-oriented Web service composition (AO4BPEL) is presented by Charfi et al. [9] to address the issue of crosscutting concerns in Web service composition and how to modularise them using *aspects.* It is an aspect-oriented extension to BPEL to support dynamic adaptation of composition at runtime. However, its syntactic weaving method did not suitable for contexts weaving. It lacks the semantic weaving mechanism as discussed in our paper. Moreover, the focus of AO4BPEL aims at using AOP to improve the modularity and increases the flexibility of Web service composition, whereas the main focus of our work is supporting automatic service composition with a systematic approach. In saying so, we study how to efficiently generate a new automaton given an automaton and the context.

5   Conclusion

We proposed the use of Aspect-oriented programming to cope with context-aware Web service composition. Technically, we discussed how to detect the context and how to semantically weave it into composition. The focus of our work is on composing Web services with context on the fly. The most interesting feature of our approach is that it provides a systematic way to compose context-aware Web services.

References

1. Alonso, G., Casati, F., Kuno, H.A., Machiraju, V.: Web Services - Concepts, Architectures and Applications. Data-Centric Systems and Applications. Springer, Heidelberg (2004)
2. Medjahed, B., Bouguettaya, A., Elmagarmid, A.K.: Composing web services on the semantic web. VLDB J. 12, 333–351 (2003)
3. Satyanarayanan, M.: Pervasive computing: Vision and challenges. IEEE Personal Communications 8 (August 2001)
4. Schilit, B.N., Theimer, M.M.: Disseminating active map information to mobile hosts. IEEE Network 8, 22–32 (1994)
5. Dey, A.K., Abowd, G.D., Wood, A.: Cyberdesk: a framework for providing self-integrating context-aware services. Knowl.-Based Syst. 11, 3–13 (1998)
6. Mostéfaoui, S.K., Hirsbrunner, B.: Towards a context-based service composition framework. In: Zhang, L.J. (ed.) Proceedings of the International Conference on Web Services, ICWS 2003, June 2003, pp. 42–45. CSREA Press (2003)
7. Maamar, Z., Benslimane, D., Thiran, P., Ghedira, C., Dustdar, S., Sattanathan, S.: Towards a context-based multi-type policy approach for web services composition. Data Knowl. Eng. 62, 327–351 (2007)
8. Kiczales, G., Lamping, J., Mendhekar, A., Maeda, C., Lopes, C.V., Loingtier, J.M., Irwin, J.: Aspect-oriented programming. In: Aksit, M., Matsuoka, S. (eds.) ECOOP 1997. LNCS, vol. 1241, pp. 220–242. Springer, Heidelberg (1997)
9. Charfi, A., Mezini, M.: AO4BPEL: An aspect-oriented extension to bpel. World Wide Web 10, 309–344 (2007)
10. Ceri, S., Daniel, F., Matera, M., Facca, F.M.: Model-driven development of context-aware web applications. ACM Trans. Interet Technol. 7, 2 (2007)
11. Kiczales, G., Hilsdale, E., Hugunin, J., Kersten, M., Palm, J., Griswold, W.G.: An overview of AspectJ. In: Knudsen, J.L. (ed.) ECOOP 2001. LNCS, vol. 2072, pp. 327–353. Springer, Heidelberg (2001)
12. Gruber, T.R.: A translation approach to portable ontology specifications. Knowl. Acquis. 5, 199–220 (1993)
13. Paolucci, M., Sycara, K.P., Kawamura, T.: Delivering semantic web services. In: WWW (Alternate Paper Tracks) (2003)
14. Sirin, E., Parsia, B., Hendler, J.A.: Filtering and selecting semantic web services with interactive composition techniques. IEEE Intelligent Systems 19, 42–49 (2004)
15. Sycara, K.P., Paolucci, M., Ankolekar, A., Srinivasan, N.: Automated discovery, interaction and composition of semantic web services. J. Web Sem. 1, 27–46 (2003)
16. Benatallah, B., Sheng, Q., Dumas, M.: The self-serve environment for web services composition. IEEE Internet Computing 7, 40–48 (2003)
17. Berardi, D., Calvanese, D., Giacomo, G.D., Hull, R., Mecella, M.: Automatic composition of transition-based semantic web services with messaging. In: Böhm, K., Jensen, C.S., Haas, L.M., Kersten, M.L., Larson, P.Å., Ooi, B.C. (eds.) Proceedings of VLDB 2005, pp. 613–624. ACM, New York (2005)
18. Casati, F., Ilnicki, S., Jie Jin, L., Krishnamoorthy, V., Shan, M.-C.: Adaptive and dynamic service composition in eFlow. In: Wangler, B., Bergman, L.D. (eds.) CAiSE 2000. LNCS, vol. 1789, pp. 13–31. Springer, Heidelberg (2000)
19. Fan, W., Geerts, F., Gelade, W., Neven, F., Poggi, A.: Complexity and composition of synthesized web services. In: PODS 2008: Proceedings of the twenty-seventh ACM SIGMOD-SIGACT-SIGART symposium on Principles of database systems, pp. 231–240. ACM, New York (2008)

20. Baldauf, M., Dustdar, S., Rosenberg, F.: A survey on context-aware systems. IJAHUC 2, 263–277 (2007)
21. Medjahed, B., Atif, Y.: Context-based matching for web service composition. Distributed and Parallel Databases 21, 5–37 (2007)
22. Gu, T., Pung, H.K., Zhang, D.: A service-oriented middleware for building context-aware services. J. Network and Computer Applications 28, 1–18 (2005)
23. Mrissa, M., Ghedira, C., Benslimane, D., Maamar, Z., Rosenberg, F., Dustdar, S.: A context-based mediation approach to compose semantic web services. ACM Trans. Interet Technol. 8, 4 (2007)
24. Maamar, Z., Mostéfaoui, S.K., Yahyaoui, H.: Toward an agent-based and context-oriented approach for web services composition. IEEE Trans. Knowl. Data Eng. 17, 686–697 (2005)
25. Pawlak, R., Seinturier, L., Duchien, L., Florin, G.: JAC: A flexible solution for Aspect-oriented programming in java. In: Yonezawa, A., Matsuoka, S. (eds.) Reflection 2001. LNCS, vol. 2192, pp. 1–24. Springer, Heidelberg (2001)
26. Sato, Y., Chiba, S., Tatsubori, M.: A selective, just-in-time aspect weaver. In: Pfenning, F., Smaragdakis, Y. (eds.) GPCE 2003. LNCS, vol. 2830, pp. 189–208. Springer, Heidelberg (2003)
27. Bachmendo, B., Unl, R.: Aspect-based workflow evolution. In: Proc. of the Workshop on Aspect-Oriented Programming and Separation of Concerns (2001)
28. Schmidt, R., Assmann, U.: Extending aspect-oriented-programming in order to flexibly support workflows. In: Proceedings of the ICSE Aspect-Oriented Programming Workshop (April 1998)
29. Baumeister, H., Knapp, A., Koch, N., Zhang, G.: Modelling adaptivity with aspects. In: Lowe, D.G., Gaedke, M. (eds.) ICWE 2005. LNCS, vol. 3579, pp. 406–416. Springer, Heidelberg (2005)
30. Courbis, C., Finkelstein, A.: Towards aspect weaving applications. In: ICSE 2005: Proceedings of the 27th international conference on Software engineering, pp. 69–77. ACM, New York (2005)
31. Verheecke, B., Cibrán, M.A., Vanderperren, V., Suvee, D., Jonckers, V.: Aop for dynamic configuration and management of web services. International Journal of Web Services Research 1, 25–41 (2004)
32. Ortiz, G., Herandez, J., Clemente, P.J.: How to deal with non-functional properties in web service development. In: Lowe, D.G., Gaedke, M. (eds.) ICWE 2005. LNCS, vol. 3579, pp. 98–103. Springer, Heidelberg (2005)

Multi-synchronous Collaborative Semantic Wikis

Charbel Rahhal, Hala Skaf-Molli, Pascal Molli, and Stéphane Weiss

INRIA Nancy-Grand Est
Nancy University, France
{skaf,molli,charbel.rahal,weiss}@loria.fr

Abstract. Semantic wikis have opened an interesting way to mix Web 2.0 advantages with the Semantic Web approach. However, compared to other collaborative tools, wikis do not support all collaborative editing mode such as offline work or multi-synchronous editing. The lack of multi-synchronous supports in wikis is a problematic, especially, when working with semantic wikis. In these systems, it is often important to change multiple pages simultaneous in order to refactor the semantic wiki structure. In this paper, we present a new model of semantic wiki called Multi-Synchronous Semantic Wiki (MS2W). This model extends semantic wikis with multi-synchronous support that allows to create a P2P network of semantic wikis. Semantic wiki pages can be replicated on several semantic servers. The MS2W ensures CCI consistency on these pages relying on the Logoot algorithm.

1 Introduction

Wikis have demonstrated how it is possible to convert a community of strangers into a community of collaborators producing all together valuable contents. Semantic wikis [7,14,15,3] by introducing semantic annotations within wiki pages, have opened an interesting way to mix Web 2.0 advantages with the Semantic Web approach. However, compared to other collaborative tools, wikis do not support all collaborative editing mode such as offline work or multi-synchronous editing [5,10]. It is not possible to work with a wiki as it is possible to work with popular distributed version control systems (DVCS) [1] such as Git and Mercurial. The lack of multi-synchronous support in wikis is a problematic, especially, when working with semantic wikis. In these systems, it is often important to change multiple pages simultaneous in order to refactor the semantic wiki structure. Without multi-synchronous support all incremental changes will be visible to both end users and semantic request engines. Therefore, they can observe inconsistent states of the wiki as in a database system without transactional support. We can say that existing wikis do not support transactional changes. Moreover, the lack of multi-synchronous support prevents users to work insulated [6] and also prevents semantic wikis to support dataflow oriented workflow. One approach to solve this problem is to synchronize a network of semantic wikis using distributed version control systems. Unfortunately, DVCS do not support data types used in semantic wikis and do not ensure the CCI consistency

G. Vossen, D.D.E. Long, and J.X. Yu (Eds.): WISE 2009, LNCS 5802, pp. 115–129, 2009.

model [16] required for distributed collaborative environment. Another approach is to integrate the DVCS collaboration model into a semantic wikis and manage synchronization of wikis using a CCI preserving algorithm. This can be achieved by deploying a network of semantic wikis. Every node of the network replicates a subset of semantic wiki pages. Any node of the network can be connected to another using a publish/subscribe model. A node that publishes changes just push operations representing these changes in a feed. A node that subscribed to this feed can pull operations at any time and re-execute remote operations locally. In this paper, we present a new model of semantic wikis called Multi-Synchronous Semantic Wiki (MS2W). This model extends semantic wikis with multi-synchronous support that allows to create a P2P network of semantic wikis based on declarative collaborative community. Semantic wiki pages can be replicated on several semantic servers. The MS2W ensures CCI consistency on these pages relying on the Logoot algorithm [18]. In this paper, we define a MS2W ontology and algorithms. This ontology can be used to compute awareness metrics for working in multi-synchronous environment [11]. Finally, we demonstrate that combining these algorithms with the Logoot algorithm allow to preserve the CCI consistency model.

The paper is organized as follows. Section 2 presents background and related works. Section 3 gives an overview of the multi-synchronouns semantic wikis (MS2W) and shows scenarios of new collaboration mode in semantic wikis. Section 4 develops the data model, the algorithms for MS2W and presents the correction of our algorithms. Section 5 presents the implementation of the MS2W. The last section concludes the paper and points to some directions for future works.

2   Background and Related Work

This section gives a brief overview of semantic wikis and shows their drawbacks. Then, it presents the definition and the principals of multi-synchronous collaboration. Finally, it presents the CCI consistency model.

2.1   Semantic Wikis

Semantic wikis such as Sematic MediaWiki [7], IkeWiki [14], SweetWiki [3] and SWooki [15] are a new generation of collaborative editing tools, they allow users to add semantic annotations in the wiki pages. These semantic annotations can then be used to find pertinent answers to complex queries. Semantic wikis can be viewed as an efficient way to better structure wikis by providing a means to navigate and answer questions or reason, based on annotations. Semantic wikis are an extension of wiki systems that preserve the same principles of wikis such as simplicity in creating and editing wikis pages. Semantic wikis embed semantic annotations in the wiki content by using Semantic Web technologies such as RDF and SPARQL. In semantic wikis, users collaborate not only for writing the wiki pages but also for writing semantic annotations. Traditionally, authoring semantics and creation ontologies has mainly been in the hand of "ontologists" and knowledge management experts. Semantic wikis allow mass collaboration for creating and emerging ontologies. Some existing semantic wikis allows the emergence of the ontology, MediaWiki(SMW) [7] and SweetWiki [3]. Others use the wikis as a collaborative ontologies editors. IkeWiki [14] aims to create an instance of existing ontologies, while OntoWiki [2] aims the creation of ontology schema. In a semantic wiki, users add semantic annotations to wiki page text to represent relations and properties on this page. In SMW users choose their own vocabularies to type links. For instance, a link between the wiki pages "France" and "Paris" may be annotated by a user as "capital".

Content of wiki page of "France"	Content of semantic wiki page of "France"
France is located in [Europe]	France is located in [locatedIn::Europe]
The capital of France is [Paris]	The capital of France is [hasCapital:: Paris]

These annotations express semantic relationships between wikis pages. Semantic annotations are usually written in a formal syntax so they are processed automatically by machines and they are exploited by semantic queries. In spite of their success, semantic wikis do not support a multi-synchronous work mode. Their current model provides only one copy of a semantic wiki page. The state of a semantic wiki page is always the current visible one on the server, intermediate inconsistent states are always visible. Consequently, transactional changes are not be supported neither the isolated work mode nor off-line editing mode. In previous work, we proposed SWooki [15] the first P2P semantic wiki. It combines the advantages of P2P wikis and semantic wikis. It is based on an optimistic replication algorithm that ensures the CCI consistency model. It supports the off-line work mode and transactional changes. Its main limitations are the total replication and the collaboration model. Every peer of the network hosts a replica of wiki pages and a replica of the semantic store. Users cannot choose the pages that they want to replicate neither the period of synchronization. Modifications are propagated on page saving. The collaborative community is implicit. Users cannot choose to whom propagate modifications. Changes propagation is under the control of system and not the users. All connected peers receive and integrate changes. A disconnected peer will receive the modifications of the others at reconnection thanks to the anti-entropy algorithm.

2.2 Multi-synchronouns Collaboration

Dourish wrote [5], *"The notion of multiple, parallel streams of activity, is a natural approach to supporting this familiar pattern of collaborative work. Working activities proceed in parallel (multiple streams of activity), during which time the participants are disconnected (divergence occurs); and periodically their individual efforts will be integrated (synchronization) in order to achieve a consistent state and progress the activity of the group".*

Multi-synchronous applications are different from synchronous and asynchronous ones by managing multiple streams of activities instead of giving the illusion of one stream. In standard collaborative applications, when a modification is made by one user, it is immediately visible by others. However, in multi-synchronous applications, modifications made by one user is not visible by others. It becomes visible only when a user validates his modifications (commits his changes). A visible change does not imply immediate integration by other activities streams. Concurrent modifications will be integrated only when users will decide it. Allowing deferred validation of changes and divergence have several important advantages and impacts [11]: Parallelization of activities, privacy, invisibility of partial changes and experimental changes. Multi-synchronous authoring tools [5,10] allow simultaneous work in isolation and later integration of the contributions. They are characterized by their abilities to support divergence *i.e* parallel steam of activities on replicated data. SAMS [12] allows team members to work in synchronous, asynchronous or multi-synchronous mode while ensuring the coherence of the shared data. It uses an operational transformation algorithm to maintain the consistency of the shared data. Although it is independent of shared objects types, SAMS requires the design of transformation functions that depend on the type of the shared object. Design of transformation functions is a hard task and errors prone. Currently, there are no transformation functions designed for semantic wiki pages. Distributed Version Control Systems[1] such Git manage files and directories. They are not used to track changes in semantic wiki pages. They ensure causal consistency, this implies that concurrent write operations can be seen in a different order on different machines. In this case, if two sites observe 2 write operations in different order then copies on both sites can diverge. DVCS systems are aware of this problem and delegate the problem to external merge algorithms for managing concurrent operations. However, as existing merge algorithms are not intrinsically deterministic, commutative and associative so convergence cannot be ensured in all cases.

2.3   CCI Consistency Model

A distributed collaborative system is composed of unbounded set of peers P. Objects modified by the system are replicated into a set of replicas R (with $0 < |R| \leq |P|$). Every replica has the same role and hosted on one peer. A peer can host replicas of different objects. Peers can enter and leave the network arbitrary. Every peer has a unique comparable identifier. The modifications applied on a replica are eventually delivered to all other replicas, then, they are applied locally. According to [16], the system is correct if it ensures the CCI consistency model.

– **Causality:** This criterion ensures that all operations ordered by a precedence relation, in the sense of the Lamport's *happened-before* relation [8] will be executed in same order on every site.

– **Convergence:** The system converges if all replicas are identical when the system is idle (eventual consistency).

– **Intention and Intention preservation:** The intention of an operation is the effects observed on the state when the operation was generated. The effects of executing an operation at all sites are the same as the intention of the operation.

Many algorithms that verify the CCI model have been developed by the Operational Transformation community [16] such as SOCT2, GOTO, COT etc. But only few of them (MOT2 [4]) support the join and leave constraint of P2P network. However, MOT2 algorithm suffers from a high communication complexity. WOOT [13] is the first synchronization algorithm that ensures the CCI consistency and respects the P2P constraints. WOOT is used in Wooki [17] a peer-to-peer wiki and an modified version of WOOT that takes in consideration semantic data is implemented in SWooki [15]. Recently, an optimized version of WOOT called Logoot is published in [18], it ensures convergence and preserves the intentions, if the causality is preserved.

3   Multi-synchronous Semantic Wiki Approach

Multi-synchronous semantic wikis allow users to build their own cooperation networks. The construction of the collaborative community is declarative, in the sense, every user declares explicitly with whom he would like to cooperate. Every user can have a multi-synchronous semantic wiki server installed on her machine. She can create and edit her own semantic wiki pages as in a normal semantic wiki system. Later, she can decide to share or not these semantic wiki pages and decide with whom to share.

3.1   Multi-synchronous Collaboration Model

The replication of data and the communication between servers is made through *channels* (feeds). The channel usage is restricted to few servers with simple security mechanisms that requires no login and complex access control. Capabilities fit perfectly these requirements [9]. The key point is that channels are read-only for consumers and can be hosted on hardware of users. When a semantic wiki page is updated on a multi-synchronous semantic wiki server, it generates a corresponding operation. This operation is processed in four steps: (1) It is executed immediately against page, (2) it is published to the corresponding *channels*, (3) it is pulled by the authorized servers, and (4) it is integrated to their local replica of the page. If needed, the integration process merges this modification with concurrent ones, generated either locally or received from a remote server.

The system is correct if it ensures the CCI (Causality, Convergence and Intention Preservation) consistency model. Multi-synchronous semantic wikis use the Logoot synchronization algorithm   [18] to integrate modifications. Logoot ensures the CCI consistency model. More precisely, Logoot ensures convergence and preserves the intentions of operations if the causality of the operations is preserved.

3.2   Collaboration Scenarios

This section presents two scenarios of collaboration in multi-synchronouns semantic wikis. We suppose several professors collaborate together through a semantic wiki to prepare lectures, exercises and exams. Later, they want to make lectures available for students and they want to integrate relevant feedbacks from students.

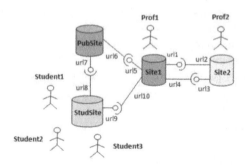

Fig. 1. Multi-synchronous semantic wikis scenario

Scenario 1: Collaboration among professors For simplicity, we suppose there are two professors $prof_1$ and $prof_2$ (see figure 1). Every professor has her own multi-synchronous semantic wiki, $site_1$ for $prof_1$ and $site_2$ for $prof_2$, respectively.

1. $prof_1$ edits three semantic wiki pages $lesson_1$, $exercises_1$ and $exam_1$ on her site $site_1$. For instance, the page $lesson_1$ edited by $prof_1$ has three lines:

   ```
   Introduction:
   In "multi-synchronous" work, parties work independently in parallel.
   [Category::Lesson] [forYear:2009]
   ```

2. $prof_1$ wants to publish her modifications on $lesson_1$ to $prof_2$. Therefore, she creates a *feed* url_1 that contains change set. Finally, she communicates the address of the feed to $prof_2$.
3. $prof_2$ subscribes to this channel and creates a feed url_2 to pull modifications. The result is a local semantic wiki page $lesson_1$ that has the same content as $lesson_1$ of $prof_1$.
4. $prof_2$ edits his local copy of the $lesson_1$ page. $lesson_1$ has now five lines:

   ```
   Introduction:
   In "multi-synchronous" work mode, parties work independently in parallel.
   [Category::Lesson] [forYear:2009]. This mode is based on divergence and
   synchronization phases.
   ```

5. In her turn, $prof_2$ shares his modifications on $lesson_1$ with $prof_1$. He creates a feed and publishes his modifications. $prof_1$ subscribes to the feed and pulls the modifications published by $prof_2$ and finally integrates these modifications on her local copy of $lesson_1$. The integration process merges the remote modifications with concurrent ones, if any, generated locally by $prof_1$. The integration process has to ensure the convergence of all copies on $lesson_1$ if all generated operations on $site_1$ and $site_2$ are integrated on both sites.

Table 1. Multi-synchronous collaboration scenario

$Site_1$	$Site_2$
Edit($lesson_1$)	
Edit($exercises_1$)	
Edit($exam_1$)	
CreatePushFeed(f_1,q_1)	
	CreatePullFeed(f_1, f_2)
Edit($lesson_1$)	Edit($lesson_1$)
Push(f_1)	
	CreatePushFeed(f_3,q_2)

The advantages of this collaboration model are, on the one hand, there is no need for centralized server to cooperate. On the other hand, every professor works on her or his own copy in isolation, publishes and pulls changes whenever she wants, *i.e.* the changes propagation is under the control of the user. This collaboration process is not supported in classical semantic wikis. The table 1 represents a part of the scenario.

Scenario 2: Collaboration among professors and students In this scenario, $prof_1$ wants to make $lesson_1$ available for her students while she continues to make corrections and minor modifications on $lesson_1$. In order to provide her students with the courses, $prof_1$ publishes them on a public site *pubSite* that can be either her proper public wiki site or the site of the university. *pubSite* is accessible by the students for read only to maintain the courses consistency. However, $prof_1$ manages to integrate relevant feedbacks from students provided by the students sites.

Professor can make continuous improvement of the lessons and can make continuous integration of the modifications and make only consistent modifications visible. Without multi-synchronous support all incremental changes will be visible to both end users and to semantic request engines. Every participant professor and student want to control the visibility of their modifications and want to control the integration of others' modifications.

4   Multi-synchronous Semantic Wiki System

This section presents the data model and the algorithms for multi-synchronous Semantic Wiki systems (M2SW). The data model is defined an ontology. Therefore, it is possible to querying and reasoning on the model itself and make future extension. For instance, it is possible to make queries like: (1) "list all unpublished changes", (2) "list all published changes on a given channel", (3) "list unpublished change set of a given semantic wiki page", (4) "list all pulled change sets", etc.

4.1   MS2W Ontology

The M2SW ontology is defined as an extension of existing ontologies of semantic wikis [3]. In this section, we present the M2SW ontology and detail only its new vocabulary and their properties.

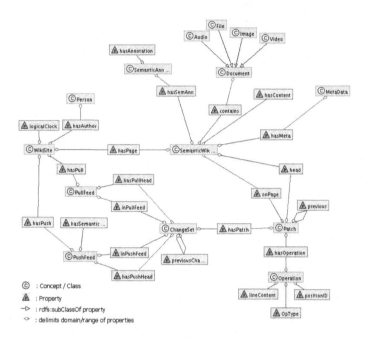

Fig. 2. Multi-synchronous ontology

- **WikiSite:** this concept corresponds to a semantic wiki server. A site has the following properties:
    - *siteID* : this attribute contains the *URL* of the site.
    - *logicalClock* : this attribute has a numeric value. Every semantic wiki server maintains a logical clock, this clock is used to identify patches and operations in an unique way in the whole network.
    - *hasPush, hasPull* and *hasPage* : the range of these properties are respectively a push feed, a pull feed and a semantic wiki page. A wiki site has several push feeds, pull feeds and several pages .
- **SemanticWikiPage:** this concept corresponds to a normal semantic wiki page. It has the following properties:
    - *pageID* : this attribute contains the *URL* of the page.
    - *hasContent* the range of this property is a String, it contains text and the semantic data embedded in the semantic wiki page.
    - *head* : this property points to the *last patch* applied to the page.

- **Operation:** this concept represents a change in a line of a wiki page. In our model, there are two editing operations : *insert* and *delete*. An update is considered as a delete of old value followed by an insert of a new value. An operation has the following properties:
  - *operationID*: this attribute contains the unique identifier of the operation. *operationID* is calculated by: $operationID = \text{concat}(Site.siteID, Site.logicalClock + +)$, the *concat* function concatenates two strings.
  - *opType*: this attribute contains the type of the operation, it can be either an *insert* or a *delete*.
  - *positionID*: denotes the position of the line in the wiki page. This identifier is calculated by the *Logoot* algorithm[18].
  - *lineContent*: is a string representing text and the semantic data embedded in the line.
- **Patch:** a patch is a set of operations. A patch is calculated during the save of the modified semantic wiki page using the Logoot algorithm. A patch has the following properties:
  - *patchID*: is a unique identifier of the patch. Its value is calculated by : $patchID = \text{concat}(Site.siteID, Site.logicalClock + +)$
  - *onPage*: the range of this property is the page where the patch was applied.
  - *hasOperation*: this property points to the operations generated during the save of the page.
  - *previous*: points to the precedent patch.
- **ChangeSet:** a change set contains a set of patches. This concept is important in order to support transactional changes. It allows to regroup patches generated on multiple semantic wiki pages. Therefore, it is possible to push modifications on multiple pages. *ChangeSet* has the following properties:
  - *changSetID*: is a unique identifier of a change set. Its value is calculated as : $changeSetID = \text{concat}(Site.siteID, Site.logicalClock + +)$
  - *hasPatch* property points to the patches generated since the last push.
  - *previousChangeSet*: points to the precedent change set.
  - *inPushFeed*: the range of this property is *PushFeed*. This property indicates the *PushFeed* that publishes a *ChangeSet*.
  - *inPullFeed*: the range of this property is *PullFeed* . This property indicates the *PullFeed* that pulls a *ChangeSet*.
- **PushFeed:** this concept is used to publish changes of a *WikiSite*. It is a special semantic wiki page. It inherits the properties of the *SemanticWikiPage* concept and defines its own properties:
  - *hasPushHead* : this property points to the *last* published *changeSet*.
  - *hasSemanticQuery*: this property contains a semantic query. This query determines the content of the push feed. For instance, the query can be "find all Lessons", this will return all the pages in the class (category) Lessons. To answer *hasSemanticQuery*, reasoning and querying capabilities of semantic wikis are used.

- **Pull Feed:** this concept is used to pull changes from a remote *WikiSite*. A pull feed is related to one push feed. In the sense that it is impossible to pull unpublished data. A pull feed is also a special semantic wiki page. It inherits the properties of the *Semantic Wiki Page* concepts and defines it own properties:

  - *hasPullHead*: this property points to the last pulled change set pulled.
  - *relatedPushFeed*: this property relates a pull feed to the *URL* of its associated push feed.

We can extend and build on *MS2W* ontology. The *MS2W* ontology is maintained by the *MS2W* developers. It is defined in OWL DL allowing to querying and reasoning on the patches, ChangeSet, PushFeed, etc. SPARQL can be used to query the MS2W data. For instance, it is possible to list all published patches on a push feed:

$$Published \equiv \exists(hasPatch^{-1}).\exists(inPushFeed^{-1}).PushFeed$$

4.2   Algorithms

As any semantic wiki server, a multi-synchronous semantic wiki server defines a *Save* operation which describes what happens when a semantic wiki page is saved. In addition, we define special operations : *CreatePushFeed, Push, CreatePullFeed, Pull* and *Integrate* for the multi-synchronous semantic wiki. We use the Logoot algorithm [18] for the generation and the integration of the *insert* and *delete* operations. In the following, detail these operations for a semantic wiki server called *site*.

Save Operation. During the saving a wiki page, the *Logoot* algorithm computes the difference between the saved and the previous version of the page and generates a patch. A *patch* is a set of delete and insert operations on the page ($Op = (opType, operationID, positionID, lineContent)$). *Logoot* calculates the *positionID*, *lineContent* and the *opType* of the operation. These operations are integrated locally and then eventually published on a push feed.

```
On Save(page : String, p̄āḡē:String) :
  Patch(pid=concat(site.siteID, site . logicalClock + +))
  foreach op ∈ Logoot(page, p̄āḡē) do
    Operation(opid=concat(site.siteID, site . logicalClock + +))
    hasOperation(pid,opid)
  endfor;
  previous(pid,page.head)
  head(page,pid)
  onPage(pid,page)
```

CreatePushFeed Operation. The communication between multi-synchronouns semantic wiki servers is made through feeds. The *CreatePushFeed* operation creates of a push feed. A push feed is a special semantic wiki page that contains a query that specifies the pushed data. It is used to publish changes of a wiki server. Authorized sites can access the published data. *CreatePushFeed* operation calls the *Push* operation.

```
On CreatePushFeed(name:String,request:String):
    PushFeed(name)
    hasSemanticQuery(name,request)
    hasPush(site,name)
    call Push(name)
```

Push Operation. This operation creates a change set corresponding to the pages returned by the semantic query and adds it to the push feed. Firstly, the semantic query is executed, then the patches of the pages returned by the query are extracted. These patches are added to the change set if they have not been published on this push feed yet.

```
On Push(name:String):
    ChangeSet(csid=concat(site.siteID,site . logicalClock ++))
    inPushFeed(csid, name)
    let published  ← { ∃x ∃y ∧ inPushFeed(y,name) ∧ hasPatch(y,x) }
    let patches ← { ∃x ∀p ∈ execQuery(name.hasSemanticQuery) ∧ onPage(x,p)}
    foreach patch ∈ {patches − published} do
        hasPatch(csid, patch)
    endfor
    previousChangeSet(csid, name.hasPushHead)
    hasPushHead(name,csid)
```

CreatePullFeed Operation. As the replication of data and the communication between multi-synchronouns semantic wiki servers are made through feeds, pull feeds are created to pull changes from push feeds on remote peers to the local peer (cf figure 3). A pull feed is related to a push feed. In the sense that it is impossible to pull unpublished data.

```
On CreatePullFeed(name:String, url:URL)
    PullFeed(name);
    relatedPushFeed(name,url)
    call Pull(name);
```

```
On ChangeSet get(cs : ChangeSetId ,url)
    if ∃x previousChangeSet(cs,x)
        return x
    else  return null;
```

Fig. 3. CreatePullFeed operation   **Fig. 4.** get a ChangeSet operation

Pull Operation. This operation fetches for published change sets that have not pulled yet (cf figure5). It adds these change sets to the pull feed and integrate them to the concerned pages on the pulled site.

get Function. This function allows to retreive a ChangeSet (cf figure 4).

Integration Operation. The integration of a change set is processed as follows (cf figure 6). First all the patches of the change set are extracted. Every operation in the patch is integrated in the corresponding semantic wiki page thanks to the Logoot algorithm.

```
On Pull(name:String):
    while ((cs ← get(name.headPullFeed,
        name.relatedPushFeed) ≠ null)
    let p  ← {∃x ∧ inPushFeed(x,name)}
    if cs ∉ {p} then
        inPullFeed(cs,name)
        call Integrate(cs)
    endif
    hasPullHead(name,cs)
    endwhile
```

```
Integrate(cs:ChangeSet):
    foreach patch ∈ cs do
        previous(patch,patch.onPage.head)
        head(patch.onPage,patch)
        foreach op ∈ hasOperation.patch
            do call logootIntegrate(op)
        endfor
    endfor
```

Fig. 5. Pull Operation   **Fig. 6.** IntegrateOperation

4.3   Correction Model

Theorem 1. *Our algorithms ensure the causality.*

proof. A site always respects the causality of its own operations since it generates these operations alone, so these operations placed in the push feed are causal. In the following, we take an hypothesis that a site S pulls from N sites that ensure the causality and we want to prove that the site itself ensures the causality. We will prove that the site S cannot violate the causality through the contradiction proof. Let us consider that the site S violates the causality, i.e. in the content of its push feed there is an operation op_2 that depends causally (Lamport dependence) on an operation op_1 and op_2 is placed before op_1 in that feed. The operations in a push feed has two different sources either they are local generated by the site itself or the site had received them from other sites. Let us study both cases (1) *local operations*: the local operations always respect the causality, so a site is not going to violate the causality. (2) *remote operations:* In order to get the operation op_2 placed at the position N in the push feed of site S, S must pull, i.e. copy all the operations that precedes op_2. Getting op_2 without having op_1 means that op_1 was not among the $N - 1$ operations that precedes op_2 in the push feed which violates the hypothesis that the site S pulls only from N sites that respect the causality. Consequently, it is not possible to find op_2 before op_1. Therefore, a site always respects the causality alone. If this site pulls from N sites that ensure the causality, it ensures the causality itself. In recurrence, all site ensure the causality for any N, where N is an integer. Hence, our algorithm ensures the causality for all the sites in the network.

Theorem 2. *Our algorithms ensure the CCI model (Causality, Convergence, Intention).*

proof. Our algorithm is based on Logoot algorithm for the generation and the integration of the operations. It is proved in [18], that the *Logoot* algorithm ensures the convergence and preserves the intentions, if the causality is preserved. Since our algorithms ensure the causality (theorem 1), hence it ensures also the convergence and preserves the intentions.

5   Implementation

We are currently implementing the MS2W model as an extension of Semantic MediaWiki [7]. Feeds, ChangeSets and Patches are represented as special semantic wiki pages. They stored in a special namespace to prevent user modification. The Logoot algorithm has been implemented in PHP and integrated in Mediawiki relying on the hook mechanism. The push, pull, createPushFeed and createPullFeed operations are available in special administration pages of MediaWiki as shown in figure 7. This extension is designed to respect the simplicity of the wikis while supporting the MS2W model and the result is an easy way to construct a P2P network of semantic wikis based on Semantic MediaWiki.

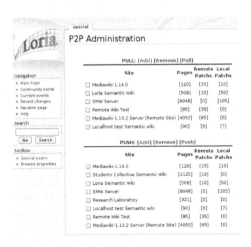

Fig. 7. MS2W Administration page

6   Conclusion and Future Work

In this paper, we propose a new model of semantic wikis called Multi-Synchronous Semantic Wiki (MS2W). MS2W extends a semantic wiki with multi-synchronous capabilities. Multi-synchronous semantic wikis allow users to build their own cooperation networks. The construction of the collaborative community is declarative. Every user declares explicitly with whom he would like to cooperate. The replication of the wiki pages on semantic wikis servers and the synchronization periods are variant and under the control of the users. The MS2W model enhances the existing semantic wikis by supporting transactional changes and the off-line work mode. Hence, multiple dataflow oriented workflows can be supported. In addition, the model takes natural advantages of a P2P network, i.e. faults-tolerance, better scalability, infrastructure cost sharing and better performance. In the paper, we develop an ontology for MS2W. Each ontological element in this wiki is exploitable, consequently advanced reasoning and querying capabilities are provided. We develop also a set of algorithms for the creation and the replication of semantic wiki pages and for the propagation and the synchronization of changes between the peers. The MS2W algorithm ensures the CCI consistency on the pages. We are currently implementing the MS2W model as an extension of Semantic MediaWiki. As for future works, we want to support the MS2W with two crucial features: (1) an undo mechanism to facilitate the undo of undesired merge results, (2) an advanced mechanism for divergence metrics based on querying the semantic annotations.

References

1. Allen, L., Fernandez, G., Kane, K., Leblang, D., Minard, D., Posner, J.: ClearCase MultiSite: Supporting Geographically-Distributed Software Development. In: Software Configuration Management: Scm-4 and Scm-5 Workshops: Selected Papers (1995)
2. Auer, S., Dietzold, S., Riechert, T.: OntoWiki – A tool for social, semantic collaboration. In: Cruz, I., Decker, S., Allemang, D., Preist, C., Schwabe, D., Mika, P., Uschold, M., Aroyo, L.M. (eds.) ISWC 2006. LNCS, vol. 4273, pp. 736–749. Springer, Heidelberg (2006)
3. Buffa, M., Gandon, F.L., Ereteo, G., Sander, P., Faron, C.: Sweetwiki: A semantic wiki. Journal of Web Semantics 6(1), 84–97 (2008)
4. Cart, M., Ferrie, J.: Asynchronous reconciliation based on operational transformation for p2p collaborative environments. In: International Conference on Collaborative Computing: Networking, Applications and Worksharing (2007)
5. Dourish, P.: The parting of the ways: Divergence, data management and collaborative work. In: 4th European Conference on Computer Supported Cooperative Work (1995)
6. Estublier, J., et al.: Impact of the research community on the field of software configuration management: summary of an impact project report. SIGSOFT Softw. Eng. Notes 27(5), 31–39 (2002)
7. Krötzsch, M., Vrandecic, D., Völkel, M., Haller, H., Studer, R.: Semantic wikipedia. Journal of Web Semantic 5(4), 251–261 (2007)
8. Lamport, L.: Times, Clocks, and the Ordering of Events in a Distributed System. Communications of the ACM 21(7), 558–565 (1978)
9. Levy, H.: Capability-Based Computer Systems. Butterworth-Heinemann Newton, MA (1984)
10. Molli, P., Skaf-Molli, H., Bouthier, C.: State Treemap: an Awareness Widget for Multi-Synchronous Groupware. In: Seventh International Workshop on Groupware - CRIWG. IEEE Computer Society, Los Alamitos

11. Molli, P., Skaf-Molli, H., Oster, G.: Divergence awareness for virtual team through the web. In: Integrated Design and Process Technology, IDPT (2002)
12. Molli, P., Skaf-Molli, H., Oster, G., Jourdain, S.: Sams: Synchronous, asynchronous, multi-synchronous environments. In: Seventh International Conference on CSCW in Design (2002)
13. Oster, G., Urso, P., Molli, P., Imine, A.: Data Consistency for P2P Collaborative Editing. In: Conference on Computer-Supported Cooperative Work (2006)
14. Schaffert, S.: IkeWiki: A Semantic Wiki for Collaborative Knowledge Management. In: 1st Workshop on Semantic Technologies in Collaborative Applications (2006)
15. Skaf-Molli, H., Rahhal, C., Molli, P.: Peer-to-peer semantic wikis. In: DEXA 2009: 20th International Conference on Database and Expert Systems Applications (2009)
16. Sun, C., Jia, X., Zhang, Y., Yang, Y., Chen, D.: Achieving Convergence, Causality Preservation, and Intention Preservation in Real-Time Cooperative Editing Systems. ACM Transactions on Computer-Human Interaction 5(1) (1998)
17. Weiss, S., Urso, P., Molli, P.: Wooki: A P2P wiki-based collaborative writing tool. In: Benatallah, B., Casati, F., Georgakopoulos, D., Bartolini, C., Sadiq, W., Godart, C. (eds.) WISE 2007. LNCS, vol. 4831, pp. 503–512. Springer, Heidelberg (2007)
18. Weiss, S., Urso, P., Molli, P.: Logoot: a scalable optimistic replication algorithm for collaborative editing on p2p networks. In: ICDCS. IEEE, Los Alamitos (2009)

Facing the Technological Challenges of Web 2.0: A RIA Model-Driven Engineering Approach

Francisco Valverde and Oscar Pastor

Centro de Investigación en Métodos de Producción de Software, Universidad Politécnica de Valencia, Spain
{fvalverde,opastor}@pros.upv.es

Abstract. One of the main reasons for the success of Web 2.0 is the improvement in user experience. This improvement is a consequence of the evolution from HTML User Interfaces (UI) to more usable and richer UI. The most popular Web 2.0 applications have selected the Rich Internet Application (RIA) paradigm to achieve this goal. However, the current Web Engineering methods do not provide the expressivity required to produce RIA interfaces. This work presents a RIA Metamodel to deal with the new technological challenges that have arisen with Web 2.0 development. This metamodel supports two main perspectives: 1) the definition of the UI as a combination of widgets from a selected RIA technology; and 2) the specification of the UI interaction as a consequence of the events produced by the user. In order to illustrate how this RIA Metamodel can be used in a Model-driven Engineering (MDE) method, this work also presents the integration of the RIA Metamodel with the OOWS method.

Keywords: Rich Internet Applications, Model-driven Development, Web User Interfaces.

1 Introduction

Nowadays, Web 2.0 is a topic that has significant influence in the Web Development community. However, Web 2.0 is still an imprecise concept because it has been defined [18] in comparison with the common practices of "Web 1.0" that were unsuccessful. From the authors' point of view, Web 2.0 can be defined from two complementary perspectives: a social one and a technological one.

From the social perspective, in "Web 1.0" websites, the end-user was a passive consumer of information that had been defined by the Webmaster. This situation has changed considerably with the arrival of Web 2.0. Today end-users not only define the website content (news, reviews, images, etc.), but they also decide which content is the most interesting. The first consequence of this role reversal has been an exponential growth of the content created by end-users on the Web.

From the technological perspective, the evolution of Web development technologies has been decisive in encouraging the end-user involvement. When the UI from the most popular Web 2.0 sites are analyzed, a high level of usability is

G. Vossen, D.D.E. Long, and J.X. Yu (Eds.): WISE 2009, LNCS 5802, pp. 131–144, 2009.

detected. To achieve this improvement in usability, the evolution of Web technologies has played an essential role. This technological evolution has defined a new application paradigm called Rich Internet Applications (RIA) [5]: a Web application in which the UI is processed on the client side and the Business logic is defined by a services backend. Examples of technologies for developing RIA are Javascript frameworks, which use AJAX calls to perform functionality requests on-demand; and specific RIA platforms such as Microsoft Silverlight or Adobe Flex [1], which introduce their own languages to define complex UI. This new application paradigm has also led to new research discussions. One of the most interesting topics that have been raised is the possibility of developing RIA from a Model-driven Engineering (MDE) approach. Since several Web 2.0 applications are currently being developed using RIA technologies, providing methods, models and tools to deal with these complex technologies has become an attractive research area.

In recent years, the Web Engineering community has defined several methods with the goal of improving the development of Web applications. These methods have mainly focused on the most common domains from the early part of this decade: e-commerce and data-intensive applications. To develop "Web 1.0" interfaces, several Web Engineering methods such as WebML [5], OOHDM [23], WSDM [26], OOWS [12], and others [22] have proposed conceptual models to deal with the Web UI specification. These models have provided interesting results for defining traditional HTML interfaces in which navigation and data retrieval are the main interactions between the user and the system. However as some authors have already addressed, these methods must be extended in order to provide the new required expressivity in the RIA domain [21][7].

Even though the models proposed by these methods are essential, UI models that address more complex UI are still required. First, RIA technologies provide a wide array of UI components to define complex interaction. Also, current UI models are limited to defining the static view (layout and aesthetic properties), while Web 2.0 also requires the specification of the reactions to user events, i.e. the dynamic view. Another issue to address is the technological heterogeneity that surrounds Web 2.0 because of the different RIA technologies that are currently available. For these reasons is not a viable task to defining an all-encompassing model that covers all the available technologies.

The main contribution of this paper is to establish the foundations for supporting the UI technological perspective of the Web 2.0 in a MDE scenario. Applying the MDE principles, the technological complexity of RIA development is abstracted to the analysts. To achieve this goal the first step is the definition of a RIA Metamodel to support the new expressivity required: 1) the definition of a UI as the composition of richer widgets; and 2) the definition of the reactions of the UI as a consequence of the events triggered by end-users. The strategy for defining this metamodel is based on the analysis of different Web 2.0 applications. The most frequently used widgets and interactions (those cannot be defined using the traditional methods) have been selected. The metamodel that has been defined is generic enough to be extended and related to different MDE methods. Furthermore, it can be used as a basis to define concrete UI metamodels to address the UI modeling for different RIA technologies. To illustrate how this RIA metamodel can be applied, the integration with the OOWS Web Engineering method is also discussed.

The paper is organized as follows: Section 2 introduces the RIA Metamodel by presenting both the static view, which specifies the UI layout and composition, and the dynamic view, which defines the UI interaction. Section 3 explains the integration of the RIA Metamodel with the OOWS Web Engineering method. Section 4 presents several related works that also deal with the Model-driven development of RIA. Finally, section 5 presents conclusions and future work.

2   Defining a RIA Metamodel for Supporting Web 2.0 Applications

As stated in the introduction, there is a close relationship between Web 2.0 and the RIA domain. RIA technologies have mainly introduced changes to develop richer UI. Since the usability of the UI is a key requirement, many Web 2.0 applications have used RIA technologies to improve it. RIA technologies have introduced two main concerns that must be supported at the UI modeling level:

1. *Richer UI widgets:* The main difference between the UI produced using HTML and RIA technologies is the set of available UI widgets. Traditionally, the HTML language is constrained to a small set of elements that can be used to build an UI. This is because HTML was designed to show and to hyperlink documents rather than as an UI language. Due to the evolution of Web interfaces, HTML has become obsolete for designing UI. RIA technologies have solved this issue by migrating a lot of UI widgets (such as Datagrids or Menu Controls) from Desktop environments. RIA technologies also include specific UI widgets for multimedia visualization (images and videos) and rich editors to create the content for Web 2.0 applications.
2. *Event-driven interaction:* RIA technologies provide highly interactive UI in order to improve user experience. This interaction is triggered by the events that are performed by the end-user over the UI widgets (for instance, a mouse click). The possible responses or reactions to these events range from a change in the UI to the request for data from the Business Logic. This event-driven paradigm is not completely original because it has already been widely applied in Desktop environments. However, it has not been adopted on the Web due to the small number of events that are supported by the HTML language. RIA technologies can provide a wide set of UI events and specific programming languages to solve this issue.

Following sections present, a RIA Metamodel to support the above-mentioned concerns: the modeling of the UI as a composition of richer widgets, and the definition of the response to the UI events.

2.1   Modeling the RIA Interface

A common agreement is to define a UI as a composition of widgets: visual components of the UI to provide the data and to hold the interaction with the user [15][30]. From the analysis of several Web 2.0 applications that use RIA technologies, widgets can be categorized into five non-excluding groups according to their interactive function:

1. *Dataview widgets*: these widgets are used to show a set of structured data retrieved from the system. The *Table* widget is the most common widget used for this task. In the RIA domain, widgets of this kind of widgets have evolved considerably to show multimedia data and to provide advanced data manipulation or retrieval.
2. *Input widgets*: these widgets handle the input of the data. Depending on the analysis performed, there is a strong relationship between the type of the data and the input widget. For instance, string values are input using the *Text Input* widget, while boolean values are introduced using the *Checkbox* widget. In Web 2.0 applications like wikis or blogs, the *Rich Text Editor* widget is widely used to introduce formatted text.
3. *Navigation widgets*: these widgets are used to change the point from which the UI is perceived. The *Link* is the most common navigation widget on the Web, but RIA has introduced alternatives such as *Tab Navigations.*
4. *Service widgets:* these widgets start the execution of a service from the Business Logic. The *Button* is the default widget of this category. RIA technologies have introduced several widgets for this task such as *Icons* or *Contextual Menus.*
5. *Layout widgets*: these widgets are useful for arranging other widgets, even though they do not provide any direct interaction with the user. Layout widgets are also required to group 'child' widgets in order to perform interaction over the whole group (e.g. to hide the widgets at the same time). Examples of these widgets are *Form, Panel* or *Vertical Box.*

These are the most common functions but there are also widgets that match two or more categories. One example is the *Editable Datagrid,* which can be used for visualization, input of data and invocation of an update service. From the analysis performed in this study, two main ideas are pointed out for the definition of a UI using a RIA technology:

- The UI has been extended mainly by using widgets that are common in desktop environments. However, specific RIA widgets have also been provided to visualize multimedia data and to simplify the creation of content.
- The UI is highly coupled to the target RIA technology. For instance, JavaScript frameworks do not provide the same set of widgets as Adobe Flex.

The first idea implies the extension of the Web Engineering method models, using the set of widgets that is required. However, that extension should not be defined in the models that address the navigation of the Web application in order not to mix different concerns. In recent years, the HCI community has addressed UI modeling defining two levels of abstraction [4]: an Abstract level, in which the UI is defined without taking into account any technological details; and a Concrete level, in which the Abstract level is extended using the information related to the target technology. This approach can be applied in current Web Engineering methods. As a matter of fact, the navigation and presentation models proposed by the Web Engineering methods can be reused to define some of the expressivity of the Abstract UI level. This can be mainly justified since these models are not tightly coupled to a specific technology even though they are Web-oriented. Thus by including a Concrete UI level, the new technological requirements can be addressed and these models can be preserved without mixing different concerns.

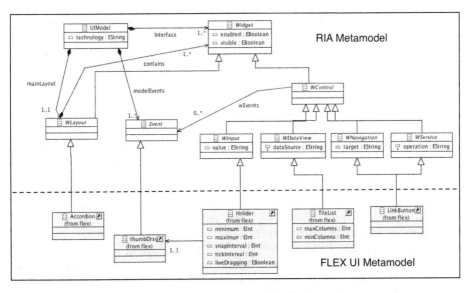

Fig. 1. The RIA Metamodel: UI view

The second idea implies the definition of a Concrete UI metamodel for each RIA technology. This set of technological-specific metamodels will define the Concrete UI models, so the advanced UI features of each technology can be introduced into the development process. Summarizing, a suitable solution requires: 1) the definition of the UI modeling at two levels of abstraction (Abstract and Concrete); and 2) the definition of one metamodel for each technology introduced into the code generation process.

Our approach proposes a RIA Metamodel to define the models of the Concrete UI level and their relationships with the models of the Abstract level (see Fig. 1). This metamodel is made up of a set of abstract modeling entities (depicted in white) from which the technological modeling entities (depicted in gray) can be defined by means of specialization relationships. This approach resembles how the UI frameworks have traditionally been developed. These abstract modeling entities are the parent entities used to create a metamodel for each specific RIA technology. Afterwards, these technology-specific metamodels are used to model the UI of the Web application for a specific RIA technology, so he analyst can define models to address all the features that a specific RIA technology can provide.

The main advantage of this approach is that the link between the Abstract level, which is made up of the Navigational Models, and Concrete level is performed using those abstract modeling entities that are common to all the technological metamodels. A suitable relationship is created between each modeling entity, which is used for defining the UI, from the Abstract level, and an abstract modeling entity from the RIA metamodel. Therefore the links between the Abstract and the Concrete levels can be reused among different technologies.

The main entity of the RIA Metamodel is a UI Model that is made up of Widgets that abstract a specific UI component. A Widget is defined by a set of Properties, which are specified in the metamodel as meta-attributes. For instance, two properties that are common to any Widget are visible (to show or hide a specific widget in the UI) and enabled (to allow or disable the interaction with the user). The interactions that users can perform over a widget are described as Events. Widgets are divided into two types depending on whether or not they can receive Events: *Layout Widgets* (WLayout entity), which are used to arrange and to contain other widgets; and *Control Widgets* (WControl entity), which can be associated to Events in order to define reactions to the user interaction. The entity WControl is also specialized into four abstract modeling entities: WDataview, WInput, WService, and WNavigation. Each entity represents the widgets that can perform one of the specific interactive functions described above. Events are related to the UI Model entity because they are reused among the different control widgets by means of association relationships.

A technology-specific metamodel must be defined using these abstract modeling entities. For instance, if the Adobe Flex platform [1] is selected as RIA technology, a Flex UI metamodel must be defined. In order to create this new metamodel, each widget provided by Flex is defined as a child entity from one or more entities of the RIA Metamodel. Flex provides a rich UI framework that enables the implementation of complex RIA. Since this framework is built around two main concepts very close to the RIA Metamodel (interface components and containers), the specialization relationships are straightforward. The different containers are defined as specializations from the WLayout entity whereas the interface components are specialized from a suitable WControl entity depending on their function.

For example, Figure 1 (bottom) shows a brief view of the Flex UI metamodel. The *Accordion* widget is a child entity of WLayout, and *TileList* or *Hslider* are child entities of WDataview and WInput, respectively. Another example is the *LinkButton* that can be used for both navigation and service execution purposes. From these technological widget entities the Events and the Properties are created. For example, in the *Hslider* widget, the property *snapInterval* defines the increment of the slider bar, whereas the *thumbDrag* event is triggered when the user moves the slider to a new position. The final result of this process is a metamodel from which a UI for the Flex platform can be modeled.

2.2 Modeling the Event-Driven Interaction

In section 2.1, a metamodel to specify the static view of a UI has been defined. However, the UI is not only a static entity because it reacts according to the interaction with the user. This interaction is perceived as events that occur over a specific widget. This dynamic view must also be included in order to develop interactive Web 2.0 applications. To define this dynamic view, several Web 2.0 applications have been analyzed by the authors, in order to select the most common reactions to events. The selected reactions are classified as follows:

1. *Changes to the UI*: a common reaction to events is a change of the UI properties perceived by the user. For example, when the user clicks on tab a new group of widgets is shown.
2. *Request for data on-demand*: the result of this reaction is a request for information from the server. Usually, only the data that has not been previously retrieved and stored is requested.

3. *Functionality execution*: this reaction implies a request-response communication with the Business Logic. When the response is received, a feedback message is presented to the user to inform about the result.

4. *Input Validation*: this reaction informs the user about mistakes and suggests a solution. When the end-user introduces a value, mistakes are common: from syntactic errors (e.g. a date with an incorrect format), to more complex ones that involves the Business Logic (e.g. to check whether or not the login provided has already been created).

5. *Navigation*: A navigation changes the current point from which the application UI is perceived by the user and the interactions available. RIA has included animation effects to highlight this reaction.

The event rule concept is introduced to describe this dynamic view made up of reactions. An event rule is defined by an Event from a source widget that triggers a Reaction associated with a target widget. This approach resembles the definition of *Event-Condition-Action* (ECA) rules proposed by the HCI community to perform the same goal [14]. The modeling entities to define the event rules are defined in the RIA Metamodel as Figure 2 illustrates.

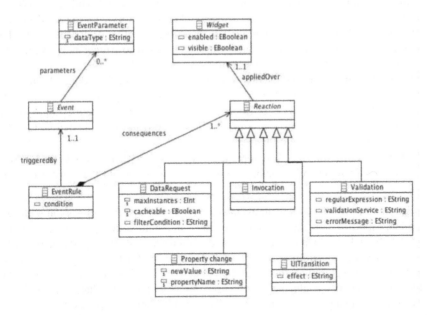

Fig. 2. The RIA Metamodel: Dynamic View

Event rules are defined over the widgets from a technological UI model specialized from the RIA Metamodel. The scope of the event rules is the layout container where are defined the widget that triggers the event and the widget that receives the reaction. Hence, an event rule can generate a reaction to several widgets as long as they are defined in the same parent layout. Additionally, the widget that produces the event and the target widget that performs the reaction can be the same. Optionally, events can include parameters with additional information to configure the reaction. Each event rule is also associated to at least one reaction of the five described above. Each reaction is represented by a modeling entity in the RIA metamodel, and it is also linked to the specific type of widget that supports the expected behavior. These five reaction entities are described below:

- *Property change:* this entity represents a change of the current value of any property of the target widget. By applying this reaction the state of a widget can be controlled according to the triggered events. Since all widgets are described using properties, this reaction can be associated to any widget.
- *Data Request*: this entity represent a request of data from the Business Logic in order to populate a Dataview widget. This reaction can be parameterized by means of the following attributes: the cacheable attribute, which provides a mechanism to avoid having to request previously retrieved data; the max instances attribute, which defines the maximum number of instances to be retrieved; and the filter condition attribute, which selects the data depending on a logic formula.
- *Invocation*: this entity represents an asynchronous service execution from the Business Logic. The user can interact with the rest of the UI while the service is being executed. This reaction is always linked to a Service widget. Moreover, this reaction triggers by default an event to inform whether or not the service has been successfully executed. That event can be used to trigger new event rules that take into account the service results.
- *Validation*: this reaction verifies whether or not the data introduced by the user is correct. The validation can be defined using a regular expression to be satisfied by the input or a Boolean service that receives the input as an argument. If the regular expression or the service result is evaluated as false, an error message is shown to the user.
- *UI Transition*: this reaction represents a transition that is associated with a Navigation widget. Additionally, a visual effect to highlight the transition can be defined.

As an example to illustrate how an event rule can be defined the suggestion pattern is used: when inputting new data, (event) the client-side automatically retrieves (without refreshing the UI) the values that match the input text. In this pattern, two Flex widgets are required to define the UI: a Text Input, and a List widget to show the suggestions. A Data request entity is associated to the List widget and the filter condition of this entity is changed as the user inputs a new text value. This event rule is defined below using a textual notation (for exemplification purposes) that conforms to the metamodel entities presented:

```
SET  RequestReacton TO List:
     RequestReaction.cacheable = true;
ON:
     TextInput.dataChange(newValue)
DO:
     RequestReaction.filterCondition = "LIKE " + newValue;
     List.Request();
```

3   RIA Modeling in the OOWS Web Engineering Method

The RIA metamodel proposed in Section 2 has been defined without taking into account a specific method. Therefore, the main issue is how the new RIA models are introduced and linked with the previous models of the method. This section presents a strategy to deal with this integration. As a proof of concept, this strategy has been applied to the OOWS Web Engineering method [12].

OO-Method [19] is an automatic code generation method that produces an equivalent software product from a system conceptual specification. OOWS was defined to extend OO-Method with the principles proposed by the Web Engineering community. To achieve this goal, OOWS introduces a new set of models for supporting the interaction concern between the user and a Web application (See Figure 3). These models are:

- *User Model*: This model is a user diagram to specify the types of users that can interact with the system.
- *Navigational Model:* This model defines the system navigational structure for each type of user by means of a Navigational Map. This map is depicted by means of a directed graph whose nodes represent Navigational Contexts and whose arcs represent navigational links that define the valid navigational paths. The different Navigational Contexts are described as an aggregation of one or more Abstract Interaction Patterns (AIP). An AIP defines the interaction in terms of two main communication flows between the user and the system: a) a population retrieval flow, which provides information from the system to the user; and b) a service execution flow started by the user, which performs a change of the state of the Information System. Two main AIP, Population and Service, are defined. These AIP are linked to the data and functionality represented by the OO-Method models. In order to constrain the behavior and/or to refine these two main interactions more accurately, auxiliary interaction mechanisms are also introduced.

Currently OOWS generates the Web Application code from these abstract models Further details about the OOWS models and the code generation process can be consulted in [28] and [29] respectively. In order to extend OOWS with the RIA Metamodel, the modeling phase is divided in two levels: an Abstract level made up of the current OOWS models and a new Concrete UI level. This new level adds a new methodological step that is highlighted in Fig. 3. In this new step (Concrete UI modeling), the analyst can choose between the modeling of a traditional HTML interface or a Flex UI. The following subsection explains how the link between the models of the two levels is established.

3.1   Integrating the RIA Metamodel with the OOWS Method

Current abstract models proposed by Web Engineering methods provide information that must be taken into account when the final UI code is generated. For instance, these models provide the data structures that must be shown using a Dataview widget. Since in the approach presented, the UI is defined using the RIA Metamodel, the integration with the previous OOWS models must also be addressed.

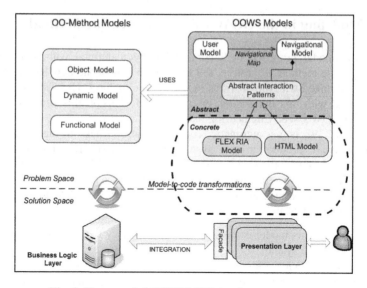

Fig. 3. The extended OOWS MDE development process

A common strategy in a MDE environment is to define a model-to-model (M2M) transformation from an abstract model to a more technological one. Hence, the technological model replaces the previous one and provides the additional expressivity required. However, the use of M2M transformations has two main disadvantages: 1) since the technological models must include all the expressivity from the abstract model they are complex to define; and, 2) since in practice, each abstract modeling entity can be represented in the UI using different RIA widgets, the number of M2M transformations to be defined is high.

To overcome these issues, the solution proposed in this work is to create relationships instead of transformations between the method metamodel and the RIA metamodel. To capture relationships of this type, weaving models have been applied in other works [6]. A weaving model [11] establishes the relationship between the modeling entities of two models that are not directly related. Weaving models are defined conforming to a weaving metamodel that defines the two metamodels to be connected and the set of relationships between the modeling entities. Therefore, neither of the two metamodels is modified because all the knowledge about the relationships between them is defined in the weaving metamodel.

For this work, a weaving metamodel has been defined between the RIA metamodel and the OOWS method metamodel. First the two metamodels were defined using the Eclipse Modelling Framework [3] because Eclipse tools such as the Atlas Model Weaver [8] and the Epsilon plug-in [10] can be used to implement the weaving metamodel. Figure 4 shows a set of relationships defined in the OOWS weaving metamodel. The main function of these relationships is to establish which widget type is going to represent an OOWS modeling entity. For instance, in OOWS the Population AIP defines the set of data to be shown to the user in a web page. Each Population AIP defined in an OOWS model must be related to a Dataview widget. When the analyst creates the weaving model, a Flex widget, which is specialized from

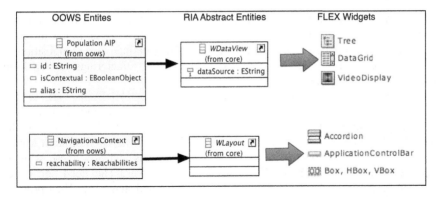

Fig. 4. Weaving relationships between the OOWS Metamodel and the RIA Metamodel

the DataView entity, must be selected for each Population AIP. The same line of reasoning is applied to the rest of the OOWS modeling entities that must be reflected in the UI.

The main advantage of this approach is that the weaving metamodel is defined between the specific method and the abstract entities of the RIA metamodel. Therefore, if another RIA technology is selected, the weaving metamodel does not need to be modified because the relationships are established with the abstract entities instead of the Flex technological entities. Furthermore, it is easier to create and maintain several weaving models than different sets of M2M transformation rules.

Once the analyst has defined the RIA model, event rules are specified using the dynamic view of the metamodel presented in section 2. In order to support the definition of these rules in the OOWS method, the XText framework has been used [17]. This framework creates an Eclipse metamodel to support the definition of a given textual grammar. Therefore, that metamodel has been included in the RIA Metamodel and related with the correspondent Event and Reaction entities.

Finally, the OOWS model compiler must be redefined because the new input models are: 1) an OOWS model that describes the interaction of the user with the system; 2) a RIA model that specifies the UI and the event rules; and, 3) a weaving model that establishes the relationships between these two models. Taking these three models as input, the final code (for instance, a Flex UI) is generated by means of model-to-code transformations. The specification of this code generation process is out of the scope of this paper.

4 Related Work

Several works in the Web Engineering field have proposed methodological extensions to support RIA development. First, Bozzon and Comai [5] have extended the WebML method to support RIA modeling. The proposed extension determines the definition at the modeling level which data, operations, hypertext links, and page contents must be processed by the client side. Additionally, this work proposes a code generation process to obtain the final application using a RIA technology. In the context of the OOHDM method, Urbieta et al. [27] propose an approach for designing RIA interfaces, taking into account the separation of the interface structure from the behavior. That work proposes an aspect-oriented perspective to combine different concerns related to the UI composition. Hence, the UI is defined as a composition of several interface atoms. They also propose [24] a set of refactorings to transform conventional Web interfaces to RIAs.

The OOH method has also been extended defining the OOH4RIA approach [15] in which two models are defined: a Presentation Model and an Orchestration Model. The Presentation Model has been defined using the Google Web Toolkit (GWT) as the technological framework to define the metamodel entities. The Orchestration Model [20] defines the interaction dependencies between widgets and how these widgets should be grouped to improve the requests to the server. The need for better interaction models has also been pointed out by Dolog and Stage [9]. They propose the use of UML statechart diagrams to support the synchronization between the client side and the server side of a RIA as well as between widgets.

The common agreement in the works mentioned above is that the current Web Engineering methods must be extended at the conceptual level in order to deal with Web 2.0 development. Our work proposes a generic RIA metamodel that has been specifically defined to be method-independent. This metamodel combines both the static and dynamic view of the RIA UI that previous works have addressed using different method-specific models. Furthermore, the previous works have mainly focus on how to model the logic and data persistence on the client side of a RIA application. Even though this issue is relevant, in our view the main advantage of RIA is the improvement in the UI usability. Our approach also considers that the methodological extension required cannot be achieved only by extending the current method models. A new methodological phase must be included in order to deal with the Concrete UI specification.

Furthermore, several works have addressed the RIA development from a HCI perspective. A metamodel is proposed by Ruiz [25] for defining a RIA UI from an Abstract Interface Model. In that work, a clear relationship is established between the abstract and the concrete UI that represents the interaction. Another interesting approach is the RUX-method [13]. This method proposes how to define at the concrete level the time-related behaviors (Temporal Presentation) and the event-response actions (Interaction Presentation) in order to define RIA interface components. The main difference between our proposal and these works is the expressivity provided by the concrete UI level. Their concrete models are defined with a set of widgets that are common to different RIA technologies. As a consequence, is not possible to take full advantage of the advanced features of a specific RIA technology.

5 Concluding Remarks

In this paper, a model-driven UI development approach for Web 2.0 has been presented. Because RIA technologies are very common in the Web 2.0 development, a metamodel for dealing with the UI of this application paradigm has been proposed. Several lessons have been learned during the development of this approach: The first lesson is that Web Engineering methods provide suitable models that can also be reused for Web 2.0 development. However, problems arise when specific technological details must be introduced. Therefore, a UI model-driven development process for Web 2.0 must consider the target technology. The second lesson is that the clear separation of abstraction levels proposed by HCI approaches can be easily adopted. Finally, the third lesson is that defining a single UI model to support every technology in Web 2.0 is an unfeasible task. The approaches to support RIA development must be flexible enough to be easily adapted to different technologies.

It should be pointed out that the manual definition of the weaving model might be a tedious and error-prone task, if the number of entities in the model is very large. A potential solution to this issue is the use of patterns. These patterns can abstract several best practices in an understandable way and be reused to avoid the full definition of the weaving model.

Further work will address full tool support of the Web 2.0 development process presented in this work. Currently, the RIA Metamodel and several model-to-code transformation rules for the Adobe Flex platform have been defined for validation purposes. A Web 2.0 application for research management is being developed using the ideas presented in this paper. However, the final goal is to apply these ideas in an industrial tool. Finally, integration with other Web Engineering methods besides OOWS must be analyzed in order to validate the flexibility of the RIA Metamodel.

Acknowledgments. This research work has been developed with the Spanish MEC support under the project SESAMO TIN2007-62894 and the FPU grant AP2005-1590.

References

1. Adobe Flex Developer Center, http://www.adobe.com/devnet/flex/ (accessed April 2009)
2. Bozzon, A., Comai, S.: Conceptual Modeling and Code Generation for Rich Internet Applications. In: 6th International Conference on Web Engineering (ICWE), California, United States (2006)
3. Budinsky, F., Merks, E., Steinberg, D., Ellersick, R., Grose, T.J.: Eclipse Modeling Framework. Addison-Wesley Professional, Reading (2003)
4. Calvary, G., Coutaz, J., Thevenin, D., Limbourg, Q., Bouillon, L., Vanderdonckt, J.: A Unifying Reference Framework for multi-target user interfaces. Interacting with Computers 15, 289–308 (2003)
5. Ceri, S., Fraternali, P., Bongio, A., Brambilla, M., Comai, S., Matera, M.: Designing Data-Intensive Web Applications. Morgan Kaufmann, San Francisco (2003)
6. Cetina, C., Fons, J., Pelechano, V.: Applying Software Product Lines to Build Autonomic Pervasive Systems. In: Proceedings of the 2008 12th International Software Product Line Conference. IEEE Computer Society, Los Alamitos (2008)
7. Comai, S., Carughi, G.T.: A Behavioral Model for Rich Internet Applications. In: 7th International Conference in Web Engineering, Como, Italy (2007)
8. Del Fabro, M., Bézivin, J., Valduriez, P.: Weaving Models with the Eclipse AMW plugin. In: Eclipse Summit Europe, Esslingen, Germany (2006)
9. Dolog, P., Stage, J.: Designing Interaction Spaces for Rich Internet Applications with UML. In: Baresi, L., Fraternali, P., Houben, G.-J. (eds.) ICWE 2007. LNCS, vol. 4607, pp. 358–363. Springer, Heidelberg (2007)
10. Epsilon, http://www.eclipse.org/gmt/epsilon/ (accessed May 2009)
11. Fabro, M.D.D., Valduriez, P.: Semi-automatic model integration using matching transformations and weaving models. In: Proceedings of the 2007 ACM symposium on Applied computing. ACM, Seoul (2007)

12. Fons, J., Pelechano, V., Albert, M., Pastor, O.: Development of Web Applications from Web Enhanced Conceptual Schemas. In: Song, I.-Y., Liddle, S.W., Ling, T.-W., Scheuermann, P. (eds.) ER 2003. LNCS, vol. 2813, pp. 232–245. Springer, Heidelberg (2003)

13. Linaje, M., Preciado, J.C., Sánchez-Figueroa, F.: Engineering Rich Internet Application User Interfaces over Legacy Web Models. IEEE Internet Computing, 53–59 (2007)

14. Mbaki, E., Vanderdonckt, J., Guerrero, J., Winckler, M.: Multi-level Dialog Modeling in Highly Interactive Web Interfaces. In: 7th International Workshop on Web-Oriented Software Technologies, vol. 445, pp. 38–43. WS-CEUR, New York (2008)

15. Meliá, S., Gómez, J., Pérez, S., Díaz, O.: A Model-Driven Development for GWT-Based Rich Internet Applications with OOH4RIA. In: Eight International Conference on Web Engineering. IEEE Computer Society, New York (2008)

16. Noda, T., Helwig, S.: Rich Internet Applications - Technical Comparison and Case Studies of AJAX, Flash, and Java based RIA. In: Best Practice Reports University of Wisconsin-Madison, vol. 2008 (2005)

17. OpenArchitectureWare. Xtext Reference Documentation, http://wiki.eclipse.org/Xtext/Documentation (accessed April 2009)

18. Oreilly, T.: What is Web 2.0? Design Patterns and Business Models for the Next Generation of Software (2005), http://www.oreillynet.com/pub/a/oreilly/tim/news/2005/09/30/what-is-web-20.html (accessed April 2009)

19. Pastor, O., Molina, J.C.: Model-Driven Architecture in Practice. In: A Software Production Environment Based on Conceptual Modelling. Springer, Heidelberg (2007)

20. Pérez, S., Díaz, O., Meliá, S., Gómez, J.: Facing Interaction-Rich RIAs: the Orchestration Model. In: Eight International Conference on Web Engineering, pp. 24–37. IEEE Computer Society, New York (2008)

21. Preciado, J.C., Linaje, M., Sánchez, F., Comai, S.: Necessity of methodologies to model Rich Internet Applications. In: 7th IEEE International Symposium on Web Site Evolution, pp. 7–13. IEEE, Budapest (2005)

22. Rossi, G., Pastor, O., Schwabe, D., Olsina, L. (eds.): Web Engineering: Modelling and Implementing Web Applications. Springer, Heidelberg (2008)

23. Rossi, G., Schwabe, D., Lyardet, F.: User interface patterns for hypermedia applications. In: Proceedings of the working conference on Advanced visual interfaces, pp. 136–142. ACM Press, Palermo (2000)

24. Rossi, G., Urbieta, M., Ginzburg, J., Distante, D., Garrido, A.: Refactoring to Rich Internet Applications: A Model-Driven Approach. In: Eight International Conference on Web Engineering, pp. 1–12. IEEE Computer Society, New York (2008)

25. Ruiz, F.J.M.: A Development Method for User Interfaces of Rich Internet Applications. DEA Thesis. Université catholique de Louvain, Louvain, Belgium (2007)

26. Troyer, O., Casteleyn, S., Plessers, P.: WSDM: Web Semantics Design Method. In: Web Engineering: Modelling and Implementing Web Applications, pp. 303–352. Springer, Heidelberg (2008)

27. Urbieta, M., Rossi, G., Ginzburg, J., Schwabe, D.: Designing the Interface of Rich Internet Applications. In: Fifth Latin American Web Congress (LA-WEB), Santiago de Chile (2007)

28. Valverde, F., Panach, I., Aquino, N., Pastor, O.: Dealing with Abstract Interaction Modelling in an MDE Development Process: a Pattern-based Approach. In: New Trends on Human-Computer Interaction, pp. 119–128. Springer, London (2009)

29. Valverde, F., Valderas, P., Fons, J., Pastor, O.: A MDA-Based Environment for Web Applications Development: From Conceptual Models to Code. In: 6th International Workshop on Web-Oriented Software Technologies, Como, Italy, pp. 164–178 (2007)

30. Vanderdonckt, J., Limbourg, Q., Michotte, B., Bouillon, L., Trevisan, D., Florins, M.: USIXML: a User Interface Description Language for Specifying Multimodal User Interfaces. In: WMI 2004, Sophia Antipolis, Greece (2004)

Intent-Based Categorization of Search Results Using Questions from Web Q&A Corpus

Soungwoong Yoon, Adam Jatowt, and Katsumi Tanaka

Graduate School of Informatics, Kyoto University
Yoshida Honmachi, Sakyo, Kyoto 606-8501, Japan
{yoon,adam,tanaka}@dl.kuis.kyoto-u.ac.jp

Abstract. User intent is defined as a user's information need. Detecting intent in Web search helps users to obtain relevant content, thus improving their satisfaction. We propose a novel approach to instantiating intent by using adaptive categorization producing predicted intent probabilities. For this, we attempt to detect factors by which intent is formed, called intent features, by using a Web Q&A corpus. Our approach was motivated by the observation that questions related to queries are effective for finding intent features. We extract set of categories and their intent features automatically by analyzing questions within Web Q&A corpus, and categorize search results using these features. The advantages of our intent-based categorization are twofold, (1) presenting the most probable intent categories to help users clarify and choose starting points for Web searches, and (2) adapting sets of intent categories for each query. Experimental results show that distilled intent features can efficiently describe intent categories, and search results can be efficiently categorized without any human supervision.

Keywords: User intent detection, Intent-based categorization.

1 Introduction

The continuous growth of the Web has made it increasingly important in our lives, yet it is still difficult to find appropriate information we intend to seek. Search engines are the most frequently used 'gateways' for entering the territory of the Web, and conventional search engines return pages that are most relevant to queries issued under the practical assumption that users' search needs have been explicitly represented by the search queries. However, queries are generally insufficient to fully describe a user's information needs as they contain very short keyword phrases [7], which may be ambiguous. Moreover, users modify their search needs frequently on viewing the search results or browsing Web pages.

A user's information need is defined as intent [1]. The *Intent Detection* on Web searching is a kind of 'holy grail' for search engines as it promises better user experience and improved satisfaction. There were several studies for detecting intent within queries by analyzing query logs [1,8,10]. However, detecting the complete user intent is not easy and is actually often impossible, because the user's search intent is

G. Vossen, D.D.E. Long, and J.X. Yu (Eds.): WISE 2009, LNCS 5802, pp. 145–158, 2009.
© Springer-Verlag Berlin Heidelberg 2009

generally very subjective and ambiguous. The precise intent may even be difficult for the users themselves to determine.

As an alternative, conventional approaches focused on categorizing search results using external knowledge and click-through data [2,9]. However, as shown in Fig. 1(a), these techniques prejudge the fixed number of intent-category pairs, rather than generate a set of exhaustive intent possibilities using the query. Moreover, they attempt to detect the statistically dominant intent of each search result, which means they overlook the fact that queries can represent many variations of intent.

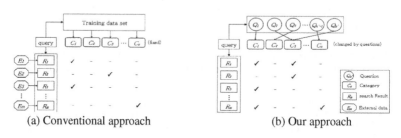

(a) Conventional approach   (b) Our approach

Fig. 1. Comparison of search results' categorization

Different to the conventional approaches, we propose a novel method of representing the most probable intent possibilities for users to improve their Web experience. Our method relies on extracting factors through which intent is formed, called intent features, using Web Q&A corpus, since the questions contain useful and typical expressions that reveal the questioner's intent.

In the proposed approach depicted in Fig. 1(b), intent features of queries are extracted using question phrases and their categories[1] appearing in Web Q&A corpus. Next, using common categories of such questions, we can determine the candidate intent features of a user query represented by a set of categories, called intent categories, without any human supervision. Moreover, these intent categories are adaptively changed according to the query, because there are numerous kinds of categories in Web Q&A corpus[2]. Finally, we categorize search results into one or more intent categories by calculating their matches with intent features of the query. We present such categorized search results to the users in real time as an alternative to a conventional ranking of search results returned by current search engines.

The advantages of our intent-based categorization of Web search results are that users should be able to more easily determine their own search needs and satisfy their search goals by seeing the categorized search results. More precisely, the advantages are two-fold: (1) presenting the most probable intent categories to help users clarify

---

[1] For example, for the query 'Kyoto' there are many question phrases related to this query in Web Q&A corpus such as 'Where is the cheapest hotel in Kyoto?', 'How to go to Kyoto?' or 'When will United-States sign the Kyoto Protocol?'. These question phrases are manually assigned within Web Q&A corpus to their corresponding categories such as 'Travel', 'Japan' or 'Health' for the above examples, respectively.

[2] For example, Yahoo! Answers (http://answers.yahoo.com), one of useful Web Q&A corpora, contains 26 top level categories and 1,640 sub-categories.

and choose starting points for Web searches, and (2) adapting sets of intent categories for each query.

Our main contribution is as follows: (a) we propose intent-based categorization of Web search results by using Web Q&A corpus to the problem of intent detection and (b) we show the method for such categorization based on linguistic analysis of questions and (c) we evaluate it through experiments.

The reminder of this paper is organized as follows. Related work and the background are presented in Section 2. We explain our methodology in Section 3 and present the experimental results and a discussion in Section 4. The conclusion and future research directions are given in Section 5.

2 Related Research

2.1 Intent Discovery

Research on search intent discovery originated from the analysis of click-through data and query-intent categorization. Following the well-known query classification first proposed by Broder [1], Jansen et al. [8] stated that user intent can be categorized into three general intent classes: navigational, transactional and informational intent. The characteristics of user intent have been conventionally defined by analyzing click-through data [1,8,10]. Using large amounts of data containing evidence of user search-related activities made it possible to not only understand user needs, but also to depict user behavior in browsing Web search results [6] or support non-informational search intent on the Web [11].

However, the usefulness of these categorizations is limited by the data sets used and the efficiency of post-processing. There is a risk of the over-generalization being reflected in mismatches in classification between automatic and manual categorization. This is because the above researches were based on their own rigid classification schemes, and biased by the data sets they used. Furthermore, the previously proposed methods often have failed to represent the actual user intent as the scope of possible intents may simply be too large and too heterogeneous to be accurately reflected in any fixed taxonomy. Moreover, one should realize that the information needs of Web users are constantly changing and so does the Web itself.

In this study, we take a different approach. Rather than conjecturing likely user search intent with fixed categorization choices, we allow users themselves to choose the search categories that they may be interested in. To achieve this, we use Web Q&A corpus that reflect typical needs of users in Web searches. With this kind of data at hand we categorize search results returned by conventional search engines allowing pages to be assigned to multiple categories. As a result, users receive categorized search results that can serve as starting points to continue search processes. We think that this kind of presentation of search results should help users to better organize their search intent space and to more effectively reach search results that truly reflect their search needs.

Our method is somewhat similar to the notion of Navigation-Aided Retrieval (NAR) proposed by Pandit and Olson [14] as a kind of post-query user navigation. They presented starting points for Web navigation using the information scent model based on a hyperlink structure within the neighborhoods of returned search results and an original query. We do not employ a link structure analysis in our work but rather focus on query semantics and possible intent categories (distilled from Web Q&A corpus) that Web users may have in relation to their queries.

2.2   Feature Extraction and Categorization of Web Search Results

Feature extraction is an essential task for categorizing texts and is, in fact, the basis of its efficiency. Detecting salient features may however be sometimes very difficult especially for short documents. Therefore, previous approaches to feature extraction from documents have sometimes also employed additional resources. Such extensions have involved acquiring lexical meanings from dictionaries or using external knowledge bases like WordNet[3] [13], Open Directory Project (ODP)[4] [4] and Wikipedia[5] [3].

Manual classification of Web pages such as the one done in ODP and Yahoo! Directory[6] is another simple solution that depends on human intervention. Although manual classification guarantees a high precision, it cannot be scaled to accommodate the Web. Therefore, automatic classification has been proposed. Clusty.org is an example of a clustering-based search engine that groups related Web search results based on their content. Other information can also be utilized to automatically group pages. For example, Chaker and Ounelli [2] used URLs and logical and hyperlink structure to capture various genres – the content, form and functionality – of Web pages, and Hu et al. [7] used a concept graph based on distilled concepts from Wikipedia and its link structures.

In this work, we use Web Q&A corpus as a training set, because questions concerned with query terms are effective expressions of the potential user intent that is hidden behind these terms. Web Q&A corpus also supports quick matching of terms and provides ready categories for questions, which enables very efficient adaptive categorization.

3   Find Intent Features and Categorize Search Results

There is an overview of our approach shown in Fig. 2. First, a user issues a query to a conventional search engine for which search results are obtained. The same query is also sent to Web Q&A corpus. Our system receives questions relevant to the query and their categories, and characterizes each category with its associated questions by head noun extraction and term scoring using the well-known term frequency–inverse document frequency (TFIDF) weighting scheme. Next, the returned search results are compared against the categories using intent features. Finally, a user receives categorized search results that s/he can browse and utilize to modify subsequent queries.

---

[3] WordNet, a lexical database for English language. Princeton University, http://wordnet.princeton.edu
[4] http://dmoz.org
[5] http://www.wikipedia.org
[6] http://dir.yahoo.com

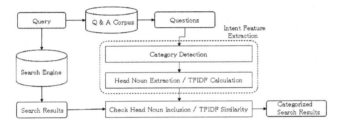

Fig. 2. Overview of our proposed system

3.1 Multiple User-Intent Model

Intent is linguistically defined as a 'purpose' or 'aim.' These meanings in the Web-search environment are restricted by the constraint 'user,' such as *'the perceived need for information that leads to someone using an information retrieval system in the first place'* [1], *'user goals in Web search'* [10], or *'the type of resource desired in the user's expression to the system'* [8].

With the above definitions we can assume that user intent in a query can be formed with words and sentences. In other words, a user can form his/her intent using words and sentences on the Web. Even though there may be many possible implicit directions, the best explicit form of intent is the query itself, which gives strength to the general assumption of the query's importance.

Suppose that there are numerous, but limited kinds of intent in a query. In the simplest case, the dominant search need of a user is the same as the query itself. However, we often face the situation when there is implicit intent hidden behind the query that cannot be directly deduced. For example, we can easily guess that the dominant intent of the query 'kyoto travel' is some kind of 'general information about travel to Kyoto city.' However, the implicit user intent may actually be more complex such as the need for 'the cheapest way to travel to Kyoto city,' or for more specific information on Kyoto such as 'hotels in Kyoto.' We regard these differences in the starting points of the same query as the *Multiple User-Intent Model*. Even though the query is the same, the user's starting points of Web search can be different (varying intent for the same query). To use our model, we made two assumptions.

- **Assumption 1.** User has always some intent behind issued query[7]. S/he can express her/his search intent by using text. We assume that users have intent in all queries, which means that their queries contain explicit intent expressions described directly by query terms, as well as implicit expressions that can be represented by query synonyms or coordinated terms.

- **Assumption 2.** The Web is sufficient to discover user intent. We assume that when the user browses information on the entire Web, s/he can find intended search results, because the Web is the largest corpus of knowledge.[8]

---

[7] Exceptional cases such as input mistakes, confusion, or spelling corrections are omitted.

[8] This assumption has been used implicitly in all intent researches, such as ones based on utilizing user click histories or using words and phrases in language models.

If the user already has a certain amount of knowledge, the query may contain his/her actual intent and the probability of finding meaningful Web information increases. However, when the user is a novice or has no idea about the query, s/he may want to realize her/his actual information need or its clue(s) by browsing search results.

3.2 Extracting Intent Features

The main problem is how to efficiently estimate set of possible intent choices for a given query. Conventional search engines deduce a user's intent by using additional information on the query such as the context of search results or its log data. They then present search results after having conducted prior preprocessing steps such as query expansions or spell corrections. The returned search results are not, however, grouped according to their meaning or potential intent-based categories. They are only arranged by ranking the search results according to pages' relevance scores.

We have chosen Web Q&A corpus in our research as a reference knowledge base. Aggregated user questions related to the query are strong evidence of typical search intentions behind the query and can be effectively used for analyzing possible intent. By sending a query to Web Q&A corpus, we can receive useful hints and topics connected to questions that are basis of our intent prediction process.

Fig. 3. Example of sending a query to Yahoo! Answers

In the example in Fig. 3 we show results obtained for the query 'kyoto travel' from Yahoo! Answers. The question 'What is the cheapest way to go to Kyoto?' is included in the category 'Japan'. It is an example of a particular possible intent that users interested in travelling to Kyoto may have. We can then use not only the category 'Japan' but also the expression 'cheapest way,' which is the core meaning of the question and is directly connected with category 'Travel' for describing this particular user intent.

Using a query, questions $Q = [q_{1'}, q_{2'},... q_{n'}]$ with their matched categories extracted from Web Q&A corpus, $C' = [c_{1'}, c_{2'},... c_{n'}]$, are collected. Next, we filter a set of unique categories appearing in C' expressed as $C = \{c_1, c_2,... c_n\}$, as well as distilled sets of questions by category, $S = \{s_1, s_2,... s_n\}$ with $n \leq n'$. Here s_i denotes the set of questions included in category c_i. From now on we will call categories $C = \{c_1, c_2,... c_n\}$ as intent categories.

We propose two methods of extracting the features for each intent category.

- **Head-noun set of questions:** The main noun phrase of a sentence contains the focus of the sentence, and the headword can be thought of as the 'important' noun within the phrase [12]. In our study, a question is an ordinary sentence and the head noun of a question within a certain intent category is regarded as a key factor of intent feature of that category. We extend the methodology of Metzler et al. [12] to extract the meanings of head nouns as the main foci of questions, called head-noun sets, as follows.

Pseudo code for extracting head-noun set of question q in question set s_j of category c_j

```
Foreach q in s_j
  POS tagging q to q[1],q[2],… q[o]
  Foreach q[i] where 1 ≤i ≤o
    If (q[i] is Noun)
      If (q[i+1] is Noun)          hn_q = q[i] + q[i+1]
      Else                          hn_q = q[i]
      End If
      If (q[i-1] is Adjective)  hn_q = q[i-1] + hn_q
      End If
    End If
    Break Foreach
    Stemming hn_q to hn_q'
    Insert hn_q' into HN_cj with count
End Foreach
```

We assume the first noun or noun phrase is the head-noun phrase for each question and extract the adjective of that phrase if there is any. The collected head-noun phrases are assumed to be head-noun sets after stemming. For example, head-noun phrases 'cheap way' in the topic 'Travel' and 'cheap ways' or 'cheapest way' are treated the same. Finally, the jth intent category has l head-noun sets $HN_{cj} = \{hn_{cj,1}, hn_{cj,2},... hn_{cj,l}\}$. These head noun sets are later used for computing their inclusion within the Web search results.

- **TFIDF vector of a question set:** We distill nouns by POS tagging and calculate TFIDF vectors of the question set for each intent category. As each question in an intent category is treated as a document in the traditional TFIDF scheme, the total number of documents corresponds to the total number of questions in this category. We call this adaptation of traditional TFIDF weighting scheme, a question-TFIDF.

$$qtfidf_{c_j,m} = \frac{n_{j',m}}{\sum_m n_{j',m}} * \log_e \frac{|\{s_{j'} \mid s_{j'} \in c_j\}|}{|\{s_{j'} \mid t_{j',m} \in s_{j'} \ and \ s_{j'} \in c_j\}|} \qquad (1)$$

where $qtfidf_{cj,m}$ is the question-TFIDF value for the mth noun of the jth intent category, $t_{j',m}$ is m^{th} noun in the j'^{th} question, $n_{j',m}$ is the number of occurrences of $t_{j',m}$, $s_{j'}$ is the j'^{th} question and c_j is the j'^{th} intent category.

The question-TFIDF vectors of jth intent category $qTFIDF_{cj} = [qtfidf_{cj,1}, qtfidf_{cj,2},... qtfidf_{cj,m}]$ are later used to compute their similarity with the Web search results.

3.3 Intent Score

For search results $R = [r_1, r_2,..., r_k]$ of a given query, the set of intent scores of each ith search result $I_i = [I_i(c_1), I_i(c_2),..., I_i(c_n)]$ is calculated using either head noun inclusion or cosine similarity between TFIDF weighted vectors. Here the intent score $I_i(c_j)$ of a given search result i and intent category j defines the correspondence of that search result to the particular intent category. We use two methods for intent score calculation:

- Counting the exact matches of head-noun sets in the jth intent category with the ith search result using HN_{sj} and normalizing by the number of head-noun sets in the jth intent category.

$$Score_{HN}(r_i,c_j) = \frac{|\{term_{i',r_i} \mid term_{i',r_i} \in HN_{c_j}\}|}{|HN_{c_j}|} \quad (2)$$

where $term_{i',ri}$ is the i'^{th} noun term in i^{th} search result.

- Measuring the cosine similarity between the term vector of r_i and j^{th} intent category vector $qTFIDF_{cj}$.

$$Score_{TFIDF}(r_i,c_j) = \frac{\vec{r}_i \cdot \vec{c}_j}{\|\vec{r}_i\| \cdot \|\vec{c}_j\|} = \frac{\vec{r}_i \cdot qTFIDF_{c_j}}{\|\vec{r}_i\| \cdot |qTFIDF_{c_j}|} \quad (3)$$

Finally, the intent score is represented by a weighted sum of HN and $qTFIDF$ scores. It indicates the inclusion strength of the ith result in the jth intent category. Parameter α is used to control the influence of HN and $qTFIDF$ factors.

$$I_i(c_j) = \alpha \cdot Score_{HN}(r_i,c_j) + (1-\alpha) \cdot Score_{TFIDF}(r_i,c_j) \quad (4)$$

The ith search result can be included in multiple intent categories by using intent score $I_i(c_j)$. Search results are categorized according to their intent scores and head-noun sets. For example in Fig.4(a), suppose we have 4 search results returned for query 'kyoto travel'. Using questions of Web Q&A corpus, we find out two intent categories, 'Japan' and 'Hotels', and distill HN_{Japan} / HN_{Hotels} sets and $qTFIDF_{Japan}$ / $qTFIDF_{Hotels}$ vectors. In Fig. 4(b), each search result is categorized by its intent score, and both 'Japan' and 'Hotels' category include 1st search result.

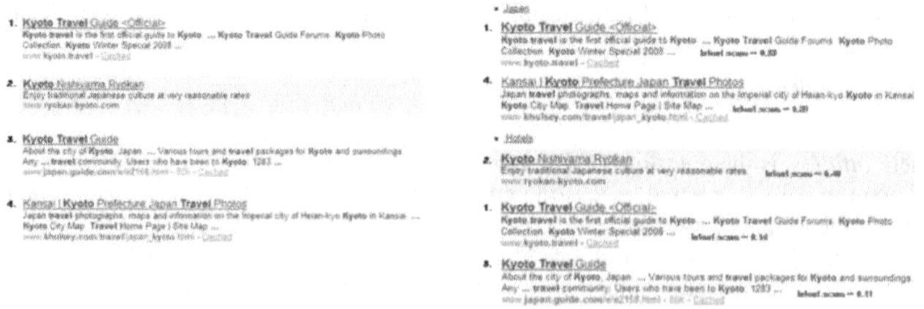

(a) Search results   (b) Search result categorization

Fig. 4. Categorization example

4   Experiments

To collect questions, we use Yahoo! Answers, which is a large corpus of user questions and answers started in December 2005. As a popular Internet reference, Yahoo! Answers has more than 10 million questions, multiple answers to each question with their validation scores, 24 top-level categories (TLCs) and their numerous sub-categories[9] [5]. This data set is useful for connecting a certain term with its corresponding questions and answers. Yahoo! Answers API[10] enables instant access by query and provides XML-formatted response. All experimental data was collected and the experiments were done in April 2009.

We use AOL 500K User Session Collection[11] to obtain queries used for evaluation. This query log contains 10,154,742 unique queries issued from March 1 to May 31 in 2006. 20 queries are randomly chosen from the top 50 most frequent AOL queries for our experiments. Table 1 lists the chosen queries together with average search results by Yahoo! and questions by Yahoo! Answers returned for these queries.

Table 1. Queries and their characteristics

Query	american idol, bank of america, ebay, google, internet, mapquest, myspace, weather, yahoo, southwest airlines, walmart, orbitz, home depot, horoscopes, yellow pages, cingular, craigslist, msn, myspace layouts, sears	
Average Yahoo! hits	Average Yahoo! Answers hits	Average number of intent categories in 200 questions
65,635,117	175,931	38

4.1   Choosing Number of Questions

First, we have to choose the number of questions to be taken from Yahoo! Answers API for each query. The higher is the number of questions extracted, the higher is the resulting number of categories, however, at the same time, the amount of noise increases and consequently the system's performance diminishes. Therefore, it is important to choose the appropriate number of questions to be analyzed.

For estimating the appropriate number of questions, we take the top 50 most frequent AOL queries excluding duplicates. We then collect 20, 50, 100, 200, 500 and 1000 questions (six question sets) including their categories obtained by sending the top 50 AOL queries to Yahoo! Answers API. Then we extract the unique categories in each question set to create the list of unique categories within each question set. We next compare the overlap of unique categories in the 1000 question set with the ones in the remaining question sets treating the former as ground truth data. In this way we calculate the precision and recall of the question sets. F_β measure is used for choosing the number of questions as follows. As precision is more important than recall for showing intent possibilities to user, we set $\beta = 0.5$ in our experiment.

---

[9] Yahoo! Answers have 26 TLCs, 326 second-level sub-categories and 1,314 third-levels with duplications in April 2009. These categories are assumed to be changed continuously in the future.

[10] http://developer.yahoo.com/ answers/

[11] http://www.gregsadetsky.com/aol-data/

$$F_\beta = (1 + \beta^2) \cdot precision \cdot recall / (\beta^2 \cdot precision + recall) \tag{5}$$

As shown in Fig. 5, we have found that a 200-question set is optimal. Conse-quently, we decided to use 200 questions for each query to detect intent features.

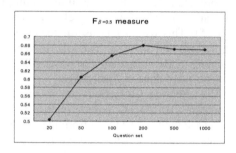

Fig. 5. $F_{\beta=0.5}$ measure result

4.2   Evaluation

From the 200 questions for each query returned by Yahoo! Answers, we extract head-noun sets *HN* and calculate the *qTFIDF* vectors of each intent category using an English morphological analyzer[12] and the Porter stemmer [15].

The terms within the 50 search results returned by Yahoo! for each query are extracted from the returned titles and snippets. Using these terms the search results are then categorized based on their intent scores. Table 2 shows an example of categorization results for query 'southwest airlines'.

Table 2. Categorization example (query: southwest airlines)

Intent Category	Head-noun set	Search result	Intent score
Air Travel	Airlines	50. Southwest Airlines	0.2389
		46. Southwest Airlines – Mahalo	0.2363
		42. Southwest Airlines	0.2338
		45. Southwest Airlines – Flight, Airfare, ...	0.2210
		49. Southwest Airlines Raises Fares – cbs11tv	0.2191
	Flight	4. Southwest Vacations – Vacation Packages...	0.0985
		1. Southwest Airlines	0.0939
		2. Southwest Airlines Reservations	0.0893
Corporations	Southwest airlines	26. Southwest Airlines News	0.3164
		10. Southwest Airlines – Wikipedia	0.2964
		40. Southwest Airlines – USATODAY.com	0.2933
		28. The Southwest Airlines Chinese New Year...	0.2903
		46. Southwest Airlines – Mahalo	0.2900
Packing & Preparation	Baggage	42. Southwest Airlines	0.4138
		23. Southwest Airlines Flight 1455 – Wikipedia	0.4043
		11. Southwest Airlines Information	0.3986
		46. Southwest Airlines – Mahalo	0.3939
		29. AIRLINE BIZ Blog I The Dallas News	0.3892

---

[12] An English part-of-speech tagger with bidirectional interface, Tsujii Laboratory, University of Tokyo: http://www-tsujii.s.u-tokyo.ac.jp

To check the efficiency of *HN* and *qTFIDF* factors, parameter α is used in three different ways: (1) *qTFIDF* only (α= 0): In this case, we use only *qTFIDF* score. (2) *HN* only (α= 1): In this case, we use only the *HN* score. (3) *Hybrid* (α= 0.75): In this case, we use both *qTFIDF* and *HN* scheme, but head-noun sets are used here more than *qTFIDF* for assessing the relevant intent categories of search results.

Search result's inclusion into each intent category is assessed in two different ways: (a) with threshold: We use the threshold of the intent score equal to 0.25. Here, the number of intent categories is reduced as some intent categories were not collected if their assigned search results had their calculated intent scores below 0.25. (b) without threshold: We collect all intent categories that have any search results assigned.

We assume that less than or equal to 20 intent categories are convenient to be shown for a query, which is actually same as the requirement for convenient presentation of search results mentioned in [10]. There is a trade-off in that showing fewer intent categories is more convenient for users, but naturally this may increase the omission ratio of potentially relevant intent categories. To check how close the number of collected intent categories is to 20, we use a one-sided optimum deviation – a standard deviation whose mean number of intent categories is substituted by 20 excluding the cases with fewer than 20 intent categories. The larger the one-sided optimum deviation is, the more difficult it is for users to recognize useful intent categories.

To evaluate category extraction efficiency, we use the precision of intent categories expressed as the count of correct intent categories within all intent categories collected for each query. We decided whether the assigned intent categories are correct or not after manually checking page content.

Fig. 6(a) and (b) show the number of intent categories and one-sided optimum deviation. We can see that the cases of using threshold are generally approaching 20 categories and deviate less than the cases without threshold.

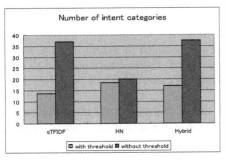
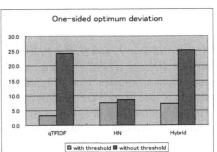

(a) Number of intent categories   (b) One-sided optimum deviation

Fig. 6. Result of category analysis

As seen in Fig. 7, the precision of extracting intent categories from Yahoo! Answers generally exceeds 0.7 and reaches a maximum of 0.784 in the case of *HN* used only with threshold. This means that questions in Yahoo! Answers are useful for extracting relevant intent categories of queries. The precision decreases for the case of not using threshold in both the *qTFIDF* and *hybrid* settings.

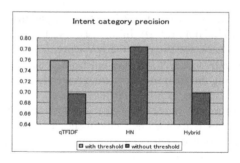

Fig. 7. Intent category precision

Next, we use the mean average precision (MAP) to evaluate the intent-based categorization of search results. We employ a binary decision to check whether search results are correctly included in given intent categories, and MAP@1 and @5 are used to compare intent-based categorization efficiency.

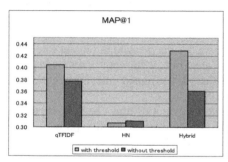 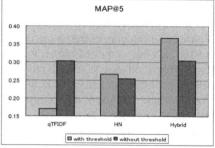

Fig. 8. Results for MAP@1   **Fig. 9.** Results for MAP@5

As seen in Fig. 8 and 9, the best accuracy is obtained in *hybrid* method, which means the *HN* and *qTFIDF* mixed case yields search results better matched to their correct intent categories. Generally, using threshold cases result in a better precision except for a case of *qTFIDF* for MAP@5.

To sum up, the case of hybrid setting with threshold produces the most relevant set of intent categories and reaches the best performance of search results' categorization.

4.3 Discussion

- **Recall of intent category extraction:** Frequency-based category distillation has defects in that it sometimes excludes valuable questions which relatively rarely occur in Web Q&A corpus. On the other hand, the categories may sometimes be too precise for a query. For example, the query 'mapquest' has various kinds of geographical categories such as 'United States,' 'Canada,' and 'Boston' in Yahoo! Answers. Even though this information is still partially useful to recognize the actual query intent categories (e.g. mapquest software covers all geographic locations), we should apply an efficient aggregation methodology in this case.

- **Efficiency of extracted intent categories:** Some distilled intent categories may not correspond to any search results. For example, the query 'bank of america' produces the 'Law & Ethics' or 'Elections' categories, which are concerned with the current events of Bank of America due to the world economic crisis and the policies of the US government. However, there are actually no search results that are relevant to these categories within 50 top search results despite that these categories are correct. On the other hand, some distilled intent categories may not have any assigned search results. In such a case user cannot find pages within top 50 search results that would directly correspond to his search intent and satisfy his information needs. To solve this problem we may need to incorporate other methods such as query expansion by adding intent features derived from the empty intent categories.

  Using only titles and snippets may sometimes be insufficient to generate the precise results when users have a definite meaning basis with query. For example, the query 'google' has a dominant intent which is navigational, and this primary intent cannot be explained linguistically, but only with head-noun set extractions.

- **Precision of intent-based categorization:** Certain intent categories may have too many search results. In this case, we can hardly see any meaningful results. Sometimes all 50 results are included. In another case, there are wrongly categorized pages for the query 'Bank of America' such as 'http://www.bankofamerica store.com/', a souvenir shop page of Bank of America. Such pages decrease the overall categorization precision. For making intent categories more useful, we treat intent scores and threshold carefully to get well-assigned search results.

- **Linguistic problems:** Sometimes there are no matches between search results and the head-noun sets of a certain category. This problem is caused by the characteristics of the Yahoo! Answers corpus, which has mainly been compiled by English speakers. We can obtain more accurate matching if we use a localized Q&A corpus, such as Yahoo! Answers Japan with Japanese queries.

5   Conclusion and Future Directions

We show a novel approach to categorization of search results called intent-based categorization. Such categorization groups search results returned for user query according to their correspondence to the most probable search intents that users can have when issuing the query. By arranging returned Web search results into the main intent categories we believe that users can better find the information that directly matches their actual search needs. In our method we extract intent features from a large corpus of online questions in order to form key intent categories for a given user query. We then use these features for categorizing search results by three methods, Head-noun set extraction, TFIDF-based vector similarity comparison and a hybrid method. The evaluation of our approach indicates high efficiency in distilling key intent categories (70% precision) and shows the potential for categorizing search results according to possible user intents (MAP@1 = 43% and MAP@5 = 37%).

As it is the first attempt of intent-based categorization, in the future, we need to increase the overall precision of the proposed method. For this, we plan to consider more deeply the actual semantics of queries. Furthermore, other aspects of data in Web Q&A corpus could be used to more precisely extract user intent features such as answers of questions, timestamps of questions and best answer votes. We also intend to employ our general intent-based approach for other purposes. For example, one can imagine an intent-based re-ranking application for Web search results or intent-based browsing and navigation enhancement in the Web. Lastly, we plan to investigate the usefulness of Yahoo! Q&A corpus for large scale usage on the Web by analyzing the number of questions and categories as well as their distribution for most popular queries in current query logs.

Acknowledgments. This research was supported in part by the National Institute of Information and Communications Technology, Japan, by Grants-in-Aid for Scientific Research (No. 18049041) from MEXT of Japan, and by the Kyoto University Global COE Program: Informatics Education and Research Center for Knowledge-Circulating Society.

References

1. Broder, A.Z.: A taxonomy of web search. SIGIR Forum 36(2), 3–10 (2002)
2. Chaker, J., Ounelli, H.: Genre Categorization of Web Pages. In: Proceedings of the 7th IEEE International Conference on Data Mining Workshops, pp. 455–464 (2007)
3. Gabrilovich, E., Markovitch, S.: Computing Semantic Relatedness Using Wikipedia-based Explicit Semantic Analysis. In: Proceedings of the 20th International Joint Conferences on Artificial Intelligence, pp. 1606–1611 (2007)
4. Gabrilovich, E., Markovitch, S.: Feature generation for text categorization using world knowledge. In: Proceedings of the 18th International Joint Conferences on Artificial Intelligence, pp. 1048–1053 (2005)
5. Gyöngyi, Z., Koutrika, G., Pedersen, J., Garcia-Molina, H.: Questioning Yahoo! Answers. In: Proceedings of QAWeb 2008 (2008)
6. Guo, Q., Agichtein, E.: Exploring mouse movements for inferring query intent. In: Proceedings of the 31st International SIGIR Conference on Research and Development in Information Retrieval, pp. 707–708 (2008)
7. Hu, J., Wang, G., Lochovsky, F., Chen, Z.: Understanding User's Query Intent with Wikipedia. In: Proceedings of the 18th International Conference on World Wide Web, pp. 471–480 (2009)
8. Jansen, B.J., Booth, D.L., Spink, A.: Determining the informational, navigational, and transactional intent of Web queries. Information Process and Management 44(3), 1251–1266 (2008)
9. Kules, B., Kustanowitz, J., Shneiderman, B.: Categorizing Web Search Results into Meaningful and Stable Categories Using Fast-Feature Techniques. In: Proceedings of the 6th ACM/IEEE Joint Conference on Digital Libraries, pp. 210–219 (2006)
10. Lee, U., Liu, Z., Cho, J.: Automatic identification of user goals in Web search. In: Proceedings of the 14th International Conference on World Wide Web, pp. 391–400 (2005)
11. Li, Y., Krishnamurthy, R., Vaithyanathan, S., Jagadish, H.V.: Getting work done on the Web: Supporting transactional queries. In: Proceedings of the 29st International SIGIR Conference on Research and Development in Information Retrieval, pp. 557–564 (2006)
12. Metzler, D., Croft, W.B.: Analysis of Statistical Question Classification for Fact-based Questions. Information Retrieval 8(3), 481–504 (2004)
13. Nastase, V., Sayyad-Shirabad, J., Sokolova, M., Szpakowicz, S.: Learning Noun-Modifier Semantic Relations with Corpus-based and WordNet-based Features. In: Proceedings of American Association for Artificial Intelligence (2006)
14. Pandit, S., Olson, C.: Navigation-Aided Retrieval. In: Proceedings of the 16th International Conference on World Wide Web, pp. 391–400 (2007)
15. Porter, M.F.: An algorithm for suffix stripping. Program 14(3), 130–137 (1980)

TermCloud for Enhancing Web Search

Takehiro Yamamoto, Satoshi Nakamura, and Katsumi Tanaka

Department of Social Informatics, Graduate School of Informatics, Kyoto University,
Yoshida-Honmachi, Sakyo, Kyoto 606-8501 Japan
{tyamamot,nakamura,tanaka}@dl.kuis.kyoto-u.ac.jp

Abstract. We previously proposed a reranking system for Web searches based on user interaction. The system encouraged users to interact with terms in search results or with frequent terms displayed in the tagcloud visualization style. Over 20,000 interaction logs of users were analyzed, and the results showed that more than 70% of users had interacted with the terms in the tagcloud area. Therefore, this visualization style is thought to have great potential in supporting users in their Web searches. This visualization style is referred to as *TermCloud* in this paper. We describe how TermCloud can increase the effectiveness of users' Web searches, and we propose a technique to generate a more useful TermCloud than the frequency-based TermCloud. Then, we show the usefulness of our method based on the experimental test.

Keywords: Tagcloud, TermCloud, user interaction, information retrieval.

1 Introduction

Web search engines have become essential tools to find desired information. Conventional Web search engines, however, do not always satisfy the information needs of users. There are four major problems, as follows:

Difficulty in creating an appropriate query: It is difficult for average users to create queries that adequately reflect their information needs. In particular, this task is more difficult when a user does not have a clear search intention [1].

Difficulty in judging how appropriate an input query is: Because conventional Web search engines display search results as a ranked list, a user has to scroll down a large result page that contains many search results and actually browse several search results to judge the relevancy of his input query.

Difficulty in finding relevant low-ranked search results: Due to limitations of the ranked list, users frequently only check high-ranked search results [2]. Therefore, even if low-ranked search results might be more relevant to users, they usually cannot reach those results.

Limited interaction to indicate search intention: The only way for users to inform their search intentions is to input queries to the search engine. Therefore, search engines have to estimate their intentions by only checking their queries. As a result, it is difficult for them to understand the user context, and they consequently fail to return suitable search results that adequately reflect the users' search intentions.

To solve these problems, we previously proposed a system that enabled users to rerank search results through simple user interaction [3]. In this system, users can

G. Vossen, D.D.E. Long, and J.X. Yu (Eds.): WISE 2009, LNCS 5802, pp. 159–166, 2009.

rerank search results with two interactions: emphasis and deletion. By using these interactions, users can inform the search engine of their intentions, for example, "*I want to check results that contain the emphasized term,*" or "*I don't want to check results that contain the deleted term,*" without recreating any queries. The system also displays frequent terms that appear in search results in the *tagcloud* visualization style to support reranking. Users can also rerank search results by clicking and emphasizing/deleting terms in the tagcloud area. Using the system, users can easily browse low-ranked search results by reranking the results.

We launched this system as a Web service for one year and collected about 20,000 interaction logs from users. An analysis of the reranking logs showed that over 70% of users performed reranking operations from the tagcloud area. We therefore think that tagclouds have enormous potential to elicit the hidden interests of users. In this paper, we refer to this visualization style as *TermCloud*.

We describe here how TermClouds can support a Web search. A TermCloud enables users to grasp what topics are related to an input query. Therefore, the user can judge whether the input query is appropriate or not. In the meantime, the user can indicate their intent by interacting with terms that appear in the TermCloud. By interacting with various terms, the user can obtain more diverse search results.

In addition, we propose an idea to enhance TermCloud to provide more useful terms in order to support Web searches. Our conventional TermCloud is generated depending on the frequencies of terms. This frequency-based TermCloud is not sufficient to support Web searches because the terms in the TermCloud are often too general to appeal to users. To generate a more useful TermCloud, we have focused on the parts of speech of terms, such as adjectives, adjectival verbs, and proper nouns. We expect that terms in such parts of speech will be useful in providing an interesting aspect for browsing search results. We conducted a user experiment to evaluate how useful these terms were in supporting a Web search.

2   TermCloud for Web Search

2.1   Difference between TermCloud and Tagcloud

A tagcloud is a visual depiction of a set of tags. A tag is usually a term that is assigned to certain information resources. To represent certain features (e.g., popularity) of tags, text attributes such as the *font size* or *color* can be used. Tagclouds have recently become a familiar visualization style in social Web services such as Flickr and Delicious. Tagclouds can serve as a tool to navigate the underlying content and to summarize a large set of tags that users have added to the content.

Among the features of conventional tagclouds, it is important to consider how to visualize a set of tags. We must define the number of tags to be displayed and the text features of these tags, such as the font size, font weight, and color. The ordering of tags (e.g., alphabetical order, popularity-based order, etc.) must also be considered. These features affect the usability of tagclouds [4], as well as the impression formation of tagclouds [5].

When we consider supporting Web searches with TermCloud, however, the *extraction from the search results of the terms to be displayed in a TermCloud* is much more important than the visualization of the TermCloud. In conventional tagclouds, the tags to be displayed are almost entirely defined by their popularity, and thus, there is no problem selecting which tags to display. In contrast, all the terms that appear in the search results for a query can be candidate terms for a TermCloud. The terms in a TermCloud directly influence its effectiveness in revealing a user's search intent or its ability to provide diverse terms that might pique the user's hidden interest.

2.2   Effects of TermCloud

The effects of a termCloud in a Web search can be divided into two aspects: *summarization* and *suggestion*.

Search Result Summarization

As displayed in the previous system, a TermCloud is a summarization of a large set of search results. A term displayed with a larger font size indicates that many search results contain the term. Therefore, the user can instantly check which topics related to the input query are major and which are minor simply by checking a TermCloud. Because of this effectiveness, users can easily judge how appropriate their queries are for their search intentions without actually checking several search results. For example, if the user wants to know about "Katsumi Tanaka," who is a professor at Kyoto University, by searching the Web and therefore inputs "Katsumi Tanaka" as a query to the Web search engine, the frequency-based TermCloud displays terms such as "professor," "pianist," "poet," and so on. Therefore, the user can see instantly that the search results clearly contain irrelevant results related to other people, such as a pianist or poet, with the same name. In a conventional Web search, the user must actually check several search results before noticing that the results for "Katsumi Tanaka" are related to several different people.

Suggestion

In our system, users can rerank search results by clicking terms in the TermCloud. As with conventional query suggestions in Web search engines, TermCloud provides a lot of suggested terms for reranking search results. The effects of suggestion can be divided into two aspects:

- **Improving the relevancy of the top k search results:** If a user wants to know about the professor named "Katsumi Tanaka" by searching the Web and inputs "Katsumi Tanaka" as a query to a Web search engine, the search results will contain many irrelevant results as described above. When the user wants to eliminate irrelevant search results, he has to modify the query to something like "Katsumi Tanaka −pianist" in conventional Web search engines. Creating such advanced queries, however, is difficult for non-advanced users. On the other hand, with a TermCloud the user can easily obtain similar results simply by clicking an irrelevant term such as "pianist" and then clicking the delete button.

- **Increasing opportunities to obtain diverse search results:** When the search intentions of users are not clear, it is important for users to browse various search results and acquire diverse knowledge. For example, if a user wants to travel to Poland, he has to gather various kinds of information about Poland, such as its history, culture, hotels, famous sights, and so on. To obtain such information, the user needs to create many queries in order to cover the different topics related to Poland. In such a search task, however, it is hard for the user to create or modify his queries, because of a lack of knowledge about Poland. Therefore, the user usually checks a few search results from a limited number of queries and thus might miss some important topics or interesting details about Poland. In contrast, a TermCloud consists of a mass of query suggestions. The TermCloud displaying many terms might provide some serendipitous terms, such as unexpected or unknown terms that the user might be interested in. TermCloud thus enables users to discover their hidden interests.

We regard the role of increasing the opportunities to obtain diverse search results as TermCloud's most important function, since a ranked result list by itself does not effectively support this kind of search. Some major commercial search engines provide some query suggesions for users to modify their queries. Their suggestions are useful when users want to improve the relevancy of search results. However, in terms of diversifying the search results, these suggestions are not sufficient because the number of suggestions is limited. Moreover, these suggestions offer such popular queries that it is difficult for users to provide unexpected queries.

3   Enhancing TermCloud Using Parts of Speech

3.1   Basic Idea

As we discussed above, the effects of TermCloud are both summarization and suggestion. However, the frequency-based TermCloud is just one possible implementation to support users' Web searches. In this section we propose an idea to enhance the effectiveness of TermCloud. When we extract terms according to their frequencies in search results, most of them are nouns, especially general nouns. These terms seem to be useful for summarizing Web search results. For some queries, however, we think that specific kinds of terms are much more effective for suggestion. For example, if a user wants to cook dinner and inputs "pork pepper" as a query, frequent terms in the search results include "cooking," "recipe," and so on. These terms indicate that many search results contain them and so serves as a summarization of the search results. In terms of suggestion, however, these terms are less meaningful because they are too common for users. Even if the user reranks search results by emphasizing "recipe," the user cannot obtain more interesting or unexpected information from the reranked search results than from the original search results. In contrast, if we focus on parts of speech, such as *adjectives* or *verbs*, we find terms that seem to be more attractive, such as "spicy," "sweet-sour," "quick," "tender," "boil," "burn," and so on. These terms are characteristic for cooking and might spark the user's imagination and reveal some hidden interests. Although users might seldom use such terms as queries in Web searches, we believe that these terms are useful as suggestions. Fig. 1 shows an image of a TermCloud that displays not only frequent terms but also other adjectives (the TermClouds displayed in the rest of this paper have been translated from Japanese into English, and colors and sizes of terms were manually set by the authors.) The TermCloud includes terms related to taste (e.g., salty-sweet and delicious) or textures (e.g., tender). These terms provide new viewpoints that seem to be useful for reranking search results.

As another example, if a user wants to know about Prof. Katsumi Tanaka and inputs "KatsumiTanaka KyotoUniversity" as a query to a Web search engine, frequent terms in the search results are "information," "research," etc. For a person's

Fig. 1. Example of TermCloud enhanced by adjectives for query "pork green pepper"

Fig. 2. Example of TermCloud enhanced by person names for query "KatsumiTanaka KyotoUniversity"

name used as a query, we think that proper nouns, especially personal names or organization names are useful as suggestions. The TermCloud in Fig. 2 displays not only frequent terms but also other personal names in the search results. By displaying the personal names in the TermCloud, users can instantly understand who has a strong relationship with Prof. Katsumi Tanaka. For example, if "Yahiko Kambayashi" appears many times in the search results of the query, the term "Yahiko Kambayashi" is displayed in a larger font. Therefore, the user can instantly understand who has a relationship with Prof. Katsumi Tanaka, as well as how strong that relationship is, simply by checking the TermCloud. We think these kinds of terms are more informative for obtaining information about Prof. Katsumi Tanaka than more general frequently used terms such as "research" and "professor.".

In this way, for certain queries, certain kinds of terms would be important for enhancing a Web search, especially for providing interesting or unexpected viewpoints about queries.

3.2 Experiments

In the previous subsection we proposed an idea to utilize parts of speech of terms to enhance the TermClouds. To evaluate what kinds of terms users prefer for reranking and the usefulness of TermCloud after enhancement with parts of speech, we conducted user experiments.

In the experiments, we compared four types of TermClouds; one was a frequency-based TermCloud (referred to as FreqCloud), and the other three were TermClouds that were enhanced by *adjectives*, *adjectival verbs*, or *proper nouns* (we call these part-of-speech-enhanced TermClouds PosClouds).

To generate four TermClouds, we first obtained the top 200 search results of a given query by using Yahoo! API. Then we morphologically analyzed the titles and summaries in the search results, calculated the frequency of terms, and obtained their parts of speech by using the Japanese morphological analyzer, MeCab. All the TermClouds contained 20 terms. The FreqCloud contained the top 20 frequent terms regardless of the part of speech. The PosClouds contained the top 10 frequent terms whose part of speech was the one specified, and the 10 remaining frequent terms whose part of speech was different from the specified one. Fig. 3 shows an example of a PosCloud enhanced by proper nouns for the query "Kyoto world heritage." (Red terms are proper nouns. Colors of terms were set manually only for this paper.).

Table 1. Queries used in the experiments

category	query
Cooking	pork green pepper
	avocado recipe
	curry recipe
Personal	KatsumiTanaka KyotoUniversity
Name	napoleon bonaparte
	TaroAso PrimeMinister
Location	Kyoto travel
	Poland sightseeing
	Kyoto world heritage
Product	camera
	iPhone
	LCD televisions
Disease	flu
	pollen allergy
	hangover

UNESCO Nijo-Castle
Old-City Otsu Nara Uji
Byoudou-Temple
information culture
cultual-assets travel Japan
East-Temple history
Kiyomizu-Temple regist
shrine introduction
sightseeing Kinkaku-ji

Fig. 3. An example of PosCloud (proper nouns) for the query "Kyoto world heritage"

We expected the usefulness of the types of terms given for suggestions to depend on the category of the query. Therefore, we prepared five categories and came up with three queries for each category. The 15 queries used in the experiment are shown in Table 1. To evaluate which of the four TermClouds was preferred by users, seven subjects were asked to perform the following task for each query:

(1) We showed a query and the top 10 search results of the query and four TermClouds (FreqCloud and three types of PosCloud) that had been printed on a sheet of paper. On the paper, the four TermClouds were aligned near each other on the right side of the search results. Four TermClouds were placed randomly for each query, and all the terms in the four TermClouds were displayed in the same size and the same color in order to prevent biased judgments from the subjects.

(2) After viewing the paper, for all of the terms in the four TermClouds, each subject was asked to check a term if it seemed to be unexpected and useful for re-searching by adding the term to the query.

After finishing the tasks, we interviewed the subjects. We note here that the experiment was conducted in Japanese, and the results were translated into English.

Fig. 4 shows the average ratio of the four TermClouds that contained the most terms that the subjects judged to be unexpected and useful for each category of queries. Fig. 5 shows the average ratio of the four TermClouds that contained the most terms that the subject judged to be unexpected and useful for each subject.

From Figs. 4 and 5, we found that the types of terms that subjects preferred depended on both the category of a query and the subjects' own preferences. From Fig. 8, when the queries included proper nouns, such as a location or a personal name category, many subjects chose proper nouns. For example, when the query was "Kyoto world heritage," many subjects chose proper nouns, such as "Kiyomizu Temple" and "Nijo Castle.". They chose these terms because they could not think up these terms for use as queries until they actually saw them in the TermCloud. They said these terms would provide important information about "Kyoto travel." In contrast, when the queries were related to disease, FreqCloud contained the most terms chosen by subjects. For example, five of the seven subjects chose the most

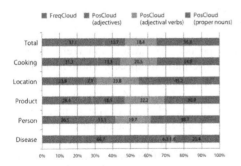

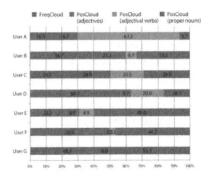

Fig. 4. Average ratios of TermClouds that contained the most terms that the subjects judged to be unexpected and useful

Fig. 5. Average ratios of TermClouds that contained the most terms that individual subjects judged to be unexpected and useful

terms from the FreqCloud in queries of "pollen allergy" and "handover." Although the subjects actually chose some adjectives, adjectival verbs, or proper nouns in those queries, those chosen terms were also contained in FreqCloud. Other adjectives, adjectival verbs, or proper nouns were seldom chosen by the subjects. As a result, the FreqCloud contained the most preferred terms in the disease category.

As shown in Fig. 5, the criteria of whether a term was unexpected and useful strongly depended on user preference. For example, users A, B, and C preferred adjectives and adjectival verbs, while users F and G seldom chose those kinds of terms. We analyzed the individual experimental results and found the following:

- User A chose many adjectival verbs as unexpected and useful terms for many queries independent of their categories, for example, "colorful" and "rich-tasting" in cooking queries, and "noble," "accessible," and "casual" in location queries. In the interview, this user mentioned that these terms made a very appealing impression, and he had seldom input them as queries to conventional Web search engines.
- User E did not choose adjectives or adjectival verbs. In the interview, he mentioned that even if he added these terms to the query, he did not think that he would obtain the desired information, and thus he did not think these kinds of terms were useful for Web searches.

The results showed that in some queries some users preferred adjectives and adjectival verbs. Because many users seldom use these kinds of terms in queries, conventional search engines cannot provide them as query suggestions to users as effectively as the frequency-based TermCloud can. Therefore, by showing these kinds of terms, we can provide other viewpoints related to the query that neither conventional Web search engines nor a frequency-based TermCloud can provide.

To generate a TermCloud that adapts user preferences, we have to personalize it. For example, user A prefers adjectival verbs in many queries. Therefore, when this user is searching, TermCloud should enhance adjectival verbs for him. In addition to personalizing TermClouds for users, the experimental results also indicate that we can use common preferences of many users. For example, when the queries are related to location names, many subjects preferred proper nouns. Therefore, if users input a query that contains a location name, the TermCloud enhanced by proper nouns is likely to be useful for most users.

4 Conclusion and Future Work

We have described the potential of TermClouds for supporting Web searches. We explained the effectiveness and the technical aspects of TermClouds in Web searches and proposed enhancing TermClouds with specific parts of speech. Though our user study was small, we found that not only the frequency of terms, but also other kinds of terms can be useful for supporting users' Web searches. In this study, we manually created an enhanced TermCloud. In the future, we plan to devise a method to automatically detect what kinds of terms are important for specific queries.

One problem with our TermCloud is that it cannot display terms that are related to the query but that do not appear in the search results of the query. In our current system, users can rerank search results but cannot modify their queries through user interactions. Therefore, TermClouds are generated only from the search results of the query. To provide a greater variety of terms in TermCloud and to enable users to browse more diverse information, we plan to generate a TermCloud by combining terms that appear in the search results and those that do not appear in the search results. In addition to achieving such a TermCloud, we also need to develop a method to combine reranking and re-searching seamlessly in our system.

In this paper, we proposed the TermCloud for supporting Web searches. We think we can apply TermClouds with other types of search results, such as searches for images, research papers, products, hotels, and so on. The challenging issue here is how to summarize non-textual information, such as price, year, color, shape, and other such factors, which must be converted to a verbal form. If we can solve this problem effectively, TermClouds can be applied to summarize and support more effective browsing of these kinds of search results.

Acknowledgement

This work was supported in part by Grant-in-Aid for JSPS Fellows, "Informatics Education and Research Center for Knowledge-Circulating Society" (Project Leader: Katsumi Tanaka, MEXT Global COE Program, Kyoto University), and by MEXT Grant-in-Aid for Scientific Research on Priority Areas: "Cyber Infrastructure for the Informationexplosion Era", "Contents Fusion and Seamless Search for Information Explosion" (Project Leader: Katsumi Tanaka, A01-00-02, Grant#: 18049041).

References

1. White, R.W., et al.: Supporting Exploratory Search. Communications of the ACM 49(4), 36–39 (2006)
2. Nakamura, S., Konishi, S., Jatowt, A., Ohshima, H., Kondo, H., Tezuka, T., Oyama, S., Tanaka, K.: Trustworthiness Analysis of Web Search Results. In: Kovács, L., Fuhr, N., Meghini, C. (eds.) ECDL 2007. LNCS, vol. 4675, pp. 38–49. Springer, Heidelberg (2007)
3. Yamamoto, T., Nakamura, S., Tanaka, K.: Rerank-By-Example: Efficient Browsing of Web Search Results. In: Wagner, R., Revell, N., Pernul, G. (eds.) DEXA 2007. LNCS, vol. 4653, pp. 801–810. Springer, Heidelberg (2007)
4. Rivadeneira, A.W., Gruen, D.M., Muller, M.J., Millen, D.R.: Getting our head in the clouds: toward evaluation studies of tagclouds. In: Proc. of CHI 2007, pp. 995–998 (2007)
5. Halvey, M.J., Keane, M.T.: An assessment of tag presentation techniques. In: Proc. of WWW 2007, pp. 1313–1314 (2007)

Seeing Past Rivals: Visualizing Evolution of Coordinate Terms over Time

Hiroaki Ohshima, Adam Jatowt, Satoshi Oyama, and Katsumi Tanaka

Graduate School of Informatics, Kyoto University
Yoshida-Honmachi, Sakyo-ku, 606-8501
Kyoto, Japan
{ohshima,adam,oyama,tanaka}@dl.kuis.kyoto-u.ac.jp

Abstract. In this paper, we describe an approach for detection and visualization of coordinate term relationships over time and their evolution using temporal data available on the Web. Coordinate terms are terms with the same hypernym and they often represent rival or peer relationships of underlying objects. We have built a system that portrays the evolution of coordinate terms in an easy and intuitive way based on data in an online news archive collection spanning more than 100 years. With the proposed method, it is possible to see the changes in the peer relationships between objects over time together with the context of these relationships. The experimental results proved quite high precision of our method and indicated high usefulness for particular knowledge discovery tasks.

1 Introduction

Automatically extracting knowledge from large textual data collections has been a popular research area for quite a long time. Researchers captured different kinds of knowledge such as semantic relationships between terms, news or any temporal patterns in text. The usual approach was to scan the stored data in search for evidences supporting particular knowledge patterns. However, the access to many collections is limited through online search interfaces due to their large size or proprietary character. Consequently, the type of knowledge that could be obtained from such repositories is somewhat limited. Therefore some researchers have recently proposed knowledge extraction from online repositories by multiply querying them through their search interfaces. For example, Bollegala et al. [2] demonstrated semantic similarity estimation between arbitrary terms that takes into account the number of search results and the content of snippets returned from Web search engines.

This kind of approach, however, can be directly applied to the collections of temporally-invariant data for which there is a simple textual interface. In contrast, in this research we attempt to focus on repositories of temporal data such as news archives. Such digital collections often allow issuing structured queries composed of search terms and a selected time period, which specifies the temporal constraints for returned data. Due to the temporal character of the data different kinds of longitudinal type knowledge can be captured.

G. Vossen, D.D.E. Long, and J.X. Yu (Eds.): WISE 2009, LNCS 5802, pp. 167–180, 2009.
© Springer-Verlag Berlin Heidelberg 2009

In this paper, we propose a method for detecting coordinate terms to a user-issued query together with their context and for visualizing their changes over time [10]. Our approach is based on data queried from online collections of news articles. Coordinate terms are bound by the fact of having the same direct hypernym term. Hypernym relation of terms is the relation represented by the pattern "is a kind of". In other words, these are terms that are on the same (semantic) hierarchy level and that often indicate peer or even rival relationships between real-world objects represented by terms. For example, Toyota, Mitsubishi and Honda are coordinate terms representing similar automobile companies in Japan, or Norway, Sweden and Finland are coordinate terms indicating countries in Scandinavia. The application that we demonstrate detects coordinate terms from an online repository of news articles over arbitrary time periods and visualizes them in form of an interactive, dynamic network. We believe that the proposed method could be applied for educational purposes at schools or other teaching facilities. Through exploratory search students could serendipitously discover relations between requested objects over time. In addition, the detected knowledge could be used as an input for subsequent processes in more complex application frameworks; for example, in automatically building histories of real-world objects such as companies, persons or countries and their inter-relationships over time.

In summary, in this paper, we (a) propose a method of detecting and visualizing coordinate terms as well as their contexts over time, (b) demonstrate an interactive application for visualization and exploration of the retrieved data and (c) evaluate it on example queries and through user studies.

The remainder of this paper is as follows. In the next section, we discuss the background and the related research. Section 3 describes our method and application for detecting and visualizing coordinate terms over time. Section 4 provides the experimental evaluation. We conclude the paper in the last section.

2 Background and Related Research

2.1 Knowledge Search from Search Engines

According to an online survey that we conducted in Japan in February 2008 on the group of 1000 respondents, 50.2% of users perform some kind of knowledge search using conventional search engine interfaces. By this, we mean the activity that is different from a usual search for arbitrary Web documents. According to the results of the survey, at least once in a month, users try to a) learn the correct spelling of input phrases (22.4% respondents), b) search for exact information such as location names returned for query "the origin of tulips is" (26.7%), c) determine the meaning of acronyms (26.7%), d) search for related terms (21.4%) or e) investigate the popularity of real-world objects (23.3%). In general, 89.8% users perform an object-level search that is a search for the information about concrete instances of persons, institutions or objects using the interfaces of standard search engines. Regarding the temporal aspect of information on the Web, 86.2% of the respondents declared that they would like to know the age of information they encounter. In the view of these results we can assume that there is a need for applications that would facilitate knowledge extraction from search engine repositories. Also, users should benefit from applications that help to estimate the age and temporal characteristics of certain information.

2.2 Related Research

Several techniques have been proposed for the purpose of discovering relations between terms. For example, in the context of coordinate term detection problem, Hearst [8] proposed discovering hypernyms through pattern matching in news articles, while Shinzato and Torisawa [12] acquired coordinate terms from HTML documents. In the latter work, coordinate terms were the ones appearing in the same levels of DOM structure such as itemized lists.

However, currently, it is difficult to freely scan the whole content of large data repositories such as collections of news articles, digitalized books or Web search engine indices. This is usually due to their huge size, proprietary character or access restrictions. Consequently, effective ways for mining data collections through their search interfaces have been proposed [2,6,10]. Bollegala et al. [2] measured inter-term similarity by analyzing Web search results. Cilibrasi and Vitányi [6] proposed Google Normalized Distance based on WebCount values in order to use it for such tasks as hierarchical clustering, classification or language translation. None of these works, however, focused on mining data collections of temporal character through their search interfaces.

Several proposals have been also made for analyzing and mining temporal document collections [1,9,13]. Topic Detection and Tracking (TDT) [1] initiative is probably best-known effort of detecting, classifying, and tracking events and story topics in historical news corpora. In addition, several methods for temporal weighting of terms have been proposed [9]. Nevertheless, the above approaches worked by scanning whole collections and required unrestricted access to every document, while our method relies on accessing the collections only through their search interfaces.

In a preliminary report [10] we have outlined a basic part of the coordinate term extraction method and shown initial system snapshots. In this paper, we a) enhance the term extraction and agglomeration method by adding additional linguistic patterns and by applying smoothing of extracted results, b) extend the context detection method and c) perform the experimental evaluation of the coordinate term extraction accuracy as well as conduct user studies on the overall system.

Our approach to visualizing the evolution of coordinate terms is related to topics of visualizing network evolution. Displaying evolution of network structure over time is quite a challenging task involving such issues as efficient indication of changes or preservation of their context [4]. There are basically two ways for visualizing graph changes over time. The first one relies on displaying sequence of graph snapshots chronologically in separate planes [3,7], while the second one uses various animation effects [4,5]. We use the latter visualization technique providing users with several additional interaction capabilities and attempting at decreasing users' cognitive overload when observing the evolution of term relationships.

3 Detecting and Visualizing Coordinate Terms over Time

In this section, we present our method of mining online news article collections for detection and visualization of changes in coordinate terms over time. The proposed application retrieves data from Google News Archive[1] search interface. Google News

---

[1] http://news.google.com/archivesearch

Archive is a service for online searching in archived collections of newspapers over the last 200 years. The service allows entering temporally structured query composed of keywords and a desired time period. It ranks results taking into account the full text of each article, its publication venue, timestamp and other factors.

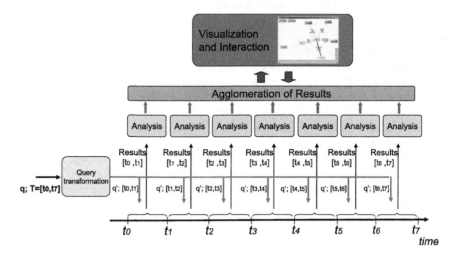

Fig. 1. Outline of the proposed method

The overview of our method is shown in Figure 1. First, a user enters query q with a certain selected time period T. The query is then transformed and sent to Google News Archive search as a series of queries for mutually exclusive and consecutive unit time segments within T. The time granularity can be also decided by the user (by default it is equal to $T/10$), although, the user should be aware of the fact that increasing the number of unit time periods raises the time cost. The system then collects the top results returned over each unit segment and detects coordinate terms using certain lexico-synactical patterns. The detected terms are then agglomerated in order to provide an interactive presentation. In addition, context of each relation between the terms is retrieved. Coordinate terms are shown in the form of a network, in which nodes represent terms and the edges represent the strength of coordinate relationships between the terms together with their contextual descriptions. User can drag the slide bar in order to see the changes in the graph structure for different time units.

3.1   Detection of Coordinate Terms

3.1.1   Coordinate Term Detection in Unit Time Segment
We describe here the method for detecting coordinate terms within a unit time period. When a query is issued it is converted to specially crafted "pattern queries" (denoted as q' in Figure 1), whose objective is to estimate the support of coordinate relationships between the query term and detected candidate terms. There are two pattern queries for each unit time period: one containing expression "q or" and containing

expression "or q". The returned 100 snippets for each of these pattern queries are then analyzed for the occurrence of both syntactical patterns. Terms that frequently appear before or after the pattern queries (i.e., "q or x", "x or q", where x is a discovered candidate term) are deemed to be coordinate terms to the query term. We use such bi-direct patterns in our method for the purpose of determining the necessary cut points for terms [11]. Otherwise the system could not detect the lengths of noun phrases that are composed of more than one term (e.g., Hong Kong). Thus only the terms that appear at least once in each of the pattern are taken into account. In addition, extracted terms are considered to be coordinate terms to the query term if the geometric average of their both pattern frequencies within returned snippets is higher than some predefined threshold[2]. The system also rejects common terms via a stop word list.

Additionally, an option is also provided that extends the above query patterns with a contextual term. For example, one could search for coordinate terms to query "apple" in the context of computer companies rather than fruits by appending a contextual term "computer".

Lastly, pattern queries "q vs.", "vs. q", "q and", "and q" are also used instead of the one with conjunctive "or" for returning more pronounced rival-type relationships.

3.1.2 Aggregation of Coordinate Terms over Time

After coordinate terms have been found for each individual time segment the system aggregates them over time. This allows for determining the relative strengths of coordinate relationships within the whole time period by comparing their pattern frequencies. Weighted smoothing is done in order to decrease the volatility of term relationships. This is because sometimes a given relationship occurs during a long time frame, yet it ceases to be detected in a short time period (e.g., one or two time units) that is s sub-period of that time frame. This may happen due to the lack of newspaper articles mentioning one of the terms for certain time units. To alleviate this effect the system uses window of a predefined length (three time units by default) with adjustable weights equal to 0.2, 0.6 and 0.2[3]. Thus, with this weight setting 60% of the smoothed value of a given relation in a certain time unit comes from the actual support for this relation in that time unit, while the remaining 40% comes from the supports for the relation in the both adjacent time units.

3.2 Detecting the Context of Coordinate Relationships

As mentioned above the system also detects and visualizes the context of each coordinate relationship. This is because real world objects can be rivals (or peers) within their different contexts. For example, countries like India and China can be listed as Asian countries, the most populous countries or emerging economic powers. We determine the context of coordinate relationship by using the set of modified versions of *TF*IDF* weighting scheme (Equations 1-4) that take into account the distribution of terms in a single time window or in the whole time period of analysis.

---

[2] By default the threshold is equal to 1, which means that coordinate terms should appear at least once in each of the both patterns ($\sqrt{1}*\sqrt{1}=1$).

[3] Both the weights and the window size can be adjusted by the system operator, for example, to further decrease the volatility.

The simplest way is to consider only the amount of returned snippets that contain the coordinate terms inside a unit time period (Equation 1).

$$S(a, p_b; t_i) = SF(a, p_b; t_i) \tag{1}$$

Here $S(a, p_b; t_i)$ is weight of a context term a of a relationship p_b, which bounds the query and coordinate term b, in a time period t_i. $SF(a, p_b; t_i)$ is the number of snippets that support p_b (contain lexical patterns binding the query and term b) and also contain the term a within time period t_i.

Next we can also consider the total number of snippets that contain the term a within t_i (Equation 2). If this number is high then the weight of a context term a will be low since the term appears in many snippets and thus may not be representative for the particular relationship p_b.

$$S(a, p_b; t_i) = SF(a, p_b; t_i) * \log_2\left(\frac{M(t_i)}{DF(a; t_i)} + 1\right) \tag{2}$$

$M(t_i)$ denotes here the count of snippets in t_i and $DF(a; t_i)$ is the number of snippets containing a in t_i. Another way is to take into account all the snippets returned over the whole time frame.

$$S(a, p_b; t_i) = SF(a, p_b; t_i) * \log_2\left(\frac{M(T)}{DF(a, p_b, T)} + 1\right) \tag{3}$$

Here, $M(T)$ denotes the count of snippets within the whole time period T and $DF(a, p_b, T)$ is the number of snippets supporting p_b that also contain term a within T. Lastly, the combined approach is used (Equation 4).

$$S(a, p_b; t_i) = SF(a, p_b; t_i) * \sqrt{\log_2\left(\frac{M(t_i)}{DF(a; t_i)} + 1\right) * \log_2\left(\frac{M(T)}{DF(a, p_b, T)} + 1\right)} \tag{4}$$

The three terms that have the highest values of weights according to one of Equations 1- 4 are then chosen as the context of the coordinate relation between the query and term b within t_i. We apply Equation 4 as a default method.

3.3 Visualization

Visualization of the results is done through an interactive, animated graph (Figures 2-3), in which nodes represent terms, and edges represent coordinate relationships with the thickness of an edge indicating the strength of the relationship. Each edge is also annotated with the top three contextual words. First, a user enters a query term and then by dragging the horizontal slider she or he can sequentially observe coordinate terms over different time periods. The length of a unit time segment is chosen by users. At any time point, the user can click on a selected node in the graph. This sends another query that contains the term in the clicked node. Consequently, the coordinate terms to both the query and the term in the clicked node will be shown in the ex-panded graph (see right-hand side example in Figure 2).

We have used a spring-type graph in which nodes' positions are determined on the basis of attraction/repulsion forces acting between the nodes. The former occurs between any two nodes bound by a coordinate relationship, while the latter is applied to the nodes that do not have such a relationship. The equilibrium position of all nodes in the graph is determined by the situation in which all acting forces are balanced. Users can freely interact with the network by changing positions of any nodes.

From a temporal viewpoint, noticing and understanding changes in the graph structure is rather difficult as it poses high cognitive overload for users. In order to facilitate the change understanding we decided to make several enhancements (see Figure 2 for example). First, the node of a query term is coloured in orange and placed in the central position. Second, the nodes whose underlying terms cease to have coordinate relationship with a query term in the next consecutive time unit are shown in gray colour. In contrast, the newly added nodes are coloured in red. In addition, due to the spring type of the graph, the new nodes move towards each other until they are stopped in their equilibrium positions and bound by edges. On the other hand, the nodes whose terms cease to have coordinate relationships in the next time unit are released from their edges and are pushed away from each other until they move outside the range of any acting forces. This colouring and animation schemes help users with noticing changes in co-ordinate relationships between the consecutive time units.

3.3.1 Summary Viewing Mode

As the above working mode shows only micro-scale changes in terms' relationships, a macro-scale overview should be also useful for users. Naturally, users could simply decrease the time granularity when interacting with a graph; for example, by changing the duration of time units from 1 to 4 years. However, a summarized overview of coordinate terms in a single snapshot would make it easier for users to obtain a rough overview of graph's evolution (Figure 3). In this kind of visualization, the width of edges indicates the overall relationship strength measured as the average pattern frequency over all the unit time segments. Each edge is annotated with its main relationship context, which is expressed as the top 3 contextual terms that occur most frequently over the whole time period for that relationship. Lastly, we also indicate the age of relationships by varying the thickness of node frames. The thick frame indicates terms that have been coordinate for a relatively long time, while the thin one denotes the recent coordinate terms.

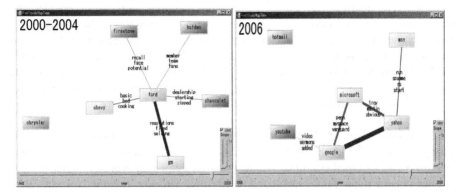

Fig. 2. Coordinate terms to the query "ford" and "google/yahoo"

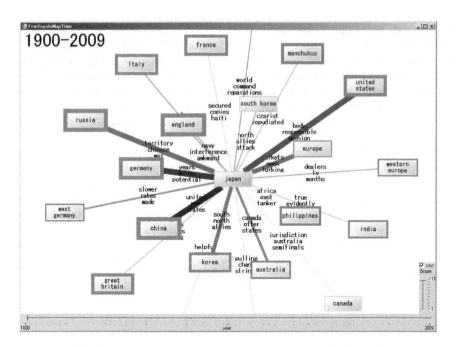

Fig. 3. Summary view of coordinate terms to the query "japan"

4 Experimental Evaluation

In this section we report on the results of the evaluation of our method and the implemented system which consists of measuring the precision of coordinate term extraction and performing user study.

4.1 Evaluation of Co-ordinate Term Detection

We have chosen a set of 20 queries for evaluation of the precision of coordinate term extraction. The queries were grouped into four categories: persons, companies and institutions, places and others (ex. physical objects or concepts). Table 1 shows the queries chosen for the evaluation. For the coordinate term extraction we have used three lexical patterns with conjunctives "or", "vs." and "and". We have applied a threshold equal to 1 which means that a given term was deemed to be a coordinate one in a certain time unit if among the results obtained over this time unit there were at least one pattern "q or x" and one pattern "x or q" for the case of the conjunctive "or".

For each query we have checked the correctness of their coordinate terms by consulting Wikipedia[4] and the Web. For example, for the queries "Ford" and "Jack Nicholson" we assumed coordinate terms to be correct if they represent other companies that operate in the same market and other movie actors or directors, respectively.

---

[4] Wikipedia: http://www.wikipedia.org

Table 1. Queries used for the evaluation with their corresponding time periods and granularities shown in parentheses

Groups	Queries			
Persons	Barry Bonds (1986-2009; 2 years)	Hillary Clinton (2000-2009; 1 year)	Barack Obama (2000-2009; 1 year)	Michael Jordan (1986-2009; 2 years)
	Ronaldinho (2000-2009; 1 year)	Ayrton Senna (1986-2009; 2 years)	Nick Faldo (1986-2009; 2 years)	Jack Nicholson (1986-2009; 2 years)
Places	Japan (1900-2009; 10 years)		Poland (1900-2009; 10 years)	
Companies, institutions	Google (2000-2009; 1 year)	IBM (1940-2009; 5 years)	Ford (1940-2009; 5 years)	NASA (1940-2009; 5 years)
	Harvard (1900-2009; 10 years)		Toyota (1940-2009; 5 years)	
Others	baseball (1900-2009; 10 years)	dollar (1900-2009; 10 years)	TV (1940-2009; 5 years)	Internet Explorer (2000-2009; 1 year)

Table 2 shows the average numbers of detected coordinate terms in unit time segments and precision values for different lexical patterns. We found out that the lexical pattern containing the conjunction "or" results in the highest precision (0.890). The lexical pattern containing the conjunction "vs." achieves also reasonably high precision (0.875). However, in this case the average number of retrieved coordinate terms within single time segments is very low (0.06) as this pattern is rarely used (ex. mostly in sports news). Both conjunctions "or" and "and" are on average more useful as producing higher number of results. Although, the pattern with the conjunctive "or" achieves higher precision (0.890) than the one with the conjunctive "and" (0.825), the latter produces on average about 35% more correct results.

Next, we investigated how the precision changes for different query groups. Table 3 lists the results of each query group for the lexical pattern using conjunctive "or". We have obtained the average precision on about 0.890 for all the query groups. The system achieved the highest precision for the queries denoting person and place names (0.969 and 0.942, respectively), while the lowest precision was obtained for "others" category (0.808). The latter was probably due to many different meanings and functions of the objects indicated by these queries. We also noticed that the queries representing place names resulted in the highest average number of correct coordinate terms within a unit time segment (5.18) and the queries in the "others" group has the lowest number (2.18).

Note that we have evaluated the correctness of coordinate terms extraction irrespectively of time periods of their occurrence. The evaluation of time-based precision (i.e. correctness of coordinate term extraction in particular time segments) is however quite difficult as finding past coordinate terms is non-trivial. Instead, we have

Table 2. Results for different conjunctives

	Conjunctive "or"	Conjunctive "vs."	Conjunctive "and"
Average number of correct results for single time unit	2.91	0.06	4.45
Precision (correct/returned results)	0.890 (683/767)	0.875 (14/16)	0.825 (1045/1266)

Table 3. Results for different query groups

	Persons	Places	Companies, institutions	Others	Average
Average number of correct results for single time unit	3.12	5.18	2.51	2.18	**2.91**
Precision	0.969	0.942	0.810	0.808	**0.890**

superficially checked whether there are any coordinate terms that should not be reported in particular time periods. On average, most of the coordinate terms appeared to occur within their correct periods. If there were any mistakes they usually resulted from too coarse granularity applied. For example, when using 10 years as the length of a unit time period our system reported "Soviet Union" and "Czechoslovakia" to be co-ordinate terms of Poland from 1900 to 2000. This is only partially correct as actually, the Soviet Union has been disestablished in December 26, 1991[5] and Czechoslovakia dissolute in December 31, 1992[6].

In the above evaluation, we have not calculated recall as it is rather difficult considering the large number of potential coordinate terms for the selected query words. Instead, to gauge the overall performance, we have plotted the precision rates against the average number of correct coordinate terms detected in unit time segments with different threshold values (see Figure 4). The different threshold levels are indicated on the graph by numbers. This allowed us to see how many correct coordinate terms have been on average dropped when the threshold is increased and how the precision changes in such cases. We can see that using the lexical pattern with the conjunctive "or" results in the best performance closely followed by the one with the conjunctive "and". The line denoted by "all" indicates the case when the results of all the lexical patterns are considered together.

4.2 User study

We now show the results of an experimental evaluation of our system on a group of users. We have asked 14 subjects who are computer science students to interact with our system. First, we have briefly explained the way to operate the system. Next, the subjects had to complete 3 tasks each lasting 5 minutes. Prior to conducting each task

---

[5] http://en.wikipedia.org/wiki/Soviet_Union
[6] http://en.wikipedia.org/wiki/Czechoslovakia

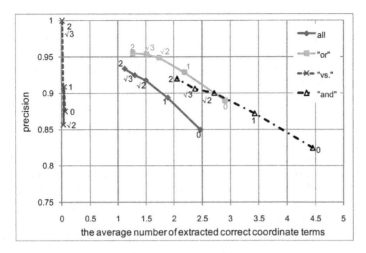

Figu. 4. Precision against the average number of extracted correct coordinate terms in unit time segments over different threshold levels (the values of the threshold levels are indicated on the graph)

with our system they were also asked to attempt to do the tasks by using conventional Web search engine within 5 minutes. Below we briefly describe the tasks:

1. For "Ford" query find 2 past (but not present) and 2 present rivals/peers as well as 2 entities that were rivals in the past and continue to be rivals now. Set the time frame ranging from 1940 until the present with a unit time period of 5 years when using the proposed system.
2. Do the same for query "Japan" with the time frame spanning from 1900 until the present with a unit time period of 10 years.
3. Do the same for "Google" and "Yahoo" terms (time frame: 1995 until the present, 2 years unit time period) and find also their common, present rivals.

As expected, the users could not find the rivals or peers of the query terms within only 5 minutes using any conventional Web search engines or even the Google News Archive Search interface itself. On the other hand, they could successfully complete all the tasks within the required time using our proposed system. Note that the tasks were still easy in the sense that we did not ask subjects to find coordinate terms within specific, shorter time periods.

After completing the tasks, we asked questions shown below in order to check user's impressions and collect comments for the further improvement of the system.

1. Is it easy to complete tasks using conventional Web search engines? ("very", "so so", "I do not know", "not so", "not at all")
2. Is it easy to complete tasks using the proposed system? ("very", "so so", "I do not know", "not so", "not at all")
3. Please comment on good and bad aspects of the normal viewing mode and the summary viewing mode.
4. What aspects of the system are good and what bad?

5. What would you like to change or add in the system?
6. For what kind of objects do you want to find coordinate terms using the system (e.g., countries, companies, persons)?
7. What kind of other historical knowledge would you like to obtain (e.g., other relations between objects)?

The results for the first and second questions are shown in Figures 5 and 6. They indicate the general usefulness of our system and its advantage for past coordinate term detection over conventional Web search engines.

For the 3rd question, the subjects generally appreciated the availability of a macro and micro-scale viewing modes. The good points in the summary viewing mode were providing an overall impression and showing entities that are in general rivals/peers. In addition, there was no need for any manual interaction as the results were presented directly in a single frame. However, the respondents reported some problems with understanding the information that is conveyed through the summary viewing mode. Normal viewing mode was considered as useful for seeing changes over time and interacting with the system.

For the 4th question the users generally agreed that it is interesting to visualize the changes of relationships over time and that the system can show rivals to an entity represented by a given query. Three subjects wrote that it is thus possible to better understand the history of certain objects. However, the same number of subjects agreed that the way to operate the system is somehow complicated mostly due to the confusion with the meanings of colors and width of edges in the graph. This was especially difficult in the summary viewing mode. Thus there is still room for improvement at the interface level. Also, one user complained about the occurrence of synonyms presented as different nodes in the graph (e.g., "alta vista" and "altavista", "soviet" and "russia") and one about coordinate terms appearing and disappearing unexpectedly. The former issue could be improved by employing more complex NLP techniques, while the latter could be alleviated by the suitable choice of weight settings in the smoothing. In addition, users told us that the system sometimes showed friendship relations rather than rival ones making it hard to distinguish between the both, even when their context was provided. This was especially true for the entities that the users did not know much about.

For the next question the users proposed improving contextual description of relations, for example, by providing larger textual summaries, and showing changes more clearly and directly. Some other interesting comments were: to show precisely when relationships start and end, to make automatic slideshow mode, and to implement the system in multi-touch panels. In addition, one subject wanted to use the system on the Web as an online service.

For the 6th question, persons and products were the most often selected answers (5 users) followed by companies (4 users). Some of users also expressed wishes to see the history of the rival relationships of academic societies, musicians, countries, diseases, songs, foreign words and sport teams. However two subjects stated that there are not many objects for which we could get interesting results and, they may actually, rarely want to know any rival relationships.

In the last question, the users expressed wishes for knowing various different types of historical knowledge such as the historical reputation of objects, historical values

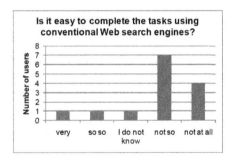

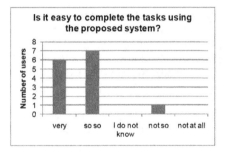

Fig. 5. Answers to Question 1

Fig. 6. Answers to Question 2

of stock prices, different types of past relationships among persons and companies, personal histories with their related information, historical wars, enemies and old buzz terms. An interesting comment was to display the information on the past common sense which cannot be currently captured using conventional techniques.

5 Conclusions

In this paper, we have proposed a method for the detection and visualization of changes in coordinate terms over time from online news article collections. This is an example of mining search engine interfaces that allow for temporally structured queries in order to extract knowledge of temporal character. Using the proposed system users can discover terms that represent rival objects for a given query and a specified time span. This kind of historical knowledge can serve educational purposes and can support understanding of the present relations between terms. The experimental results have indicated high effectiveness of the proposed approach of extracting coordinate terms over time and confirmed the usefulness of our visualization approach.

Acknowledgments

This research was supported in part by the National Institute of Information and Communications Technology, Japan, by Grants-in-Aid for Scientific Research (Nos. 18049041, 21700105, and 21700106) from MEXT of Japan, by the Kyoto University Global COE Program: Informatics Education and Research Center for Knowledge-Circulating Society, and by a Microsoft IJARC CORE4 project: Toward Spatio-Temporal Object Search from the Web.

References

[1] Allan, J. (ed.): Topic detection and tracking: event-based information organization. Kluwer Academic Publishers, Norwell (2002)
[2] Bollegala, D., Matsuo, Y., Ishizuka, M.: Measuring semantic similarity between words using web search engines. In: WWW 2007, pp. 757–766. ACM Press, New York (2007)

[3] Brandes, U., Corman, S.R.: Visual unrolling of network evolution and the analysis of dynamic discourse? Information Visualization 2(1), 40–50 (2003)

[4] Chen, C.: Information Visualization. Springer, Heidelberg (2006)

[5] Chen, C., Morris, S.: Visualizing Evolving Networks: Minimum Spanning Trees versus Pathfinder Networks. In: INFOVIS 2003 (2003)

[6] Cilibrasi, R., Vitányi, P.M.B.: The Google Similarity Distance. IEEE Trans. Knowl. Data Eng. 19(3), 370–383 (2007)

[7] Erten, C., Harding, P.J., Kobourov, S.G., Wampler, K., Yee, G.: Exploring the computing literature using temporal graph visualization. In: Proceedings of SPIE. Visualization and Data Analysis, vol. 5295 (2004)

[8] Hearst, M.A.: Automatic Acquisition of Hyponyms from Large Text Corpora. In: COLING 1992, pp. 539–545 (1992)

[9] Kleinberg, J.: Temporal dynamics of on-line information streams. In: Garofalakis, M., Gehrke, J., Rastogi, R. (eds.) Data Stream Management: Processing High-Speed Data Streams. Springer, Heidelberg (2005)

[10] Ohshima, H., Jatowt, A., Oyama, S., Tanaka, K.: Visualizing Changes in Coordinate Terms over Time: An Example of Mining Repositories of Temporal Data through their Search Interfaces. In: Proceedings for the International Workshop on Information-explosion and Next Generation Search (INGS 2008), IEEE CS Digital Library, pp. 61–68 (2008)

[11] Ohshima, H., Oyama, S., Tanaka, K.: Searching Coordinate Terms with Their Context from the Web. In: Aberer, K., Peng, Z., Rundensteiner, E.A., Zhang, Y., Li, X. (eds.) WISE 2006. LNCS, vol. 4255, pp. 40–47. Springer, Heidelberg (2006)

[12] Shinzato, K., Torisawa, K.: A Simple WWW-based Method for Semantic Word Class Acquisition. In: RANLP 2005, pp. 493–500. Springer, Heidelberg (2005)

[13] Swan, R., Allan, J.: Automatic generation of overview timelines. In: Proceedings of the 23rd Conference on Research and Development in Information Retrieval, Athens, Greece, pp. 49–56. ACM Press, New York (2000)

A Novel Visualization Method for Distinction of Web News Sentiment

Jianwei Zhang[1], Yukiko Kawai[1], Tadahiko Kumamoto[2], and Katsumi Tanaka[3]

[1] Kyoto Sangyo University
{zjw,kawai}@cc.kyoto-su.ac.jp
[2] Chiba Institute of Technology
kumamoto@net.it-chiba.ac.jp
[3] Kyoto University
ktanaka@i.kyoto-u.ac.jp

Abstract. Recently, an increasing number of news websites have come to provide various featured services. However, effective analysis and presentation for distinction of viewpoints among different news sources are limited. We focus on the sentiment aspect of news reporters' viewpoints and propose a system called the *Sentiment Map* for distinguishing the sentiment of news articles and visualizing it on a geographical map based on map zoom control. The proposed system provides more detailed sentiments than conventional sentiment analysis which only considers positive and negative emotions. When a user enters one or more query keywords, the sentiment map not only retrieves news articles related to the concerned topic, but also summarizes sentiment tendencies of Web news based on specific geographical scales. Sentiments can be automatically aggregated at different levels corresponding to the change of map scales. Furthermore, we take into account the aspect of time, and show the variation in sentiment over time. Experimental evaluations conducted by a total of 100 individuals show the sentiment extraction accuracy and the visualization effect of the proposed system are good.

1 Introduction

Recently, the number of online news websites, such as those associated with the Los Angeles Times [1], USA Today [2], and the New York Times [3], has increased with the spread of the Internet. In addition, an increasing number of portal news sites, such as Google News [4], Yahoo! News [5], and MSNBC [6], have been designed to collect and integrate similar news articles from various news sites. These portal sites provide browsing, keyword search, and various personalized services. Users can thus acquire the information they want by accessing a single portal site, instead of several dispersed news sites. Google News [4] is a search engine that searches many of the world's news sources and can aggregate news articles related to a specific topic from different news sites. Yahoo! News [5] allows users to select rankings of news articles based on various aspects, such as readers' comments, blogger attention, and number of bookmarks. MSNBC [6] provides personalization and a customized layout based on the interests of users.

G. Vossen, D.D.E. Long, and J.X. Yu (Eds.): WISE 2009, LNCS 5802, pp. 181–194, 2009.

These existing services are useful. However, there has been little research on distinguishing the viewpoints of different Web sources. News reporters working for different websites may report a same event with different opinions and sentiments. For example, different news sites may support different political parties, so that their opinions on a certain policy proposed by a political party may be in conflict. The results of baseball games are often reported with different sentiments by different newspapers, depending on where the newspaper is based. The present paper examines the effective analysis and differentiation of the viewpoints of different news websites. In particular, we focus on the sentiment aspect.

To solve this problem, we propose a system called the *Sentiment Map*, which can extract and visualize sentiment tendencies for different news websites. When a user enters one or more query keywords, the proposed system first retrieves news articles related to the specified topic, and then calculates sentiment tendencies for each news site using a pre-constructed sentiment dictionary. Finally, the proposed system generates a sentiment map that visually distinguishes the sentiment among different news sites. When users interactively change the scale of the sentiment map, the sentiment tendencies of news articles can automatically be reaggregated for the new geographical scale based on map zoom control. Furthermore, the proposed system also shows the sentiment variation with time. Unlike conventional positive/negative analysis of sentiment, we define more detailed sentiment vectors of four dimensions: Joy ⇔ Sadness, Acceptance ⇔ Disgust, Anticipation ⇔ Surprise, and Fear ⇔ Anger. The sentiment map helps users acquire an intuitive image of the sentiments of different news sources.

Figure 1 shows an example of a sentiment map for the query "Iraq war", presenting the sentiment distinction at the continent level for this war. This map summarizes the sentiment tendencies of news articles on the topic of the Iraq war based on the unit of each continent. The horizontal axis of each sentiment graph attached to the geographical map represents the period during which news articles are retrieved for the sentiment analysis (In this example, the period is three days from October 5 to October 7, 2008), and the vertical axis represents the average sentiment values of news articles published in each continent. Default presentation of a sentiment graph is positive and negative polarities, averaged by sentiment values of four dimensions. When the mouse moves over a sentiment graph (e.g., North America), more detailed sentiments of four dimensions are separately displayed. Using this sentiment map, a user can obtain a general perspective of the various sentiments held by different continents with respect to the war before further reading the contents of news articles. When the user zooms in to or out of the map, domains (city level, region level, country level, or continent level) are recalculated automatically. Figure 2 shows the sentiment distinction of news articles on the Iraq war at the state level.

The proposed sentiment map enables the following:

- sentiments of news articles beyond positive/negative analysis are extracted
- sentiment tendencies of news sources are distinguished and visualized with different geographical scales
- sentiment variation are shown with respect to time

In the present paper, we describe the concept and implementation of the sentiment map and evaluate the proposed system through several experiments. Section 2 provides an overview of the sentiment map generation. Section 3 describes the offline processing of the proposed system, including the main procedure, the construction of the sentiment dictionary, and the generation of sentiment vectors for news articles. Section 4 describes the online processing. Section 5 discusses the evaluation of the sentiment map conducted by a total of 100 individuals. Section 6 reviews related research. Section 7 concludes the paper and describes areas for future study.

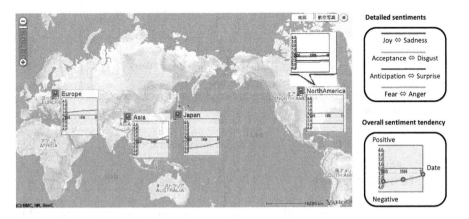

Fig. 1. Example of a sentiment map at the continent level for the query "Iraq war"

Fig. 2. Example of a sentiment map at the state level for the query "Iraq war"

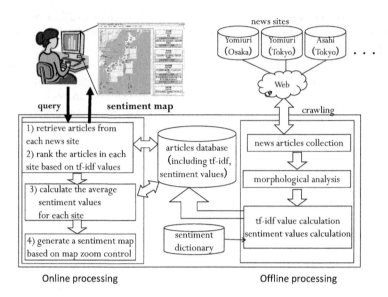

Fig. 3. Flow of sentiment map generation

2   System Overview

Figure 3 shows an overview of the system for generating a sentiment map. This system consists of two parts: offline processing (right-hand side of Figure 3) and online processing (left-hand side of Figure 3).

Collection and analysis of news articles are pre-processed offline, before online retrieval from a user. First, news articles from various news sites are crawled. Then, a morphological analysis of the collected articles is conducted to extract the words with specific parts of speech, and their $tf \cdot idf$ values are calculated. We construct a sentiment dictionary in which the entries include sentiment values of words. A sentiment vector of four dimensions is attached to each news article by looking up the sentiment values of words appearing in the article from the sentiment dictionary and averaging these values. The collected news articles, the $tf \cdot idf$ values of the extracted words, and the sentiment vectors of news articles are stored in a database.

When a user enters one or more query keywords, the proposed system first retrieves relevant news articles from the database. The system then groups the articles by news sites and ranks the articles in each site based on $tf \cdot idf$ values. Then, for each news site, the average sentiment values of news articles are calculated. Next, sentiment graphs are generated for each news site and attached to a geographical map. We call this generated map a sentiment map. The distinction of sentiment tendencies among different news sites can be compared visually. The user can also browse the sentiment summarization at different levels by zooming in to or out of the sentiment map. The proposed system also presents the sentiment variation with time of the news articles for an event.

3   Offline Processing

In preprocessing, news articles are first collected and analyzed as follows:

1. n news articles (P_1, ..., P_i, ..., P_n) are crawled from several specified news sites.
2. HTML tags are eliminated from the crawled news articles.
3. The articles are morphologically analyzed to extract proper nouns, general nouns, adjectives, and verbs.
4. The weight $tf \cdot idf(w, P_i)$ of each extracted word w in news article P_i is calculated:

$$tf \cdot idf(w, P_i) = \frac{C(w, P_i)}{N(P_i)} \cdot log \frac{N}{N(w)}, \tag{1}$$

   where $C(w, P_i)$ is the number of times that word w appears in article P_i, $N(P_i)$ is the number of words extracted from P_i, N is the number of all collected news articles, and $N(w)$ is the number of articles in which word w appears.
5. A sentiment dictionary in which the entries indicate the correspondence of a target word and its sentiment value is constructed.
6. A sentiment vector of four dimensions is generated for each article by averaging the sentiment values of words that appear in the article.

The following sections describe in detail the construction of the sentiment dictionary (step 5) and the generation of sentiment vectors for news articles (step 6).

3.1   Sentiment Dictionary Construction

We consider sentiment values of four dimensions for news articles: Joy ⇔ Sadness, Acceptance ⇔ Disgust, Anticipation ⇔ Surprise, and Fear ⇔ Anger. These four dimensions are designed based on the eight basic elements of human emotion, as proposed by psychologist Plutchik [7]. His theory is one of the most influential approaches for classifying emotion. The issue of comparing it with other models of emotion [8,9] is our future challenge. A sentiment dictionary is constructed to extract the sentiment values of these four dimensions for words by analyzing the Nikkei Newspaper Full Text Database from 1990 to 2001, which consists of two million articles in total. The basic idea is to compare the co-occurrence of target words with two groups of original sentiment words for each dimension. The original sentiment words for the four dimensions are listed in Table 1. Each dimension e ($e \in \{a, b, c, d\}$) has two opposite sets e_1 and e_2 of original sentiment words. For example, for the dimension a of Joy ⇔ Sadness, $a_1 = \{pleasure, be pleased, ..., bless\}$ and $a_2 = \{sad, feel sorry, ..., sorrow\}$.

   Each entry of the sentiment dictionary (Table 2) consists of a target word w and its sentiment values (including a scale value $S_e(w)$ and a weight $M_e(w)$) of four dimensions.

Table 1. Original sentiment words for four dimensions (translated from Japanese)

Dimensions (e)	Original sentiment words $(e_1 \Leftrightarrow e_2)$
a: Joy	pleasure, be pleased, glad, happy, enjoy, blessing, bless
$\Leftrightarrow$ Sadness	$\Leftrightarrow$ sad, feel sorry, sadness, sorrow
b: Acceptance	agreement, agree, consent, acknowledgment, acknowledge, acceptance, accept
$\Leftrightarrow$ Disgust	$\Leftrightarrow$ disgust, dislike, hate, be unpleasant, antipathy, have an antipathy, evasion, evade
c: Anticipation	expectation, expect, anticipation, anticipate, forecast
$\Leftrightarrow$ Surprise	$\Leftrightarrow$ surprise, be surprised, astonishment, astonish, admiration, admire
d: Fear	fear, be scary, misgivings, have misgivings, be frightened
$\Leftrightarrow$ Anger	$\Leftrightarrow$ anger, get angry, resentment, resent, rage, enrage

The scale value $S_e(w)$ of one dimension is calculated using the following procedure. First, considering the Y (year) edition of the Nikkei newspaper, let the number of articles that include any word in the set e of original sentiment words (Table 1) be $df(Y, e)$, and let the number of articles that include both target word w and any word in e be $df(Y, e\&w)$ [1]. The joint probability $P(Y, e\&w)$ of e and w is then calculated as follows:

$$P(Y, e\&w) = \frac{df(Y, e\&w)}{df(Y, e)} \qquad (2)$$

Next, considering the two opposite sets e_1 and e_2 of original sentiment words, the interior division ratio $R_{e_1 \Leftrightarrow e_2}(Y, w)$ of $P(Y, e_1\&w)$ and $P(Y, e_2\&w)$ is calculated as follows:

$$R_{e_1 \Leftrightarrow e_2}(Y, w) = \frac{P(Y, e_1\&w)}{P(Y, e_1\&w) + P(Y, e_2\&w)} \qquad (3)$$

where $R_{e_1 \Leftrightarrow e_2}(Y, w) = 0$ if the denominator is 0.

Finally, the scale value $S_e(w)$ is calculated as the mean value of all editions,

$$S_e(w) = \sum_{Y=1990}^{2001} R_{e_1 \Leftrightarrow e_2}(Y, w) \Bigg/ \sum_{Y=1990}^{2001} T_{e_1 \Leftrightarrow e_2}(Y, w) \qquad (4)$$

where $T_{e_1 \Leftrightarrow e_2}(Y, w)$ is 0 if both $df(Y, e_1\&w)$ and $df(Y, e_2\&w)$ are 0, and $T_{e_1 \Leftrightarrow e_2}(Y, w)$ is 1 otherwise. The introduction of the denominator tends to assign a relatively large $S_e(w)$ to those words that appear only during specific years (rather than every year) but are strongly related to specific sentiment words,

---

[1] We compared our methods which counted co-occurrence on a document level with those on a paragraph or sentence level in our preliminary experiments. The results showed that the processing time of the methods on a paragraph or sentence level increased dramatically but the improvement of precision was not remarkable. Thus, the document-level co-occurrence was chosen in our current implementation.

e.g., "Olympics". The scale value $S_e(w)$ of a word w is between 0 and 1. This value is close to 1 if w appears in many articles together with the original positive words in e_1, and is close to 0 if w and the original negative words in e_2 often appear in the same articles.

For different words, the numbers of editions in which they appear and the total number of occurrences may vary greatly. Therefore, we introduce the weight $M_e(w)$ of w, which is calculated as follows:

$$M_e(w) = \log_{12} \sum_{Y=1990}^{2001} T_{e_1 \Leftrightarrow e_2}(Y, w) \times \log_{144} \sum_{Y=1990}^{2001} (df(Y, e_1 \& w) + df(Y, e_2 \& w))$$

(5)

$M_e(w)$ is proportional to the number of editions and the number of occurrence, which means words that appear multiple times and in several editions are assigned large weights. Specifically, the words, $M_e(w)$ of which are 0, are not appended to the sentiment dictionary. Since we use a large corpus, the number of such words is actually small and the coverage of words in the sentiment dictionary is high.

Table 2. Examples of sentiment dictionary entries (translated from Japanese)

Entry word w	Joy $\Leftrightarrow$ Sadness		Acceptance $\Leftrightarrow$ Disgust		Anticipation $\Leftrightarrow$ Surprise		Fear $\Leftrightarrow$ Anger	
	$S_a(w)$	$M_a(w)$	$S_b(w)$	$M_b(w)$	$S_c(w)$	$M_c(w)$	$S_d(w)$	$M_d(w)$
childcare	0.604	1.273	0.336	1.199	0.285	1.346	0.404	1.105
dispatch	0.531	1.312	0.775	1.625	0.493	1.653	0.549	1.386
get angry	0.274	1.300	0.170	1.179	0.107	1.304	0.021	1.622
ghost	0.395	0.869	0.416	0.617	0.338	0.849	0.793	0.803
new year's present	0.897	0.877	0.516	0.456	0.393	0.877	0.564	0.348
smell	0.485	1.309	0.098	1.205	0.133	1.304	0.469	1.113
strong	0.575	1.270	0.190	1.221	0.397	1.489	0.422	1.159
travel	0.659	1.675	0.442	1.499	0.309	1.737	0.425	1.405

3.2 Sentiment Vector Generation for News Articles

The sentiment vector $O(P)$ of a news article P has the form $(O_a(P), O_b(P), O_c(P), O_d(P))$. Consider P as a set of words extracted from it by the morphological analysis. A sentiment value $O_e(P)$ of article P on dimension e is calculated by averaging and inclining the sentiment values of words that appear in P. The calculation equation, which assigns a sentiment value between 0 and 1 to a news article, is as follows:

$$O_e(P) = \sum_{w \in P} S_e(w) \times |2S_e(w) - 1| \times M_e(w) \bigg/ \sum_{w \in P} |2S_e(w) - 1| \times M_e(w) \quad (6)$$

where the scale value $S_e(w)$ and weight $M_e(w)$ of each word w that appears in P can be looked up in the sentiment dictionary constructed as described above. Many general words may be independent of the sentiment of the text, and the scale values $S_e(w)$ of these words are approximately 0.5. The $|2S_e(w) - 1|$ term of these words approach 0, so that the effect of the emotionless words is removed.

4   Online Processing

When a user enters one or more query keywords, the proposed system performs the following procedure and returns a sentiment map.

1. The news articles that include the keywords are retrieved from the article database.
2. The retrieved articles are grouped by news sites, and the news articles of each site are ranked in the descending order of the $tf \cdot idf$ values of the query keywords in each news article.
3. Sentiment vectors for each news site are generated by averaging the sentiment vectors of news articles in that site, which are generated as described in Section 3.2.

   Each element of a sentiment vector is a value $\in (0, 1)$. For the symmetry of the sentiment graphs which will be generated in the next step, we normalize it to a value $\in$ (-5, 5) by subtracting 0.5 from it and multiplying the result by 10.
4. Sentiment graphs are generated for each news site based on the sentiment vectors and are attached to a geographical map for the purpose of generating a sentiment map.

   We use a graph creating library JpGraph [10] to generate sentiment graphs for news sites. A sentiment graph corresponds to a summarization of sentiment values of news articles related to the query keyword for a new site. Sentiment graphs for news sites are mapped to news site locations on a geographical map using the Yahoo! Map API [11]. This geographical map with sentiment graphs is referred to as a "sentiment map."
5. When the user changes the scale of the sentiment map, the geographical scale is recalculated based on map zoom control, and sentiment values are resummarized corresponding to the new scale.

   The presentation scale of the sentiment map can be automatically adjusted based on map control, which includes functions such as zoom in and zoom out. The largest scale of the sentiment map is the world map, and the smallest scale of the sentiment map is a news website. When the sentiment map is presented at the world map level, the sentiment tendencies are aggregated for each continent. When the sentiment map is presented at the Japanese map level, sentiment graphs are generated for each region of Japan (e.g., Kanto area, Kansai area, etc.). When the map scale is zoomed in to the Japanese prefecture level, the sentiment summarization level is the individual news site.

5   Experiments

We implement a prototype [12] of sentiment map that extracts sentiments from news articles and visualizes the sentiments on a geographical map. The collected news sites and their geographical regions are shown in Table 3. Section 5.1 presents the interface of the proposed system. To evaluate our system, 100 individuals are asked to provide their judgments about the accuracy of sentiment extraction (Section 5.2), the effect of visualization (Section 5.3), and some comments on the overall system (Section 5.4).

Table 3. News websites considered in the experiments

Country	Region	Prefecture	News site	URL
Japan	Hokkaido-Tohoku	Hokkaido	Hokkaido Shimbun	http://www.hokkaido-np.co.jp/
		Iwate	Kahoku Online Network	http://www.kahoku.co.jp/
	Kanto-Tokai	Tokyo	Tokyo Web	http://www.tokyo-np.co.jp/
		Aichi	Chunichi Web	http://www.chunichi.co.jp/
	Kinki-Chugoku	Hyogo	Kobe Shimbun	http://www.kobe-np.co.jp/
		Hiroshima	Chugoku Shimbun	http://www.chugoku-np.co.jp/
	Kyushu-Okinawa	Nagasaki	Journal Nagasaki	http://www.nagasaki-np.co.jp/
		Okinawa	Okinawa Times	http://www.okinawatimes.co.jp/
Europe			asahi.com	http://www.asahi.com/international/europe.html
America			asahi.com	http://www.asahi.com/international/namerica.html
Asia			asahi.com	http://www.asahi.com/international/asia.html

5.1   System Interface

Figure 4 shows the interface of the proposed system. News sites from which news articles are collected and the dates on which the news articles were crawled are presented on the initial retrieval page. The user can input one or more query keywords and select the period of news articles that he/she wishes to browse (i.e., to analyze the sentiments thereof).

Figure 5 shows the retrieval result for the query keyword "China" during the period from September 8 to September 10 of 2008. The upper-right frame shows the headlines of the top five news articles, the $tf \cdot idf$ values of the query keyword in which are the highest for each site. By clicking the headlines, the user can browse the contents of corresponding news articles. The lower-right frame displays the sentiment graph of the selected news article, as well as the 10 words with the highest $tf \cdot idf$ values, which tend to represent the topic of the news article. A sentiment graph in the lower-right frame is a bar graph, in which four bars respectively represent four kinds of sentiments of a news article. A sentiment graph in the left frame is a line graph, in which the horizontal axis represents time and the vertical axis represents the average sentiment values of four dimensions for a news site. When the mouse moves over a sentiment graph in the left frame, a sentiment graph with more detailed sentiments of four dimensions is displayed. For a retrieval, a sentiment map at Japanese region level is initially shown respectively for four representative Japanese geographical regions. By zooming in, a sentiment map at the news site level can be regenerated. By zooming out to a world map, the sentiment tendencies can be summarized for each continent.

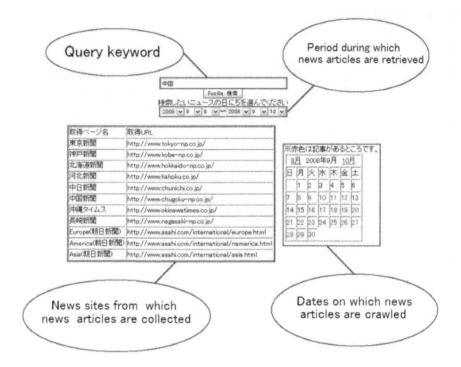

Fig. 4. System interface

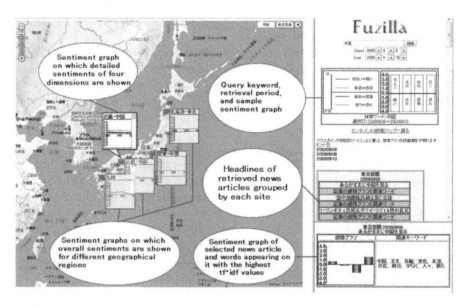

Fig. 5. Retrieval result

5.2   Evaluation of Sentiment Extraction Accuracy

This section reports the accuracy of sentiment values extracted by the proposed system. Given a query keyword, the proposed system retrieves related news articles grouped by each news site, and calculates the sentiment values of four dimensions for each news site by averaging the sentiment values of the 10 news articles with the highest $tf \cdot idf$ values of the query keyword in each news site.

To evaluate the error between the sentiment values calculated by the proposed system and the sentiment values decided by individuals, questionnaires were filled out by 100 individuals. We selected five query keywords and for each keyword selected 10 news articles with the highest $tf \cdot idf$ values in a specific news site. These individuals read the 10 news articles and evaluated the sentiment tendency on four dimensions. For a news article and a dimension, e.g., Joy $\Leftrightarrow$ Sadness, the individuals assigned the news article one of five levels: joy, close to joy, neither joy nor sadness, close to sadness, and sadness. n_1, n_2, n_3, n_4, and n_5 ($\sum_{i=1}^{5} n_i = 100$) were the numbers of the individuals who gave the five levels. We converted the evaluation of the individuals to a numerical value using the following scoring system: joy = 1, close to joy = 0.75, neither joy nor sadness = 0.5, close to sadness = 0.25, and sadness = 0. The sentiment value of a news article on a dimension evaluated by the 100 individuals was $(n_1 * 1 + n_2 * 0.75 + n_3 * 0.5 + n_4 * 0.25 + n_5 * 0)/100$. Finally, the sentiment values of the 10 news articles were averaged as the sentiment values for the news site.

The error of sentiment values between the proposed system and the user evaluation is shown in Table 4. For most of query keywords and most of sentiment dimensions, the sentiment values averaged by the 100 individuals' judgments and those calculated by the proposed system are similar. For example, the sentiment value of the news articles related to the query "Beijing" for the dimension of Joy $\Leftrightarrow$ Sadness which our system calculates is 0.5110, which is a value close to the users' average 0.5203. The average errors of all the query keywords are small, between 0.068 and 0.105, which indicates that the proposed system can extract sentiment values that are similar to those decided by individuals.

Table 4. Evaluation of the error of sentiment values between sentiment values calculated by the proposed system and sentiment values decided by individuals

Query keyword		Average sentiment values of news articles related to the keyword			
		Joy $\Leftrightarrow$ Sadness	Acceptance $\Leftrightarrow$ Disgust	Anticipation $\Leftrightarrow$ Surprise	Fear $\Leftrightarrow$ Anger
Beijing	user	0.5203	0.5815	0.5368	0.5165
	system	0.5110	0.5255	0.3766	0.5566
teacher	user	0.2533	0.3230	0.3528	0.7560
	system	0.4639	0.5135	0.4430	0.4952
Hashimoto	user	0.5080	0.5590	0.5115	0.5075
governor	system	0.4236	0.5244	0.5238	0.4571
Kyoto	user	0.4733	0.5903	0.5135	0.5120
	system	0.5299	0.5440	0.3983	0.5587
Fukuda	user	0.4418	0.4825	0.4453	0.5800
premier	system	0.4208	0.4692	0.4957	0.4519
Average error		0.07638	0.06814	0.08566	0.10522

5.3   Evaluation of Visualization Effect

In this section, we describe the visualization effect about how helpful the senti-ment map is to understand the sentiment distinction. A total of 100 individuals also evaluated the visualization effect of the proposed system using the senti-ment map. For each of three given query keywords, our system provided the sentiment map which presented the sentiment distinction at three geographical scales: the smallest scale of news sites, larger scale of Japanese geographical re-gions, and the largest scale of world's continents. The individuals were asked to provide their comprehension level about how conscious they were of the sen-timent distinction among the different news sites, among the different regions, or among the different continents. The evaluation was ranked on a five-level scale: understand, somewhat understand, neither clear nor unclear, somewhat unclear, and unclear. Figure 6 shows the evaluation results for the three query keywords and the three geographical scales. The percentage of individuals who indicated that they could "understand" or "somewhat understand" the senti-ment map was 40% to 50%, whereas the percentage of individuals who indicated that the sentiment map was "somewhat unclear" or "unclear" was 25% to 35%. This indicates that the proposed sentiment map is useful for clarifying the news sentiments.

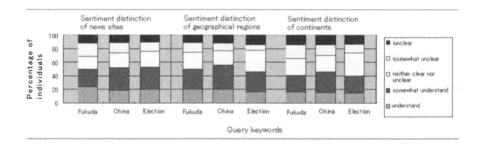

Fig. 6. Evaluation of visualization effect

5.4   Some Comments on the Overall System

A total of 100 individuals were also asked to provide an evaluation of the overall system and arbitrary comments. Individuals, who described the proposed sys-tem as being satisfactory, made comments such as, "I became interested in the contents of the news articles and wanted to read them further", and "I could understand the sentiment tendencies of the news sites even without having read the articles". On the other hand, there were also some complaints. For exam-ple, dissatisfied individuals reported that the sentiment maps were generated too slowly and that sentiment graphs were sometimes difficult to browse. These aspects will be improved in the future.

6   Related Research

There have been a number of studies on Web news systems, considering information collection, categorization, integration, and recommendation. Google News [4] collects news articles from approximately 4,500 websites and provides similar articles. Yahoo! News [5] uses a ranking technology based on various aspects so that specific types of news are displayed prominently. MSNBC [6] recommends personalized news articles to users by analyzing their browsing history. Although these news sites provide useful services, the aspect of news writer sentiment is not considered.

Sentiment analysis [13,14,15] is increasingly important in the areas of NLP and text mining, which extracts sentiments from text such as movie reviews, book reviews, and production evaluations. Turney [16] proposed a method for classifying reviews into two categories: recommended and not recommended based on mutual information. Pang et al. [17] extracted only the subjective portions of movie reviews and classified them as "thumbs up" or "thumbs down" by applying text-categorization techniques. Esuli et al. [18] presented a method for determining the orientation of subjective terms based on quantitative analysis of the glosses of such terms. However, these methods only consider positive and negative sentiments. Unlike these methods, the proposed method captures more detailed sentiment aspects of four dimensions: Joy ⇔ Sadness, Acceptance ⇔ Disgust, Anticipation ⇔ Surprise, and Fear ⇔ Anger. Furthermore, we visualize the different sentiments of different news sources. Except for the model of emotion proposed by Plutchik [7] which is used by our current research, there also exist other models. Russell [8] proposed a two-dimensional space where the horizontal dimension was pleasure-displeasure, and the vertical dimension was arousal-sleep. The remaining four variables: excitement, depression, contentment, distress, were their combination, not forming independent dimensions. Pitel et al. [9] considered 44 paired emotion directions and created a sentiment dictionary for French using a SVM classifier. Extension based on these models is one of our future work.

7   Conclusions and Future Work

In the present paper, we described a novel method called the Sentiment Map for distinguishing and visualizing the sentiment tendencies of Web news. The proposed method can dynamically summarize the sentiments of news sources for different scales of geographical regions. Sentiment graphs are generated for news sources and are attached to a geographical map, so that users can intuitively distinguish the sentiments of news writers. We implemented a prototype system and, through experimental evaluations, demonstrated that the accuracy of sentiment extraction and the effect of visualization were good.

The proposed method has been applied to analyze the sentiments of news writers. However, research on extracting the sentiments of news readers is also needed, and we plan to construct a system that can recommend news articles that match the sentiments of news readers.

Acknowledgments

This work was supported in part by the National Institute of Information and Communications Technology, Japan, and by the MEXT Grant-in-Aid for Young Scientists (B) (#21700120, Representative:Yukiko Kawai).

References

1. Los Angeles Times, http://www.latimes.com/
2. USA Today, http://usatoday.com/
3. The New York Times, http://www.nytimes.com/
4. Google News, http://news.google.co.jp/
5. Yahoo! News, http://headlines.yahoo.co.jp/
6. MSNBC, http://www.msnbc.msn.com/
7. Plutchik, R.: The Emotions. Univ Pr. of Amer (1991)
8. Russell, J.A.: A Circumplex Model of Affect. Journal of Personality and Social Psychology 39(6), 1161–1178 (1980)
9. Pitel, G., Grefenstette, G.: Semi-automatic Building Method for a Multidimensional Affect Dictionary for a New Language. In: LREC 2008(2008)
10. JpGraph, http://www.asial.co.jp/jpgraph/
11. Yahoo! Map API, http://developer.yahoo.co.jp/webapi/map/
12. Sentiment Map, http://klab.kyoto-su.ac.jp/~zjw/cgi-bin/Fuzilla/News/
13. Strapparava, C., Mihalcea, R.: Task 14: Affective Text. In: SemEval 2007 (2007)
14. Pang, B., Lee, L.: Opinion Mining and Sentiment Analysis. Foundations and Trends in Information Retrieval 2(1-2), 1–135 (2007)
15. Wright, A.: Our Sentiments, Exactly. Communications of the ACM 52(4), 14–15 (2009)
16. Turney, P.D.: Thumbs Up or Thumbs Down? Semantic Orientation Applied to Unsupervised Classification of Reviews. In: ACL 2002, pp. 417–424 (2002)
17. Pang, B., Lee, L.: A Sentiment Education: Sentiment Analysis Using Subjectivity Summarization Based on Minimum Cuts. In: ACL 2004, pp. 271–278 (2004)
18. Esuli, A., Sebastiani, F.: Determining the Semantic Orientation of Terms through Gloss Classification. In: CIKM 2005, pp. 617–624 (2005)

Visually Lossless HTML Compression

Przemysław Skibiński

University of Wrocław, Institute of Computer Science,
Joliot-Curie 15, 50-383 Wrocław, Poland
inikep@ii.uni.wroc.pl

Abstract. The verbosity of the Hypertext Markup Language (HTML) remains one of its main weaknesses. This problem can be solved with the aid of HTML specialized compression algorithms. In this work, we describe a visually lossless HTML transform that, combined with generally used compression algorithms, allows to attain high compression ratios. Its core is a transform featuring substitution of words in an HTML document using a static English dictionary, effective encoding of dictionary indexes, numbers, and specific patterns.

Visually lossless compression means that the HTML document layout will be modified, but the document displayed in a browser will provide the exact fidelity with the original. The experimental results show that the proposed transform improves the HTML compression efficiency of general purpose compressors on average by 21% in the case of gzip, achieving comparable processing speed. Moreover, we show that the compression ratio of gzip can be improved by up to 32% for the price of higher memory requirements and much slower processing.

Keywords: HTML compression, HTML transform, semi-structural data compression.

1 Introduction

Since the origin of World Wide Web, the Hypertext Markup Language (HTML) is a standard for Internet web pages. HTML has many advantages. One of its main advantages is that it is a textual format, what means that HTML is human-readable and can be edited by any text editor. The textual format of HTML is also one of its main disadvantages as it introduces verbosity. Nevertheless verbosity can be coped with by applying data compression.

In this work we will present our specialized algorithm for HTML compression, which achieves much higher compression than the state-of-the-art LSHT algorithm. It also uses a fixed English dictionary. The algorithm is designed in four variants for proper general-purpose algorithms.

The map of the paper is as follows. Section 2 contains a short review of existing HTML compression methods thus putting our work in a proper context. In Section 3 we describe step-by-step our HTML transform, its main ideas, and its most significant details. The next section presents details about optimizations for back-end

G. Vossen, D.D.E. Long, and J.X. Yu (Eds.): WISE 2009, LNCS 5802, pp. 195–202, 2009.

compression algorithms used with our transform. Section 5 contains implementation details, description of files used for experiments, and experimental results. Section 6 gives our conclusions.

2 Related Work

HTTP compression [11] is the technology used to compress contents from a web server (an HTTP server) and to decompress them in an user's browser. HTTP compression is a recommendation of the HTTP 1.1 protocol specification as it reduces network traffic and improves page download time on slow networks [12]. It is especially useful when size of the web pages is large.

The popular LZ77-based gzip was intended to be the HTTP compression algorithm. Currently, HTTP servers and clients supports also LZ77-based deflate format. Lighttpd server supports also BWT-based bzip2 compression, but this format is only supported by lynx and some other console text-browsers. Deflate, gzip, and bzip2, however, are general-purpose compression algorithms and much better results can be achieved with a compression algorithm specialized for dealing with HTML documents.

In our previous work [14] we have presented the first two specialized HTML compression algorithms called SDHT and LSHT. These methods are related to text compression [16] as they use respectively a semi-static dictionary of the most frequent words in the document or a static English dictionary. These methods are also related to XML compression [17] as both formats, HTML and XML, are SGML-based. SDHT and LSHT use several techniques from our XML compressor [17] as e.g., effective encoding of numbers, dates and times.

3 HTML Transform

In this section we present our Visually Lossless Static HTML Transform (VLSHT). We introduce subsequent parts of our algorithm step by step.

3.1 End Tag Encoding

In a well-formed HTML document, every end tag must match a corresponding start tag. This can hardly be exploited by general-purpose compression algorithms, as they maintain a linear, not stack-alike data model. The compression ratio can then be increased by replacing every matching end tag with merely an element closing flag.

Our transform puts elements on a stack when a start tag has appeared. The last inserted element is removed from a stack when an end tag has appeared. The problem with HTML is that not all elements must have a closing tag. It can be solved by ignoring elements that allow an end tag omission. The second problem with HTML is that some tags (e.g. <p>) should have corresponding end tags, but human editors skip these closing tags. Moreover, web browsers do not report errors on documents of this kind. Therefore our transform allows non-valid HTML documents. The above-mentioned problems do not occur in XHTML.

3.2 Quotes Modeling

Attributes of HTML elements usually contain neighboring *equal* and *quotation mark* characters (e.g. `attribute="value"`). Sometimes attributes are encoded using *equal* and *apostrophe* characters (e.g. `attribute='value'`). We have found that replacing these two characters with a flag improves compression performance. We made the same with *quotation mark* and *angle right bracket* (*greater*) characters that closing start tags with attribute(s) (e.g. `<element-name attribute="value">`).

3.3 Number Encoding

Numbers appear very often in HTML documents. We found that storing numbers as text is ineffective. Numbers can be encoded more efficiently using a numerical system with base higher than 10.

In our transform every decimal integer number n is replaced with a single byte whose value is $\lceil \log_{256}(n+1) \rceil + 48$. The actual value of n is then encoded as a base-256 number. A special case is made for sequences of zeroes preceding a number – these are left intact.

Our transform encodes in a special way also other numerical data that represent specific information types. Currently our transform recognizes the following formats:

- dates between 1977-01-01 and 2153-02-26 in YYYY-MM-DD (e.g. "2007-03-31", Y for year, M for month, D for day) and DD-MMM-YYYY (e.g. "31-MAR-2007") formats;
- years from 1900 to 2155 (e.g. "1999", "2008")
- times in 24-hour (e.g., "22:15") and 12-hour (e.g., "10:15pm") formats;
- value ranges (e.g., "115-132");
- decimal fractional numbers with one (e.g., "1.2") or two (e.g., "1.22") digits after decimal point.

3.4 Static Dictionary

Our transform uses a static dictionary, which is embedded in the compressor and the decompressor. There are two advantages of a static dictionary over a semi-dynamic dictionary: there is no need to make the first pass over the input data to create the semi-dynamic dictionary and there is no need to store the semi-dynamic dictionary within processed data to make decompression possible.

On the other hand a static dictionary is limited to some class of documents e.g. English language. The dictionary must be spread with the compressor and the decompressor. Moreover, a semi-dynamic dictionary contains words that are actually frequent in the document, not words that could potentially be frequent, as it is in the case of a static dictionary. Nevertheless according to [14] for HTML documents a static English dictionary usually gives a better compression ratio than a semi-dynamic dictionary.

3.5 Visually Lossless Optimization

HTML documents are usually displayed in a browser. The browser ignores the document layout, therefore tabulators, end of line symbols, and runs of spaces can be replaced with a single space symbol or even removed. The one exception are <PRE> and <STYLE> tags, which should be left intact. We call this technique visually lossless optimization. This technique is well-known from HTML optimizers.

From the other side visually lossless compression is lossy. The lossy compression means in this case that layout, which may be useful for human editors of a document will be modified. Moreover the exact fidelity of the decompressed document with the original required in order to verify the document integrity using a cyclic redundancy check or hash functions will not be supported. If we can accept these disadvantages we will get a high improvement from visually lossless compression.

4 Back-End Compression

Succinct word encoding appears to be the most important idea in Visually Lossless Static HTML Transform (VLSHT). There are four modes of encoding, chosen depending on the attached back-end compression algorithm: LZ77-based [20], LZMA/BWT-based [3], PPM-based [5], and PAQ-based [10]. In all cases, dictionary references are encoded using a byte-oriented prefix code, where the length varies from one to four bytes. Although it produces slightly longer output than, for instance, Huffman coding [7], the resulting data can be easily compressed further, which is not the case with the latter. Obviously, more frequent words have assigned shorter codewords.

The LZ77 and PPM optimized transform contain of the biggest possible alphabet for codewords: byte values from 128 up to 255 and most values in range 0–31, plus a few more. These symbols are very rarely used in most HTML documents. If, however, one of these symbols occurs in the document, and is not part of an encoded word, the coder marks it with a special escape symbol. In the LZMA/BWT and PAQ optimized transform the codeword alphabet consists of fewer symbols, because it uses only 128 symbols with byte values from 128 up to 255.

5 Experimental Results

This section presents implementation details of the VLSHT algorithm. It also contains description of files used for experiments and discussion on experimental results of the VLSHT algorithm with four different back-end compression methods.

5.1 Implementation Details

The VLSHT implementation contains a fast and simple HTML parser built as a finite state automaton (FSA), which accepts proper words and numerical (including date and time) expressions. The parser does not build any trees, but treats an input HTML document as one-dimensional data. It has small memory requirements, as it only uses a stack to trace opening and closing tags. The parser supports the HTML 4.01 specification (e.g. allowed an end tag omission for some tags).

The VLSHT implementation uses a static English dictionary with about 80.000 words. In this dictionary, words are sorted with the relation to their frequency in a training corpus of more than 3 GB English text taken from the Project Gutenberg library. The words are stored in lower case as VLSHT implements the capital conversion method to convert the capital letter starting a word to its lowercase equivalent and denote the change with a flag. Additionally, VLSHT uses another flag to mark a conversion of a full uppercase word to its lowercase form.

VLSHT is lossy in a sense that the HTML document layout will be modified, but the document displayed in a browser will provide the exact fidelity with the original. The transforms can handle any HTML documents with 8-bit (ISO-8859 and UTF-8) or 16-bit (Unicode) encodings. VLSHT was implemented in C++ and compiled with MS Visual C++ 2008.

5.2 HTML Corpus

In compression benchmarking, proper selection of documents used in experiments is essential. To the best of our knowledge, there is no publicly available and widely respected HTML corpus to this date. Therefore, we have based our test suite on HTML files (without images, etc.) downloaded from common Internet web sites. The resulting corpus represents a wide range of real-world HTML documents.

Detailed information for each group of the documents is presented in Table 1; it includes: URL address, number of files and total size of files. The size of a single file spans from 1 up to 296 KB.

Table 1. Basic characteristics for the HTML corpus used in the experiments

Name	URL address	no. files	Total size
Hillman	hillmanwonders.com	781	34421 KB
Mahoney	www.cs.fit.edu/~mmahoney/	11	596 KB
MaxComp	maximumcompression.com	61	2557 KB
STL	www.sgi.com/tech/stl/	237	2551 KB
TightVNC	tightvnc.com	21	289 KB
Tortoise	tortoisesvn.net	393	5342 KB
Travel	travelindependent.info	69	3841 KB

5.3 Compression Ratio

The primary objective of experiments was to measure the performance of our implementation of the VLSHT algorithm. For comparison purposes, we included in the tests general-purpose compression tools: gzip 1.2.4, LZMA 4.43, PPMVC 1.2, and FastPAQ8, employing the same algorithms at the final stage of VLSHT, to demonstrate the improvement from applying the HTML transform.

Table 2. Compression results for HTML datasets in output bits per input character

	HufSyl	LZWL	gzip	StarNT+gzip	WRT+gzip	mPPM
Hillman	2.95	2.13	1.51	1.42	1.44	1.34
Mahoney	3.31	3.23	2.72	2.54	2.49	2.30
MaxComp	3.03	2.39	1.86	1.79	1.80	1.55
STL	3.48	3.22	2.19	1.97	1.95	2.31
TightVNC	3.44	3.26	2.34	2.17	2.13	2.24
Tortoise	3.37	3.13	2.27	2.08	2.06	2.23
Travel	2.88	2.72	2.34	2.06	1.97	1.95
Average	2.808	2.510	1.904	1.754	1.730	1.740
Improvement				7.88%	9.13%	

	gzip	LSHT +gzip	VLSHT +gzip	LZMA	LSHT +LZMA	VLSHT +LZMA
Hillman	1.51	1.23	1.17	1.29	1.13	1.07
Mahoney	2.72	2.26	2.17	2.35	2.08	2.00
MaxComp	1.86	1.47	1.45	1.53	1.38	1.36
STL	2.19	1.85	1.74	2.13	1.79	1.69
TightVNC	2.34	2.09	1.95	2.23	1.99	1.86
Tortoise	2.27	2.02	1.93	2.17	1.92	1.84
Travel	2.34	1.84	1.69	2.13	1.74	1.60
Average	1.904	1.595	1.513	1.729	1.504	1.428
Improvement		16.22%	20.55%		13.02%	17.43%

	PPMVC	LSHT +PPMVC	VLSHT +PPMVC	FPAQ	LSHT +FPAQ	VLSHT +FPAQ
Hillman	1.19	1.06	1.00	1.14	1.01	0.96
Mahoney	2.09	1.92	1.86	2.01	1.83	1.77
MaxComp	1.41	1.30	1.28	1.36	1.24	1.22
STL	1.91	1.71	1.62	1.90	1.67	1.58
TightVNC	1.96	1.86	1.76	1.96	1.82	1.71
Tortoise	1.93	1.83	1.76	1.92	1.77	1.70
Travel	1.79	1.60	1.49	1.79	1.56	1.44
Average	1.535	1.410	1.346	1.510	1.363	1.298
Improvement		8.14%	12.30%		9.77%	14.07%

As we are aware of just two specialized algorithms for HTML compression [14] we have also compared our algorithm to well-know word-based text compression techniques: StarNT [18], WRT [16], HufSyl [8], LZWL [8], and mPPM [1]. We have also tried to use XMLPPM [4] and SCMPPM [2], which work well with XHTML files, but it do not support HTML files.

The first part of Table 2 contains results of word-based text compression algorithms. For each program and group of HTML documents a bitrate is given in output bits per input character, hence the smaller the values, the better. The last but one row includes an average bitrate computed for all the seven groups of documents. The last row presents the average improvement of preprocessors for all documents compared to the general purpose algorithms result.

The next parts of Table 2 contain compression results of the introduced HTML corpus using gzip, LZMA, PPMVC, FastPAQ, and our implementation of the VLSHT algorithm combined with gzip, LZMA, PPMVC, and FastPAQ.

VLSHT with gzip achieves compression results better than all word-based text compression algorithms, including a PPM-based mPPM. Compared to the general-purpose compression tools, VLSHT improves compression of the introduced HTML corpus on average by 21% in the case of gzip, over 17% for LZMA, over 12% in the case of PPMVC and about 14% for FastPAQ. Compression and decompression speed of VLSHT in comparison to general-purpose compression algorithms is a little bit lower as there is a need to read a fixed English dictionary. VLSHT, however, allows to read the dictionary only once and processes all HTML documents in one run.

6 Conclusions

HTML has many advantages, but its main disadvantage is verbosity, which can be coped with by applying data compression. HTML is usually used in combination with gzip compression, but gzip is a general-purpose compression algorithm and much better results can be achieved with a compression algorithm specialized for dealing with HTML documents.

In this paper we have presented the VLSHT transform aiming to improve HTML compression in combination with existing general purpose compressors. The main disadvantage of VLSHT algorithm is a fixed English dictionary required for compression and decompression.

VLSHT is lossy in a sense that the HTML document layout will be modified, but the document displayed in a browser will provide the exact fidelity with the original. Thanks to the VLSHT transform, however, compression ratio of the introduced HTML corpus was improved by as much as 21% in the case of gzip, 17% for LZMA, 12% in the case of PPMVC and 14% for FastPAQ. VLSHT with FastPAQ gives the best compression effectiveness, which is 32% better than gzip without any transform. Moreover, VLSHT gives over 4% improvement over the state-of-the-art LSHT algorithm for all tested general-purpose compression algorithms.

VLSHT has many nice practical properties. It is implemented as a stand-alone program, requiring no external compression utility, no HTML parser, thus avoiding any compatibility issues.

References

1. Adiego, J., de la Fuente, P.: Mapping Words into Codewords on PPM. In: Crestani, F., Ferragina, P., Sanderson, M. (eds.) SPIRE 2006. LNCS, vol. 4209, pp. 181–192. Springer, Heidelberg (2006)
2. Adiego, J., de la Fuente, P., Navarro, G.: Using Structural Contexts to Compress Semistructured Text Collections. Information Processing and Management 43(3), 769–790 (2007)

3. Burrows, M., Wheeler, D.J.: A block-sorting data compression algorithm. SRC Research Report 124. Digital Equipment Corporation, Palo Alto, CA, USA (1994)
4. Cheney, J.: Compressing XML with multiplexed hierarchical PPM models. In: Proceedings of the IEEE Data Compression Conference, Snowbird, UT, USA, pp. 163–172 (2001)
5. Cleary, J.G., Witten, I.H.: Data compression using adaptive coding and partial string matching. IEEE Trans. on Comm. 32(4), 396–402 (1984)
6. Deutsch, P.: DEFLATE Compressed Data Format Specification version 1.3. RFC1951 (1996), http://www.ietf.org/rfc/rfc1951.txt
7. Huffman, D.A.: A Method for the Construction of Minimum-Redundancy Codes. In: Proc. IRE 40.9, September 1952, pp. 1098–1101 (1952)
8. Lánský, J., Žemlička, M.: Text Compression: Syllables. In: Proceedings of the Dateso 2005 Annual International Workshop on DAtabases, TExts, Specifications and Objects. CEUR-WS, vol. 129, pp. 32–45 (2005)
9. Mahoney, M.: About the Test Data (2006), http://cs.fit.edu/~mmahoney/compression/textdata.html
10. Mahoney, M.: Adaptive Weighing of Context Models for Lossless Data Compression. Technical Report TR-CS-2005-16, Florida Tech., USA (2005)
11. Nielsen, H.F.: HTTP Performance Overview (2003), http://www.w3.org/Protocols/HTTP/Performance/
12. Radhakrishnan, S.: Speed Web delivery with HTTP compression (2003), http://www-128.ibm.com/developerworks/web/library/wa-httpcomp/
13. Shkarin, D.: PPM: One Step to Practicality. In: Proceedings of the IEEE Data Compression Conference, Snowbird, UT, USA, pp. 202–211 (2002)
14. Skibiński, P.: Improving HTML Compression. To appear in Informatica (2009)
15. Skibiński, P., Grabowski, S.z.: Variable-length contexts for PPM. In: Proceedings of the IEEE Data Compression Conference, Snowbird, UT, USA, pp. 409–418 (2004)
16. Skibiński, P., Grabowski, S.z., Deorowicz, S.: Revisiting dictionary-based compression. Software – Practice and Experience 35(15), 1455–1476 (2005)
17. Skibiński, P., Grabowski, S.z., Swacha, J.: Effective asymmetric XML compression. Software – Practice and Experience 38(10), 1027–1047 (2008)
18. Sun, W., Zhang, N., Mukherjee, A.: Dictionary-based fast transform for text compression. In: Proceedings of international conference on Information Technology: Coding and Computing, ITCC, pp. 176–182 (2003)
19. Wan, R.: Browsing and Searching Compressed Documents. PhD dissertation, University of Melbourne (2003), http://www.bic.kyoto-u.ac.jp/proteome/rwan/docs/wan_phd_new.pdf
20. Ziv, J., Lempel, A.: A Universal Algorithm for Sequential Data Compression. IEEE Trans. Inform. Theory 23(3), 337–343 (1977)

Enhancing Web Search by Aggregating Results of Related Web Queries

Lin Li[1,*], Guandong Xu[2], Yanchun Zhang[2], and Masaru Kitsuregawa[3]

[1] School of Computer Science & Technology, Wuhan University of Technology, China
cathylilin@whut.edu.cn
[2] School of Engineering & Science, Victoria University, Australia
{guandong.xu, Yanchun.zhang}@vu.edu.au
[3] Institute of Industrial Science, University of Tokyo, Japan
kitsure@tkl.iis.u-tokyo.ac.jp

Abstract. Currently, commercial search engines have implemented methods to suggest alternative Web queries to users, which helps them specify alternative related queries in pursuit of finding needed Web pages. In this paper, we address the Web search problem on related queries to improve retrieval quality by devising a novel search rank aggregation mechanism. Given an initial query and the suggested related queries, our search system concurrently processes their search result lists from an existing search engine and then forms a single list aggregated by all the retrieved lists. In particular we propose a generic rank aggregation framework which considers not only the number of wins that an item won in a competition, but also the quality of its competitor items in calculating the ranking of Web items. The framework combines the traditional and random walk based rank aggregation methods to produce a more reasonable list to users. Experimental results show that the proposed approach can clearly improve the retrieval quality in a parallel manner over the traditional search strategy that serially returns result lists. Moreover, we also empirically investigate how different rank aggregation methods affect the retrieval performance.

1 Introduction

Search engines are widely used on the Web and they are making more information easily accessible than ever before. However, the difficulties in finding only those which satisfy an individual's information goal increase due to the continued rapid growth in data volume of the Web and Web users' inexpert in phrasing query. Recent research studies [2,14,23,26] have grown interests in finding past related search queries to improve Web search. Furthermore, commercial search engines have implemented methods to suggest alternative queries to users, such as *Related search terms* in Google, *Search Assist* in Yahoo!, and *Related Searches* in Live Search. The purpose of these query suggestion methods is to help users easily specify alternative related queries for more relevant search

---

* The work was done when Lin Li was a Ph.D. student at the University of Tokyo.

G. Vossen, D.D.E. Long, and J.X. Yu (Eds.): WISE 2009, LNCS 5802, pp. 203–217, 2009.
© Springer-Verlag Berlin Heidelberg 2009

results. However, the current utilization of query suggestion is still naïve. After getting suggestion, a user usually has to submit these recommended queries one by one to find the results matching her information need. Moreover, she sometimes has to frequently navigate through the result pages because she is not sure whether the recommended queries are exactly matching her need before she reads the actual contents of Web pages. Obviously, this is tedious for the user to manipulate several search windows. In addition, if a single query is deficient in accurately representing her information need, the set of recommended related queries may have a higher possibility to provide a broader search converge over Web pages, thereby more likely including the information the user wants.

In this paper we address this search problem and devise a novel enhanced web search approach by aggregating results of related Web queries, which aims at facilitating locating the information need of a user. Our search system takes a couple of related queries as search inputs and outputs a final search result list which is the aggregation of the result lists of these input queries. The strength of the combined query collections can substantially enhance the utilization of query suggestion to improve Web search quality.

The technical issue addressed in our system is the rank aggregation of the search result lists given a set of queries. Various rank aggregation methods have been studied and employed in many applications [10,19,24,27]. In this paper we propose a generic framework of rank aggregation based on random walk by constructing a so-called Win/Loss graph of Web pages. Random walk on the Win/Loss graph determines the aggregated rank of each page in the final result list by using the voting rule. In particular two kinds of competition rules are studied to determine the Win/Loss relationship between two nodes in the graph. One is based on *pairwise* contest that chooses the next Web page based on the number of pairwise contests (within all the lists) the page won. The other one is based on *pairwise majority* contest that decides the next Web page by the number of pairwise majority contests the page won. The advantage of the proposed framework is that it takes into account not only the number of wins that an item won, but also the quality of the competitor items. In addition, the proposed framework on the two kinds of Win/Loss graphs generalizes two main schools of solutions in rank aggregation spearheaded by Borda [5] and Copeland [8] which also lay down a foundation of Markov Chain based methods [10,11,19]. Experimental results show that the proposed approach can clearly improve the retrieval quality in a parallel manner over the traditional search strategy that serially returns result lists. In addition, we experimentally compare the effectiveness of four typical rank aggregation methods that are used in our framework.

In summary, this paper aims to make contributions on a) enhancing Web search by the aggregation of the search results of related queries (Section 2), b) devising a generic rank aggregation framework based on random walk and discussing how to employ various rank aggregation methods in the proposed framework (Section 3), and c) providing empirical evidences as to demonstrate how result aggregation improves search quality and how different rank aggregation methods affect system

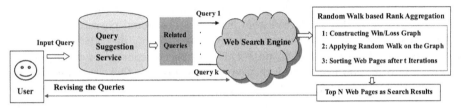

Fig. 1. Our search system overview

performance (Section 4). Last, we review related work in Section 5 and conclude our work in Section 6.

2   Our Search System Overview

In this section, we give an overview of our search system. As illustrated in Figure 1, its flowchart includes two important components, query suggestion (leftmost cylinder) and rank aggregation (rightmost box). Given a query input by a user, we first need its related queries. In this paper, we are mainly interested in how to make use of related queries to enhance Web search, not how to find related queries. Therefore, we assume that related queries are already available. Our idea can be supported not only by the popular query suggestion service in commercial search engines, but also by other approaches of finding related queries [2,14,23,26]. For example, one of our ongoing research is to blend the QUBiC approach proposed in [14] into our system. After a set of related queries is selected by the user, we get their search results from a search engine (e.g., Google). Last, we aggregate these search results. As shown in the rightmost box of Figure 1, the aggregation is implemented by three steps: 1) constructing Win/Loss graph where order relationship among search results is encoded, 2) applying random walk on Win/Loss graph to assign a new score to each search result, and 3) sorting nodes (search results) in the graph based on the standing probability distribution of the random walk. The technical details will be discussed in the next section.

3   Our Generic Rank Aggregation Framework

Suppose that we have some related queries given an input query, our goal is to combine their search result lists returned by search engines and generate a single final list of Web pages to users. In this section, we propose a generic rank aggregation framework for combining search lists.

3.1   Preliminary

In the field of rank aggregation, let U be a set of items and a rank list (or simply ranking) τ w.r.t. U is an ordering of a subset of U. Also, if $i \in U$ is present in τ, written $i \in \tau$, let $\tau(i)$ denote the position or rank of the i item in the list. A highly ranked or preferred item has a low-numbered position in the list, which means if $\tau(i) < \tau(j)$, i is more highly ranked than j in τ. If τ contains all the item in U, then τ is said to be a *full list*. In the context of our problem, given an information need, the k related queries $(Q_1, \cdots, Q_k)$ are submitted to a search engine. We let τ_i denote the top N (say, N=100) results of the search engine w.r.t. the query Q_i and U be the set of all Web pages returned by these k queries. Since τ_i is most surely only a subset of U, we have an inequality $|\tau_i| \leq |U|$. Such lists that rank only some of the items (Web pages) in U are called partial lists. Clearly the pages in U that are not present in the list τ_i can be assumed to be ranked below N by the search engine.

Given several search lists, traditional rank aggregation methods directly re-order an item based on its positions on the lists. Usually they count the number of wins that the item gets according to a position-based competition rule [5,8,25]. For example, Condorcet condition [25] specifies that if an item (e.g., p) wins or ties with every other item (e.g., q) in a pairwise competition, i.e., $\tau_i(p) \leq \tau_i(q)$ for p,q=1, $\cdots$, $|U|$ and i=1,$\cdots$, k, the item as the winner will be put in the first position of the final fused list. The traditional aggregation methods mainly consider the number of wins that an item won (or the positions of competitors), but ignore the effect of the quality of items that the item won.

In the field of random walk, let G=(V, E) be a connected directed graph where V represents the set of nodes and E is the set of edges. Consider a *random walk* on G: a random walker starts at an arbitrary node v_0 randomly selected from V; if after several steps the random walker is at a node v_t, she uniformly moves to the neighbor of v_t with probability $1/O(v_t)$ where $O(v_t)$ represents the outdegree of v_t. A sequence of nodes visited by the random walker $(v_t : t$=0, 1, $\cdots)$ constitutes state transitions in a Markov chain and the edges connecting those nodes are unweighted. If the state transition of a Markov chain is not uniform (edges are differently weighted), we can treat it as a random walk with some transition probability. In both unweighted and weighted cases, the standing probability distribution of a random walk on the graph naturally generates an ordering list of all the nodes in V. The random walk based rank mechanism has been widely used especially in the area of Web search, e.g., PageRank [18].

The aforementioned two research paradigms were developed independently but still correlated to each other. The representative work on Markov chain based rank aggregation is Dwork et al. [10] who proposed four specific methods. However, the relationship among the four methods and traditional rank aggregation methods is not clearly presented by the authors. For each method, whether its transition probability is reasonable needs theoretical analysis for further improvement. Therefore, we are encouraged to devise a generic rank aggregation framework which combines the traditional and random walk based rank aggregation into a unified manner. Upon the unified framework, we can theoretically and empirically study how we can employ various rank aggregation methods, and which of them is the most effective for solving our problem.

3.2   Three Steps for Rank Aggregation

Based on the order relationship between two search results among these individual lists, we need a rank mechanism to score each search result (i.e. Web page) and re-sort them according to their assigned scores. Our idea is that the traditional rank aggregation can be used as a rule to determine the probability of state transition or the weight of an edge connecting two nodes on a connected directed graph. Then, the random walk based rank mechanism iteratively refines the ordering to extend the traditional competition-based rank aggregation methods by considering not only the number of wins that an item won, but also the quality of the competitor items. For example, if a won b in one competition, a got one point; if a won c and c' points are more than b's, a got more than one point (e.g., two points).

Step 1: Constructing Win/Loss Graph. We first give the definition of Win/Loss graph, and then describe two kinds of competition rules to construct it (e.g., the probability of state transition between nodes).

Win/Loss Graph: Web pages and Win/Loss relationship are modeled as a directed graph $G(V, E)$ where nodes in V represent Web pages and a directed edge $< p, q >$ in E corresponds to a Win/Loss relationship between p and q. Specifically speaking, if p wins q according to a competition rule, the link direction is from q to p (q-> p); if p is defeated by q and loses the competition, the link direction is from p to q (p-> q).

Based on the definition of Win/Loss graph, the number of inlinks of a node (e.g., q) means how many times the node won other nodes in the competition and the number of outlinks of a node means how many times the node was defeated by other nodes and lost in the competition. Here we produce the connection between Win and Inlink (Loss and Outlink), which closely resembles PageRank where a good page have many good inlinks (pages). Furthermore, we can use a variety of competition rules to determine the Win/Loss (Inlink/Outlink) relationship between nodes. In this paper, we mainly study two popular competition rules, i.e., pairwise contest and pairwise majority contest.

Win/Loss Graph on Pairwise Contest: the competition rule using pairwise contest is as follows:

In the rank list τ_i w.r.t the query Q_i ($i = 1, \cdots, k$) and two Web pages q and p, (a) if $\tau_i(p) < \tau_i(q)$, i.e., p wins q in this pairwise contest, q is treated as an inlink of p (q-> p); (b) if $\tau_i(p) > \tau_i(q)$, i.e., p is defeated by q in this pairwise contest, q is treated as an outlink of p (p-> q).

Notice that $\tau_i(q)$ cannot be the same as $\tau_i(p)$ in an individual list. The duplicate inlinks and outlinks will be omitted as a post-processing step. The indegree of p is the number of pairwise contests with all other pages in U that p won.

Win/Loss Graph on Pairwise Majority Contest: the competition rule using pairwise majority contest is as follows:

In the rank list τ_i w.r.t the query Q_i ($i = 1, \cdots, k$), let *the number of the lists* where $\tau_i(p) < \tau_i(q)$ be *wins* of the page p over the page q and *the number of the lists* where $\tau_i(p) > \tau_i(q)$ be *losses* of p over q;
(a) if *wins* > *losses*, i.e., p wins q in this pairwise majority contest, q is treated as an inlink of p (q–> p);
(b) if *wins* < *losses*, i.e., p is defeated by q in this pairwise majority contest, q is treated as an outlink of p (p–> q);
(c) if *wins* = *losses*, there is *NO* link between p and q because they are level.

The indegree of p is the number of pairwise majority contests p won. After constructing Win/Loss graph, we can apply a PageRank-like iterative method to sort the nodes (Web pages) in the graph.

Step 2: Applying Random Walk on Win/Loss Graph. In the above descriptions of two competition rules, we utilize the ordering relationship between two Web pages which appear in a same list τ_i to construct our Win/Loss graph. The order of two pages appeared in a same list τ_i is an explicit relationship. However, as we discussed in Section 3.1, each list τ_i in our problem is a partial list which means that there are some pages in U left unranked by τ_i. Clearly the pages that are not present in the list τ_i can be assumed to be ranked below $|\tau_i|$, which is an implicit ordering relationship. We will argue that a random walk behavior on the Win/Loss graph naturally reflects both explicit and implicit ordering relationships between two pages.

We model a random walk on a Win/Loss graph as follows. If a walker is at the page p now, the walker has two choice:

(a) she may walk to the next page q chosen from p's outlinks uniformly or based on the edge's weights. The main idea is that in each step, we move from the current page p to a better page q since q wins p. This walk behavior indeed represents an explicit ordering relationship in a list according to a competition rule;
(b) or she may also jump to the next page q uniformly chosen from the set of pages which appear in a list where p is not in. The reason is that we assume that the pages (e.g., p) that are not present in a list are ranked below that all the pages in the list (e.g., q). This jump behavior models the implicit ordering relationship based on the reasonable assumption.

We rank nodes corresponding to the standing probability distribution (i.e. score) of the walker on the graph. Thus, we have

$$r^{(t)}(q) = \frac{(1 - \alpha)}{|J_q|} + \alpha \sum_{p \in I(q)} r^{(t-1)}(p) w(p, q) \,, \tag{1}$$

where $r^{(t)}(q)$ is the rank score of node q after t iterations, $|J_q|$ is the number of pages which appear in a list where q is not in. $I(q)$ is the indegree of q. $w(p, q)$ is the weight of the edge (p–> q). We tune up the walk behavior and the jump behavior by a mixing parameter α, $0< \alpha <1$. From this formula we determine the overall score of a target node by counting *both* the number of nodes linking to a target node *and* the relative quality of each pointing node. Note that in computation we also include a small uniform probability *epsilon trnasitions* from every node to every other node, to overcome a sort of trap in the Win/Loss graph, called a *rank sink* by Brin and Page [18]. In addition, the Win/loss graph assumes that each node has at least one outlink, which, however, may be not always true. These *epsilon trnasitions* modify the Web pages with no outlinks in the Win/Loss graph to include virtual links to all other pages in the graph, which guarantees convergence to a unique rank score distribution of nodes [4]. At last, we can ensure a smooth, complete ranking on all the items in $|U|$ (the number of nodes in the graph). This smoothing technique was used in a number of random walk based ranking methods, including Google PageRank [18].

Step 3: Sorting Nodes after t Iterations. After constructing the Win/Loss graph and applying the random walk on it, we can sort the nodes by their ranks using Equation 1. The recursive running of Equation 1 gives the probability distribution that the walker is on page q after t iterations. When t equals to 1, no heuristic is used, while t is large enough, $r^{(t)}(q)$ will relatively converge to a stationary distribution. Then, the distribution induced on the state transitions of all the pages in the Win/Loss graph produces a final ranking of these pages. In other words, the ranked position of each page represents its relative significance matching the information need of users. Usually, the initial state is chosen uniformly at random because in general the initial value will not affect final values, just the rate of convergence [18].

3.3 Discussions

Here we discuss how to incorporate typical rank aggregation methods, i.e., Borda Count(BC) [5], Copeland Method(CM) [8] and four specific random walk methods proposed by Dwork et al. [10], i.e.,$MC1$, $MC2$, $MC3$, and $MC4$, into our proposed framework. The differences of their parameter settings are listed in Table 1. Using the proposed generic framework, we find that the four random walk based methods generalize BC and CM and further extend them by considering the quality of items in the competitions.

(1)Generalization of Borda Count. The random walk on Win/Loss graph using pairwise contest is a generalization of Borda Count method. BC is a popular rank fusion method and also widely discussed in [1,19]. For each list, the topmost item receives $n - 1$ points, the second item receives $n - 2$ points, and so on. The item with the maximal points will be put in the first position of the fused list. In fact, we can view the points received by an item in a list as the number of pairwise contest it won against all other items in this list, and the items are ranked in a decreasing order of total points obtained in all lists.

Table 1. The generic rank aggregation framework

	α	$w(p, q)$	$r^{(0)}(p)$	rule	iteration
BC	0.5	the number of lists where q is ranked higher than p	$O(p)$	pairwise contest	1
CM	0.5	the value *wins-losses* of each pairwise majority contests q won	$O(p)$	pairwise majority contest	1
$MC1$	1	unweighted	randomly	pairwise contest	t ($t > 1$)
$MC2$	1	the number of lists where p is	randomly	pairwise contest	t ($t > 1$)
$MC3$	1	the number of lists where q is ranked higher than p	randomly	pairwise contest	t ($t > 1$)
$MC4$	1	unweighted	randomly	pairwise majority contest	t ($t > 1$)
PW-1	0.85	unweighted $1/O(p)$	randomly	pairwise contest	1
PW-t	0.85	unweighted $1/O(p)$	randomly	pairwise contest	t ($t > 1$)
PWM-1	0.85	unweighted $1/O(p)$	randomly	pairwise majority contest	1
PWM-t	0.85	unweighted $1/O(p)$	randomly	pairwise majority contest	t ($t > 1$)

Following the direction of BC, in our framework, if the weight of the edge between q and p ($w(p, q)$) is based on the number of lists where q is ranked higher than its inlinked nodes (e.g., p), on this weighted Win/Loss graph, t iterations and one iteration produce similar aggregation results to that calculated by $MC3$ and BC respectively. On the other hand, the total points of an item in all lists may include duplicate pairwise comparisons. For example, if the page q is ranked higher than the page p in two lists, BC adds two points for q. In an unweighted Win/Loss graph on pairwise contest, we assign only one point for q in the pairwise comparisons between q and p of all the lists, which means we do not consider how many lists where q wins p, but whether q wins p. In this case, therefore, $w(p, q)$ is set to be $1/O(p)$ where $O(p)$ is the outdegree of p. On this unweighted Win/Loss graph, t iterations generate similar aggregation results with $MC1$.

Moreover, $MC2$ utilizes a different weighting strategy from $MC3$ so that the distribution induced on its states produces a ranking of the pages such that q is ranked higher than p if the geometric means of the ranks of q is lower than that of p. Generally speaking, $MC2$ and $MC3$ can be regarded as the different weighted versions of $MC1$.

(2)Generalization of Copeland Method. Similar to Win/Loss graph on pairwise contest, the random walk on Win/Loss graph using pairwise majority contest generalizes Copeland's suggestions of sorting the items by the number of pairwise majority contests they won. This amounts to sorting nodes by their indegrees in the Win/Loss graph using pairwise majority contest. If the initial probability of a node p is set to $O(p)$, i.e., $r^{(0)}(p) = O(p)$, the random walk on this unweighted graph after one iteration exactly models CM which is also popular in the literature of rank aggregation [17]. $MC4$ is based on the above defined graph with t iterations. Other parameters are also given in Table 1. In addition, the edges in the Win/Loss graph can be weighted by the value *wins-losses* of each pairwise majority contest a node won, thus generating a weighted version for $MC4$.

(3)Four Methods Used in Our Generic Framework. As shown in Table 1, we find that most existing methods are very different in several aspects, thus having difficulties in comparing them without a unified framework. We outline three aspects of a rank aggregation method involved in our framework: 1) competition rule for the Win/Loss relationship of competitor items, 2) iterative computation for the quality of competitor items, and 3) weighting strategy for enhancing the Win/Loss relationship. Due to the space limit, in this paper we only focus on the first two aspects (i.e., unweighted graph).

We investigate which kind of competition rules (pairwise contest or pairwise majority contest) is the most effective in our system and whether the iterative computation can improve our system performance. We will experimentally discuss four methods on unweighted Win/Loss graph, i.e., PW-1, PW-t, PWM-1, and PWM-t in Table 1. PW (PW-1 and PW-t) is based on pairwise contest and similar to $MC1$. PWM (PWM-1, and PWM-t) is based on pairwise majority contest and similar to $MC4$. We assign equal weights to all edges which means we uniformly choose the next page from p's outlinks, i.e., $w(p, q)$ is set to be $1/O(p)$ as shown in Table 1. Note that $MC2$ and $MC3$ can be regarded as weighted versions of $MC1$.

From the above discussions, we know that BC(pairwise contest) and CM(pairwise majority contest) directly rank items by the number of wins in their contests, while random walk on a directed graph propagates the indegree (wins) of a node over the whole Win/Loss graph, inducing an iterative computation for combining rankings. The random walk based methods show that a node which has more highly ranked nodes as its inlinks will be ranked higher. For evaluation, we conduct experiments on two kinds of computation. One has only one iterative computation (i.e., PW-1 and PWM-1). The other has t (t>1) iterative computations (i.e., PW-t and PWM-t).

4   Experiments

In this section, we present experimental evaluation results: we will first explore how the aggregation of the search results is able to greatly improve the search quality in comparison to the traditional retrieval methods which return Web pages query by query, and then we will investigate the impact of incorporating different rank aggregation methods into our framework on the search quality.

4.1   Experimental Setup and Evaluation Measure

First we need a collection of queries that reflect various users' information needs and each kind of information need consists of a chain of specific queries for the purpose of experiments. Here we use the original queries collected by Shen et al. [20] as a seed set where those queries labelled by a same topic number are considered semantically related (30 topics and 146 queries in total). We use the topic number to represent one information need of a user. For example, there is a topic representing the information need of buying a surveillance equipment including queries of "bug", "bug spy", and "bug spy security", and the three queries within this topic are submitted search engines to get their initial search results. We then evaluate the retrieval performance of the proposed approaches in terms of relevant page precision. In a word, given *an information need* we evaluate the retrieval performance of different methods.

The top 100 search results of each query are retrieved from Google Directory Search, and the number of total returned search results is 12103 given 146 queries. Furthermore, we also obtained various topical category information of search results corresponding to each topic number (i.e. information need), which is provided by Google Directory Search. For evaluation we have to judge where a search results is relevant to its information need (represented by a topic number). Here an automatic judgment method is introduced rather than manually viewing each search result by human expert. It works as follows: we assume that one identified topical category with a maximal occurrence frequency among all the categories of these search results is the category indicative to this information need. Therefore, the search results exactly matching this topical category indicative will be considered as relevant ones. Therefore, in evaluation we can know the relevant Web pages of each topic number. A parameter in our automatic judgment method is the relevant result size. We set its lower bound to be M. In parameter study, if the number of search results matching the topical category indicative, is smaller than the lower bound, then the category with the second maximal occurrence frequency will be selected as the category indicative. This process continues, until the size reaches the lower bound.

Mean Average Precision (MAP) is an evaluation metric for evaluating ranking methods [15]. In our problem, our object is information need not query. Given an information need ID_i, its average precision (AP) is defined as:

$$AP_i@N = \frac{\sum_{j=1}^{N}(P@j * pos(j))}{\# \ of \ relevant \ Web \ pages \ in \ ID_i}, \tag{2}$$

where N, as an evaluation parameter, is the number of top Web pages evaluateded (e.g., 10), $P@j$ is the precision score of the returned search result at position j, and $pos(j)$ is a binary function to indicate whether the Web page at position j is relevant to ID_i. Then, we obtain MAP scores by using the average value of the AP values of all the evaluated information needs.

4.2   Results and Discussions

We did evaluations when M (relevant result size) varies from 10 to 40 with a step of 10. The experiment results are shown in Figure 2. *Google* is our baseline in which Google's MAP score averaged by all the related queries within a topic number is calculated. It is seen that the four random walk based methods, i.e. PW-1, PW-t, PWM-1 and PWM-t generally produce higher MAP scores than the baseline at different values of N and M. For example, when M=30, the improvements of these four methods at N=5 are 5.43%, 5.43%, 20.83%, 25.15%,

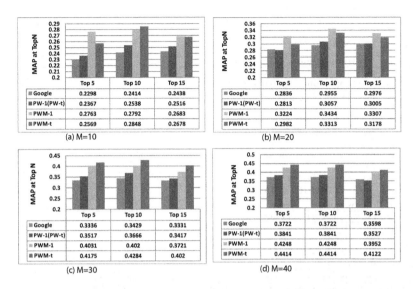

Fig. 2. MAP@5, 10, 15 when M varies from 10 to 40 with a step of 10

respectively. The experiment results validate the effectiveness and importance of making good use of the query collective to achieve the performance improvement. In other words, we conclude that the proposed rank aggregation algorithm can outperform the traditional search methods in terms of retrieval quality.

In addition, we want to identify which rank aggregation method is the most effective to retrieval quality. First, the pairwise majority contest based approaches (PWM) exhibit better results than the pairwise contest based approaches (PW). For example, when $M=10$ and $N=10$, PWM-1 and PWM-t outperform PW-t $(PW$-t) by 10.00% and 12.21% respectively. An interesting observation is that PW-1 and PW-t (two random walk models on pairwise contest with different iterations) have the same MAP scores in Figure 2. After checking the rank aggregation values, we found that although the values were different, the ordering produced by these values did not change. This means that more iterations (e.g. $t=40$) just give more convergence of values rather a new ordering. However, different iterations used by PWM-1 and PWM-t (two random walk models on pairwise majority contest) change both values and ordering.

We also compare PWM-1 with PWM-t. PWM-1 produces the highest MAP scores at $M=10$ and 20, while PWM-t shows best performance at $M=30$ and 40. M represents the number of relevant Web pages corresponding to an information need. When the information need is simple like finding a website with relative small size of answers, PWM-1 looks more effective than PWM-t in such cases. When the information need covers several aspects and the size of answers is relatively large, PWM-t seems more useful than PWM-1. In such cases, t iterative computation can further improve the search performance since t iterative computation has an effect on the coverage of the whole results by considering not only the number of wins that an item won, but also the quality

Table 2. Search results of individual queries and our search system

	Query 1: MOUSE
1.	**http://en.wikipedia.org/wiki/mouse** (Highly Relevant)
2.	http://en.wikipedia.org/wiki/computer_mouse
3.	http://www.apple.com/mightymouse/
4.	http://www.apple.com/keyboard/
5.	http://www.mousebreaker.com/
	Query 2: HOUSE MOUSE
1.	http://www.house-mouse.com/
2.	http://www.house-mouse.com/eeek-mail/
3.	http://psc.disney.go.com/abcnetworks/toondisney/shows/hom/
4.	http://psc.disney.go.com/abcnetworks/toondisney/games/pack_the_house/index.html
5.	**http://en.wikipedia.org/wiki/mus_musculus** (Highly Relevant)
	Query 3: HOUSE MOUSE BIOLOGY
1.	**http://www.pestproducts.com/mice.htm** (Highly Relevant)
2.	**http://www.pestproducts.com/rodents.htm** (Relevant)
3.	**http://en.wikipedia.org/wiki/mus_musculus**(Highly Relevant)
4.	http://www.ipm.ucdavis.edu/pmg/pestnotes/pn7483.html
5.	**http://doyourownpestcontrol.com/mice.htm**(Highly Relevant)
	Our search system
1.	**http://en.wikipedia.org/wiki/mus_musculus** (2,3) (Highly Relevant)
2.	**http://www.nsrl.ttu.edu/tmot1/mus_musc.htm** (2) (Highly Relevant)
3.	**http://www.house-mouse.com/** (2)
4.	**http://en.wikipedia.org/wiki/mouse** (1) (Highly Relevant)
5.	**http://animaldiversity.ummz.umich.edu/site/accounts/information /mus_musculus.html**(3) (Highly Relevant)

of its competitor items. From these results we can say that different retrieval mechanisms are appropriate for different kinds of information need for the high retrieval quality. This is consistent with the results given by Fujii at. [12] which first classified queries into informational and navigational ones and then used different retrieval models for the two kinds of queries.

4.3   Case Study

Here, we also present a case study of finding more relevant web pages via the proposed rank aggregation framework. Table 2 lists the top five search results corresponding to an information need which consists of three queries, i.e., **mouse**, house mouse, house mouse biology. The URLs of Web pages are given but the titles and snippets are omitted due to the space limit. The judgments are manually given by our analyst. The highly relevant and relevant pages are shown in bold fonts and the number in a round bracket following each URL denotes which queries retrieve this URL. The aggregation scores are calculated by $PWM\text{-}t$.

From Table 2, we observe that the number of highly relevant pages at the top five produced by our system is more than the initial query (mouse) issued by a user, and any recommended query (house mouse, house mouse biology). Moreover, our system covers broad search results derived from different queries, which increases the diversity of the fused search result list. For example, " http://www.nsrl.ttu.edu/tmot1/mus_musc.htm" comes from the query "house mouse"(query #2), one of search results of "http://en.wikipedia.org/wiki/mouse", is from the query "mouse" (query #1) and the query "house mouse biology" (query #3) includes "http://www.pestproducts.com/mice.htm". In contrast to current search engines which are able to efficiently retrieve results for a single query, thus, our system provides an alternative and useful way to produce more relevant Web pages by using parallel search strategy with related queries.

5   Related Work

Many rank aggregation methods have been proposed in the literature. They can be classified based on whether: 1) they rely on score (value) [16,19,21]; 2) they rely on rank (order) [1,10,13,17,27]; 3) they require training data or not [19]. The performance of some rank-based methods are comparable to score-based methods [19], which is useful in the context of Web search since scores are usually unavailable from search engines. Certainly, it is reasonable for us to guess the approximate relevance values, but this topic is out of the scope of this paper. In this paper, we propose a generic rank aggregation framework based random walk. Various representative rank aggregation methods can be applied in our framework, as listed in Table 1. This generic rank aggregation framework lays down the foundation for researchers to theoretically and empirically compare different rank aggregation methods them under a unified framework.

Metasearch is orthogonal to our work, which submits a query to several search engines to obtain several lists of search results. We assume that we could get useful search contexts from related queries and do searches on a search engine. On the other hand, query expansion is also an alternative to improve search quality [6,7,9,22]. Most query expansion techniques suggest terms used extracted from Web pages. However, some terms are difficult to be suggested because of their high document frequencies. Moreover, query expansion generates artificial queries while in this paper we focus on rank aggregation of search results can improve retrieval quality. Terms in related queries are actually input by previous users and reflect their search intents. Query expansion using related queries would be an interesting topic in our future work.

6   Conclusions and Future Work

In this paper, we studied how to utilize related Web queries to improve Web search. To find the effective method of rank aggregation, we proposed a generic rank aggregation framework which applies random walk on a novel Win/Loss graph as our rank mechanism. The proposed Win/Loss graph can utilize a variety of competition rules to determine its edge direction and weights. In addition, we discussed how some representative rank aggregation methods are integrated into our framework and empirically showed how different methods affect on the retrieval quality of our search system. Experimental results verify that our system is quite effective in facilitating users' locate relevant information. In the future, incorporating the title and content of a URL to our approach and differently weighting the edges in the Win/Loss graph are probably two interesting and promising topics.

References

1. Aslam, J.A., Montague, M.H.: Models for metasearch. In: Proc. of SIGIR, pp. 275–284 (2001)
2. Baeza-Yates, R.A., Hurtado, C.A., Mendoza, M.: Improving search engines by query clustering. JASIST 58(12), 1793–1804 (2007)
3. Beeferman, D., Berger, A.L.: Agglomerative clustering of a search engine query log. In: Proc. of KDD, pp. 407–416 (2000)
4. Bianchini, M., Gori, M., Scarselli, F.: Inside pagerank. ACM Trans. Interet Technol. 5(1), 92–128 (2005)
5. Borda, J.: Mémoire sur les élections au scrutin. Comptes rendus de l'Académie des sciences 44, 42–51 (1781)
6. Chirita, P.-A., Firan, C.S., Nejdl, W.: Personalized query expansion for the web. In: Proc. of SIGIR, pp. 7–14 (2007)
7. Collins-Thompson, K., Callan, J.: Query expansion using random walk models. In: Proc. of CIKM, pp. 704–711 (2005)
8. Copeland, A.: A reasonable social welfare function. Mimeo, University of Michigan (1951)
9. Cui, H., Wen, J.-R., Nie, J.-Y., Ma, W.-Y.: Query expansion by mining user logs. IEEE Trans. Knowl. Data Eng. 15(4), 829–839 (2003)
10. Dwork, C., Kumar, R., Naor, M., Sivakumar, D.: Rank aggregation methods for the web. In: Proc. of WWW, pp. 613–622 (2001)
11. Farah, M., Vanderpooten, D.: An outranking approach for rank aggregation in information retrieval. In: Proc. of SIGIR, pp. 591–598 (2007)
12. Fujii, A.: Modeling anchor text and classifying queries to enhance web document retrieval. In: Proceedings of WWW, pp. 337–346 (2008)
13. Lebanon, G., Lafferty, J.D.: Cranking: Combining rankings using conditional probability models on permutations. In: Proc. of ICML, pp. 363–370 (2002)
14. Li, L., Yang, Z., Liu, L., Kitsuregawa, M.: Query-url bipartite based approach to personalized query recommendation. In: Proc. of AAAI, pp. 1189–1194 (2008)
15. Manning, C.D., Raghavan, P., Schutze, H.: Introduction to Information Retrieval. Cambridge University Press, Cambridge (2008)
16. Montague, M.H., Aslam, J.A.: Relevance score normalization for metasearch. In: Proc. of CIKM, pp. 427–433 (2001)
17. Montague, M.H., Aslam, J.A.: Condorcet fusion for improved retrieval. In: Proc. of CIKM, pp. 538–548 (2002)
18. Page, L., Brin, S., Motwani, R., Winograd, T.: The pagerank citation ranking: Bringing order to the web. Technical report, Stanford Digital Library Technologies Project (1998)
19. Renda, M.E., Straccia, U.: Web metasearch: Rank vs. score based rank aggregation methods. In: Proc. of the 2003 ACM Symposium on Applied Computing (SAC 2003), pp. 841–846 (2003)
20. Shen, X., Tan, B., Zhai, C.: Context-sensitive information retrieval using implicit feedback. In: Proc. of SIGIR, pp. 43–50 (2005)
21. Shokouhi, M.: Segmentation of search engine results for effective data-fusion. In: Amati, G., Carpineto, C., Romano, G. (eds.) ECIR 2007. LNCS, vol. 4425, pp. 185–197. Springer, Heidelberg (2007)
22. Sun, R., Ong, C.-H., Chua, T.-S.: Mining dependency relations for query expansion in passage retrieval. In: Proc. of SIGIR, pp. 382–389 (2006)

23. Wen, J.-R., Nie, J.-Y., Zhang, H.: Query clustering using user logs. ACM Trans. Inf. Syst. 20(1), 59–81 (2002)
24. Yang, Z., Li, L., Kitsuregawa, M.: Efficient querying relaxed dominant relationship between product items based on rank aggregation. In: Proc. of AAAI, pp. 1261–1266 (2008)
25. Young, H.P.: Condorcet's theory of voting. American Political Science Review 82(4), 1231–1244 (1988)
26. Zhang, Z., Nasraoui, O.: Mining search engine query logs for query recommendation. In: Proc. of WWW, pp. 1039–1040 (2006)
27. Zhu, S., Fang, Q., Deng, X., Zheng, W.: Metasearch via voting. In: Liu, J., Cheung, Y.-m., Yin, H. (eds.) IDEAL 2003. LNCS, vol. 2690, pp. 734–741. Springer, Heidelberg (2003)

Extracting Structured Data from Web Pages with Maximum Entropy Segmental Markov Model

Susan Mengel and Yaoquin Jing

Texas Tech University, Computer Science,
Box 43104, Lubbock, TX
susan.mengel@ttu.edu, jing.andy@gmail.com

Abstract. Automated techniques can help to extract information from the Web. A new semi-automatic approach based on the maximum entropy segmental Markov model, therefore, is proposed to extract structured data from Web pages. It is motivated by two ideas: modeling sequences embedding structured data instead of their context to reduce the number of training Web pages and preventing the generation of too specific or too general models from the training data. The experimental results show that this approach has better performance than Stalker when only one training Web page is provided.

Keywords: HTML extraction, Markov Model.

1 Introduction

As part of the Semantic Web effort, finding a way to extract structured data from Web pages and integrating the data with uniform schemes would assist Web users with common tasks, such as searching and product comparisons. Because the source file of a Web page consists of a sequence of content, such as structured data and tags, the problem addressed in this paper can be defined as follows: given the source file of a Web page, find the subsequences which contain structured data, and then extract these data from the original Web page and from similar Web pages.

2 Approaches for Structured Data Extraction

The approaches for extracting structured data from Web pages can be classified into three categories: manual, semi-automatic, and automatic. As the manual approaches [1] need users to write extraction rules in the special rule languages after investigating the characteristics of the Web pages embedding structured data, they are time-intensive and error-prone. Therefore, researchers currently focus on the approaches belonging to the latter two categories. Semi-automatic approaches [2], [3], [4] adopt machine learning technologies, such as instance-based learning or inductive learning, to generate extraction rules based on the

G. Vossen, D.D.E. Long, and J.X. Yu (Eds.): WISE 2009, LNCS 5802, pp. 219–226, 2009.

provided training examples, which contain extracted structured data labeled by users. One limitation of these approaches is that their performance depends on the coverage of the training Web pages for a set of Web pages embedding similar structured data; the more training Web pages, the better performance of the approaches. However, more training Web pages means more work for users. The automatic approaches [5], [6], [7] are based on the assumption that the similar structured data are embedded with similar sequences of tags and content on Web pages. Hence, structured data can be automatically found by searching the similar subsequence of a Web page without the users involvement. One limitation of these approaches is that they only process the Web pages containing at least two similar structured data. In addition, unexpected structured data can be extracted by these approaches and users still need to post-process them.

Learning extraction rules also exists in developing general purpose information extraction systems for natural language text using Markov models [8], [9], [10]. The model presented in this paper is based on these models.

3 Extracting Structured Data Using a Maximum Entropy Segmental Markov Model

The new approach is based on the following two initial ideas: unlike other semi-automatic approaches based on the inductive learning paradigm, which generate extraction rules based on the context of structured data (or data items) of a Web page, it constructs a model to describe the sequence (instead of its context) of embedded structured data (or data items). Secondly, as the semi-automatic approaches based on the instance-based learning paradigm usually generate templates by combining differences among the training data, the learned templates may be too general or specific to extract structured data from similar Web pages correctly. The cause of this problem is that extra assumptions are made from training data. For example, one training data contains a distinct symbol not existing in other ones; a learned template containing this symbol makes an assumption that all sequences embedding similar structured data contain this symbol. This problem can be solved by enforcing a model only describes the characteristics of training data without extra assumptions. To satisfy the requirements of the above two ideas, a maximum entropy segmental Markov model approach is proposed to extract structured data from Web pages.

3.1 Maximum Entropy

The principle of maximum entropy [11] is a framework to estimate the distribution of data. Its underlying principle is that the best model for data is the one satisfying certain constraints derived from training data with the fewest possible assumptions. More explicitly, given a set of training data, the probability distribution p should be consistent with the known evidence or partial information and maximize the entropy

$$H(a) = -\sum_{x \in \epsilon} p(x) \log p(x) \tag{1}$$

where ϵ is the event space, such as all sequences of similar Web pages embedding similar structured data.

To apply the maximum entropy principle to estimate the distribution of data, a critical step is the representation of the facts (or evidences) about data. For example, how to represent the known fact that student names embedded on Web pages are enclosed with $< table >$ and $< /table >$ tags. In most applications, this fact is represented with a binary function $f_i : \epsilon \rightarrow \{0, 1\}$, called a feature (function). For example, the feature function $f_{<table>}(x)$ denotes a sequence enclosed by the $< table >$ and $< /table >$ tags.

3.2 MESMM

To establish an maximum entropy segmental Markov model (MESMM) for sequences embedding structured data, users are asked to highlight one structured data on a Web page. The approach then automatically generates training data, which are used to generate a segmental Markov model (SMM). For each state in the SMM, feature functions are generated based on its training data. At the same time, the generalized iterative scaling (GIS) procedure [12] is used to learn the state transition distribution based on the maximum entropy principle. When a query Web page is submitted, the approach first determines if this Web page is similar to the training Web pages based on their Kullback-Leibler distance. If the Web page is similar, the corresponding MESMM model is applied to find the sequences embedding structured data and their optimal segmentations with the inference algorithm. If the query Web page is not similar to any model's training Web pages, users are required to highlight structured data and a new model is generated accordingly.

The maximum entropy segmental Markov model (MESMM) has a segment of observations instead of one observation for each state. Fig. 1 illustrates the graphical structure of the MESMM, where K is the length of a state sequence except s_0, which denotes a "start" state, and $1 \leq K \leq T$.

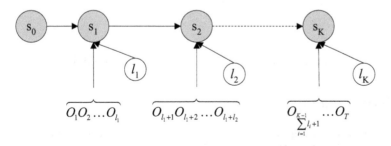

Fig. 1. The graphical structure of the MESMM

The pseudocode of the inference algorithm is shown in Figure 2 and is similar to the Viterbi algorithm [13], but differs in that it also stores the length of the current observation segment. The algorithm first creates two matrices, δ and φ, with the size $T \times |M|$ (lines 2-3), where T is the length of an observation sequence and $|M|$ is the number of distinct states in the MESMM. Note that each state is indexed with a number between zero and $|M| - 1$. Furthermore, the "start" state is assigned with the index zero. bGiven a position t in an observation sequence, the algorithm finds the maximal value of δ_t for each possible current state by enumerating segments with the length from one to t (lines 13-29). This step runs iteratively for each position in the sequence. The time complexity of this algorithm is $O(|M|^2 T^2)$ and the space complexity is $O(|M|T)$. Further details of the operation of the MESMM may be found in [14].

Algorithm OptimalSegmentation (In: O, Q; Out: φ)
// O is an observation sequence; Q is the MESMM. φ is the matrix storing related values.
{
1.   T=O's length;
// $|M|$ the number of distinct states in Q.
2.   Create the matrix δ with the size $T \times |M|$;
3.   Create the matrix φ with the size $T \times |M|$;
// A "start" state is indexed with '0'.
4-6. $\delta[0,0] = 1$; $\varphi[0,0].Length = 0$; $\varphi[0,0].Prev = 0$;
7.   For $i = 0$ To $|M| + 1$
8-10. $\delta[0,i] = 0$; $\varphi[0,i].Length = 0$; $\varphi[0,i].Prev = 0$;
11.   EndFor
12.   For $t = 1$ To T
13.   For $i = 1$ To $|M|$
14. $v = 0$; //store the maximum probability;
15. $s = 0$; //store the previous state;
16. $n = 0$; //store the length of a segment;
17.   For $n = i$ To 1
18.   For $j = 1$ To $|M|$
19.   If $\delta[t - l, j] \times p(s = i|s' = j, O_{t-l+1}O_{t-2+2} \ldots O_t) > v$ then
20-22. $v = \delta[t - l, j] \times p(s = i|s' = j, O_{t-l+1}O_{t-2+2} \ldots O_t)$; $s = j$; $n = l$;
23.   EndIf
24.   EndFor
25.   EndFor
26-28. $\delta[t, i] = v$; $\varphi[t, i].Length = n$; $\varphi[t, i].Prev = s$;
29.   EndFor
30.   EndFor
}

Fig. 2. The inference algorithm for the MESMM

4   Experiments

One critical issue in designing experiments is to choose an appropriate approach to compare with the MESMM approach. The semi-automatic approaches definitely have better performance than the manual or automatic approaches, so it is meaningless to select a manual or automatic approach to be compared with the MESMM approach. Among all semi-automatic approaches, Stalker has the best performance and its idea has been adopted by the commercial product, Fetch [15]. Hence, Stalker is selected to be compared with the MESMM approach on performance.

Another issue is the collection of experimental data. As no standard experimental data is available in this field, each approach constructs its data by directly selecting Web pages on the Internet. To avoid the bias of some special Web pages on performance, experimental data is constructed by selecting Web pages from those Web sites used in published papers. There are two requirements on selecting Web sites. One is that a Web site still exists on the Internet; another is that the MESMM approach requires at least two similar Web pages, one for learning and another for extracting, to evaluate its performance.

The principal goal of the MESMM approach is to keep the high accuracy with fewer training web pages. To achieve this goal, the experiment is performed in the following way: for each web site, one web page is selected as the training example, which is used to generate the MESMM model and to learn the corresponding state transition distributions. Then, the model is used to extract structured data from the remaining similar web pages.

4.1 Evaluation Metric

Three types of errors exist for an approach to extract structured data from a web page. The first type, denoted as m, is missed expected data items; the second type, denoted as w, is wrong expected data items; the third type, denoted as e, is extra (or unexpected) data items (note that errors are represented with data items instead of structured data). Based on three types of errors, a metric, error rate, is proposed to measure the performance of an approach extracting structured data from a Web page.

$$r = \frac{n_u}{N_E} \qquad (2)$$

where N_e is the number of expected data items to be extracted from a Web page; n_u is the number of erroneous items extracted from a Web page and $n_u = m + w + e$. Besides the error rate, another metric is the precision of an approach which may be derived as one minus the error rate.

4.2 Results

The experimental results are listed in Tab. 1. While more pages were used (30 Web sites each with 4 or 5 similar pages), due to space limitations, the data shown includes all Web pages where the MESMM approach had errors or where Stalker had an average error of .5 or above. Most of the Web pages had four to 20 pieces of structured data each with 2 or 3 items (www.ubids.com had upwards of 662 pieces of structured data). The MH column indicates the approach utilized to extract structured data from Web pages, where the Stalker and the MESMM approaches are denoted with S and M, respectively. The error rate is calculated according to Eq. 2. The average error rate of a Web site is calculated based on the error rates of its similar Web pages. From the table below, the overall average error rate for Stalker is 0.64 (0.37 with all 30 Websites) and for the MESMM, 0.14 (0.08 with all 30 Websites).

The performance difference between Stalker and the MESMM approach can be justified by investigating their underlying mechanisms. Stalker uses context symbols to discover the boundaries of sequences embedding structured data or data items. The MESMM approach, however, takes sequences themselves to determine if they embed expected structured data. This way is consistent with the basic assumption on extraction systems that similar structured data are embedded on similar sequences. Secondly, Stalker chooses common symbols occurring in the contexts of embedding sequences to locate structured data. However, it is very difficult to find those common symbols with fewer training examples. In this situation, Stalker would consider the symbols specific to the training web page as common symbols. As a result, the generated extraction rules are too specific to extract structured data from similar web pages. In the MESMM approach,

Table 1. Experimental Result Error

Website	MH	Page 1	Page 2	Page 3	Page 4	Avg
www.asiatravel.com	S	0.0	0.0	0.0	0.0	0.0
	M	1.0	1.0	1.0	1.0	1.0
www.barnesnoble.com	S	1.0	1.0	1.0	1.0	1.0
	M	0.0	0.0	0.0	0.0	0.0
www.bestbuy.com	S	0.11	0.38	0.89	0.78	0.54
	M	0.01	0.02	0.11	0.0	0.04
www.borders.com	S	0.5	0.67	0.57	0.57	0.58
	M	0.0	0.0	0.0	0.0	0.0
www.compusa.com	S	0.97	0.93	0.93	0.88	0.93
	M	0.0	0.0	0.0	0.0	0.0
www.coolhits.com	S	0.0	0.0	1.0	1.0	0.5
	M	0.0	0.0	0.0	0.0	0.0
www.epicurious.com	S	1.0	1.0	0.25	1.0	0.81
	M	0.0	1.0	0.0	0.5	0.38
www.etoys.com	S	1.0	1.0	1.0	1.0	1.0
	M	0.0	0.0	0.0	0.0	0.0
www.flipdog.com	S	0.0	1.0	0.0	0.05	0.26
	M	0.0	0.0	0.0	0.0	0.0
www.grijins.com	S	1.0	1.0	1.0	1.0	1.0
	M	0.0	0.0	0.0	0.0	0.0
www.newegg.com	S	1.0	1.0	1.0	1.0	1.0
	M	0.0	0.0	0.0	0.0	0.0
www.overstock.com	S	0.07	0.0	0.08	1.0	0.29
	M	0.0	0.0	0.0	1.0	0.25
www.qualityinks.com	S	0.0	0.0	0.0	0.0	0.0
	M	0.0	1.0	0.0	0.0	0.25
www.radioshark.com	S	0.33	0.38	0.38	1.0	0.52
	M	0.0	0.0	0.0	1.0	0.25
www.scistore.cambridgesoft.com	S	0.75	0.74	0.74	74.0	0.74
	M	0.0	0.0	0.0	0.0	0.0
www.ubids.com	S	1.0	1.0	1.0	1.0	1.0
	M	0.02	0.12	0.07	0.06	0.07

the model takes all features of an embedding sequence into account. Since most of features of similar sequences are approximately identical, specific features of the training web page have minor impact on determining the similarity of a sequence.

One weakness of the MESMM approach compared with Stalker is the time complexity of its inference algorithm. Given a sequence with the length n, Stalker takes almost linear time $O(n)$ to locate a subsequence with extraction rules. However, the MESMM approach takes $O(Cn^2)$ time to determine if a sequence is similar, where C is the number of states of the model.

5   Conclusions and Future Work

The primary contribution of this paper is a new semi-automatic approach for extracting structured data from Web pages, which maintains good performance with fewer training Web pages. The experimental results demonstrate that this approach has far better performance than Stalker when there is only one training Web page. However, there still exists room to improve the MESMM approach and extend its application. The improvement to the inference algorithm becomes very crucial when the approach is applied to process very long sequences. One solution is that the inference algorithm takes a chunk of contiguous symbols with the same state instead of taking each single symbol one time at a time. For example, if a tag node is assigned with a state, all its sub-nodes are assigned with the same state. The current implementation of the MESMM approach needs to be extended to process Web pages where data items from structured data are interleaved.

References

1. Feldman, R., Aumann, Y., Finkelstein-Landau, M., Hurvitz, E., Regev, Y., Yaroshevich, A.: A Comparative Study of Information Extraction Strategies. In: Gelbukh, A. (ed.) CICLing 2002. LNCS, vol. 2276, pp. 349–359. Springer, Heidelberg (2002)
2. Chang, C.-H., Kuo, S.-C.: OLERA: Semisupervised Web Data Extracion with Visual Support. IEEE Intelligent Systems 4(6), 56–64 (2004)
3. Zhai, Y., Liu, B.: Extracting Web Data Using Instance-Based Learning. In: Proceedings of 6th International Conference on Web Information System Engineering (2005)
4. Hogue, A., Karger, D.: Thresher: Automating the Unwrapping of Semantic Content from the World Wide Web (2005)
5. Lemma, K., Getoor, L., Minton, S., Knoblock, C.: Using the Structure of Web Sites for Automatic Segmentation of Tables. In: Proceedings of the 2004 ACM SIGMOD International Conference on Management of data, pp. 119–130 (2004)
6. Zhai, Y., Liu, B.: Web Data Extraction Based on Partial Tree alignment. In: Proceedings of the 14th International World Wide Web in Chiba, Japan (2005)
7. Liu, B., Zhai, Y.: NET- A System for Extracting Web Data from Flat and Nested Data Records. In: Proceedings of 6th International Conference on Web Information Systems Engineering (2005)

8. Rabiner, L.R.: A Tutorial on Hidden Markov Models and Selected Applications in Speech Recognition. Proceedings of the IEEE 77(2), 257–285 (1989)
9. McCallum, A., Freitag, D., Pereira, F.: Maximum Entropy Markov Models for Information Extraction and Segmentation. In: Proceedings ICML 2000, pp. 591–598 (2000)
10. Ge, X.: Segemental Semi-Markov Models and Applications to Sequence Analysis. PhD. Thesis, University of California, Irvine (2002)
11. Good, I.J.: Maximum Entropy for Hypothesis Formulation, Especially for Multidimensional Contingency Tables. The Annals of Mathematical Statistics 34, 911–934 (1963)
12. Darroch, J.N., Ratcliff, D.: Generalized Iterative Scaling for Log-Linear Models. The Annals of Mathematical Statistics 43(5), 1470–1480 (1972)
13. Viterbi, A.J.: Error Bounds for Convolutional Codes and an Asymptotically Optimal Decoding Algorithm. IEEE Transactions on Information Theory IT-13, 260–269 (1967)
14. Jing, Y.: Extracting Structured Data from Web Pages with Maximum Entropy Segmental Markov Models. Texas Tech University, Computer Science, Doctoral Dissertation (2007)
15. Fetch Technologies, Inc. (2009), http://www.fetch.com

Blog Ranking Based on Bloggers' Knowledge Level for Providing Credible Information

Shinsuke Nakajima[1], Jianwei Zhang[1], Yoichi Inagaki[2], Tomoaki Kusano[2], and Reyn Nakamoto[2]

[1] Kyoto Sangyo University
nakajima@cse.kyoto-su.ac.jp, zjw@cc.kyoto-su.ac.jp
[2] kizasi Company, Inc
{inagaki, kusano, reyn}@kizasi.jp

Abstract. With the huge increase of recently popular user-generated content on the Web, searching for credible information has become progressively difficult. In this paper, we focus on blogs, one kind of user-generated content, and propose a credibility-focused blog ranking method based on bloggers' knowledge level. This method calculates knowledge scores for bloggers and ranks blog entries based on bloggers' knowledge level. Bloggers' knowledge level is evaluated based on their usage of domain-specific words in their past blog entries. A blogger is given multiple scores with respect to various topic areas. In our method, blog entries written by knowledgeable bloggers have higher rankings than those written by common bloggers. Additionally, our system can present multiple ranking lists of blog entries from the perspectives of different bloggers' groups. This allows users to estimate the trustworthiness of blog contents from multiple aspects. We built a prototype of the proposed system, and our experimental evaluation showed that our method could effectively rank bloggers and blog entries.

1 Introduction

Recently, user-generated content websites such as blogs and social networking services have become established as popular online pastimes. Being user-generated, the amount of data created and subsequently available on the Web has grown exponentially. This, combined with the widely varying quality of user-generated content, makes it increasingly difficult to find credible information. When searching for information on the Web, a user usually makes use of a search engine such as Google. Google's PageRank algorithm [1] does an excellent job of reflecting the general popularity and authority of Web pages. However, traditional search engines do not fare as well with user-generated content due to their differing information characteristics. Particularly, user-generated content is rapidly and frequently updated, thus not effectively evaluated by PageRank, which relies heavily on incoming links. Credibility-focused search and ranking methods for user-generated content are strongly required.

In this paper, we specifically focus on blogs. In this area, there exist several blog-specific search and ranking engines today. These engines usually take one of

G. Vossen, D.D.E. Long, and J.X. Yu (Eds.): WISE 2009, LNCS 5802, pp. 227–234, 2009.

two approaches: (1) ranking the individual entries, (2) ranking the entire blogs as a whole. Approach 1 often uses a keyword-based search and then sorts the results by the entries' post date. Google Blog Search [2] belongs to this type. However, this type of blog search engine does not effectively assess the entry contents, which lowers the credibility of the results. Approach 2 usually uses some combination of link count, access count, as well as voting. Technorati [3] is such a search engine. Although it can find relevant bloggers based on their entry history, it does not guarantee that the latest relevant entries will be returned due to their site-based ranking. Given that blog contents are heavily focused on the latest happenings, this is an unfortunate drawback.

We propose a credibility-focused blog ranking method based on bloggers' knowledge level. Our method assumes that a person who has high knowledge of a certain topic is more credible than a person with a low level of knowledge. Figure 1 shows the relationship between a knowledgeable person and credible information. By analyzing bloggers' past entries and ranking bloggers by their knowledge level, we can provide more credible blog entries to the end user.

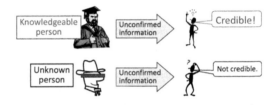

Fig. 1. Relationship between knowledgeable people and credible information

In our method, we first extract topic areas and create a term dictionary which provides domain-specific words for each of these topic areas. We then evaluate a blogger's knowledge level based on the blogger's usage frequency of these domain-specific words. Generally, a blogger's knowledge level varies with respect to different topic areas. A person may be an expert in one field, while (s)he may know little to nothing about another field. For example, a blogger who is familiar with automobiles may lack the basic knowledge on computers. Thus, in our research, a blogger's knowledge scores are calculated for multiple topics. We next rank blog entries based on their bloggers' knowledge scores. Blog entries written by knowledgeable bloggers are highly ranked. In addition, given search keywords, our method can provide multiple ranking lists of blog entries from the perspectives of different bloggers' groups. For example, when a user searches for the "Java" information, our system presents multiple ranking lists from the different aspects, such as "programming", "education", and "examination". Thus, our system is very helpful for users to find credible information by presenting a varied set of topic rankings and highly ranking blog entries written by knowledgeable bloggers.

2   Related Work

Recently, the number of blog search websites, such as Google Blog Search [2] and Technorati [3], has increased with the spread of Web 2.0. These blog search engines index blogs and provide ever useful search functions. These commercial services maintain our motivation on the research of blog ranking.

There is much ongoing academic research into blog search and ranking methods. Fujimura et al. [4] proposed an algorithm for ranking blog entries by weighting the hub and authority scores of a blogger. Kritikopoulos et al. [5] presented a method for ranking blog entries based on a link graph consisting of explicit links and implicit links. Both of these methods focus mainly on link analysis, while our method ranks bloggers and blog entries based on blogs' contents. Links between blog entries are helpful to further improve our blog ranking system, and effective use of this kind of information is a future direction of our current research.

In terms of credibility and trust related research, Gil et al. [6] introduced several factors that users should consider when deciding whether to trust Web contents or not. Adler et al. [7] presented a content-driven reputation system for Wikipedia which could extract authors with a high reputation. Andersen et al. [8] provided a trust-based recommendation system by making use of social network structures. Our work focuses on another type of Web resources, blogs. Our method can identify credible bloggers by analyzing their past blog entries, and subsequently find credible blog entries.

3   Estimating Bloggers' Knowledge Level

In this section, we explain how we estimate a blogger's knowledge level. It is divided into three main parts:

1. Constructing a dictionary of "Knowledgeable Bloggers' Groups (KBGs)", representing topic areas and their domain-specific words.
2. Identifying "Knowledgeable Bloggers (KBs)" for each KBG, assigning bloggers to their relevant topic areas.
3. Calculating KBs' knowledge scores for his/her KBG.

3.1   Constructing a Dictionary of KBGs

Generally, bloggers have their specific interests and post blog entries related to specific topic areas. We call a blogger who is familiar with a topic area as a "Knowledgeable Blogger (KB)" for this topic area. A set of knowledgeable bloggers for a topic area is marked as a "Knowledgeable Bloggers' Group (KBG)" for this topic area. We first extract some keywords representing the topic areas daily discussed in blogs. Each keyword becomes the title of the topic area, and also represents the name of the KBG familiar with the topic area. We then extract frequently used words for each topic area, and create a dictionary, which summarizes the topic areas and their domain-specific words. The detailed process of constructing a dictionary is shown as follows:

1. We perform a regular Web search by using the search keywords such as "expert", "fan", and "mania", and extract the keywords which occur before and after these search keywords.
2. The keywords with occurrence frequency below a certain threshold are filtered.
3. We browse the keywords with occurrence frequency above the threshold, and remove duplicate and inappropriate ones. The remaining keywords are appended to the dictionary as the selected topic areas. In our current implemented system, about 14,000 keywords are registered on the dictionary.
4. For each keyword (i.e., the title of each extracted topic area), we extract the top n words which have high co-occurrence frequency with it from a large blog entry corpus. Specifically, n is 400 in our current system. These words which are domain-specific for their corresponding topic areas are also registered on the dictionary.

Figure 2 is an example of the dictionary. The column g shows the titles of the extracted topic areas (i.e., KBGs' names). Each row shows each topic area's domain-specific words and their corresponding co-occurrence frequency β. For example, the keyword "computer" is extracted as the representative title of the "computer" topic. It is also the name of the KBG who has high level of knowledge related to the "computer" topic. This topic area has its domain-specific words, such as "windows", "desktop" and "company". Additionally, the dictionary is re-constructed periodically, since blog entries are frequently updated and the words co-occurring with a topic vary with respect to time.

g	$j = 1$		2		...		400	
computer	windows	$\beta_{1,1}$	desktop	$\beta_{1,2}$	...	...	company	$\beta_{1,400}$
Obama	president	$\beta_{2,1}$	crisis	$\beta_{2,2}$	...	...	white	$\beta_{2,400}$
⋮	⋮	⋮	⋮	⋮	⋮	⋮	⋮	⋮

Fig. 2. Dictionary of KBGs

3.2   Identifying KBs for Each KBG

For the purpose of finding the relevant set of bloggers for each topic area, we next assign bloggers to their relevant topic areas. It is possible that a blogger is assigned to more than one KBGs. We regard a blogger who continues writing blog entries related to a topic area as a KB of this KBG. We list up several conditions by which it is decided that whether a blogger should be assigned to a KBG. These conditions focus on two aspects: the number of bloggers' entries containing the title of the topic area or its domain-specific words, and the period in which bloggers continue writing such entries. An example is "the blogger is identified as a KB of a KBG, if (s)he wrote twenty or more entries containing domain-specific words related to the KBG over a three month period".

3.3   Calculating KBs' Knowledge Scores for the KBG

We now calculate KBs' knowledge scores, which indicates how knowledgeable a KB is for a topic. Basically, scores are calculated based on how often as well as how in-depth a blogger writes blog entries related to a certain topic. If a blogger has an extensive use of the domain-specific words of a topic, high knowledge scores are attached to the blogger.

We first calculate $score_g(e)$, the score of an individual entry e with respect to the topic g as follows:

$$score_g(e) = \sum_{j=1}^{n} \alpha_j \cdot \beta_j \cdot \gamma_j \tag{1}$$

where $n = 400$ is the number of the domain-specific words, $\alpha_j = \frac{n-j}{n}$ is the weight of word j which decreases as j increases, β_j is the co-occurence frequency of word j, and γ_j is a binary value which indicates whether entry e contains word j or not.

Once we have the individual entries' scores, we next calculate $score_g(b)$, the score of a blogger b with respect to the topic g:

$$score_g(b) = \frac{l}{n} \cdot \frac{log(m)}{m} \cdot \sum_{i=1}^{m} score_g(e_i) \tag{2}$$

where e_i is an entry which blogger b wrote, m is the number of entries which blogger b has posted within a given period, $n = 400$ is the number of the domain-specific words, and l is the number of the domain-specific words which occurred in all the entries written by blogger b. $\frac{l}{n}$ indicates the coverage ratio of the domain-specific words which blogger b has used. $\frac{log(m)}{m}$ reduces the effect that a blogger frequently writes a large amount of entries, but most of them are unrelated entries.

4   Ranking Blog Entries Based on Bloggers' Knowledge Level

We now explain the process of blog search and ranking. When an end user enters one or more search keywords, our system does the following steps:

1. Blog entries which contain the search keywords are retrieved. These entries will be grouped and ranked by our system.
2. The system then identifies the bloggers of these entries, and finds the KBGs which the bloggers belong to. As mentioned before, a blogger may belong to multiple KBGs.
3. The KBGs are sorted in the descending order by the numbers of bloggers in each group.
4. Blog entries retrieved by Step 1 are assigned to the corresponding KBGs, according to the affiliation of their bloggers. Since a blogger may belong to multiple KBGs, it is possible that a blog entry is grouped to multiple KBGs.

5. For a KBG, the entries in this group are ranked in the descending order by
   the knowledge scores of their bloggers. That is to say, the entries written by
   bloggers with high knowledge scores are given higher rankings than those
   written by bloggers with low knowledge scores.

We built a prototype of blog search engine [9] based on the previously described
method. The beta version of this system was released in September, 2008. As
of April 20, 2009, our system contains about 174,000,000 blog entries collected
from about 7,422,000 bloggers. The number of KBGs is about 14,000 and the
number of KBs for all the KBGs is about 100,000.

Figure 3 is a snapshot of the implemented system prototype. The KBGs are
presented in the left part of Figure 3. The end user can freely select the topic they
are interested in, and then the entries in this group are presented in the right
part of Figure 3. In this way, various aspects from different ranking lists can be
provided to the end user. The user can then browse the entries from the aspects
they are concerned about. Thus, the user can better acquire knowledge, since
entries are organized by different perspectives and more credible information is
highly ranked.

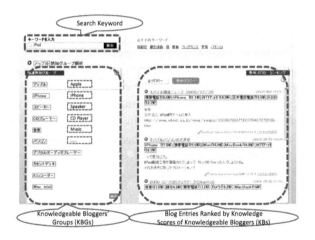

Fig. 3. A snapshot of the system prototype

5 Experiments

We randomly selected 20 search keywords, and four individuals were asked to
evaluate our implemented system about the precision of KBG, KB, and blog
entries.

5.1 KBG's Precision

Given a search keyword, our system returned some KBGs. Each individual
checked the top 5 KBGs and decided whether the name of each KBG was related

to the search keyword. The precision is the ratio of the number of relative ones
to all the top 5 KBGs. Figure 4 shows the results. k represents a search keyword,
each bar for $k1$ to $k20$ is the precision average of four individuals for each search
keyword, and the bar for $ave20$ is the precision average of 20 search keywords.
The fact that the precision is about 1 indicates that most of the KBGs returned
by our system are related to the corresponding search keywords.

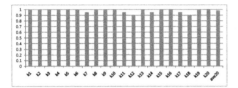
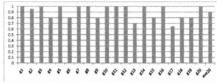

Fig. 4. KBG's precision   **Fig. 5.** KB's precision

5.2   KB's Precision

The four individuals were also asked to evaluate KBs. We selected the top KBG
for each of 20 search keywords, and subsequently acquired 20 KBGs. For each
KBG, the top 5 bloggers were evaluated by each individual. The individual
browsed bloggers' entries and judged whether they were appropriate as a KB
with respect to the KBG in question. The precision is the ratio of the number
of appropriate KBs in all the top 5 bloggers. The results are shown in Figure 5.
The average precision of 0.91 indicates most of the bloggers highly ranked by
our method are exactly knowledgeable.

5.3   Blog Entries' Precision

For a search keyword and a KBG, the top 5 blog entries in the ranking list of
each KBG were browsed by the four individuals. If a blog entry was related to
the search keyword and KBG in question, and also regarded as credible, it was
marked as appropriate. The precision is the ratio of the number of appropriate
ones to the top blog entries. Figure 6 shows the precision considering the top 3
KBGs. In this case, for a search keyword, 15 entries (5 entries in each of 3 KBGs)
were evaluated. Figure 7 shows the precision in the case that the 25 entries in
the top 5 KBGs were evaluated. The average precision is about 75% and 67%,
which are high in the field of blog search. This indicates that our method can
extract related and credible entries.

6   Conclusions and Future Work

We proposed a credibilty-focused blog ranking method based on bloggers' knowledge level. The results of this study include: (1) a relationship between knowledgeable people and credible information, (2) a method for estimating bloggers'

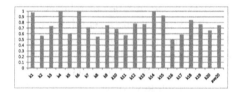 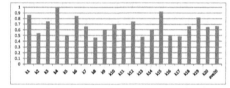

Fig. 6. Blog entries' precision for the top 3 KBGs

Fig. 7. Blog entries' precision for the top 5 KBGs

knowledge level based on their usage of domain-specific words in his or her past blog entries, (3) a prototype system of blog ranking based on bloggers' knowledge scores, which can provide multiple ranking lists for various topic areas.

In future work, we plan to improve our system by developing more powerful methods for filtering spam, further improving the method for calculating bloggers' knowledge scores, and investigating more aspects for providing information with high credibility.

Acknowledgments

This work was supported in part by the National Institute of Information and Communications Technology, and MEXT (Grant-in-Aid for Young Scientists (B) #20700089).

References

1. Brin, S., Page, L.: The Anatomy of a Large-Scale Hypertextual Web Search Engine. Computer Networks 30(1-7), 107–117 (1998)
2. Google Blog Search, `http://blogsearch.google.co.jp/`
3. Technorati, `http://www.technorati.jp/`
4. Fujimura, K., Inoue, T., Sugisaki, M.: The EigenRumor Alogorithm for Ranking Blogs. In: WWW 2005 2nd Annual Workshop on the Weblogging Ecosystem: Aggregation, Analysis and Dynamics (2005)
5. Kritikopoulos, A., Sideri, M., Varlamis, I.: BlogRank: Ranking Weblogs Based on Connectivity and Similarity Features. In: AAA-IDEA (2006)
6. Gil, Y., Artz, D.: Towards Content Trust of Web Resources. In: WWW, pp. 565–574 (2006)
7. Thomas Adler, B., de Alfaro, L.: A Content-driven Reputation System for the Wikipedia. In: WWW, pp. 261–270 (2007)
8. Andersen, R., Borgs, C., Chayes, J.T., Feige, U., Flaxman, A.D., Kalai, A., Mirrokni, V.S., Tennenholtz, M.: Trust-based Recommendation Systems: An Axiomatic Approach. In: WWW, pp. 199–208 (2008)
9. Kizasi Blog Search, `http://kizasi.jp/labo/fansearch/index.py`

Multi-source Remote Sensing Images Data Integration and Sharing Using Agent Service

Binge Cui[1], Xin Chen[1], Pingjian Song[2], and Rongjie Liu[2]

[1] College of Information Science and Engineering, Shandong University of Science and Technology, 266510Qingdao, China
`cuibinge@yahoo.com.cn`
[2] First Institute of Oceanography, S.O.A. Xianxialing Road 6#, 266510 Qingdao, China

Abstract. Remote sensing images have been utilized fully in disaster detection and other domains. However, many researchers cannot find and access the appropriate remote sensing images as they needed. In this paper, we proposed an effective approach to integrate and share the image resources over the Web. Firstly, the image metadata are exposed based on Grid services and the standard metadata specification; secondly, Agent service is introduced to discover and invoke the metadata services dynamically; thirdly, researchers can query and browse or locate the remote sensing images through the service interface. We have developed a service-oriented remote sensing images integration platform, which supports the parallel query and browse of multi-source remote sensing images. Moreover, it can provide better availability and extensibility.

Keywords: Remote Sensing Images, Data Integration, Resource Sharing, Grid Service, Agent Service.

1 Introduction

Satellite remote sensing technologies are developed rapidly in recent years. Remote sensing images have four basic characteristics: large-area, quasi-synchronous, multi-temporal and low-cost. Due to such benefits, remote sensing images have been utilized extensively in disaster detection, meteorological prediction, resources investigation, environment protection [1]. Remote sensing images are usually stored and managed by different departments, which is difficult for researchers to access or to acquire them [2]. In order to promote the research in ocean sciences, it is urgent for us to integrate and share the remote sensing images over the Web [3].

Remote sensing image metadata describe the important characteristics of image files, such as the longitude and latitude, coordinate system, projection method, sensor mode, orbit number [4]. All metadata are extracted from the image files or header file. Based on the image metadata, users can determine whether the remote sensing images satisfy their requirements. If we can integrate the image metadata distributed in different departments and share them, then researches will know where the remote sensing images that they needed are located. If users have the access privileges, they can even download the image files from the corresponding stations.

G. Vossen, D.D.E. Long, and J.X. Yu (Eds.): WISE 2009, LNCS 5802, pp. 235–246, 2009.

In this paper, we proposed an approach to integrate and share the remote sensing images over the Web. The image providers extract and store the image metadata into the metadata repository using the Metadata Extracting and Archiving service. And then, the image metadata are exposed using the Metadata Retrieving service. In order to eliminate the semantic conflicts of the images metadata among different stations, we have defined a standard metadata specification. Each Grid service should be published in the service community. In order to enable researches to access multiple remote sensing images stations simultaneously, we have designed an Agent service to take over users' queries and invoke the corresponding Grid services. All remote sensing images and metadata are stored in the local servers of each department, which assures full security for the remote sensing images. We developed a platform for the integration of remote sensing images.

The rest of this paper is organized as follows. Section 2 introduces the conceptual model for remote sensing images integration. Section 3 describes the Metadata Retrieving service as well as the standard metadata specification. Section 4 introduces the Agent service to discover and invoke all deployed Metadata Retrieving services dynamically. Section 5 describes the architecture for the remote sensing images integration platform. Section 6 discusses related work. Finally, the conclusion is given in Section 7.

2   Conceptual Model for Remote Sensing Images Integration

Metadata integration and sharing is the foundation and precondition of the remote sensing images integration. In this paper, we proposed a novel conceptual model for metadata integration and servicing as shown in Figure 1.

In Figure 1, the conceptual model is comprised of five modules:

1. Resource Providers: Each department owns and manages a lot of remote sensing data, including image files, metadata and micro-images. Among them the image files are acquired from some toll stations or network, metadata are extracted or computed from image files, micro-images are made by researchers manually based on the remote sensing images.
2. Metadata Processing Services: These services are deployed on the local application server of each department. Among them Retrieving service retrieves image metadata according to users' queries, Extracting service extracts image metadata from the header files, and Archiving service stores the metadata into the metadata repository. Other services include Metadata Management service, Cloud Cover Computing service, etc.
3. Redirecting Services: Agent service acts as an agent between users (or administrators) and the individual Grid services. For example, users want to query the remote sensing images within a certain zone. When Agent service receives such a request, it will search all available Retrieving services by referring to the service community, and invoking them to return the image metadata. For Extracting service and Archiving service, their WSDL (Web Service Description Language) are discovered and bound dynamically according to the locations of administrators.

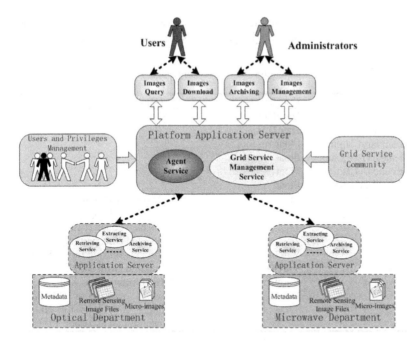

Fig. 1. Conceptual Model for Metadata and Images Integration

4. Grid Service Community: It will answer for the description, organization, storage and management of Grid services. Currently, we use a datasheet to store the registration information of all services. The service community is accessed through the Grid Service Management service.

5. Users and Privileges Management: The system users are classified into four roles: platform administrator, data administrators, registered users and public users. Here, platform administrator is in charge of the registration and management of users and data administrators, as well as the performance monitor of the integration platform. Data administers answer for the archiving and management of remote sensing data, the registration of Grid services, and the access privileges control. Registered users can query and browse the image metadata and micro-images. Moreover, they can download the authorized remote sensing images. Public users can only query and browse the limited image metadata and micro-images.

3   Metadata Retrieving Service and Metadata Specification

Remote sensing images can be queried through the common query interface of the integration platform. However, some users want to search the remote sensing images by specifying the range of longitudes and latitudes; others want to specify the location using paths and rows. Moreover, users want to query the metadata for multiple satellites and sensors at one time, and they want to specify different parameter sets for each satellite or sensor. To meet the above requirements, we defined two search operations with extensible parameters based on XML schema. One operation is "MetadataSearchByLL", and its input parameters are shown in Table 1.

Table 1. Input Parameters for the Service Operation "MetadataSearchByLL"

Parameter Name	Date Type	Comment
StartDateTime	DateTime	
EndDateTime	DateTime	
WestBoundaryLongitude	Float	
EastBoundaryLongitude	Float	
NorthBoundaryLatitude	Float	
SouthBoundaryLatitude	Float	
ResultSetScope	Int	0: Images within the selected zone wholly; 1: Images center within the selected zone; 2: Images within the selected zone partially or wholly.
Source	Varchar	Remote Sensing Image Source
OrbitNumber	Varchar	Satellite Orbit Number
SpecialParams	Varchar	Its format is a XML document, which will store the additional query conditions for all selected satellites and sensors.

The input parameters for the operation "MetadataSearchByPR" is shown in Table 2. It uses paths and rows instead of longitudes and latitudes to describe the images location. Moreover, it needn't the parameter "ResultSetScope" for each image corresponds to one unique path and row.

Table 2. Input Parameters for the Service Operation "MetadataSearchByPR"

Parameter Name	Date Type	Comment
StartDateTime	DateTime	
EndDateTime	DateTime	
PathMin	Int	Minimum Path Number
PathMax	Int	Maximum Path Number
RowMin	Int	Minimum Row Number
RowMax	Int	Maximum Row Number
Source	Varchar	Remote Sensing Image Source
OrbitNumber	Varchar	Satellite Orbit Number
SpecialParams	Varchar	Its format is a XML document, which will store the additional query conditions for all selected satellites and sensors.

An example for the format for the parameter "SpecialParams" is as follows:

```
<SpecialParams>
  <SpecialParam>
    <SatName>LANDSAT-5</SatName>
    <SensorName>TM</SensorName>
```

```
    <CloudCover>
      <MinValue>0</MinValue>
      <MaxValue>10</MaxValue>
    </CloudCover>
  </SpecialParam>

</SpecialParams>
```

The output of the operation "MetadataSearchByLL" is also a XML document. Each section of the document corresponds to the result set returned from one metadata table. A typical example for the output parameter is as follows:

```
<DataSets>
  <DataSet SatName = "LANDSAT-5" SensorName = "TM">
    <Records>
      <Record>
        <Path> 400 </Path>
        <Row> 22 </Row>
        <OrbitNumber> 95874 </OrbitNumber>
        <AverageCloudCover> 0 </AverageCloudCover>
        <SceneStartTime> 2002-3-11 4:06:18
</SceneStartTime>
        <SceneEndTime> 2002-3-11 4:06:43 </SceneEndTime>
        ......
      </Record>
    </Records>
  </DataSet>

</DataSets>
```

The output of the operation "MetadataSearchByLL" contains multiple datasets as usual, and each dataset has different data structure. Thus, it is impossible to define the output of the operation using simple data types. By introducing the XML schema for the input and output parameters, we can extend the operation interface optionally. Other client programs can process and display the output results based on the XML schema.

To eliminate the heterogeneities among various types of remote sensing data, we defined the standard metadata specification for optical images and microwave images, and built the mappings between the image metadata and the standard metadata. A partial mapping file is as follows:

```
<Satellite satname = "LANDSAT-5" sensorname = "TM"
  <Parameters>
    <Parameter>
      <ColumnName> Landsat4WRSPath </ColumnName>
      <DataType> int </DataType>
      <MappingColumn> TrackNumber </MappingColumn>
    </Parameter>
    <Parameter>
      <ColumnName> Landsat4WRSRow </ColumnName>
      <DataType> int </DataType>
      <MappingColumn> FrameNumber </MappingColumn>
    </Parameter>
```

```
<Parameter>
  <ColumnName> OrbitNumber </ColumnName>
  <DataType> int </DataType>
  <ColumnSize> 4 </ColumnSize>
  <MappingColumn> OrbitNumber </MappingColumn>
</Parameter>
<Parameter>
  <ColumnName> NumberofRows </ColumnName>
  <DataType> int </DataT ype>
  <ColumnSize> 4 </ColumnSize>
  <MappingColumn> Lines </MappingColumn>
</Parameter>
<Parameter>
  <ColumnName> NumberofColumns </ColumnName>
  <DataType> int </DataT ype>
  <ColumnSize> 4 </ColumnSize>
  <MappingColumn> Samples </MappingColumn>
</Parameter>
  </Parameters>

</Satellite>
```

In the above XML document, Landsat4WRSPath and Landsat4WRSRow are the field names defined in the header file of LANDSAT-5; TrackNumber and FrameNumber are the field names defined in the standard metadata specification. The query condition and query result are described in the standard metadata, which assures the independence of the upper layer applications.

4 Agent Service and Dynamic Invocation of Grid Service

In practice, remote sensing data are distributed in different departments for management and system reasons. In order to improve the access efficiency and data security, most Grid services are deployed on the local application server of each department. Thus, there may be multiple identical Grid services on the Web. Which Retrieving service will be invoked when users submit a metadata query? We believe that all available Retrieving services should be invoked simultaneously. Which Extracting and Archiving service will be invoked when users want to archive one scene remote sensing image? We believe that only the Grid services deployed on the same department as the administrator should be invoked. In this paper, we proposed and implemented an Agent service to implement the dynamic discovery and invocation of Grid services.

Firstly, the Grid services deployed on every application server should be registered using the Grid Service Management service; secondly, Agent service discovers the WSDL address for the Grid service with the specific service name and station identifier; thirdly, Agent service receives and processes the input parameter set for the Grid services, and then invokes the Grid service with these parameters. At last, Agent service takes over the outputs of the invoked Grid service, and returns them to the upper layer Web applications. If the invoked service is Retrieving service, then Agent service should merge the result set firstly. The input for Agent service is shown in Table 3.

Table 3. Input Parameters for Agent Service

Parameter Name	Date Type	Comment
ServiceName	Varchar	Grid Service Name
Operation	Varchar	Operation Name
Station	Varchar	It denotes the station that users belong to. For public or registered users, the value should be an empty string.
InputParams	Varchar	Its format is a XML document, which will store the input parameters for the invoked Grid service.

In Table 3, "ServiceName" denotes the invoked service; "Operation" denotes the operation name of the service. "Station" is used to identify the one and only Grid service that should be invoked. For example, an administrator worked in the optical department can only invoke the Extracting service and Archiving service running on the optical application server. If "Station" is assigned a null string, then all related Grid services running on every application server should be invoked, such as for meta-data retrieving operation.

Assume that the invoked service is Extracting service. An example for the "InputParams" is as follows:

```
<InputParams>
  <InputParam datatype = "Varchar"
    <ParamName> Satellite </ParamName>
    <ParamValue> LANDSAT-5 </ParamValue>
  </InputParam>
  <InputParam datatype = "Varchar"
    <ParamName> Sensor </ParamName>
    ParamValue> TM </ParamValue>
  </InputParam>
  <InputParam datatype = "Varchar"
    <ParamName> Station </ParamName>
    <ParamValue> OP </ParamValue>
  </InputParam>
  <InputParam datatype = "Varchar"
    <ParamName> HeaderFile </ParamName>
    <ParamValue> ftp://192.168.130.231/p121r34˙5t19920824.met
    </ParamValue>
  </InputParam>

</InputParams>
```

In C-Sharp, we add a Web reference to the Agent service with the reference name "Agent", and invoke the Extracting service based on the Agent service as follows:

```
Agent.AgentService as = new Agent.AgentService();
as.ServiceInvoke("ExtractingService", "Extract", "OP","
<InputParams>");
```

The effect of these statements is equivalent to that of the following statements:

```
Extracting.ExtractingService es = new
Extracting.ExtractingService();
es.Extract("LANDSAT-5", "TM", "OP",
"ftp://192.168.130.231/p121r34'5t19920824.met");
```

If the invoked service is Retrieving service, an example for the "InputParams" is as follows:

```
<InputParams>
  <InputParam datatype = "DateTime"
    <ParamName> StartDateTime </ParamName>
    <ParamValue> 2007-12-21 23 : 00 : 00 </ParamValue>
  </InputParam>
  <InputParam datatype = "DateTime"
    <ParamName> EndDateTime </ParamName>
    <ParamValue> 2007-12-21 23 : 10 : 00 </ParamValue>
  </InputParam>
  <InputParam datatype = "Float"
    <ParamName> WestBoundaryLongitude </ParamName>
    <ParamValue> 116.74 </ParamValue>
  </InputParam>
  <InputParam datatype = "Float"
    <ParamName> EastBoundaryLongitude </ParamName>
    <ParamValue> 120.41 </ParamValue>
  </InputParam>
  <InputParam datatype = "Float"
    <ParamName> NorthBoundaryLatitude </ParamName>
    <ParamValue> 34.64 </ParamValue>
  </InputParam>
  <InputParam datatype = "Float"
    <ParamName> SouthBoundaryLatitude </ParamName>
    <ParamValue> 32.26 </ParamValue>
  </InputParam>
  <InputParam datatype = "Int"
    <ParamName> ResultSetScope </ParamName>
    <ParamValue> 0 </ParamValue>
  </InputParam>
  <InputParam datatype = "Varchar"
    <ParamName> Source </ParamName>
    <ParamValue> All </ParamValue>
  </InputParam>
  <InputParam datatype = "Varchar"
    <ParamName> OrbitNumber </ParamName>
    <ParamValue> 84252 </ParamValue>
  </InputParam>
  <InputParam datatype = "Varchar"
    <ParamName> SpecialParams </ParamName>
    <ParamValue>
      <SpecialParams>
        <SpecialParam>
```

```
          <SatName> LANDSAT-5 </SatName>
          <SatType> Optical </SatType>
          <SensorName> TM </SensorName>
          <CloudCover>
             <MinValue> 0 </MinValue>
             <MaxValue> 10 </MaxValue>
          </CloudCover>
        </SpecialParam>
      </SpecialParams>
    </ParamValue>
  </InputParam>

</InputParams>
```

In C-Sharp, we can invoke the Retrieving service based on the Agent service as follows:

```
Agent.AgentService as = new Agent.AgentService();
as.ServiceInvoke("RetrievingService",
"MetadataSearchByLL", "", " <InputParams>");
```

The effect of these statements is equivalent to that of the following statements:

```
Retrieving.RetrievingService rs = new
Retrieving.RetrievingService();
rs.MetadataSearchByLL("2007-12-21 23 : 00 : 00", "2007-12-21 23 :
10 :00", 116.74, 120.41, 34.64, 32.26, 0, "All", "84252", "
<SatName>LANDSAT-5</SatName><SatType>Optical</SatType>
<SensorName>TM</SensorName><CloudCover><MinValue> 0
</MinValue><MaxValue>10 </MaxValue></CloudCover>");
```

Based on the above discussion we can see that, by using Agent service, Grid service can be discovered, bound and invoked dynamically. Thus, any remote sensing data can be accessed and processed through the integration platform as long as they are encapsulated using Grid services and registered in the service community. Moreover, Agent service provides parallel queries and faults tolerance to improve the efficiency and reliability of the Web applications.

5 Remote Sensing Images Integration Platform Architecture

In order to implement the organization, storage, management and sharing of remote sensing data, we designed a deployment architecture for the integration platform. The guiding idea of the design is to improve the performance and availability of the platform, and to assure the security of the remote sensing data that possessed by different departments.

In Fig. 2, Agent service and Grid Service Management service are deployed on the platform application server. The SQL Server 2000 database is deployed on the platform server, which will store the registration information for Grid services, users and

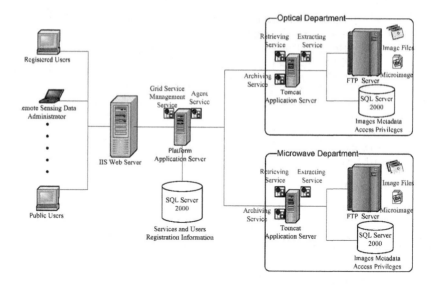

Fig. 2. Deployment Architecture for the Integration Platform

administrators. In practice, the IIS Web server, platform application server and data-base are deployed on the same server to reduce the hardware cost and to improve the system performance.

Retrieving service, Extracting service, Archiving service and other metadata services are deployed on the Tomcat application server in each department. Remote sensing image files and micro-images are stored on the FTP server, which provides strict access control and high security. The images access privileges and metadata are stored in the SQL Server 2000 database. Each user can be granted the access privileges to each kind of remote sensing images. Tomcat application server and database are deployed on the same server, but FTP server is usually a separate physical server to maximize the security of remote sensing images.

Registered users and public users can query the remote sensing image through the integration platform. The query result includes the image metadata and micro-images, and the user interface is similar to the book information list in Amazon. Registered users can also download the remote sensing image files with appropriate privileges. Data administrators use the integration platform to archive and manage their remote sensing images. The metadata are extracted and stored during the archiving process, and they are integrated and shared through the Retrieving services. The five-tier deployment architecture not only assures the availability and extensibility of the platform, but also improves the performance for the remote sensing images access.

6 Related Works

OGSA-DAI is a middleware product which supports the exposure of data resources, such as relational or XML databases, onto grids [5]. Various interfaces are provided and many popular database management systems are supported. The software also includes a collection of components for querying, transforming and delivering data in different ways, and a simple toolkit for developing client applications. The only short-coming for OGSA-DAI is that it doesn't support the parallel query of multi-source data, and our integration platform can query the metadata of multiple satellites from the distributed departments.

Wang Na proposed three-tier architecture based on J2EE platform to implement the real-time publication of ocean remote sensing data [6]. In this architecture, remote sensing image files are stored in the large-scale relational database, and they are ac-cessed using ArcSDE spatial database engine. The real-time remote sensing data publication system provides the functions of querying, browsing and downloading. How-ever, users can only query the remote sensing data within one department, and they cannot browse and compare the image data among multiple departments. In other words, there is no integration platform to associate one image provider with another.

Lin Yu-xian et al. proposed architecture for the sharing of remote sensing data in digital city, which consists of data layer, service layer and application layer [7]. In the service layer, it provides data service interface and resource directory. Resource directory provides navigation, retrieving and locating of remote sensing data resources. The sharing and service platform builds a central node to synchronize the resource directory on each embranchment node. The service platform can support the city application system through the data service interface. The design of the platform doesn't consider the archiving of remote sensing images and metadata, which is the foundation and prerequisite of the sharing of remote sensing data.

Du Xiao et al. investigated rapid importing of remote sensing images and metadata acquiring system [8]. They transformed the remote sensing images into a user-defined file, which can be handled by the operation system. Metadata information of images can be extracted and stored into the relational database with each metadata item corresponding to a user-defined file. The storage of the user-defined file is implemented through a shared directory built on the server, which has weaker security and narrower scope of application than relational database or FTP server.

7 Conclusions

In this paper, we designed and implemented a remote sensing data integration and sharing platform. The image metadata are extracted and exposed using Grid services, and all services are managed by the service community. We proposed an Agent service, which can discover, bind and invoke the corresponding Grid service dynamically in a large-scale, open and ever-changing Grid environment. The partial input and output parameters are described using XML document, which enhances the extensibility of the user interface for service operations. Our work differs from those existing systems in that the integration platform supports the parallel query of multi-source remote sensing images. We also discussed the standard metadata specification for metadata integration and query. In the next phrase, we will consider the description and location of remote sensing data via domain ontology.

Acknowledgments. This Work is supported by Project of "Taishan Scholar" Funded by Government of Shandong Province and Research Project of "SUST Spring Bud".

References

1. Wang, X., Wang, S., Wang, W.: Study on Remote Sensing Image Metadata Management and Issue. In: IEEE International Geoscience and Remote Sensing Symposium (2005)
2. Zhu, F., Turner, M., Kotsiopoulosc, I., et al.: Dynamic Data Integration: A Service-Based Broker Approach. Int. J. Business Process Integration and Management 1(3), 175–191 (2006)
3. Yu, J., Han, Y.: Service Oriented Computing - Principles an Applications, pp. 261–298. Qinghua University Press, Beijing (2006)
4. China Remote Sensing Satellite Ground Station: Online Catalogue System (2004), http://cs.rsgs.ac.cn/csen/query/querymap.asp
5. OGSA: The OGSA-DAI Project (2005), http://www.ogsadai.org.uk/
6. Na, W.: Design and Implementation of Real-Time Publication System of Ocean Remote Sensing Data. [Master Thesis]. Zhejiang University, Hangzhou (2006)
7. Lin, Y., Li, Q.: The Services Sharing of Remote Sensing Data in Digital City. Computer Science 34(4), 121–125 (2007)
8. Du, X., et al.: Researches on the Rapid Importing Of Remote Sensing Images and Meta-data Acquiring System. In: Remote Sensing for Land and Resources, pp. 80–84 (2006)

An Integrated Declarative Approach to Web Services Composition and Monitoring

Ehtesham Zahoor, Olivier Perrin, and Claude Godart

LORIA, INRIA Nancy Grand Est Campus Scientifique,
BP 239, 54506, Vandoeuvre-lès-Nancy Cedex, France
{ehtesham.zahoor,olivier.perrin,claude.godart}@loria.fr

Abstract. In this paper we propose a constraint based declarative approach for Web services composition and monitoring problem. Our approach allows user to build the *abstract composition* by identifying the participating entities and by providing a set of constraints that mark the boundary of the solution. Different types of constraints have been proposed to handle the composition modeling and monitoring. *Abstract composition* is then used for instantiating the *concrete composition*, which both finds and executes an instantiation respecting constraints, and also handles the process run-time monitoring. When compared to the traditional approaches, our approach is declarative and allows for the same set of constraints to be used for composition modeling and monitoring and thus allows for refining the *abstract composition* as a result of run-time violations, such as service failure or response time delays.

1 Introduction

Traditional Web services composition approaches (such as WS-BPEL and WS-CDL) tackle the composition problem by focusing on the control flow of the composition process. Although control over the composition process is critical, in some cases it must be relaxed to some extent to make the process flexible, but flexibility and control on the composition process are conflicting requirements. We detail in this paper a sample crisis management scenario that highlights the importance of proper balance between control and flexibility of the composition process. A problem of traditional service composition approaches is that they are procedural and as proposed in [14] they over constrain the composition process making it rigid and not able to handle the dynamically changing situations. Further the focus on data, temporal aspects and other non-functional requirements is not thoroughly investigated. Another important aspect is the run-time monitoring of the composition process and although it is tightly coupled with the composition process, it is not well integrated to the traditional composition approaches. Proposed solutions introduce a new layer for the composition monitoring and thus does not provide the important execution time violations feedback to the composition process. Finally, the scalability of the composition process is an important factor as the number of available services to choose from

G. Vossen, D.D.E. Long, and J.X. Yu (Eds.): WISE 2009, LNCS 5802, pp. 247–260, 2009.

is increasing rapidly. As a result, exploring all possible solutions to the composition problem may not be a feasible option and some choices should be made at different stages to avoid the solution explosion of the composition process.

In this paper we propose a constraint based declarative approach for Web services composition and monitoring problem. Our approach allows user to build the *abstract composition* by identifying the participating entities and by providing a set of constraints that mark the boundary of the solution. Different types of constraints have been proposed to handle the composition modeling and monitoring. *Abstract composition* is then used for instantiating the *concrete composition*, which both finds and executes an instantiation satisfying constraints, and also handles the process run-time monitoring.

When compared to the traditional approaches, our approach is declarative and allows for the same set of constraints to be used for composition modeling and monitoring and thus allows for refining the composition model as a result of run-time violation. Moreover, our approach models both the data and control flow and the constraints include both the functional and non-functional specifications (such as security and temporal aspects on both control and data). Further, in contrast to the procedural approaches, we propose a declarative approach to model the composition process. Then, our approach aims to target the conflicting requirements of flexibility and control on the composition process. At one hand, user can loosely constrain the composition process to provide the composition engine the flexibility to choose the solution. On other hand user can over constrain the composition process to focus on the control. Further, to handle the scalability requirements our approach allows for one best matched (user chosen) Web service as a result of node instantiation and handles the case when the service selection choice needs to be backtracked based on dependency between services and allows for propagation of newly chosen solution.

2   Motivation and Related Work

The motivation for our work stems from the process modeling and monitoring in a crisis situation and we present a crisis management scenario that highlights the benefits of the approach. A crisis situation is, by nature, a dynamic situation especially in its first phases. It also demands for a composition that is characterized by temporal constraints, uncertainty, multiple and changing goals, coordination of multiple services and multiple data sources, and require the composition process to be more flexible to adapt to continuously changing environment. The situations these ad hoc compositions are dealing with are complex, ambiguous, and very dynamic. Information arrives from multiple sources, with varying degrees of reliability and in different formats. Information that was treated at time t may be superseded by new information at time t+1.

The interesting concept with a crisis scenario is that it brings together two related dimensions: *organization* and *situation. Organization* encompasses the design time composition modeling which involves identifying activities and control and data flow between them. There have been many approaches to model this dimension. Most of these approaches can be divided into Workflow composition and AI planning based approaches, as discussed in [10]. The composition result can be regarded as a workflow because it includes the atomic Web services and the control and data flow between these services. *Static* workflow composition approaches require an *abstract composition* to be specified and the selection and binding is performed automatically by the Web services composition process, while the *dynamic* workflow composition approaches require to both build the *abstract composition* and select atomic service automatically based on user request as proposed in [11]. The composition process can also be regarded as a AI planning problem assuming that each Web service can be specified by its pre-conditions and effects (using situation calculus [5,8], rule-based planning [6], theorem proving [15] or other approaches including [13]).

The problem of traditional approaches (such as WS-BPEL or WS-CDL) is that all what is not explicitly modeled is forbidden. These approaches have in common that they are highly procedural, i.e., after the execution of a given activity the next activities are scheduled. Seen from the viewpoint of an execution language their procedural nature is not a problem [14]. However, unlike the modules inside a classical system, Web services tend to be rather autonomous and an important challenge is that all parties involved need to agree on an overall global process. Moreover, this way of modeling renders difficult to model complex orchestrations, i.e. those in which we need to express not only functional but also non-functional requirements such as cardinality constraints (one or more execution), existence constraints, negative relationships between services, temporal constraints on data or security requirements on services (separation of duties for instance). With current approaches, the designer should explicitly enumerate all the possible interactions and in turn over-constrain the orchestration. In case of multiple constraints, the problem becomes even more difficult. Moreover, the flexibility of the obtained model is really low as modifying one aspect (e.g. temporal) has important side effects on other aspects (e.g. control flow or security). A more detailed discussion can be found in [9]. When compared to other declarative approaches [14,9], our approach allows for the same set of constraints to be used for both process modeling and monitoring.

The second dimension a crisis situation focuses on is the *situation*. The composition process to handle the crisis should be able to measure and to adapt to continuously changing situation. This leads to the problem of Web services monitoring and the approaches for dealing with Web services monitoring include [1,2,4]. The problem with current monitoring approaches is that they are mostly proposed as a new layer to the procedural approaches such as WS-BPEL. As a result, they are unable to bridge the gap between organization and situation in a way that it is not possible to learn from run-time violations and to change the process instance (or most importantly process model) at execution time.

The need of observability (the feedback that provides insight of a composition), the support of dynamicity (ability to change resources, services, and ordering as situations change and evolve), the support of focus change (ability to reorient focus in a dynamic environment), and the support of various perspectives (ability to consider the organization given different points of view - control, data,...) guide the motivation of our approach. We believe that the declarative approach appears to be well adapted rather than the traditional imperative approach. Using a declarative language allows to concentrate on the "what" rather than the "how" and it is more flexible as you specify only the boundaries of the composition rather than its precise execution (reducing the over-specification associated with the imperative method). Then, the monitoring of the composition is largely facilitated as the same constraints can be used for both the definition, the instantiation, and the execution of the composition.

3   Motivating Example

Let us consider a sample scenario when the emergency landing of the plane carrying important government officials has resulted in serious injuries to the passengers. An emergency center has been set up in the remote region for handling patients. In a typical SOA based setup, the emergency center works by contacting the Web services provided by different systems. Depending on the condition of each patient the emergency center may either opt for nearby initial checkup center or for the detailed checkup center, for providing patient emergency treatment and to examine the nature of injuries to the patient. The emergency center may also decide to transfer the patient to some nearby hospital (not known in advance), this choice will be made using the Web services provided by different hospitals and will also be based on certain constraints such as the hospitalization and surgery facilities availability and some non-functional properties such as reliability, temporal requirements and others. The chosen hospital Web service can then be used to schedule operation theatre, allocate surgery team and to provide critical data to the hospital.

The composition process may also decide to discover and communicate with the ambulance service (or SAMU[1] service for serious injuries) to transfer the patient to the selected hospital and again, as the Web service is not known in advance, some constraints may be specified to discover the service.

Due to high-profile passengers, contacting Police department for assistance may be needed. Further the access to the patient information file from the Web service provided by the social security system may also be needed. Finally, the emergency center may also discover and contact some blood bank service to arrange additional blood supply for the patient (if patient blood type is rare).

4   Proposed Framework

Our proposal aims to provide a declarative framework for addressing the Web services composition and monitoring problem, such as the one presented in the motivating example. In this section we will briefly discuss the main concepts related to our approach and will detail them in the sections to follow. Our proposed

---

[1] SAMU (Service d'Aide Médicale d'Urgence) is the French hospital based emergency medical service.

framework has two main stages, *abstract composition* and the *concrete composition*. Each stage has a set of constraints targeted to handle the organization (composition modeling) and the situation measurement dimension (monitoring). This gives our framework the flexibility to use the same set of constraints for bridging the gap between organization and situation measurement (see figure 1).

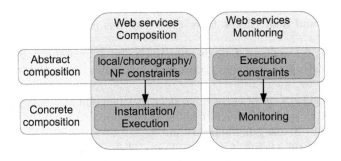

Fig. 1. Proposed framework components

The composition process starts when the user specifies the *abstract composition*, using a user friendly interface, allowing her/him to drag and drop components and provide constraints. Various related concepts include:

- *Web services* - The user can specify the concrete Web services instances known in advance, to be used within the composition process.
- *Nodes* - If the Web service instance is not known in advance, the user can specify the Web service node which has a unique type such as Hospital.
- *Constraints* - Constraints specify the boundaries for the solution to the composition process and different type of constraints can be added to the *abstract composition* process for handling modeling and monitoring dimensions. The constraints related to composition modeling include the *local,choreography* and *non-functional* constraints while the constraints for handling composition monitoring include *execution* constraints (see figure 1).

The *abstract composition* specified by the user is used to instantiate the *concrete composition* phase. As similar to the *abstract composition*, the *concrete composition* process also has different stages for handling composition modeling and monitoring. Local and choreography constraints are used for nodes instantiation and process execution while the execution constraints are handled at run-time monitoring phase of the *concrete composition*.

In order to model the *abstract composition*, our approach relies on the Event Calculus (EC) [3,7]. The choice of EC is motivated by several reasons. First, EC integrates an explicit time structure (this is not the case in the situation calculus) independent of any sequence of events (possibly concurrent). Then, given the abstract composition specified in the EC, an event calculus reasoner can be used to instantiate the concrete composition. Further, EC is very interesting as the same logical representation can be used for verification at both design time (static analysis) and runtime (dynamic analysis and monitoring).

The EC is a first-order logic that comprised the following elements: $\mathcal{A}$ is the set of *events* (or actions), $\mathcal{F}$ is the set of fluents (fluents are *reified*[2]), $\mathcal{T}$ is the set of time points, and $\mathcal{X}$ is a set of objects related to the particular context. In EC, events are the core concept that triggers changes to the world. A fluent is anything whose value is subject to change over time. EC uses predicates to specify actions and their effects. Basic event calculus predicates are:

- *Initiates*(e, f, t) - fluent f holds after timepoint t if event e happens at t.
- *Terminates*(e, f, t) - fluent f does not hold after timepoint t if event e happens at t.
- *Happens*(e, t) is true iff event e happens at timepoint t.
- *HoldsAt*(f, t) is true iff fluent f holds at timepoint t.
- *Initially*(f) - fluent f holds from time 0.
- *Clipped*(t_1, f, t_2) - fluent f was terminated during time interval $[t1, t2]$.
- *Declipped*$(t1, f, t2)$ - fluent f was initiated during time interval $[t1, t2]$.

Further, some event calculus axioms are available that relate the various predicates together. Using EC, we are able to represent both the organization, i.e. the *abstract composition* of services, and the situation, i.e. the verification that everything goes as planned at execution time.

5   Abstract Composition

5.1   Constraints

The constraints added to the *abstract composition* serve as the boundaries for the acceptable solution to the composition problem. These constraints can be divided into following categories:

- **Local Constraints** are the constraints added to the Web service nodes in the composition process. These constraints specify the properties that should be respected while binding the Web service nodes to concrete Web service instances and as our approach aims to choose the best matched solution for the node instantiation, the local constraints specify one specific path (solution) to choose from all available paths (solutions) for the Web services composition process. Local constraints can be in the form of non-functional requirements such as security, reliability, quality requirements. They can also be in the form of some domain specific functional properties (hospitalization, surgery facilities availability for the motivating example). Formally, local constraints are translated as predicates in EC. For instance, service s_1 is reliable would be written with the following formula: $reliable(s_1, value)$ where *value* is true.

---

[2] Fluents are first-class objects which can be quantified over and can appear as the arguments to predicates.

- **Choreography constraints** specify the constraints regarding the control flow of the composition process and express the order and execution sequence of the participating activities. Some examples of choreography constraints include *before*, *after*, *if-then-else*, *choice* and others. Choreography constraints are also guided by the dependency between the participating entities, specifying that a service s_1 has a dependency on service s_2 will require s_1 to be executed before the service s_2. Formally, following EC formula specifies that service s_1 must be executed before service s_2:
  $Initially(forbidden(s_2, f)) \wedge Terminates(s_1, forbidden(s_2, f), \_)$.

- **Non-functional constraints** specify the constraints independent of the functional aspect of the web service composition. It can be for instance security requirements. Formally, if we want to model a specific security rule stating for instance that once a service s_1 has been executed, the service s_2 cannot be executed for the next 20 minutes, we write:
  $Initiates(s_1, forbidden(s_2, f), t_1) \wedge Declipped(t_1, forbidden(s_2, f), t_2) \wedge (t_1 + 20 \leq t_2)$.

- **Execution constraints** specify the constraints to be validated at run-time. These constraints take the form of *monitors*, which have a associated monitoring event/condition and actions to perform if the condition to be monitored is encountered. We will take a detailed look on monitors in section-7.

5.2   Example

Let us now review the motivating example and discuss how the *abstract composition* can be specified, introducing the associated constraints. The *abstract composition* is specified using abstract-refine approach, the base *abstract composition* for the motivating example can be specified as:

  initialCheckupWS, detailedCheckupWS, Hospital(?h), Ambulance(?a), SAMU(?s), regionalPoliceWS, someSocialSecurityWS, BloodBank(?b)

The presentation syntax above is used to describe the participating Web services in the composition process, the question mark (?) operator marks the variables, i.e. the Web service nodes that have not yet instantiated. The syntax also specifies the type of participating nodes.

The base *abstract composition* has no constraints added to it, i.e. all that is specified is the invocation (or instantiation and invocation for Web service nodes). To mark the boundaries of the abstract composition, we start by adding the different type of constraints to the *abstract composition*. The *initialCheckup* is a concrete (already known) web service and thus has no local constraints. For the choreography constraints, we consider the service to be invoked *before* the *hospital* and *detailedCheckup* service and that if the *initialCheckup* service is executed then the *detailedCheckup* service is also executed. Further, the service has data dependency on the patient information from the *socialSecurity* Web service. As part of execution constraints, we consider that the data validity from the service is for 1 hour and the response time of the service should be less that 5 ms. Finally, for the cardinality constraints, which are part of the choreography constraints, we consider that the service can be executed zero or one times during the process execution. This marks the service to be optional and thus can be skipped for some instance (for all other participating services cardinality is exactly one). Below we present the event calculus formalization for the associated constraints to the *initialCheckupService* (ICS), we will detail the execution constraints later in section-7:

Choreography constraints:
before hospital - $Initially(forbidden(Hospital(h), true)) \land Terminates(ICSInvoked, forbidden(Hospital(h), true), \_)$
If ICS then detailedCheckup - $Initiates(ICSInvoked, HoldsAt(invoke(detailedChekup, true), t_2), t_1) \land t_1 < t_2$
data dependency on socialSecurityWS - $Initially(forbidden(ICS, true)) \land Terminates(socialSecurityWSInvoked, forbidden(ICS, true), \_)$

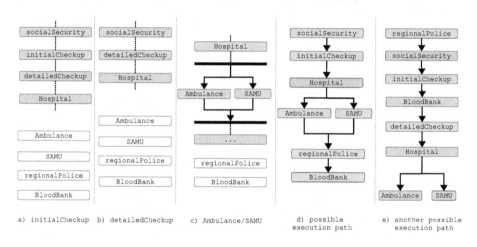

a) initialCheckup   b) detailedCheckup   c) Ambulance/SAMU   d) possible execution path   e) another possible execution path

Fig. 2. Abstract composition for the motivating example

The choreography constraints associated with the *initialCheckupWS* also guide the partial control structure of the composition process (see figure 2-a), specifying constraints such as *before hospital* does not mark that the *hospital* service will immediately follow but specifies that there may be zero or many steps (services) between them. We can then have the similar constraints for the *detailedCheckup* service, excluding the constraint the if *detailedCheckup* is executed then the *initialCheckup* in also executed. This refines the partial control flow induced by the *initialCheckup* service (see figure 2-b). Next, for the hospital node we have some local constraints such as reliable, secure Web service and that the selected hospital must provide hospitalization and surgery facilities. Further the hospital service has data dependency on initialCheckup and detailedCheckup Web services, below we present constraints modeling using EC, we will leave the discussion of execution constraint (in case of service failure re-instantiate hospital node) until section-7:

Local Constraints: $reliable(Hospital(h), true) \land providesSurgery(Hospital(h), true)$
Choreography Constraints: Similar to EC model for *initialCheckup* service

For the ambulance and SAMU nodes, we have some local constraints and the choreography constraint that they cannot coexist. Further, they have data dependency constraint on the Hospital node and this refines the partial control flow by stating that in any solution to the composition process either of two services should be chosen after the hospital service invocation (see figure 2-c).

Local Constraints:
$reliable(Ambulance(a), true) \land providesAirServices(Ambulance(a), true)$
Choreography Constraints:
$Initiates(ambulanceServiceInvoked, forbidden(SAMUService, true), \_) \land$
$Initiates(SAMUServiceInvoked, forbidden(ambulanceService, true), \_)$

Then, for the *BloodBank* node, we can have some local constraints for service discovery and it has data dependency on the *socialSecurity* service. Finally, *regionalPolice* service is unconstrained and this gives the flexibility to invoke the service anywhere in the composition process. These constraints mark the boundary of the possible solution to the composition process but intentionally do not over-constraint the composition process providing the flexibility for process execution (see figure 2-d and 2-e for possible execution paths).

6   Concrete Composition

The event calculus model for the abstract composition specified by the user can then be used to instantiate the concrete composition using the event calculus reasoner, below we highlight the various related concepts. The *concrete composition* process is divided into three phases; the *instantiation* phase handles the instantiation of Web service nodes to concrete Web service instances. The *execution* phase follows, which executes the instantiated Web services composition process, finally the *monitoring* phase handles the composition process monitoring during execution. In this section we will detail the instantiation phase and in the next section will discuss the monitoring phase of the composition process.

Instantiation. The instantiation process is responsible for binding the Web service nodes to concrete Web service instances. The process starts by using the *local constraints* added to the *abstract composition*, that highlight the user preferences for the Web service discovery. These constraints are used to query the Web services repository for identifying the services satisfying these constraints however, in case of a loosely constrained node, the result set can be very large. Our proposal thus aims to choose the best matched Web service either selected manually by the user or based on some user-specified criteria such as the quality rating for the Web service, by assuming that some trusted third-party has quality ratings assigned to services. For the instantiation process, we may also have to consider the choreography constraints associated to a Web service node in order to identify if the service has data dependency on the some already instantiated node. This will further constrain the Web service node to consider only the instantiations that respect the dependency between nodes. For the motivating example, the hospital node has data dependency on the initialCheckup service and thus may require to consider only the hospital Web services which can handle compatible data, this leads to a set of service composability rules which space limitations restrict us to detail.

If the instantiation result set for a node is empty then we have following possibilities. If some constraint is unsatisfied, user can be given option if she/he wants to relax the constraint. For example the user can decide to relax the reliability constraint in an attempt to discover new instances. Further, if the dependency between nodes is unsatisfied, we need to backtrack to the results of previous node to select some other instantiation solution and then proceed to finding solution for the current node. The process continues until all backtrack solutions have been explored. Finally when none of above two situations hold, the composition process fails with notifying the user of the intermediate results.

Then, an important aspect of our proposal concerns the ability for the instantiation to be modified at execution. Let us consider for instance that a node has been statically instantiated. At runtime, if the service fails, the node can be re-instantiated with a new service in order to continue the execution.

Backtracking. The backtracking process involves finding an alternative to some previously chosen node instantiation solution. Backtracking is needed when the dependency between nodes is unsatisfied resulting in empty result set.

For the motivating example, the Ambulance node has data dependency on the Hospital node and lets consider the Hospital node has been instantiated to *someHospitalService* providing data in JSON format, then instantiating the Ambulance node will require us to consider only the Ambulance services requiring data in JSON format. Further, consider that there is no service available for the Ambulance node which can handle JSON data (however all can handle XML), this will require us to backtrack to the Hospital node to choose some other service, say *someOtherHospitalService* which may be providing XML data.

Propagation. Once the backtracking process execution terminates, resulting in a newly chosen solution (instance), the composition solution must be recomputed and may require the propagation of newly chosen solution. This would likely be the case when a (partial) solution to the composition process has already been determined and backtracking to some higher node (in hierarchal order) may result in propagating the new solution. Further, propagation may also be needed when the user fine tunes the solution by manually selecting some other Web service after the instantiation process. In reference to the motivating example scenario discussed for the backtracking process, the reinstantiation result i.e. *someOtherHospitalService* should be propagated to the Ambulance node.

7   Composition Monitoring

The composition monitoring phase works by using the execution constraints, called monitors, attached to the abstract composition. Below we first briefly discuss the Event Processing Network (EPN) framework on which we will base our proposed monitoring framework.

7.1   Event Processing Network

Event processing network[12] is defined to be a pattern promoting the production, detection, consumption and reaction to events. An EPN model consists of four components, event producers (EP), event processing agents (EPA), consumers (C) and connection channels, called event channels (EC), for communication between other components. The EPA has following three stages, Pattern detection - responsible for selecting events matching a particular pattern, Processing - for applying processing functions to events detected and thus resulting in derived events and Emission - for emission of derived events.

Regarding proposed framework, the events generated by the composition process include the process startup, termination, and messages exchanged between the composition process and the services. Each event has associated header information which indicates the event meta-data including its source, type (such as inputMessage, outputMessage), time stamp and other similar information. In context of our proposed model, the composition process and participating Web services can be termed as the *event producers*. The produced events will then be processed by the EPA, which in our case is the *event listener* attached to the composition process.

7.2   Monitors

Monitors specify the execution constraints added to the abstract composition and each monitor has a set of activation conditions and associated actions.

Activation Condition. Each monitor has a set of activation conditions and the associated actions. The monitor activation conditions are based on the pattern detection stage of the EPN, below we discuss different activation stages.

- *Context* specifies the context of events that will be used for evaluating the event conditions. *Temporal* context can be specified to handle the conditions where monitoring is based on invocation history, as an example consider that we need to monitor the average response time for a Web service in last 24 hours. *Spatial* context can be specified, for example to monitor events originating from Web service in certain geographical region. Finally *semantic* based context can be used to handle cases when generated events have relevance through mutual object or entity, as an example consider the case when we are willing to monitor the response time of all the Web services related to (or have the same type of) a particular Web service. The context can also be specified as of value *null*, requiring all the events to be processed.

- *Policies* can include decisions to either use first, last or each of event (within specified context) in stream for pattern detection. They can also apply further constraints to only include the events satisfying a predicate on their attributes or by specifying expiry time for events.

  As an example consider that only output messages from some service s, should be used for monitoring; we can thus specify the policy to consider all the events having type as *message* and *source* as service s in their meta-data.
- *eventConditions* as similar to the patterns in an EPN model, the events conditions specify the conditions to be checked for events conforming policies and that are within specified context. Event conditions are specified using event calculus and some common types of event conditions include verifying data values within messages being sent and received by the composition process, overall time taken by the composition process and others.
- *Directives* specify the directives for reporting monitoring violations to the actions stage. The monitoring process may decide to report the monitoring violations as they are observed by specifying the directive as *immediately*, this would likely be the case of a service failure. However, the monitoring process can also decide to delay the reporting by specifying directive as *delay - timeValue* to delay the reporting in an attempt to give the service some time to recover from the violation, this would likely be the case of exceeding response time for the Service.

Actions. Once the eventCondition specified for the monitor is satisfied, associated actions specify the actions to be taken. Some common actions include terminate/ignore/reinstantiate and others. The re-instantiation function has an important application to the Web services monitoring process. In case of a service failure or a tardy service having a significant delay in the response time, to a service chosen as the result of the instantiation process, the monitoring process can add directives to re-instantiate the Web service node. The current service is added to the set of already used services for the node and a newly chosen service can then be used. This leads to the run-time composition of the Web services and a detailed discussion is beyond the scope of this paper.

The re-instantiation and then propagation to dependent nodes can be expensive, if the services are already in execution but it prevents the complete failure. Another important aspect is the handling of (partial) execution results of the service; if the service hasn't yet been invoked and no data is available, the re-instantiation is safe. If there are some intermediate result, they can either be discarded or passed to the newly instantiated service.

7.3   Example

Let us now review the motivating example and see how composition monitoring works using proposed framework. For the *initialCheckup* service we can specify some execution constraints that the data validity period for the service response is one hour and that the response time for the service should be less than 2 seconds. For the response time, the monitor below can be attached to the composition process as part of execution constraints of the service.

```
monitor: initialCheckup_responseTime
activation:
  context: none - every event should be taken into account
  policies: last request/response message, service = initialCheckup
  eventCondition:
  HoldsAt(requestSent(ICService, true), t) ∧
  HoldsAt(responseReceived(ICService, true), t') ∧ t + 2 > t'
  directives: immediate
action: send response time alert message
```

The monitor above, added to abstract composition, can then be used by the event listener attached to the composition process for runtime handling. The monitor requires event listener to listen for the messages sent/received by the composition process that are within specified context (specified as none and thus listens for every event) and those conforming policies (last request/response messages from the *initialCheckup* service). Once the messages within specified context and conforming to policies is detected by the event listener, event conditions are checked (time difference between request/response messages greater than 2 seconds) and in case of conditions become true, directives (immediately) are observed to identify when to report this violation to actions stage. The actions stage can then take the appropriate actions (send notification message). Then for monitoring the data validation, the monitor below can be specified:

```
monitor: initialCheckup_dataValidation type: Message
activation:
  context: none
  policies: last response message, service = initialCheckup
  eventCondition:
  Declipped(t, available(checkupWSData, true), t') ∧ (t + 60 > t')
  directives: immediate
action: send data expiry alert message
```

Every service that is using the data of *initialCheckup* can then have a monitor to listen for the data expiry message of *initialCheckup* service and to take the corresponding actions. We can then also have a monitor to handle the Hospital node re-instantiation in case of service failure, omitted due to space limitations.

8   Conclusion

In this paper, we present a constraint based declarative approach for Web services composition and monitoring problem. Our approach allows user to build the *abstract composition* by identifying the participating entities and by providing a set of constraints that mark the boundary of the solution. Different types of constraints have been proposed to handle the composition modeling and monitoring; local, choreography and non-functional constraints guide the composition design, while the execution constraints, called monitors and are based on Event Processing Architecture, are used for process monitoring during execution.

The *abstract composition* can then be used for the *concrete composition*, which involves instantiating the Web service nodes to the concrete Web service instances respecting local constraints associated with the nodes. The instantiation process then executes the composition and attaches the event listener to the composition process for handling run-time monitoring based on execution constraints. We have also presented a sample Crisis Management scenario, that highlights our approach.

References

1. Barbon, F., Traverso, P., Pistore, M., Trainotti, M.: Run-time monitoring of instances and classes of web service compositions. In: ICWS, pp. 63–71 (2006)
2. Baresi, L., Guinea, S., Kazhamiakin, R., Pistore, M.: An integrated approach for the run-time monitoring of BPEL orchestrations. In: Mähönen, P., Pohl, K., Priol, T. (eds.) ServiceWave 2008. LNCS, vol. 5377, pp. 1–12. Springer, Heidelberg (2008)
3. Kowalski, R.A., Sergot, M.J.: A logic-based calculus of events. New Generation Comput. 4(1), 67–95 (1986)
4. Mahbub, K., Spanoudakis, G.: Run-time monitoring of requirements for systems composed of web-services: Initial implementation and evaluation experience. In: ICWS, pp. 257–265 (2005)
5. McIlraith, S.A., Son, T.C.: Adapting golog for composition of semantic web services. In: KR, pp. 482–496 (2002)
6. Medjahed, B., Bouguettaya, A., Elmagarmid, A.K.: Composing web services on the semantic web. VLDB J. 12(4) (2003)
7. Montali, M., Chesani, F., Mello, P., Torroni, P.: Verification of choreographies during execution using the reactive event calculus. In: WS-FM 2008 (2008)
8. Narayanan, S., McIlraith, S.A.: Simulation, verification and automated composition of web services. In: WWW, pp. 77–88 (2002)
9. Pesic, M., van der Aalst, W.M.P.: A declarative approach for flexible business processes management. In: Business Process Management Workshops, Austria (2006)
10. Rao, J., Su, X.: A survey of automated web service composition methods. In: Cardoso, J., Sheth, A.P. (eds.) SWSWPC 2004. LNCS, vol. 3387, pp. 43–54. Springer, Heidelberg (2005)
11. Schuster, H., Georgakopoulos, D., Cichocki, A., Baker, D.: Modeling and composing service-based and reference process-based multi-enterprise processes. In: Wangler, B., Bergman, L.D. (eds.) CAiSE 2000. LNCS, vol. 1789, pp. 247–263. Springer, Heidelberg (2000)
12. Sharon, G., Etzion, O.: Event-processing network model and implementation. IBM Systems Journal (2008)
13. Sirin, E., Hendler, J., Parsia, B.: Semi-automatic composition of web services using semantic descriptions. In: Web Services: Modeling, Architecture and Infrastructure workshop in ICEIS 2003, pp. 17–24 (2002)
14. van der Aalst, W.M.P., Pesic, M.: Decserflow: Towards a truly declarative service flow language. In: The Role of Business Processes in Service Oriented Architectures (2006)
15. Waldinger, R.J.: Web agents cooperating deductively. In: Rash, J.L., Rouff, C.A., Truszkowski, W., Gordon, D.F., Hinchey, M.G. (eds.) FAABS 2000. LNCS (LNAI), vol. 1871, pp. 250–262. Springer, Heidelberg (2001)

Formal Identification of Right-Grained Services for Service-Oriented Modeling*

Yukyong Kim and Kyung-Goo Doh**

Dept. of Computer Science & Engineering, Hanyang University, Ansan, 426791,
South Korea
{yukyong,doh}@hanyang.ac.kr

Abstract. Identifying the right-grained services is important to lead the successful service orientation because it has a direct impact on two major goals: the composability of loosely-coupled services, and the reusability of individual services in different contexts. Although the concept of service orientation has been intensively debated in recent years, a unified methodic approach for identifying services has not yet been reached. In this paper, we suggest a formal approach to identify services at the right level of granularity from the business process model. Our approach uses the concept of graph clustering and provides a systematical approach by defining the cost metric as a measure of the interaction costs. To effectively extract service information from the business model, we take activities as the smallest units in service identification and cluster activities with high interaction cost into a task through hierarchical clustering algorithm, so as to reduce the coupling of remote tasks and to increase local task cohesion.

Keywords: Service identification, service granularity, business process model, UML activity diagram, graph clustering.

1 Introduction

The basic idea of Service-Oriented Architecture (SOA) is the restructuring of the information technology (IT) systems or IT landscapes into loosely coupled, independent services. These services should allow the reuse of existing IT functionality in order to shorten the time between design and implementation when business requirements change [1]. The key challenges in developing the service-oriented systems are the refinement and eventually the mapping of business processes to the existing service infrastructure. However, the existing services do not immediately fit the requirements elicited during business process modeling. We consider this problem as the identification of reusable services at the right level of granularity that can bring on a mismatch between the business process models and the

---

* This work is supported by the Engineering Research Center of Excellence Program of Korea Ministry of Education, Science and Technology (MEST)/Korea Science and Engineering Foundation (KOSEF), grant number R11-2008-007-01003-0.
** Corresponding author.

G. Vossen, D.D.E. Long, and J.X. Yu (Eds.): WISE 2009, LNCS 5802, pp. 261–273, 2009.
© Springer-Verlag Berlin Heidelberg 2009

available services. In this paper, we focus on how the right level of service abstraction and granularity could be provided based on business process models specifying the business requirements.

A business process is a collection of business functions required to achieve its ultimate business goals or objectives. In practice, the business functions are connected with each other to represent the execution sequence or execution pattern with various control constructors, such as serial, parallel, alternative, and so on, which are used in modeling a business process. A business function, also called a business activity, has its corresponding participant which completely supports its task and is ultimately materialized as a service. Thus a service is essentially a business component, which implements an autonomous business concept or business process.

Note that the coverage of a service depends on the system implementation policy. That is, a single service can support the role of a single business activity, several business activities or even a whole business process. This is the problem of service granularity. Because a business process is composed of a set of business activities realized by a set of services, service granularity is related with determining both the number of services required to fulfill a business process and the coverage of a service. Hence, identifying the right-grained services is to discover and determine needed services to achieve the business processes designed from the business requirements. The problem of identifying appropriate services has not been addressed in the literature. No formal methodology and tools that allow the designer to generate and evaluate alternative designs based on a set of managerial design goals exist [2]. This paper describes a formal approach to identify services of right granularity.

Our goal is to determine the service coverage to fit the business processes and then expose a reasonable number of services. We solve the problem of determining the right coverage of service using the cost metric of interactions between business activities. Suggested cost metric is to evaluate amount of interactions and to determine which activities are covered by a service. Several researches have suggested as the service modeling approach that can identify and specify service components [3–5]. However, because they provide only descriptive guidelines to define services, it is less obvious and objective to apply those approaches, and then it much relies on experience and intuition. The major contribution of our work is a formal and systematical approach using metrics which are expected to be clear, objective and efficient for identifying services of the right abstraction level. This article is organized as follows: First, we briefly mention the related work in Section 2. Section 3 describes terms and basic principles used in our paper. Section 4 presents our service identification method along with a running example. After analyzing and discussing the results of validation in Section 5, we summarize and conclude the paper including some future works in Section 6.

2 Related Works

The development and integration of services resemble Component Based Software Development (CBSD), where pre-built parts, known as business components, are assembled into larger scale applications [6, 7]. In 2005, T. Erl introduced a service modeling process to produce service and operation candidates. This process provides steps and guidelines for the modeling of a SOA consisting of application, business, and orchestration service layers [3]. IBM introduced Service-Oriented Modeling and Architecture (SOMA) [4]. SOMA illustrates the activities for service modeling and the importance of activities from service consumer and provider perspectives. It is an enhanced, interdisciplinary service modeling approach that extends existing development processes and notations such as object-oriented analysis and design, Enterprise Architecture (EA) frameworks, and Business Process Modeling (BPM). In [5], Web Services Modeling Framework (WSMF) was defined to provide a rich conceptual model for the development and the description of Web services. The philosophy of WSMF is based on the maximal de-coupling principle. A model in WSMF consists of four main elements: ontology that provide the terminology used by other elements; goal repositories that define the problems that should be solved by web services; web services descriptions that define various aspects of a web service; and mediators which bypass interoperability problems.

In [2], H. Jain et al. described a formal approach to web services identification, which takes an analysis level object model, representing a business domain, as input and generates potential web service designs, in which the classes in the object model are grouped into appropriate web services based on static and dynamic relationships between classes. An initial hierarchical grouping of classes is derived using a maximum spanning tree algorithm. In [8], M. Bell suggested the conceptual service identification process based on six best practices that can assist with identifying organizational concepts, establishing conceptual services, founding service associations, and forming service structures. Those six best practices are concept attribution, concept classification, concept association, concept aggregation, concept generalization, and concept specification. To discover abstractions and derive conceptual services, he used the decision tree. The attribution analysis process yields sets of recommended attributes that are essential inputs into most categorization activities. Conceptual services are derived from those attributes by applying their corresponding business rules.

These approaches have key limitations: One is that they lack details about how to identify and define services from the business domain. Even though the decision tree is used in [8], they provide only descriptive guidelines instead of using a formal approach to modeling services. The other is that they are based on object models or component models. To remedy these limitations, they usually employ classes and component grouping techniques to identify services. To resolve these limitations in this paper, we formalize the service identification problem on the graph, and directly derive services from the business requirements rather than object or component models.

3 Preliminaries

As shown in Figure 1, the service model in between business model and implementation model is a key factor that can help achieve the service orientation. The service model provides a logical place to define the contracts that ensure that the business side of the organization is aligned with the IT side from a requirement

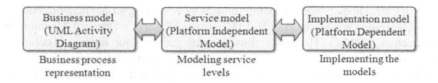

Fig. 1. Three part model of service orientation

perspective [9]. Service models play an important role during service-oriented analysis and service-oriented design phases. We aim at identifying services from the business model at the proper abstraction level. The identified services are the base for building a service model written in WSDL.

Once the business process is defined and modeled, and the business functionality is understood, then the service identification step starts. As previously stated, a business process is a sequence of activities that are ordered according to a set of procedural rules. Activity diagrams of UML (Unified Modeling Language) have been widely adopted into the business process modeling [10]. Based on activity diagrams, the modeling for communication specification and process logic of inter-organizational processes can be unified to the same modeling language. An activity diagram is used to define the execution logic of business process. Difference roles in business process and their communication structures can be defined based on the swim-lane notation.

Definition 1. An activity diagram G is a tuple $(A, D, S, R, F, AS, AF, SL)$, where

1. A is a finite set of activity nodes.
2. D is a finite set of decision nodes. D_b is the set of branch nodes and D_m is the set of merge nodes. D_b and D_m is a partition of D, i.e., $D_b \cap D_m = \emptyset$ and $D_b \cup D_m = D$.
3. S is a finite set of synchronization nodes. S_f is the set of fork nodes and S_j is the set of join nodes. S_f and S_j is a partition of S, i.e., $S_f \cap S_j = \emptyset$ and $S_f \cup S_j = S$.
4. A_S is the set of start nodes of G and A_F is the set of end nodes of G.
5. R is the set of business entities or organizational units of G.
6. $SL: A \cup D \cup S \rightarrow R$ is the mapping function from diagram elements to business entities or organizational units.
7. $F \subseteq (A_S \times A) \cup ((A \cup D \cup S) \times (A \cup D \cup S)) \cup (A \times A_F)$ is a set of edges. F is partitioned into two subsets F_L and F_R. F_L is the set of intra-flow edges connecting nodes within the same business entity, i.e., $F_L = \{(v_1, v_2) \mid (v_1, v_2) \in F \wedge SL(v_1) = SL(v_2)\}$. F_R is the set of inter-flow edges interconnecting different business entities, i.e., $F_R = \{(v_1, v_2) \mid (v_1, v_2) \in F \wedge SL(v_1) \neq SL(v_2)\}$.

Activity diagrams for business process must be prescribed under the following three constraints:

C1. There are only one start node denoted by a solid circle and one or more end nodes shown by bull's eye symbols in an activity diagram. The start node has only one post-activity node and the end node has one pre-activity node.

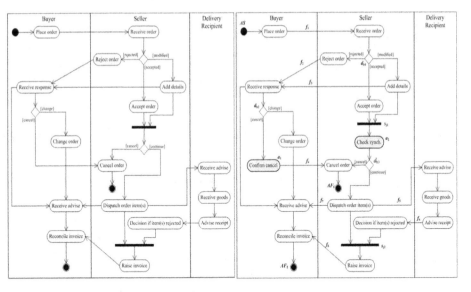

(a) An original activity diagram   (b) An activity diagram for business process

Fig. 2. Example: activity diagram for business process

C2. Every node connected to inter-flow edges must be either an activity node or a synchronization node. For example, the activity a_1 in the Buyer swim-lane in Figure 2 (b) is a newly introduced activity node to fulfill this constraint.

C3. No edge is allowed between non-activity nodes. For example, the activity a_2 in the Seller swim-lane in Figure 2 (b) is introduced to satisfy this constraint.

The execution of business process is modeled by the behaviors of its activity diagrams. The behaviors are described in terms of the set of all execution paths from start node to end node.

Definition 2. Let $G = (A, D, S, R, F, A_S, A_F, SL)$ be an activity diagram for business process. An *execution path* in G is the sequence of *a* start node, followed by one or more nodes, and followed by an end node. $a_i \leq_p a_k$ denotes that an activity a_i occurs before an activity a_k in a path p.

For example, Figure 3 shows a path, $<AS, a_1, a_2, d_{b1}, a_5, S_{j1}, a_{10}, d_{b3}, a_{11}, a_{12}, a_{13}, a_{17}, S_{j2}, a_{18}, a_{16}, AF_2>$ is an execution path in Figure 2.

Generally, a *task* and an *activity* can be treated with no difference in the business process. In this paper, however, we discriminate a task from an activity. To identify a service, we may attempt to map an activity to a service because service orientation treats the activities performed by the business process as services. According to the concept of SOA, however, a service must describe a business workflow. Because an activity is the smallest unit of work that makes sense to a user, it might not describe a complete business flow. Thus we might have to consider the case of a service consisting of several activities. To express the related activities in activity diagrams, we need a logical unit that eventually corresponds to a service.

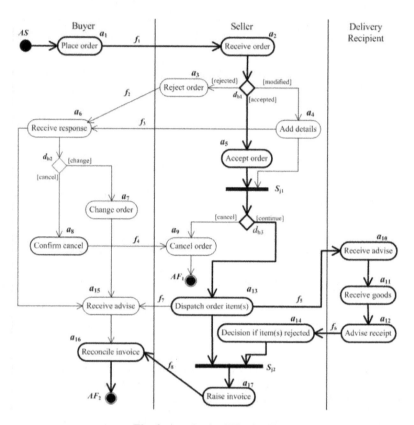

Fig. 3. A path p1 of Fig. 2–(b)

Definition 3. For $G = (A, D, S, R, F, A_S, A_F, SL)$, an *activity* is the smallest unit of work in the business process and is represented by a node in $A \cup D \cup S$. Especially, every activity node in A is given a weight which is the number of paths the activity state belongs to.

Definition 4. For $G = (A, D, S, R, F, A_S, A_F, SL)$, a *task* is a logical group of related activities in $A \cup D \cup S$, being clustered together in G.

A service includes a sequence of business workflow, and services are executed across a network. However, operations internal to the service communicate directly with each other within a single machine, not across a network connection. Thus a service cannot be located across several roles. From these points of view, defining a task as to minimize the amount of interactions between activities has an effect on identifying a service of the right granularity. Thus we establish the task clustering principle as follows: for every activity in $A \cup S \cup D$ in G, activities are clustered into a task where they are all connected with intra-flow edges.

A service itself can be coarse-grained or fine-grained. The level of granularity for services tends to be coarser than the level of granularity for objects or components. A service typically exposes a single, discrete business process [11]. Coarse-grained services require less network roundtrips as the execution state is contained in the message. Consequently service granularity refers to how much functionality the service covers. In our view, defining right-grained services is determining a task so as to include an adequate number of activities. There are three possible ways for determining a task:

1. *One-to-One*: One activity could be directly mapped to only one task.
2. *All-to-One*: Activities in a role becomes a cluster in its entirety.
3. *Many-to-Many*: Activities in the same role are decomposed into several clusters, each of which could be mapped to a task.

In *One-to-One* mapping, each activity would only model a single task. For example, we can recognize 17 tasks from 17 activity nodes in Figure 2-(b). However, as previously mentioned, a task may have to comprise a sequence of activities. Moreover, even if an activity can conceptually be an atomic service fully describing a business workflow, too many fine-grained services may lead to heavy traffic between the service providers and consumers. In *All-to-One* mapping, the number of tasks is equivalent to the number of roles. In the example of Figure 2-(b), we can identify 3 tasks from 3 roles. In this case, services are coarse-grained, giving benefits of decreasing network overhead. However, services may not be flexible enough so that reuse may be very hard or not even be possible at all. It is easy to see that the smaller the size of a service is, the higher the chance for its reuse becomes. Hence, it is desirable to decompose tasks properly in order to maximize the reusability and the composability of service components. Therefore, *Many-to-Many* mapping is the best candidate that provides the opportunities to decompose tasks in proper granularity. Because the number of services directly affects the performance and network overheads, we present in the next section the mechanical way of decomposing tasks based on a cost metric that assesses the amount of interactions between tasks.

4 Service Identification

In this section, we present how to identify tasks on G to define services at the right level of abstraction. We formalize the identification problem and define the cost metric.

4.1 Problem Definition

The approach we propose for identifying services uses an activity diagram G as input. Because services are defined from tasks in our method, we mainly focus on the approach of task identification on G. We formalize the task identification as the activity allocation problem on the graph under the task clustering principle of the previous section. We consider G as a weighted graph in which each branch and node is given a numerical weight by Definition 5.

Definition 5. Given an activity diagram $G = (A, D, S, R, F, A_S, A_F, SL)$, each activity node a in A has a weight value $freq(a)$ representing how many paths a belongs to. Each arc (a_i, a_j) in F also has a weight value $cost(a_i, a_j)$ which is the interaction cost overhead between nodes a_i and a_j. The interaction cost is usually determined by the system environment.

Our goal is to cluster activities and determine a task to minimize the cost of interactions. Then the task identification can be concretely seen as the *minimal activity distribution* (MAD) problem on a weighted directed graph G that represents business processes. The MAD problem is to allocate activities to tasks such that the total cost of remote interactions is minimized. The followings are assumptions made for the MAD problem.

Assumption 1 For each activity, the cost of executing its own set of operations is constant regardless of the number of operations.
Assumption 2 The remote interactions cost more than the local ones.

Definition 6. For G, each activity or task a_i has a weight $freq(a_i)$ as an initial value. Each edge $e = (a_i, a_j) \in F$ has a weight $cost(a_i, a_j)$ as an initial value. Then the interaction cost of a pair of tasks a_i and a_j, $cost(a_i, a_j)$, is calculated iteratively as follows:

$$cost(a_i, a_j) = \min\left(freq(a_i), freq(a_j)\right) * cost(a_i, a_j)$$

Here, we define the total interaction cost $Tcost(G)$ of G is the sum of cost of all tasks.

$$Tcost(G) = \sum_{i,j=1,i \neq j}^{n} \left(cost(a_i, a_j)\right)$$

4.2 Service Identification

The problem of service identification from an activity diagram of business workflow is formalized as the MAD problem determining tasks in the activity diagram in Section 4.1. In this subsection, we present the way to identify tasks at the right level of abstraction. The identification process consists of two steps: activity clustering and activity allocation. Activities are clustered in such a way that the total cost of communications is minimized. Each cluster is then mapped to a task. The next step is to organize tasks into the initial set of services by allocating activities to the corresponding task and defining operations for each task. Then each task becomes a service that can be described in Web Services Description Language (WSDL).

(1)   Clustering activities into tasks

In graph clustering, when an edge e is joined to v_i and v_j, and two vertices v_i and v_j are merged into a new cluster v_k, every edges incident to v_i or v_j except e is incident to the vertex v_k. Activity clustering is similar to the graph clustering and starts by placing each activity in a task by its own, creating $|A|$ tasks in G. Tasks are then repeatedly combined in such a way that the total cost of communications is minimized. The following shows how to calculate the weight for a new task:

Rule 1. When adjacent two tasks are merged, one of their incident edges having the largest weight is selected first.

Rule 2. Once an edge is selected, the edge cannot be selected again in each repetition.

Rule 3. When tasks are merged, a new edge is created and its weight is calculated.

Rule 4. When adjacent two tasks are combined into a new task, the weight of the new task is the maximum weights of two tasks.

Based on rules *Rule 1* and *Rule 2*, we determine which tasks are merged. The graph **G** is reconstructed by adjusting edges on *Rule 3* and assigning the weight newly to each task on *Rule 4*. The following Figure 4 shows activity clustering steps for Figure 2-(b) using above rules.

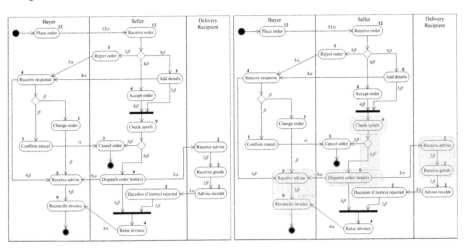

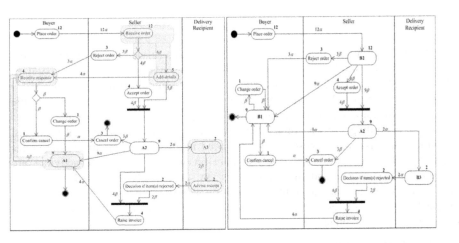

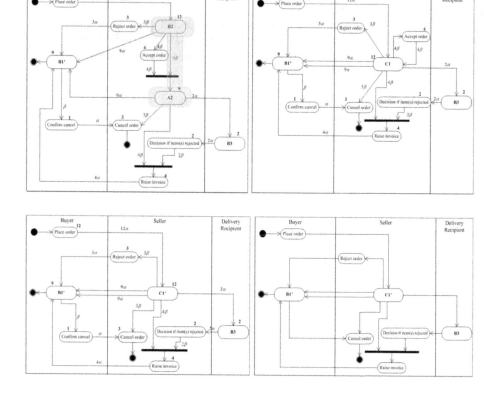

Fig. 4. Clustering steps for Fig. 2-(b)

(2)   Organizing tasks into initial set of services

The ideal scenario is one in which the cohesion within a service is maximized and the coupling between services is minimized. Finding a service design that maximizes intra-service cohesion and minimizes inter-service coupling is formalized as the MAD problem in this paper. Now we organize identified tasks into services to derive the service specification. Graph clustering provides a good way for grouping the vertices in a graph according to their connections. We then generate a structure of the tasks. Activities in a task are suggested to be included in a service. This method provides potential designs with different levels of inter-service coupling where activities are organized into services, and smaller services are successively integrated into bigger ones. This leads the initial solution based on the preferred size of services and reasonable number of services desired for the business domain. The initial set can be further refined based on heuristics.

(3)   Service description

For identified services, a set of attributes to describe and document the capability of each service is defined. Some of the key attributes include: Who owns it? Who is its customer? What are the inputs and outputs? This rich description of the capabilities can be passed to development teams who can use the information to help select the appropriate implementation technologies, hosts, and deployment topologies. The service description is easily derived from tasks and activity descriptions provided by the business model. A WSDL document defines services as collections of network endpoints, or ports. In WSDL, the abstract definition of endpoints and messages is separated from their concrete network deployment or data format bindings. This allows the reuse of abstract definitions: *messages*, which are abstract descriptions of the data being exchanged, and *port types* which are abstract collections of operations [12]. We can gain *<data type>* from activities and their interaction scheme and *<port type>* from operations included in the activity.

5   Evaluation

Comparison of approaches: A variety of heterogeneous approaches have been proposed as shown in Table 2. Approaches especially vary in terms of service hierarchies and analysis objectives. Thus, methods are proposed to identify services by utilizing the information systems in place in a bottom-up approach or follow a

Table 1. Comparison of approaches regarding service identification

Approach (Year) Criteria	Jain et al. (2004)	T. Erl (2006)	M. Bell (2008)	Proposed approach (2009)
Background & starting point	Bottom-up. Analysis of current IS and their functionality	Meet-in-the-middle. Parallel analysis of business processes and IS	Bottom-up. Analysis of current IS	Top-down. Business processes are decomposed
Service classification scheme	Implicit distinction of elemental and composed services	11 service types are proposed (partially orthogonal)	6 categories for conceptual services	3 service hierarchies: service, task, activity
Covering of SOA design phases	Focus on service development, service identification is a minor stage	All SOA phases	Service categorization and specification	Service identification and specification
Characteristics	7 phases, short documentation	Exhaustive documentation, case studies, guidelines	Decision tree	Formal criteria, WSDL description
Application of process models for service identification	Functional areas only to enable code reengineering	Initially decomposed into service candidates	–	Process model divided into service candidates

procedure of analyzing business requirements in a top-down approach. Other approaches integrate both perspectives into a hybrid strategy, referred to as 'meet-in-the-middle' approach. Compared to those approaches, the procedure presented in this paper introduces a strong business perspective into the derivation of service candidates. This is done by integrating business partners as important participants when deriving services from business process models.

Analysis of the clustering algorithm: We first analyze the time complexity of clustering algorithm. Suppose n activities are obtained from the business model, then there are n^2 pairs of activities or cluster candidates. Select the pair with greatest cost from n^2 pair of activities, with time complexity of $O(n^2)$. The time complexity processing all possible activity pairs is $O(n^2)$ and suppose the average time complexity to compute the interaction cost of a activity pair is $O(m)$, then the time complexity for the whole process is approximately $O(m*n^2)$. To compute cost between two activities, suppose the number of activities in every tasks is T/n and suppose every activity contains L operations in average and then the time complexity to compute $cost()$ between tasks is $2*(T/n)*L$, i.e. $O(L*T/n)$. Therefore, the number n of activities has great influence on the clustering algorithm.

Case study: The results of this work are currently being validated at a simplified version of the actual procedure that deals with requests for student grants in a LMS (Learning Management System). To have control over granularity is one of the major concerns in their migration to SOA. The validation of this work is that the presented identification process is adopted by the LMS. This means that the impact of each service under development is verified with respect to each type of granularity, *One-to-One, All-to-One,* and *Many-to-Many*. For each type of the granularity, we evaluate the total interaction cost between activities. Although the simplified use on the LMS, *Many-to-Many* mapping is appropriate in the given context.

6 Conclusion and Future Work

Although the concept of SOA has been intensively debated in recent years, a unified methodical approach for identifying services has not yet been reached. Service granularity, the scope of functionality that is exposed by a service, is a crucial issue in designing SOA. Every SOA needs to have well designed services in order to gain the predicted benefits, such as flexible business processes and low development costs. However, while many literature sources suggest architects to choose the right level of granularity of services, none of these studies goes into detail about how to do this.

In this paper, we attempted to discuss service granularity. Although the importance of coarse-grained services is stated, the enterprise architecture nowadays has to deal with a broad spectrum of possible service granularity levels. From this perspective, we defined a formal method of right-grained service identification based on the business model, using the graph clustering technique. To effectively extract service information from the business model, we proposed an activity clustering approach based on cost metrics. This approach takes activities as the smallest units in service identification, takes the cost metric as a measure of connectivity between activities, and clusters activities with high interaction cost into a task through hierarchical clustering algorithm, so as to reduce the coupling of remote tasks and to increase local task cohesion.

This approach still needs further improvement. Such as, it does not take into account the concept of service category which is based on the nature of the logic they encapsulate and the manner in which they are typically utilized within SOA. Moreover, certain thresholds in the identification process shall be given by experienced engineers to have expected effect which may be in the selection of center points during the process of clustering is not ideal. As part of further research, we will propose concrete metrics and rules to determine which granularity levels are appropriate in a particular context. Now we are developing a tool for service design based on business modeling.

References

1. Adam, S., Doerr, J.: How to better align BPM & SOA. LNCS, vol. 5074, pp. 49–55. Springer, Heidelberg (2008)
2. Jain, H., Zhao, H., Chinta, N.: A Spanning Tree Based Approach to Identifying Web Services. International Journal of Web Services Research 1(1), 1–20 (2004)
3. Erl, T.: Service-Oriented Architecture: Concepts, Technology, and Design. Prentice-Hall, New York (2005)
4. Arsanjani, A.: Service-Oriented Modeling and Architecture (SOMA), IBM white paper (2005)
5. Fensel, D., Bussler, D., Ding, Y., Omelayenko, B.: The Web Service Modeling Framework WSMF. In: Electronic Commerce Research and Applications, vol. 1(2), pp. 113–137. Elsevier B.V., Amsterdam (2002)
6. Herzum, P., Sims, O.: Business Component Factory: A Comprehensive Overview of Component-Based Development for the Enterprise. John Wiley & Sons Inc., Chichester (2000)
7. Vitharana, P., Zahedi, F., Jain, H.: Component-based Software Development: Design, Retrieval, and Assembly. Communications of the ACM 46(11), 97–102 (2003)
8. Bell, M.: Service-Oriented Modeling: Service Analysis, Design, and Architecture. John Wiley & Sons Inc., Chichester (2008)
9. Sehmi, A., Schwegler, B.: Service Oriented Modeling for Connected Systems (Part 1). Microsoft Architect Journal (7) (2006)
10. Zhijun, Y.: Consistency Analysis of Interorganizational Processes Based on Activity Diagrams. In: Proceedings of the IEEE International Conference on e-Business Engineering (ICEBE 2005), pp. 187–190. IEEE Computer society, Los Alamitos (2005)
11. Hanson, J.: Coarse-grained Interfaces Enable Service Composition in SOA. JavaOne article (2003)
12. Christensen, E., Curbera, F., Meredith, G., Weerawarana, S.: Web Services Description Language (WSDL) 1.1, W2C Note (2001)

Start Trusting Strangers? Bootstrapping and Prediction of Trust⋆

Florian Skopik, Daniel Schall, and Schahram Dustdar

Distributed Systems Group, Vienna University of Technology
Argentinierstr. 8/184-1, A-1040 Vienna, Austria
{skopik, schall, dustdar}@infosys.tuwien.ac.at

Abstract. Web-based environments typically span interactions between humans and software services. The management and automatic calculation of trust are among the key challenges of the future service-oriented Web. Trust management systems in large-scale systems, for example, social networks or service-oriented environments determine trust between actors by either collecting manual feedback ratings or by mining their interactions. However, most systems do not support bootstrapping of trust. In this paper we propose techniques and algorithms enabling the prediction of trust even when only few or no ratings have been collected or interactions captured. We introduce the concepts of *mirroring* and *teleportation* of trust facilitating the evolution of cooperation between various actors. We assume a user-centric environment, where actors express their opinions, interests and expertises by selecting and tagging resources. We take this information to construct tagging profiles, whose similarities are utilized to predict potential trust relations. Most existing similarity approaches split the three-dimensional relations between users, resources, and tags, to create and compare general tagging profiles directly. Instead, our algorithms consider (i) the understandings and interests of actors in tailored subsets of resources and (ii) the similarity of resources from a certain actor-group's point of view.

1 Introduction

Trust and reputation systems are essential for the success of large-scale Web systems. In such systems usually information, provided by users or obtained during their interactions, is collected to detect beneficial social connections, mostly leading to trust between their members. While many trust-, recommendation- and reputation systems have been described, including there underlying models and modes of operation [1,2,3], one particular problem has been mostly neglected: How to put the system into operation, i.e., how to bootstrap trust between users to let them benefit from using the system; even if there is not yet much, or even no, collected data available.

⋆ This work is supported by the European Union through the FP7-216256 project COIN.

G. Vossen, D.D.E. Long, and J.X. Yu (Eds.): WISE 2009, LNCS 5802, pp. 275–289, 2009.

Our prior work [4] describes, an environment comprising humans and services, in which interactions spanning both kinds of entities are monitored. We strongly believe that trust can only be based on the success and outcome of previous interactions [4,5]. Without having knowledge of prior (observed) interactions, we argue that trust between users cannot be determined in a reliable manner. Therefore, we propose an approach for *trust prediction* that aims at compensating the issue of bootstrapping trust. We consider influencing factors stimulating the evolution of trust. In various environments, such as collaborative systems, trust is highly connected to interest similarities and capabilities of the actors. For instance, if one actor, such as a human or service, has the capabilities to perform or support a collaborative activity reliably, securely and dependably, it may be sensed more trustworthy than other actors. Moreover, we argue, that if actors have interests or competencies similar to well-known trusted actors, they may enjoy initial trust to some extend.

The contributions of this paper are as follows. First, we introduce our concepts to trust prediction, and model the application environment. Second, we present our approach for creating and comparing tagging profiles based on clustering, and a novel method for trust prediction using similarity measurements. Third, we evaluate our algorithms using real world data sets from the tagging community `citeulike`[1], and show a reference implementation of our approach.

The remainder of the paper is organized as follows. Sect. 2 is about the motivation and concepts of trust prediction. In Sect. 3 we model the tagging environment, and describe our approach in Sect. 4. The results of the evaluation are depicted in Sect. 5. In Sect. 6 we introduce the architecture of a framework utilizing our new approach. Related work is listed in Sect. 7. We conclude and show our future plans in Sect. 8.

2   Towards Prediction of Trust

Trust between entities can be managed in a graph model (for example, see [6]). The graph is defined as $G = (V, E)$ composed of the set V of vertices defining entities trusting each other and the set E of directed edges denoting trust relations between entities. This model is known as the *Web of Trust*.

In Fig. 1 four different scenarios are depicted, which show concepts for trust determination in a web of trust. We assume a situation where trust from entitiy a to entitiy c is to be determined. The first case in Fig. 1(a) visualizes the optimal case, in which a trust relation from a to c can be inferred directly, e.g., based on previous interactions [4]. In the second case in Fig. 1(b), no direct trust relation could be determined, however trust can be propagated if we assume transitivity of trust relations [2], enabling b to recommend c to a. The third case in Fig. 1(c) depicts, that there is neither a direct nor a propagated trust relation from a to c. However, unrelated third party entities d and e may provide a weaker, but acceptable, notion of trust in c through the means of reputation. For our work the fourth use case in Fig. 1(d) is the most interesting one, which demonstrates

---

[1] http://www.citeulike.org

the limitations of the web of trust. If no one interacted with c in the past and no one has established trust to c, our trust prediction approach needs to be applied.

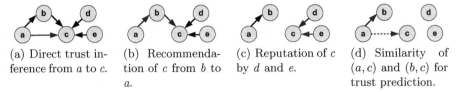

(a) Direct trust inference from a to c.

(b) Recommendation of c from b to a.

(c) Reputation of c by d and e.

(d) Similarity of (a, c) and (b, c) for trust prediction.

Fig. 1. trust(a,c)=?: The need for trust prediction in a web of trust

We distinguish the following both modes of trust prediction:

- **Trust Mirroring.** Depending on the environment, interest and competency similarities of people can be interpreted directly as an indicator for future trust. This is especially true in environments where actors have the same or similar roles (e.g., online social platforms). There is strong evidence that actors "similar minded" tend to trust each other more than any random actors [7,8]; e.g., movie recommendations of people with same interests are usually more trustworthy than the opinions of unknown persons. In Fig. 1(d), this means measuring the similarity of a's and c's interests, allows, at least to some extent, trust prediction (dashed line).
- **Trust Teleportation.** As depicted by Fig. 1(d), we assume that a has established a trust relationship with b in the past, for example, based on b's capabilities to assist a in work activities. Therefore, others having similar interests and capabilities as b may become similarly trusted by a in the future. In contrast to mirroring, trust teleportation is applied in environments comprising actors with different roles. For example, a manager might trust a developer belonging to a certain group. Other members in the same group may benefit from the existing trust relationship by being recommended as trustworthy as well. We attempt to predict the amount of future trust from a to c by comparing b's and c's interests and capabilities.

Sophisticated profile similarity measurements are needed in both cases to realize our vision of trust prediction.

3   Tagging Environment

According to our concepts of trust prediction, we need models to manage the interests and competencies of humans, and features of resources, e.g., services, respectively. In contrast to traditional centralized approaches where, one instance such as the human resource department, manages a catalog of competencies, we follow a **dynamic self-managed user-centric approach**. We assume an environment where each actor tags different types of resources s/he is interested in, such as bookmarks, scientific papers and Web services. Based on the kind

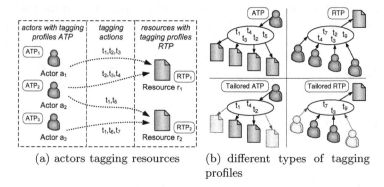

(a) actors tagging resources

(b) different types of tagging profiles

Fig. 2. Description of the tagging environment

of resource tagged and the tags assigned, we can infer the centers of interest, expressing to some extent their knowledge areas and capabilities; but from a community's view also the features or preferred usage of tagged resources. By utilizing this knowledge and applying our concepts of *trust mirroring* and *trust teleportation*, we think it is possible to predict trust relations potentially emerging in the future.

We model the environment as depicted in Fig. 2(a) which consists of:

- a set of actors A, having different interests reflected by actor-tagging-profiles (ATP). These profiles are derived from tags $T' \subseteq T$ used by $a_i \in A$ on a subset of resources $R' \subseteq R$.
- a set of resources R, having different properties (covering actor interests) reflected by resource-tagging-profiles (RTP). These profiles are derived from tags $T' \subseteq T$ used by a subset of actors $A' \in A$ on $r_j \in R$.
- a set of tagging actions $T = \{t_x\}$, where each t_x is created by an actor $a_i \in A$ for a resource $r_j \in R$.

3.1 Modes of Profile Similarity Measurement

We determine *tagging profiles* for both actors (ATP) and resources (RTP) (Fig. 2(b)). ATPs express independent from particular resources, which tags are frequently used by actors and therefore, their centers of interest. RTPs describe how a particular resource is understood in general, independent from particular actors. According to our motivating scenario depicted in Fig. 1(d), ATP similarities can be either interpreted as *trust mirroring* or *trust teleportation*. In contrast to that, RTP similarities are mostly only meaningful for *trust teleportation* (e.g., Actor a trusts a resource r_j, thus s/he might trust a very similar resource r_k as well.)

Compared to general profile similarity, and common profile mining approaches, e.g. in recommender systems [9], we do not only capture which actor uses which tags (ATP) or which resource is tagged with which tags (RTP). We rather consider how an actor tags particular subsets of resources. Using such *Tailored ATPs* we can infer similarities of tag usage between actors $a_i, a_j \in A$, and therefore similarities in understanding, using, and apprehending the same specific resources $R' \subseteq R$. Furthermore, we capture how two resources $r_i, r_j \in R$ are tagged by the same group of actors $A' \subseteq A$. Such *Tailored RTPs* can be utilized to determine similarities between resources and how they are understood and used by particular groups of actors (Fig. 2(b)).

4   Similarity-Based Trust Prediction

Similarities of actors' tag usage behavior can be directly calculated if an agreed restricted set of tags is used. There are several drawbacks in real-life tagging environments that allow the usage of an unrestricted set of tags. We identified two major influencing factors prohibiting the direct comparison of tagging actions. First, synonyms cause problems as they result in tags with (almost) the same meaning but being differently treated by computer systems, e.g., football v.s. soccer. Second, terms, especially combined ones, are often differently written and therefore not treated as equal, e.g., social-network v.s. socialnetwork.

Due to the described drawbacks of comparing tagging actions directly, we developed a new approach, which measures their similarity indirectly. This approach to similarity measurement and *trust prediction*, is depicted in Fig. 3. Three steps are performed: (i) *Clustering.* Identifying tagging actions, each consisting of an actor $a_i \in A$ tagging a resource $r_j \in R$ using tags $T' = \{t_x\}, T' \subseteq T$, and hierarchically clustering tags in global interest areas (*interests tree*). (ii) *Mapping.* Mapping of actor interests and resource properties to the created tree, to construct tagging profiles. (iii) *Predicting.* Calculating similarities of ATPs and RTPs, and applying trust prediction to determine potential trust relations.

4.1   Hierarchical Clustering of Global Interest Areas

The advantage of clustering related tags is twofold: (i) we are able to identify widely used synonyms and equal, but differently written, tags (including singular/plural forms), and (ii) we are able to identify tags with similar meanings or

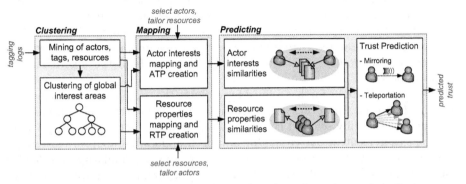

Fig. 3. An approach to trust prediction based on clustering and similarity

tags mostly used in combination. To this end, we build from the captured tagging actions a global interests tree by applying hierarchical clustering. This interests tree reflects which tags are generally applied to resources in combination, and therefore, their relatedness.

The utilized concepts are well-known from the area of information retrieval (see for instance [10]), however, while they are normally used to determine the similarities of documents based on given terms, we apply them in the opposite way. This means we determine term, i.e., tag, similarities based on given tag sets, forming kinds of documents.

The tag frequency vector t_x^2 (1) describes the frequencies f the resources $R = \{r_1, r_2 \ldots r_j\}$, are tagged with tag $t_x \in T$ globally, i.e., by all actors A.

$$t_x = \langle f(r_1), f(r_2) \ldots f(r_j) \rangle \ . \tag{1}$$

The tag frequency matrix tfm (2), built from tag frequency vectors, describes the frequencies the resources R are tagged with tags $T = \{t_1, t_2 \ldots t_x\}$.

$$tfm = \langle t_1, t_2 \ldots t_x \rangle_{|R| \times |T|} \ . \tag{2}$$

The popular tf^*idf model [10] introduces tag weighting based on the relative distinctiveness of tags (3). Each entry $tf(t_x, r_j)$ in tfm is weighted by the log of the total number of resources $|R|$, divided by the amount $n_{t_x} = |\{r_j \in R \mid tf(t_x, r_j) > 0\}|$ of resources the tag t_x has been applied to.

$$tf^*idf(t_x, r_j) = tf(t_x, r_j) \cdot \log \frac{|R|}{n_{t_x}} \ . \tag{3}$$

Finally, the cosine similarity, a popular measure to determine the similarity of two vectors in a vector space model, is applied (4).

$$\mathrm{sim}(t_x, t_y) = \cos(t_x, t_y) = \frac{t_x \cdot t_y}{||t_x|| \cdot ||t_y||} \ . \tag{4}$$

We perform hierarchical clustering to the available tag vectors. This clustering approach starts by putting each tag vector t_x into a single cluster, and compares cluster similarities successively. Tag clusters are then merged bottom-up when the similarity measurement result exceeds predefined thresholds. The output of clustering is a hierarchical tree structure, i.e., a dendrogram, reflecting global interest areas and their similarity (Fig. 4). The details of the algorithm are shown in Sect. 6.

The approach can be further refined by applying the concept of latent semantic indexing (LSI) [11]. However, very common in information retrieval, this method demands for carefully selected configuration parameters not to distort the similarity measurement in our case. Our approach applies hierarchical clustering, which means tag clusters are merged based on varying similarity thresholds. Thus, we do not necessarily need a further level of fuzziness introduced by LSI.

---

[2] bold printed symbols denote vectors.

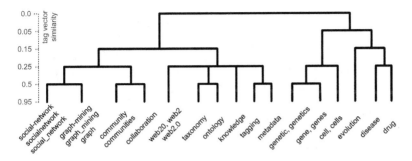

Fig. 4. A small part of the citeulike global interests tree

4.2 Tagging Profile Creation

As mentioned earlier, we create tagging profiles for both actors and resources. While ATPs describe the interests of actors, RTPs reflect features and properties of resources. The performed steps to create either kind of tagging profile are almost identical. Therefore we show exemplary the construction of ATPs in Fig. 5. For RTPs the transposed tagging matrices are used.

The upper part of the left picture (Fig. 5(a)) depicts the tree of global interests, created in the previous step. The lower part describes tagging matrices of three actors, e.g., actor a_1 tags resource r_{11} with tag t_1. In Fig. 5(b), these tagging activities are weighted and mapped to the *bottom* clusters of the interests tree (here: level 2). For this purpose, the impact w of each tag t_x on a_i's ATP is calculated by (5), assuming that the sum runs over all resources $R_{a_i} \subseteq R$ that are tagged by a_i with tag $t_x \in T_{r_j}$. Therefore, the more tags are assigned to one resource $r_j \in R_{a_i}$, the less impact one tag t_x has on the description of the resource. The assigned weights to each cluster build the ATP vectors $\boldsymbol{p_{a_i}}$ (see Fig. 5(b)).

$$w(a_i, t_x) = \sum_{\forall r_j \in R_{a_i}} \frac{1}{|T_{r_j}|} \cdot \qquad (5)$$

In the next steps the ATP vectors are aggregated and propagated to the upper levels, by simply building the average of all weights assigned to child clusters. Hence, new ATP vectors on a higher and more abstract level are built. Finally, the root of the interests tree is reached according to Fig. 5(b).

For each actor either all tagged resources or a representative subset (e.g., the most frequently tagged resources) is used to create the ATP. Such a general ATP reflects an actor's general interests. The same can be applied to resources, where RTPs describe their general use. Instead, tailored ATPs reflect the actor's understanding and apprehension of a particular and carefully selected subset of resources. For instance, in the case of trust prediction in a collaborative environment, resources might be selected according to their importance in an ongoing task. According to Fig. 5, this means each actor tags exactly the same resources, i.e., $r_{x1} = r_{x2} = r_{x3} \, \forall x \in \{1, 2, 3\}$. On the other hand, tailored RTPs can be used

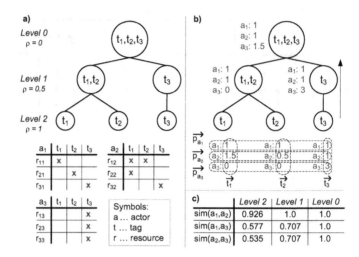

Fig. 5. An example for tag mapping and ATP comparison: a) interest tree and actor tagging actions. b) creating ATPs by mapping tagging actions to the tree. c) calculating ATP similarities on different tree levels.

for trustworthy replacing one resource with another one, on which a particular subset of actors have similar views.

4.3 Trust Prediction

The similarity of two actors a_i and a_j is determined by the cosine of the angle between their ATP vectors $\boldsymbol{p_{a_i}}$ and $\boldsymbol{p_{a_j}}$ (cosine similarity). This similarity can be calculated for each level of the global interests tree, whereas the similarity increases when walking from the bottom level to the top level. Fig. 5(c) shows the similarities of ATP vectors on different levels for the given example.

However, the higher the level and the more tags are included in the same clusters, the more fuzzy is the distinction of tag usage and therefore the similarity measurement. Thus, we introduce the notion of reliability ρ (6) of a tagging profile similarity measurement.

$$\rho(\text{sim}(a_i, a_j)) = \frac{level}{numLevels} . \tag{6}$$

For mirrored trust τ_M (7), as defined in Sect. 2, only profile similarities and their reliability are used to predict a level of potential trust.

$$\tau_M(a_i, a_j) = \text{sim}(a_i, a_j) \cdot \rho(\text{sim}(a_i, a_j)) . \tag{7}$$

Teleported trust τ_T (8) means an existing directed trust relation $\tau(a_i, a_k)$ from actor a_i to a_k is teleported to a third actor a_j depending on the similarity of a_k and a_j. This teleportation operation $\otimes$ can be realized arithmetically or rule-based.

$$\tau_T(a_i, a_j) = \tau(a_i, a_k) \otimes (\text{sim}(a_k, a_j) \cdot \rho(\text{sim}(a_k, a_j))) . \tag{8}$$

5   Evaluation and Discussion

We evaluate and discuss our new tagging profile creation and similarity measurement approach using real-world data sets from the popular `citeulike`[3] community. `Citeulike` is a platform where users can register and tag scientific articles. But before we used this tagging data, we performed two refactoring operations: (i) removing tags reflecting so-called stop words, e.g., `of`, `the`, `in`, `on` etc., resulting from word groups which are sometimes separately saved; (ii) filtering of tags reflecting ambiguous high level concepts such as `system`, `paper`, `article`; (iii) deleting tags not related to the features or properties of resources, including `toread`, `bibtex-import`, `important`. These steps reduce the available 'who-tagged-what' data entries from 5.1 million to 4.4 million.

5.1   Interests Tree Creation

For the later following ATP and RTP creation, all actor or resource tags are mapped to the same global interest tree. Therefore, the tree must be broad enough to contain and cover the most common tags. Due to the huge size of the data set, we picked the 100 articles to which most distinct tags have been assigned, and use all tags which have been applied to at least five of these articles.

In `citeulike` users are free to add arbitrary self-defined tags, raising the problem of differently written tags reflecting the same content. For instance the tag `social-network` appears written as `socialnetwork`, `social_networks`, `social-networks` etc., all meaning the same. To realize their equality, we start by clustering tags with a comparably high similarity (≥ 0.95), and consider these clusters as our initial cluster set. As long as differently written, but equally meant tags are similarly frequently used and distributed among the resources, we can capture their potential equality, otherwise the impact of alternative tags is comparably low and negligible. Then, we compare tag clusters applying much lower similarities (≤ 0.50) to capture tags reflecting similar concepts.

Table 1 summarizes the tagging data properties used to construct the interests tree. This tree consists of six levels, starting with 760 clusters on the lowest one (see Fig. 4 in Sect. 4). The utilized algorithm is detailed in the next section.

Table 1. Data properties for constructing the global interests tree

Metric	Filtered data set	Interests tree
Number of articles	1020622	100
Number of articles recognized by more than 50 users	25	21
Number of distinct tags	287401	760
Number of distinct tags applied by more than 500 users	272	-
Number of distinct users	32449	-
Average number of tags per article	1.2	157
Average number of users per article	3.5	37

---

[3] http://www.citeulike.org/faq/data.adp

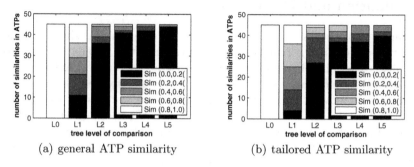

(a) general ATP similarity   (b) tailored ATP similarity

Fig. 6. ATP similarity in `citeulike` on different levels

5.2   Profile Mapping and Trust Prediction

We determine (i) for 10 highly active users the similarities of their general ATPs, and (ii) for 10 users in the area of the *social web* their tailored ATPs. For the first test we select the 10 articles which have been tagged with most distinct tags. Then, for each of these articles, we picked the user who applied most tags to it. Therefore, we get users, who tag highly recognized but different articles. We create the ATPs by retrieving all tags, that each of the selected users applied to his/her 10 most tagged articles (between 50 and 300 tags per ATP). We compare all ATPs with each other (in total 45 comparisons) on each level of the interests tree. The results are depicted in Fig. 6(a). As expected, level 5 comparisons result mostly in no similarity, only two ATPs have a similarity of 0.42 on this level. The amount of similar ATPs in different similarity classes increases when we compare them on higher levels of the interests tree. On level 0, of course, all ATPs are equal, because all tags are merged in the same cluster. These results show, that our approach of indirect similarity measurement provides distinguishable similarity results on different levels of the interests tree.

In a second experiment we measure similarities of tailored ATPs. We restrict the tags used for ATP creation to a subset of resources, and consider only tags assigned to articles in the field of the *social web*. We filter all articles, which are not linked to the `citeulike` groups *Semantic-Social-Networks*[4], *social_navigation*[5], and *Social Web*[6]. The ATP similarity results for the 10 most active users spanning these groups are depicted in Fig. 6(b). Obviously, due to the restricted tag set and a common understanding of tag usage, ATP similarities, especially on level 2 to 4, are significantly higher than in the general comparison before. Furthermore, we compare two sets of users, interested in computer science, but only members of one set participate in *social web* groups. Their general ATPs are largely similar on level 1 to 3, because all users assigned many general tags related to computer science. However, if we compare both groups' ATPs tailored

---

[4] http://www.citeulike.org/groupfunc/328/home (82 users, 694 articles)

[5] http://www.citeulike.org/groupfunc/1252/home (20 users, 507 articles)

[6] http://www.citeulike.org/groupfunc/3764/home (27 users, 444 articles)

to the *social web*, there is nearly no remarkable similarity before level 1. We conclude, that tailored profiles are a key to more precise trust prediction.

6   Implementation

In this section we introduce the architectural components of the trust management framework. Our architecture has been implemented on top of Web service technology suitable for distributed, large-scale environments. Furthermore, we detail the clustering algorithm by showing the steps needed to create hierarchical, tag-based interests trees.

6.1   Reference Architecture

The architecture evolved from our previous efforts in the area of trust management in service-oriented systems (see [4] for details on the VieTE framework).

Our architecture consists of the following main building blocks:

- **Tagging and Social Network Web Services** facilitate the integration of existing systems and the usage of external data sources. Tagging and social networks, for example, interaction graphs, can be imported via Web services.
- **Data Provisioning** comprises a set of **Providers**. We separated these providers in resource-centric (e.g., *Tag, Resource, Actor*) and trust-centric blocks. Providers enable access to **Tagging Data** and **Social Network Data** using the messaging system JMS[7]. We use the WS-Resource Catalog (WS-RC) specification[8] to manage resources in the system.
- **Trust Prediction** components consist of **Management** support, responsible for the ATP/RTP creation and tailoring of tagging profiles, and **Measurement** support used for various algorithmic tasks such as trust prediction and similarity calculation.
- **Trust Prediction Web Service** enables access to predicted trust in a standardized manner. We currently support SOAP-based services but plan to enhance our system by adding RESTful services.

6.2   Clustering Algorithm

We detail our clustering approach to interests tree creation as illustrated by Algorithm 1. The clustering starts by putting each tag vector t_x (see (1) in Sect. 4) into a single cluster, and comparing cluster similarities successively. After comparing each cluster with each other, all clusters having cosine similarities above a predefined threshold ϑ and have not been merged yet, are combined to single clusters. Then, ϑ is lowered and the algorithm compares again all available clusters. Finally, all tag vectors are merged in one single cluster, resulting in a tree structure, that reflects the global interests (Fig. 4 in Sect. 4). The function *getSimilarity()* implements an average similarity measurement by comparing artificial tag vectors that are based on the averages of all vectors within respective clusters.

---

[7] http://java.sun.com/products/jms/
[8] http://schemas.xmlsoap.org/ws/2007/05/resourceCatalog/

Algorithm 1. Hierarchical clustering of global interest areas

```
/* create tag frequency matrix */
⟨A, R, T⟩ = retrieveTaggingDataFromDB()
tfm = ∅
for each tₓ ∈ T do
    tₓ = createTagFrequencyVector(tₓ, ⟨A, R, T⟩)
    addToTagFrequencyMatrix(tfm, tₓ)
end for
/* weight single tag entries */
for each tₓ ∈ T do
    for each rⱼ ∈ R do
        tf(tₓ, rⱼ) = extractValue(tfm, tₓ, rⱼ)
        updateValue(tfm, tf(tₓ, rⱼ) * idf(tₓ, rⱼ))
    end for
end for
/* perform hierarchical clustering */
ϑ[] = {0.95, 0.5, 0.25, 0.15, 0.05, 0.0}
Cluster[][1] = createClusterForEachTag(tfm)
for i = 1 → |ϑ[]| do
    for u = 1 → |Cluster[][i]| do
        Cᵤ = Cluster[u][i]
        if ¬isMerged(Cᵤ) then
            Cₛᵢₘ[] = {Cᵤ}
            for v = u + 1 → |Cluster[][i]| do
                Cᵥ = Cluster[v][i]
                if ¬isMerged(Cᵥ) and getSimilarity(Cᵤ, Cᵥ) ≥ ϑ[i] then
                    addToClusterArray(Cₛᵢₘ[], Cᵥ)
                end if
            end for
            Cₘ = mergeClusters(Cₛᵢₘ[])
            addToClusterArray(Cluster[][i + 1], Cₘ)
        end if
    end for
end for
```

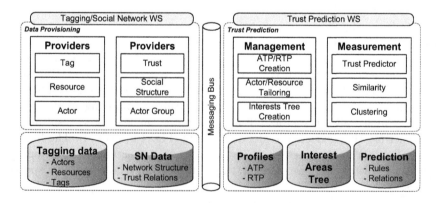

Fig. 7. Reference architecture enabling trust prediction in social network platforms

7   Related Work

Recently, trust in collaborative environments and service-oriented systems has become a very important research area. Several EU-funded projects such as COIN[9] focus on, for example, trusted collaboration in networked enterprises. Some surveys of trust related to computer science have been performed [2,3,6], which outline common concepts of trust, clarify the terminology and show the most popular trust models. Trust management systems for service-oriented-environments [12,13] as well as for mixed systems [14], comprising humans and services, such as the VieTE framework [4], are a focus of current research. VieTE aims at collecting interaction data in collaborations of humans and services, and facilitating the emergence of trust among collaboration participants. For bootstrapping such systems we introduced two concepts of trust prediction. Both concepts model the inference of trust based on interest similarities as studied in [7,8]. Other approaches to trust prediction do not necessarily address the cold-start problem. They focus more on the forecast of trust evolvement based on earlier determined trust relations [15], or on the prediction of non-existing trust relations applying transitive trust propagation [16].

Tagging and its meaning has been widely studied in [17]. Several approaches have been introduced, dealing with the construction of hierarchical structures of tags [18,19], generating user profiles based on collaborative tagging [9,20], and collaborative filtering in general [21].

Determining profile similarities has not been addressed well in previous works. Therefore, we applied the concepts of tailored tagging profiles, and indirect similarity measurement. Our approach uses various mathematical methods from the domain of information retrieval, including term-frequency and inverse document frequency metrics [10], measuring similarities, and hierarchical clustering [22].

8   Conclusion and Future Work

In this paper we introduced concepts for trust prediction, i.e., *trust mirroring* and *trust teleportation* which address the cold-start problem and facilitate bootstrapping trust management systems. As these concepts are based on profile similarities, we described a novel approach to compare interests and capabilities of entities within Web-based environments. The application of this approach has been evaluated with real data sets, gathered from a community which has similar characteristics as our proposed tagging environment. We found out that our approach of indirect tagging profile similarity measurement provides adequate results for trust prediction.

Our future plans are twofold. First, we plan to apply the presented bootstrapping mechanisms in our VieTE [4] trust management system for service-oriented environments, and study their influences on trust determination and improvements from the users' point of view. Second, we will test the extended version of VieTE in real cross-enterprise collaboration scenarios of the COIN project.

---

[9] http://www.coin-ip.eu

References

1. Grandison, T., Sloman, M.: A survey of trust in internet applications. IEEE Communications Surveys and Tutorials 3(4) (2000)
2. Jøsang, A., Ismail, R., Boyd, C.: A survey of trust and reputation systems for online service provision. Decision Support Systems 43(2), 618–644 (2007)
3. Ruohomaa, S., Kutvonen, L.: Trust management survey. In: Herrmann, P., Issarny, V., Shiu, S.C.K. (eds.) iTrust 2005. LNCS, vol. 3477, pp. 77–92. Springer, Heidelberg (2005)
4. Skopik, F., Schall, D., Dustdar, S.: The cycle of trust in mixed service-oriented systems. In: Euromicro SEAA (2009)
5. Skopik, F., Truong, H.L., Dustdar, S.: Trust and reputation mining in professional virtual communities. In: ICWE, pp. 76–90 (2009)
6. Artz, D., Gil, Y.: A survey of trust in computer science and the semantic web. J. Web Sem. 5(2), 58–71 (2007)
7. Ziegler, C.N., Golbeck, J.: Investigating interactions of trust and interest similarity. Decision Support Systems 43(2), 460–475 (2007)
8. Matsuo, Y., Yamamoto, H.: Community gravity: Measuring bidirectional effects by trust and rating on online social networks. In: WWW, pp. 751–760 (2009)
9. Shepitsen, A., Gemmell, J., Mobasher, B., Burke, R.: Personalized recommendation in social tagging systems using hierarchical clustering. In: RecSys, pp. 259–266. ACM, New York (2008)
10. Salton, G., Buckley, C.: Term-weighting approaches in automatic text retrieval. Information Processing and Management 24(5), 513–523 (1988)
11. Deerwester, S., Dumais, S., Furnas, G., Landauer, T., Harshman, R.: Indexing by latent semantic analysis. Journal of the American society for information science 41(6), 391–407 (1990)
12. Conner, W., Iyengar, A., Mikalsen, T., Rouvellou, I., Nahrstedt, K.: A trust management framework for service-oriented environments. In: WWW (2009)
13. Malik, Z., Bouguettaya, A.: Reputation bootstrapping for trust establishment among web services. IEEE Internet Computing 13(1), 40–47 (2009)
14. Schall, D., Truong, H.L., Dustdar, S.: Unifying human and software services in web-scale collaborations. IEEE Internet Computing 12(3), 62–68 (2008)
15. Chang, E., Dillon, T.S., Hussain, F.K.: Trust and reputation for service-oriented environments: technologies for building business intelligence and consumer confidence. Wiley, Chichester (2006)
16. Massa, P., Avesani, P.: Trust-aware collaborative filtering for recommender systems. In: CoopIS, DOA, ODBASE, pp. 492–508 (2004)
17. Golder, S.A., Huberman, B.A.: The structure of collaborative tagging systems. The Journal of Information Science (2006)
18. Heymann, P., Garcia-Molina, H.: Collaborative creation of communal hierarchical taxonomies in social tagging systems. Technical Report 2006-10, Computer Science Department (April 2006)
19. Eda, T., Yoshikawa, M., Yamamuro, M.: Locally expandable allocation of folksonomy tags in a directed acyclic graph. In: Bailey, J., Maier, D., Schewe, K.-D., Thalheim, B., Wang, X.S. (eds.) WISE 2008. LNCS, vol. 5175, pp. 151–162. Springer, Heidelberg (2008)

20. Michlmayr, E., Cayzer, S.: Learning user profiles from tagging data and leveraging them for personal(ized) information access. In: Proceedings of the Workshop on Tagging and Metadata for Social Information Organization, WWW (2007)
21. Herlocker, J.L., Konstan, J.A., Terveen, L.G., Riedl, J.T.: Evaluating collaborative filtering recommender systems. ACM Trans. Inf. Syst. 22(1), 5–53 (2004)
22. Romesburg, H.C.: Cluster Analysis for Researchers. Krieger Pub. Co. (2004)

Finding Comparative Facts and Aspects for Judging the Credibility of Uncertain Facts

Yusuke Yamamoto[*] and Katsumi Tanaka

Graduate School of Informatics, Kyoto University,
Yoshida-Honmachi, Sakyo, Kyoto, Japan
{yamamoto, tanaka}@dl.kuis.kyoto-u.ac.jp

Abstract. Users often encounter unreliable information on the Web, but there is no system to check the credibility easily and efficiently. In this paper, we propose a system to search useful information for checking the credibility of uncertain facts. The objective of our system is to help users to efficiently judge the credibility by comparing other facts related to the input uncertain fact without checking a lot of Web pages for comparison. For this purpose, the system collects comparative facts for the input fact and important aspect for comparing them from the Web and estimates the validity of each fact.

Keywords: Support of credibility judgment, Mining of comparative facts and aspects for comparison, Web mining, Credibility.

1 Introduction

Nowadays, there is a great deal of information on the Web and people can easily obtain it. As the Web increases in popularity, however, problems with the credibility of Web information have emerged. Most of Web information is anonymous and not authorized unlike conventional mass media. This is why people often encounter uncertain facts. For example, many Japanese Web pages report the uncertain fact that "soybeans are effective for weight loss" without any evidence. As another example, the question "Which country makes the most famous beer?" has a variety of answers on the Web, such as "Mexico is famous for beer" and "Germany is famous for beer", on Yahoo! Answers[1], a well-known question answering (QA) site. In a case like this, users can have difficulty judging which answers are correct or incorrect because some answers have little evidence and other comparative answers may be given on other Web sites. If users are unaware of such information credibility, they can easily be misled. Therefore, a system is needed for analyzing or helping users judge the credibility of information on the Web.

For this purpose, we have developed a system called *Honto Search* to help users judge the credibility of uncertain facts ("Honto?" means "Is it true?" in Japanese) [1, 2]. The aim of Honto Search is to enable a user to judge the credibility of an uncertain

---

[*] He also works as a Research Fellow (DC2) of the Japan Society for the Promotion of Science.
[1] The question "Which Country Makes The Best Beer?" in Yahoo! Answers:
http://answers.yahoo.com/question/index;_ylt=AgY58h8jhIJVGArKDTlYu5966xR.;_ylv=3?
qid=20080329195454AAGTWWC&show=3#yan-answers

G. Vossen, D.D.E. Long, and J.X. Yu (Eds.): WISE 2009, LNCS 5802, pp. 291–305, 2009.
© Springer-Verlag Berlin Heidelberg 2009

Fig. 1. Example of a Honto Search 2.0 result

fact by comparing related facts and checking the information in each fact. After the user inputs an uncertain fact and a verification target within the fact into Honto Search, the system collects alternative or countervailing facts from the Web and shows the temporal changes of each fact's popularity and sentiment. The system is imperfect, however, for credibility judgment. First, it often fails to collect enough comparative facts for comparing the input uncertain fact. Secondly even if the system collects enough comparative facts, it unexpectedly also extracts unrelated facts as well. Thirdly, temporal analysis and sentiment analysis are not always useful. The really desired function is to notice aspects necessary for checking the credibility of uncertain facts and to enable the user to check the information about a fact in terms of the aspects.

In this paper, we propose an improved, real-time system for more substantial credibility judgment of uncertain facts. This system extends Honto Search, and we call it *Honto Search 2.0*. A target fact in Honto Search 2.0 is an uncertain fact whose credibility can be judged by comparison with other related facts. To judge the credibility of such facts, the system has two functions:

- **Comparative Fact Finding:** The system collects only comparative facts for judging the credibility of the uncertain fact and estimates the validity of each fact by using a Web search engine.
- **Aspect Extraction for Checking the Fact Credibility:** The system also extracts aspects necessary to check the credibility of facts in detail from the Web.

Fig.1 illustrates one example of *Honto Search 2.0* where the user has checked whether Germany is more famous for beer than any other country. Given the two types of inputs, the system returns several comparative facts, such as "Belgium is famous for beer", "Cologne is famous for beer", and "Munich is famous for beer". At the same time, the system estimates the validity each fact on the Web. In this example, the system estimates the fact "Belgium is famous for beer" as the most valid comparative fact in the comparative facts including the fact "Germany is famous for beer". In addition, the system shows several aspects for checking credibility, such as "color", "bitterness", and "weissbier". By doing a Web search with these aspects and each fact, the user can check Web pages describing them. In this way, the system enables users to judge the credibility of uncertain facts.

The remainder of the paper is organized as follows. In the next section, we discuss related work. Section 3 provides a system overview of Honto Search 2.0, while Section 4 discusses the details of our method to extract valid comparative facts from the Web. In Section 5, we explain the proposed method to collect aspects for judging the credibility of facts. In Section 6, we report experimental results obtained using our system. The last section concludes the paper and outlines our future research directions.

2 Related Work

There are previous studies focused on the credibility of information. Fogg et al. studied various metrics to evaluate Web site credibility from the viewpoint of users [3] and analyzed the effectiveness of all these metrics by doing a large-scale experiment [4]. Nakamura et al. surveyed around 1000 participants on their attitudes toward the credibility of Web search engines [5]. Few such projects, however, have proposed concrete methods of evaluation or applications. We proposed a system, Honto Search, to support assessment of the credibility of uncertain facts [1, 2]. Kobayashi et al. proposed the method to judge whether a product name is a brand name or a glorified term [6].

There are various works on comparative search and browsing in the Web research field. Sun at el. proposed a system named *CWS* for searching Web page sets that are appropriate for comparing two specified topics [7]. Nadamoto at el. developed a system, called a comparative web browser (CWB), for comparing one Web page with another on the same topic [8, 9]. The CWB has two browser windows and concurrently displays two Web pages in a way that enables the page contents to be automatically synchronized. Nakamura et al. proposed the system named *SyncRerank* to enable users to simultaneously rerank two kinds of search results when users compare two search results [10]. These works are based on the assumption that users need to specify comparative topics or aspects for comparison. On the other hand, our system can automatically find the comparative topics and the aspects for comparison.

Many works have examined Web mining of comparative objects or information for such comparison. Kurashima et al. proposed a method to rank the entities in a specific category by using comparative sentences like "The quality of X is better than Y" [11]. Liu et al. proposed a system called *Opinion Observer* [12]. Once several product names are input to the system, it extracts aspects for comparing products and aggregates the review information about each product from the viewpoint of each aspect. Zhai at el. proposed a generative probabilistic mixture model to extract aspects for comparing topics [13]. Ohshima et al. proposed a method to find coordinate terms of a given term by using a Web search engine in real time [14]. Most of these approaches, however, have focused only on entities like products, people, and so on. Moreover, they assume off-line data processing. On the other hand, our proposed method extracts comparative facts in the form of phrases from the Web and does not depend on any specific domains. Moreover, our method can extract comparative facts and aspects for comparison in real time.

3 System Overview

In this section, we describe an overview of our system, *Honto Search 2.0*. The purpose of Honto Search 2.0 is to enable users to compare an uncertain fact with related facts for judging the credibility of the uncertain fact in real time. Fig. 2 shows a flowchart of the operation of Honto Search 2.0.

The system requires two kinds of inputs. One is an uncertain fact whose credibility a user wants to check. This fact is input to the system as a phrase. The other input is a specific part of the uncertain fact, which we call a *verification target*. For example, if a user wants to know whether Germany is famous for beer as compared with other regions, the user inputs the phrase "Germany is famous for beer" as the uncertain fact and "Germany" as the verification target. After that, it collects comparative fact candidates from the Web in order to check the credibility of the input fact. The comparative fact candidates are extracted by applying syntactic pattern mining to Web search indexes. In the next step, from among the collected fact candidates, the system selects only meaningful facts for comparison with the input fact. Examples of such comparative facts are "Belgium is famous for beer", "The Czech Republic is famous for beer", and so on. At the same time, the validity of each fact is estimated by using statistical information on the Web. The collected comparative facts and the input fact are thus ranked according to validity scores.

To enable the user to check the credibility of facts in more detail, the system also gives the user viewpoints for comparison between facts. We call these viewpoints *aspects*. Possible aspects corresponding to the example fact above, i.e., "Germany is famous for beer", are *taste, amount of consumption, brand, manufacturing method*, and so on. The system also provides a function to link to Web pages that describe each fact and specific aspect. As a result, the user can easily check the details of each fact in terms of each aspect.

Our system collects all necessary data for analysis by using a conventional Web search engine and analyzing the search engine's indexes in real time. That is, the system contains no data of its own. Therefore, it can flexibly deal with a wide variety of input facts.

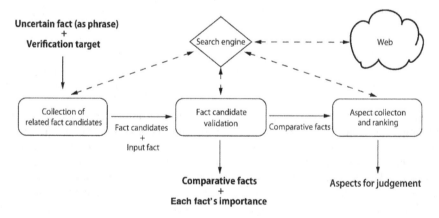

Fig. 2. Flowchart of the operation of Honto Search 2.0

4 Finding Comparative Facts

The objective of our system is to enables users to judge the credibility of an uncertain fact by comparing related facts. In this section, we propose a method to achieve this goal by finding comparative facts and estimating their validity.

4.1 Model and Task Definition

When a user enters an uncertain fact, as a phrase, and a verification target, within the fact, into our system, it collects several comparative facts from the Web. In the case of the uncertain fact given above, "Germany is famous for beer", with the term "Germany" as the verification target, the previous version of our system extracted sentences matching the pattern "(*) is famous for beer" from Web pages. Here, we regard the fact "Germany is famous for beer" as a *proposition* generated from a certain *predicate*. Moreover, we regard the verification target "Germany" as an *object* for the *variable* of the predicate. If we use these ideas, we can consider that the operation of inputting an uncertain fact and specifying its verification essentially consists of identifying the predicate. For example, if we define the predicate *FamousBeerPlace(x)* to mean that x is famous for beer, then our system's first task is to find a set of candidate objects $X = \{x \mid FamousBeerPlace(x)$ *could be true}*.

The second task of our system is to estimate the validity of each of the collected fact candidates. In the case of "Germany is famous for beer", we need to estimate the importance or validity of comparative facts such as "Belgium is famous for beer", "The Czech Republic is famous for beer", and so on. We suggest that this operation means evaluating the strength of the relation between the predicate *FamousBeerPlace(x)* and various objects for the variable x, like *Germany, Belgium, Czech Republic*.

Hence, in this section, we formally define our system's tasks as the following:

- **Task1: Comparative fact Candidate Extraction:** First, given an uncertain fact u and a verification target x, we find a predicate p such that $p(x)$ is equivalent to u. Next, to collect as many comparative facts as possible, we extract other possible predicates $P' = \{p'_1, p'_2,..., p'_n\}$ from the Web, where each $p'(x)$ is semantically similar to $p(x)$. After that, we extract a set of *comparative objects $X = \{ x \mid the$ predicate $p(x)$ or $p'(x)$ in P' can be true }* from the Web. We define each $p(x)$ for x in X as a *comparative fact candidate*.
- **Task2: Precise Estimation of Fact Validity:** To estimate the validity of each fact, we evaluate the strength of the relation between the predicate p and each comparative object x.

4.2 Extraction of Syntactic Patterns to Find Comparative Facts

In the previous version of our system, users often fail to get enough comparative facts to check the credibility of an uncertain fact, because the system used just one predicate (syntactic pattern) for collecting comparative facts. If the predicate does not appear on the Web, we cannot extract any comparative facts from the Web. To increase the variety of comparative facts, we need to collect several predicates representing the semantics of the original predicate.

Our basic strategy for achieving this goal is to extract several important keywords from the uncertain fact and then collect patterns, which include all of the keywords, as new predicates. The actual procedure is defined as follows:

1. The system does morphological analysis of the input fact. It then extracts only nouns, adjectives, and verbs (other than the verb "to be"). We denote the extracted terms as $T = \{t_1, t_2,..., t_n\}$. In the case of "Germany is famous for beer", the system extracts *{Germany, famous, beer}* as *T*.
2. The system issues the query "t_1 AND t_2 AND ... AND t_n" to a Web search engine and gets the top-N Web search results.
3. The system first collects sentences containing all of the keywords in *T* from each result's snippet, and then extracts substrings with arbitrary keywords at both ends. Examples of such substrings are *"famous beer in Germany"*, *"Germany developed world famous beer"*, *"Germany famous for beer"*.
4. The system replaces the verification target in each substring with *<variable>*. For the above examples, this gives *"famous beer in <variable>"*, *"<variable> developed world famous beer"*, and *"<variable> famous for beer"*.
5. The system ranks the resulting patterns by considering their lengths and their frequencies in the search results collected in step 2. We assume that the more frequent and shorter a pattern is, the appropriately it works as an alternative predicate. The score for pattern ranking is defined as the following:

$$score(pattern) = freq(pattern) * \log \frac{C}{length(pattern)} \tag{1}$$

Here, *freq(pattern)* is the frequency of *pattern* appearing in the search results, and *length(pattern)* is the number of terms in *pattern*, and *C* is a constant number.

6. Finally, the system selects the top N patterns from the ranked patterns as the set of other possible predicates, *P'*. It also replaces the verification target in the input fact with *<variable>* and denotes the resulting predicate as *p*.

4.3 Finding Comparative Fact Candidates

Next, we collect comparative fact candidates for checking the credibility of the input fact. In this step, we collect Web pages about each predicate by using a Web search engine and then extracting comparative fact candidates from the search results. We then select the final comparative fact candidates by using the assumption that comparative facts can concurrently appear in documents including the input fact. The procedure is as follows:

1. The system converts each predicate to a query for extracting comparative fact candidates. If the predicate has the form *"<pattern1> <variable> <pattern2>"*, like *"beer cup features many of <variable>'s famous"*, then the system generates the query *"<pattern1> AND <pattern2>"*. Otherwise, the system eliminates *<variable>* from the predicate and uses the rest of the predicate as a query. For example, the predicate *"<variable> is famous for beer"* is converted to the query *"is famous for beer"*.

2. The system issues each query to a Web search engines and gets the to-N search results. The system extracts the parts of result snippets that matches *<variable>* of the predicate p or one of the predicates in P' from the snippets of the results.
3. The system checks whether the part of speech (POS) of each extracted term is the same as the POS of the verification target. If they are the same, the term can be an object candidate c for the variable of the predicate p.
4. Finally, the system collects the top N Web pages including the input fact by using a search engine. If an object candidate c is included in some of the collected pages, the system regards $p(c)$ as a final comparative fact candidate.

4.4 Verification of Candidates as Comparative Fact

To estimate the validity of a fact $p(c)$, our previous system issued each fact as a phrase to a Web search engine and used the page counts as a query to the search engine. Phrase search is so strict, however, that we could not often get a page count for a fact. Moreover, comparing the page count of an uncertain fact with the page counts of comparative facts was too rough for estimating the validity of the uncertain fact. We instead need to estimate fact validity more precisely.

We can assume that the validity of a fact $p(c)$ is given by the strength of the relation between the object candidate c and the predicate p. Applying this assumption, we use the WebPMI [15] to estimate the fact validity. The WebPMI is one kind of point-wise mutual information and is estimated by calculating the co-occurrence degree between two terms on the Web. We define the fact validity *FactValidity(c, p)* of the fact $p(c)$ by using the WebPMI as follows:

$$FactValidity\,(c,p) = \log(\frac{H(c \wedge p)}{H(c)H(p)}) \qquad (2)$$

Here, $H(q)$ means the page count for query q in a Web search engine.

By using this definition, the system estimates the fact validity for all comparative fact candidates collected by the procedure given in Section 4.3. Only if the fact validity of a comparative fact candidate is greater than zero, we regard the candidate as a comparative fact. Finally, the system shows the comparative facts and their scores to the user.

5   Extraction of Aspects for Judging Credibility of Facts

In checking the credibility of an uncertain fact, it is insufficient to compare related facts from the viewpoint of fact validity. The credibility of a fact often depends on specific aspects in comparing facts. In addition, the most important issue in judging credibility is to understand why a fact is credible or not. When a user checks the credibility of an uncertain fact, if the user knows specific aspects necessary to check the credibility, there is no problem. At that time, the user can search for clues to check the credibility on his or her own. Users do not always know, however, which aspects are important in checking the credibility of uncertain facts. In this section, we describe an approach to extract aspects for judging the credibility of an uncertain fact from the Web.

5.1 Collection of Aspect Candidates

When an uncertain fact is described in terms of an aspect in a document, certain assessment words are often used around the aspect. For example, in the case of the fact "Germany is famous for beer", phrases such as "amount of consumption is high" and "good taste" can be found in documents about this fact, and we can thus select "amount of consumption" and "taste" as aspects. For the purpose of finding aspects, one possible method is to collect pages including the uncertain fact and extract frequently neighboring assessment terms such as adjectives. Although this method cannot collect enough aspects and not all of them are useful, the collected aspects can be used as candidates. Therefore, we apply this method to first collect aspect candidates.

In this paper, we have focused on uncertain facts whose credibility is checked by comparison with other, related facts. In this case, the necessary aspects depend on the facts with which users want to compare the uncertain fact. For example, one user might want to check the credibility of the fact "Germany is famous for beer" by comparison with the fact "Belgium is famous for beer", while another user might want to compare with the fact "Germany is famous for sausage". That is, the extracted aspects depend on the predicate for the uncertain fact. Therefore, we use the predicate to collect aspect candidates. The procedure for aspect extraction is described as follows:

1. The system converts the predicate for the uncertain fact to a phrase query, as described in Section 4.3. The system then issues the phrase query to a Web search engine and collects the top-N search results.
2. The system extracts phrases with the following syntactic patterns from each search result snippet: "*<Adjective> <Noun phrase>*" or "*<Noun phrase> <the verb "to be"> <Adjective>*". In this step, we use a morphological analyzer to identify each term's POS.
3. The system extracts <Noun phrases> as aspect candidates from the collected phrases. At this time, aspect candidates that appear in a stopword list are eliminated from the list of aspect candidates.

5.2 Aspect Ranking by Using Comparative Facts

In the case of using only adjectives as clues for extracting aspect candidates, inappropriate terms can appear as aspects. Therefore, we need to estimate the appropriateness of aspect candidates and distinguish worthless candidates.

The simplest approach is to calculate the probability for each aspect candidate, $Pr(a|p)$, that the aspect candidate a appears given a predicate p. Unexpectedly, however, inappropriate terms can have a high probability of appearing as appropriate aspects, because candidates are collected by using a simple syntactic rule. To solve this problem, we introduce another hypothesis. Because expected aspects are useful for comparing an uncertain fact with related facts, we suppose that the more useful an aspect is, the more facts appear with it in Web pages, as illustrated in Fig. 3. By using this assumption, we determine the probability $Pr(a|p)$. Let C be a set of comparative terms that are objects for the variable of the predicate p and are collected by the method proposed in Section 4. The probability $Pr(a|p)$ can be defined as follows:

$$\Pr(a \mid p) = \frac{\Pr(a, p)}{\Pr(p)}$$

$$= \frac{\sum_{c \in C} \Pr(a, c, p)}{\Pr(p)}$$

$$= \frac{\sum_{c \in C} \Pr(a \mid c, p) \Pr(c, p)}{\Pr(p)}$$

$$= \sum_{c \in C} \Pr(a \mid c, p) \Pr(c \mid p) \tag{3}$$

Here, $Pr(a|c,p)$ means the probability that aspect a appears in Web pages containing the comparative fact $p(c)$, while $Pr(c|p)$ means the probability of occurrence of the comparative term c if predicate p is specified. Hence, $Pr(c|p)$ is the co-occurrence degree between c and p, which we estimate as the following:

$$\Pr(c \mid p) = \frac{FactValidity(c, p)}{\sum_{c' \in C} FactValidity(c', p)}, \tag{4}$$

where the function *FactValidity* was defined in Section 4. To enhance the validity in calculating the probability $Pr(a|c,p)$, we introduce a semantic factor into the calculation, as with the syntactic patterns shown in the previous subsection. We redefine $Pr(a|c,p)$ as the probability of occurrence of aspect term a in Web pages containing fact $p(c)$, where a appears in the form "<Adjective> <a>" or "<a> <the verb "to be"> <Adjective>". In fact, it is difficult to collect all Web pages containing the fact $p(c)$ and then calculate $Pr(a|c,p)$. Therefore, we calculate $Pr(a|c,p)$ approximately by using the top-N Web search results collected with the query "p AND c".

By using these definitions, we can finally calculate the probability $Pr(a|p)$ for all aspect candidates collected as described in Section 5.1. The system orders all aspect candidates by score and reports the top N terms to the user as important aspects for judging the credibility of an uncertain fact.

6 Evaluation

We conducted two kinds of evaluations for our algorithm. The first was for evaluating the performance of the algorithm in collecting comparative facts. The second was for evaluating how many meaningful aspects were collected by the algorithm for comparison. For these experiments, we prepared 20 pairs of uncertain facts and verification targets as a test set for evaluation. These pairs are listed in Table 1. The pairs in the test set were categorized into 6 groups. As described above, the credibility of the uncertain facts is supposed to be checked by comparison with other related facts, such as the examples of comparative facts given in the table. These experiments were conducted in Japanese, and then the results were translated into English. Constant number C was set to 30.

6.1 Validity and Variety of Collected Facts

To evaluate the performance of comparative fact collection, we used our algorithm with all pairs listed in Table 1. We set the system to use Google as the Web search engine and to collect the top 100 search results. In this experiment, we ordered the collected comparative facts by fact validity and evaluated the number of collected facts that is appropriate for comparison with the top 3, top 5, top 10, and all results. The adequacy of the facts was judged by checking whether they were reported in Wikipedia. In addition, we evaluated the processing time of our algorithm. The algorithm proposed in our previous work was used as a baseline, and the previous results were compared with the results of our new algorithm.

Table 1. Test set for the experiments

Fact type	Input fact	Verification target	Example of comparative facts
Local product of nation	Germany is famous for beer	Germany	Belgium, Denmark
	Germany is famous for beer	beer	sausage, wine, car
	Poland is famous for amber	Poland	Lithuania, Russia
	Poland is famous for amber	amber	escargot, rye
Compound's effectiveness	Anthocyanin helps eyestrain	anthocyanin	polyphenol
	Anthocyanin helps eyestrain	eyestrain	atherosclerosis, cyanocobalamin
Geographic characteristic of nation	England is a rainy country	England	Thailand, Malaysia
	Italy is an earthquake-prone country	Italy	Japan, Armenia, Turkey
	Japan has many volcanoes	Japan	Indonesia, Guatemala
	Drought often happens in India	India	Australia
Social characteristic of nation	Agriculture is important in Poland	Poland	China, Australia, France
	Moscow is an expensive city	Moscow	Tokyo, London
	London has a large population	London	Mumbai, Tokyo, New York
Leading country for sport	Japan is strong in judo	Japan	France, Netherlands
	Japan is strong in baseball	Japan	United States, Korea, Cuba
	Argentina is strong in football	Argentina	Brazil, England, Spain
	Japan is strong in volleyball	Japan	Cuba, Brazil
Common religion of nation	Buddhism is common in Japan	Japan	Thailand, Korea
	Islamism is common in Indonesia	Indonesia	Egypt, Turkey
	Hinduism is common in India	India	Nepal, Bangladesh

Table 2 summarizes the results of the two algorithms. The proportion of appropriate comparative facts obtained by the proposed method was higher than the proportion obtained by the previous method in all cases except the top-3 results. In the case of all results, the proportion obtained by the proposed method was about 5% higher than obtained by the previous method. As shown in Table 2, there was little difference between the proposed method and the previous one from the viewpoint of the validity of collected comparative facts. From these results, both methods can be expected to perform well in collecting valid comparative facts.

When focusing on the variety of collected comparative facts, however, we find a significant difference between the algorithms' performances. The number of valid comparative facts collected by the proposed method was 26.1% greater than that collected by the previous method, on average. The proposed method was slower than the previous method, because the system must access a Web search engine three times for one calculation of the WebPMI, but we think this extra time is necessary for better judgment of the credibility of uncertain facts.

For the detail study, we pick up some examples of comparative fact extraction. Table 3 illustrates the results. When we focused on the predicates used in fact extraction, we found a problem. In case an input uncertain fact does not often appear on the Web, the system fails to find alternative predicates for collecting comparative facts and to collect comparative facts. One of the examples is the fact "Poland is famous for <amber>". In such a case, we need to transform the input fact to another expression before applying our proposed method. Actually, when we uses the query "<Amber> is a specialty product of Poland" by substitutes the term "famous" with "specialty product", we got vodka, mushroom, hot pepper, chess, etc. as comparative terms. On the other hand, in case the input uncertain fact often appears to some extent on the Web, the system succeeded in increasing the amount of valid comparative facts. The most typical case is the input "<Germany> is famous for beer". In the case of this input, the previous algorithm collected 5 valid comparative facts while the proposed method collected 9 valid comparative ones. "Ireland", "United States", "Thailand", "Korea" were collected by our proposed method as additional valid comparative facts.

Table 2. Results of using Honto Search 1.0 (previous method) vs. Honto Search 2.0 (proposed method) for comparative fact collection

Algorithm	Proportion of valid comparative facts in top-N results				Average of processing time(s)	Increase in number of valid comparative facts
	@1	@3	@5	All		
Proposed method	85.0%	70.4%	69.1%	70.9%	11.53	26.1%
Previous method	85.0%	80.0%	63.3%	65.6%	2.57	-

Table 3. Examples of comparative fact extraction. The term between brackets is the verification target in the uncertain fact. The number in parenthesis is the fact validity score. Underlined terms are valid terms as variable of the predicate for the input fact.

Input fact (verification target)	Result
<Germany> is famous for beer	Belgium(2.97), Cologne(2.78), Munich(2.77), Czech Republic(2.53), Denmark(2.43), Ireland(2.42), United States(2.03), Thailand(2.02), Germany(1.97), Korea(1.93), England(1.91)
Agriculture is important in <Poland>	Macedonia(4.00), Poland(3.39), Rumania(3.30), Spain(2.54), Thailand(2.15), Japan(1.15), China(0.58)
Drought often happens in <India>	Australia(3.52), India(3.18)
<Japan> is strong in baseball event	Cuba(3.20), Korea(2.16), Asia(2.04), Osaka(1.41), Hokkaido(1.28), Japan(0.96), Ehime(0.95), Wakayama(0.90), Taiwan(0.52)
<Japan> is strong in judo event	Nederland(2.70), France(1.83), Japan(1.01)
Poland is famous for <amber>	amber(0.31)

We also need to improve the validity calculation of extracted comparative facts. For example, when we input the fact "<Japan> is strong in baseball event" to the system, we got 9 comparative facts, but only 3 facts of them were valid. The invalid comparative facts are superclass or subclass objects of Japan such as Asia, Osaka prefecture, and Hokkaido prefecture. For solving this problem, it is effective to use the ontological information of the verification target as well as the POS information.

6.2 Aspect Extraction

Next, we evaluated the performance of aspect extraction for judging the credibility of uncertain facts. We applied our aspect extraction algorithm with all pairs listed in Table 1. As described in Section 6.1, we collected the top 100 search results in analyzing Web pages. In this experiment, we ordered the extracted aspects for each uncertain fact by the probability $Pr(a|p)$ in formula (3) and extracted the top-10 aspects as the final ones. Then, we evaluated how many aspects were meaningful for comparing the collected comparative facts with each input fact and judging its credibility. We manually judged whether the extracted aspects were meaningful.

Table 4. Three best cases of aspect extraction. The term between brackets is the verification target in the uncertain fact. The underlined terms are appropriate aspects.

Uncertain fact (verification target)					
<Germany> is famous for beer		Agriculture is important in <Poland>		Drought often happens in <India>	
amount of consumption	0.03907	vegetable	0.19545	snow	0.47420
color	0.03654	fruit	0.05869	climate	0.47420
weissbier	0.02200	future	0.05639	wildfire	0.17527
bitterness	0.01579	industry	0.04210	weather	0.08000
japan	0.01279	production	0.02950	rain	0.07052
ferment	0.01253	nature	0.02666	amount	0.05897
Pilsner Urquell	0.01183	region	0.01837	influence	0.04000
culture method	0.01142	amount of crop	0.01809	region	0.03897
restaurant	0.00960	amount	0.01809	green	0.03052
street	0.00897	land	0.01548	problem	0.03052

Table 5. Three worst cases of aspect extraction. The term between brackets is the verification target in the uncertain fact. The underlined terms are appropriate aspects.

Input fact (verification target)					
Poland is famous for <amber>		<Japan> is strong in judo		<Japan> is strong in baseball	
soup	0.02000	player	0.06868	high school	0.03087
-		news	0.03756	team	0.03049
-		feelings	0.03290	game	0.02993
-		gossip	0.02567	school	0.02541
-		rugby	0.02315	impression	0.02278
-		factor	0.02000	awareness	0.02179
-		think	0.01951	feelings	0.02132
-		fighting sport	0.01685	reason	0.01827
-		Tokyo	0.01190	United States	0.01379
-		opponent	0.01025	foundation	0.01336

In the case of applying our algorithm to all pairs in the test set, the average number of meaningful aspects was 4.75. We assume that our system would show 10 aspects for an uncertain fact and the user could then select specific ones to check detailed information about those aspects of the uncertain fact on the Web. Therefore, we consider the performance of our system in this experiment to be adequate.

To more intuitively understand the results, we studied some specific cases of aspect extraction. Table 4 summarizes the three best cases, in terms of obtaining many meaningful aspects, among the pairs of an uncertain fact and a verification target. When we input the fact "Germany is famous for beer" and specified "Germany" as the verification target, we obtained 7 appropriate aspects. In this case, we assume that a user would want to check the credibility of the fact by comparing Germany with other countries famous for beer, such as Belgium. Therefore, aspects like "amount of consumption", "color", and "bitterness" would be useful for judging the credibility of the fact. Most of the collected aspects for the other pairs were also regarded as useful. The common features in these uncertain facts are that we could obtain many comparative facts for any pair and that they were appropriate facts for comparison.

For example, of the 11 comparative facts collected for the uncertain fact "<Germany> is famous for beer", 9 were appropriate.

Table 5 summarizes the three worst cases of aspect extraction. We could not collect any meaningful aspects for the uncertain fact "Poland is famous for <amber>, with only one aspect collected at all. This was because there were few pages including the fact, and therefore, the system could not extract syntactic patterns for collecting comparative facts. As for the facts "<Japan> is strong in judo" and "<Japan> is strong in baseball", the system could obtain only a few meaningful aspects, although it did extract a several number of aspects for each fact. In the case of the former fact, the number of extracted comparative facts was very small. Therefore, we think that the quality of the extracted aspects was low. In the case of the latter fact, we actually obtained many comparative facts, but the system could not collect many meaningful aspects. This was because most of the comparative facts were not valid. We expected that, ideally, the comparative facts of the latter fact should represent which countries are other leading baseball countries. However, most of the collected comparative facts represented that specific Japanese prefectures are strong in baseball event. This is why we need a certain number of valid comparative facts to collect meaningful aspects.

7 Conclusion

In this paper, we developed the system to help users to judge the credibility of the uncertain facts by showing comparative facts and important aspects for judgment of the credibility. Evaluations showed that our proposed method could find comparative facts and important aspects for comparison from the Web if input facts are relatively often seen on the Web.

However the technique of our proposed method is immature. First, if descriptions about uncertain facts do not appear to an extent on the Web, the system fails to collect comparative facts and aspects for comparison. In such a case, we need to modify input facts to collect as many Web pages for analysis as possible. Moreover, we need to consider how to extract comparative facts with negative polarity such as "Soy bean is totally not effective for weight loss" against "Soy bean is effective for weight loss". As a more substantial problem, ideally, users expect the system to directly check whether the input uncertain fact is true or not and to estimate which comparative fact is the most credible. Our system estimates each comparative fact using WebPMI, but this estimation is still based on the statistical relation between the variable and the predicate. We have the assumption that the credibility of a fact involves various factors and should be estimated by considering all of them. We proposed the method to find aspects for checking the credibility of uncertain facts. We have a plan to estimate the credibility of uncertain facts by using these aspects as parameters.

There is a lot of unreliable information on the Web. Especially, Web 2.0 contents are critical. Lately, Web 2.0 contents such as Yahoo! Answer and Wikipedia are getting more attention as collective knowledge. However, most of them are not authorized. Our proposed method can be useful from the viewpoint of estimating the credibility of Web 2.0 contents by aggregating Web 1.0 contents. In the future, we plan to estimate the credibility of Web 2.0 contents and support users to judge the credibility by using our proposed method.

Acknowledgment

This work was supported in part by a MEXT Global COE Program "Informatics Education and Research Center for Knowledge-Circulating Society" (Project Leader: Katsumi Tanaka), a MEXT Grant-in-Aid for Scientific Research on Priority Areas "Cyber Infrastructure for the Information-explosion Era", Planning Research "Contents Fusion and Seamless Search for Information Explosion" (Project Leader: Katsumi Tanaka, A01-00-02, Grant#: 18049041), the National Institute of Information and Communications Technology, and a MEXT Grant-in-Aid for JSPS Fellows (Project Leader: Yusuke Yamamoto, Grant#: 211243).

References

1. Yamamoto, Y., Tezuka, T., Jatowt, A., Tanaka, K.: Honto? Search: Estimating Trustworthiness of Web Information by Search Results Aggregation and Temporal Analysis. In: Dong, G., Lin, X., Wang, W., Yang, Y., Yu, J.X. (eds.) APWeb/WAIM 2007. LNCS, vol. 4505, pp. 253–264. Springer, Heidelberg (2007)
2. Yamamoto, Y., Tezuka, T., Jatowt, A., Tanaka, K.: Supporting Judgment of Fact Trustworthiness Considering Temporal and Sentimental Aspects. In: Bailey, J., Maier, D., Schewe, K.-D., Thalheim, B., Wang, X.S. (eds.) WISE 2008. LNCS, vol. 5175, pp. 206–220. Springer, Heidelberg (2008)
3. Fogg, B.J., Tseng, H.: The elements of computer credibility. In: Proc. of CHI 1999, pp. 80–87 (1999)
4. Fogg, B.J., Marshall, J., Laraki, O., Osipovich, A., Varma, C., Fang, N., Paul, J., Rangnekar, A., Shon, J., Swani, P., Treinen, M.: What makes web sites credible? A report on a large quantitative study. In: Proc. of CHI 2001, pp. 61–68 (2001)
5. Nakamura, S., Konishi, S., Jatowt, A., Ohshima, H., Kondo, H., Tezuka, T., Oyama, S., Tanaka, K.: Trustworthiness analysis of web search results. In: Kovács, L., Fuhr, N., Meghini, C. (eds.) ECDL 2007. LNCS, vol. 4675, pp. 38–49. Springer, Heidelberg (2007)
6. Kobayashi, T., Ohshima, H., Oyama, S., Tanaka, K.: Evaluating Brand Value on the Web. In: Proc. of WICOW 2009, pp. 67–74 (2009)
7. Sun, J.T., Wang, X., Shen, D., Zeng, H.J., Chen, Z.: CWS: A Comparative Web Search System. In: Proc. of WWW 2006, pp. 467–476 (2006)
8. Nadamoto, A., Tanaka, K.: A Comparative Web Browser (CWB) for Browsing and Comparing Web Pages. In: Proc. of WWW 2002, pp. 727–735 (2002)
9. Nadamoto, A., Qiang, M., Tanaka, K.: Concurrent Browsing of Bilingual Web Sites by Content-Synchronization and Difference-Detection: In Proc. of WISE 2003, pp. 189—199 (2003)
10. Nakamura, S., Yamamoto, T., Tanaka, K.: SyncRerank: Reranking Multi Search Results Based on Vertical and Horizontal Propagation of User Intention. In: Bailey, J., Maier, D., Schewe, K.-D., Thalheim, B., Wang, X.S. (eds.) WISE 2008. LNCS, vol. 5175, pp. 120–135. Springer, Heidelberg (2008)
11. Kurashima, T., Bessho, K., Toda, H., Uchiyama, T., Kataoka, R.: Ranking entities using comparative relations. In: Bhowmick, S.S., Küng, J., Wagner, R. (eds.) DEXA 2008. LNCS, vol. 5181, pp. 124–133. Springer, Heidelberg (2008)
12. Liu, B., Hu, M., Cheng, J.: Opinion Observer: Analyzing and Comparing Opinions on the Web. In: Proc. of WWW 2005, pp. 342–351 (2005)

13. Zhai, C., Veliveli, A., Yu, B.: A Cross-Collection Mixture Model for Comparative Text Mining. In: Proc. of SIGKDD 2004, pp. 743–748 (2004)
14. Ohshima, H., Oyama, S., Tanaka, K.: Searching Coordinate Terms with Their Context from the Web. In: Aberer, K., Peng, Z., Rundensteiner, E.A., Zhang, Y., Li, X. (eds.) WISE 2006. LNCS, vol. 4255, pp. 40–47. Springer, Heidelberg (2006)
15. Bollegala, D., Matsuo, Y., Ishizuka, M.: Measuring Semantic Similarity between Words Using Web Search Engines. In: Proc. of WWW 2006, pp. 757–766 (2006)

Query Evaluation on Probabilistic RDF Databases

Hai Huang and Chengfei Liu

Faulty of ICT, Swinburne University of Technology, Australia
{hhuang,cliu}@groupwise.swin.edu.au

Abstract. Over the last few years, RDF has been used as a knowledge representation model in a wide variety of domains. Some domains are full of uncertainty. Thus, it is desired to process and manage probabilistic RDF data. The core operation of queries on an RDF probabilistic database is computing the probability of the result to a query. In this paper, we describe a general framework for supporting SPARQL queries on probabilistic RDF databases. In particular, we consider transitive inference capability for RDF instance data. We show that the *find* operation for an atomic query with the transitive property can be formalized as the problem of computing path expressions on the transitive relation graph and we also propose an approximate algorithm for computing path expressions efficiently. At last, we implement and experimentally evaluate our approach.

1 Introduction

The Resource Description Framework (RDF) is the proposal of the W3C for a standard metadata model to describe resources on the semantic web. An increasing amount of data is becoming available in RDF format. In real applications, there are many domains that are full of uncertainty. We face large volumes of data generated with uncertainty. For example, in biology science, probabilistic links between concepts can be obtained from various prediction techniques and probabilistic links are mutually independent [1]. Thus, it is desired to process and manage probabilistic RDF data.

To process and manage probabilistic RDF data, the central problem is query evaluation on RDF probabilistic databases. In a traditional database system, the answer to a query q is distinctive. However, in a probabilistic database, the system computes the answers and for each answer computes a probability score representing the confidence. Query evaluation on the probabilistic relational databases [2, 3, 4] and probabilistic XML databases [5, 6] has been studied. However, this problem has not been addressed in RDF databases. In this paper, we propose a framework for supporting SPARQL queries on the probabilistic RDF database. And we also consider query evaluation on RDF data with transitive properties.

For example, in Fig.1, a SPARQL query is posed on a probabilistic diseases database. The database consists of RDF triples with probabilities showing the confidence about the relationship. The query asks for the diseases that are associated with cough and cause of fatigue. We add the superscript "t" to mean "transitive". Thus, "AssociatedWith^t" denotes that this property is transitive. Now the problem is how to compute the probability of each answer. We will interpret this example in detail for introducing the main concepts and techniques of this paper.

G. Vossen, D.D.E. Long, and J.X. Yu (Eds.): WISE 2009, LNCS 5802, pp. 307–320, 2009.
© Springer-Verlag Berlin Heidelberg 2009

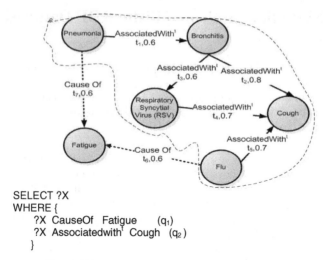

SELECT ?X
WHERE {
    ?X CauseOf Fatigue   (q₁)
    ?X Associatedwith' Cough   (q₂)
}

Fig. 1. SPARQL query on a probabilistic RDF database

We define the RDF probabilistic diseases database based on possible worlds semantics. A database instance is any subset $I \subseteq triples(R)$ (the set of all triples in the database) with a certain probability. In this paper, we assume that all the triples in the database are independent probabilistic events. It implies that $Pr(t_1, t_2, ..., t_n) = Pr(t_1) \cdot Pr(t_2) \cdot ... \cdot Pr(t_n)$. For instance, in table 1, $I_1 = \{t_1\}$, $Pr(I_1) = Pr(t_1) \cdot (1 - Pr(t_2)) \cdot (1 - Pr(t_3)) \cdot (1 - Pr(t_4)) \cdot (1 - Pr(t_5) \cdot (1 - Pr(t_6)) (1 - Pr(t_7)) = 0.000288$.

Table 1. Database instances

$I_0 = \{\}$	$(1 - Pr(t_1)) \cdot (1 - Pr(t_2)) \cdot (1 - Pr(t_3)) \cdot (1 - Pr(t_4)) \cdot (1 - Pr(t_5)) \cdot (1 - Pr(t_6))(1 - Pr(t_7)) = 0.000192$
$I_1 = \{t_1\}$	$Pr(t_1) \cdot (1 - Pr(t_2)) \cdot (1 - Pr(t_3)) \cdot (1 - Pr(t_4)) \cdot (1 - Pr(t_5)) \cdot (1 - Pr(t_6)) (1 - Pr(t_7)) = 0.000288$
.....	.....
$I_{127} = \{t_1, t_2, t_3, t_4, t_5, t_6, t_7\}$	$Pr(t_1) \cdot Pr(t_2) \cdot Pr(t_3) \cdot Pr(t_4) \cdot Pr(t_5) \cdot Pr(t_6) \cdot Pr(t_7) = 0.190512$

We now illustrate query evaluation on the probabilistic RDF database. We adopt the intentional query evaluation [2] that associates each triple with a probabilistic event. The intermediate and result tuples are associated with a complex event through $find(\sigma)$, $join(\Theta)$ and $project(\pi)$ operations.

Consider the query in Fig.1 that consists of two atomic queries (triple patterns): $q_1(?X, CauseOf, Fatigue)$ and $q_2(?X, Associatedwith', Cough)$. We first do the $find(\sigma)$ operation which extracts all triples that match the atomic queries. For query $q_1(?X, CauseOf, Fatigue)$, it is clear that triples t_6 and t_7 match q_1 and we get the tuples "Pneumonia" and "Flu" with events t_7 and t_6 respectively (shown in Fig.2(a)).

The second atomic query $q_2(?X, Associatedwith', Cough)$ is distinguished by the transitive property "Associatedwith' ". Note that there are two transitive triple paths $t_1 \rightarrow t_3 \rightarrow t_4$, $t_1 \rightarrow t_2$ between resources "Pneumonia" and "Cough". The tuple

"Pneumonia" is obtained only when $t_1 \wedge t_3 \wedge t_4$ or $t_1 \wedge t_2$ is true. So we assign the complex event $(t_1 \wedge t_2) \vee (t_1 \wedge t_3 \wedge t_4)$ to the tuple "Pneumonia". Similarly, there are four tuples that match q_2 associated with events (shown in Fig.2(b)). We can observe that if two nodes are strongly connected, the event expression would be huge. We will discuss how to process the *find* operation efficiently in Section 4.

$q_2.?x$	event
Pneumonia	$(t_1 \wedge t_2) \vee (t_1 \wedge t_3 \wedge t_4)$
Flu	t_5
RSV	t_4
Brochities	$t_2 \vee (t_3 \wedge t_4)$

(b) $\sigma(?X, \text{Associatedwith}^t, \text{Cough})$

$q_1.?x$	event
Pneumonia	t_7
Flu	t_6

(a) $\sigma(?X, \text{CauseOf}, \text{Fatigue})$

Fig. 2. Tuples that match the atomic queries

Then we join the tuples from two atomic queries using the logic operator "$\wedge$", if the two tuples have the same value on the shared attributes.

?x	event
Pneumonia	$t_7 \wedge ((t_1 \wedge t_2) \vee (t_1 \wedge t_3 \wedge t_4)) = (t_7 \wedge t_1 \wedge t_2) \vee (t_7 \wedge t_1 \wedge t_3 \wedge t_4)$
Flu	$(t_6 \wedge t_5)$

Fig. 3. $\sigma(q_1) \Theta (\sigma(q_1))$

At last, we obtain two possible answers "Pneumonia" and "Flu" associated with events $(t_7 \wedge t_1 \wedge t_2) \vee (t_7 \wedge t_1 \wedge t_3 \wedge t_4)$, $(t_6 \wedge t_5)$ respectively. The probabilities of answers are obtained by adding the probabilities of database instances that make events true. For example, database instance $I_{127} = \{t_1, t_2, t_3, t_4, t_5, t_6, t_7\}$ can make the events of two answers true, so the probability of I_{127} should be added to the probabilities of two answers. Given the probabilistic distribution over database instances, computing the probability of event expressions is an NP-hard problem. We will employ binary decision diagram (BDD) [8] for computing the probabilities of event expressions.

In this paper, we discuss the problem of evaluating SPARQL queries on probabilistic RDF databases. To the best of our knowledge, there is no work done on this problem. We claim the following contributions in this paper:

(1) We propose a framework for supporting SPARQL query on probabilistic RDF databases.

(2) We consider transitive inference capability on RDF instance data. We show that the *find* operation for the atomic query with the transitive property can be formalized as the problem of computing path expressions on the transitive relation graph, in which case we propose an approximate algorithm for computing path expressions efficiently.

The remainder of this paper is organized as follows. Some preliminary is given in Section 2. Section 3 describes the query evaluation on RDF probabilistic databases. In Section 4, we design the approximate algorithms on the transitive relation graph. Section 5 presents an experimental evaluation of our approach. Section 6 discusses related work.

2 Preliminary

An **RDF term** is an URI or a literal or a blank node. An **RDF triple** (s, p, o)$\in (U \cup B) \times U \times (U \cup B \cup L)$ is called an RDF triple, where U is a set of URIs, B a set of blank nodes and L a set of literals. In a triple, s is called subject, p the property (or predicate), and o the object. An **RDF triple pattern** (s, p, o) $\in (U \cup V) \times (U \cup V) \times (V \cup U \cup L)$, where V is a set of variables disjoint from the sets U, B and L.

We also assume the following: Indvs $\subseteq U$ is a set of individuals (instances); C$\subseteq$U is the set of classes; Props$\subseteq$U is the set of properties. Props$^t \subseteq$ Props is a set of transitive properties and Props$^n \subseteq$ Props is a set of normal properties. We have Props$^t \cup$ Props^n= Props and Props$^t \cap$Props^n=$\varnothing$.

An **RDF tuple** is a partial function from variables to RDF terms. Note that an RDF tuple is different from an RDF triple (a statement implying a semantic relation between resources). Conversely, an RDF tuple does not carry meaning and it just maps some variables to some RDF terms.

Definition (RDF Relation). An RDF relation is a set of RDF tuples. It can also be represented as a table. Each row corresponds to an RDF tuple and each column is an attribute named by a variable. For instance, in Fig.2(a), q_1.?x is the variable of the relation containing tuples "Pneumonia" and "Flu".

Definition (Probabilistic RDF Database). A probabilistic RDF datatabse D is a finite set of probabilistic triples. We denote triples(D) as all triples in the database. Each triple t is associated with a probability value and a unique identifier. The triple t has the form <s, p, o, Pr(t), $\tau(t)$> where s$\in$ Indvs, p$\in$ Props $\cup$ {rdf : type}, o$\in$ Indvs $\cup$ L $\cup$ C. s, p and o are subject, property and object of triple t. Pr: triples(D)$\rightarrow$[0,1] is a probability function and τ: triples(D)$\rightarrow$Strings is a mapping form each t to a unique identifier which we call the *event* of triple t in this paper.

We interpret the RDF probabilistic database D in terms of possible   worlds. A database instance is any subset $I_i \subseteq$triples(D). I_1, I_2, ..., I_n are called possible worlds. $Pr(I_i) = \prod_{t \in I_i} Pr(t) \cdot \prod_{t \notin I_i} (1 - Pr(t))$. The sum of all probabilities of possible instances is 1, i.e., $\sum_{I_i} Pr(I_i) = 1$.

A set of RDF triples can be represented as a graph. Now we give the concept of probabilistic RDF graph as follows:

Definition (Probabilistic RDF Graph). A probabilistic RDF graph is a labeled directed graph denoted by G=(N, E, ℓ_E, τ, Pr) where:

(1) N$\subseteq$Indvs is a set of nodes.
(2) E={edge$_{s,p,o}$: (s, p, o)$\in$ G}

(3) ℓ_E is a labeling function such that $\ell_E(\text{edge}_{s,p,o})=p$.

(4) $\tau : E \rightarrow$ Strings, is a mapping from edges to a unique identifier (event).

(5) Pr: $E \rightarrow [0,1]$ is a mapping from edges to a probability value.

For example, Fig.1 shows the probabilistic RDF graph for the diseases RDF databases.

Definition (Probabilistic Transitive Relation Graph). A probabilistic transitive relation graph $G^t=(N^t, E^t, \ell_E, \tau, Pr)$ for transitive property p^t is a subgraph of the probabilistic RDF graph G, where $N^t \subseteq N$, $E^t \subseteq E$ and $\forall \text{edge}_{s,p,o} \in E^t$, we have $\ell_E(\text{edge}_{s,p,o})=p^t$.

For example, in Fig.1, the probabilistic transitive relation graph for the transitive property *AssociatedWith^t* is the part surrounded with dashed lines.

Since in probabilistic transitive relation graph G^t, the property p^t is fixed, we denote an edge as (s, o) instead of (s, p^t, o) for brevity. Now we define the concept of *path* and *reachbality* on G^t. A *path ps* from node n_1 to n_k is a sequence of edges $\text{edge}_1(n_1, n_2) \cdot \text{edge}_2(n_2, n_3) \cdot \ldots \cdot \text{edge}_{k-1}(n_{k-1}, n_k)$. We say that n_k is *reachable* from n_1 if there exist a path from n_1 to n_k denoted by $n_1 \mapsto n_k$, else $n_1 \not\mapsto n_k$. Given a path *ps* from *s* to *v*, we define the path expression $\lambda(ps)$ as the conjunction of events of all edges in the path.

$$\lambda(ps) = \bigwedge_{edge_i \in ps} \tau(edge_i)) \tag{1}$$

Given two nodes *s* and *v* on G^t, We also define the path expression $T(s, v)$ from node *s* to *v* as the disjunction of expressions of paths connecting s to v:

$$T(s,v) = \bigvee_{ps \in PS} \lambda(ps) \tag{2}$$

where PS is the set of paths connecting *s* to *v*.

Definition (Query Semantics). Let q be a query over the probabilistic RDF database D. The database is given by a probability distribution over database instances. We denote $Answers_q(I_j)$ as the set of results of q over the database instance I_j. For any result tuple *ans*, we have: $\text{Pr}(ans) = \sum_{I_j} \text{Pr}(I_j)$ where I_j is any database instance s.t.

$ans \in Answers_q(I_j)$.

3 Query Evaluation

We have shown the concepts of a probabilistic RDF database and we now address the problem of how to compute the answers with probabilities given a SPARQL query. We restrict our discussion to conjunctive SPARQL query with the rule form $Q \leftarrow q_1, q_2, \ldots, q_n$, where Q is the head of the query and $q_1, q_2, \ldots, q_n$ are atomic queries (triple patterns). We use var(Q) to denote the variables in Q. For example, the SPARQL query in Fig.1 can be written as the rule: $Q(?X) \leftarrow (?X, \text{CauseOf}, \text{Fatigue}), (?X, \text{Associatedwith}^t, \text{Cough})$.

3.1 Intentional Query Evaluation

We adopt intentional query evaluation of [2]. The basic idea of this approach is to associate each triple with a basic probabilistic event. When processing the query, the intermediate and result tuples are associated with a complex event that is the combination of basic events through *find* (σ), *join* (Θ), and *project* (π) operations. We use ee(t) to stand for the complex event of tuple t and show how three operations associate the tuples with complex events as follows:

- **Find** (σ)

The *find* operation (σ) takes an atomic query q (triple pattern) and returns all tuples that match the atomic query. *q* is of the form (s, p, o) where each term is either an RDF resource or literal or a don't care. There are two cases:

Case1: If a predicate term in q is a normal property then σ copies the events of input triples which satisfy the query q to the output tuples .i.e. if $q(t) = t'$, then

$$ee_{\sigma(q)}(t') = \tau(t)$$

where t' is the output tuple induced by triple t. An example of *find* operation is shown in Fig.2(a).

Case2: In this case, the predicate term in the atomic query is a transitive property. The atomic query is of three possible forms $(a, p', ?obj)$ or $(?sub, p', b)$ or $(?sub, p', ?obj)$ where a and b are constants and p' is a transitive property. We will show that the *find* operation can be formalized as the problem of computing the path expression between nodes on the transitive relation graph.

Let $G^t = (N^t, E^t, \ell_E, \tau, Pr)$ be the probabilistic transitive relation graph for   property p^t. If tuple b_k matches $(a, p', ?obj)$, there must exist a path ps_i: $edge_1(a, b_1)$, $edge_2(b_1, b_2)$,..., $edge_{k-1}(b_{k-1}, b_k)$ from node a to b_k in G^t. It also implies that if events $\tau(edge_1(a, b_1))$, ..., $\tau(edge_{k-1}(b_{k-1}, b_k))$ all are present, then the event $ee(b_k)$ of tuple b_k is present. From Formulas (1) and (2), we get the path expression from node a to b_k:

$$T(a, b_k) = \bigvee_{ps \in PS} \lambda(ps) = \bigvee_{ps \in PS} (\bigwedge_{edge_i \in ps} \tau(edge_i))$$

where PS is the set of paths connecting a to b_k. Obviously, $ee(b_k) = T(a, b_k) = \bigvee_{ps \in PS} (\bigwedge_{edge_i \in ps} \tau(edge_i))$. So the *find* operation on the transitive graph can be

formalized as the *single source path expression* problem on G. Similarly, computing the event of tuple a that matches $(?sub, p', b)$ or the event of tuple (a, b) that matches $(?sub, p', ?obj)$ can also be formalized as the *single sink path expression* problem or the *all pairs path expression* problem.

Generally, if the predicate term in the atomic query is a transitive property, the *find* operation can be formalized as computing the path expression $T(s, v)$ between nodes s and v on the transitive relation graph. We will discuss on how to compute $T(s, v)$ efficiently in Section 4. An example of an atomic query with a transitive property is shown in Fig. 2(b).

– **Join (⊖)**

The join (⊖) operation joins two relations on their shared attributes. $R_1 \ominus R_2$ contains all combinations of a tuple from relation R_1 and a tuple from R_2 where they shared attributes are equal.

$$ee_{R_1 \ominus R_2}(t, t') = ee_{R_1}(t) \wedge ee_{R_2}(t')$$

An example of join operation is shown in Fig.3.

– **Project (π)**

The project operation (π) restricts an RDF relation to a subset of its attributes. A tuple belongs to the result relation if at least one of its origin tuples belongs to the argument relation. The event expression of result tuple t' can be represented as the disjunction of the complex events of original tuples:

$$ee_{\pi_{(A)}}(t') = \bigvee_{t : \pi_{(A)}(t) = t'} ee(t)$$

3.2 Representing Answers of Queries as DNF

In this section, we will show that the answers of a query can be represented as a disjunctive normal formula (DNF). Given a conjunctive query $Q \leftarrow q_1, q_2, \ldots, q_n$, where Q is the goal and $q_1, q_2, \ldots, q_n$ are subgoals. For obtaining answers, we do the *find* operation for every atomic query first and then do the join operation $(q_1 \ominus q_2 \ominus \ldots \ominus q_n)$ between subgoals; we can get tuples with the form of $\bigwedge_i t_i$ where t_i is one of the answers of q_i. We do the final project $\prod_{Var(Q)} (q_1 \ominus q_2 \ominus \ldots \ominus q_n)$ at the end, which groups tuples based on the values of attributes $Var(Q)$. Thus, the result tuples can be represented as the disjunctive normal formula $\bigvee_j C_j$, where C_j is the conjunctive clause.

So our problem can be transferred to evaluate the probabilities of DNFs. Note that if a predicate term in the atomic query q_i is a transitive property then the event expressions of answers t_i may be the complex events i.e. DNFs. In this case, we need to convert the formulas to DNF formulas with $O(mn)$ where m is the maximal number of clauses in t_i for q_i and n is the number of result tuples.

3.3 Computing the Probability of DNF Formula (BDD)

It is known that computing the probability of DNF formula is an #P-hard problem, even if all variables are independent, as they are in our case. Some methods such as Monte Carlo method [7] is proposed for computing the probability of DNF. In this paper, we adopt the binary decision diagrams (BDDs) [8] method which is used widely in digital-system design and combinatorial optimisation.

A binary-decision diagram represents a DNF formula as a rooted directed acyclic graph. Each non-terminal vertex v is labeled by a variable $var(v)$ and has arcs directing toward two children: $lo(v)$ (shown as a dashed line in Fig.4) corresponding to the case where the variable is assigned 0; $hi(v)$ (shown as a solid line) corresponding to the case where the variable is assigned 1. Each terminal vertex is labeled 0 or 1. For a given assignment to the variables, the probability value yielded by the DNF formula is determined by tracing a path from the root to a terminal vertex, following the branches indicated by the values assigned to the variables. The algorithm for computing the probability of DNF formula using BDD is given in *Algorithm ComProbability* [8].

DNF formula
$d=(t_1 \wedge t_2) \vee (t_1 \wedge t_3 \wedge t_4)$

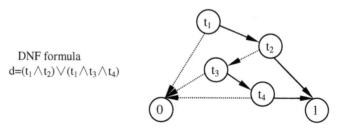

Fig. 4. DNF formula and the corresponding BDD

Algorithm ComProbability
input: BDD vertex v;
output: Probability
1   If v is the 1-terminal **Then Return** 1;
2   **Else**
3   **If** v is the 0-terminal **Then Return** 0
4   **Else** // v is a non-terminal vertex
5   lo=the low children of n;
6   hi=the high children of n;
7            $\Pr(hi) :=$ ComputeProb(hi);
8            $\Pr(lo) :=$ ComputeProb(lo);
9   **Return** $\Pr(v)\cdot\Pr(hi) + (1- \Pr(v)) \cdot\Pr(lo)$

4   Evaluation of Atomic Query with Transitive Property

In Section 3.1, we have shown that if the predicate term in the atomic query is a transitive property p^t, then the *find* operation can be formalized as computing the path expression between two nodes on the transitive relation graph. In this section, we will discuss how to process the *find* operation on the transitive relation graph efficiently.

4.1   Storing the Transitive Relation Graph

We define transitive relation $\prec_{pt}$ as a partial order relation of node pairs on G^t. Each directed edge (x, y) in G^t implies $x \prec_{pt} y$. According to transitive property, if there exists a path from node x to z in G^t, i.e. $x \mapsto z$, then we have $x \prec_{pt} z$ such that x is the *ancestor* of z and z is the *descendant* of x. For example, in Fig.5(a), node a is the ancestor of node g and $a \prec_{pt} g$.

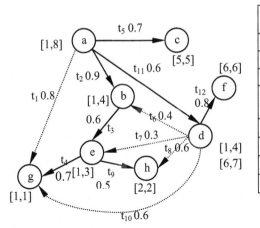

node	Immediate Successors	encoding
a	{b, d, g, c}	[1,8]
b	{e}	[1,4]
c	∅	[5,6]
d	{b, e, h, g, f}	[1,4] [6,7]
e	{g, h}	[1,3]
f	∅	[6,6]
g	∅	[1,1]
h	∅	[2,2]

Fig. 5 (a). A sample of transitive relation graph **(b).** Encoding for nodes

To accelerate the *find* operation, we pre-compute the transitive closure of relation $\prec_{pt}$ and store it. Some previous work has been done on storing the transitive closure relation [9, 10]. Agrawal et.al [11] proposed to assign a node multiple intervals that encapsulate reachability information for its descendant nodes. Nodes of the graph can be covered by a spanning tree. Each node is assigned with an integer interval [start, end] according to the visited orders in a depth-first traversal such that the integer "start" is the postorder number of the node and the integer "end" is the lowest postorder number among its descendants. The relation $\prec_{pt}$ between node pairs can be checked by their overlapping intervals. a node x is an ancestor of a node y, only if y.start>x.start and y.end<x.end.

For example, every node in Fig.5(a) is assigned integer intervals as shown in Fig.5(b). The dashed arcs are non-spanning tree arcs in the graph. Given two nodes a and e, since the interval [1, 4] of node e is overlapped by the interval [1, 8] of node a, we have $a \prec_{pt} e$ and $a \mapsto e$.

4.2 Find Operation on Transitive Relation Graph

In this section, we discuss the *find* operation (σ) on the transitive relation graph. As shown in Section 3.1, if the predicate term in the atomic query is a transitive property, the *find* operation can be formalized as computing the path expression $T(s, v)$ from nodes s to v in the transitive relation graph. We assume no cycles contained in the transitive relation graph.

We first consider the exact algorithm of *find* operation on the transitive relation graph. It finds all paths from s to v for computing $T(s,v)$ by depth-first search. Since the reachability information between nodes is known (according to the encoding of nodes), it is possible to avoid transversing the whole graph. The algorithm first expands all successors v_i of node s. If $v_i \mapsto v$, it implies that there exists at least one path from s to v through v_i and the algorithm should expand the successors of v_i.

Conversely, if $v_i \not\mapsto v$ it implies that there is no path from s to v through v_i and the algorithm could stop expanding the successors of v_i. The reachability information here is a kind of heuristic information used to focus searching on promising paths from s to v. Worst case space and time complexity of the algorithm are $O(h)$ and $O(b^h)$ respectively, where h is the maximum length of the simple path from nodes s to v and b is the branching factor of nodes.

When pairs of nodes are connected by multiple paths, it fails to discard substantial paths using reachability information. Furthermore, the path expression $T(s,v)$ would be large, which becomes computationally infeasible to compute the probability of the path expression. For example, in Fig.5(a) since node a and node g are strongly connected, it almost traverses all edges in the graph to compute $T(a,g) = t_1 \vee (t_2 \wedge t_3 \wedge t_4)$ $\vee (t_{11} \wedge t_6 \wedge t_3 \wedge t_4) \vee (t_{11} \wedge t_7 \wedge t_4) \vee (t_{11} \wedge t_{10})$.

To improve the efficiency of computing $T(s,v)$, we propose an approximate algorithm. The basic idea is trying to obtain the incomplete path expression (denoted by $\tilde{T}(s,v)$) between two nodes, which is smaller than the complete one with approximate probability. The approximate algorithm will estimate the error of incomplete path expression. If the estimated error is smaller than the approximation threshold ε, then the algorithm will stop and return the incomplete path expression.

Note that the path expression between nodes s and v is a DNF formula $\bigvee_{i=1}^{k} \lambda(ps_i)$, where k is the number of paths from s to v and $\lambda(ps_i)$ is the conjunctive clause representing the path expression of path ps_i. Now we give the definition of ε-approximation path expression as follows:

Definition (ε-approximation path expression) Given the path expression $T(s,v) = \bigvee_{ps_i \in PS} \lambda(ps_i)$ where PS is the set of all paths from s to v, we say that $\tilde{T}(s,v)$ is the ε-approximation of $T(s,v)$ if :

1) $\Pr(T(s,v)) - \Pr(\tilde{T}(s,v)) \leq \varepsilon$
2) $\tilde{T}(s,v) = \bigvee_{ps_i \in A} \lambda(ps_i)$, such that $A \subseteq PS$

For example, in Fig.5(a), given $T(a,b) = t_2 \vee (t_{11} \wedge t_6)$, $\tilde{T}(a,b) = t_2$ and $\varepsilon = 0.03$, we can compute $\Pr(T(a,b)) = \Pr(t_2 \vee (t_{11} \wedge t_6)) = 0.924$, $\Pr(\tilde{T}(a,b)) = \Pr(t_2) = 0.9$, $\Pr(T(a,b)) - \Pr(\tilde{T}(a,b)) = 0.024 \leq 0.03$. So $\tilde{T}(a,b)$ is 0.03-approximation of $T(a,b)$.

We employ the iterative-deepening search to find the paths from s to v. Iterative-deepening search combines breadth-first optimality with the low space complexity of depth-first search. In this way, we find the paths from s to v by running depth-first search repeatedly with a growing search depth. For each given search depth h, we define *FoundedPaths* as the set of paths from s to v we have founded. We construct the incomplete path expression: $\tilde{T}_h(s,v) = \bigvee_{ps_i \in FoundedPaths} \lambda(ps_i)$. We also define

PromisingPaths as the set of paths $ps(s, v_i)$ in the search tree that are cut off such that the length of $ps(s, v_i)$ is equal to depth h and $v_i \mapsto v$.

Now the problem is how to bound the error of incomplete path expression $\tilde{T}_h(s,v)$ for each search depth h. We construct two DNF formulas d_{lower} and d_{upper} to represent the lower bound and upper bound for $\tilde{T}_h(s,v)$:

$$d_{lower} = \bigvee_{ps_i \in FoundedPaths} \lambda(ps_i) \ ; \quad d_{upper} = \bigvee_{ps_i \in FoundedPaths \cup Promisin gPaths} \lambda(ps_i)$$

d_{lower} is the disjunction of expression of founded paths from s to v and d_{upper} is the disjunction of path expression of founded paths and promising paths from s to v. For each depth h, we have: $\Pr(d_{lower}) \leq \Pr(\tilde{T}_h(s,v)) \leq \Pr(d_{upper})$.

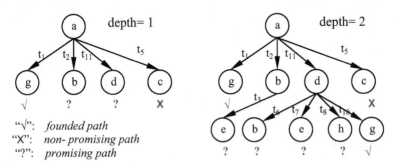

"√": founded path
"X": non- promising path
"?": promising path

Fig. 6. Approximate find algorithm on the Transitive Relation graph

Now we give the approximate *find* algorithm as follows:

Approximate Find Algorithm

Input: nodes v_{org}, $v_{dest,}$, path ps, approximation ε;
Output: $\tilde{T}(v_{org}, v_{dest})$

1   **Initial** Upper = 1, Lower = 0; FoundedPaths={ }; PromisingPaths={ };
2   *depth*=1; ps=Λ(empty path); Candidates={ };
3   **While** (Upper- Lower>ε) **Do**
4   **Expand** v_{org}'s immediate successors $(v_1, v_2, \ldots, v_n)$;
5   **For** i:= 1 to n do **Search**$(v_i, v_{dest}, ps ,depth)$;
6   Lower= ComProbability($\bigvee_{ps_i \in FoundedPaths} \lambda(ps_i)$);
7   Upper=ComProbability($\bigvee_{ps_i \in FoundedPaths \cup Ptomi sin gPaths} \lambda(ps_i)$);
8   *depth*=*depth*+1;
9   **End While**
10   **Return** $\tilde{T}(v_{org}, v_{dest}) = \bigvee_{ps_i \in FoundedPaths} \lambda(ps_i)$

11   **Procedure Search** $(v_k, v_{dest}, ps, depth)$
12   **Initial** h:=0;
13   **If** (h< =*depth*) or (Candidates<>∅) **Then**
14   **Add** v_k's immediate successors $(v_{k1}, v_{k2}, \ldots, v_{kn})$ in to Candidates;
15   **For** i:= 1 to n **Do**
16   **If** $v_{ki}= v_{dest}$ **Then**
17   ps=ps· edge(v_{ki}, v_{dest});
18   **Add** ps into FoundedPaths; **Remove** v_{ki} from Candidates;

19	**If** (v_{ki}.[start] < v_{dest}.[start]) and (v_{ki}.[end]> v_{dest}.[end]) **Then**
20	ps= ps·edge(v_{ki},v_{dest})); **Remove** v_{ki} from Candidates;
21	**If** (h=$depth$) **Then Add** ps into PromisingPaths;
22	**Else Search**(v_{ki}, v_{dest}, ps, h+1);
23	**Else Remove** v_{ki} from Candidates; //$v_{ki}\nrightarrow v_{dest}$
24	**End For**
25	**End Procedure**

For example, to obtain the 0.01-approximation of $T(a,g)$ in transitive relation graph (shown in Fig.5(a)), the algorithm sets search depth=1 first (shown in Fig.6), we then get $FoundedPath$={(a, g)}, $PromisingPaths$={(a, b); (a, d)}. So d_{lower}= t_1, d_{upper} = ($t_1 \vee t_2 \vee t_{11}$), Pr(d_{lower})=Pr(t_1)=0.8, Pr(d_{upper})=Pr($t_1 \vee t_2 \vee t_{11}$)=0.92. Since Pr(d_{upper})-Pr(d_{lower}) =0.012 > 0.01, we need to increase the search depth to 2.

When depth=2, we get $FoundedPath$={(a, g); (a, d)·(d, g)}, $PromisingPaths$={(a, b)·(b, e); (a, d)·(d, b); (a, d)·(d, e); (a, d)·(d, h)}. So d_{lower}= $t_1 \vee (t_{11} \wedge t_{10})$, d_{upper} = ($t_1 \vee (t_{11} \wedge t_{10}) \vee (t_{11} \wedge t_{16}) \vee (t_{11} \wedge t_8) \vee (t_{11} \wedge t_7)$). Since Pr($d_{upper}$)-Pr($d_{lower}$)<0.01, we can obtain $\tilde{T}_{(a,g)}$ = $t_1 \vee (t_{11} \wedge t_{10})$ is the 0.01-approximation of $T(a,g)$.

5   Experiments

We generate the dataset based on the Lehigh University Benchmark LUBM [12]. Probability scores are assigned to each triples. They are treated as mutually independent events. We modify the data generator UBA1.7 and add a transitive property pre-$requisite^t$. The domain and range of pre-$requisite^t$ are both class $Course$. The triples with a predicate pre-$requisite^t$ are generated randomly. All algorithms are implemented in Java 1.5 and run on a windows XP professional system with P4 3G CPU and with 1G RAM. We use PSEpro from objectStore (http://objectstore.net) as the storing engine for storing the encoded probabilistic transitive relation graph. We also use JavaBDD (http://javabdd.sourceforge.net/) for BDD operations.

Table 2. Queries for experiments

$Q1$: Q(x):-(?x,type GraduateStudent)(?x,takesCourse,?y)
$Q2$: Q(x,y):-(?x,advisor,?y)(?x,type,FullProfesr)
$Q3$: Q(z):-(?x,teacherOf,?z)(?x,type,AssistantPrpfessor)
$Q4$:Q(x):(?x,pre-requisite^t,GraduateCourse0)(?y,type,FullProfessor)(?y, teacherOf,?x)
$Q5$: Q(x):-(?x,pre-requisite^t,?y)(?z,researcInterest, 'Research12')(?z, teacherOf,?y)

In the first experiment, we measure the running time for five queries developed (Shown in Table 2). $Q4$ and $Q5$ contain transitive property pre-$requisite^t$. We pre-compute the transitive closure of relation $\prec_{pre-requisite^t}$ and store the encoded transitive relation graph. We use the exact $find$ algorithm for $Q4$ and $Q5$. The running time for five queries is shown in Fig.7(a). It shows that the running time of queries with transitive property increases significantly compared with those of the queries without

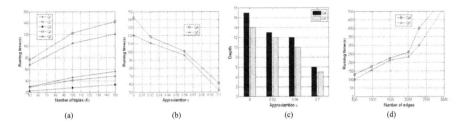

Fig. 7. Running time and iterative depth of queries

transitive property, since most of the time is spent in the *find* operation on the transitive relation graph. This suggests it is desired to optimize the *find* operation on the transitive relation graph.

In the next experiment, we verify the efficiency of *Algorithm Approximate Find* on the transitive relation graph. The dataset contains 150k triples and the transitive relation graph for *pre-requisite*[t] consists of 657 edges and 311 nodes. We vary ε from 0.02 to 0.1. The running time and iterative depth of $Q4$ and $Q5$ is shown in Fig.7(b) and (c). Note that it applies the exact *find* algorithm when ε=0 and the approximate *find algorithm* when ε>0. From Fig.7(b), it shows that *Algorithm Approximate Find* brings considerable time savings, since iterative depth decreases significantly (shown in Fig.7(c)) and path expression generated is relatively small. It suggests that if the users have demands of time restriction, the system could set an appropriate ε for speeding up processing of the queries with transitive property.

We also evaluate our approximate find algorithm on the transitive relation graph with edges ranging from 500 to 3000. The error ε is fixed to 0.01. From Fig.7(d), we can see that the running time increases dramatically when the number of edge is more than 2000. It indicates that we need more efficient algorithms in the case where the transitive relation graph is huge and dense, which is also our future work.

6 Related Work

Query evaluation on the probabilistic relational database [2, 3, 4] and probabilistic XML database [5, 6] has been studied. There is also some research about uncertainty in logic and Web languages. In terms of representation, Fukushige [13] provided a comprehensive method for representing probabilistic relations in RDF. In terms of probabilistic extensions to logic and ontology languages, Koller et. al [14] and Giugno et al. [15] proposed probabilistic extensions of description logics; Costa et al. [16] extended OWL with uncertainty based on first-order Bayesian logic. Our work focused mostly on query evaluation on RDF databases based on possible worlds semantics. In [17], the authors propose the pRDF language and discuss the query evaluation only for the atomic query. In this paper we developed a framework for evaluating SPARQL conjunctive queries on RDF probabilistic databases and we also discussed the approximate query evaluation on the atomic with transitive property.

7 Conclusion

This paper addressed the issue of supporting SPARQL queries on the probabilistic RDF databases. Query evaluation framework is developed based on possible world semantics. We also considered transitive inference on RDF instance data. To accelerate the *find* operation for the atomic query with transitive property, the approximation algorithm is proposed on the transitive relation graph. The future work includes designing more powerful *find* algorithms; developing advanced probabilistic models.

Acknowledgments. This work was partially supported by the Australian Research Council Discovery Project under the grant number DP0878405.

References

1. Raedt, L.D., Kimmig, A., Toivonen, H.: ProbLog: A Probabilistic Prolog and Its Application in Link Discovery. In: IJCAI 2007, pp. 2462–2467 (2007)
2. Fuhr, N., Rölleke, T.: A Probabilistic Relational Algebra for the Integration of Information Retrieval and Database Systems. ACM Trans. Inf. Syst. 15(1), 32–66 (1997)
3. Grädel, E., Gurevich, Y., Hirsch, C.: The Complexity of Query Reliability. In: PODS 1998, pp. 227–234 (1998)
4. Dalvi, N.N., Suciu, D.: Efficient query evaluation on probabilistic databases. VLDB J. 16(4), 523–544 (2007)
5. Abiteboul, S., Senellart, P.: Querying and updating probabilistic information in XML. In: Ioannidis, Y., Scholl, M.H., Schmidt, J.W., Matthes, F., Hatzopoulos, M., Böhm, K., Kemper, A., Grust, T., Böhm, C. (eds.) EDBT 2006. LNCS, vol. 3896, pp. 1059–1068. Springer, Heidelberg (2006)
6. Hung, E., Getoor, L., Subrahmanian, V.S.: PXML: A Probabilistic Semistructured Data Model and Algebra. In: ICDE 2003 (2003)
7. Karp, R.M., Luby, M.: Monte-Carlo Algorithms for Enumeration and Reliability Problems. In: FOCS 1983, pp. 56–64 (1983)
8. Bryant, R.E.: Graph-Based Algorithms for Boolean Function Manipulation. IEEE Trans. Computers 35(8), 677–691 (1986)
9. Aït-Kaci, H., Boyer, R.S., Lincoln, P., Nasr, R.: Efficient Implementation of Lattice Operations. ACM Trans. Program. Lang. Syst. 11(1), 115–146 (1989)
10. Caseau, Y.: Efficient Handling of Multiple Inheritance Hierarchies. In: OOPSLA 1993, pp. 271–287 (1993)
11. Agrawal, R., Borgida, A., Jagadish, H.V.: Efficient Management of Transitive Relationships in Large Data and Knowledge Bases. In: SIGMOD Conference 1989, pp. 253–262 (1989)
12. Guo, Y., Pan, Z., Heflin, J.: An evaluation of knowledge base systems for large OWL datasets. In: McIlraith, S.A., Plexousakis, D., van Harmelen, F. (eds.) ISWC 2004. LNCS, vol. 3298, pp. 274–288. Springer, Heidelberg (2004)
13. Fukushige, Y.: Representing Probabilistic Relations in RDF. In: ISWC-URSW 2005, pp. 106–107 (2005)
14. Koller, D., Levy, A.Y., Pfeffer, A.: P-CLASSIC: A Tractable Probablistic Description Logic. In: AAAI/IAAI 1997, pp. 390–397 (1997)
15. Giugno, R., Lukasiewicz, T.: P-SHOQ(D): A Probabilistic Extension of SHOQ(D) for Probabilistic Ontologies in the Semantic Web. In: Flesca, S., Greco, S., Leone, N., Ianni, G. (eds.) JELIA 2002. LNCS (LNAI), vol. 2424, pp. 86–97. Springer, Heidelberg (2002)
16. da Costa, P.C.G., Laskey, K.B., Laskey, K.J., Pool, M.: International Semantic Web Conference, ISWC-URSW 2005, pp. 23–33 (2005)
17. Udrea, O., Subrahmanian, V.S., Majkic, Z.: Probabilistic RDF. In: IRI 2006, pp. 172–177 (2006)

Recommending Improvements to Web Applications Using Quality-Driven Heuristic Search

Stephane Vaucher[1], Samuel Boclinville[2], Houari Sahraoui[1], and Naji Habra[2]

[1] DIRO, Université de Montréal, Québec, Canada
{vauchers, sahraouh}@iro.umontreal.ca
[2] PReCISE Research Center, FUNDP, University of Namur, Belgium
samuel.boclinville@student.fundp.ac.be, nhag@info.fundp.ac.be

Abstract. Planning out maintenance tasks to increase the quality of Web applications can be difficult for a manager. First, it is hard to evaluate the precise effect of a task on quality. Second, quality improvement will generally be the result of applying a combination of available tasks; identifying the best combination can be complicated. We present a general approach to recommend improvements to Web applications. The approach uses a meta-heuristic algorithm to find the best sequence of changes given a quality model responsible to evaluate the fitness of candidate sequences. This approach was tested using a navigability model on 15 different Web pages. The meta-heuristic recommended the best possible sequence for every tested configuration, while being much more efficient than an exhaustive search with respect to execution time.

1 Introduction

Successful Web applications (WAs) not only satisfy the need of their users for interesting features, but also provide a pleasant user experience as well. Quality problems (eg. bad navigability) can have a negative impact on this experience, and should therefore be corrected. For a manager planning out the maintenance tasks, identifying which task can best correct such problems can be daunting since its impact on quality is generally unknown beforehand.

Many quality characteristics can be defined in a model that evaluates the extent to which an application conforms to a set of non-functional requirements. Such a model typically includes quality rules/standards and is refered to as a *quality model*. While the use of (implicit or explicit) quality models should be part of any improvement process, quality models do not allow, by themselves, to determine what specific changes should be implemented to improve the quality of an application. This is reflected in the literature. There are many contributions focussing on the quality *assessment* of Web applications, yet to the best of our knowledge there is little or no work focussing on its improvement, or more exactly, how to achieve a certain level of quality given resource limitations. What work exists is not specific to Web applications, but rather to general software development [1,2,3].

G. Vossen, D.D.E. Long, and J.X. Yu (Eds.): WISE 2009, LNCS 5802, pp. 321–334, 2009.

In this article, we present a method to propose improvements to a Web application on the basis of a quality model. Given a model, a set of possible transformations and an estimate of available resources, our method will propose an optimised sequence of transformations to apply to an application. To find the exact sequence is generally intractable since it is not solvable in polynomial time. We therefore propose the use of meta-heuristics to find a suitable approximation. The method is implemented using the *simulated annealing* meta-heuristic and is tested in a study that serves as a proof of concept. The study evaluates improvements proposed to the navigability of 15 Web pages. The proposed method is shown to identify the optimal solution in constant time relative to the number of transformations considered. The method is therefore deemed to be well-suited for this problem.

The paper is organised as follows. In the next Section, we present related work in both Web quality assessment and quality improvement by refactoring. Section 3 presents an overview of the proposed method. The quality model used for the study is presented in Sect. 4. Section 5 details the meta-heuristic algorithm (simulated annealing) and the transformations used. Finally, Sect. 6 presents the case study.

2   Related Work

Our work crosscuts two research domains Web quality and refactoring. We present work related to our problem in both domains.

To evaluate WA quality, several contributions have proposed guidelines, principles, checklists, evaluation methodologies and automatic assessment tools. We present some of these contributions. Nielsen and Loranger [4] propose advice on how to address Web usability issues. Boldyreff et al. [5] present a set of metrics to assess WA quality and particularly WA evolvability. Deluze [6] discusses WA performance with respect to existing Internet technologies. These contributions give principles but do not explicitly show how to use them to evaluate the quality of a WA.

Some authors proposed quality assessment methods or models such as WebQEM (Web Quality Evaluation Methodology) by Olsina et al. [7] or FMSQE (Fuzzy Model for Software Quality Evaluation) by Albuquerque et al. [8] . Like many others, these contributions define quality in tree-like, hierarchical models inspired by the ISO 9126 software product standard. The evaluation of a high-level notion of quality is done by aggregating the evaluations of more concrete (and more measurable) sub-factors.

Directly related to this work, Malek et al. [9] proposed a method for building WA quality models using Bayesian networks. Following this method, they produced a model to measure the navigability of Web pages, presented in [15]. In an controlled experiment, they showed that the model could accurately measure the notion of navigability as perceived as by a user. We therefore reused this model to go beyond simple quality assessment and suggest actual improvements to pages. The model is briefly described in Sect. 4. The approach of Malek et al. was also used by Caro et al. [10] for the particular case of Web portal data quality.

Some work has been done to bridge the gap between quality assessment and improvement, mostly in the field of object-oriented (OO) software development. In particular, the focus was put on the impact of refactoring on OO metrics (as in Sahraoui et al. [1] and Dubois et al. [11]). The effect on quality is however implicit (e.g. lower coupling is good) and does not take into consideration a precise and complete evaluation according to a quality model. The determination of refactoring sequences using heuristic-search methods was studied for OO programs (e.g. Seng et al. [3], and Harman and Tratt [12]). In general, the objective is to determine the transformation sequences that best improve some design metrics. This work is however done without knowing whether or not this metric selected is indeed a measure of quality.

Finally, for Web refactoring, Olsina et al. [2] propose refactoring patterns that can be applied to design models with the perspective of improving quality. Ping and Kontogiannis [13] propose a refactoring approach that addresses specifically WA architecture, *i.e.,* dependencies between Web pages. For both contributions, the link between refactoring and quality is implicit, and yet again, the notion of quality is based on best practices instead of on a well-defined notion of quality as provided by a quality model.

3   Recommending Improvements

Any recommendation should be the result of a cost-benefit analysis which compares the *cost* of implementing a change with the *benefit* measured in terms of quality improvement. Although managers should be accustomed to estimating the cost of a change, it is less obvious to estimate its effect on a quality. In fact, most modifications (e.g. refactoring) have a theoretical impact on one or several quality criteria, but it is difficult to decide which of a set of possible modifications is the most appropriate given a specific context. Furthermore, this decision process is even more complicated when these modifications are combined. In this Section, we present how our approach solves these problems.

3.1   Global Overview

At the heart of the proposed approach is the concept of transformations. A transformation is a simple modification to a WA that corresponds to a well-defined developer activity. This activity has a cost and affects the state of a Web page. The objective is to select, out of a domain of possible transformations, the best sequence to apply to a given Web page. In the proposed approach, the cost is determined using an experts estimation of work while the impact of a given solution is left to a quality model.

The proposed approach is illustrated in Fig. 1. It includes two processes used for recommendation: first, the evaluation of quality and second, the suggestion of transformation. The evaluation process judges a page in a given state: the current state, or the state after a sequence of transformations. This process is used by the suggestion process to find an optimal solution.

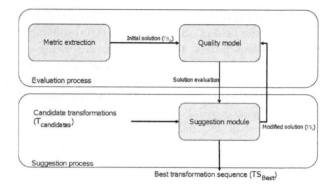

Fig. 1. The global process for the improvement of Web application quality

3.2   Quality Evaluation Process

To evaluate the quality of a page, we rely on a quality model (QM). There are many advantages to relying on a QM. First, it automates the judgment of an expert and can decide objectively even in the presence of contradictory information (ex: clutter vs functionality). Second, as presented in Sect. 2, there are many existing models documented present in the literature. It is thus possible to reuse previous work.

If we take the example of a transformation that adds a search engine to a Web site. The model would not only consider a search functionality has been added, but would likely also consider the effect of the new links/forms necessary to access the the search page. The effect of applying this transformation on the quality of a Web page is not obvious. If we consider a QM that models navigability, adding a search engine might improve navigability in a Web site, but can also add clutter to an interface, decreasing the navigability of a page. In these cases, QMs automates the decision of whether or not the quality has been globally improved.

A model uses metrics as inputs describing the state of a Web page and outputs a score. If we consider a vector of metric values $m = (m_1, m_2, ...)$ used as inputs to a model, the quality model is basically a function $q(m)$.

3.3   Suggestion Process

This process is responsible for suggesting the best sequence of transformations (called solution) that can be applied to a Web page. The fitness of a solution is judged by its effect on its quality as measured by the quality model. Since the model uses metrics as inputs, transformations are defined according to their effects on these metric. Finally, there is a cost constraint limiting the transformations that can be considered.

Measuring Quality Improvement. Let TS be a transformations sequence $TS = (t_1, t_2, ..., t_n)$ *i.e.*, an ordered sequence composed of elements taken from a set of available transformations ($T_{candidates}$). The impact of such a transformation sequence can be expressed as a function that modifies the vector of metric values m by cumulating the effect of the transformations $t_1, t_2, ..., t_n$ in that order.

This function, $apply\_transform$ (1), computes new inputs metrics given a transformation sequence TS. Each individual transformation t_i in TS, is associated to a metric transformation function tr_met_i corresponding to the effect of applying that transformation on the Web page. The output of $apply\_transform$ is the successive application of the functions of the transformations it contains. The modified metrics (m') are then used by the QM to evaluate the global score of the modified page ($q(m')$).

$$m' = apply\_transform(TS, m) = tr\_met_n(tr\_met_{n-1}(\cdots tr\_met_1(m))) \qquad (1)$$

Selecting Solutions. The suggestion process should identify the best solution (TS_{best}) which maximises the quality improvement (Equation 2) given a cost constraint (W).

$$\forall(TS_i) : q(apply\_transform(TS_{best}, m_0)) > q(apply\_transform(TS_i, m_0)) \qquad (2)$$

Each transformation t_i of TS has a cost associated to it, $cost(t_i)$ that should reflect the cost of implementing the transformations. The global cost of a transformation sequence is the sum of the costs of the different transformations composing the sequence and should be inferior to a cost constraint W.

$$Cost(TS) = \sum_{1}^{n} cost(t_i) < W \qquad (3)$$

Searching for the Best Solution. To find an optimal solution, the suggestion process needs to consider every possible solution. Without the cost constraint, the search space is nearly infine because some transformations can be repeated. Even with the cost constraint, the search space cannot be explored in polynomial time. If we were to simplify the problem and consider that every possible transformation can be applied or not (binary decision), with no ordering, the number of solutions to consider is $\in O(2^n)$. Furthermore, since there is no direct relationship between a transformation and its effect on quality, we cannot limit the search space. There are however meta-heuristics that can find nearly optimal solutions by guiding the exploration of the large search space in a reasonnable amount of time [14].

4   Assessing Web Quality

In this Section, we present the kind of quality model used by the suggestion process to evaluate proposed transformation sequences. This general description is accompanied by the description of a model focussing on the evaluation of a major attribute, the navigability of Web pages.

4.1   Quality Model

Quality models are built to systematize a qualitative judgment by a stakeholder of a phenomenon. For these QM to be useful, they should be as automated as possible. Generally, they use metrics to quantitatively describe an observable state as perceived by an expert and output a judgment as either a predicted category (e.g. good vs. bad) or a predicted value (e.g. score).

For use in the proposed approach, a QM must return a global score which can be used to compare different solutions. Furthermore, its judgment process must be fully automated, requiring no information beyond the initial description of a Web page.

4.2   Navigability Model

To illustrate our recommendation approach, we use the QM presented in [15]; it evaluates the navigability of Web pages. The QM is built using Bayesian Belief Networks (BBNs). BBNs organise an evaluation process as a graph. The graph contains links which indicate causal or descriptive relationships and nodes which indicate metrics or decisions. The metrics are the inputs to the model and are represented using probability distributions. Nodes with incoming links are decisions (intermediate or final) and are represented using conditional probability tables.

Figure 2 presents the evaluation procedure for navigability. The model has 13 inputs which are described in Table 1. The decision of whether or not a page is navigable (navigability node) directly depends on three sub-characteristics: the ability of a user to *locate* a desired page, his ability to find information on the desired page (bind) and the download speed. Both the locate and bind nodes are intermediate decision nodes which depends on other sub-characteristics.

The operational details of the QM including the precise process to convert metrics into probability distributions is described in [15]. In a nutshell, binary

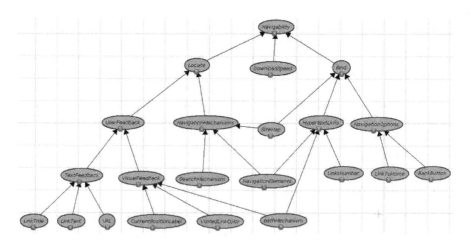

Fig. 2. The navigability model

metrics are converted into probabilities of 0 or 1 if the metric is respectively false or true. Numeric metrics are converted into discrete probabilities distributions (e.g. for $P(low)$, $P(medium)$ or $P(high)$) in two steps. First, fuzzy clustering is used to identify significant thresholds for the metrics values (a threshold for every possible discrete value). Second, when evaluating a Web page, the probability distribution for input nodes is interpolated using the distance of the metrics extracted with the neighbouring thresholds.

The output node (Navigability) corresponds to the probability that a user would consider the navigability satisfactory. The more likely users are satisfied, the better the quality of the page.

Table 1. Inputs to the navigability model

Metric	Node	Type
Download speed	DownloadSpeed	measure (count s.)
Ratio of links with titles (LTitle)	LinkTitle	measure ($[0,1]$)
Ratio of links with text (LTxt)	LinkText	measure ($[0,1]$)
Presence of a search engine (SE)	SearchMechanism	binary
Presence of a site map (SM)	SiteMap	binary
Presence of a menu (Nav)	NavigationElements	binary
Indication of location in Web site (CPL)	CurrentPositionLabel	binary
Visited links change color (VLC)	VisitedLinkColor	binary
Breadcrumbs (BRC)	PathMechanism	binary
Number of links in page (NoL)	LinkNumber	measure (count)
Link to home (Home)	LinkToHome	binary
Support for Back Button (BB)	BackButton	binary

5 Suggesting Improvements

In this Section, we present the suggestion process; this process is illustrated using the example of recommending improvements to navigability. To begin, transformations are defined with respect to their effect on the inputs of the navigability QM presented earlier. Then, we present how to select the best sequence of transformations to improve the quality of a Web page. Considering every possible solution when there are many possible transformations is intractable. We therefore rely on a meta-heuristic algorithm: *simulated annealing*.

5.1 Transformations for Navigability

To improve quality, it is necessary to first identify the set of candidate transformations ($T_{candidates}$) and define their effects on the inputs of the QM. Let T_{NAV} be the set of candidate transformations available to improve navigability. These transformations can be general changes used to improve quality like refactorings or quality-specific changes (e.g. adding a search engine). In Table 2, we define a set of transformations applicable to improving navigability of a Web page. They

Table 2. Selected transformations (T_{NAV}) and their effects on metrics(Table 1))

Transformation	Metric variation
Add/Remove site map	NoL +/- 1, SM := true/false
Add/Remove search engine	NoL +/- 1, SE := true/false
Add/Remove URL*	NoL +/- 1
Add/Remove link to Home	NoL +/- 1, Home := true/false
Add/Remove menu	NoL +/- a, Nav := true/false
Add/Remove current position label	NoL +/- b, CPL := true/false
Add/Remove breadcrumbs	NoL +/- c*, BRC := true/false
Enable/Disable back button support	BB := true/false
Add/Remove visited colour link	VLC := true
Divide/Merge page*	NoL := NoL $\div/\times$ 2 +/- d*
Correct link text	LTxt := 100%
Correct/Remove link titles	LTitle := 100%/0%

are defined according to their effect on the 12 metrics of the navigability QM. Those which can be repeated multiple times are identified by an asterisk.

Some transformations like adding/removing breadcrumbs affect a variable number of links (variables a, b, c and d) which depends on the Web applications themselves. The exact number of links need to be evaluated empirically.

5.2 Simulated Annealing

A naive approach to suggestion would consider every possible transformation sequence given a cost constraint. Although the small size of T_{NAV} allows for an exploration of every possible solution in reasonnable time, it would not scale if we were to consider a larger set of transformations.

Simulated annealing(SA) is a meta-heuristic algorithm inspired by the metallurgic process of annealing. It guides an exploration of a large search space to find a mear optimal solution. It follows the steps described in Algorithm 1. It reflects a cooling process where a temperature Trs_0 decreases geometrically by a factor α at every iteration. Every iteration, a solution is compared to Nrs neighbouring solutions. When a neighbouring solution is better, as judged by a fitness function, it is retained for the next iteration. If the neighbour is not better, it can still be retained if, but only with a probability that depends on the current temperature. This element of randomness exists to avoid stagnating at a locally optimal solution. As the algorithm temperature drops, there however are fewer weaker solutions accepted as $e^{-\Delta/T_{rs}}$ decreases. Finally, the algorithm ends when until a specified number of iterations has passed. As with all meta-heuristics, SA is a general algorithm which is adapted to specific problems. Three elements are required to adapt SA: the problem's search space, the neighbourhood function and the fitness function.

Solution Space and Representation. T_{NAV} defines the transformations available for any given page evaluated by the navigability QM. When evaluating a page, not all transformations are however applicable. Excluding these transformations limits the size of the search space and improves performance. For example, it is useless to consider correcting link titles for a page where the links are all correct. We therefore limit the domain of valid transformations for a specific Web page $T_{Page} \subset T_{NAV}$ and solutions are vectors of transformations $s = (t_1, t_2, ..., t_n)$ where $t_i \in T_{Page}$.

Neighbourhood Function. The initial state is an empty sequence of transformations and the neighbourhood function(NF) is responsible to iteratively modify it until a satisfactory final solution is found. For every iteration of the SA algorithm, the neighbourhood function chooses randomly to either add a new transformation to the solution or remove a transformation already contained in s. Possible additions are however limited to those that will preserve the coherence of the overall solution. The set of acceptable transformations is $T_{neigh} \subset T_{page}$ where $t_i \in T_{neigh} \wedge coherent(s, t_i)$ for a solution s. The coherence function serves not only to ensure that a solution returned makes sense to a user, but also to reduce the search space.

Two possible situations can lead to incoherent sequences: *redundant* transformations and *opposite* transformations. Some transformations affect discrete values of metrics of a quality model (e.g. adding a search engine). It would be redundant for these types of transformation to be reapplied twice. Some groups of transformations have opposite effects (e.g. merging and splitting a page). A candidate transformation is deemed incoherent with an existing solution if the solution already contains an opposite transformation. The only way it can be inserted is if all the opposite transformations are deleted first.

Fitness Function. For any given solution, a QM acts as a fitness function to evaluates how "good" is a solution. Since the SA algorithm requires a single value for the fitness evaluation of a solution, the fitness function needs to combine the notions of cost and quality improvement. Our fitness function (4) penalises a solution if it does not respect the cost constraint. A higher QM score solution which does not respect the cost constraint (W) will always yield a lower fitness value than any solution that respects it.

$$fitness(s) = \begin{cases} 0.5 + Nav\_Impr * 0.5 & \text{if } cost(s) \leq W \\ Nav\_Impr * 0.5 & \text{if } cost(s) > W \end{cases} \qquad (4)$$

where Nav_Impr corresponds to the quality improvement: the relative variation between the current QM score and the initial score.

6 Case Study

In this Section, we present a study to evaluate the feasibility of applying the proposed approach in an industrial context.

```
SIMULATED ANNEALING(Trs0 ,Nrs, . . .) ;
Choose s₀                                      /* Chose initial solution */ ;
Trs := Trs₀                                    /* Initialise temperature */ ;
STOP := false ;
BestSol := s := s₀                             /* Initialise Best Solution */ ;
while !STOP do
    for i := 1 to Nrs do
        Generate s′ ∈ N(s)                     /* Generate neighbour */ ;
        Δfitness := fitness(s′) − fitness(s)   /* Fitness function */ ;
        if ΔC ≥ 0 then
            s := s′                            /* accept the solution */ ;
        else
            Generate random number r ∈ [0, 1] ;
            if r ≤ e^{−ΔC/Trs} then
                s := s′                        /* Accept with small probability */ ;
            end
        end
        if C(s′) ≤ C(BestSol) then
            BestSol := s′ ;
        end
    end
    Trs := α.Trs                               /* Lower the temperature */ ;
    if StopCriteria then
        STOP := True ;
    end
end
return BestSol ;
```

Algorithm 1. Simulated Annealing

6.1 Objectives

The goal of the study is to verify the usefulness of the proposed recommendation approach from the perspective of manager facing quality problems. The approach is evaluated according to two objectives:

- Verify if the meta-heuristic finds the optimal solution;
- Measure if the execution uses a reasonable amount of time and resources. This is particularly important since the evaluation of a Web application would depend on the evaluation of every Web page.

We used the QM and the transformation set respectively presented in Sects. 4 and 5. For the first objective, we compared the quality improvement of the solution returned by an exhaustive search to that of the best solution of the SA algorithm. For the second objective, we compared their execution times. It was possible to compare our approach to an exhaustive search types because of the small number of possible transformations (T_{NAV}) considered in this case.

Table 3. Transformation domain and initial quality of studied pages

# Page	1	2	3	4	5	6	7	8	9	10	11	12	13	14	15
$|T_{Page}|$	21	17	17	15	13	13	15	15	9	11	13	11	9	11	9
q_{NAV}	13%	19%	24%	25%	68%	69%	73%	73%	76%	77%	83%	84%	84%	84%	85%

6.2 Study Setup

The comparison is performed on a set of 15 randomly selected Web pages. These pages are of different quality (q_{NAV}) and have different search spaces ($|T_{Page}|$) as shown in Table 3. As expected, the pages with fewer possible transformations generally have better navigability scores.

In order to collect metrics on the Web pages, we developed a Web application. Most metrics could be extracted automatically by using htmlunit[1], a Java library generally used to test Web sites. The metrics which required human intervention were entered using a Web interface. This interface also allows a user to filter out transformations that should not be considered and define T_{Page}.

The SA algorithm was initialised with the following parameters: $Trs = 10$, $Nrs = 30$ and $\alpha = 0.8$. The Trs value can be considered a typical value considering the size of the search space. At every iteration. the algorithm selects 30 random neighbours. The α value chosen is relatively low, as normal values are closer to 0.9. This parameter limits the number of iterations used.

Table 4. Transformation costs

Transformation	Cost
Add/Remove site map	3
Add/Remove search engine	6
Add/Remove URL	2
Add/Remove link to Home	1
Add/Remove menu	6
Add/Remove current position label	5
Add/Remove breadcrumbs	6
Enable/Disable back button support	1
Add/Remove visited colour link	2
Divide/Merge page	8
Correct link texts	5
Correct/Remove all the link titles	6/4

Setting Costs. To compare the quality solutions found (first objective), Web pages are evaluated according to four different cost constraints (W): $< 0.25W_{MAX}$, $< 0.5W_{MAX}$, $< 0.75W_{MAX}$ and $< W_{MAX}$, where W_{MAX} is the maximum cost of

---

[1] http://htmlunit.sourceforge.net

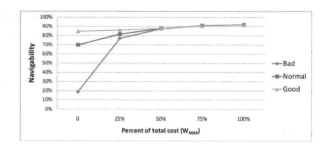

Fig. 3. Quality for different cost constaints

a solution. This cost is computed by adding the cost of all transformations $\in T_{Page}$. The costs of the different transformations, are set according to our expected level of difficulty. The costs are presented in Table 4. Whether these costs are realistic or not, should not affect the validity of the results since they affect both compared search types (SA and exhaustive) equivalently.

6.3 Results

For every Web page considered and for every cost constraint, the SA algorithm found the best solution. This verifies the first objective of the study. Fig. 3 summarises the quality improvement for each cost step. In this plot, pages are grouped together according to their initial quality scores to minimise visual clutter. There are pages with bad navigability ($q_{NAV} \leq 25\%$, pages 1-4), normal navigability (pages 5-10), and good navigability ($> 80\%$, pages 11-15).

After the first cost constraint (25% of total cost), quality is improved for all pages, most significantly for bad and normal pages (increase of 70% and 10% respectively) The reason for this is simple, the most cost-effective transformations are identified and executed first. The worst pages tend to improve much more than good pages at this step because they are more ways they can be transformed positively than good pages. Another explanation is that their sets T_{Page} tend to be larger and thus W_{MAX} (and consequently $0.25W_{MAX}$) is much

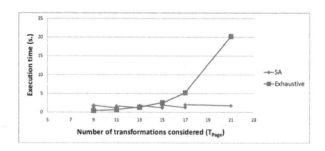

Fig. 4. Execution time vs. number of transformations considered

larger than that of better pages. From the second constraint on (50% of total cost), the quality of all pages becomes less and less discriminable as it gradually converges to the best possible quality level (92%), attained when $(W = W_{MAX})$.

Figure 4 shows the difference in execution time. The number of considered candidate transformations is on the X axis, while the execution time is on the Y axis. The Figure shows that SA requires constant (1.5 s.) time to find the best solution while the exhaustive search quickly become inefficient (over 20 seconds to consider 21 transformations). We conclude that SA is capable to find good solutions in a reasonable amount of time.

7   Conclusion

We proposed an approach to recommend improvements to Web applications. This is based on the idea of leveraging existing work on quality assessment and refactoring. Given a quality model and a set of possible transformations defined with respect to the QM, the approach searches for the best transformations to implement considering cost constraints.

The approach consists of two processes: a suggestion process which uses a meta-heuristic algorithm to propose transformation sequences and a solution evaluation process which uses a QM as a black-box to evaluate these sequences. The approach is general since the exact choice of QM depends on the quality characteristic that needs to be improved. Furthermore, both general and quality-specific transformations can be considered.

We illustrated the approach using a QM evaluating the *navigability* of Web pages. We also presented a set of transformations defined according to their effects on this QM. In a feasibility study, we showed that the proposed approach managed to find the optimal sequence of improvements to 15 different Web pages while being scalable.

It is possible to apply this technique to every page contained in a Web application, but some transformations affect more than one page (e.g. adding a search engine). In future work, we plan on investigating how to propose the best improvements for a whole application instead of treating pages individually.

References

1. Sahraoui, H.A., Godin, R., Miceli, T.: Can Metrics Help to Bridge the Gap between the Improvement of OO Design Quality and its Automation? In: Proceedings of the 16th International Conference on Software Maintenance, pp. 154–162 (2000)
2. Olsina, L., Rossi, G., Garrido, A., Distante, D., Canfora, G.: Incremental Quality Improvement in Web Applications Using Web Model Refactoring. In: Weske, M., Hacid, M.-S., Godart, C. (eds.) WISE Workshops 2007. LNCS, vol. 4832, pp. 411–422. Springer, Heidelberg (2007)
3. Seng, O., Stammel, J., Burkhart, D.: Search-based Determination of Refactorings for Improving the Class Structure of Object-oriented Systems. In: Cattolico, M. (ed.) Proceedings of the 2006 GECCO conference companion on Genetic and evolutionary computation, pp. 1909–1916. ACM, New York (2006)

4. Nielsen, J., Loranger, H.: Prioritizing Web Usability. New Riders, Berkeley (2006)
5. Boldyreff, C., Warren, P., Gaskell, C., Marshall, A.: Web-SEM Project: Establishing Effective Web Site Evaluation Metrics. In: Proceedings of the 2nd International Workshop on Web Site Evolution, Washington, DC, USA, pp. 17–20. IEEE Computer Society, Los Alamitos (2000)
6. Deleuze, C.: Some Points Affecting Web Performance. In: Cordeiro, J.A.M., Pedrosa, V., Encarnação, B., Filipe, J. (eds.) Proceedings of the 2nd International Conference on Web Information Systems and Technologies, pp. 242–245. INSTICC Press (2006)
7. Olsina, L., Lafuente, G., Rossi, G.: Specifying Quality Characteristics and Attributes for Websites. In: Murugesan, S., Desphande, Y. (eds.) Web Engineering. LNCS, vol. 2016, pp. 266–278. Springer, Heidelberg (2001)
8. Albuquerque, A.B., Belchior, A.D.: E-Commerce Websites: a Qualitative Evaluation
9. Malak, G., Sahraoui, H.A., Badri, L., Badri, M.: Modeling Web-Based Applications Quality: A Probabilistic Approach. In: Aberer, K., Peng, Z., Rundensteiner, E.A., Zhang, Y., Li, X. (eds.) WISE 2006. LNCS, vol. 4255, pp. 398–404. Springer, Heidelberg (2006)
10. Caro, A., Calero, C., de Salamanca, J.E., Piattini, M.: Refinement of a Tool to Assess the Data Quality in Web Portals. In: Proceedings of the7th International Conference on Quality Software, pp. 238–243. IEEE Computer Society, Los Alamitos (2007)
11. Du Bois, B., Demeyer, S., Verelst, J.: Does the "Refactor to Understand" Reverse Engineering Pattern Improve Program Comprehension? In: Proceedings of the 9th European Conference on Software Maintenance and Reengineering, Washington, DC, USA, pp. 334–343. IEEE Computer Society, Los Alamitos (2005)
12. Harman, M., Tratt, L.: Pareto Optimal Search Based Refactoring at the Design Level. In: Lipson, H. (ed.) Proceedings of the 2007 GECCO conference companion on Genetic and evolutionary computation, pp. 1106–1113. ACM, New York (2007)
13. Ping, Y., Kontogiannis, K.: Refactoring Web sites to the Controller-Centric Architecture. In: Proceedings of the 8th European Conference on Software Maintenance and Reengineering, pp. 204–213. IEEE Computer Society, Los Alamitos (2004)
14. Ferland, J.A., Costa, D.: Heuristic search methods for combinatorial programming problems. Technical report, Université de Montréal (2001)
15. Haydar, M., Malak, G., Sahraoui, H., Petrenko, A., Boroday, S.: Anomaly Detection and Quality Evaluation of Web Applications. In: Handbook of Research on Web Information Systems Quality. IGI Global (2008)

A Web Recommender System for Recommending, Predicting and Personalizing Music Playlists

Zeina Chedrawy and Syed Sibte Raza Abidi

Faculty of Computer Science, Dalhousie University, Halifax, Canada
{chedrawy,sraza}@cs.dal.ca

Abstract. In this paper, we present a Web recommender system for recommending, predicting and personalizing music playlists based on a user model. We have developed a hybrid similarity matching method that combines collaborative filtering with ontology-based semantic distance measurements. We dynamically generate a personalized music playlist, from a selection of recommended playlists, which comprises the most relevant tracks to the user. Our Web recommender system features three functionalities: (1) *predict* the likability of a user towards a specific music playlist, (2) *recommend* a set of music playlists, and (3) *compose* a new personalized music playlist. Our experimental results will show the efficacy of our hybrid similarity matching approach and the information personalization method.

Keywords: Web personalization, Web recommender systems, music recommendation, semantic similarity matching.

1 Introduction

Access to and consumption of relevant information is paramount to Web users, especially given the sheer volume of information now available over the Web. A key approach to overcome cognitive overload faced by users is the development of *user-centric systems*—termed as Web recommender systems, adaptive or personalized information retrieval systems—that retrieve/recommend Web-based information artifacts such as documents and Websites based on the user's preferences and goals. The idea is that a *one size fits all* model for Web information retrieval is non-optimal, rather the individualistic nature of each user should be taken into account to provide the user with a personalized Web experience [12,13]. This brings to relief the need to pursue *intelligent information personalization* by working with the 'semantics' of the information through the use of Semantic Web technologies [15].

In this paper, we present a Web recommender system for recommending, predicting and personalizing music playlists based on a user model. We have developed an item and user matching approach that combines the Web 2.0 notion of peer wisdom and Web 3.0 concept of semantic relationships between items/users. Our similarity matching approach is a hybrid of collaborative filtering (CF) and semantic distance measurement methods. Our music recommender system offers the functionality to dynamically compose a personalized music playlist by selecting the most relevant individual tracks from a list of recommended playlists, and then

G. Vossen, D.D.E. Long, and J.X. Yu (Eds.): WISE 2009, LNCS 5802, pp. 335–342, 2009.
© Springer-Verlag Berlin Heidelberg 2009

aggregating them to generate a personalized playlist. Our Web recommender system features three functionalities: (1) predict the likability of a user towards a specific music playlist, (2) recommend a set of music playlists that are potentially of interest to a user, and (3) compose a new personalized music playlist. Our experimental results will show that (1) the use of semantic descriptions of information items combined with the multi-attribute CF improves the accuracy of predictions and the quality of recommendations; and (2) the application of our compositional adaptation method allows fine-tuning of existing information items to make them more personalized vis-à-vis the user model. Fig. 1 shows the schematic of our Web-based music recommender system.

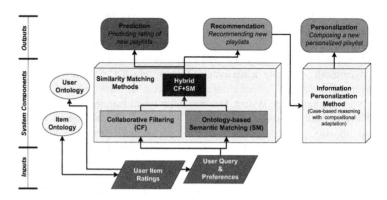

Fig. 1. A schematic of our Web-based recommender system

2   Web Recommender Systems for Information Personalization

Web recommender systems can be categorized into the following three categories (a) Standard Content/Collaboration Based Systems; (b) Hybrid Systems; (c) Semantics Based Systems. Recommender Systems employing the *content-based filtering* approach recommend information artifacts based on their relevance to existing user profiles and on the descriptions of the artifacts [1,2]. The limitation of the content-based approach is that recommendation is limited to the description within the user profile, thus other interesting and/or related information artifacts that do not match the user profile are not recommended. Recommender Systems using *collaborative-filtering* (CF) approach take a community-based approach by computing the similarities between the profiles of multiple users and then recommend information artifacts that are preferred by the community closest to a given user [3,10]. CF based recommender systems on the one hand may recommend surprising information artifacts, whereas on the other hand, they may miss out on information artifacts that are uniquely of interest to a specific user but not necessarily to his/her community. To address the limitations of content and CF based recommender systems, the next generation of recommender systems employed a hybrid of both content and collaborative approaches [4,8,9]. To improve the information search and the matching of information items and users, the recent trend is to exploit the semantic information associated with user and item descriptions. Typically, ontologies are created to represent the user model and the information item by incorporating salient concepts and their relationships. A semantic matching algorithm can look beyond simple keyword search by traversing an RDF graph to find both specializations and generalizations of a given concept. Examples of such systems are [5,14].

From the literature review it is clear that there is an abundance of Web recommender systems that are apt at recommending information artifacts based on user and/or community model. However, these systems are not able to further adapt the available information artifacts to compose a *personalized information artifact*—the recommended artifact may have some elements that are of no use to the user. Our work is an extension of the abovementioned systems as we pursue to dynamically compose a personalized music playlist by selecting music objects from multiple Web sources and then aggregating them in a meaningful manner to yield a composite information artifact that is more pertinent to the user's interest.

3 Our Hybrid Item-Based Similarity Matching Method

For the purposes of predication, recommendation and personalization of playlists, the first step is to establish similarities between existing items/users. We have extended existing methods to develop a hybrid item-based similarity matching method.

Item-Based Collaborative Filtering Multi-Attribute Similarity: We have extended traditional single-attribute CF approach [6] by developing a multi-attribute rating scheme that allows users to rate a music playlist along five attributes (*lyrics, rhythm, tunes, performance,* and *overall likability*). The algorithm is described below:

Step 1- Specify user preferences. The user assigns the weight values (W_A) to each attribute along which similarities between information items are to be computed.
Step 2- Compute the similarity between items with respect to every attribute. For every attribute A, the similarity between information items I and J as given by [6]:

$$Sim_A(I,J) = \frac{\sum_{U \in Users}(R_A(U,I) - \bar{R}_A(U))(R_A(U,J) - \bar{R}_A(U))}{\sqrt{\sum_{U \in Users}(R_A(U,I) - \bar{R}_A(U))^2}\sqrt{\sum_{U \in Users}(R_A(U,J) - \bar{R}_A(U))^2}}. \qquad (1)$$

Where $R_A(U,I)$ denotes the rating of user U on item I with respect to attribute A; $\bar{R}_A(U)$ is the average rating of user U as per attribute A.
Step 3- Compute the CF multi-attribute similarity between items

$$MultSim(I,J) = \frac{\sum_{A=1}^{5} W_A \cdot Sim_A(I,J)}{\sum_{A=1}^{5} W_A}. \qquad (2)$$

Item-Based Semantic Similarity: In this method, we calculate the similarities between two items based on their semantic descriptions given in an ontology. The similarity between items I and J is based on the ratio of the common/shared RDF descriptions between I and J (*count_common_desc(I,J)*) to their total descriptions (*count_total_desc(I,J)*) as proposed by [7] and is given by:

$$SemSim(I,J) = \frac{count\_common\_desc(I,J)}{count\_total\_desc(I,J)}. \qquad (3)$$

We argue that our semantic similarity approach helps to bootstrap Web recommender systems in case not enough ratings are available on a particular item (cold-start problem), and also provides explanations about why a particular information artifact has been recommended or not.

Hybrid Item-Based Semantic-CF Similarity: Using (Eq.2 and Eq.3) we calculate the hybrid Semantic-CF similarity using a linear weighted approach as:

$$Sim(I,J) = W_M * MultSim(I,J) + W_S * SemSim(I,J). \qquad (4)$$

Where W_M and W_S are the weights assigned to CF multi-attribute and semantic similarities respectively.

4 Prediction, Recommendation and Personalization of Playlists

Prediction. Given a user U, an instance in the user ontology containing the ratings on music playlists, and a playlist P (not yet rated by U), our recommender system predicts the rating of U on P using the method provided in [6], where the similarity between items is replaced by our hybrid similarity (Eq.4).

Recommendation. The recommendation of a list of music playlists to a user is based on his/her past ratings and the playlists' ratings of other peers. The algorithm for recommending a list of playlist most similar to the user is the standard CF algorithm by [6] with the extension of using our hybrid Semantic-CF similarity (Eq.4).

Personalization. Typically, Web recommender systems recommend the complete information artifact even if it comprises multiple components—for instance a book comprises chapters, and a music playlist comprises individual songs. We have developed a component-level recommendation approach that allows the dynamic selection of components from artifacts, as per their relevance to the user model, and aggregating them to compose a personalized information artifact. It may be noted that, our approach is only applicable when the multiple independent components do not have any inter-relationships between them and are simply part of a larger artifact [12].

Given S_N as the set of the N playlists recommended to the user, we recommend a personalized playlist as follows:

Step 1- Compute the similarity of the individual tracks within S_N with the user model. Let $Sim(P_i,U)$ $(i=1 \ to \ N)$ be the similarity of playlist P_i to user U (i.e. similarity of playlist P_i to the set of playlists preferred by U as derived in [6]). Let $Sim_1(T,U)$ be the similarity of track T to U. Because the same track may belong to multiple playlists, therefore we define the similarity of a track to the user model over all the playlists in S_N that have the track T as follows:

> For every Track $T \in P_i$,
>> For every Playlist $P \in S_N$,
> If $T \in P$ then $Sim_1(T,U) = Sim_1(T,U) + Sim(P_i,U).$ \qquad (5)

Step 2: Compute the genre-based similarity between individual tracks and the user model. Each playlist and track has a list of music genres assigned to it (i.e. Rock). Each user is also assigned a list of genres that represent the genres of the playlists he has listened to. We represent users and tracks as vectors in the g-dimensional genre space and use the cosine between these vectors as a measure of their similarity. Let $\vec{U}_U$ and $\vec{R}_T$ be the vectors of g dimensions for user U and track T respectively, where g corresponds to the number of genres available. Then the cosine similarity $cos\_sim(T,U)$ between U and T is:

$$cos\_sim(T, U) = cos\left(\vec{R}_T, \vec{U}_U\right) = \frac{\vec{R}_T.\vec{U}_U}{\|\vec{R}_T\|_2 \|\vec{U}_U\|_2} = \frac{\Sigma_g (m_g n_g)}{\sqrt{\Sigma_g m_g^2}\sqrt{\Sigma_g n_g^2}} \ . \qquad (6)$$

Where n_g is the number of playlists of genre g that user U has listened to; m_g is the number of times the track T has been assigned genre g. We apply the sigmoid function to the cosine similarity to scale it within the range [-1,1]. Genre similarity between a user U and a track T is given as:

$$Sim_2(T, U) = \frac{1}{1 + e^{cos\_sim(T,U)}} \ . \qquad (7)$$

We compute the overall similarity of each track with the user model as follows:

$$Sim(T, U) = Sim_1(T, U) * Sim_2(T, U) \ . \qquad (8)$$

Step 3: Select tracks that are most similar to the user model by sorting them based on their similarity values and selecting the top M tracks ($M=15$).

5   Experimental Results and Evaluation

In this Section, we evaluate the performance of our Web based music recommendation system in terms of (1) the impact of semantic similarity towards improving the accuracy and quality of predictions and recommendations, (2) the appropriateness of the personalized playlist towards the user model.

The music data is taken from the Website *Lastfm* (http://www.last.fm) that is a radio station which uses CF to recommend a radio stream to its listeners. The data set contains 215 users having 46850 album ratings distributed across five attributes of an album. In total we have 4426 albums, where each album contains a number of tracks. For testing purposes, we divide the user ratings dataset into *training* (80%) and *testing* sets (20%). We perform a 5-fold cross validation and results are averaged over the 5 cycles of execution. We conducted a set of experiments using four different scenarios. *Scenario 1* uses the CF method only, *Scenario 2* uses the semantic similarity method only, *Scenario 3* uses a hybrid of CF and semantic similarities methods with equal contribution (both have a weight of 0.5), and *Scenario 4* uses a hybrid of CF and semantic similarities with different weights ($W_S=0.7$; $W_M=0.3$).

Evaluating Prediction. We evaluate prediction based on the rating along the *overall likability* attribute only; the same evaluation can be applied to the other attributes. This experiment takes as input test users and their items for which a predicted rating value is desired, and the respective weights assigned to the rating

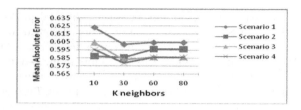

Fig. 2. MAE values for predictions with varying neighborhood sizes

attributes of these users. We use the *Mean Absolute Error (MAE)* [6] to measure the accuracy of our predictions. We initially set all test users' weights to $W_{lyrics} = 0.2$; $W_{performance} = 0.3$; $W_{tunes} = 0.4$; $W_{rhythm} = 0.1$; $W_{overall\ likability} = 0.9$ for all four scenarios. Fig. 2 shows the values of MAE obtained with various neighborhood sizes. It may be noted that $K=30$ is the optimal neighborhood size for all scenarios.

Table 1 shows the MAE values for the four scenarios with neighborhood size $K=30$. It may be noted that *Scenario 4* produces the least MAE.

Table 1. Prediction MAE values for the four scenarios *(K=30)*

	Scenario 1	Scenario 2	Scenario 3	Scenario 4
MAE	0.60192	0.58563	0.58257	0.57878

Next, we aim to understand the contribution of the semantic similarity method to the overall hybrid similarity matching approach. We modulate the contribution of the semantic similarity method towards the calculation of the overall similarity with $K=30$ (Fig. 3). We note that when $W_S=0$ (*Scenario 1*), MAE = 0.60192; when $W_S =1$ (*Scenario 2*), MAE = 0.58563. Fig. 3 shows that MAE reaches its minimum when the contributions are $W_M=0.3$ and $W_S=0.7$, thus highlighting the significant impact of our semantic similarity approach to the overall similarity value.

Evaluating Recommendation. We evaluate the recommendation accuracy of our music recommender system using the *HITS' number* as in [11]. We set $N = 15$ top recommendations, $M = 15$ tracks/playlist. We set $K=30$, $W_s= 0.7$, $W_M=0.3$.

From Table 2 it may be noted that there is a clear advantage (i.e. number of HITS) when we combine the semantic and CF similarities thus vindicating the efficacy of our hybrid similarity matching approach.

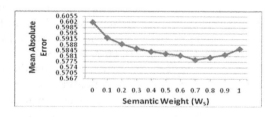

Fig. 3. Impact of the semantic similarity approach on the overall prediction

Table 2. HITS' number for CF and Semantic-CF recommendations for all test sets

Test Set		1	2	3	4	5
Semantic-CF Recommendation	*Hits*	13	10	20	17	12
CF Recommendation		2	7	4	6	2

Evaluating Personalized Playlists. We measure the quality of our personalized playlists in terms of (1) the similarity between the personalized playlist and the user model with respect to an *Appropriateness Factor (AF)*; and (2) the *Matching Genre Ratio (MGR)* of the personalized playlist to the preferred genre(s) of the user model. For each track in the personalized playlist, we compute the *MGR* as:

$$\tag{9}$$

Where *MGcount(U,T)* is the number of matching genres between user U and track T of the personalized playlist P; *Gcount(T)* is the number of genres for track T. We test our personalization approach by taking 20% of test users from every test dataset.

For all test users in each test dataset, we generated personalized playlists based on the N playlists that were earlier recommended to them. We compared the *AF* of the personalized playlist with the corresponding user model. Table 3 shows the percent increase in *AF* for all test users for every test dataset. On average, the increase in the *AF* over all 5 test datasets is 71.55%.

Our results show that by averaging the *MGR* over all test users in the test datasets, 74.43% of the genres associated with the personalized tracks match the user models (see Table 3). Therefore, we conclude that the personalized playlist is closer to the user's interests as compared to the original N recommended playlists.

Table 3. Impact of the personalization on the recommendations in terms of *AF* and *MGR*

	Test Set 1	Test Set 2	Test Set 3	Test Set 4	Test Set 5
AF % Increase	88.55 %	57.31%	81.38 %	66.59 %	63.93 %
Average	71.55 %				
MGR	68.69 %	78.34 %	72.63 %	75.32 %	77.18 %
Average	74.43 %				

6   Discussion and Concluding Remarks

Our work has demonstrated the potential of using semantic relationships to match items and individuals improves the search results, as opposed to the use of traditional collaborative filtering methods. Our information personalization approach generates improved web experiences for users in terms of providing them personalized information as opposed to the entire artifact.

As part of our future work, we plan to further extend our semantic similarity matching technique beyond using just the semantic attributes to compare items and we plan to develop a new semantic similarity measure that takes into account explicit relationships between information items that can be reasoned over to infer information items that are better correlated with the user model.

References

1. Billsus, D., Pazzani, M., Chen, J.: A Learning Agent for Wireless News Access. In: Proc. of the Intl. Conf. on Intelligent User Interfaces, pp. 33–36 (2002)
2. Cano, P., Koppenberger, M., Wack, N.: An industrial-Strength content-based Music Recommendation System. In: Proc. 28th Intl. ACM SIGIR Conf. on Research and Development in Information Retrieval, Salvador, Brazil (2005)
3. Shani, G., Chickering, M., Meek, C.: Mining Recommendations from the Web. In: Proceedings of the 2nd Intl. Recommender Systems Conference, RecSys (2008)
4. Debnath, S., Ganguly, N., Mitra, P.: Feature weighting in content based recommendation system using social network analysis. In: Proc. 17th Intl. Conf. on World Wide Web, Beijing, China, pp. 1041–1042 (2008)
5. Katakis, I., Tsoumakas, G., Banos, E., Bassiliades, N., Vlahavas, J.: An adaptive personalized news dissemination system. Journal of Intelligent Information Systems 32, 191–212 (2009)
6. Sarwar, B., Karypis, G., Konstan, J., Riedl, J.: Item-Based Collaborative Filtering Recommendation Algorithms. In: Proc. of the 10th Intl. WWW Conference (2001)
7. Hau, J., Lee, W., Darlington, J.: A Semantic Similarity Measure for Semantic Web Services. In: Web Service Semantics: Towards Dynamic Business Integration (2005)
8. Resnick, P., et al.: GroupLens: An Open Architecture for Collaborative Filtering of Netnews. In: Proc. of ACM Conf. on Computer Supported Cooperative Work, pp. 175–186. Chapel Hill, NC (1994)
9. Celma, O., Ramrez, M.H.P.: Foafing the music: A Music Recommendation System Based on RSS Feeds and User Preferences. In: Proc. 6th Intl. Conf. on Music Information Retrieval (2005)
10. Cotter, P., Smyth, B.: PTV: Intelligent Personalized TV Guides. In: Proc. 12th Conf. Innovative Applications of Artificial Intelligence, pp. 957–964. MIT Press, Cambridge (2000)
11. Sarwar, B., Karypis, G., Konstan, J., Riedl, J.: Analysis of Recommendation Algorithms for e-commerce. In: 2nd ACM conf. on Electronic Commerce, pp. 158–167 (2000)
12. Abidi, S.S.R.: Designing Adaptive Hypermedia for Internet Portals: A Personalization Strategy Featuring Case Base Reasoning With Compositional Adaptation. In: Garijo, F.J., Riquelme, J.-C., Toro, M. (eds.) IBERAMIA 2002. LNCS (LNAI), vol. 2527, Springer, Heidelberg (2002)
13. Abidi, S.S.R.: Intelligent Information Personalization; From Issues to Strategies. In: Germanakos, P. (ed.) Intelligent User Interfaces: Adaptation and Personalization Systems and Technologies. IGI Global Press (2008)
14. Mobasher, B., Jin, X., Zhou, W.: Semantically Enhanced Collaborative Filtering on the Web. In: Berendt, B., Hotho, A., Mladenič, D., van Someren, M., Spiliopoulou, M., Stumme, G. (eds.) EWMF 2003. LNCS (LNAI), vol. 3209, pp. 57–76. Springer, Heidelberg (2004)
15. Spivack, N.: The Third-Generation Web is Coming,
   http://www.KurzweilAI.net/
16. Schafer, J., Frankowski, D., Herlocker, J., Sen, S.: Collaborative Filtering Recommender Systems. In: Brusilovsky, P., Kobsa, A., Nejdl, W. (eds.) Adaptive Web 2007. LNCS, vol. 4321, pp. 291–324. Springer, Heidelberg (2007)

Verification of Composite Services with Temporal Consistency Checking and Temporal Satisfaction Estimation

Azlan Ismail, Jun Yan, and Jun Shen

School of Information Systems and Technology, University of Wollongong,
Wollongong, NSW, 2522, Australia
{ai423, jyan, jshen}@uow.edu.au

Abstract. This paper aims to address the issue of consistency and satisfaction of composite services with the presence of temporal constraints. These constraints may cause conflict between services and affect the estimation over composition requirements. Existing verification approaches have not adequately addressed this issue. Therefore, this paper contributes to the verification method with temporal consistency checking and temporal satisfaction estimation. A set of checking rules and estimation formulae are presented according to workflow patterns and temporal dependencies. The method will lead to three major outcomes; consistent with satisfactory combination, consistent with unsatisfactory combination and inconsistent with unsatisfactory combination.

Keywords: composite service, temporal consistency, temporal constraints, temporal satisfaction, verification.

1 Introduction

A business process in the Web services environment contains a set of services that are composed using compositional language such as WS-BPEL[9]. The composed services may invoke external parties which offer required functionality based on certain quality criteria with some additional constraints.

This work focuses on the temporal constraints that can be attached together with the offered values. The temporal constraints can be utilized to restrict a period of time (e.g., execution duration, availability) or time points (e.g., start time operation, finish time operation, setup time operation) or both. In the Web services environment, these constraints can be extracted from Service Level Agreement(SLAs). Recently, a specification of SLA namely WS-Agreement [2] has been proposed and some recent works have used and extended it.

In our previous work [7], we have shown that temporal constraints may cause violation to individual temporal constraint of services when they are analyzed collaboratively. Thus, it is vital to check the temporal consistency and ensure that only consistent combinations are considered for the satisfaction estimation.

To address these problems, we propose a verification method which takes several major inputs including temporal constraints to perform consistency checking

G. Vossen, D.D.E. Long, and J.X. Yu (Eds.): WISE 2009, LNCS 5802, pp. 343–350, 2009.

and temporal satisfaction estimation. This method utilises workflow patterns [15] as the basis to explore the process model. A set of consistency checking rules are proposed based on the temporal relation [1] [16] and temporal constraints verification in workflow [13] [4]. The temporal estimation formulae are proposed based on the QoS aggregation of service composition [3] [8]. The method will lead to three distinct outcomes; consistent with satisfactory combination, consistent with unsatisfactory combination and inconsistent with unsatisfactory combination.

The rest of the paper is organised as follows. Section 2 describes the data required for enabling the checking and estimation procedure. Section 3 presents the verification method with a set of checking rules and formulae as well as summarising them as an algorithm. Section 4 remarks some related works. Finally, section 5 summarises this paper and discusses some future work.

2   Capturing Related Information

The temporal consistency checking and the temporal satisfaction estimation requires various data as inputs. Information related to the execution order can be extracted from a composition model described using one of the composition languages such as WS-BPEL. The information related to QoS, temporal and composition requirement can be extracted from Web service level agreement specification such as WS-Agreement. Formally, the verification model involves a set of elements (P, F, T, U, G) where each of them is described as follows:

- P is a process represented as a graph with two elements (A, E). A is a set of activities $(s_1, ..., s_n)$ where each s_i refers to an individual service that provides one or more operations. E is a set of edges that define the relations between services, $E \subseteq A$ x A. In WS-BPEL, services can be identified through $< partnerlink >$. Furthermore, their relations can be determined by the control structure activities such as $< sequence >$, $< flow >$, etc.
- F is a function that retrieves a pattern as a subset of the process, S. For the sake of simplicity, this paper focuses on two types of patterns;
  - Sequential pattern which is comparable to $< sequence >$ in WS-BPEL. When the pattern type is sequential, S contains a pair of services, such as $(s_i \prec s_j)$.
  - Parallel pattern which is comparable to $< flow >$ in WS-BPEL. When the pattern type is parallel, S contains a partial set of services, such as $(s_i \prec (s_{i+1}, ..., s_{i+m}) \prec s_k)$.
- T is a function that retrieves temporal constraints information of a component service $s_i \in A$. We focus on two types of temporal constraints as follows:
  - start-after-time constraint sa; it constrains the time for a service $T_{sa}(s_i)$ to start executing.
  - finish-before-time constraint fb; it constrains the time for a service $T_{fb}(s_i)$ to finish executing.

These constraints can be referred to the time period defined in WS-Agreement specification. Recent works such as [14] has discussed and proposed some extension to WS-Agreement. For instance, an agreement can be defined by two dates; start date and finish date. A start date does not mean an operation must start on the date, but rather states it can start at any time from this date. Similar interpretation can be given to the finish date. Obviously, these two dates can be translated into sa as the start date and fb as the finish date.

In addition to the agreement period, an agreement may also have a validity period for specific quality attribute. This data can be extracted through $< QualifyingCondition >$. For instance, a duration time of 2 hours can only be executed within office hour, 9am to 5pm. In regards to the temporal constraints, we may translate 9am as sa and 5pm as fb.

- U is a function that retrieves duration value of a component service $s_i \in A$, given as $U_d(s_i)$. A duration represents an interval value such as 10 minutes, 1 hour, etc. The value can be obtained from $< ServiceLevelObjective >$.
- G is a set of composition requirements. Since we are interested in time, the requirement would be any time-related requirement. In this work, we focus on the total time to be spent by the composed services.

3   Verification Approach

The following subsections provide the details of the temporal consistency checking and temporal satisfaction estimation which lead to the outcomes.

3.1   Temporal Consistency Checking

This procedure contains a set of rules which are based on the following:

- *Temporal relation* - As mentioned in [11] there are thirteen types of temporal relations formalised by [1] as interval relations and followed by [16] as point relations. For the sake of simplicity, we focus only on *before* and *overlap* temporal relations. Furthermore, we analyse the relation between temporal constraints based on point relations.
- *Estimation of Completion Time* - The estimated completion time will be computed and checked against fb. We utilize the works from temporal verification of workflow such as [13] [4]. However, in our work, the temporal constraint verification is meant to support determination of consistent combination between services.

With these rules, two distinct decisions can be defined, as follows:

Consistent Combination, CON -
   It is determined when any of the following rule is satisfied, given as follows:

1. R_1: The fb of preceding service maintains the *before* type relation with the sa of succeeding service.
2. R_2: The addition of estimated completion time of the preceding service and the duration of succeeding service does not violate the fb of succeeding service.

These rules are applied to check the consistency of sequential, splitting and merging patterns. For the sequential pattern with a pair of services $(s_i \prec s_j)$, consistent combination, given as CON_{seq}, is determined when it satisfies the following:

$$R_1(T_{fb}(s_i) < T_{sa}(s_j)) \vee R_2(T_{sa}(s_i) + U_d(s_i) + U_d(s_j) <= T_{fb}(s_j)) \quad (1)$$

For the splitting pattern with a set of services $(s_i \prec (s_{i+1}, ..., s_{i+m}))$, consistent combination, given as CON_{split}, is determined when it satisfies the following, $\forall j = \{1, ..., m\}$:

$$R_1(T_{fb}(s_i) < T_{sa}(s_j)) \vee R_2(T_{sa}(s_i) + U_d(s_i) + U_d(s_j) <= T_{fb}(s_j)) \quad (2)$$

For the merging pattern with a set of services $((s_{i+1}, ..., s_{i+m}) \prec s_k)$, consistent combination, given as CON_{merge}, is determined when it satisfies the following, $\forall j = \{1, ..., m\}$:

$$R_1(T_{fb}(s_j) < T_{sa}(s_k)) \vee R_2(T_{sa}(s_j) + U_d(s_j) + U_d(s_k) <= T_{fb}(s_k)) \quad (3)$$

Combination of splitting and merging determine the consistency of the parallel pattern. Therefore, for the parallel pattern, given as CON_{par}, consistent combination is determined when it satisfies this rule:

$$CON_{split} \wedge CON_{merge} \quad (4)$$

Inconsistent Combination, INC -
It is determined when the combination violates R_1 AND R_2 for any pattern. The rules can be summarized as follows:

$$\neg CON_{seq} \vee \neg CON_{split} \vee \neg CON_{merge} \quad (5)$$

3.2 Temporal Satisfaction Estimation

This procedure will eventually lead to the overall conclusion namely; (i) consistent with satisfactory combination, (ii) consistent with unsatisfactory combination and (iii) inconsistent with unsatisfactory combination. We adopt the work from QoS aggregation of service composition [3] [8] to design the formulae. With the given formulae, the estimated time to be spent can be accumulated based on QoS workflow reduction techniques such as the one proposed in [3]. However, as discussed in our previous work [7], the temporal constraints may cause some waiting time. In this work, we define it as follows:

Definite Waiting Time, dwt -
It is determined when the fb of preceding service maintains the *before* type relation with the sa of succeeding service. Therefore, for the sequential pattern, the definite waiting time is computed as follows:

$$dwt_{seq} = T_{sa}(s_j) - T_{fb}(s_i) > 0 \quad (6)$$

For the splitting pattern, the definite waiting time is computed as follows:

$$dwt_{split} = \min(T_{sa}(s_{i+1}), ..., T_{sa}(s_{i+m})) - T_{fb}(s_i) > 0 \qquad (7)$$

For the merging pattern, the definite waiting time is computed as follows:

$$dwt_{merge} = T_{sa}(s_k) - \max(T_{fb}(s_{i+1}), ..., T_{fb}(s_{i+m})) > 0 \qquad (8)$$

For the parallel pattern, the definite waiting time is computed as follows:

$$dwt_{par} = dwt_{split} + dwt_{merge} \qquad (9)$$

With this definition and formulae, the temporal satisfaction estimation for the total time to be spent can be obtained as follows:

Estimated Time Spent, $EstS$ -
For the sequential pattern, the estimated time spent is formulated as follows:

$$EstS_{seq} = U_d(s_i) + U_d(s_j) + dwt \qquad (10)$$

For the parallel pattern, the estimated time spent is formulated as follows:

$$EstS_{par} = U_d(s_i) + \max(U_d(s_{i+1}), ..., U_d(s_{i+m})) + U_d(s_k) + dwt \qquad (11)$$

By applying the workflow reduction technique, the estimated time to be spent can be accumulated. Therefore, the overall conclusion can be defined as follows:

Consistent with Satisfactory Combination, $CON_{satisfy}$ -
Given a process P, consistent with satisfactory combination is determined as follows:

$$for\ any\ patterns,\ (CON_{seq} \wedge CON_{par}) \wedge (EstS_{seq} + EstS_{par} \leq G) \quad (12)$$

Consistent with Unsatisfactory Combination, $CON_{unsatisfactory}$ -
Given a process P, consistent with unsatisfactory combination is determined as follows:

$$for\ any\ patterns,\ (CON_{seq} \wedge CON_{par}) \wedge (EstS_{seq} + EstS_{par} > G) \quad (13)$$

Inconsistent with Unsatisfactory Combination, $INC_{unsatisfactory}$ -
Given a process P, inconsistent with unsatisfactory combination is determined as follows:

$$for\ any\ patterns,\ (INC_{seq} \vee INC_{par}) \vee (EstS_{seq} + EstS_{par} > G) \quad (14)$$

3.3   The Algorithm

This section presents the algorithm for verifying composite services with temporal consistency checking and temporal satisfaction estimation as depicted in (1). The algorithm begins by extracting a pattern from P (line 1). It is followed by an iterative verification based on sequential or parallel pattern (lines 3-9 and 10-17). For both, the verification performs the temporal consistency checking (lines 4 and 11). If consistent, then it moves to the estimation (lines 5 and 12). Consistent services are then combined towards atomic service (lines 5 and 12-13). For the successful iteration, the algorithm checks whether the process can satisfy the composition requirement which leads to consistent with satisfactory or consistent with unsatisfactory (lines 22 and 24). For the unsuccessful iteration, the outcome is inconsistent with unsatisfactory combination (line 27).

Require: (P, F, T, U, G)
Ensure: (CSC, CUC, IUC)
1: $F_{type}(S) \leftarrow$ get the first pattern in P
2: **while** P is not an atomic service **do**
3:     **if** the pattern is $F_{seq}(s_i \prec s_j)$ **then**
4:         **if** consistency checking is CON_{seq} **then**
5:             $U_d(s_i) \leftarrow EstS_{seq}$ and $s_i = s_i + s_j$ and Update P with new s_i
6:         **else**
7:             Mark as inconsistent and break
8:         **end if**
9:     **end if**
10:    **if** the pattern is $F_{par}(s_i \prec (s_{i+1}, ..., s_{i+m}) \prec s_k)$ **then**
11:        **if** consistency checking is CON_{par} **then**
12:            $U_d(s_i) \leftarrow EstS_{par}$ and $s_i = s_i + (s_{i+1}, ..., s_{i+m}) + s_k$ and
13:            Update P with new s_i
14:        **else**
15:            Mark as inconsistent and break
16:        **end if**
17:    **end if**
18:    $F_{type}(S) \leftarrow$ get the next pattern in P
19: **end while**
20: **if** P is an atomic service **then**
21:    **if** satisfaction checking is $CON_{satisfy}$ **then**
22:        **return** CSC
23:    **else**
24:        **return** CUC
25:    **end if**
26: **else**
27:    **return** IUC
28: **end if**

Algorithm 1. Verification Algorithm

4   Related Works

Verification of composite services is gaining attention from researchers. The taxonomy proposed in [5] is utilised for presenting this section. In relation to our work, two perspectives are involved, namely the performance perspective and temporal perspective.

From the performance perspective, the aim is typically to predict the satisfaction of QoS values over the performance metric. In the context of web service composition, existing work such as [3] [8] proposed measurement methods based on workflow structures such as sequential, parallel, etc. Our work adopts this direction by emphasizing the needs to check for temporal constraint consistency which may give impact to the prediction. Moreover, it is worth to highlight recent work that addressed the integration of composition specification and QoS-related specification to support performance prediction. In [6], an extension of WSDL was proposed to describe and integrate QoS information into BPEL processes. In addition, [17] addressed the integration of information gathered from BPEL and SLA and used the simulation technique to verify against performance metric.

From the temporal perspective, the aim is to ensure the given temporal constraints are consistent when combining with the composition specification. Within the web service composition, [10] addressed verification of BPEL process with temporal constraints which was presented as finite-state machine equipped with a set of clock variables. Then, the verification of temporal constraints was implemented by using a model checker. In addition, [12] proposed temporal constraints that were defined in OWL-S by using time ontology. Then, an extension of Petri Nets was proposed and used to verify the temporal constraints. In contrast to [10] [12], we consider different types of temporal constraints that can be extracted from SLAs. Furthermore, we utilised workflow-based pattern instead of formal method.

5   Conclusion and Future Work

In this paper, we have presented a verification method that utilises various information including temporal constraints and structural dependencies to perform the checking and estimation procedure. The method will lead to three major outcomes. In addition, it can contribute to the analysis of the behavior of composite services from the temporal consistency and satisfaction perspective. Obviously, there is no point of making a prediction if services are actually inconsistent between each other.

Future work will focus on the evaluation of the effectiveness of the approach. Furthermore, we will explore other properties such as related to resource that contribute to the consistency checking and satisfaction estimation. This will expand the method to cater from different perspectives.

Acknowledgments. This research is partly supported by the Australian Research Council Discovery Project Scheme under grant number DP0663841 and University of Wollongong Small Research Grant.

References

1. Allen, J.F.: Maintaining knowledge about temporal intervals. Commun. ACM 26(11), 832–843 (1983)
2. Andrieux, A., Czajkowski, K., Dan, A., et al.: Web services agreement specification (ws-agreement). In: Open Grid Forum (2007)
3. Cardoso, J., Sheth, A., Miller, J., et al.: Quality of service for workflows and Web service processes. Web Semantics: Science, Services and Agents on the World Wide Web 1(3), 281–308 (2004)
4. Chen, J., Yang, Y.: Temporal dependency for dynamic verification of temporal constraints in workflow systems. In: Jin, H., Pan, Y., Xiao, N., Sun, J. (eds.) GCC 2004. LNCS, vol. 3251, pp. 1005–1008. Springer, Heidelberg (2004)
5. Chen, J., Yang, Y.: A taxonomy of grid workflow verification and validation. Concurrency and Computation: Practice and Experience 20(4), 347–360 (2008)
6. D'Ambrogio, A., Bocciarelli, P.: A model-driven approach to describe and predict the performance of composite services. In: Proc. WOSP 2007, pp. 78–89 (2007)
7. Ismail, A., Yan, J., Shen, J.: Dynamic service selection for service composition with time constraints. In: Proc. ASWEC 2009, pp. 183–190 (2009)
8. Jaeger, M.C., Rojec-Goldmann, G., Muhl, G.: Qos aggregation for Web service composition using workflow patterns. In: Proc. EDOC 2004, pp. 149–159 (2004)
9. Jordan, D., Evdemon, J., Alves, A., et al.: Web services business process execution language version 2.0. OASIS (2007)
10. Kazhamiakin, R., Pandya, P., Pistore, M.: Representation, Verification, and Computation of Timed Properties in Web Service Compositions. In: Proc. ICWS 2006, pp. 497–504 (2006)
11. Koubarakis, M.: Temporal CSPs. In: Handbook of Constraint Programming, pp. 665–697. Elsevier, Amsterdam (2006)
12. Liu, R., Dai, G., Hu, C., et al.: A Verification Method for Temporal Consistency of Service Flow. In: Proc. COMPSAC 2008, pp. 1187–1192 (2008)
13. Marjanovic, O.: Dynamic verification of temporal constraints in production workflows. In: Proc. ADC 2000, pp. 74–81 (2000)
14. Müller, C., Martín-Díaz, O., Ruiz-Cortés, A., Resinas, M., Fernández, P.: Improving temporal-awareness of WS-agreement. In: Krämer, B.J., Lin, K.-J., Narasimhan, P. (eds.) ICSOC 2007. LNCS, vol. 4749, pp. 193–206. Springer, Heidelberg (2008)
15. van der Aalst, W.M.P., Hofstede, A.H.M.T., Kiepuszewski, B., et al.: Workflow patterns. Distributed and Parallel Databases 14(1), 5–51 (2003)
16. Vilain, M., Kautz, H.: Constraint propagation algorithms. In: Proc. AAAI 1986, pp. 377–382 (1986)
17. Xiao, H., Chan, B., Zou, Y., et al.: A Framework for Verifying SLA Compliance in Composed Services. In: Proc. ICWS 2008, pp. 457–464 (2008)

Adaptive Rich User Interfaces for Human Interaction in Business Processes

Stefan Pietschmann, Martin Voigt, and Klaus Meißner

Technische Universität Dresden
Faculty of Computer Science, Chair of Multimedia Technology
01062 Dresden, Germany
{Stefan.Pietschmann, Martin.Voigt, Klaus.Meissner}@tu-dresden.de

Abstract. In recent years, business process research has primarily focussed on optimization by automation, resulting in modeling and service orchestration concepts implying machine-to-machine communication. New standards for the integration of human participants into such processes have only recently been proposed [1,2]. However, they do not cover user interface development and deployment. There is a lack of concepts for rich business process UIs supporting flexibility, reusability and context-awareness. We address this issue with a concept for building human task presentations from service-oriented UIs. Those *User Interface Services* provide reusable, rich UI components and are selected, configured and exchanged with respect to the current context.

1 Introduction

Over the past years, the Internet has evolved to a stable and popular application platform. This is especially true for business applications, which heavily employ Web Services to provide functionality in a technology-independent, reusable way. Usually, those applications represent business processes (BPs) that are executed in a service-oriented fashion based on a composition description, the most prominent composition language being WS-BPEL [3]. BPEL focuses on machine-to-machine communication and a fully automatic process execution.

Although BP research stems from the modeling and automation of originally human-centered workflows, current process engines and standards like BPEL do not reflect the undisputed importance of human interactions. Common human activities in processes involve data input and validation as well as decision making. Consequently, several vendors like IBM and Oracle provide proprietary BPEL extensions in their engines to support such "human tasks". Of course, their use entails interoperability and portability problems [4]. Promising recent proposals like BPEL4People (B4P) [1] and WS-HumanTask [2] allow for a standardized integration of human-based activities in BPEL processes.

Problems that persist with these specifications are the development and deployment of the human task user interfaces. Mature standards and tools have been developed for BP modeling, specification and execution, but no comparable efforts have addressed the presentation layer.

G. Vossen, D.D.E. Long, and J.X. Yu (Eds.): WISE 2009, LNCS 5802, pp. 351–364, 2009.

To adequately support human tasks, sophisticated user interfaces are needed. They should, for example, include advanced data visualization techniques (e. g., interactive tables and graphs), allow for multimedia integration (e. g., image slide shows and rich text editors), support collaboration functionality, etc.

In prevalent solutions, UIs are usually generated from proprietary markup code. First and foremost, vendor-specific UI definitions contradict portability and interoperability of human task specifications. Furthermore, resulting user interfaces do not meet the necessary requirements. They are usually simplistic, form-based and lead to media disruptions. As an example, users need to open external applications to write a report or look up a route, while the same kind of functionality could be included in a more interactive and intelligent task UI.

All in all, there is a lack of concepts for the definition and deployment of flexible and reusable rich UIs in business processes. Thus, development and maintenance of human-involved BPs are time-consuming and costly. Since processes can be accessed from different contexts (user roles and preferences, device characteristics), context-awareness of UIs in this domain poses an additional challenge.

To address the above-mentioned problems, we show how to utilize service-oriented user interfaces at the presentation layer of human tasks. Therefore, we propose a concept for coupling a service-oriented UI integration and composition system developed within the CRUISe[1] project and presented in [5,6] with existing business process engines.

The remainder of this paper is structured as follows. In Section 2 we present a motivating example and discuss both advances in the integration of human tasks in business processes, as well as strategies for providing the corresponding user interfaces. After giving a brief overview of the CRUISe system in Section 3, our concept for the integrated, declarative UI composition description, the dynamic UI composition based on CRUISe, and the interface between the presentation layer and the underlying human task (engine) are presented in Section 4. Section 5 describes our prototypical implementation with the help of the exemplary process and its corresponding user interface. In Section 6 we conclude this paper and outline future work.

2   Human Interaction in Business Processes

The problem domain of human interaction in BPs can be divided into two parts (cf. Figure 2): (1) Human Task Integration and (2) Human Task Rendering. The former refers to the formal and practical integration of human activities in BPEL-based BPs, including data and role management. The latter deals with issues regarding the UI description, generation and deployment for such human tasks, as well as with its interface to the task engine. We will briefly discuss related work

[1] The CRUISe project is funded with means of the German Federal Ministry of Education and Research under promotional reference number 01IS08034-C.

concerning both parts after introducing an exemplary human-involved process which illustrates the necessity of rich UIs for human tasks.

2.1 An Exemplary Business Process

Together with an industry partner we designed a business process which serves as a motivating example and use case for our implementation. To reduce complexity we limited the process to a sequence of essential (human) tasks. It is without doubt, that in the real-world, it would include additional system tasks, which are independent of our concept, though.

Our use case represents an insurance process (Figure 1). It is started by an incoming notification of claim from a customer (1), which is reviewed by an insurance employee in a human task (2). If the claim is accepted, it is forwarded to a field worker for planning an on-site-inspection (3). When he has finished his inspection and handed in the results (4), the case can be decided on by an insurance employee (5).

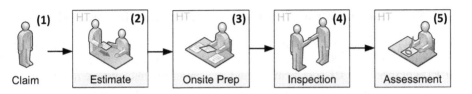

Fig. 1. Human-Involved Insurance Process

As can be seen, upon activation this process includes at least four human tasks. Every one of them needs to provide a corresponding user interface to allow the different people involved to input data needed. In task (2), it needs to be decided whether the claim is denied, or which field worker it is assigned to, alternatively. The task UI for (3) should provide information on the case and how to get to the customer. The UI for task (4) has to provide means for data input from the inspection, e. g., for photos and a textual report. Finally, the employee has to be provided with preprocessed, visualized data in (5) to support his decision-making.

We identified several UI parts that are very common in business processes and would significantly simplify human task interaction. They relate to often-needed input data. As an example, instead of putting in color codes, users can be offered a color picker. In our example, maps can be used to visualize the route to the customer for field workers, and to show service providers nearby that may repair damages. Field workers can be provided a rich text editor for their reports, and media integration, such as an image uploader and browser. For insurance employees, we can utilize rich UI components that provide sophisticated data visualization, such as interactive graphs. In contrast to prevalent solutions, we argue that such rich UI components can make business processes including human tasks much more efficient and thereby more profitable.

2.2   Integration of Human Tasks in BPs

Following a whitepaper by IBM and SAP, in 2007 all major BP engine vendors jointly released two specifications for standardization by OASIS: BPEL4People [1] (B4P) and WS-HumanTask [2] (WS-HT).

B4P introduces a `PeopleActivity` in BPEL that allows for the integration of human interactions. Those are specified based on WS-HumanTask, which provides an XML syntax for modeling human tasks and notifications. Furthermore, WS-HT defines an API for accessing task instances and controlling their life cycle from a client (often referred to as *Task List Client*, TLC). According to [7], both specifications show a fair support of common workflow resource patterns.

Definition, generation and deployment of a concrete user interface for human interactions within a business process are not covered by WS-HumanTask. It does define a `rendering` element which is supposed to enclose UI-specific markup, but its content is unspecified. Thus, related efforts regarding process and task UIs are discussed in the next section.

2.3   Strategies for Providing User Interfaces for Human Tasks

Research has covered different aspects of human-involved BPs, e. g., model-driven development [8,4], user access control [9] and integration with existing BPEL engines [10]. UI specification and provision in this context has been neglected, so far. Since WS-HT does not cover human task rendering either, we will present alternative strategies for service or BP UIs in the following, and discuss how they relate to the requirements specified in Section 1.

A pragmatic approach for UIs in SOA are **Dedicated Client Applications**. They are built with Java, .NET, or the like, and offer a "perfect-fit" UI at best. Service orchestration is either defined implicitly in the program code or facilitated by an underlying process engine. Since the user interface and its process-binding are completely custom, this method does not meet our requirements of a reusable, standards-compliant UI provision.

Another popular approach to SOA UIs are **Web Portals** [11], where local or remote portlets (WSRP) include the services' presentation. Usually, each portlet is developed like a client application. Yet, alternative approaches like WSUI employ UI generation techniques, which are discussed later. Portal-based solutions imply the setup of a heavy infrastructure and entail poor practical reusability due to proprietary vendor-specific extensions. Furthermore, the binding of portals to process engines as offered by SAP and IBM is not standardized at all.

With the advent of "Web 2.0", mashups have become an alternative SOA composition principle [11]. In the business world, they are referred to as **Enterprise Mashups** – applications which form a *"user-centric micro-combination of standards-based internal and external data sources"* [12]. Prominent tools and platforms, e. g., from Serena, JackBe and Corizon, offer visual composition mechanisms and widget-based UIs, but do not provide standardized integration with BPEL engines. Research efforts from the workflow point of view cover mashup-like, "Web-centric" composition models [13,14]. However, none of these approaches focus on the development and deployment of a corresponding (context-aware) web user interface for the resulting mashup application.

A popular strategy for SOA UIs is automatic **UI Generation** from service descriptions. It usually employs UI-specific extensions to WSDL, such as GUIDD [15]. While research has mainly focused on mobility, multimodality [16] and adaptivity [17] of resulting service UIs, some works propose to integrate such techniques with business processes, e. g. the *XML Interaction Service* presented in [18], and the model-to-code transformation in [19]. In commercial systems, like the ActiveVOS engine (cf. Section 5), XSLT is used. UI generation often results in rather simplistic HTML or XForms which lack desired interactivity and flexibility. More advanced UIs are not supported by existing solutions and would dramatically complicate UI description and the underlying generation logic. In contrast to these system, our approach uses the declarative UI description to integrate existing, distributed, rich UI components for human interaction.

It is clear to see, that no current approach allows for a standards-compliant integration of rich, reusable, interactive user interfaces for human tasks in BPEL-based BPs. Component-based web UIs lack a standardized process binding, while integrated, generation-based approaches do not facilitate UIs that are as rich and flexible as needed. Thus, in the next section we will present a promising alternative for providing rich UIs in different application domains.

3   CRUISe: Service-Oriented UI Composition

As can be seen from the last section, standardization for integration of human tasks in BPs is actively driven by several major vendors of BPEL engines. Yet, definition and deployment of the corresponding UIs are largely unspecified and based on proprietary solutions. In this paper we propose the coupling of BPEL processes with the service-oriented user interface management system CRUISe [5] to facilitate rich, flexible and reusable user interfaces for human interaction in BPs. While BPEL allows for the orchestration of back end services, CRUISe

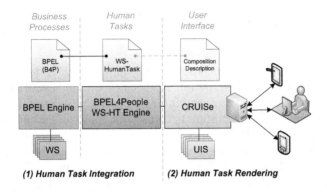

Fig. 2. Conceptual idea of a CRUISe-based task UI

realizes the orchestration of *User Interface Services* (UIS) that provide the presentation layer for human tasks, as illustrated in Figure 2.

Concept, architecture and related work of CRUISe have been presented and discussed in [5,6]. In the following, we will briefly outline relevant parts of CRUISe to illustrate its convenience for the provision of human task UIs.

We argue that web applications can be solely based on services that provide data, business logic and **user interfaces** – we focus on the latter. By using distributed services for the dynamic composition of a web application UI we can exploit advantages of service-oriented architectures, like reusability, customizability, and technology-independence, at the presentation layer.

Figure 3 gives an overview of CRUISe. Its core concepts are *User Interface Services* (UIS) that encapsulate generic, reusable web UI components. They are dynamically selected, configured and integrated into a homogeneous, web-based UI with help of the *Integration Service*, which supports different *Integration Contexts*. This means, that the integration can be carried out on the server as well as on the client (Figure 3 shows the server-side integration).

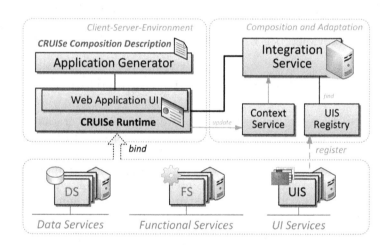

Fig. 3. Architectural overview of CRUISe

In CRUISe, the presentation layer of web applications is described declaratively in a *Composition Description*. It specifies the orchestration of several UIS, i. e., their configuration, layout, binding to back end services, and the event flow between them. This description is transformed into an executable web application containing UI placeholders by the *Application Generator*. Input and output of this generation process are technology-specific and independent from the overall concept. In the case of the prototype presented in [5], the composition description is based on JSP, and the transformation results in a servlet.

Generated applications run in the *CRUISe Runtime*, which controls event- and data-flow specified in the composition description and allows for homogeneous binding of services providing business logic and data. The location of the Runtime may be server- or completely client-side.

At application initialization, that is, when a client sends a request, the UI placeholders are dynamically filled by embedding integration code for User Interface Services. Therefore, the Runtime calls the *Integration Service* which is responsible for finding UIS in a *UIS Registry* that match the given application requirements and context. Those are ranked by their accuracy of fit, and the integration code for the most suitable UIS is returned and dynamically included into the application. As mentioned above, integration code can be, for instance, JSP, portlet, or client-side JavaScript code.

When the integration process is finished, UI services are initialized and may load remote UI code or content. Again, this UIS binding can be carried out on the server (by downloading UI components to the web server) or on the client (by loading remote UI components with JavaScript, comparable to Google's APIs).

Overall, this architecture has numerous benefits: it allows for easy, declarative authoring of a web application UI, it facilitates the composition of web UIs from reusable, configurable, rich components that are provided "as-a-service" and can thus be integrated dynamically with the help of their interface. Since application and Integration Service are decoupled, the latter can be used in different integration contexts, i. e., by different types of applications. Finally, the integration at run time allows for context-aware configuration and exchange of UIS and thereby adaptive user interfaces.

In the next chapter we will show how rich UI components can be provided for human interaction in BPs. Thereby, WS-HT clients form a specific integration context that can benefit from the CRUISe Integration Service.

4   Service-Oriented User Interfaces for BPEL-Based Business Processes

This section covers our concept of binding BPEL engines, responsible for the orchestration of back end services, with the CRUISe system orchestrating User Interface Services. This solutions offers a separation of concerns between task and UI management and simplifies authoring and maintenance while offering rich and adaptive UIs for human tasks. On a side note, it proves the seamless integration and practicability of CRUISe for human-involved processes.

An overview of the concept is given by Figure 4. It comprises three interrelated concerns: (1) the definition of a CRUISe-based human task UI, (2) the integration of User Interface Services as task UIs at run time, and (3) the communication between the UIS-based presentation layer and the underlying human task (engine). All three aspects are discussed in more detail in the following.

4.1   Composing the Human Task UI

Our concept integrates seamlessly into the authoring process of a human task. As usual, an author needs to define a task with the means of WS-HumanTask. As

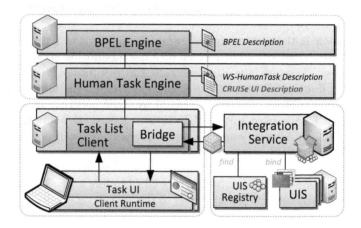

Fig. 4. Integration of CRUISe with a business process infrastructure

mentioned in Section 2.2, WS-HT defines an element named `rendering` whose content is not covered by the specification and is supposed to contain an XML-based description of the task's user interface. Figure 5 shows that multiple renderings may be defined, and that we add a CRUISe-specific one (line 2). Because of its declarative, XML-based nature, we can embed a CRUISe Composition Description (CCD) there.

```
 1<htd:renderings>
 2    <htd:rendering type="cruise">
 3        <uis:component xmlns:uis="..." name="route_on_map">
 4            <uis:properties>
 5                ...
 6                <uis:mode>route</uis:mode>
 7            </uis:properties>
 8            <uis:data>
 9                <uis:startLoc>Poststr. 27, Dresden, Germany</uis:startLoc>
10                <uis:destLoc>
11                    <xsl:value-of select="$request/ns1:objectAddress" />
12                </uis:destLoc>
13            </uis:data>
14            <uis:datachannels>..</uis:datachannels>
15            <uis:href>http://uisprovider.com/UISGoogleMaps</uis:href>
16            ...
17        </uis:component>
18    </htd:rendering>
19    <htd:rendering type="xsl"> ...</htd:rendering>
20</htd:renderings>
```

Fig. 5. CRUISe UI definition in WS-HumanTask rendering

The CCD, i.e., the UI description, contains "hot spots" which are later filled with UI components provided by User Interface Services. Those hot spots are defined with the help of specific tags (`uis:component`). In Figure 5 the CCD contains a single UIS declaration (line 3). It contains properties of the UI component to integration, e. g., the mode "route" of a map (lines 4–7), initialization data (lines 8–13), subscriptions for incoming and outgoing events (line 14), the UIS location (line 15) and further configuration data for the UI component, e. g., an API key. Usually, this hot spot would be embedded in a complete, declarative UI description, whose language is not stipulated by CRUISe. Depending on the server environment, i. e., the technology used by the Task List Client, it can be XHTML, JSP, PHP, XAML, or the like.

Line 11 exemplifies access to task instance data: In this example from our prototype (cf. Section 5), the driving directions from an insurance company to a customer are visualized by a UIS. Therefore, the customer's address is made available in the task instance, and accessed from the UI composition via an XPath expression. This mechanism allows for run time access to relevant task instance data from the task's presentation layer.

4.2   Integration of User Interface Services

WS-HT defines the *Task List Client* (cf. Section 2.2) as an interface between task engine and client. With its help users can list, view, and execute human tasks. To this end, the TLC makes use of the task engine's standardized web service interface to retrieve and update task instance data.

Figure 4 shows, how CRUISe (cf. Figure 3) and the business process infrastructure blend in. As can be seen, the TLC is extended with the server-side CRUISe Runtime. Conforming to the concept presented in Section 3, it contains communication functionality to establish a connection with the CRUISe Integration

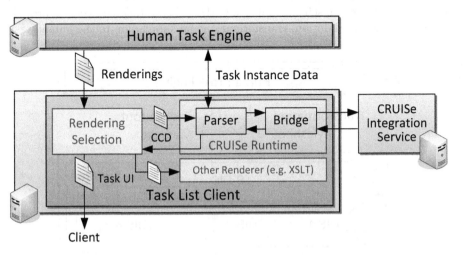

Fig. 6. TLC-CRUISe-Binding

Service (CIS). For the CIS, the TLC is yet another web application with a specific integration context.

Details of the TLC extension and the binding with the Integration Service are shown in Figure 6. The server-side CRUISe Runtime contains a *Parser* and a *Bridge* component. At run time, the TLC requests presentation markup (the `renderings`) from the task engine. In case of a CRUISe rendering, the CCD is processed by the Parser, which extracts all UIS definitions. After resolving expressions that refer to task instance data, the integration process is executed as described in Section 3. The Bridge forwards UIS definitions to the Integration Service which returns integration code for the appropriate UIS. Once all integration code has been loaded and composed to a complete task UI by the Runtime, it is returned to the TLC and sent to the client.

UIS Binding takes place on the client. The UIS integration code is executed when the task UI is initialized in the browser, and loads remote UI components from UIS servers. This mechanism is comparable to loading a Google Map from remote. Event flow between integrated UI components is controlled by the CRUISe Runtime, based on the wiring specified in the CCD.

4.3 UI-HT-Interaction

In WS-HT, every human task has an incoming (from the BP) and an outgoing message (back to the BP). Both need to conform to a given XML schema defined during the modeling of the process. The compliance of the incoming message is assured by the BP engine and not in our responsibility. Its data can be accessed from the UI via XPath expressions as mentioned in Section 4.1.

The consolidation and validation of the outgoing message, though, is a challenge for the presentation layer. As user-generated data resides in different UI components (provided by different UIS), it needs to be combined and prepared to conform to the given schema. Thus, a CRUISe-based task UI needs to provide means for data consolidation, transformation and submission to the human task

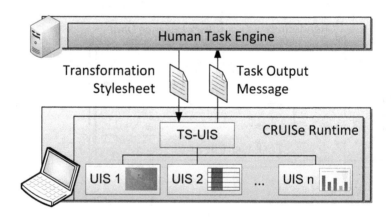

Fig. 7. Data Processing by the TaskSubmission-UIS

engine. For this purpose, a task author includes a specific UIS in the task UI: the *TaskSubmission-UIS* (TS-UIS). Its structure is illustrated in Figure 7.

At design time, the TS-UIS is specified by the task author as data sink for UI components providing task-relevant data. At runtime, it collects all data and stores it in a temporary DOM. For this purpose, the TS-UIS includes additional transformation logic to XML, as JSON is typically used for client-side information exchange. This data aggregation and transformation functionality is fully transparent to the user. The visual representation of the TS-UIS contains a status indicator, which shows if all information necessary has been supplied by the user, and means to complete the task, e. g., a button.

On task completion, aggregated UI data is mapped to a valid task output message for the human task. This mapping is based on a transformation stylesheet provided by the task author.

4.4 Context-Aware Task UIs

As mentioned in Section 1, an additional requirement for web-based process UIs are heterogeneous usage contexts, e. g., different devices (PDA vs. desktop PC) and different situations (private vs. public) it is accessed from. Instead of integrating UI adaptation logic in the task description, our concept supports the separation of concerns between task management (task engine, TLC) and management of the (adaptive) UI (CRUISe).

Context-awareness in CRUISe can be attained in different ways. For one, context data can directly influence UIS configuration, e. g., as initialization parameters. In addition, context parameters can impact the UIS selection process. For instance, the availability of necessary plug-ins on the client (e. g., Flash) can be taken into account when deciding which UI component to integrate.

Beside usage, user and device context, the process context plays an important role with regard to BPs. Since task instance data can be referenced in the composition description, they can affect the contextualization, as well. As a result, we can adapt the UI depending on the task status or relevant process data.

In this paper we do not specifically focus on UI adaptation for human tasks. Yet, by decoupling BP engines from these aspects by using the CRUISe system and its adaptation mechanisms, context-aware user interfaces can be provided for any standards-compliant task engine.

5 Implementation

To verify our concepts we integrated the CRUISe Integration Service with a BPEL4People engine and tested it with an exemplary business process containing several human tasks. In the following we will present details of our implementation, the process and its corresponding CRUISe-based task UIs.

Of the two commercially available BPEL engines that claim support for B4P and WS-HT – Intalio Tempo and Active Endpoints ActiveVOS – we found that only Active Endpoints' product was completely standards-compliant.

Thus, we decided to base our proof-of-concept prototype on their BPEL engine `ActiveBPEL 5` and the corresponding TLC, which are available as open source. It constitutes a minimally invasive integration, because it only affects the ActiveBPEL TLC and relies on the task engine's interface standardized in WS-HT. Hence, our solution works for any standards-compliant human task engine.

In our prototype the composition description is defined as XHTML containing placeholders for UIS (cf. Section 4.1), and processed by an XSLT style sheet used by ActiveBPEL to generate the user interface.

We extended the ActiveBPEL TLC – a Java web application – with the *Rendering Parser* and the *CRUISe Bridge* as described in Section 4.2. Conceptually, both form the server-side CRUISe Runtime. Web service communication with the Integration Service is based on Apache Axis, a framework already used by the TLC. It was necessary to bypass the client-side "same origin policy" [20] for the interaction between TaskSubmission-UIS and task engine. Therefore, we added a REST and a SOAP proxy mechanism to the Integration Service and extended it with "JSON with Padding" functionality – a mechanism commonly employed for client-side access to content from external domains.

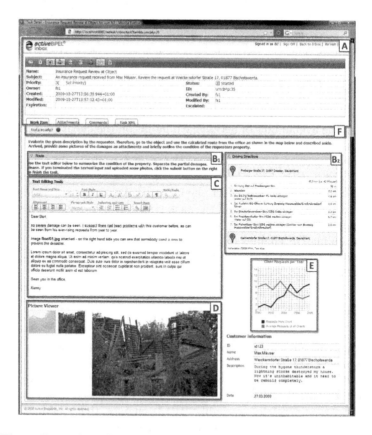

Fig. 8. Screenshot of a CRUISe-based UI within the ActiveBPEL TLC

To test our implementation we designed the business process presented in Section 2.1 with the help of the ActiveVOS Designer, and used it with the extended TLC. One of the resulting human task UIs is shown in Figure 8.

It is embedded in the TLC frame (A), which provides additional information about the task. The CRUISe-based task UI below differs a lot from prevalent, form-based interfaces and offers more interactive and "rich" UI components. For instance, it includes a map (B_1 and B_2), a rich text editor (C), a picture browser (D) and a charting UI component (E) – all of them realized and integrated as fully configurable and reusable UIS. The reusability is exemplified by the map UIS being integrated twice in different modes, i.e., configurations: B_1 (minimized) is visualizing a route on a map, while B_2 provides textual directions. The TS-UIS on top (F) indicates that data is missing for task submission. Once it has been entered and validated, a button for task completion appears.

With the help of our prototype we could prove the practicability of our concept. The resulting UIs are more useful, effective and context-aware compared to those of existing systems at stable authoring cost.

6   Conclusion and Future Work

Our paper describes how the user interface management system CRUISe can be utilized to provide rich, reusable UIs for human tasks in BPEL processes. The concept presented fills the gap of *UI Rendering* for human interaction in current standards. By integrating service-oriented UIs, development and reuse of human task presentations is greatly simplified, and resulting UIs become richer and context-aware. Since our approach relies on existing standards and decouples UI management and process execution, CRUISe-based UIs can be reused with different WS-HT-compliant BP engines. Apart from these benefits, our concept and prototype show the applicability of CRUISe in different integration contexts – in this case the server-side integration in a WS-HT Task List Client.

In the future we plan to investigate into UIS of higher granularity, so that one UIS may provide a complete human task UI. We are further interested in combining multiple human tasks into one, integrated user interface, and to incorporate collaboration techniques. In CRUISe we are focusing on the context-aware selection and configuration of UIS by improving context monitoring and incorporating Semantic-Web-based service matching mechanisms.

References

1. Agrawal, A., et al.: WS-BPEL Extension for People (BPEL4People) Version 1.0. (June 2007),
   http://www.ibm.com/developerworks/webservices/library/specification/ws-bpel4people/
2. Agrawal, A., et al.: Web Services Human Task (WS-HumanTask) Version 1.0. (June 2007),
   http://www.ibm.com/developerworks/webservices/library/specification/ws-bpel4people/

3. Alves, A., et al.: Web Services Business Process Execution Language Version 2.0. (April 2007), http://docs.oasis-open.org/wsbpel/2.0/wsbpel-v2.0.pdf
4. Link, S., Hoyer, P., Schuster, T., Abeck, S.: Model-Driven Development of Human Tasks for Workflows. In: Proc. of the 3rd Intl. Conf. on Software Engineering Advances (ICSEA 2008), October 2008, pp. 329–335 (2008)
5. Pietschmann, S., Voigt, M., Meißner, K.: Dynamic Composition of Service-Oriented Web User Interfaces. In: Intl. Conf. on Internet and Web Applications and Services (ICIW 2009), Mestre/Venice, Italy, pp. 217–222. IEEE CPS, Los Alamitos (2009)
6. Pietschmann, S., Voigt, M., Rümpel, A., Meißner, K.: CRUISe: Composition of Rich User Interface Services. In: Proc. of the 9th Intl. Conf. on Web Engineering (ICWE 2009), San Sebastian, Spain. Edition 5648, pp. 473–476. Springer, Heidelberg (2009)
7. Russell, N., van der Aalst, W.M.: Work Distribution and Resource Management in BPEL4People: Capabilities and Opportunities. In: Bellahsène, Z., Léonard, M. (eds.) CAiSE 2008. LNCS, vol. 5074, pp. 94–108. Springer, Heidelberg (2008)
8. Holmes, T., Tran, H., Zdun, U., Dustdar, S.: Modeling Human Aspects of Business Processes – A View-Based, Model-Driven Approach. In: Schieferdecker, I., Hartman, A. (eds.) ECMDA-FA 2008. LNCS, vol. 5095, pp. 246–261. Springer, Heidelberg (2008)
9. Thomas, J., Paci, F., Bertino, E., Eugster, P.: User Tasks and Access Control over Web Services. In: IEEE Int. Conf. on Web Services (ICWS 2007), Salt Lake City, USA, pp. 60–69. IEEE, Los Alamitos (2007)
10. Holmes, T., Vasko, M., Dustdar, S.: VieBOP: Extending BPEL Engines with BPEL4People. In: 16th Euromicro Conf. on Parallel, Distributed and Network-Based Processing (PDP 2008), February 2008, pp. 547–555 (2008)
11. Steger, M., Kappert, C.: User-facing SOA. Java Magazine, 65—77 (March 2008)
12. Crupi, J., Warner, C.: Enterprise Mashups Part I: Bringing SOA to the People. SOA Magazine (XVIII) (May 2008)
13. Pautasso, C.: Composing RESTful services with JOpera. In: International Conference on Software Composition 2009, Zurich, Switzerland. LNCS, vol. 5634, pp. 142–159. Springer, Heidelberg (2009)
14. Curbera, F., Duftler, M., Khalaf, R., Lovell, D.: Bite: Workflow composition for the web. In: Krämer, B.J., Lin, K.-J., Narasimhan, P. (eds.) ICSOC 2007. LNCS, vol. 4749, pp. 94–106. Springer, Heidelberg (2007)
15. Kassoff, M., Kato, D., Mohsin, W.: Creating GUIs for Web Services. IEEE Internet Computing 7(5), 66–73 (2003)
16. Steele, R., Khankan, K., Dillon, T.: Mobile Web Services Discovery and Invocation Through Auto-Generation of Abstract Multimodal Interface. In: Intl. Conf. on Information Technology: Coding and Computing, vol. 2, pp. 35–41 (2005)
17. He, J., Yen, I.L.: Adaptive User Interface Generation for Web Services. In: Proc. of the IEEE Intl. Conf. on e-Business Engineering (ICEBE 2007), Washington, DC, USA, pp. 536–539. IEEE CS, Los Alamitos (2007)
18. Kuo, Y.S., Tseng, L., Hu, H.C., Shih, N.C.: An XML Interaction Service for Workflow Applications. In: Proc. of the ACM Symposium on Document Engineering (DocEng 2006), pp. 53–55. ACM Press, New York (2006)
19. Torres, V., Pelechano, V.: Building Business Process Driven Web Applications. In: Dustdar, S., Fiadeiro, J.L., Sheth, A.P. (eds.) BPM 2006. LNCS, vol. 4102, pp. 322–337. Springer, Heidelberg (2006)
20. Jackson, C., Bortz, A., Boneh, D., Mitchell, J.C.: Protecting Browser State from Web Privacy Attacks. In: Proc. of the 15th Intl. Conf. on World Wide Web (WWW 2006), Edinburgh, UK, pp. 737–744. ACM, New York (2006)

Personalizing the Interface in Rich Internet Applications

Irene Garrigós[1], Santiago Meliá[1], and Sven Casteleyn[2]

[1] Universidad de Alicante, Campus de San Vicente del Raspeig, Apartado 99 03080
Alicante, Spain
{igarrigos, santi}@dlsi.ua.es
[2] Vrije Universiteit Brussel, Department of Computer Science, WISE, Pleinlaan 2, 1050
Brussel, Belgium
Sven.Casteleyn@vub.ac.be

Abstract. Recently, existing design methodologies targeting traditional Web applications have been extended for Rich Internet Application modeling support. These extended methodologies currently cover the traditionally well-established design concerns, i.e. data and navigation design, and provide additional focus on user interaction and presentation capabilities. However, there is still a lack of design support for more advanced functionality that now is typically offered in state-of-the-art Web applications. One yet unsupported design concern is the personalization of content and presentation to the specific user and his/her context, making use of the extra presentational possibilities offered by RIAs. This article addresses this concern and presents an extension of the RIA design approach OOH4RIA, to include presentation personalization support. We show how to extend the RIA development process to model the required personalization at the correct level of abstraction, and how these specifications can be realized using present RIA technology.

1 Introduction

Due to the growing demand for Web applications offering a rich user experience, traditional Web applications are being replaced by the so-called Rich Internet Applications (RIAs), which provide an interface, interaction and functionality capabilities similar to desktop applications. RIA development has new requirements and concerns come into play [17], complicating the task of a Web engineer. The Web engineering community is well-aware of these difficult challenges, extending the design methodologies that target traditional Web 1.0 applications to also support RIAs (e.g. WebML [3], RUX [13], OOHRIA[9], OOHDM [16]). However, due to their relative youthfulness, these new methodologies do not yet cover all design concerns usually encountered in state-of-the-art Web applications. One yet unsupported aspect is the personalization of content and presentation to the specific user and his/her context, specifically for RIAs. RIA UIs are typically dependent on the context device rendering them and vulnerable to the limitations they impose: limited screen size, more difficult interaction and poorer multimedia support. In this paper, we aim to overcome some of these problems by personalizing the UI depending on the specificities of the device (i.e. the device context). To do so, we adapt the UI in two ways: (1) an interface re-organization to fit the UI layout to the

G. Vossen, D.D.E. Long, and J.X. Yu (Eds.): WISE 2009, LNCS 5802, pp. 365–378, 2009.
© Springer-Verlag Berlin Heidelberg 2009

device dimensions, and (2) the transformation of some origin widgets into specific widgets that work more efficiently on the target device.

In this paper, we thus extend the existing RIA design method OOH4RIA [9,12] to support the personalization of the RIA user interface for different devices. Based on a set of models and transformations, OOH4RIA defines a model-driven development process that allows to easily introduce new concerns to RIA development. In this paper, we extend the OOH4RIA process by (1) introducing a user model, a device model and a presentation model marking and a widget mapping, (2) defining transformations able to generate presentations for different devices, reducing the effort to redefine new presentation models for each device and (3) integrating a new role in the engineering process called the personalization designer, in charge of defining the personalization models and artifacts. This extended process allows us to obtain different device-aware versions of the same RIA project. The remainder of this paper is organized as follows. Section 2 presents the extensions done in OOH4RIA to integrate personalization. Section 3 presents the main contribution of the paper: the personalization of the RIA user interface to different contexts. Section 4 shows a running example to illustrate the proposal. Section 5 points out how personalization for RIA's and for traditional Web applications differs, and outlines related approaches. Finally, Section 6 provides conclusions and future research lines.

2   Integrating Personalization in the OOH4RIA Development Process

OOH4RIA [9] is a proposal whose main target is to cover all the phases of the Rich Internet Application (RIA) lifecycle development. It defines a model-driven process that specifies the artifacts to obtain an almost complete RIA for a GWT framework [7]. This paper presents an extension of the OOH4RIA development process with activities and artifacts that allow us to introduce the personalization concern into RIA development. To represent this extended process (see Fig. 1) we use the OMG standard called Software Process Engineering Metamodel (SPEM)[11]. Specifically, we have selected the SPEM Activity Diagram because it allows us to introduce the sequence of activities with their input and output work products as well as separating the responsibilities of different process roles. However, the model-driven discipline defines a new kind of automatic activities, artifacts and roles that are not represented by the standard SPEM notation. For this reason, we have extended the SPEM profile introducing a *ProcessRole* stereotype able to represent transformation engines called "Model Transformer" and defines a set of stereotypes of the metaclass activity to represent different MDA transformations such as PIMToPIM, PIMToPSM, PIMToCode, PSMToCode, etc.

The OOH4RIA process starts when the *OOH designer* defines the OOH domain model in order to represent the domain entities and the relationships between them. This model is the starting point of the three main subprocesses in which this process is split: (1) the definition of the RIA server side where the *GWT Server side* transformation generates the business logic and persistence from the domain and navigational entities, (2) the RIA user interface that begins with the *Define OOH Navigation Model* activity where *OOH designer* represents the navigation through the domain concepts and establishes the visualization constraints using the navigation model. The process continues transforming the navigation model into the presentation model by means of the PIM2PSM transformation called *Nav2Pres* which establishes the different screenshots, which represent spatial distributions of the widgets rendered in a given moment, of the presentation model. After obtaining the container screenshots of the presentation model, the *User Interface designer* completes by placing the widgets, defining the style and establishing the spatial configuration by means of Panels.

The personalization extension introduced by this work presents two initial activities, which can be performed order-independent. The first is the activity *Define Device Model* carried out by the *Personalization Designer* where the domain, navigation and presentation models are the input work product of this activity. In the device model, for each targeted device, a set of widget mappings is specified, which specify the transformation of a particular widget type to another widget type, more suitable for the targeted device type. These mappings can be selected (i.e. re-used) from a predefined set of widget mappings (stored in the so-called Widget Mappings Repository), or newly defined. Depending on the user browsing device, a set of transformation rules defined inside the *Press2DevicePres* transformation (explained in the next paragraphs) will be triggered performing the corresponding widget mappings. The second activity is *Define User Model*, during which the personalization designer specifies the user model. This model represents the dynamic data structures where the information about the user and his/her context is stored which is used to base the personalization on (e.g., device type).

The next step in the personalization process consists of marking the presentation model. The goal of this activity is to mark which elements will be subject to spatial rearrangement, and to provide the necessary details for the subsequent transformation. This process (i.e. marking) has to be repeated for each target device. The markings are defined using the marking technique defined by the MDA guide [10]. This activity produces different sets of markings defined over the presentation model (i.e. marked presentation model), that together with the user model and the widget mappings specified in the device model, are the inputs of the *Pres2DevicePres* transformation.

The personalization process is concluded by the execution of a (fixed) set of transformation rules, part of the OOH4RIA personalization approach. In this work, we focus only on rules referring to presentation issues; content personalization rules are outside the scope of this paper. These transformation rules produce a device-specific presentation model. Concretely, the rules transform the user interface elements that were previously defined in the user interface models in two steps. First, the location of the user interface elements in the target application is transformed, according to the markings made by the personalization designer. Second, widgets are transformed, according to the mappings specified by the personalization designer.

Since the RIA possesses a rich interactive user interface similar to desktop applications, the static features of widgets must be completed with a model that will allow us to specify the interaction between these widgets and the rest of the system. This model has been called orchestration model and is represented as a UML profile of state machine diagram. The orchestration model does not have to be defined from scratch because a model-to-model transformation called *Pres&Nav2Orch* allows us to obtain the skeleton, where after the designer completes the orchestration model introducing the events, operations and triggers of different states. The orchestration model and the personalized presentation model are the input of the *Orch2DeviceOrch* transformation, which generates a new orchestration model personalized to a specific device, corresponding to re-organized layout and widgets.

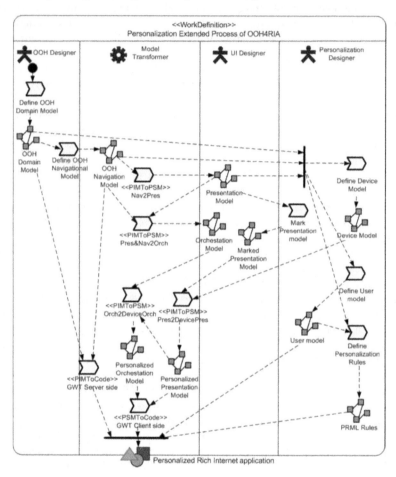

Fig. 1. Simplified Personalization Extended Process of OOH4RIA

Afterwards, the user model together with the domain, navigation and presentation models are the input that permits to realize the activity *Define Personalization Rules*. This activity defines the personalization rules that establish the different personalization strategies that will personalize the website to the user preferences, goals and context. To define these rules we use the PRML language [6] which was defined in the context of OOH to extend it with personalization support. These rules can be modified at runtime to modify the personalization strategies (this is out of the scope of the present work).

The last step consists of defining the model-to-text transformations that will grant us the personalized RIA implementation. The *GWT Server Side* transformation generates the server code from the OOH domain and the navigation models, while the *GWT client side* transformation generates the client side code using a specific GWT framework. These model-to-text transformations are written in the MOFScript language which follows the OMG ModelToText RFP for the representation of model-to-text transformations.

3 Device Context Adaptation of the Presentation Model

In this work, we are focused on the device context personalization of the presentation layer of a RIA, and for this purpose, we must reorganize the layout widgets in the user interface depending on the screen size, and some widgets may need to be transformed into others that better fit the targeted device screen dimensions.

In OOH4RIA, the RIA presentation elements and their layout is represented by the presentation model. As explained, the OOH4RIA presentation model is based on the GWT framework, which is composed of widgets and panels (i.e. layout widgets) where the widgets are placed. For personalization purposes, the designer has to specify how these panels and widgets are transformed and/or reorganized for the target application (i.e. specific device). For instance, one screenshot element (which represent spatial distributions of the widgets rendered in a given moment) specified in the original presentation model may be split into different screenshots in a mobile screen device. As already explained, we allow the personalization designer to add device dependency support using a mark-and-transform approach. By providing pre-defined mappings, and supporting the overall personalization transformation process in the OOH4RIA development process, we significantly reduce the effort for the designer.

The OOH4RIA device context adaptation is made up of following steps:

- *Defining the User Model*, containing user and context variables (e.g., device type), to store runtime information on the user and his/her context. Personalization will be based on the runtime information stored in the user model (e.g., the device type).
- *Defining the Device Model*, by selecting and instantiating existing widget mappings from the Mapping Repository or defining custom mappings. A widget mapping specifies how to transform one widget type (e.g., a Tree) to another widget type (e.g., a MenuBar). The device model consists of different sets of mappings, each targeting a particular device type.
- *Marking the Presentation Model*, in order to determining the spatial arrangement of the panels in the target presentation. As for the widget mappings, different sets markings are specified, each containing markings targeting one particular device type.
- *Perform personalization transformations*, by executing a pre-defined set of transformation rules. The personalization transformation takes as input the presentation model, the user model, the device model and the markings, to generate the personalized presentation model. This transformation is fully automated, and can be performed at runtime (depending on the device type of the user), or at design time, pre-transforming *n* personalized presentation models, one for each targeted device. In our implementation, we elected the latter approach, to avoid runtime performance overhead.

We now discuss the different steps in more detail.

a) *Defining the User Model*

In the user model, information regarding the user characteristics, interest, preferences or context is stored. In our case, as we focus on device dependency, we store information regarding the device context of the user in order to select, at runtime, which presentation model variant is to be used in the Web application.

b) *Marking the Presentation Model*

In the following step, the designer marks the presentation model in order to indicate how the elements will be reorganized. For each targeted device type, a new marked presentation model is defined. These sets of markings together with the device model data will drive the transformation rules (explained next), which modify the spatial arrangement of the elements, and transform widgets from one type to another.

To allow the designer marking the elements, the metamodel of the presentation model is extended: each of the panels has a new attribute called *Location* which indicates whether the panel will be placed in a new screenshot or it will be shown in an existing one (in Section 5 we can see an example on marking a presentation model). The location attribute can have different values:

- **Inherits:** this is the default value for all the panels. The panels are nested, all the nested panels will be placed in the same screenshot as their upper panel unless the designer specifies a different value.
- **New:** in this case the designer specifies that the panel will be placed in a separate screenshot.
- **None:** this value is assigned when the designer wants to exclude the panel, so it will not be visible (and all what is contained in it) from the target application.
- **All:** the designer assigns this value when he wants to include this panel in all the screens of the target application.
- **Containerid:** this value denotes another concrete panel (designated by its containerID) in which the current panel should be nested.

c) *Defining the Device Model*

In order to deal with the personalization at widget level, the personalization designer selects widget mappings from a predefined set of mappings, and instantiates them, complementing them with the necessary details for the specific presentation model (e.g., height and width of an element), If needed, he can define new, custom widget mappings. This results in several sets of mappings, each targeting a specific device type. Each mapping specifies the conversion of a widget (type) to another widget, giving it similar functionality in the target device. In Fig. 3 we can see one set of mappings, targeting a vertical type mobile device for the running example RIA of Section 5.

d) *Performing the Personalization Transformation*

The activity diagram represented in Fig. 3 establishes the general execution workflow of transformation rules that constitute the *Pres2DevicePres* transformation introduced in the OOH4RIA process (see Fig. 1). A fixed set of transformation rules automatically transforms the presentation model to a personalized presentation model. The input of the transformation is the defined set of widget mappings for a specific device and a marked presentation model, which steer the generic transformation process indicating which widgets to transform, and how to relocate panels. As there are *n* sets of widget mappings, and *n* presentation markings, the *Pres2DevicePres* transformation is performed *n* times, each producing a specific personalized presentation model for a specific targeted device type.

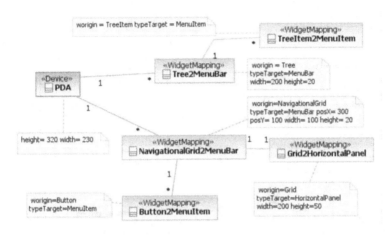

Fig. 2. The Device Model of GWT Mail application

The execution starts with the root rule called *CreatingPresModelForEachDevice* which creates the presentation model element for each device defined in the device model. When the dimensions (height and width) of the device are larger than the definition, the transformation invokes the *CreatingIdenticalScreenShot* rule, which creates Screenshots identical to the destination model. On the contrary, if the device dimensions are smaller, than the *CreatingScreenShotFromRoolPanel* rule establishes a Screenshot from the container panel with the dimensions adjusted to the device.

Here begins the reorganization of the containers or panels where the transformation checks whether the root panel contains inside panels. If it does, the *CheckingContainedPanels* rule is executed and it decides the destination of the panel according to the value of the location attribute. (1) If location is equals to *new* then the panels requires a new Screenshot, thus executing the *CreatingNewScreenshot* rule. (2) If the location is equal to the *ID* of a pre-existing panel or is equal to intherits then a new Screenshot will be created within it. (3) However, if we want to eliminate the panel (location equal to *none*), we execute *RemovingContainedPanel* rule. (4) Finally, if we want the panel to appear in all the Screenshots (location equal to *All*), the *PlacingPanelScreenshot* rule is executed.

Figure 4 gives specific details of the rule *CreatingNewScreenShot* using the QVT graphical notation. There are two checkeable domains, i.e. two metamodels are checked to see if these domain patterns comply with them.

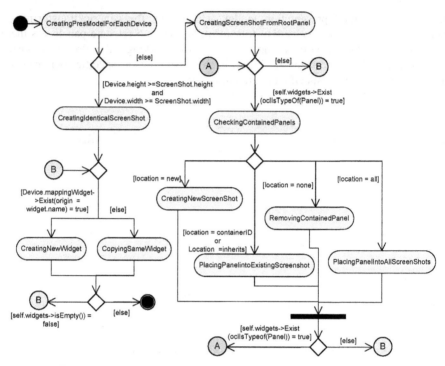

Fig. 3. Rule Map of the ObtainSpecificDevicePres QVT Transformation

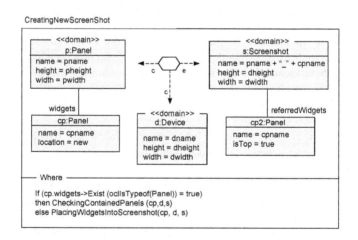

Fig. 4. Example of Pres2Device: CreatingNewScreenShot QVT Transformation Rule

On the one hand, the rule confirms that there is a *p* panel containing a *cp* panel, its location attribute being new. Also, it confirms that there is a Device element in the device model, from which we request name and dimensions. A Screenshot element is now created in the enforceable domain, with the name derived from the panel and its contained-panel (pname + "_"+ cpname). Additionally, the rule creates a root panel called cp2 inside this Screenshot containing the elements of the original Screenshot. Finally, the rule executes the where part which checks whether the panel in its turn contains other panels. If this is the case, the rule recursively invokes the *CheckingContainedPanel*s rules; otherwise, the workflow goes to point B starting the simple Widgets transformation side.

Point B in the *Pres2DevicePres* transformation is where the widget transformations start. Here, the transformation checks if there is a WidgetMapping into the device model for the current Widget. If it does not, the original Widget is copied into the target presentation model by the *CopyingSameWidget* rule. If it does, the *CreatingNewWidget* rule is executed, which transforms the widget according to the corresponding mapping from device model.

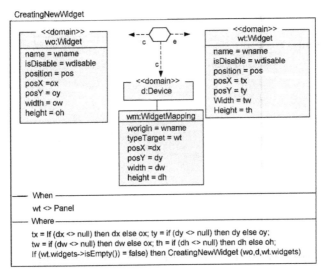

Fig. 5. CreatingNewWidget QVT Transformation Rule

Figure 5 presents the *CreatingNewWidget* rule, converting one widget into another one by gathering the information from the WidgetMapping defined in the device model. Firstly, this rule checks that the source Widget is not a panel in the *When* sentence. From here, the rule creates a new widget that maintains the same name, position and isDisable properties. However, the rule introduces the personalization information from the device model (see Fig. 2), where the WidgetMapping defines a new Widget by means of the typeTarget attribute, and establishes the new location of the widget with the posX and posy, and the new dimension with height and width attributes. Finally, the rule checks if the Widget contains other nested Widgets in the Where clause of the QVT rule, in this case, this rule is invoked recursively in order to transform the contained widgets.

In the next section we present the different artifacts generated during the process applying them to a clear and simple case study: the GWT Mail application [12]. In essence, this case study demonstrates how to construct a relatively complex user interface, similar to many common email applications, and how to easily adapt this user interface to a smaller device such as PDA.

4 Running Example

Figure 6 shows the presentation model for the GWT Mail case study. This example was also used in [9] where a complete description of all the design models is presented. In this paper we only focus on the presentation model and we are going to adapt this model so it is suitable for a mobile device. To model the needed device personalization the designer has to follow the steps explained in Section 3:

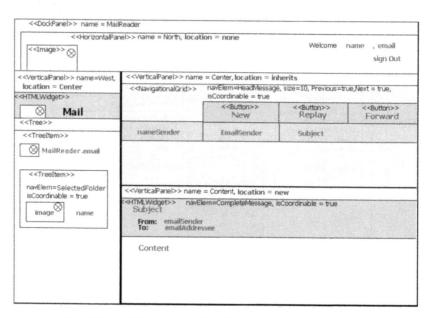

Fig. 6. Marked Presentation Model of the GWT Mail application

a) Defining the User Model
The user model is defined storing information regarding the device context of the user in order to select, at runtime, which presentation model variant is to be used in the Web application. In our case, the user model contains a variable "DeviceType", storing the device type of the user.

b) Marking the Presentation Model
Following the OOH4RIA development process, the designer marks, for the targeted device, the different panels depending on where he wants to locate them in the target application. In this case, the designer decides the *north* panel will be eliminated in the target website; the *center* panel will inherit[1] the location of its upper panel (in this case the rootpanel called *MailReader*). The *content* panel will be located in a new screenshot. Finally, the *west* panel is relocated in the same screenshot as the *center* panel (so the location value is its containerID, *e.g center*). The marked presentation model for the running example is shown in Fig.6.

---

[1] As explained before *inherits* is the default value so it is not needed to explicitly specify it, but we show it here for clarity purposes.

c) Defining the Device Model

After marking the presentation model, the designer specifies the transformations for the desired widgets. In our example, he instantiates the existing TreeToMenuBar mapping from the Mapping Repository and specifies the target position of the widgets (in the target panels) and their size. Furthermore, he defines a custom mapping to transform a NavigationalGrid to a MenuBar.

The device model for this case study is shown in Fig 2. In this case two main *WidgetMapping* classes are specified, namely *Tree* (originated from the Mapping Repository) and *NavigationalGrid*. These classes represent the *tree* widget located in the vertical panel called *west* of the source presentation model and the *navigationalGrid* widget located in the vertical panel called *Center* of the same model respectively. In the case of the *tree* widget the designer specifies that it is transformed into a *MenuBar* widget. In the same way, the widgets contained in the *tree* (i.e. *TreeItems*) are mapped into *MenuItems*. In the case of the *NavigationalGrid* widget, the designer specifies its target widget as a *MenuBar* widget. The *NavigationalGrid* is a custom widget (the reader can consult the metamodel of the presentation model in [8]), and in this case it contains other widgets to be mapped: *buttons* which are mapped as *MenuItems*, and a *Grid* that is mapped into a *Horizontal* panel.

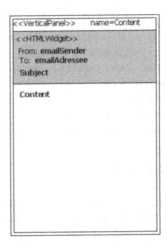

Fig. 7. Screenshots of the Presentation Model of the GWT Mail for PDA

d) Performing the Personalization Transformation

Given the marks done in the presentation model and having the device and user models specified, the set of transformation rules specified in Fig. 3 is executed. First, as the screen of the target device is smaller than the one of the source device, a new screenshot is created from the root panel called *MailReader* (*CreatingScreenShotFromRootPanel* rule). The next step checks the panels of the source presentation model based on the marks done by the designer. For the upper panel (i.e. *north*) the location is *none*, so the *RemovingContainedPanel* rule is executed. This panel will not be present in the target application. As such, the marks of all panels are inspected, applying the appropriate transformation rules. For example, the panel called *content* has location=*new* which means that the rule *CreatingNewScreenShot* is performed, creating a new screenshot where the panel *content* is placed.

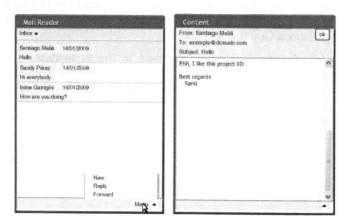

Fig. 8. ScreenShots of the implementation of the GWT Mail for PDA

The vertical panel called *center* inherits its location from the upper panel (*MailReader*) so it is placed in the same screenshot (already created). Finally the vertical panel called *west* is also located in the same screenshot because its location is the same as the *center* panel (*i.e. containerID=center*).

After the transformation of panels is performed, widgets are checked. In this case the indicated widgets (*Tree* and *NavigationalGrid*) are transformed in the device model performing the *CreatingNewWidget* rule. In Fig. 7 we see the generated presentation model and in Fig.8 two screenshots of the generated application.

5   Related Work

Personalization has been intensively studied in traditional Web application methods. Typically, content, navigation and presentation are personalized to tailor to the specific user based on his/her preferences, characteristics, context and browsing behavior. Traditional Web applications limit the possibilities to track the user browsing to the requests performed to the server. RIAs provide new client-side capacities, new presentation features and different communication flows between the server and client side. These differences with respect to traditional Web applications must be taken into account in RIAs design, as well as in the specification of personalization strategies. Moreover due to the richer set of events that can be contemplated (e.g. drag and drop, scroll, mouse over, etc...) interaction with the user gets richer too and as a consequence, new and more accurate personalization possibilities arise.

In this paper, we focus on the presentation layer, where a RIA website gets more distinctive from a traditional website. In the context of traditional Web applications we can find several approaches treating the personalization of the interface [1, 4, 5, 8]. We highlight two approaches: [1] and [5] in which the layout is personalized depending on the user access device. As explained, presentation in traditional websites is very limited. RIA applications provide richer and more interactive user interfaces, similar to desktop applications. They offer multimedia native support and support animations. As a consequence, from a personalization point of view, the layout and look-and-feel of the application can be personalized but also system reaction to user interaction has to be specified accordingly. Recently, existing Web design methodologies were extended to also support RIAs. The most relevant ones are (1) OOHDM[16] which provides the use of ADVcharts to model widget interaction[14]. (2) WebML which extends its conceptual modeling primitives for RIA's [3] and provides support for distributed event-driven RIA's and specific interaction patterns typically occurring in RIA's[2]. (3) RUX [13], a method independent presentation framework for RIA's, allowing it to tackle presentational specificities of RIA's. RUX has been applied to WebML and UWE, lending its presentational capabilities to these approaches and (4) OOH4RIA which we will elaborate and use as a framework in this article.

To the best knowledge of the authors, there is only one approach [15] that provides personalization support specifically targeting Rich Internet Applications. This approach is not in the context of Web engineering and performs on-the-fly adaptation over AJAX pages. The authors combine ontologies to annotate RIAs and adaptation rules which are derived from semantic Web usage mining techniques. This approach however, does not contemplate the personalization of the presentation features, which is exactly the focus of this paper. We thus present a personalization approach founded in a Web application method, and specifically focus on the RIA-specific elements of the presentation layer.

6   Conclusions and Future Work

In this paper, we presented an approach that allows achieving device-dependence in Rich Internet Applications, by extending the existing Web design method OOH4RIA with personalization support. We herein focused on the enhanced presentational capabilities of RIA's. We positioned the personalization design activity in the overall RIA design process, and explained it in detail. Our approach consists of two main steps. During the first step, the personalization designer marks the presentation model for spatial rearrangement of widgets in the targeted device. This marking needs to be done for each targeted device. The second step consists of the definition of the device model, by specifying widget mappings: one set of mappings for each device, specifying which and how the different widgets should be mapped onto other widgets for a targeted device. The designer does so either by selecting existing widget mappings, and instantiate them for particular use (i.e., specifying concrete values for generic parameters, such as height or width), or creating custom ones. Based on the markings and the mappings, specific (device-dependent) presentation models are automatically derived. This is done by a set of transformations specified as part of the OOH4RIA development process.

Our approach was illustrated using a case study, consisting of GWT mail application, which we personalized for (small screen) PDA devices.

Currently, we are integrating the personalization transformation in the OOH4RIA tool, which is based on the Eclipse Graphical Modelling framework (GMF) and supports the overall development process. Furthermore, we are currently working on defining the transformation rules that should be performed over the orchestration model to complement the work described here.

References

1. Carughi, G.T., Comai, S., Bozzon, A., Fraternali, P.: Modeling Distributed Events in Data-Intensive Rich Internet Applications. In: Benatallah, B., Casati, F., Georgakopoulos, D., Bartolini, C., Sadiq, W., Godart, C. (eds.) WISE 2007. LNCS, vol. 4831, pp. 593–602. Springer, Heidelberg (2007)
2. Comai, S., Carughi, G.T.: A Behavioral Model for Rich Internet Applications. In: 7th International Conference on Web Engineering (2007)
3. Dolog, P., Stage, J.: Designing Interaction Spaces for Rich Internet Applications with UML. In: Baresi, L., Fraternali, P., Houben, G.-J. (eds.) ICWE 2007. LNCS, vol. 4607, pp. 358–363. Springer, Heidelberg (2007)
4. Fiala, Z., Frasincar, F., Hinz, M., Houben, G.J., Barna, P., Meissner, K.: Engineering the presentation layer of adaptable web information systems. In: Koch, N., Fraternali, P., Wirsing, M. (eds.) ICWE 2004. LNCS, vol. 3140, pp. 459–472. Springer, Heidelberg (2004)
5. Garrigós, I.: A-OOH: Extending Web Application Design with Dynamic Personalization, Phd thesis, University of Alicante (2008)
6. Google. Google Web Toolkit (GWT), http://code.google.com/webtoolkit
7. Houben, G.J., Van der Sluijs, K., Barna, P., Broekstra, J., Casteleyn, S., Fiala, Z., Frasincar, F.: Hera. Web Engineering: Modelling and Implementing Web Applications. Human-Computer Interaction Series (2007)
8. Martínez, F.J., Muñoz, J., Vanderdonckt, J., González, J.M.: A First Draft of a Model-Driven Method for Designing Graphical User Interfaces of Rich Internet Applications. In: 4th Latin American Web Congress (LA-Web) (2006)
9. Meliá, S., Gómez, J., Pérez, S., Diaz, O.: A Model-Driven Development for GWT-Based Rich Internet Applications with OOH4RIA. In: Eighth International Conference of Web Engineering, Yorktown Heights, USA (2008)
10. Object Management Group (OMG). MDA Guide (version 1.0.1). Published (June 2003), http://www.omg.org/docs/omg/03-06-01.pdf
11. Object Management Group (OMG). Software Process Engineering Metamodel, version 1.1. Published (2005), http://www.omg.org/docs/formal/05-01-06.pdf
12. Pérez, S., Díaz, O., Meliá, S., Gómez, J.: Facing Interaction-Rich RIAs: The Orchestration Model. In: 8th International Conference of Web Engineering, USA (2008)
13. Preciado, J.C., Linaje, M., Comai, S., Sánchez- Figueroa, F.: Designing Rich Internet Applications with Web Engineering Methodologies. In: 6th International Conference on Web Engineering (2006)
14. Rossi, G., Urbieta, M., Ginzburg, J., Distante, D., Garrido, A.: Refactoring to Rich Internet Applications. A Model Driven Approach. In: 8th International Conference of Web Engineering, USA (2008)
15. Schmidt, K., Stojanovic, L., Stojanovic, N., Thomas, S.: On Enriching Ajax with Semantics: The Web Personalization Use Case. In: Franconi, E., Kifer, M., May, W. (eds.) ESWC 2007. LNCS, vol. 4519, pp. 686–700. Springer, Heidelberg (2007)
16. Urbieta, M., Rossi, G., Ginzburg, J., Schwabe, D.: Designing the Interface of Rich Internet Applications. In: 5th Latin American Web Congress (2007)
17. Wright, J.M., Dietrich, J.B.: Requirements for Rich Internet Application Design Methodologies. In: Bailey, J., Maier, D., Schewe, K.-D., Thalheim, B., Wang, X.S. (eds.) WISE 2008. LNCS, vol. 5175, pp. 106–119. Springer, Heidelberg (2008)

Towards Improving Web Search: A Large-Scale Exploratory Study of Selected Aspects of User Search Behavior*

Hiroaki Ohshima, Adam Jatowt, Satoshi Oyama, Satoshi Nakamura, and Katsumi Tanaka

Graduate School of Informatics, Kyoto University
Yoshida Honmachi, Sakyo, Kyoto 606-8501, Japan
{ohshima,adam,oyama,nakamura,tanaka}@dl.kuis.kyoto-u.ac.jp

Abstract. Recently, the Web has made dramatic impact on our lives becoming for many people a main information source. We believe that the continuous study of user needs and their search behavior is a necessary key factor for a technology to be able to keep along with society changes. In this paper we report the results of a large scale online questionnaire conducted in order to investigate the ways in which users search the Web and the kinds of needs they have. We have analyzed the results based on the respondents' attributes such as age and gender. The findings should be considered as hypotheses for further systematic studies.

Keywords: Web search, search engines, user survey, user study.

1 Introduction

Although search engines are Web gateways, still, many times, it is difficult for users to satisfy their search needs. The reasons of lower effectiveness of Web search engines are multiple and may not always be immediately evident. We thus believe that the investigation of user search habits and the analysis of the needs they have is necessary and should be repeatedly conducted over time. This is especially important now in the view of the re-organization of the Web and the change in user focus and interest brought about by the Web 2.0 phenomenon and related technologies.

To this end we have decided to survey users for identifying the current usage patterns of search engines, related problems and necessary improvements that need to be done. The survey was administered on the group of 1000 online respondents in Japan in February 2008. We have divided users into equal or roughly equal groups considering their age and gender to analyze the results.

---

* The complete report of this study is available at:
http://www.dl.kuis.kyoto-u.ac.jp/~ohshima/
questionnaire2008_report.pdf

G. Vossen, D.D.E. Long, and J.X. Yu (Eds.): WISE 2009, LNCS 5802, pp. 379–386, 2009.
© Springer-Verlag Berlin Heidelberg 2009

The previous studies of the Web search (see [3] for survey) were often based on analyzing query logs. In [6] the authors manually classified a set of 500 queries from a query log into three basic classes: navigational, informational and resource, where each class could have some sub-classes. Since query logs contain large amounts of data, automatic approach was needed. Qiu and Cho [7] used click-through data and anchor-link distribution to correctly classify nearly 60% of queries into navigational and informational types. White and Morris [8] analyzed the searching and browsing behaviors of advanced searchers confirming that users who use advanced query syntax seem to be more efficient in search and spend more time online.

However when using anonymized query logs it is usually hard to determine the problems that average users have. This is because query and click-through data cannot always precisely answer questions on the degree to which the users had satisfied their search needs, the problems they encountered, neither their wishes or expectations they had. In addition, it is difficult to accurately interpret the data from the viewpoint of particular user attributes such as gender or age.

In this study we directly asked users about their activities related to the Web search and enhancements they would like. The objective was to make an overview of current user search activities on the Web and to identify potential problems and needs that users have when searching the Web. We have also focused on Web 2.0 sources.

Surveys made by Graphics, Visualization, & Usability Center (GVU) of Georgia Institute of Technology [4] were the first studies of the Web carried through online questionnaires. The objective of that project was to measure and describe the user population in the early years of the Web. More recently, Fogg et al. [1] reported results of an online questionnaire done in order to analyze user's perception of page credibility and to understand the key factors that influence it. The Pew Internet & American Life Project [5] is an initiative for continuous study of demographic aspects of Internet usage. Data collecting is usually done through telephone surveys. The topics of published surveys range from e-health, social communities to the impact of the Internet on politics. However, to the best of our knowledge, no similar questionnaire-based study that would directly concern the issues of Web search has been done so far. Lastly, with the advent of the so-called Web 2.0 it is becoming more appealing to analyze the activities of users in generating, utilizing and evaluating content on the Web.

2 Questionnaire Settings

The questionnaire was conducted online on a group of 1000 Web users in Japan between the 9th and 11th February 2008. The respondents volunteered for the study. For completing the survey the respondents received financial gratification. Subjects were grouped into equal size categories (250 respondents in each category) depending on their age: 20-29, 30-39, 40-49 and 50-59 years old. Also, in each category, half respondents were males and half females. Thus there was an even distribution of the four age groups for each gender. In addition, the subjects were selected so that the distribution of their living places roughly reflected the population distribution within Japan. In consequence, there were more users coming from densely populated areas (e.g., Tokyo and Osaka) than from the less populated ones (e.g., Ehime, Fukui).

We have presented the subjects with a multiple answers and top N answers' question types. The former gives the respondents the freedom to choose as many answers as they need among those provided, while the latter lets the subjects select N most significant answers. The questions and answers were written in Japanese. We show the translated results here.

We performed a chi-square significance test on the results to find significant differences between the answers of different user groups. For accuracy, we do not calculate it if answers to particular questions were chosen by less than the 5% of users.

3 Results

For each question, we first describe the aggregated results collected from all the participating users. Next, we will report statistically significant differences between particular user groups, provided there were any, in the form of an itemized list with the corresponding annotations: A (age) and G (gender). All the reported differences are with the significance strength $p<1\%$ unless stated otherwise. Due to space constraints we report here only some interesting findings.

Question on User search Activities
First, we asked a question about users' search activities on the Web via a multiple answers question (see Fig. 1). Not surprisingly, search by using standard search engines has been the most frequently chosen activity largely exceeding other choices. 93.7% users selected the Web search as one of their choices and 42.4% admitted issuing navigational search queries, that is, queries whose underlying intent is to return pointers to given pages or sites. Conventional search engines are also commonly used by users for news, image and video searches (33.3%, 22.9% and 14.8% of users, respectively). Only a relatively small number of users (about 5%) use advanced search operators such as "intitle:" or "-". This confirms the results from the previous study done by White and Morris [8]. We have also found out that many queries are issued from toolbars in Web browsers (37.5%). Also, relatively large number of subjects (14.9%) access links to copies of search results returned by search engines (e.g., when the original page cannot be accessed). This explains why major search engines provide access points to the cached copies of their search results despite risking violations of copyright laws.

A   The answer about the Web search using conventional search engines has been chosen at almost equal rates among different age groups. On the other hand, users in their 20s perform significantly more mobile search, video search, news search, image search, Q&A search and search in Wikipedia[1] than other age groups, and the decrease in the usage is inversely correlated to the age of users.

G   Searching for news and inside Wikipedia as well as searching using advanced operators are significantly more common among men than among women. On the other hand, women tend to more frequently search in Q&A sites ($p<5\%$).

---

[1] http://www.wikipedia.org

Question on Favorite Content Types and User Activity on the Web

Next, we focused on the content types on pages that users view and create on the Web (Fig. 2). We asked users what content types they viewed in the last week and what content types they created or edited in the last month on the Web through a multiple

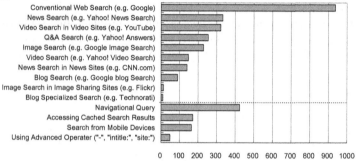

Fig. 1. Question on users' searching activities on the Web (multiple answers)

answers' question. News articles are the most frequently viewed content followed by blogs and videos from social sites like YouTube[2]. Wikipedia appears to be a highly popular destination (31.5%). Social bookmarking content in sites such as delicious[3] still remains in the interest of a rather small group of Web users. The low number of bookmarked and annotated pages appears to be one of the main problems preventing them to be used for search improvement on Web scale [2].

Considering user activity, it could be observed that majority of users do not perform any content generating/updating actions (49.5%). Actually, we have found out through additional question that the most popular activity is not social – "creating links in personal browsers" (30.6%). Users are usually less active in creating particular content type on the Web when compared to consuming it. We define an *activity indicator* of a given user group for a particular content type as the number of the users in the group that actively create the content divided by the number of the users in the group that only consume the content. If the activity indicator is 0 then the particular user group is just passively consuming the content, while the value 1 means all the users create, modify or distribute the content. Table 1 displays the activity indicators for different content types for all user groups. We can see that the activity indicator for Wikipedia is 0.08 (26/315) and 0.07 in case of video sharing sites for which only 29 users upload videos as opposed to 400 watching videos online. It is however much higher for blogs or public diaries, 0.47 (190/404). The activity indicator for blogs decreases along with the age of user groups.

A   Users in older age groups view different content types significantly less frequently than the users in younger age groups (except for the questions about reading news in news sites or through conventional Web search engines). Users in their 20s are most active in almost each content generating/editing activities when compared to the other age groups. The exceptions here are updating own

---

[2] http://www.youtube.com
[3] http://delicious.com/

Web sites, writing private blogs, making bookmarks in browsers, editing Wikipedia content. Regarding the bookmarks in browsers, the young users probably just use search engines to re-find content or navigate to particular sites. They also use social bookmarking sites such as del.ici.ous more than older users. As for editing the Wikipedia content, the young respondents may lack knowledge and confidence to write or correct articles that are often of narrow focus and require certain knowledge.

G Female users read statistically more blogs of their acquaintances, while male users read more news articles in news sites, read more Wikipedia content as well as watch more movies in video sharing sites. We also found out that men more frequently update content in Wikipedia than women do (p<5%).

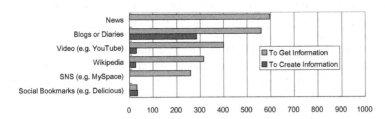

Fig. 2. Question about content types that users view and create/edit on the Web

Table 1. Activity indicators of different user groups for selected content types

Category	Sub-category	Videos	Wikipedia	Blogs
Age	20s	0.07	0.05	0.54
	30s	0.07	0.12	0.45
	40s	0.11	0.06	0.44
	50s	0.03	0.12	0.39
Gender	men	0.07	0.09	0.47
	women	0.08	0.07	0.47
All		**0.07**	**0.08**	**0.47**

Question on Context of Search Results

We have also investigated what kinds of additional information users wish to have when receiving search results besides the usual data (titles, snippets, URLs) delivered by conventional Web search engines (Fig. 3). This was a top N question type in which the respondents had to select three results in the order of their importance. Interestingly, the most often selected choice is the one about displaying typical queries for which pages in search results are usually retrieved (55.7% of users have selected it as one of their top choices). Showing snapshots, images or graphs of returned pages is the second most popular answer (42.9%). No significant differences were found for different user groups.

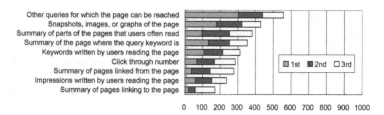

Fig. 3. Question on additional information users would like to have in Web search

Questions on Types of Searched Objects and the Problems in Person Search

We have also asked about what kinds of objects the users usually search for the information on the Web using multiple answers' question (Fig. 4). We have found out that users search for any kinds of real-world objects. Especially, searches for the information about famous persons, places or products are the most common answers. Also, about 26.5% of users issue their own names into search engines in order to track the information about them on the Web. The Pew Internet & American Life Project reported the higher occurrence of this kind of search for the group of young Web users in USA (47% of US teens issue their own names as search queries [5]). In our study this number was 33% of the users in their 20s.

A Young people submit their own names, names of other persons or their groups, whether famous or not, more frequently than the older users. On the other hand, users in their 30s submit more often names of places where they work(ed), live(ed) or learn(ed). Names of owned products are more often submitted as queries by users in their 30s and 40s than by the other age groups.

G Women statistically more frequently than men submit names of places where they live, work or learn to search engines for receiving object-related information.

Through an additional question, we have also asked users about problems that they encounter when searching for the information on persons or small groups of persons on the Web. The trustworthiness of Web information appears to be the main problem for users. They often do not trust the information they encounter on the Web (51.9% of users). In addition, many subjects admitted that there is lots of untrue information on the Web (35.2%). Thus, there is an obvious need here for further improvements of search technologies related to personal information retrieval that would take into account the credibility of results apart from their relevance. In addition, the freshness of personal information is another aspect that the users cannot easily evaluate (46%).

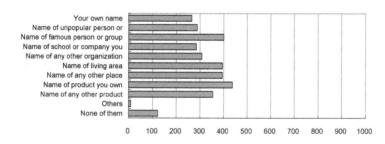

Fig. 4. Question on types of searched objects

4 Discussion

First, we briefly list some of the important results:

- Web search is very popular. When searching users often issue queries from browser toolbars, however, they rarely use advanced query operators. Cached copies of search results are relatively popular among searchers. Web search using search engines is done at the same rate independently of users' age, gender and locale. Men search and read news as well as Wikipedia content more frequently than women, while women read more blogs.
- News articles are highly popular and news reading or news searching are quite common activities. Wikipedia continues to be very popular, while social bookmarking sites still remain in the interest of few users. Younger Web users more frequently search and read various types of content on the Web when compared to older users. Women are more interested in blogs and diaries, while men prefer more Wikipedia and news content.
- Many users do not contribute to any content on the Web. The typical contribution is usually in the form of blog or diary comments. Consumers of blogs are thus more active than, for example, those of Wikipedia. The activity of users depends on age.
- Users would like to obtain information on the topics for which pages are popular on the Web. In general, there seems to be need for more additional data on search results to be provided for searchers.
- Person and product search are popular and users commonly search for information on current affiliations of persons or their reputation. Quite many users, especially the younger ones, check online information on themselves. Credibility of information and its freshness seem to be key problems in person search. Users often cannot obtain satisfactory information when searching information on persons. Person name disambiguation and credibility analysis of personal information should become important research areas.

Next we discuss some issues and implications:

- The above study has some weaknesses. First, it has been conducted within a single country making the results subject to certain cultural differences. Second, the selection of subjects was not purely random within the population, since the users volunteered for the study. Third, many problems could be only crudely identified since asking more detailed or complex questions would require presenting particular examples to users and providing them with detailed explanations.
- From the study, it appears that users require additional information on search results such as common queries issued by other users for which the results are returned. Although, the ranking algorithms applied by current search engines have been greatly improved, conventional interfaces for displaying search results seem to be still insufficient for users. Thus users have problems to find appropriate pages from results' lists using only the information on page titles and snippets. Therefore more additional information on returned pages should improve user Web search experience.
- The results of the group analysis can be used for improving personalized search and recommendation systems on the Web. For instance, female users may prefer to ob-

tain more search results from Q&A sites or blogs, while men from news sites and Wikipedia for their queries. Naturally, many users will prefer not to reveal their personal data and there are certain privacy issues here that should be considered. However, some user attributes can be actually automatically estimated to some extent. Even quite general user attributes such as age group, gender and location could already increase the effectiveness of Web search applications.

5 Conclusion

Concluding, Web search is the most common activity on the Web and it is important, although challenging, to continually measure users' satisfaction, recognize their behavioral patterns and problems they face. We believe that the effective studies should not only be done on numerical data, such as the one in query logs, but should also include direct questioning through which more complex issues can be highlighted and investigated (e.g., age, gender). To this end, we conducted an online survey on 1000 Web users focusing on general user activity on the Web.

Acknowledgements

This research was supported in part by the National Institute of Information and Communications Technology, Japan, by Grants-in-Aid for Scientific Research (Nos. 18049041 and 18049073) from MEXT of Japan, and by the Kyoto University Global COE Program: Informatics Education and Research Center for Knowledge-Circulating Society.

References

[1] Fogg, B.J., Marshall, J., Laraki, O., Osipovich, A., Varma, C., Fang, N., Paul, J., Rangne-kar, A., Shon, J., Swani, P., Treinen, M.: What makes Web sites credible?: a report on a large quantitative study. In: Proceedings of CHI 2001, pp. 61–68 (2001)

[2] Heymann, P., Koutrika, G., Garcia-Molina, H.: Can social bookmarking improve web search? In: Proceedings of WSDM 2008, pp. 195–206 (2008)

[3] Jansen, B.J., Pooch, U.: A review of Web searching studies and a framework for future research. Journal of the American Society of Infor. Science and Techn. 52(3), 235–246 (2001)

[4] Kehoe, C.M., Pitkow, J.: Surveying the Territory: GVU's Five WWW User Surveys. The World Wide Web Journal 1(3), 77–84 (1996)

[5] The Pew Internet & American Life Project, http://www.pewinternet.org

[6] Rose, D.E., Levinson, D.: Understanding user goals in web search. In: Proceedings of the WWW 2004, pp. 13–19 (2004)

[7] Qiu, F., Cho, J.: Automatic identification of user interest for personalized search. In: Proceedings of the WWW 2006, pp. 727–736 (2006)

[8] White, R.W., Morris, D.: Investigating the querying and browsing behavior of advanced search engine users. In: Proceedings of SIGIR 2007, pp. 255–262 (2007)

An Architecture for Open Cross-Media Annotation Services

Beat Signer[1] and Moira C. Norrie[2]

[1] Vrije Universiteit Brussel
Pleinlaan 2
1050 Brussels, Belgium
bsigner@vub.ac.be
[2] Institute for Information Systems, ETH Zurich
CH-8092 Zurich, Switzerland
norrie@inf.ethz.ch

Abstract. The emergence of new media technologies in combination with enhanced information sharing functionality offered by the Web provides new possibilities for cross-media annotations. This in turn raises new challenges in terms of how a true integration across different types of media can be achieved and how we can develop annotation services that are sufficiently flexible and extensible to cater for new document formats as they emerge. We present a general model for cross-media annotation services and describe how it was used to define an architecture that supports extensibility at the data level as well as within authoring and visualisation tools.

1 Introduction

With the rapid growth of Web 2.0 communities, many users are no longer simply passive readers of information published on the Web and have become actively involved in the information management process by creating new content or annotating existing resources. While web technologies have enabled the large-scale and low-cost sharing of information, annotation services allow users to integrate and augment that information in an ad-hoc manner without any pre-defined integration schemas or the need to have a local copy of that information or even update access. This allows user communities to build a knowledge layer on top of the Web through various forms of annotation services. As a result, the idea of external link metadata as introduced by the hypertext community in the form of dedicated link servers, has nowadays found its manifestation in more widely used applications in the context of Web 2.0.

The opening of information resources to third-party contributors has also been recognised by the digital library community as a way of enriching existing content with community-based annotations and associations to supplementary external resources. By bridging the gap between content managed within a digital library and digital information available outside of the library, as well as enabling annotations across digital library systems, external annotation and link services may contribute to the integration of content managed by different digital libraries.

G. Vossen, D.D.E. Long, and J.X. Yu (Eds.): WISE 2009, LNCS 5802, pp. 387–400, 2009.

The potential of knowledge sharing through collaborative annotations can only be fully exploited, if a general and sustainable *annotation fabric* can be established to ensure that annotations persist over time and can be reused and extended by future applications. Therefore, some common annotation standards and guidelines are required to make different solutions interoperable rather than producing isolated and proprietary annotation services. In the context of the Web, we have already seen first efforts to establish specific annotation standards such as the one defined by the Annotea[1] framework. The digital library community has also tried to establish annotation standards by defining digital library reference models which include annotations as information objects.

However, in addition to specifying common annotation models and standards, it is necessary to define a flexible and extensible reference architecture capable of supporting any form of cross-media annotation. It is no longer sufficient to support only textual or a fixed set of multimedia annotations. The Web is a platform with a rich and continuously evolving set of multimedia types and it is important to ensure that link and annotation services can be easily extended to cater for new media types at the data level as well as by integrating them into authoring and visualisation tools. In this paper, we present such an architecture along with the general cross-media annotation model on which it is based.

We begin in Sect. 2 by providing an overview of existing annotation systems. In Sect. 3 we introduce the concept of open cross-media annotation systems and discuss some of their requirements in terms of extensibility on both the model and architecture level. We then introduce our cross-media annotation model in Sect. 4, discussing how it supports extensibility and comparing its main features with existing annotation proposals. Details of how to realise an annotation service based on the proposed model and architecture are provided in Sect. 5. Concluding remarks are given in Sect. 6.

2   Existing Annotation Systems

Before discussing different solutions for content annotation, we consider the question of what the difference is between an annotation and a link or association with supplemental information. In our opinion, the annotation process mainly "differs" from regular linking as known from a variety of hypermedia systems through the fact that the creation of a new annotation often includes the content authoring of the annotation object itself. In contrast, link authoring usually creates associations between existing resources. We would therefore see annotation services as a specialised application of more general link services. This implies that we do not treat annotations as metadata but deal with them on the same level as any other information object. In this section, we therefore cover more general hypermedia solutions as well as specialised annotation services.

---

[1] http://www.w3.org/2001/Annotea/

The Annotea [1] project developed by the World Wide Web Consortium (W3C) provides a framework for collaborative semantic annotations and bookmarks as well as topics. Annotea makes use of the Extensible Markup Language (XML) in combination with the Resource Description Framework (RDF) to store annotation metadata about XML documents on separate servers. The W3C's Amaya[2] browser and editor uses Annotea to annotate arbitrary web pages. The Amaya editor enables parts of an HTML document to be addressed based on XPointer expressions which can then be annotated by textual information. Some of the ideas introduced by Annotea are nowadays used in social bookmarking and tagging systems. The linking (and annotating) of XML resources is also supported by the XML Linking Language (XLink) [2].

While Annotea and XLink make explicit assumptions about the type of document to be annotated, the Flexible Annotation Service Tool (FAST) [3] claims to be more flexible by providing a core annotation service with different gateways for specific information management systems. The gateway approach is a good mechanism to integrate the annotation service with different information management systems. However, FAST does not explicitly deal with extensibility issues in terms of different media types on the annotation tool and application level. For a cross-media annotation service, it is essential that new media types can be introduced without having to change already existing applications as we show in the next section.

The interoperability of link services has also been discussed by the open hypermedia community and different proposals such as the Open Hypermedia Reference Architecture (OHRA) [4] have been made. The same comments that have been given for FAST in terms of a simple extension with new media types are also valid for the OHRA architecture.

An annotation service addressing parts of documents managed by a digital library system through the concept of *marks* is presented by Archer et al. [5]. Annotations can be stored either together with the document or in an external repository. While the system provides a flexible means of addressing specific document parts, it currently supports only textual annotations.

A fixed set of multimedia annotations is supported by the web-based MADCOW [6] multimedia digital annotation system which uses a client-server architecture in combination with a browser plug-in. A good overview of MADCOW and other annotation solutions is provided in [7]. While these systems can be extended on the model level to support new types of media, we will show that there is a lack of simple extensibility on the application level. In an optimal case, there should be a clear separation of concerns not only between the media-specific annotation details on the model level but also between a general annotation authoring and management tool and its components dealing with various types of annotation resources. As a contribution of this paper, we therefore discuss some limitations of existing annotation tools and introduce an architecture for extensible cross-media annotation services.

---

[2] http://www.w3.org/Amaya/

3   Open Cross-Media Annotation

In this section, we discuss the limitations of existing digital annotation tools with respect to support of cross-media annotations and introduce the requirements for true cross-media annotation tools. Existing annotation architectures and services can be classified based on the types of resources that can be annotated as well as the potential media types that can be used in annotations. To illustrate the different types of systems, we define the *annotation matrix* shown in Fig. 1. On the horizontal axis, we mark the number of different resource types that can be annotated whereas on the vertical axis we record the number of different media types that can be used in annotating a given resource.

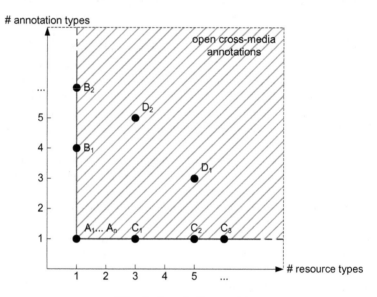

Fig. 1. Annotation matrix

The simplest type of annotation service, represented by $\mathscr{A} = \{A_1, \ldots, A_n\}$ in Fig. 1, only provides functionality for one type of resource to be annotated (e.g. text) and the annotations themselves can also be of a single type only (e.g. sound). An example of such a system is Annotea where XML documents are annotated with textual content. Some more flexibility is provided by systems where a single type of resource can be associated with annotations of different media types. For example, textual content is annotated with text notes, sounds and movies. These types of annotation services $\mathscr{B} = \{B_1, \ldots, B_n\}$ are located on the vertical line going through 1. The Stickis[3] browser toolbar is such a solution where regular webpages can be annotated with a set of rich media content. A third class of systems $\mathscr{C} = \{C_1, \ldots, C_n\}$ enables the annotation of different types of resources, but with a single annotation media type only. Those solutions can

---

[3] http://stickis.com

be found on the horizontal line going through 1. Last but not least, we have true cross-media annotation services $\mathscr{D} = \{D_1, \ldots, D_n\}$, where a set of different resource types can be linked to annotations of different media types. An example of such an annotation service is MADCOW, where a fixed set of digital resource types (i.e. text, images and videos) can be annotated with text, images, sound or videos.

Even if we have a true cross-media annotation service, there is often a limitation in terms of there being a fixed set of media types that can be annotated and used in annotations. We aim for an extensible solution where any new type of resource or annotation can be added at a later stage. We name these types of extensible solutions *open cross-media annotation systems*. Open cross-media annotation systems are not represented by a single point in our annotation matrix, but rather cover the entire shaded area. While some existing solutions such as the FAST model support this kind of extensibility on the model level—at least for digital media types—we show that there is a lack of extensibility when it comes to the architecture and application level.

To illustrate what we mean by a lack of extensibility on the annotation architecture and application level, let us have a closer look at the MADCOW [6] multimedia digital annotation system. As mentioned earlier, the authoring tool for creating new multimedia annotations has been realised as a browser plug-in. The tool currently deals with text, image and video annotations which is also reflected through different visual elements such as media-specific buttons in the MADCOW user interface. Let us consider what happens if it is decided that a new media type, for example sound, should be supported by the MADCOW annotation system. Since the authoring tool has been implemented as a single monolithic component, the user interface would have to be extended to deal with the new type of resource. This implies that for each newly introduced media type, a new version of the user interface would have to be deployed. Furthermore, since there is no flexible mechanism to dynamically extend the set of supported media types on demand, each instance of the annotation tool always has to support all existing types of resources even if a user works only with a limited subset of these media types. Last but not least, often there is not a single annotation tool but different versions (e.g. browser plug-in and standalone component) making use of the same underlying annotation model. Therefore, we have to ensure that the user interfaces of all existing annotation tools are extended individually in order to support a single new media type. This problem of extensibility on the annotation tool or application level is not something that is present in MADCOW only, but rather is common to most existing annotation solutions when faced with requirements to introduce new media types. Our solution to deal with this extensibility problem is to make sure that the visual definition of annotation anchors (selectors) for a specific resource type is no longer part of the general annotation tool but realised in separate visual plug-in components that can be automatically installed on demand.

We propose an architecture for an open cross-media annotation system based on a cross-media annotation model that supports this form of extensibility. The basic idea is that we have one or more annotation services that offer their functionality to different client applications as shown in Fig. 2. A first important thing to point out is that we make a clear distinction between the core annotation and link service and any media-specific implementation. The annotation service knows how to deal with the underlying annotation model presented in the next section but any media-specific functionality is introduced via specific *data plug-ins*. To extend the annotation service with a new media type, a data plug-in has to be provided. An annotation service might be installed with an existing set of data plug-ins, but plug-ins can also be downloaded and installed on demand from different resource plug-in repositories (see dashed arrows in Fig. 2). Since we aim for extensibility not only on the model and data layer but also on the application level, a *visual plug-in* has to be developed in addition to the data plug-in. While it seems to be obvious to separate the media-specific creation and visualisation of annotation or link anchors from the general annotation tools, is exactly the current lack of this separation of concerns that makes it difficult to flexibly extend existing annotation solutions with new media types.

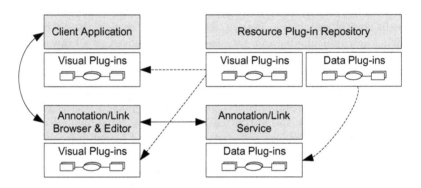

Fig. 2. Open cross-media annotation architecture

Since we do not want to force application developers to rewrite and change their entire application to make use of our annotation service, we propose a standalone annotation/link browser component that runs on the client platform. The only required communication between a client application and the annotation browser deals with information about the resource that is currently accessed within the client application. Based on a unique resource identifier, the annotation browser contacts the annotation service to get information about any additional external annotation and link data that has been defined for the given resource. The annotation browser also has to ensure that a visual plug-in for the given resource type is installed. Each visual plug-in has basically two purposes. First, it has to be able to render a specific resource type and visualise any annotation anchors (defined by selectors) that have been defined within that resource. Secondly, the visual plug-in has to provide some functionality to create and delete resources as well as selectors. After the information about the annotations has been retrieved from the annotation service, the annotation anchors will be highlighted by the visual plug-in. In the case that an annotation is selected within the annotation browser, a request is sent to the annotation server to get supplemental information for the selected annotation. As soon as another resource is accessed in the client application, the information shown in the annotation browser is automatically updated. While the communication and integration of existing applications with an annotation tool is not novel and has already been used in related approaches, again the extensibility of these annotation tools is often limited due to the fact that the application logic of the tool deals with media-specific details.

Having presented the general idea of open cross-media annotation systems along with the requirements for extensibility on both the data and application levels, we will provide some details of how extensibility is achieved on each of these levels in the next two sections.

4   Annotation Model

In this section, we start by looking at one of the proposed reference models for annotation services before going on to present our general cross-media annotation model that could be used as a basis for the implementation of such services.

Within the DELOS Network of Excellence on Digital Libraries[4], a reference model (DLRM) was defined to support more systematic research on digital libraries and serve as a foundation for comparing the functionality of different digital library implementations. We briefly outline the parts of the DELOS reference model dealing with annotations. This enables us to position our model in relation to the existing reference model as well as highlighting some of the major differences arising from the goal and intended use of the model.

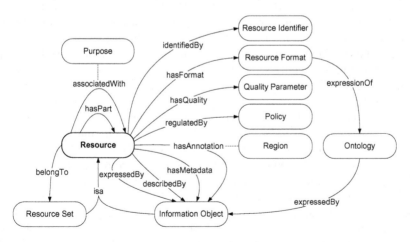

Fig. 3. Digital library resource domain concept map

---

[4] http://www.delos.info

Figure 3 shows parts of the digital library resource concept map as introduced in the DLRM document [8]. The most general concept in the reference model is the Resource which is used to represent any digital library entity. Particular instances of digital library resources (e.g. text, videos and annotations) are represented by the Information Object concept. A Resource defines some characteristics which are shared by all the different types of resources. These characteristics include a unique resource identifier, information about the resource format and quality as well as specific resource policy information.

The definition of composite resources is supported through the hasPart relation whereas the linking of different resources is enabled by the associatedWith relation. The annotation of arbitrary resources (or particular regions) with other information objects is represented by the hasAnnotation relationship between the Resource and Information Object concepts. Since we will pay special attention to the annotation mechanism while comparing our model with the reference model, we would also like to give the exact definition of an annotation as provided in the DLRM document:

> An *Annotation* is any kind of super-structural *Information Object* including notes, structured comments, or links, that an *Actor* may associate with a *Region* of a *Resource* via the *<hasAnnotation>* relation, in order to add an interpretative value. An annotation must be identified by a *Resource Identifier*, be authored by an *Actor*, and may be shared with *Groups* according to *Policies* regulating it (*Resource* is *<regulatedBy>* *Policy*). An *Annotation* may relate a *Resource* to one or more other *Resources* via the appropriate *<hasAnnotation>* relationship.
>
> Candela et al. [8]

After this very brief overview of the concepts for annotating and linking resources in the DELOS digital library reference model, we now introduce our model. The first thing to note is the fact that our model is defined using the OM data model [9] that integrates concepts from both entity relationship (ER) and object-oriented data models and is intended to bridge the gap between conceptual and implementation models. This means that our model can be mapped directly to database structures and is therefore a step closer to the realisation of annotation services than the typical reference models while still being at the conceptual level.

As explained in Sect. 2, we treat an annotation as a special type of link between two or more resources. Our annotation model is actually an application and extension of our more general resource-selector-link (RSL) model [10] for cross-media linking. The extended RSL model is shown in Fig. 4.

The OM model supports information modelling through a separation of classification and typing. While *typing* deals with entities represented by objects with attributes, methods and triggers, the *classification* through named collections deals with the semantic roles of specific object instances. In Fig. 4, collections are represented by the rectangular shapes with the membertype specified in the shaded upper right part. The OM model provides a high-level *association* construct, represented by an oval shape, which enables associations between entities to

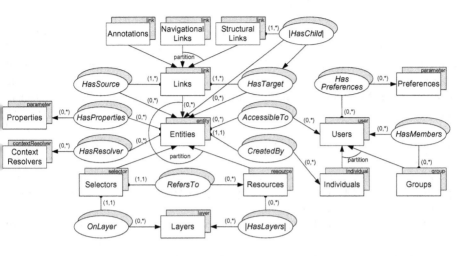

Fig. 4. RSL-based annotation model

be classified and manipulated directly. A ranking over an association is indicated by placing the association's name between two vertical lines (e.g. |HasLayers|). It is important to emphasise that OM also serves as a modelling language for a set of object-oriented data management systems and has been used to implement our link and annotation server (iServer) [11].

Similar to the Resource concept in the DLRM model, our annotation model introduces the generic notion of an entity type and all entity instances are classified and grouped by the collection Entities. As in the DELOS reference model, an entity has different characteristics which are shared among all specialisations of the entity type. Each entity is created by exactly one individual which is represented in the model by the CreatedBy association. Furthermore, access rights can be defined at entity level by the AccessibleTo association. Note that these access rights can be granted on the group level or to individuals as well as to combinations of groups and individuals. A set of contextResolver instances can be associated with each entity which defines if an instance is available within a specific context. Last but not least, arbitrary properties (parameters) in the form of key/value pairs can be associated with an entity by using the HasProperties association. This enables the extension of entities with any additional metadata required by third party applications without having to extend the core data model. To deal with complex metadata, an entity can also be associated with other entities by using the concept of a link introduced in the following paragraphs. The RSL model offers three specialisations of the abstract entity concept represented by the resource, selector and link subtypes.

The resource type represents any particular digital or physical resource that has to be managed by the annotation and link model. It is similar to the Information Object concept in the DLRM model. For each specific resource type to be supported, a new resource subtype with media-specific characteristics has to be defined via a resource plug-in mechanism.

The definition of links between different entities is supported by the link type. A link can have one or multiple source entities and point to one or more target entities which is reflected by the cardinality constraints on the HasSource and HasTarget associations. As mentioned earlier, we treat annotations as a special classification of links which is represented by the collection named Annotations in our model. Note that by treating links and annotations as first-class objects and at the same time modelling them as specialisations of the entity type, we gain some flexibility compared to the DLRM model where links are represented by the associatedWith relation. We can not only define links between resources but also create links that have other links as source or target objects. This enables us, for example, to easily add an annotation to a link; something which is not possible in the DLRM model since the hasAnnotation relationship cannot be defined over the associatedWith relation.

Often we want to link or annotate specific parts of a resource rather than entire resources. In our model, we therefore introduce the selector type as a third specialisation of the entity type. A selector is tightly coupled to a specific resource type (over the RefersTo association) and enables the selection of a specific part of a given type of resource. For example, a selector for sounds might be time-based (i.e. from time t_i to time t_j) whereas a selector for text documents could be based on character positions (i.e. from character c_i to character c_j). It is up to the developer of a new resource plug-in to not only provide an implementation for the specific resource type but also the corresponding selector. Each selector is further associated with a layer which, in the case of overlapping selectors, defines their precedence order.

How does our selector concept compare to the resource addressing functionality offered by the DLRM model? In the DLRM model, specific regions of a resource can be annotated by using the Region concept. However, the mechanism for selecting a specific region of a resource is only available for the information object to be annotated but not for the annotation itself. This means that, in DLRM, only entire information objects can be used as annotations whereas, in our RSL-based model, also parts of resources can be used to annotate other entities. Another benefit of the selector concept and the modelling of links and annotations as first-class objects becomes evident, if we revisit the concept of links provided by the associatedWith relation in the DLRM model. There, links can only be defined between entire resources whereas in our model we can use the selector concept to create links between specific parts of different resources.

As described earlier, our RSL-based annotation model defines any access rights at entity level. This has the advantage that we can not only specify if a resource is available as supported in the DLRM model by the regulatedBy and Policy concepts but also define access rights on the selector and link level. This means that we can, for example, define that a selector which is used to annotate a resource is only available for specific users whereas the resource itself may be available for everybody. We can therefore specify access rights on a very fine level of granularity and not just define if an entire resource is accessible or not.

The same flexibility that has just been described for accessing annotations, links, resources and selectors based on user profiles is also applicable to the context-specific information delivery based on the `contextResolver` concept introduced earlier in this section. This implies that an annotation or any other entity might only be accessible in a specific context. For example, some annotations might only become available if the user has already accessed specific resources beforehand.

A final remark has to be made about the representation of different types of annotations in our annotation model. In Fig. 4, only a single type of annotation, described by the `Annotations` collection, is shown. Of course it is easily possible to distinguish different types of annotation by introducing further subcollections. We can, for example, distinguish between formal and informal annotations as well as comments, explanations and other types of annotations. Since the OM model offers the possibility that an object can be a member of different collections, it is even possible that an annotation has multiple classifications at the same time as described in [12]. Annotea also offers a flexible classification of annotations via the annotation subtype concept. A slightly different approach has been chosen in FAST [7], where parts of an annotation can be classified via a specific meaning mechanism.

Our annotation model introduces some flexibility in terms of the granularity and the types of objects that can be annotated as well as used in annotations. While the model has many similarities to existing solutions, for example the DLRM model, it also shows that through generalisation and the treatment of annotations and links as first-class objects, we become more flexible in cross-annotating digital as well as physical content. While the presented model can be extended to deal with new types of media by providing specific resource and selector implementations, the management of cross-media annotation and link information is only part of the problem to be addressed. Whereas other annotation models such as the FAST model also deal with media extensions on the model level, in the next section we investigate some of the problems arising when this extensibility should be supported at the application and annotation tool level. Based on our experience in implementing solutions for different types of cross-media annotations, we propose an extensible and scalable architecture for open cross-media annotation services.

5   Extensible Annotation Tools

After highlighting the requirements for extensible cross-media annotation services and presenting our solution on the model layer, we now show how the extensibility can be dealt with on the authoring tool and visualisation level. As introduced earlier, the data plug-ins are responsible for persistently storing any additional data that is required to support a new media type. In particular, a specific implementation of the resource and selector concepts have to be provided for each new data plug-in and the interface methods to create, read, update and delete (CRUD) media-specific data have to be implemented.

The functionality of a visual plug-in is defined by an interface that has to be implemented by concrete visual plug-in instances. Each visual plug-in has to provide some functionality to define new resources as well as selectors which can then be used as annotation sources or targets by the general annotation tool. Furthermore, the interface defines a number of methods that are used by the general annotation tool to get access to the selector or resource that is currently selected within the visual plug-in. This is the only direct connection from the annotation browser introduced earlier in Fig. 2 to arbitrary visual plug-ins.

The annotation browser can not only be used to browse existing annotations but also as an authoring tool to define new cross-media annotations. In the default setting, the annotation browser shows two main windows next to each other as indicated in Fig. 5. The window on the left-hand side represents the source document whereas the one on the right-hand side is for the target document. The tool further provides functionality to create and delete annotations (CRUD) as well as to deal with more general functionality of the link model (RSL). To define an annotation for a given source document, the user first selects the specific part of the resource to be annotated in the left window and then annotates it with parts of the resource shown in the right window. Note that as part of the annotation process, the user can not only select existing resources but also create new annotation resource instances based on the editing functionality offered by the visual plug-in. After selecting the 'create annotation' command, the authoring tool gets access to the required selected entities via the visual plug-in interface. Note that since this single dependency between the authoring tool and any existing plug-ins is defined on the entity level (resources or selectors), the authoring tool does not deal with any media-specific implementation and therefore does not have to be changed at all to support a new resource type via the visual plug-in mechanism.

The default setup with two adjacent windows for the source document and its annotation is very similar to the configuration of the Memex described by Bush, where also a source and target screen are available [13]. The major difference is that in Bush's vision there is only a single resource type (microfilm) available, whereas in our case we have a potentially unlimited number of resource types represented by the set of available data and visual plug-ins. Of course the type of resources visualised in the two windows can be changed independently since each window is managed by a separate instance of a visual resource plug-in. Furthermore, different configurations of the annotation authoring tool with more than two resource windows are also imaginable.

While the use of the annotation browser and authoring tool provides access to external annotation services without any GUI changes to an existing client application, it is also possible to integrate the visualisation functionality for specific media types directly within the client application. A client application can either make use of existing visual plug-ins or the functionality defined by the visual plug-in interface can be implemented in an application-specific manner. For example, the right-hand side of Fig. 5 shows a web browser client with a visual plug-in which we developed for the XHTML resource type. The web

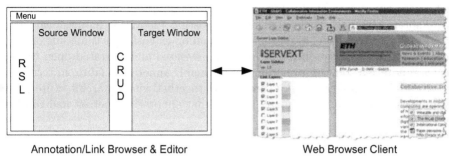

Fig. 5. Annotation browser and editor interfacing with external clients

browser client communicates with the annotation editor and can either act as a substitute for the source or target window. The important thing to note is that each resource type is treated separately through a specific plug-in. If a user selects a highlighted annotation selector within the client, it will be checked whether a visual plug-in for the linked annotation is available and, if so, the annotation is visualised. In the case that there is no client-specific visualisation available, the annotation browser will be used as a mediator to visualise the corresponding annotation. This has the major advantage that we can add new types of resources to our annotation service without the client application having to know about them. Of course, if desired, the client application can then always be extended to "natively" support the new media type as shown for the web browser extension.

In the annotation authoring process described earlier, we can not only define the selectors within the authoring tool but also directly access information from the visual plug-ins installed in external client applications. In this case, the client application informs the annotation tool about the currently active selector which has to be used as an annotation source or target. This has the advantage that, for annotation-aware client applications (with the corresponding visual plug-ins), any selections can be done directly within the application and only the command to create the annotation has to be issued by using the annotation authoring tool.

Various applications have been realised based on the presented cross-media annotation and link model. For that purpose, different plug-ins for digital resources (e.g. web pages or movies) as well as physical resources (e.g. interactive paper or RFID-tagged objects) have been implemented [11]. While our earlier applications were based on a simpler client-server architecture, we are currently implementing the described architecture which should finally result in the desired open cross-media annotation and link service.

6   Conclusions

We have presented an architecture for an open cross-media annotation system that can be dynamically extended with new media types. Through generalisation and the treatment of annotations and links as first-class objects, the presented

RSL-based annotation model introduces some flexibility in comparison to existing annotation models. While a number of existing annotation models deal with extensibility on the model level, the corresponding extensibility is missing on the authoring and visualisation level. We have presented an integrated open cross-media annotation solution providing a sustainable annotation fabric in terms of an extensible cross-media annotation model together with an architecture that guarantees future extensibility and ensures that annotations persist and can be reused over time.

References

1. Koivunen, M.R.: Semantic Authoring by Tagging with Annotea Social Bookmarks and Topics. In: Proc. of SAAW 2006, 1st Semantic Authoring and Annotation Workshop, Athens, Greece (November 2006)
2. Christensen, B.G., Hansen, F.A., Bouvin, N.O.: Xspect: Bridging Open Hypermedia and XLink. In: Proc. of WWW 2003, 12th Intl. World Wide Web Conference, Budapest, Hungary (May 2003)
3. Agosti, M., Ferro, N.: A System Architecture as a Support to a Flexible Annotation Service. In: Proc. of the 6th Thematic Workshop of the EU Network of Excellence DELOS, Cagliari, Italy (June 2004)
4. Goose, S., Lewis, A., Davis, H.: OHRA: Towards an Open Hypermedia Reference Architecture and a Migration Path for Existing Systems. Journal of Digital Information 1(2) (December 1997)
5. Archer, D.W., Delcambre, L.M.L., Corubolo, F., Cassel, L., Price, S., Murthy, U., Maier, D., Fox, E.A., Murthy, S., McCall, J., Kuchibhotla, K., Suryavanshi, R.: Superimposed Information Architecture for Digital Libraries. In: Christensen-Dalsgaard, B., Castelli, D., Ammitzbøll Jurik, B., Lippincott, J. (eds.) ECDL 2008. LNCS, vol. 5173, pp. 88–99. Springer, Heidelberg (2008)
6. Bottoni, P., Civica, R., Levialdi, S., Orso, L., Panizzi, E., Trinchese, R.: MADCOW: A Multimedia Digital Annotation System. In: Proc. of AVI 2004, Intl. Working Conference on Advanced Visual Interfaces, Gallipoli, Italy (May 2004)
7. Agosti, M., Ferro, N.: A Formal Model of Annotations of Digital Content. ACM Transactions on Information Systems (TOIS) 26(1) (November 2007)
8. Candela, L., Castelli, D., Ferro, N., Ioannidis, Y., Koutrika, G., Meghini, C., Pagano, P., Ross, S., Soergel, D., Agosti, M., Dobreva, M., Katifori, V., Schuldt, H.: The DELOS Digital Library Reference Model - Foundations for Digital Libraries (December 2007)
9. Norrie, M.C.: An Extended Entity-Relationship Approach to Data Management in Object-Oriented Systems. In: Elmasri, R.A., Kouramajian, V., Thalheim, B. (eds.) ER 1993. LNCS, vol. 823. Springer, Heidelberg (1994)
10. Signer, B., Norrie, M.C.: As We May Link: A General Metamodel for Hypermedia Systems. In: Parent, C., Schewe, K.-D., Storey, V.C., Thalheim, B. (eds.) ER 2007. LNCS, vol. 4801, pp. 359–374. Springer, Heidelberg (2007)
11. Signer, B.: Fundamental Concepts for Interactive Paper and Cross-Media Information Spaces. PhD thesis, ETH Zurich, Dissertation ETH No. 16218 (2006)
12. Decurtins, C., Norrie, M.C., Signer, B.: Putting the Gloss on Paper: A Framework for Cross-Media Annotation. New Review of Hypermedia and Multimedia 9 (2003)
13. Bush, V.: As We May Think. Atlantic Monthly 176(1) (July 1945)

Video Search by Impression Extracted from Social Annotation

Satoshi Nakamura and Katsumi Tanaka

Graduate School of Kyoto University
Yoshida-Honmachi, Sakyo, Kyoto, Japan
{nakamura,tanaka}@dl.kuis.kyoto-u.ac.jp

Abstract. This paper proposes a novel indexing and ranking method for video clips on video sharing Web sites that overcomes some of the problems with conventional systems. These problems include the difficulty of finding target video clips by the emotional impression they make, such as level of happiness, level of sadness, and so on because text summaries of video clips on video sharing Web sites usually do not contain such information. Our system extracts this type of information from comments on the video clips and generates an impression index for searching and ranking. In this work, we present analytical studies of video sharing Web site. Then, we propose an impression ranking method and show the usefulness of this method on the experimental test. In addition, we describe the future direction of this work.

Keywords: Video IR, ranking, indexing, impression, social annotation, video sharing Web sites.

1 Introduction

The popularity of video sharing Web sites has exploded over the past couple of years. *YouTube*, the main video sharing Web site in the world, had more than 80 million videos as of May 2008. *NicoNico Douga*, the main video sharing Web site in Japan, had about 2.7 million videos at the end of June 2009. On these sites, a vast number of users enjoy watching video clips. For example, *Ellacoya Networks* reported that nearly 79 million users watched more than 3 billion video clips on *YouTube* in January 2008 alone.

Video sharing Web sites have two types of users: uploaders who upload clips to the sites and viewers who view the uploaded clips. The basic procedure is that an uploader uploads a video clip with a title and a short summary. Then, the uploader and viewers add tags to the video clip to categorize it. A viewer can watch popular video clips by checking the video clip rankings and can find a target video clip by navigating with tags or by searching with keywords. However, it is not easy to find target video clips because the text information for each clip is very short. Particularly, the text information for each clip usually does not contain information about the type of emotional impression that the video clip might make happy, sad and so on.

On the other hand, people sometimes want to search video clips by impression. For example, when a user wants to lighten his mood, he may look for a funny video clip.

G. Vossen, D.D.E. Long, and J.X. Yu (Eds.): WISE 2009, LNCS 5802, pp. 401–414, 2009.

When a user wants to cry from watching a video clip, he may look for a tear-jerker. In addition, a user may want to watch video clips on subjects such as, for example, "amazing football technique" or "how to cook delicious food". However, it is too difficult to find such video clips because such impression information for each clip is sparse and conventional systems provide only popularity-based ranking mechanisms and do not provide such impression-based searching and ranking. As a result, users may be unable to find clips relevant to their desired impression.

On *YouTube* and *NicoNico Douga*, users can post comments about a video clip, evaluating it or recommending it to other users. For example, *NicoNico Douga* had about two billion comments for about 2.7 million video clips at the end of June 2009. In addition, *YouTube* and *NicoNico Douga* have an embedded video service for Web pages, while many blog services enable bloggers to easily embed such video clips into their blogs. Many bloggers thus embed video clips that they recommend to their readers. Nevertheless, *YouTube* and *NicoNico Douga* do not use such social annotation to improve their search services.

In this work, we focus on using social annotation such as Weblogs, social bookmarks, and comments to generate indexes of video clips (Fig. 1). For example, in comments and Weblogs referring to a video clip, there may be comments about the user's impression of the clip such as their evaluation of it, whether they enjoyed it, or if it made them feel sad. Such information is very useful for generating an index of video clips on video sharing Web sites for the purposes of searching and ranking.

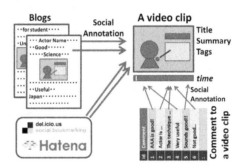

Fig. 1. Social annotation on video clips

Our ultimate goal is to develop a system for indexing and ranking video clips on video sharing Web sites that uses all relevant social annotation available on the World Wide Web such as comments on video sharing Web sites, comments on Internet bulletin boards, entries in Weblogs, tags in social bookmark services, and text on mash-up sites. As a first step, in this work, we propose a method for generating an impression index based only on comments about video clips. The impression indexing method enables users to search for or rank video clips based on feelings such as happiness, sadness, and surprise. We also developed a ranking algorithm based on the index and used a prototype system to experimentally evaluate our approach.

We first describe related work and explain the function of video sharing Web sites and social annotation. Then, we describe the results of our analytical study on the impact of social annotation on video sharing Web sites. Next, we describe our indexing and ranking methods and present the results of prototype testing, which shows the usefulness of our method. Finally, we conclude with a brief summary and a look at future work.

This work makes three significant contributions.

- It shows that comments are an important contribution to video sharing Web sites as a form of social annotation.
- It shows that impression indexing and ranking of video clips can be done by using comments found in social annotation.
- It experimentally shows that our impression index and its ranking are useful to look for target video clips depending on an emotional impression.

2 Related Work

Video indexing is a fundamental technique that enables users to search for a specific scene in a video clip or to generate a summary of a video clip. Several indexing methods have been proposed that use visual features such as color [2], camera motion [1], human faces [8], text obtained from closed captions [14], and classes and volumes of audio information [3, 4, 12]. These methods were mainly designed for use with broadcast TV programs, but they can be extended to video clips on video sharing Web sites. However, because they use only data provided by the content provider, the indexes generated basically reflect only the provider's intentions. These methods thus cannot incorporate factors such as the viewpoints and responses of viewers into the search and ranking functions for video clips.

Dimitrova et al. proposed a content-based video retrieval method that uses an example video clip [9]. The content-based approach is one method of retrieving video clips. We approach the video-retrieval problem differently. We will show the usefulness and potential of social annotation for video retrieval.

We proposed and developed a system for generating a summarizing video of a TV program by analyzing comments on an Internet bulletin board about the program [5]. This system classifies comments into the categories of delight and sorrow by pattern matching with a delight/sorrow dictionary. The system then generates an index for making a digest based on the level of delight or sorrow. *Uehara* et al. described a system for creating an attention graph from dialogues on an Internet bulletin board about a TV drama [6]. This system detects the level of viewer attention by analyzing the comments for each scene in the drama. These researches only focused on searching for specific scenes within a video clip and did not focus on searching for a video clip from a large video clip database. In addition, these researches did not address the generation of an index for searching for and ranking video clips.

Several methods have been described for using social annotation to judge the quality of content. For example, *Yanbe* et al. [15] and *Heyman* et al. [11] proposed using social bookmarks to rank Web search results. *Yanbe* et al. focused on using impression tags for Web pages to rank search results. *Boydell* et al. [10] proposed summarizing Web pages on the basis of social bookmarks. These efforts showed the potential of using social annotation for evaluating the quality of content. However, using social annotation to generate an index of video clips and to judge their quality has not been addressed.

3   Video Sharing Web Site

Millions of video clips have been uploaded to video sharing Web sites, and millions of users watch them. In the work reported here, we used *NicoNico Douga* as the video sharing site as it is the most popular video sharing Web site in Japan. It had about 10 million users as of the end of October 2008. Users can upload, view, and share video clips as they do on *YouTube* and other video sharing sites. The differences between *NicoNico Douga* and the others are the simplicity of posting comments at specific points in a video clip and a function that enables users to overlay posted comments on a video clip.

While *YouTube* users can also post comments for a video clip, it is not easy to post comments at a specific playback point. Instead, commenters include the target playback time in their posted comments such as "Watch him fall at 2:30!" When a *NicoNico Douga* user posts a comment for a video clip he is watching, the system sets the playback time of the video clip at the time the comment was posted as the target playback time of the comment. The user can easily post comments for a specific time point in a video clip with this system.

Moreover, *NicoNico Douga* overlays the comments for a video clip at the corresponding playback times. Users enjoy not only watching the video clip but also seeing the comments of others at the appropriate points in the video. This synchronicity creates a sense of a shared watching experience. This comment overlay function can be turned on and off by the user.

As mentioned, *NicoNico Douga* had more than 1.9 billion comments for 2.5 million video clips as of May 2009. There were more than 10 million comments for the most commented upon video clip! We can thus say that comments make an important contribution to video sharing Web sites as a form of social annotation. We will address their impact more specifically in the next section.

We believe that such video sharing sites will become even more popular worldwide, and that the number of video sharing sites will continue to increase. In fact, several video sharing sites have followed the lead of *NicoNico Douga* and have started providing synchronous comment services (*LYCOS mix*[1] in Japan, *AcFun*[2] in China, and so on). In addition, some mash-up sites have started to manage posted comments and overlay them on video clips that are stored on other video sharing Web sites. The alpha version of *NicoNico Douga* was also a mash-up site that used video clips stored on *YouTube*.

On *NicoNico Douga* and similar sites, the information and social annotation for each video clip usually include the following:

- Identification number of a video clip
- Title and summary of the video clip, which are written by the uploader
- Number of times viewed, number of posted comments, and number of times it has been marked as a favorite
- Upload date and length of the video clip
- Tags added by users
- Viewer comments.

[1] http://mix.lycos.jp/
[2] http://www.acfun.cn/

A viewer comment generally includes the identification number of the viewer, the comment itself, the date posted, and the corresponding playback time.

NicoNico Douga uses the number of views, comments, and favorite settings to rank video clips on the assumption that these metrics reflect popularity. While this may be sufficient in terms of determining overall popularity, it is insufficient for indicating the quality of a video clip. For example, it is not easy for users to search for tear-jerker video clips. In addition, they cannot rank video clips by the level of "tear-jerker-ness." Conventional systems do not provide such indexing or ranking systems. Our method for generating an impression index for video clips does.

4 Analytical Study

First, we created two sub-datasets of the weekly and monthly 100 most commented upon video clips to evaluate the usefulness of the number of comments about a clip in *NicoNico Douga*. Here, we manually assigned "low quality video clip" to video clips that are specifically focused on collecting comments (i.e., the uploader asks viewers to post comments), video clips that are typing games (i.e., viewers type text in response to presented text), and video clips made for greeting each other and so on. Figure 2 shows the relationship between the rankings of video clips based on the number of posted comments and the number of low quality videos. In this figure, the horizontal axis is the ranking based on the number of posted comments and the vertical axis is the number of low quality video clips.

We found that about 18% of the weekly top 100 clips and 32% of the monthly top 100 clips were low quality. In addition, there were more low quality video clips among those that ranked the highest than among the low ranked video clips based on the number of posted comments. This result indicates the number of comments is insufficient for judging the quality of video clips.

To construct a dataset for analyzing *NicoNico Douga*'s comments, we developed a comment crawler that collect the comments and some information such as the title,

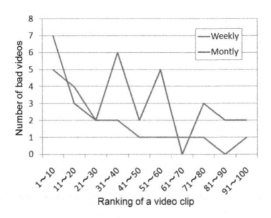

Fig. 2. The relationship between the rankings of video clips based on the number of posted comments and the number of low quality videos

summary, and tags and so on. Each *NicoNico Douga* video clip is identified by a unique number and the largest video clip identification number was just over 5,000,000 when we started to crawl them (October 21, 2008). Our crawler generates an identification number randomly from 1 to 5,000,000 to crawl them. We limited the crawling to the most recent 1,000 comments per clip because, as mentioned, a video clip can have up to 10 million comments.

We ended up with 968,721 video clips (19.4% of all clips on *NicoNico Douga*). Although the number was relatively small compared to the total number of clips, it was sufficient for analyzing the impact of social annotation.

We divided the dataset into live video clips, which users could watch, and dead video clips, which users could no longer watch because they had been deleted. There were 304,460 live video clips and 664,261 dead video clips. This means that 68.57% of the video clips in our dataset had been removed either because the uploaders had removed them or because the service had removed them due to copyright violations. On this site, copyright violation is a major reason for removal. The number of crawled comments for the live video clips in our set was 56,473,136.

The video clips in our dataset had an average length of 549.44 seconds. Moreover,

- The average number of viewings was 4072.73.
- The average number of comments was 479.88.
- The average number of times a video clip was marked as a favorite was 56.67.

Figure 3 shows the relationship between the number of posted comments and the percentage of the video clips in our dataset that had that number of comments. In this figure, the horizontal axis is the percentage of video clips in our dataset and the vertical axis is the number of posted comments per video. As shown by the plot in this figure, about 38.5% of the video clips in our dataset had more than 100 comments, and about 5% had more than 2000.

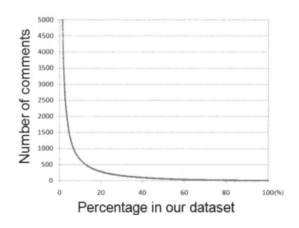

Fig. 3. Percentage of video clips with specified number of posted comments

We developed a dictionary that supported the generation of an impression index to classify comments as either positive or negative, and as indicating happiness, sadness, and surprise [16].

In this dictionary, there are 217 patterns of regular expressions to match positive comments, 232 patterns to match negative comments, 13 patterns of regular expressions to match comments expressing happiness, 30 patterns to match comments expressing sadness, and 7 patterns to match comments expressing surprise. We generated these regular expressions manually to detect the type of impression of the comments.

Here, we randomly selected 10,000 comments from our dataset to check the accuracy and coverage of extracting each factor. "Accuracy" is the percentage of extracted comments that are correct, i.e., they match the target impression. "Coverage" is the percentage of correct comments that are extracted. The correct comments were manually identified.

$$Accuracy = \frac{Num(extracted\_correct\_comment)}{Num(extracted\_comment)} \times 100$$

$$Coverage = \frac{Num(extracted\_correct\_comment)}{Num(correct\_comment\_in\_dataset)} \times 100$$

As shown in Table 1, the accuracy was a little lower for "happiness" than for other impressions. The reason for the low accuracy of detecting "happiness" comments was that viewers use the laughing symbol not only for laughing but also mockery. To solve this problem, we have to analyze comments in detail.

Table. 1. Accuracy and coverage

	Accuracy	Coverage
Positive	95.3%	97.2%
Negative	97.1%	93.7%
Happiness	85.5%	98.3%
Sadness	95.8%	97.5%

If the number of comments for a video clip is small, our system processes have lower reliability. However, 38% of video clips have more than 100 comments. We can say that their accuracy and coverage are sufficient to judge the level of impressions or to rank video clips according to impression.

We then used our dictionary to judge the impression of each comment in our dataset. On average, for each video clip, there were 22.24 positive comments, 10.25 negative comments, 71.24 comments expressing happiness, 6.32 comments expressing sadness, and 2.18 comments expressing surprise. That is, there were relatively more comments that were positive or that expressed happiness. We can say that there are many positive comments and comments expressing happiness and there are few comments expressing surprise or sadness. These average values are useful for judging the types of the impression of a video clip.

Next, to analyze the relationship between the impression comments and their corresponding playback times, we created a sub-dataset containing those video clips in the original dataset with more than 100 comments. This sub-dataset contained

117,217 video clips. In this analysis, first, our system normalizes the playback time of the video clip by dividing it into 100 units of playback time. Then, the system calculates the ratio of total comments and the ratio of each type of impression comment in each playback unit and each video clip. Finally, the system calculates the average of these in each playback unit.

Figure 4 shows the change in the number of comments by impression as video viewing progressed. The horizontal axis represents the video playback time in percentage terms. The vertical axis represents the ratio of comments for each impression.

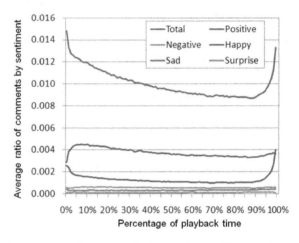

Fig. 4. Average ratio of comments by impression as video viewing processed

We found that the ratio of comments that were negative, sad, or expressed surprise, on average, was fairly evenly distributed over the playback time. In contrast, the average ratio of total comments decreased from the start to about 90% of the playback time and then sharply increased. Moreover, the ratio of positive comments decreased slightly from the start to about 90% of the playback time and then also sharply increased until the end of viewing; the ratio of positive comments at the end was twice that at the start. We can use these results to normalize the level of each impression at each point in time during playback or as a threshold for assigning one or more impressions to a video clip.

Here, we extracted 1519 enjoyable video clips that were tagged "enjoyable" or "laughter," and 560 tear-jerker video clips which were tagged "tear-jerker" or "moving" from our dataset by matching the tags. Our system normalized video clips with 20 playback units.

Figures 5 and 6 show the change in the number of comments by impression as video viewing progressed. Figure 5 relates to enjoyable video clips and Figure 6 relates to tear-jerker video clips. In these figures, the horizontal axis represents the video playback time in percentage terms and the vertical axis represents the ratio of comments for impression.

We found that tear-jerker video clips had many comments expressing sadness, more than enjoyable video clips, and more than the average of all video clips in our

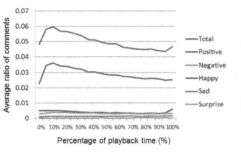

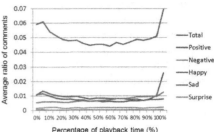

Fig. 5. Average ratio of comments by impression as video viewing processed in enjoyable video clips

Fig. 6. Average ratio of comments by impression as video viewing processed in tear-jerker video clips

dataset. In addition, we also found that the end of tear-jerker video clips had many positive comments, more than the end of enjoyable clips. We can use these differences to determine the type of video clip.

5 Our Method

5.1 Impression Indexing and Ranking

Using the results of our analyses, we developed a method for ranking video clips for impression searching.

Our system uses this method not only for ranking video clips but also for searching by impression.

Our system first normalizes the playback time of a video clip by dividing it into 100 units of playback time. Next, the system counts each type of impression comment in each playback unit using our dictionary. Then, the system calculates the impression score of the video clip using the following equation.

$$Score(v,i) = \log_{10} impression_{all} \times \frac{impression_{all}}{total_{all}} + w(s) \times \frac{\sum_{k=96}^{100} positive_k}{total_{all}}$$

where v is the target video clip, s is the target impression the user searches for, $impression_{all}$ is the total number of comments expressing target impression s, $total_{all}$ is the total number of comments to the video clip, $w(i)$ is a weight value for target impression i, and $positive_k$ is the number of positive comments in the kth playback unit. In this equation, we emphasize the positive comments at the end of the video clip based on the results shown in Fig. 4. In addition, we set $w(sadness)$ as higher than $w(happiness)$ because of the results shown in Figs. 5 and 6.

When the user searches for an impression i for a list of extracted video clips, the system calculates the score of each impression. The clips are sorted on the basis of the scores.

If a query contains an impression keyword (i.e., moving, tear-jerker, laughter, happiness, sadness, surprising, and so on) that is defined in the query modification dictionary we prepared, our system uses these terms not only for the keyword search but also for impression-based ranking.

When a user submits an impression term with other keywords as a query, our simple query modification mechanism first extracts video clips with the other keywords and then sorts by the level of the input impression.

For example, when the user inputs "tear-jerker cat story" as a query, the system extracts video clips that contain "cat story", sorts them by the level of sadness, and displays them.

5.2 Implementation

We developed our crawling system using Perl. The system crawls the video clip comments and the title, summary, tags, posted date, length, and so on and stores them in a database.

When the user inputs a query that does not contain an impression term, the system first returns a ranking of video clips based on *NicoNico Douga*'s popularity-based rankings. Then, our system enables users to rank the list of video clips on the basis of happiness, sadness, surprise, positive response, and negative response by clicking the impression button. After that, the system re-ranks the list of video clips based on the calculated impression score.

In addition, we also developed our client system as an extension of Mozilla Firefox 3.0. This system automatically generates a time-related graph for each video clip when the user accesses a ranking page showing the video search results or a video clip page. Figure 7 compares the conventional system and our system. The conventional system has no function to rerank the search results and only provides a thumbnail image, posted date, title, summary, recently posted comments, length, and some other information.

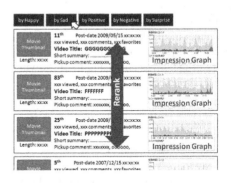

Fig. 7. The left figure is an image of a list of search results using the conventional system. The right figure is an image of a list of search results using our system. Our system shows impression graphs and has several control buttons the user can click to rerank the search results.

Figure 8 is a screen snapshot of our system. With this system, a user can easily see how the impression levels changed during viewing, enabling him or her to judge the quality of a video clip before watching it. Figure 9 shows an example of an impression graph. Figure 10 shows a screen snapshot after reranking by level of sadness. The user can use our system without stress because our system can rerank 100 search results in only two seconds.

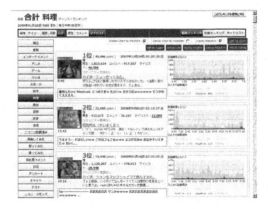

Fig. 8. Sample screen snapshot showing ranking of cooking video clips. Change in impression levels during viewing is shown on the right.

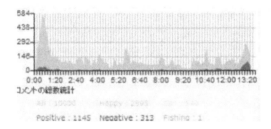

Fig. 9. An impression graph. The horizontal axis is the playback time. The vertical axis is the number of comments.

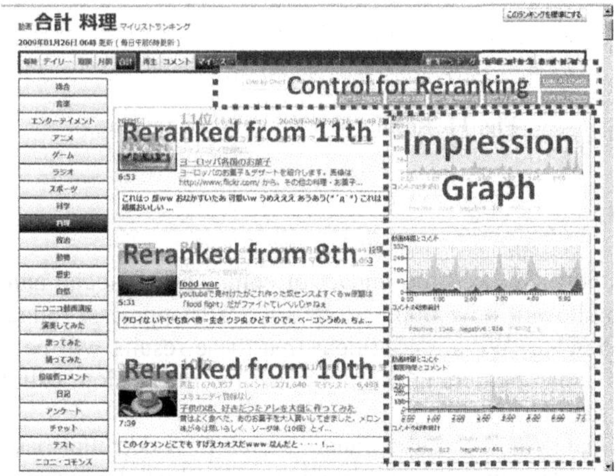

Fig. 10. Sample screen snapshot showing reranking of cooking video clips by level of sadness.

5.3 Evaluation

We evaluated our method experimentally to determine its usefulness to our system. In our evaluation, we used our collected dataset, which has 304,460 clips. In this experimental test, we conducted a user-based experiment to judge the usefulness of impression ranking.

We prepared five lists of enjoyable video clips and five lists of tear-jerker video clips, as determined by their tags. Each tag list of video clips had more than 10 video clips. We selected the top 10 most commented upon video clips in each list as a dataset. Then, we asked two users to judge the level of happiness and sadness of these video clips after watching them. They evaluated the video clips from 1 to 5. We did not inform the users of how the video clips had been ranked.

After collecting the user evaluations, we used our system to rank them according to the levels of happiness and sadness. Figure 11 plots these results. In this figure, the horizontal axis is the video clip rank based on our system and the vertical axis is the user evaluations of the video clips.

The results suggested that our system is useful for ranking video clips based on the level of sadness, but not for ranking clips based on the level of enjoyment.

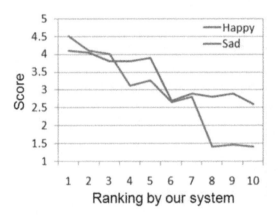

Fig. 11. Results of the impression ranking

6   Discussion

Our analytical studies showed the impact of comments as social annotation to video clips. They also showed how impressions such as happiness, sadness, and surprise change during viewing. We are confident that these results will be useful for future research in this area. Searching and ranking by impression will be one type of next-generation search system.

In a conventional system, the user cannot search for video clips based on impression information if the video clips do not contain any text about the impression, and, in fact, almost no video clips contain such impression information. Our system enables users to conduct an impression search. For example, a user can search for tear-jerker video clips, enjoyable video clips, and amazing video clips using our system.

There are many video clips that receive comments classified as indicating sadness. We asked our students to use our system and we received their feedback. We then found that high quality tear-jerker video clips had many comments expressing sadness throughout and many positive comments at the end. This knowledge supports our equation for calculating a sadness score.

Here, we focused only on happiness, sadness, surprise, positive response, and negative response. We can improve our system and develop new methods for ranking based on impression. We plan to improve our dictionary to detect additional impressions and context such as positive comments saying "thank you" and positive comments evaluating the video. If we can better utilize such comments we can improve our ranking method.

In addition, we plan to detect the senses related to posted comments (i.e., taste, sight, smell, touch, and hearing). If we can rank video clips on the basis of senses, the user can easily find video clips appealing to the sense of taste, beautiful video clips, video clips agreeable to the ear, and so on.

We did not take users or user groups into consideration. For example, users who support the *F.C. Barcelona* football team may enjoy video clips of matches lost by the *Real Madrid* football team or clips that viewers who support *Real Madrid* found disappointing. This impression is based on rivalry. There are many such situations. We thus plan to introduce group-based video ranking/recommendation.

We think that we can use posted comments to generate text indexes. For example, users post an actor name or event name to the specific playback time. Then, we can detect what happened or who acted and so on by analyzing posted comments. In addition, there have been many studies on detecting actors' actions [7] or faces by image-based retrieval [13] methods. If we can combine these methods and our impression indexing method, we can create better indexing methods of video information retrieval.

8 Conclusion

In this paper, we showed the potential of video clip comments on video sharing Web sites and proposed an indexing and ranking method for searching video clips based on emotional impression extracted from these comments. Our impression indexing and ranking methods showed the potential of our system to contribute to next-generation video search techniques.

We did not consider blogs because the size of our crawled dataset was not large. We are now crawling blog entries to generate an index of video clips, and we plan to add this to our system and evaluate its usefulness. We think that the quality of content in blog entries is better than in video comments. Once we have introduced the use of blog entries for generating an index of video clips, we will focus on the differences in quality and quantity.

Acknowledgements

This work was supported in part by the National Institute of Information and Communications Technology and by the "Informatics Education and Research Center for Knowledge-Circulating Society" (Project Leader: Katsumi Tanaka, MEXT Global COE Program, Kyoto University). This work was also supported in part by MEXT Grant-in-Aid "Contents Fusion and Seamless Search for Information Explosion" (Project Leader: Katsumi Tanaka, A01-00-02, Grant#: 18049041).

References

1. Akutsu, A., Tonomura, Y., Hashimoto, H., Ohba, Y.: Video Indexing Using Motion Vectors. In: SPIE Proc. VCIP 1992, pp. 522–530 (1992)
2. Nakagawa, A., Tanaka, Y.: Automatic Video Indexing and Full-video Search for Object Appearances. IPSJ 33(4), 543–550
3. Saur, D., Tan, Y.P., Kulkarni, S., Ramadge, P.: Automated Analysis and Annotation of Basketball Video, Databases V. SPIE, vol. 3022, pp. 167–187
4. Miyamori, H.: Automatic Annotation of Tennis Action for Content-based Retrieval by Integrated Audio and Visual information. In: Bakker, E.M., Lew, M., Huang, T.S., Sebe, N., Zhou, X.S. (eds.) CIVR 2003. LNCS, vol. 2728, pp. 331–341. Springer, Heidelberg (2003)
5. Miyamori, H., Nakamura, S., Tanaka, K.: Generation of Views of TV Content Using TV Viewers' Perspectives Expressed in Live Chats on the Web. In: Proceedings of ACM Multimedia 2005, November 2005, pp. 853–861 (2005)
6. Uehara, H., Yoshida, K.: Annotating TV Drama based on Viewer Dialogue - Analysis of Viewers' Attention Generated on an Internet Bulletin Board. In: 2005 Symposium on Applications and the Internet (SAINT 2005), pp. 334–340 (2005)
7. Laptev, I., Perez, P.: Retrieving actions in movies. In: Proc. of ICCV 2007, October 2007, pp. 1–8 (2007)
8. Smith, M., Kanabe, T.: Video Skimming and Characterization through the Combination of Image and Language Understanding Techniques. In: Bakker, E.M., Lew, M., Huang, T.S., Sebe, N., Zhou, X.S. (eds.) CIVR 2003. LNCS, vol. 2728, pp. 331–341. Springer, Heidelberg (2003)
9. Dimitrova, N., Abdel Mottaleb, M.: Content-based Video Retrieval by Example Video Clip. In: Proc. of SPIE, vol. 3022, pp. 59–70 (1997)
10. Boydell, O., Smyth, B.: From social bookmarking to social summarization: an experiment in community-based summary generation. In: Proceedings of the 12th international conference on Intelligent User Interfaces, pp. 42–51
11. Heymann, P., Koutrika, G., Garcia-Molina, H.: Can social bookmarking improve web search? In: Proceedings of the international conference on Web search and Web Data Mining, pp. 195–206
12. Intille, S., Bobick, A.: Closed-world Tracking. In: Proceedings of the Fifth International Conference on Computer Vision, pp. 672–678
13. Sivic, J., Everingham, M., Zisserman, A.: Person spotting: video shot retrieval for face sets. In: Leow, W.-K., Lew, M., Chua, T.-S., Ma, W.-Y., Chaisorn, L., Bakker, E.M. (eds.) CIVR 2005. LNCS, vol. 3568, pp. 226–236. Springer, Heidelberg (2005)
14. Nakamura, Y., Kanabe, T.: Semantic Analysis for Video Contents Extraction Spotting by Association in News Video. In: ACM Multimedia, pp. 393–401
15. Yanbe, Y., Jatowt, A., Nakamura, S., Tanaka, K.: Can Social Bookmarking Enhance Search in the Web? In: Proc. of. JCDL 2007, pp. 107–116 (2007)
16. Nakamura, S., Shimizu, M., Tanaka, K.: Can Social Annotation Support Users in Evaluating the Trustworthiness of Video Clips? In: Proc. of WICOW 2008 (2008)

Single Pattern Generating Heuristics for Pixel Advertisements

Alex Knoops[1], Victor Boskamp[1], Adam Wojciechowski[2],
and Flavius Frasincar[1]

[1] Econometric Institute
Erasmus University Rotterdam
PO Box 1738, NL-3000
Rotterdam, the Netherlands
{alex.knoops,victorboskamp}@gmail.com, frasincar@ese.eur.nl
[2] Institute of Computing Science
Poznan University of Technology
ul. Piotrowo 2, 60-965 Poznan, Poland
adam.wojciechowski@put.poznan.pl

Abstract. Pixel advertisement represents the presentation of small advertisements on a banner. With the Web becoming more important for marketing purposes, pixel advertisement is an interesting development. In this paper, we present a comparison of three heuristic algorithms for generating allocation patterns for pixel advertisements. The algorithms used are the orthogonal algorithm, the left justified algorithm, and the GRASP constructive algorithm. We present the results of an extensive simulation in which we have experimented with the sorting of advertisements and different banner and advertisement sizes. The purpose is to find a pattern generating algorithm that maximizes the revenue of the allocated pixel advertisements on a banner. Results show that the best algorithm for our goal is the orthogonal algorithm. We also present a Web application in which the most suitable algorithm is implemented. This Web application returns an allocation pattern for a set of advertisements provided by the user.

Keywords: pixel advertisements, allocation patterns, heuristic algorithms.

1 Introduction

With the Web usage still growing, Web advertising becomes a more dominant form of marketing every year. According to the Interactive Advertising Bureau, Web advertising revenues for 2008 are totaled \$23.4 billion in the U.S. only [1]. Banner advertisements have a 22 percent share in these figures.

A special form of Web advertising is *pixel advertisement*. Pixel advertisement originated in 2005 from the English student Alex Tew's "Million Dollar Homepage" [2]. The homepage holds a 1000 by 1000 pixel grid from which blocks of 10 by 10 pixels could be bought for 1 dollar per pixel. Buyers could place an image

G. Vossen, D.D.E. Long, and J.X. Yu (Eds.): WISE 2009, LNCS 5802, pp. 415–428, 2009.

on their pixels and let the image link to their website. The general idea of pixel advertising is to have a *banner* with several small advertisements in pixel blocks (i.e., multibanner), instead of just one advertisement occupying the banner.

In [3] the success of the "Million Dollar Homepage" and the failure of the many copycats that arose is analyzed. Since visitors do not return to the "Million Dollar Homepage" the paper proposes some improvements to the concept of pixel advertisement in Web pages. In [4] the authors extend the idea of pixel advertisement to placing small ads in banners. In this paper, we build upon their results, generalizing and thoroughly evaluating the proposed solutions.

Fig. 1. Sample from "Million Dollar Homepage"

The research question tackled in this paper can be defined as follows: *how to arrange rectangular pictures of different sizes and different prices for advertisement on a banner, in order to maximize revenue?* An important assumption we make is that we have a predefined set of advertisements that can be placed on the banner. This differs from the "Million Dollar Homepage" approach, where buyers just select free pixel blocks they want to purchase. In that case, there is no arrangement necessary and the problem tackled in this paper is nonexistent. Another assumption is that the banner size is given and that the set of advertisements should contain more advertisements than would fit on the banner. Note that even if the ads fit on the banner, the placement is still a problem. Furthermore, the problem we face is a static allocation problem with no dynamic dimension like time-sharing of advertisements.

Finding the optimal allocation of advertisements in a banner may be defined as a *two-dimensional, single, orthogonal, knapsack problem* [5]. The problem is NP-hard [6], making it extremely time-consuming to find the optimal solution(s) using integer programming. In this paper, we focus on applying heuristics to find adequate solutions.

We use three heuristic algorithms to allocate advertisements. For this, we experiment with sorting of advertisements and use different banner sizes. Our main objective is to find a heuristic algorithm that generates advertisement allocation patterns that maximize profit. Our secondary objective is to create a Web application. Therefore, a good performance also requires that the execution time is acceptable (i.e., within 30 seconds) to users of the Web application.

Related work on the placement of Web advertisements has been focusing on the *ad placement problem*, introduced in [7] as a variant of the bin packing problem. Despite the name, the most important feature of the ad placement problem is time scheduling of advertisements on a banner in *time slots*. Furthermore, it is concerned only with the placement of one advertisement on a banner or some advertisements side-by-side, whereby the height of the advertisements is equal to the height of the banner.

In [7], a distinction is made between the *offline* and *online* scheduling of advertisements. In the offline problem, we have a predefined set of advertisements to be scheduled. In the online problem, requests for placement arrive sequentially and we have to decide whether to accept requests without knowledge of future ones.

Another distinction made concerns the MINSPACE and MAXSPACE problems. The MINSPACE problem minimizes the banner size required for allocating a given set of advertisements in a fixed amount of time slots. The MAXSPACE problem maximizes the total profit given a fixed banner size and a fixed amount of time slots, which provide not enough free space for allocating all advertisements. For both problems, several solutions are available using polynomial time approximation algorithms [8,9,10], Lagrangian decomposition [11,12], column generation [12], and a hybrid genetic algorithm [13]. The approach presented in this paper is different from the ad placement problem, since we do not take into account time scheduling and we allocate advertisements not only side-by-side but also two-dimensional. Based on the previous classifications we are dealing here with an offline and MAXSPACE problem.

The rest of the paper is organized as follows: In Sect. 2 and 3 the simulation variables and allocation algorithms are defined. An analysis of the results is presented in Sect. 4. Section 5 discusses the implementations of our approach in a Web application. Section 6 concludes the paper and identifies future research directions.

2   Simulation

In order to obtain unbiased results in finding the most suitable environment for our purposes, we tested the allocation algorithms in a simulation using different configuration parameters, which defined the properties of each simulation cycle. These parameters consisted of 9 different banner sizes, 120 different sortings of the set of advertisements, and 6 different maximum sizes of the advertisements for each of the 3 algorithms. Each combination of configuration parameters represents a single simulation cycle. Altogether this resulted in 19440 simulation cycles. The details of these configuration parameters are described in the next few paragraphs. During each simulation cycle, one set of advertisements was allocated to one banner. The complete simulation was implemented in Matlab and run as a single batch file. All simulations were done on a Intel Core 2 Duo CPU P8400 at 2.26 GHz.

Size of the Banner. Five standard banner sizes [14], commonly used in Web advertising, have been selected to be used for each of the simulation cycles. The width W and height H of the banners are shown in Table 1. During the simulation the widths and the heights of the banners are also reverted to avoid bias towards particular sorting of the set of advertisements or banner dimensions. In total this amounts to 9 different banners (the square banner need not be reverted).

Table 1. Standard banner sizes

$W \times H$	Banner
728×90	Leader board
234×60	Half Banner
125×125	Square Button
120×600	Skyscraper
336×280	Large Rectangle

Price of the Banner. In practice, an existing banner may already generate revenue. One of the attributes of the banner is its price. This price however, will be set to a single fixed price during the simulations. This is done in order to avoid ambiguous results, in which it may not be clear if profit comes from the original banner or the allocated advertisements. During the simulations the price per pixel for the banner has been set to 4 which is much lower than the price range per pixel of the advertisements. This is done in order to avoid that no advertisements are allocated, when the banner generates more revenue than any of the advertisements.

Size of the Advertisements. For our simulation the advertisements where pseudo-randomly generated. The minimum width and height are 10 pixels, like the implementation on the "Million Dollar Homepage". In our experiment we allow the dimensions of the advertisement to vary between a minimum of 10 pixels and a variable maximum. The maximum width w_{max} and height h_{max} are defined as fraction of the banner width and the banner height. For this simulation the combinations of the maximal width and the maximal height are:

$$\{w_{max}, h_{max}\} \in \{\{1/5, 1/2\}, \{1/2, 1/2\}, \{1/3, 1/3\}, \{1/5, 1/5\}, \{1/2, 1/5\}, \{1, 1\}\}$$

Sorting of Advertisements. The heuristic algorithms iterate through the set of advertisements sequentially. The sorting of the set influences the generated pattern and is part of the heuristics. The simulation uses the following attributes of the advertisements to sort the set: (1) price per advertisement pixel p, (2) width w, (3) height h, (4) total area $w \times h$, (5) flatness w/h, and (6) the proportionality $|\log(w/h)|$, the last attribute refers to how much the rectangle resembles a square. A value of 0 for this attribute means that the rectangle is a square. Any higher value signifies that the rectangle is flat or tall. The sorting can be done in either *ascending* or *descending* order.

Once the set has been sorted based on the values of the attributes, a secondary sort is executed using one of the remaining attributes. The secondary sort has a minor influence on the resulting ordered set. Altogether the set of advertisements is sorted in 120 different ways, ($\frac{12!}{10!} - 12 = 120$, since we want to exclude the situations were the primary sort equals or is opposite of the secondary sort).

The prices of the advertisements are proportional to their dimensions. The price per pixel of an advertisement is set to 10 with random value between -1

and 1 added to this value, resulting in a uniform distribution between 9 and 11. The price of the advertisement is calculated by multiplying this price per pixel with its area.

During each cycle of the simulation, the configuration parameters are registered. For each cycle the waste rate (ratio of unallocated space over the total space in the banner) and the total profit of the generated allocation pattern are calculated. The execution time and the number of advertisements placed are also registered.

3   Heuristic Algorithms

We implemented three different heuristic algorithms: the *left justified*, the *orthogonal* algorithm, and the *GRASP constructive algorithm*.

The initialization step is identical for all algorithms. The algorithms assume a banner B with width w_B and height h_B. First the values of the primary and secondary sort, s_1 and s_2 are checked. Their values correspond to the attributes described in Sect. 2 and may be either positive or negative corresponding to an ascending and descending sorting order. There is a set A with n advertisements a_i where, $1 \leq i \leq n$. Sorting A according to s_1 and s_2 yields A_0. This is the ordered set of advertisements through which we iterate in each algorithm. Furthermore, the iterator i for the ordered set of advertisements A_0 is initialized at 1. The initiation step is given in Alg. 1.

Algorithm 1. Heuristic algorithm initialization

Ensure: $s_1 \neq s_2$ & $s_1 \neq -s_2$ {Avoid duplicate sorting in either direction}
    Sort all a_i in A first by s_1 and then by s_2
    A_0 {Ordered set A}
    $i := 1$ {Iterator for A_0}

Left Justified Algorithm. The *left justified algorithm* iterates through the ordered set of advertisements A_0. For each advertisement a_i it scans through the columns of the banner B from top to bottom. If the end of the column is reached, the iterator continues at the next column on the first row, and so on. When an available field is found and the advertisement fits on the empty location, it is placed in the banner. Advertisements are placed with the top left corner at the current field. When the end of ordered set A_0 is reached or when the banner is completely filled, the allocation pattern is returned. The details of this algorithm are shown in Alg. 2.

Orthogonal Algorithm. The *orthogonal algorithm* looks for new free locations for the current advertisement by moving diagonally from the top left corner $(r, c) = (1, 1)$ of banner B.

At each step, the algorithm searches for the next free space where the advertisement can be allocated at the location $(r, i), i \in \{1 \dots c\}$ and $(i, c), i \in \{1 \dots r\}$.

Algorithm 2. *Left justified* algorithm

$\textbf{for } i = 1 \text{ to } n \textbf{ do}$
  Select a_i from A_0
  $finished := false$
  $r := 1$ {Current row in B}
  $c := 1$ {Current column in B}
  $\textbf{while } finished = false \textbf{ do}$
    $\textbf{if } a_i$ fits on $B_{r,c}$ $\textbf{then}$
      {Allocate a_i on $B_{r,c}$}
      $\textbf{for } p = c \text{ to } c + x_i \textbf{ do}$
        $\textbf{for } q = r \text{ to } r + y_i \textbf{ do}$
          $B_{p,q} := i$
        $\textbf{end for}$
      $\textbf{end for}$
      $finished := true$
    $\textbf{else if } r + y_i > h_B \textbf{ then}$
      $\textbf{if } c < w_B \textbf{ then}$
        $c := c + 1$
        $r := 1$
      $\textbf{else}$
        $finished := true$
      $\textbf{end if}$
    $\textbf{else if } r + x_i > w_B \textbf{ then}$
      $finished := true$
    $\textbf{else}$
      $\textbf{if } r < h_B \textbf{ then}$
        $r := r + 1$
      $\textbf{else}$
        $\textbf{if } c < w_B \textbf{ then}$
          $c := c + 1$
          $r := 1$
        $\textbf{else}$
          $finished := true$
        $\textbf{end if}$
      $\textbf{end if}$
    $\textbf{end if}$
  $\textbf{end while}$
$\textbf{end for}$
$\textbf{return } B$

At the first free location closest to the border of the banner the advertisement a_i is allocated. When there is a tie we choose the one on the vertical search path. When we fail to allocate an advertisement for a certain (r, c) we continue to walk diagonally down-right by increasing both r and c by one. When the final row is reached, but there are still columns left, we only increase the column. When the final column is reached, but there are still rows left, we only increase the row. This means that after we start walking diagonally, we will eventually switch to walking either right or down, except for the situation when the banner B is a square.

Algorithm 3. *Orthogonal* algorithm

---

for $i = 1$ to n **do**
  select a_i from A_0
  $r := 1, c := 1$
  $verticalfound := false$, $horizontalfound := false$
  $verticalplace := (0,0)$, $horizontalplace := (0,0)$
  $colscomplete := false$, $rowscomplete := false$
  while $(colscompl$ && $rowscompl) = false$ **do**
    if $colscomplete = false$ **then**
      for $p = 1$ to r **do**
        if a_i fits on $B_{c,p}$ **then**
          store (c,p) in $verticalplace$, $verticalfound := true$, break
        end if
      end for
    end if
    if $rowscomplete = false$ **then**
      for $q = 1$ to c **do**
        if a_i fits on $B_{q,r}$ **then**
          store (q,r) in $horizontalplace$, $horizontalfound := true$, break
        end if
      end for
    end if
    if $horizontalfound = true$ or $verticalfound = true$ **then**
      {Select location closest to left or upper border}
      {Assume selected location is $B_{k,l}$: allocate a_i on this location}
      for $p = k$ to $k + x_i$ **do**
        for $q = l$ to $l + y_i$ **do**
          $B_{p,q} := i$
        end for
      end for
    end if
    if $r < h_B$ **then**
      $r := r + 1$
    else
      $rowscomplete = true$
    end if
    if $c < w_B$ **then**
      $c := c + 1$
    else
      $colscomplete = true$
    end if
  end while
end for
return B

When a_i is allocated, we start again in the top left corner of the banner and try to allocate the next advertisement from A_0. The details of this algorithm are shown in Alg. 3.

GRASP Constructive Algorithm. The *GRASP constructive algorithm*, is based on the constructive phase of the greedy randomized adaptive search procedure (GRASP) for the constrained two-dimensional non-guillotine cutting problem [15]. Since the algorithm was produced for the cutting stock problem, it has a somewhat different approach. We have adapted the algorithm to fit our problem.

In the GRASP algorithm, besides an ordered set of advertisements A_0, a list of empty rectangles L is maintained. Empty rectangles are parts of the banner where no advertisement is allocated yet. Initially, list L contains only the full banner. To allocate advertisements, the following procedure is followed.

First, we take the smallest rectangle of L in which an advertisement from list A_0 can fit. Then, we place an advertisement a_i from ordered set A_0 that fits in the free rectangle. Whenever an advertisement is placed in a rectangle, new empty rectangles are formed and added to L, while the original rectangle is removed from L. We always place the advertisement in a corner of the rectangle which is closest to a corner of the banner, and cut the empty space left in such a way that it yields optimal new free rectangles. In Fig. 2 the empty rectangles 1, 2, and 3 are formed by placing an advertisement. In order to obtain the optimal new empty rectangles we merge either empty rectangles 1 and 2, or 2 and 3. We choose the combination which yields the largest area for the merged rectangle. When there are no empty rectangles left (L is empty, the full banner is allocated) or no advertisements from list A_0 fits the rectangles in L, the algorithm stops.

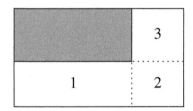

Fig. 2. Empty rectangles in GRASP algorithm

4   Analysis

The analysis of the simulation results was done with the tool R. This statistical software package allows all tasks to be automated in scripts. After the results are prepared, we normalized the profit and execution time by adding two extra columns with the profit per banner pixel $P_{pixel} = \frac{P_{total}}{BW \times BH}$ and the execution time per banner pixel $E_{pixel} = \frac{E_{total}}{BW \times BH}$. P_{total} is the total profit of the allocated pattern, E_{total} is the total execution time for the allocated pattern, BW is the banner width, BH is the banner height and w is the waste rate.

We are primarily interested in the profit per banner pixel of the allocation pattern P_{pixel}. The execution time is only relevant for the implementation of the algorithm. Since the same set of advertisements is used for all heuristic algorithms, we can evaluate their performance by comparing the normalized profits and execution times.

In Table 2 the distribution of the profit per banner pixel P_{pixel} is displayed for each of the algorithms. The *orthogonal* algorithm has resulted in a higher average profit per banner pixel and has been selected to be implemented in the Web application described in Sect. 5.

Table 2. Five point summary of the profit per banner pixel per algorithm

Algorithm	Minimum	1st Quartile	Median	Mean	3rd Quartile	Maximum
Orthogonal	6.079	8.585	9.082	8.887	9.427	10.620
Left justified	5.748	8.155	8.626	8.509	9.042	10.540
GRASP	4.730	6.978	8.044	7.962	9.083	10.600

As expected there is a strong correlation between the waste rate and the profit per banner pixel (P_{pixel}). The obtained value -0.9802 shows that a lower waste rate will result in a higher profit per banner pixel.

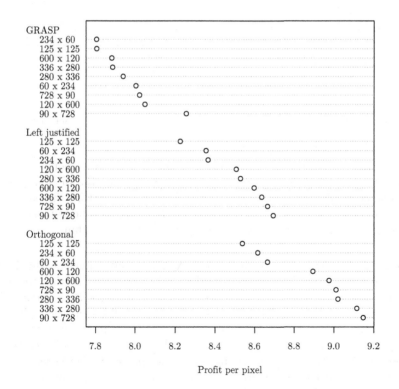

Fig. 3. Dotchart: profit per banner pixel for each banner size per algorithm

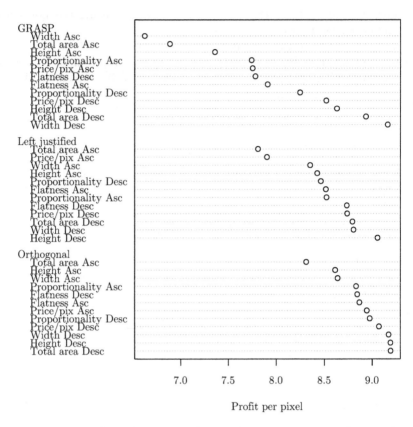

Fig. 4. Dotchart: profit per banner pixel for each primary sorting order per algorithm

Banner Size. From the dot chart in Fig. 3 the average profit per banner pixel is categorized by the dimensions of the banner. Besides the obviously better performance of the *orthogonal* algorithm, the graph shows that the banner size influences the performance of the algorithm. There is no solid evidence that a particular banner size benefits the performance of the algorithms.

Sorting. The preliminary sorting of the advertisements influences the final allocation pattern. From the dotchart in Fig. 4 it shows that sorting the advertisements based on their dimensions is of greater influence than sorting them based on their price. For each of the three algorithms, allocating the highest, the widest, or the advertisements with the largest total area first, yields the highest profit per banner pixel. This can be explained by the strong negative correlation between the waste rate and the profit per banner pixel. Furthermore, the figure shows that the *orthogonal* algorithm is less sensitive to the preliminary sorting of the advertisements, showing that the algorithm is more robust than the other ones.

Execution Times. The main interest in the execution time of the algorithm is a practical one. Though the *GRASP* algorithm shows the lowest execution times, the main issue is not to find the fastest algorithm, but merely one that is usable within the context of a Web application. Usable patterns of allocated advertisements should not come at the cost of waiting for more than 30 seconds for a result. In Table 3 the main characteristics of the execution times are displayed.

Table 3. Five point summary of the CPU time per algorithm in seconds

Algorithm	Minimum	1st Quartile	Median	Mean	3rd Quartile	Maximum
Orthogonal	0.016040	0.432000	2.632000	3.151000	4.745000	20.49000
Left justified	0.008244	0.156200	0.571000	0.956600	1.203000	17.25000
GRASP	0.003904	0.025610	0.072310	0.071180	0.099090	0.320000

Though it is clear that the *orthogonal* algorithm has the highest execution times, its outliers are only around 20 seconds of execution time. During the migration to Java for the implementation of the Web application, the execution times decreased remarkably.

Advertisement Allocator

Introduction

This is the Advertisement Allocator using the "Orthogonal" allocation algorithm. It is an implementation of a pattern-generating heuristic for a NP-hard, non-guillotine cutting-stock problem.

Advertisment

Enter the Comma Separated Values file with the required information about the advertisement. The following format with the semicolon (;) as a separator is expected:

Id; filename ; price ; url;

The Id must be unique in the list and must be a whole number larger than zero. The Filename cannot contain any spaces or other strange characters. The Price must be a valid positive number with '.' (dot) as the decimal separator. The URL can be any string without spaces.

Filename: Browse...

Enter the ZIP-file containing all the advertisements to be allocated. The ZIP-file should contain a flat list of pictures without any directories.

Filename: Browse...

Sample As an example you can use this ZIP-file with small advertisement and this corresponding pricelist.

Banner

◉ Choose a standard empty banner

728 x 90   ▾

◯ Or manually set the dimensions of the banner

Banner width: 100

Banner height: 100

◯ Or upload an existing banner, that will serve as the background for unallocated pixels

               Browse...

Optional: Specify the value of the banner.

Price of the whole banner:

Sorting

◉ Normal sort

The heuristic allocator goes through the list of advertisements sequentially. Sorting the list of ads based on their attributes significantly influences the final allocation. The default setting should yield good results, but may not be optimal. Feel free to try different combinations. Note that the secondary sort will only be taken if it applies to a different attribute.

Primary sort: Area   ▾   Descending ▾

Secondary sort: Price   ▾   Descending ▾

Send

Fig. 5. Advertisement allocator frontpage

Allocation Results

Result

Bannerwidth:	**728 pixels**	Bannerheight:	**90 pixels**
Total value allocated ads:	**41**	Total value uploaded ads:	**527**
Number of allocated ads:	**9**	Waste rate:	**9.17% (6005 of 65520 pixels)**
Execution time:	**137 ms**		

Banner as single image

Imagemap

```
<map name="banner" id="banner">
<area shape="rect" coords="0,0,181,66" href="http://www.ebay.com/"
alt="http://www.ebay.com/" /><area shape="rect" coords="181,0,400,39"
href="http://www.mailbigfile.com/" alt="http://www.mailbigfile.com/" /><area shape="rect"
coords="181,39,405,76" href="http://cloudalicio.us/" alt="http://cloudalicio.us/" /><area
shape="rect" coords="400,0,603,38" href="http://360.yahoo.com/" alt="http://360.yahoo.com/" /><area
shape="rect" coords="405,38,561,81" href="http://www.dropsend.com/"
alt="http://www.dropsend.com/" /><area shape="rect" coords="561,38,686,90"
href="http://www.skype.com/" alt="http://www.skype.com/" /><area shape="rect" coords="603,0,717,37"
href="http://www.feedblitz.com/" alt="http://www.feedblitz.com/" /><area shape="rect"
```

Fig. 6. Advertisement allocator result

5 Software

The implementation of the *orthogonal* heuristic algorithm as a Web application is available at http://headshredder.homelinux.net:8080/java/. It provides an allocation pattern for a set of advertisements using the orthogonal algorithm. A screenshot of the frontpage is displayed in Fig. 5.

Users can upload their own set of advertisements in the form of a comma separated values file and a zip file containing the pictures. The comma separated values file holds information on every advertisement in the format id; filename; price; URL;. The filename corresponds to a picture from the zip file, belonging to the advertisement. Furthermore, the user has to set parameters for the banner and the sorting criteria used. The user can select a standard banner size, manually set the dimensions, or upload an existing banner. For sorting, the user can specify the primary and secondary sorting criteria in either ascending or descending order.

The advertisement allocator provides the allocation results with some statistics. It returns the allocated banner as a single image and gives a corresponding imagemap in HTML. An imagemap is a list of coordinates relating to a picture. On the coordinates the specified URL is set. This makes it easy for Webmasters to implement their pixel advertisement banner. An example of such an result is displayed in Fig. 6.

6   Conclusion

Our main objective was to find a heuristic algorithm that generates advertisement allocation patterns that maximize profit. The best algorithm for our purposes is the *orthogonal* algorithm. Sorting the advertisements based on the width, height, and total area in descending order yields the best results. This algorithm was able to generate the patterns with the highest profit. It did not have the lowest execution times, but these were still well within the predefined time boundaries. The Java implementation showed that its performance did not influence the Web application's responsiveness.

This research also uncovers possible future work directions. Our research is limited to the allocation algorithms we have used. Better results may be achieved when using more intelligent algorithms. These algorithms should consider a few steps ahead and reach a better allocation while keeping revenue in mind. The GRASP algorithm showed great promise as an efficient algorithm with its low execution times. The implementation of the improvement phase as suggested in the original paper [15] may prove worth the effort in the future. It may also be more realistic to give different positions on a banner different prices. In our research we have a predefined set of advertisements with different prices regardless of the position they get allocated. The Eyetrack III [16] research investigates people's eye movements over Web pages. More frequently watched areas in the banner may be assigned a higher price.

In [3] is described that the "Million Dollar Homepage" concept has some weak points. The major problem of the original concept is that visitors do not return, because the content is never changed. Making the content dynamic will increase the effectiveness of pixel advertisement. Therefore, we propose further research adding time constraints to the pixel advertisement problem. Until now, related work only focused on scheduling advertisements side-by-side. Instead, it may be interesting to schedule pixel advertisement banners. This will make the present, static pixel advertisements more dynamic and increase user attention.

References

1. Interactive Advertising Bureau: Internet Advertising Revenue Report (2008), http://www.iab.net/insights/_research/530422/adrevenuereport
2. Tew, A.: Million Dollar Homepage, http://www.milliondollarhomepage.com/
3. Wojciechowski, A.: An Improved Web System for Pixel Advertising. In: Bauknecht, K., Pröll, B., Werthner, H. (eds.) EC-Web 2006. LNCS, vol. 4082, pp. 232–241. Springer, Heidelberg (2006)
4. Wojciechowski, A., Kapral, D.: Allocation of Multiple Advertisement on Limited Space: Heuristic Approach. In: Mauthe, A., Zeadally, S., Cerqueira, E., Curado, M. (eds.) FMN 2009. LNCS, vol. 5630, pp. 230–235. Springer, Heidelberg (2009)
5. Wäscher, G., Haußner, H., Schumann, H.: An Improved Typology of Cutting and Packing Problems. European Journal of Operational Research 183(3), 1109–1130 (2007)
6. Garey, M.R., Johnson, D.S.: Computers and Intractability; A Guide to the Theory of NP-Completeness. W. H. Freeman & Co., New York (1990)

7. Adler, M., Gibbons, P.B., Matias, Y.: Scheduling Space-Sharing for Internet Advertising. Journal of Scheduling 5(2), 103–119 (2002)
8. Dawande, M., Kumar, S., Sriskandarajah, C.: Performance Bounds of Algorithms for Scheduling Advertisements on a Web Page. Journal of Scheduling 6(4), 373–394 (2003)
9. Freund, A., Naor, J.S.: Approximating the Advertisement Placement Problem. Journal of Scheduling 7(5), 365–374 (2004)
10. Dawande, M., Kumar, S., Sriskandarajah, C.: Scheduling Web Advertisements: A Note on the Minspace Problem. Journal of Scheduling 8(1), 97–106 (2005)
11. Amiri, A., Menon, S.: Efficient Scheduling of Internet Banner Advertisements. ACM Transactions on Internet Technology 3(4), 334–346 (2003)
12. Menon, S., Amiri, A.: Scheduling Banner Advertisements on the Web. INFORMS Journal on Computing 16(1), 95–105 (2004)
13. Kumar, S., Jacob, V.S., Sriskandarajah, C.: Scheduling Advertisements on a Web Page to Maximize Revenue. European Journal of Operational Research 173(3), 1067–1089 (2006)
14. Interactive Advertising Bureau: Ad Unit Guidelines, http://www.iab.net/iab/_products/_and/_industry/_services/1421/1443/1452
15. Alvarez-Valdes, R., Parreño, F., Tamarit, J.M.: A GRASP Algorithm for Constrained Two-Dimensional Non-Guillotine Cutting Problems. The Journal of the Operational Research Society 56(4), 414–425 (2005)
16. Outing, S., Ruel, L.: The Best of Eyetrack III: What We Saw When We Looked Through Their Eyes. Poynter Institute, http://poynterextra.org/eyetrack2004/main.htm

Generation of Specifications Forms through Statistical Learning for a Universal Services Marketplace

Kivanc Ozonat

HP Labs
kivanc.ozonat@hp.com

Abstract. In a few business sectors, there exist marketplace sites that provide the consumer with specifications forms, which the consumer can fill out to learn and compare the service terms of multiple service providers. At HP Labs, we are working towards building a universal marketplace site, i.e., a marketplace site that covers thousands of sectors and hundreds to thousands of providers per sector. We automatically generate the specifications forms for the sectors through a statistical clustering algorithm that utilizes both business directories and web forms from service provider sites.

1 Introduction

There are a growing number of service providers, in sectors such as printing, marketing, IT and finance, with which a consumer can interact over the web to learn their service terms (i.e., information such as the price and time to delivery of their services). The service provider typically presents the consumer with a web form that includes entries on the specifications for the service. For instance, a printing services form would include entries on the size and type of paper, quantity to be printed, color and type of ink, folding, drills, proofing and perforation. The consumer makes her specifications by filling out the form, and, in response, the service provider e-mails the consumer their service terms.

There exist "marketplace" sites, such as the printindustry.com of the printing services sector and the Buyerzone.com, that provide the consumer with the ability to compare multiple service providers through specifications forms. Unfortunately, there are only a few such marketplace sites, and no site covers all the sectors. At HP Labs, we are working towards building a "universal" marketplace site, i.e., a marketplace site that covers thousands of sectors and hundreds of providers per sector. The consumer navigates through the different sector names and service providers in the site. She then selects one of the sectors, and is presented with the specifications form for that sector.

A main challenge in building the marketplace site is the generation of a specifications form for each sector. Given that there are a large number of sectors and that the specifications for some sectors may evolve over time, it is infeasible to attempt to manually generate a form for each sector.

G. Vossen, D.D.E. Long, and J.X. Yu (Eds.): WISE 2009, LNCS 5802, pp. 429–442, 2009.

In this paper, we employ a statistical clustering-based approach to generate a specifications form for each sector. For each sector, we first crawl the websites of the service providers listed under that sector in a business directory, and retrieve the service providers' web forms. The forms are distinguished from non-form content based on HTML tags. We then generate a specifications form for the sector from among the retrieved web forms.

We generate the specifications form for a given sector through a three-step process: (i) partitioning each retrieved form into questions (i.e., specifications), (ii) grouping the similar questions together, and (iii) selecting a representative question from each group to generate the specifications form.

Towards this end, we employ a statistical, iterative algorithm that, at each iteration, performs two updates: (i) the partitioning of each form into its questions based on the HTML tags in the forms, and (ii) the grouping of similar questions into clusters. We note that partitioning a form into its questions (specifications) based on the HTML tags in the form is a technical challenge since many HTML tags are *multi-purpose* tags, i.e., tags that may be used as question separators in some forms and used for entirely different purposes in other forms.

The previous work focused on related problems such as the retrieval, classification and generation of web forms [1,4,3,5,7,10,9,2]. However, the previous work did not address the problem of providing specifications forms to consumers within a marketplace setting. Further, the techniques utilized in the previous work were semi-automated, i.e., techniques that required the labeling of the attributes/concepts in the forms. While, in [11,12], these issues have been addressed, they are done so through selecting the "best form" from a repository rather than composing a new form from multiple forms. This approach has a limitation since it requires the repository to include at least one form (the "best from") that contains all of the specifications for the sector.

We apply our approach to generate specifications forms for 22 sectors. These sectors are printing, outbound telemarketing, graphic web design, direct marketing, outdoor advertisement, business insurance, payroll services, database design, corporate event planning, commercial cleaning, translation, video production, medical billing, construction (forklifts), cabling, check services, merchant accounts services, access control, alarm systems, video surveillance, window repair and human resources software. Our simulations indicate that the specifications forms generated by our approach capture the essential service specifications more accurately than alternative, manual or automated approaches to the same problem.

2   Formulation and Approach

Our goal is to generate a specifications form for any given sector. The specifications form is generated based on the forms retrieved from the service provider websites in the sector.

In section 2.1, we describe the repository of web forms, i.e., the set of all forms that we retrieve from service providers' websites. In section 2.2, we introduce a binary vector representation for the questions in the forms, and in section 2.3, we discuss how we utilize the HTML tags in the partitioning of the forms into questions.

In sections 2.4, 2.5 and 2.6, we introduce an iterative algorithm that, at each iteration, performs two updates: (i) the partitioning of each form into its questions based on the tags and form content, and (ii) the grouping of similar questions into clusters. Following the convergence of the algorithm, the specifications form is generated by selecting the most representative question from each cluster.

2.1   Repository and Notation

For any given sector, we crawl the websites of the service providers listed under that sector in a business directory (such as Yellowpages.com), and retrieve the web forms from the crawled websites. A form is distinguished automatically from non-form content through the HTML tags (in particular, the "form" tag) used in the forms. A web form typically contains the specifications that the service provider asks for from its customers. For instance, the forms retrieved from printing-related service providers might include specifications such as color, ink type, ink size, drilling, perforation and proofing.

Each service provider in the business directory is listed under one or more sectors. While some service providers are listed under only one sector, most are listed under multiple sectors as they serve more than one sector. For instance, it is not uncommon for a service provider listed under printing to be also listed under advertising. If a service provider is listed under multiple sectors, we - manually - decide which of the multiple sectors fits best to the service provider, based on the web content of the service provider.

The sector repository consists of N samples, where each sample i, $1 \leq i \leq N$, represents a retrieved form from a service provider in that sector.

We index each distinct word in the sector repository by w, and we denote the total number of distinct words used in all forms in the sector repository (except for the stopwords such as "and", "if", etc.) by W. Thus, $1 \leq w \leq W$.

2.2   Question Representation

The jth question of form i is represented by the binary feature vector $x_{i,j}$. The vector $x_{i,j}$ is a W-length vector, whose elements function as indicators for the presence of the repository words in form i. Denoting by $x_{i,j}^{w}$, the wth element of $x_{i,j}$, where $1 \leq w \leq W$,

$$
x_{i,j}^{w} = \begin{cases} 1 & \text{if word } w \text{ appears in question } j \text{ of form } i, \\ 0 & \text{if otherwise.} \end{cases} \tag{1}
$$

2.3   Tags

We define a *question separator* as an HTML tag that is used to separate two questions in a form. By manually analyzing a training set of web-based forms (a set of 50 randomly selected forms from our sector repositories), for each tag t, we record n_t, given by

$$n_t = \frac{\text{no. of times } t \text{ is used as a question separator}}{\text{no. of occurrences of } t}. \tag{2}$$

A higher value of n_t signals that the tag t is more likely to be used as a question separator in any given form. For instance, based on our training set, the listing tags, such as "li", "br" and "p", have higher values of n_t than the meta tags, such as "title", "link" and "style".

2.4   Clustering of the Questions

Consider K question clusters with each question $x_{i,j}$ being mapped to one and only one of the K clusters. We define μ_k, $1 \leq k \leq K$, to be the mean of cluster k. The cluster mean μ_k is a W-length vector such that its wth element represents the wth word in the repository. In particular, μ_k^w, the wth element of μ_k is given by

$$\mu_k^w = \frac{\text{no. of questions with word } w \text{ in cluster } k}{\text{no. of questions in cluster } k}, \tag{3}$$

thus, $0 \leq \mu_k^w \leq 1$.

We map each question $x_{i,j}$ to one of the $K << N$ clusters; each question gets mapped to the cluster with the closest cluster mean in Euclidean distance, i.e., the cluster that minimizes

$$d(x_{i,j}, k) = \min_k \sum_w (x_{i,j}^w - \mu_k^w)^2. \tag{4}$$

2.5   Partitioning of the Forms

We partition each form into its questions based on both the HTML tags in the form and the content of the form. The presence of a tag with a high value of n_t signals that the tag t could be a partitioning point in the form. On the other hand, a tag with a high n_t value by itself is not sufficient to conclude that the form should be partitioned at t. In addition to the tags, we also take into account the content in the form.

Consider the form i with J questions, and we seek to find if question $x_{i,j}$ of cluster k should be partitioned further into two questions. Let t be some tag, and denote the part of $x_{i,j}$ appearing before t by $x_{i,j,1}$ and the part of $x_{i,j}$ appearing after t by $x_{i,j,2}$. To find out if $x_{i,j}$ should be partitioned into two questions at tag t, we test if, for any pair of clusters l and m, $1 \leq l \leq K$, $1 \leq m \leq K$,

$$d(x_{i,j,1}, l) + d(x_{i,j,2}, m) < d(x_{i,j}, k), \text{provided } l \neq m. \tag{5}$$

If there exists any two clusters l and m such that (5) holds true, we partition $x_{i,j}$ further into two questions at tag t. The statement (5) implies that representing $x_{i,j,1}$ and $x_{i,j,2}$ with clusters l and m, respectively, is a better fit than representing $x_{i,j}$ with its cluster k.

The test in (5) does not take into account the tag information. Some tags are more likely to be question separators than others; we incorporate this fact into (5) by revising it as

$$n_t \times (d(x_{i,j,1}, l) + d(x_{i,j,2}, m)) < d(x_{i,j}, k), \text{provided } l \neq m, \tag{6}$$

where t is the tag that appears between $x_{i,j,1}$ and $x_{i,j,2}$. If multiple tags exist between $x_{i,j,1}$ and $x_{i,j,2}$, then we take the tag with the highest value of n_t.

2.6   Updates - Partitioning and Clustering

We implement our algorithm by iteratively applying the partitioning and clustering steps. At the initial iteration, each of the N forms is partitioned into two questions; each form is partitioned at the tag with the highest n_t value in the form. This is followed by the clustering of the questions into K clusters. At each subsequent iteration, each question, satisfying (6), is partitioned followed by the clustering of the questions.

We define the cost function as

$$\sum_{i=1}^{N}\sum_{k=1}^{K}\sum_{j \in k}\sum_{w}(x_{i,j}^{w} - \mu_{k}^{w})^2, \tag{7}$$

i.e., the sum of the costs (4) due to all questions in all N forms.

We repeat the clustering and partitioning steps until convergence, i.e., the change in (7) from one iteration to the next is less than some pre-defined ϵ.

2.7   Algorithm - Summary

For any given sector (e.g., printing, telemarketing, graphic design, etc.), we generate the specifications form for the sector as follows:

1. *Initial Partitioning*: Partition each form, i, $1 \leq i \leq N$, into two questions at the tag with the highest n_t value in the form.
2. *Iteration index*: Set iteration index $t = 1$, set K and ϵ.
3. *Clustering update*: Cluster the questions from all N forms (into K clusters) by mapping each question $x_{i,j}$ to the cluster k, minimizing (4).
4. *Partitioning update*: For each question $x_{i,j}$ and for each tag t appearing in the question, check (6). If (6) is satisfied, partition $x_{i,j}$ into two new questions at the tag t.
5. *Convergence*: If the change in (7) from iteration $t - 1$ to t is less than ϵ, go to step 6. Else, set $t = t + 1$ and go to step 3.
6. *Generate the specifications form*: For each cluster, k, find the cluster member (i.e., a question) that is closest in Euclidean distance to μ_k. The set of the closest cluster members constitutes the specifications form.

3 Related Work

The retrieval, classification and generation of web-based forms using statistical techniques have been explored in [1,4,3,5,7,10,9,2,11,12]. The approach taken in form retrieval has been the use of focused web crawlers [1,4,3,7]. A focused web crawler does not retrieve links from every visited page; instead, it estimates the probability of the visited page being relevant to the focus topic, and retrieves the links only if the probability is sufficiently high. A supervised page classifier is often used to estimate the probability that a page is relevant to the focus topic. A special case of focused web crawlers is the form-focused web crawler, which is designed to focus on and retrieve web forms [1]. The form-focused web crawler consists of a form classifier in addition to the page classifier. The form classifier is used to distinguish forms from non-forms based on form tags. It has been shown, however, that the accuracy of focused crawlers (even the form-focused crawler) is low in terms of retrieving relevant forms. For instance, in an experiment conducted for database domains, it has been shown that the accuracy of the form-focused crawler is around 16 percent [1,4,3,7].

The statistical classification of web forms based on form content and structure has been considered in [5,10,9,2]. In [5,2], web forms are classified into two classes, searchable forms and non-searchable forms, using statistical classification based on the structure of the forms. In [9,10,2], web forms are classified based on their textual content using statistical clustering methods. In [9,10], the techniques require manual pre-processing: labeling form attributes. Thus, the techniques discussed in [9] and [10] are semi-automated and not scalable. While the approach in [2] does not require a manual labeling of form attributes, it does require the manual labeling of forms to specify the categories or domains that they belong.

Statistical techniques for generating forms have been explored in [10] in the context of web-based services. In [10], a web-form has been modeled as a four-level hierarchy: service categories (e.g., books, education, travel), domains (e.g., search a book, find a school, query an airport), data types (e.g., book title, school type, destination airport), and terms (e.g., title, liberal arts, city). A statistical model has been generated for each form domain based on the terms used in the forms of that domain. This model can then be used to generate the specifications form for the domain. However, the approach is only semi-automated since the domains and data types need to be extracted and labeled manually. Further, it does not address the issue of the retrieval of the relevant forms.

The issue of providing a specifications form in a services marketplace has been addressed in [11,12]. However, in [11,12], the forms are generated through selecting the "best form" from a repository rather than composing a new form from multiple forms. This approach is limited since the repository may not include any single form that contains all of the specifications.

4   Simulations

4.1   Repository

The simulations are conducted using 22 sectors obtained from the business directory Yellowpages.com. These sectors are printing, outbound telemarketing, graphic web design, direct marketing, outdoor advertisement, business insurance, payroll services, database design, corporate event planning, commercial cleaning, translation, video production, medical billing, construction (forklifts), cabling, check services, merchant accounts services, access control, alarm systems, video surveillance, window repair and human resources software.

There are $N = 200$ service providers (or equivalently, $N = 200$ web forms) in each of the 22 sector repositories. For each of the 22 sectors, we used the specifications form for the sector from the Buyerzone.com website as the ground truth.

4.2   Comparisons

In our simulations, we compare the following five approaches:

- Random approach: For each sector, a form in the sector repository is randomly selected, and is used as the specifications form for the sector.
- Aggregate approach: For each sector, we select 20 forms randomly from the sector repository. We aggregate manually the specifications covered in the selected web forms. We restrict the number of service providers to 20 so that the amount of manual work done by the consumer to construct her specifications form by the aggregate approach is bearable.
- Supervised clustering: In this approach, for each sector, we select a specifications form from among the $N = 200$ forms in the sector repository. The approach used in the selection of the specifications form is as follows: first, calculate the mean vector of the 200 forms, then, select the form, which is closest to the mean vector in Euclidean distance, as the specifications form.
- Form generation without tag information: This is the approach described in section II except that the tag information is disregarded. It differs from the approach in section 2 in that the partitioning is done through the test in (5) instead of the test in (6).
- Form generation with tag information: This is the approach described in section 2.

4.3   Output Forms

For each of the 22 evaluated sectors, we compared the specifications forms outputted by the approaches discussed in section 4.2. The comparisons are included in Table 1. Each cell corresponds to the true detection rate for the corresponding approach and corresponding sector. The true detection rate refers to the ratio of the number ground truth specifications present in a form to the total number of ground truth specifications. Overall, the form generation with tags outperforms the remaining 4 approaches. In particular, for the printing, outbound telemarketing, graphic web design, outdoor advertising, video surveillance and human resources software sectors, the true detection rates for the forms outputted by the form generation with tags approach are 1.

4.4   Random and Aggregate Approaches

From Table 1, in each sector, the true detection rate for random approach is low compared with that of the form generation with tags approach. While the random selection provides a specifications form without much effort (i.e., just pick a service provider listed under the sector in the business directory, and use its web form), the randomly selected forms have a median true detection rate of only .22. Thus, for the sectors considered, the randomly selected forms are not very representative of the ground truth specifications.

The detection performance of the aggregate approach, with a median detection rate of .92, is comparable to that of the form generation with tags approach. The aggregate approach performs better in 6 of the sectors (direct marketing, business insurance, payroll, database design, forklifts and cabling), while the form generation with tags approach performs better in 8 of the sectors (graphic web design, outdoor advertisement, corporate event planning, commercial cleaning, medical billing, check services, merchant accounts services and access control). We should note, however, that the aggregate approach is manual; it requires one to spend considerable time and effort, including extracting terms and concepts manually from the forms in service providers' websites, and construct a list of questions manually from the terms and concepts.

4.5   False Alarms

Table 2 shows the false alarm rates for each of the sectors and for each of the approaches. The false alarm rate refers to the ratio of the number non-ground truth specifications present in a form to the total number of ground truth specifications. From Table 2, the aggregate approach performs better than the form generation with tags approach in terms of the false alarm rate. However, our observations indicate that many of the false alarms counted towards the rates in Table 2 are additional service options (which may actually be informative to the customer). For instance, for the printing sector, the form generation with tags approach outputs a specifications form that includes entries on padding, foil stamping and packaging. While these entries are not in the ground truth (and as such, they are counted towards the false alarm rate), they are additional printing service options rather than irrelevant entries.

4.6   Supervised Approach

As shown in Table 1, the detection rates for the supervised clustering approach are lower than those for the form generation with tags approach for 18 of the

Table 1. Detection Rates

Sector	Random	Aggregate	Supervised	No Tags	With Tags
Printing	.27	1.0	.49	.68	1.0
Outbound telemarketing	.29	1.0	.70	.51	1.0
Web design	.12	.59	.70	.70	1.0
Direct marketing	.26	1.0	.29	.81	.94
Outdoor ads	.12	.51	1.0	.68	1.0
Business insurance	.20	.41	.38	.36	.38
Payroll services	.14	1.0	.80	.65	.84
Database design	.15	1.0	.76	.40	.88
Corporate events	.20	.91	.91	.80	.93
Commercial cleaning	.40	.90	.60	.60	.92
Translation	.35	.75	.69	.40	.75
Video production	.14	.70	.52	.52	.70
Medical billing	.19	.68	.62	.59	.72
Forklifts	.21	.85	.75	.78	.83
Cabling	.25	.95	.80	.77	.90
Check services	.31	.91	.76	.62	.92
Merchant accounts	.19	.92	.82	.80	.95
Access control	.22	.88	.78	.66	.94
Alarm systems	.35	.86	.81	.80	.86
Video surveillance	.32	1.0	.78	.70	1.0
Window repair	.19	.94	.94	.72	.94
HR software	.26	1.0	1.0	.58	1.0
Median	.22	.92	.77	.68	.93

Table 2. False Alarm Rates

Sector	Random	Aggregate	Supervised	No Tags	With Tags
Printing	.71	.22	.28	.24	.28
Outbound telemarketing	.69	.21	.41	.47	.31
Web design	.72	.33	.32	.32	.28
Direct marketing	.53	.18	.23	.23	.23
Outdoor ads	.65	.32	.19	.27	.14
Business insurance	.62	.59	.52	.54	.34
Payroll services	.56	.20	.30	.32	.30
Database design	.59	.20	.35	.35	.35
Corporate events	.64	.09	.20	.30	.18
Commercial cleaning	.20	.10	.35	.40	.30
Translation	.18	.25	.25	.25	.25
Video production	.54	.30	.23	.23	.23
Medical billing	.45	.32	.26	.32	.25
Forklifts	.34	.23	.29	.29	.29
Cabling	.49	.38	.21	.20	.30
Check services	.36	.24	.32	.12	.22
Merchant accounts	.29	.18	.35	.29	.15
Access control	.54	.13	.20	.24	.19
Alarm systems	.50	.24	.12	.12	.18
Video surveillance	.42	.19	.14	.14	.24
Window repair	.36	.12	.12	.24	.20
HR software	.29	.08	.08	.18	.08
Median	.53	.22	.26	.27	.25

22 sectors. These 18 sectors include those sectors for which there exists no one form (in the repository) that includes all the ground truth specifications. The supervised approach can perform well only when there exists at least one form in the repository that includes all (or most) of the ground truth specifications for the sector; the outdoor advertisement sector is an example of this case.

The supervised approach leads to particularly low detection rates in five of the sectors: direct marketing, business insurance, commercial cleaning, printing and video production. We have observed that, in each of these cases, the repository did not contain a single form that included all (or most) of the ground truth specifications for the sector.

4.7 Form Generation without Tags

We partition a form into questions based on both the form content and the HTML tags. For the database design sector, the different questions (specifications) in the forms shared many common words. Thus, partitioning the database design forms into their questions based only on the content of the questions was not very accurate. This is evidenced by the relatively low true detection rate of the database design sector for the form generation without tags approach.

The inclusion of the HTML tags in the partitioning of the forms is particularly helpful in the case when the different specifications share many words in common. Using the test in (6) instead of the test in (5) improves the detection rate; for the database design sector, the form generation without tags approach leads to a true detection rate of only 0.40, while the detection rate is 0.88 when tags are included (i.e., the test in (6) is used).

4.8 Number of Clusters

A key parameter used in our simulations is K, the number of clusters. Each of the curves in Fig. 1(a) and Fig. 1(b) illustrates how the true detection rate for the form generation with tags approach varies as the number of clusters increases. Each curve in Fig. 1(a) corresponds to one of the first six sectors in Table 1, and each curve in Fig. 1(b) corresponds to one of the second six sectors of Table 1. In each curve, we plotted the detection rate for the values of K ranging from 5 to 30. When $K = 5$, the true detection rates are low, and they increase as K increases. At around $K = 25$, the true detection rates stabilize.

Each curve in Fig. 2(a) and Fig. 2(b) illustrates how the false alarm rate for the form generation with tags approach varies as the number of clusters increases. Similar to Fig. 1, each curve in Fig. 2(a) corresponds to one of the first six sectors in Table 2, and each curve in Fig. 2(b) corresponds to one of the second six sectors of Table 2. In each curve, we plotted the false alarm rate for the values of K ranging from 5 to 30. When $K = 5$, the false alarm rates are low, and they increase as K increases. Based on Fig. 1 and Fig. 2, there is a trade-off between the true detection rate and the false alarm rate, and the number of clusters can be used to adjust this trade-off.

4.9 Multiple Tags

Often, questions are separated by multiple tags instead of a single tag. As discussed in section 2, when two questions are separated by multiple tags, we take

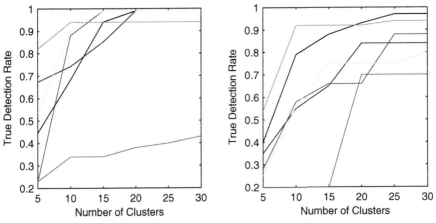

(a) Printing (blue), telemarketing (red), web design (black), direct marketing (green), outdoor ads (yellow), business insurance (magenta).

(b) Payroll services (blue), database design (red), corporate events (black), commercial cleaning (green), translation (yellow), video production (magenta)

Fig. 1. True Detection Rate vs. Number of Clusters

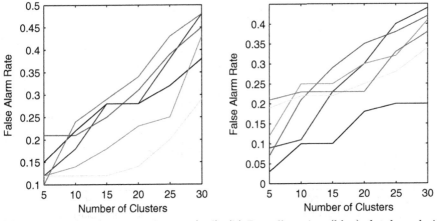

(a) Printing (blue), telemarketing (red), web design (black), direct marketing (green), outdoor ads (yellow), business insurance (magenta).

(b) Payroll services (blue), database design (red), corporate events (black), commercial cleaning (green), translation (yellow), video production (magenta)

Fig. 2. False Alarm Rate vs. Number of Clusters

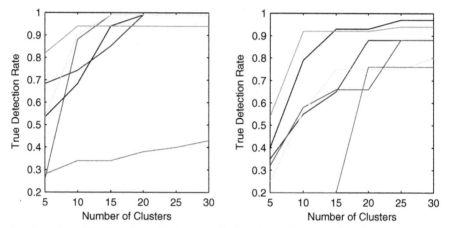

(a) Printing (blue), telemarketing (red), web design (black), direct marketing (green), outdoor ads (yellow), business insurance (magenta).

(b) Payroll services (blue), database design (red), corporate events (black), commercial cleaning (green), translation (yellow), video production (magenta)

Fig. 3. True Detection Rate vs. Number of Clusters - Vector view of tags

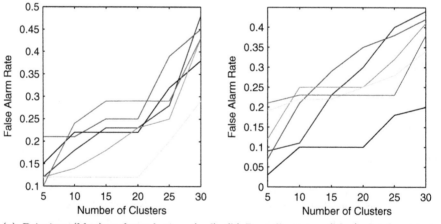

(a) Printing (blue), telemarketing (red), web design (black), direct marketing (green), outdoor ads (yellow), business insurance (magenta).

(b) Payroll services (blue), database design (red), corporate events (black), commercial cleaning (green), translation (yellow), video production (magenta)

Fig. 4. False Alarm Rate vs. Number of Clusters - Vector view of tags

into account only the tag with the highest n_t value. In Fig. 3 and Fig. 4, we took an alternative approach, and used pairs of consecutive tags instead of single tags. Thus, each time there were more than a single tag between two questions, we viewed the tags in pairs (or, equivalently as vectors of two tags).

Fig. 3 shows the true detection rates and Fig. 4 shows the false alarm rates when the tags are viewed in pairs rather than individually. Comparison of Fig. 3 and Fig. 4 with Fig. 1 and Fig. 2 indicates that, for some sectors, the true detection rates increased and the false alarm rates decreased when the tags are viewed in pairs. This might imply that taking into account the statistical relations among the tags might increase the accuracy of our approach, increasing the detection rates and reducing the false alarm rates.

5   Discussion

We are building a universal marketplace site that provides consumers with forms (with entries, questions, etc.), which consumers can fill out to make their service specifications. This would allow the consumers to interact with multiple service providers, to learn their service terms and to compare them without much effort. We expect that, for some sectors, the form may not span all the specifications, and the service providers may need to correspond with the consumer to ask for specifications beyond those covered in the form. However, even in such cases, the presence of a filled-out form, covering most of the specifications, would be helpful by reducing the time spent in the correspondence.

Generating a form by aggregating the entries and questions in multiple forms often requires multiple manual steps, including attribute-value pair extraction and labeling of the attributes [13]. We offer an alternative approach, where the HTML tags and form content are utilized jointly to partition the forms into questions without any manual labor. The partitioning is followed by the clustering of similar questions and selecting a representative question from each cluster, automating the aggregation step.

We add that our approach has multiple limitations. First, the sites, from which we retrieve the web forms, need to be machine crawlable; some sites require login, or break forms into multiple successive pages. Second, the approach is not suitable for all types of services; for instance, engaging with a professional service such as a physician requires other considerations beyond factual specifications.

References

1. Barbosa, L., Freire, J.: Searching for hidden web databases. In: WebDB (2005)
2. Barbosa, L., Freire, J.: Combining classifiers to identify online databases. In: WWW (2007)
3. Chakrabarti, S., Punera, K., Subramanyam, M.: Accelerated focused crawling through online relevance feedback. In: WWW (2002)
4. Chakrabarti, S., van den Berg, M., Dom, B.: Focused crawling: A new approach to topic-specific web resource discovery. Computer Networks (1999)

5. Cope, J., Craswell, N., Hawking, D.: Automated discovery of search interfaces on the web. In: ADC (2003)
6. Dempster, A., Laird, N., Rubin, D.: Maximum likelihood from incomplete data via the em algorithm. Journal of the Royal Statistical Society (1977)
7. Diligenti, M., Coetzee, F., Lawrence, S., Giles, C., Gori, M.: Focused crawling using context graphs. In: VLDB (2000)
8. Duda, R., Hart, P., Stork, D.: Pattern Classification. Wiley, Chichester (2001)
9. He, B., Chang, K.: Organizing structured web sources by query schemas: a clustering approach. In: CIKM (2004)
10. Hess, A., Kushmerick, N.: Automatically attaching semantic metadata to web services. In: IIWeb (2003)
11. Ozonat, K., Young, D.: A universal services marketplace over the web. In: ICAI (2009)
12. Ozonat, K., Young, D.: Towards a universal marketplace over the web: Statistical multi-label classification of service provider forms with simulated annealing. In: KDD (2009)
13. Probst, K., Ghani, R., Krema, M., Fano, A., Liu, Y.: Semi-supervised learning of attribute-value pairs from product descriptions. In: IJCAI (2007)
14. Schapire, R., Singer, Y.: Boostexter: a boosting-based system for text categorization. Machine Learning (2000)

An Urban Planning Web Viewer Based on AJAX[*]

Miguel R. Luaces, David Trillo Pérez, J. Ignacio Lamas Fonte,
and Ana Cerdeira-Pena

Database Laboratory, University of A Coruña,
Campus de Elviña s/n. A Coruña, 15071, Spain
{luaces,dtrillo,jilamas,acerdeira}@udc.es

Abstract. The *Program for Promoting the Urbanism Network* is a Spanish project promoted by *red.es*. The main goal of this project is the systematization of the urban planning of all the municipalities of the country using a single conceptual model that will end with the regional differences. The program has two main goals: first, building a *Transactional Planning Management System* based on a service-oriented architecture (SOA) of spatial services for processing the urban information, and second, providing an environment for publishing the information in the urban planning based on the standards for the creation of Spatial Data Infrastructures (SDIs). In a first phase, a collection of databases for the urban planning of different areas was generated, as well as a collection of services for the exploitation of the databases, and finally, different versions of viewers for the urban planning information. The services isolate the designers of urban data systems from the internal complexities of the data model, whereas the viewers allow final users to access the information in an easy and fast way. We show in this paper the Urban Planning Web Viewer for the Spanish municipality of Abegondo. The main features of the application are the modular architecture based on standard services, and the exclusive use of both AJAX (Asynchronous JavaScript and XML) and DHTML (Dynamic HTML) technologies in order to provide an extensible and very useful application with a high level of accessibility.

Keywords: urban planning, geographic information system, spatial data infrastructure, web viewer, service-oriented architecture, AJAX, interoperability.

1 Introduction

Red.es is the public entity within the Spanish Ministry of Industry, Tourism and Trade (MITyC) responsible for executing certain projects devoted to promote the information society. This is done in collaboration with the different autonomous

[*] This work has been partially supported by Ministerio de Educación y Ciencia (PGE and FEDER) ref. TIN2006-15071-C03-03, by Ministerio de Ciencia e Innovación ref. AP2007-02484 (FPU Program) for Ana Cerdeira-Pena, and by Xunta de Galicia ref. 2006/4 and ref. 08SIN009CT.

G. Vossen, D.D.E. Long, and J.X. Yu (Eds.): WISE 2009, LNCS 5802, pp. 443–453, 2009.
© Springer-Verlag Berlin Heidelberg 2009

communities, provincial councils and local entities of the country as well as with the private sector of the information and communication technology sector (ICT).

The *Program for Promoting the Urbanism Network* arises from a collaboration agreement between the MYTyC, the Spanish Federation of Municipalities and Provinces (FEMP) and *red.es* in order to introduce the ICT in the urban planning field of the local entities. More precisely, this program aims to define the appropriate systems, structures and technological resources to turn the urban planning information, which is usually drawn and written in paper documents, into digital information, and to use the digital information during all the life cycle of the urban planning process. That is, from the initial draft to the final application, without loss of information. The digital conversion of the information gives the urban planning process the typical advantages of information systems, that is, higher accuracy, consistency, universal access and ease of navigation through the information and reduction or even elimination of the distribution and copy costs [1].

Under this context, *red.es* proposed the definition and implementation of a *Transactional Planning Management System* using a service-oriented architecture of spatial services to deal with the urban planning information and a web-based publishing environment based on the standards for the creation of spatial data infrastructures. Therefore, three different components were generated:

1. A single conceptual model for urban planning that removes the differences between the different regions, and a collection of urban planning databases from selected areas following this conceptual model.
2. A collection of services for publishing the information stored in the urban planning databases. These services also isolate the designers of applications dealing with urban planning information from the internal complexities of the urban planning data model. Among these services, there is a *Web Map Service (WMS)* [2] that publishes the urban planning information as map images with different layers, a *Web Document Service (WS)* that provides a direct access to documents and urban planning repositories, and a *Planning Service* that provides an application programming interface (API) with different operations for the management of the urban planning database. There are operations in this API to compute the urban classification of a geographic point, to search urban planning areas by keywords, etc.
3. Different versions of web viewers for the urban planning information that allow people to access the information easily and quickly.

In this paper we present the urban planning web viewer for the Spanish council of Abegondo (in Galicia, Spain). This viewer acts as a client of the *WMS*, the *WS* and the *Planning Service* using AJAX and DHTML to provide a really useful application with a high level of accessibility.

The rest of the paper is organized as follows. In Section 2 we describe the application focusing on its main functional features. Then, Section 3 is devoted to technical features with special attention to the architecture of the system and to the interaction with external services. Finally, we conclude the paper showing the advantages of the solution and future lines of work in Section 4.

2 The Urban Planning Web Viewer: Functional Features

The Urban Planning Web Viewer is a web-based light client for browsing and querying the urban information of the council of Abegondo using the services developed by *red.es* as part of the *Program for Promoting the Urbanism Network*. These services provide the urban planning information by means of geographic information as well as alphanumeric information and documents.

Fig. 1. Urban planning web viewer interface

As it can be seen in Fig. 1, the application user interface consists of a *Map Window* and several panels and toolbars. The *Map Window* shows graphical information about the urban planning information using geographic layers provided by the *WMS*, and other external sources such as the *WMS* of the Spanish Cadastre, the *WMS* of the National Plan of Air Ortophotography (PNOA) or the *WMS* of the Geographical Information System of the Agricultural Plots (SIGPAC). Furthermore, the panels provide the users with additional information and the toolbars enable them to apply several different functions, more precisely:

1. *Navigation Toolbar*: to move the *Map Window* over the council surface. It provides functions such as: zoom in, zoom out, window zoom, zoom to initial extension, drag-based movement, movement to the four cardinal directions, and an overview map that shows the situation of the current view with respect to the municipality and that provides a quick way to move the view to a certain location.

2. *Current View Information Panel*: this panel shows dynamical information about the current view such as the coordinates of the cursor, the spatial reference system used, the displaying scale (both numeric and graphical) and the address (street and number) that is closest to the position pointed by the mouse.
3. *Content Panel*: it allows the users to select the information layers that are shown in the *Map Window*. The layers are categorized into those that deal with the urban planning (Classification, Categories, Qualification, Management, Systems, Protections, Affections and Reservations) and those which provide background information (Cadastre and Orthophotographs). The user can also set the transparency level of each one of the layers in order to display several ones at the same time.
4. *Query Tool*: this tool allows users to obtain urban information for a given point of the map. This information includes: (1) the information of the current urban planning layers, (2) the collection of documents storing the urban planning information related to that point along the time, and (3) the graphic plans for that point. Figure 2 shows an example of a query result with the tab displaying the collection of documents selected.

Urban planning layers information

Graphic plans

Documents with urban planning information

Fig. 2. Query result

5. *Geocoding Toolbar*: a toolbar with a group of tools for searching urban planning information using keywords. It also gives the option to search using the identifiers of the Spanish cadastre, or even by postal address. This toolbar is divided into several tabs, one for each kind of search, and each tab contains a form where the users can introduce the information needed (that is, a keyword, a cadastre identifier, or an address). All searches are performed in three steps: (1) the user introduces the search data and clicks on the button *Search*, (2) the application shows in the results panel the list of elements retrieved that fulfill the criteria, and finally, (3) the user selects one of the elements retrieved to automatically position the *Map Window* over that element.
6. *Measuring Toolbar*: it contains different tools to measure distances and surfaces over the *Map Window*.
7. *Map and Urban Planning Report Generation Toolbar*: these tools provide the user with an easy way to generate maps and urban reports from the current view in PDF format. The map generation tool creates urban maps using the cartography currently loaded in the *Map Window* (layers and styles associated).

With respect to the tool for the generation of urban planning reports, the user can request this functionality after performing a query. That is, the user requests this functionality from the query results window and the application creates a report with the urban planning qualification information for the given point. Furthermore, the report can also be sent by email. Figure 3 shows two examples of a report and a map generated with the application.

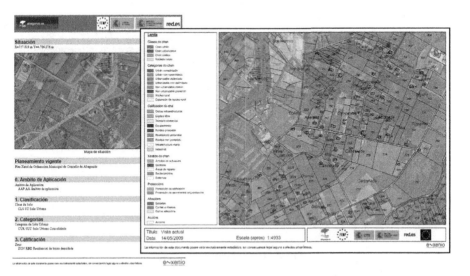

Fig. 3. Examples of a report and an urban map

3   The Urban Planning Web Viewer: Technical Features

One of the most relevant features of the Urban Planning Web Viewer of Abegondo is that it is entirely based on open source software. This assures a low cost of maintenance as well as technological independence because the application can be run on any platform.

The architecture of the application is shown in Fig. 4. Notice that it is modular and based on the standard services defined by the *International Organization for Standardization (ISO)* and the *Open Geospatial Consortium (OGC)*. This important feature ensures that the system is interoperable, it is easy to be extended, and it is easy to integrate within a spatial data infrastructure [3] following the INSPIRE directives.

With respect to the technologies used in the implementation, the exclusive use of AJAX/DHTML technologies in the client side clearly improves the accessibility of the application because the installation of plug-ins or applets is not necessary in the client for its properly performance [4].

3.1   Architecture of the Application

The Urban Planning Web Viewer follows a three-layer architecture following the Model-View-Controller architectural pattern. The client side (the View of the

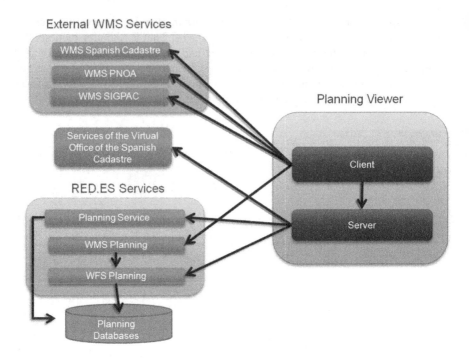

Fig. 4. Application architecture

application) has been implemented using only AJAX/DHTML, whereas the server side (the Model and the Controller) has been implemented using Java 2 Enterprise Edition (J2EE) technology.

With respect to the client side, the implementation uses the library *OpenLayers* [5] for the *Map Window* and the different tools that interact with it. *OpenLayers* is an open source library in *Javascript* for displaying maps using geographic information services as data sources. Some of the panels and toolbars of the client side (such as the *Geocoding Toolbar* or the *Content Panel*), have been implemented using *jQuery* [6]. This is a *Javascript* framework that simplifies the interaction with HTML. It also simplifies the usage of AJAX technology for handling events and adding interactivity to web applications.

In the server side, the *Spring* [7] framework has been used for implementing the Controller. This framework is an open source software as well, and it speeds up the implementation of the Controller of a MVC architectural pattern. We also use *JasperReports* [8] in the server side for the creation of the PDF maps and reports. This open source library makes the creation of paper reports very simple.

3.2   Interaction with External Services

Beyond the architecture and internal functionality of the application, the most powerful feature of the Urban Planning Web Viewer is its capability to interact with external services. This feature makes the application interoperable and extensible, and provides for an easy integration in a spatial data infrastructure. To explain this feature, we describe the main interactions of our application with the urban planning services of *red.es* and with other services.

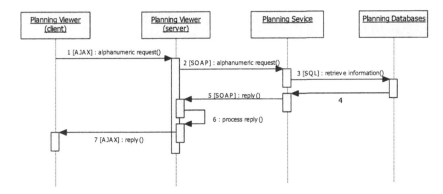

Fig. 5. Accessing urban planning alphanumeric information

To access the urban planning information, the application uses the red.es services. In order to access the alphanumerical information, the application acts as a client of the *Planning Service* provided by red.es. This service uses SOAP (Simple Object Access Protocol) as the communication protocol, and therefore, XML requests and replies are exchanged between the server side of the Urban Planning Web Viewer and the Planning Service. A sequence diagram for this process is shown in Fig. 5.

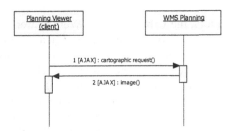

Fig. 6. Accessing urban planning geographic information

With respect to geographic information, the *WMS* service of the provided by *red.es* is used as the information source. The *WMS* service fetches the geographic information from the urban planning database and generates image maps for the information. The client side of the Urban Planning Web Viewer uses *OpenLayers* as a client of this *WMS* service. Figure 6 shows a sequence diagram that represents this situation. In order to access external *WMS* such as the one provided by the Spanish Cadastre or the one provided by the National Plan of Air Ortophotography, the client side of the Urban Planning Web Viewer uses the same strategy used for the *WMS* provided by *red.es*.

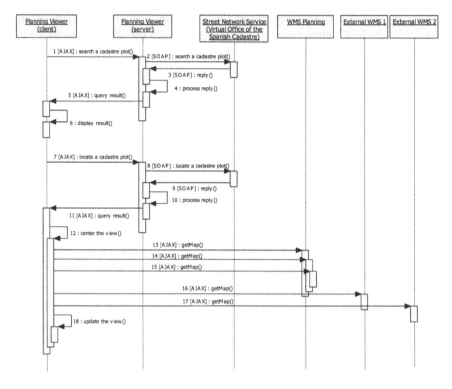

Fig. 7. Searching using the Cadastre web service

Regarding the search tool, the Urban Planning Web Viewer uses the street network service provided by the Virtual Office of the Spanish Cadastre [9]. Using this service, a client application can search the street network of the Spanish Cadastre and the information of the Cadastre that is not protected by law. The service defines a protocol that uses XML to represent the requests and the replies of the service. Figure 7 shows a sequence diagram of this process. First, the server side of the Urban Planning Web Viewer queries the external services to retrieve a list of search results that fulfill the query terms and then it displays the results to the user. When the user selects one of the query results, the Urban Planning Web Viewer uses the geographic location associated to the query result to position the *Map Window*. The client side of the application uses *OpenLayers* to center the *Map Window* and to retrieve the new maps.

A more complex use case involves using the urban planning services provided by red.es to retrieve information from the urban planning database. This process is described by the sequence diagram shown in Fig. 8. The process consists of the following steps:

1. The user types in the *Geocoding Toolbar* the information and clicks the *Search* button.

    The client side of the application sends an AJAX request to the server side of the application to retrieve the elements that fulfill the search criteria.

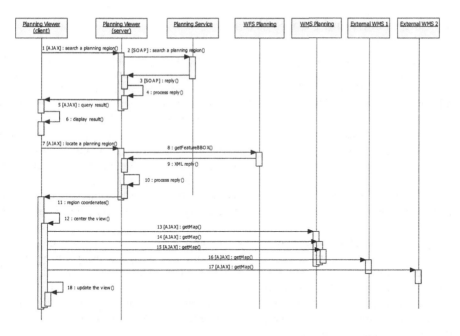

Fig. 8. Searching using the urban planning services

The server side of the application invokes the *Planning Service* using a SOAP request.

The server side of the application retrieves the reply from the *Planning Service*. The reply is processed and sent back to the client side of the application.

The client side of the application displays the search results in the results panel of the *Geocoding Toolbar*.

2. The user selects one of the search results

The client side of the application sends an AJAX request to the server side to retrieve the geographic location of the element selected.

The server side of the application performs a request to the *Web Feature Service (WFS)* [10] provided by *red.es* in order to compute the geographic location of the element selected.

The server side of the application retrieves and processes the XML response provided by the *WFS*, and sends the result back to the client side of the application.

The client side of the application uses *OpenLayers* to position the *Map Window* centered over the element. In turn, *OpenLayers* requests the required map images from the *WMS* services associated to the layers that are being displayed in the map.

452   M.R. Luaces et al.

4 Conclusions and Future Work

In this paper, we show the Urban Planning Web Viewer that we have developed for the municipality of Abegondo. This work was developed under the *Program for Promoting the Urbanism Network* funded by *red.es*. The Urban Planning Web Viewer allows the citizens of the municipality to browse and query the urban planning information. Furthermore, the application provides tools for: (1) finding easily and quickly a given Cadastre plot or an urban planning region, (2) querying the classification given by the urban planning to a specific geographic point, (3) generating paper maps and reports with the urban planning information, and (4) performing other operations such as measuring distances, surfaces, or browsing the urban planning documents. The paper also describes the architecture of the system and the interaction process between the system and the external services are described with detail.

The most important features of the system are the following: (1) it was developed using open source software, (2) the architecture was designed using the standard services defined by ISO and OGC, and the client side of the application was developed using AJAX and DHTML. These features imply that the application has a very low maintenance cost, an extensible architecture that is interoperable, and a high level of accessibility. Finally, the process of integrating the application in a spatial data infrastructure is also very easy.

As future lines of work, we are considering the following functionality:

1. Using other external services to perform searches. For instance, we plan to use the services provided by *Cartociudad* [11], which were developed by the National Geographic Institute of Spain, to be able to search using postal codes, census districts, or street names.
2. Retrieving from the Cadastre service the complete information of a land parcel and displaying this information in the user interface and in the paper reports.
3. Including *e-government* functionality such as producing urban planning certificates.

References

1. Rodríguez-Gironés, M., Brun, G., Romero, E.L.: Urbanismo y TIC en España, Recomendaciones para el impulso del urbanismo en red. Red.es (2008)
2. Open Geospatial Consortium. Web Map Service Specification. Version 1.3., http://www.opengeospatial.org/standards/wms (retrieved, August 2008)
3. Global Spatial Data Infrastructure Association (2007), http://www.gsdi.org (accessed, June 2009)
4. Brisaboa, N.R., Luaces, M.R., Paramá, J.R., Trillo, D., Viqueira, J.R.: Improving Accessibility of Web-Based GIS Applications. In: Shafer, D.F. (ed.) Proceedings of the 16th International Workshop on Database and Expert Systems Applications (DEXA 2005), pp. 490–494. IEEE Computer Society, Los Alamitos (2005)
5. OpenLayers website, http://openlayers.org (accessed, June 2009)
6. jQuery website, http://jquery.com (accessed, June 2009)
7. Spring Source website, http://www.springsource.org/ (accessed, June 2009)

8. JasperReports website, `http://jasperforge.org/projects/jasperreports` (accessed, June 2009)
9. Virtual Office of the Spanish Cadastre services, `http://www.catastro.meh.es/ws/webservices_catastro.pdf` (accessed June 2009)
10. Open Geospatial Consortium. Web Feature Service Specification. Version 1.3., `http://www.opengeospatial.org/standards/wfs` (accessed, June 2009)
11. Cartociudad website, `http://www.cartociudad.es` (accessed June 2009)

Data Center Hosting Services Governance Portal and Google Map-Based Collaborations

Jih-Shyr Yih and Yew-Huey Liu

IBM T. J. Watson Research Center
Yorktown Heights, NY 10598, USA
{jyih,yhliu}@us.ibm.com

Abstract. In the IT services business, a multi-year enterprise application hosting contract often carries a price tag that is an order of magnitude larger than that of the solution development. For hosting services providers to compete over the revenue stream, the ability to provide rapid application deployment is a critical consideration on top of the price differences. In fact, a data center is tested repeatedly in its responsiveness, as application hosting requires iterations of deployment adjustments due to business condition, IT optimization, security, and compliance reasons. In this paper, we report an enterprise application deployment governance portal, which coordinates service delivery roles, integrates system management tools, and above all keeps the clients involved or at least informed. In the data center operations such as: early engagement, requirement modeling, solution deployment designs, service delivery, steady state management, and close out; this paper illustrates how the Google Map technology can be used in representing both the target deployment architecture and delivery process. The Google map model can then be used in delivery process execution and collaborations. The resulting governance portal has been fully implemented and is in active use for the data center business transformation in IBM.

Keywords: Hosting Services, Data Center, On Boarding, Service Delivery Process, Cloud Computing, Group Wisdom, Wiki, Business Support System, Operations Support System, Google Maps, and Web. 2.0.

1 Introduction

In IT services business, an enterprise application is said to be in a "transition" phase, when the application is installed and configured onto physical machines in a hosting environment. Transitioning of an application can happen several times in its lifecycle, as it moves to different hosting services providers. Application transition is iterative in nature, involving multiple passes of adjustments to approach optimal performance. The changing business or IT requirements also trigger adjustments in deployment architecture. Poorly designed or executed transitions can result in excessive delay of production, wastes, non-compliance or down times in steady-state.

For an enterprise application owner, criteria for selecting a hosting services provider can be: 1) meeting the IT requirements, 2) having an affordable financial

G. Vossen, D.D.E. Long, and J.X. Yu (Eds.): WISE 2009, LNCS 5802, pp. 455–462, 2009.

model, and 3) demonstrating quality in execution. Requirements to a data center can be functional as well non-functional, e.g., high availability (HA), disaster recovery by migration, on-demand resource allocation and degrees of service level agreements. All of the above can affect the deployment architecture [1, 2, 3]. On the other hand, while clients are making selections, data centers are also selective in choosing application profiles to support, based on economy of scale considerations and the availability of required application supporting skills. For examples, offerings from a hosting services provider can be specialized for SAP applications only.

For financial model and cost saving considerations, an outsourcing provider's value proposition usually offers significant cost saving, say, larger than 20 percent, compared to the in-house operations, made possible by the economy of scale operated by the provider. Additionally, a client company can move hardware and facility capital off the book by outsourcing.

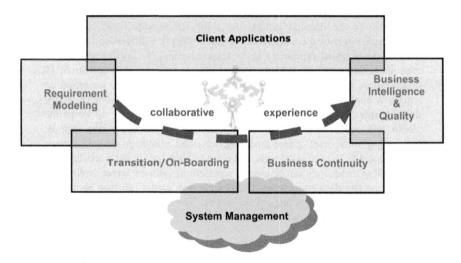

Fig. 1. Enterprise Hosting Services

When it comes to deployment, currently a typical enterprise data center takes not hours or days, but rather months, to transition a production application. A hosting service provider faces the task of orchestrating dozens of service delivery roles within a data center, as well as the need to leverage across data centers to jointly support complex applications. Fig. 1 shows the aspects of work done by the enterprise hosting services in: 1) requirement modeling, 2) transition/on-boarding, 3) business continuity, and 4) business intelligence & quality measure. This paper addresses data center operation issues in how to improve the efficiency and quality of deployment requirement execution, towards responsive and rapid on-boarding of applications to data centers. Section 2 gives a high-level list of what deployment operations are to be orchestrated inside a data center. Section 3 shows a model-driven, collaborative execution approach, in which requirement and process models are constructed based on a new collaborative technology based on Google Maps. We will show how the collaboration can be extended across data centers in Section 4, before concluding with the implementation results in Section 5.

2 Enterprise Application Deployment Operations

To explain why it takes months to deploy an enterprise application for production, in addition to the usual tasks such as, early engagement, requirement definition and solutions design, we highlight a few major activities for the rest of the deployment operations in Table 1.

Table 1. Enterprise Application Deployment Major Delivery Activities

1. Begin delivery -- Transition meetings, procure HW and SW
2. Install and configure servers -- Allocate HW, server name/IP, server configurations, build servers, ID mgmt
3. Install and configure middleware -- Application & middleware support, initial data load, configure backup
4. Deploy servers -- Security scan, enable firewall
5. UI compliance -- Corporate compliance, exceptions, hosting domain, URL taxonomy & redirect
6. Steady state readiness and preparation for future change requests
7. System integration test
8. Application performance test
9. Steady state cutover
10. Initiate billing
11. Conclude delivery -- Client checkpoint meetings, delivery survey, lessons learned, documentation
12. Steady state mgmt -- Support hosting environment -- Server/network outages, issues, problems, changes, risks, dependencies -- Server availability results -- Annual contract, workload, rates review
13. Close out

There are usually several rounds of initial engagement negotiations between a client and an engagement manager before reaching an agreement. The delivery then begins with a teaming meeting among the assigned architect, project manager, and technical specialists. Staffing and acquiring physical resources are potentially major road blocks, if the data center business model does not include adequate forward planning.

The automation of installing and configuring servers and middleware has been much discussed in Cloud Computing recently [4, 5]. Surprisingly, server installation or configuration is actually not reported as the bottleneck in the long production process. For instance, the various security scans and compliance checks could take more time, especially so if there are exceptions to be approved.

While the configured application is going through integration tests and performance tests, the client can get familiar with the process of making future change requests. Examples of change requests are: the need to move a server to a different security zone, adjust the size of a server cluster, and increase the dedicated RAM size of a logical server.

The system administrators are notified ahead of new servers coming on line, and will begin receiving the servers after passing the tests, and the transition team cuts over the applications to the steady-state team. Meanwhile, the billing process can be initiated, and the transition team needs to wrap up the delivery with client checkpoint meetings, delivery survey, lessons learned discussion, and documentation. A graphical representation of the service delivery activities with dependencies is shown in Fig. 2.

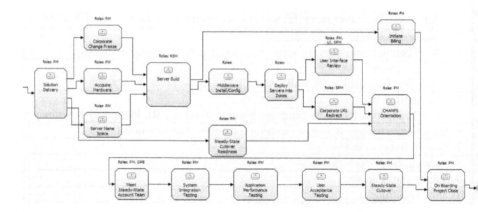

Fig. 2. Solution Delivery in Enterprise Application Deployment

The steady-state system management team is to maintain the hosting environment, recover from server/network outages, resolve issues or problems, respond to change requests while the application is on-line, and continuously identify risks or dependencies to stake holders. Finally, the account office may need to exercise the close out process, when the client discontinues the hosting services.

3   Collaborative Workflow over Google Maps

In this section, a new approach is introduced for model-driven hosting services delivery.

3.1   Hosting Services Delivery Web 2.0 Modeling

To begin, we propose a model with *deployment architecture* and *transition process* as two dimensions in modeling. An example of the two-dimensional model is given in

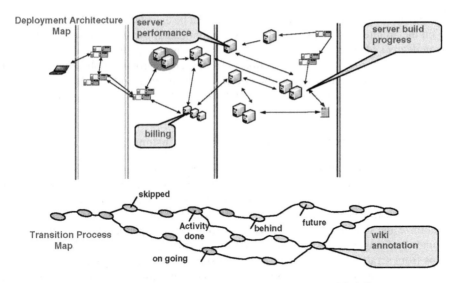

Fig. 3. Deployment Architecture and Transition Process Modeling

Fig. 3. The deployment architecture model shows the deliverables, and the transition process model shows the work orders needed to transition the application to the hosting environment. Both the architecture and process are in Google Map representation, for easy of user annotations and interactions with automated management tools.

3.2 Using Google Map Technology for Workflow Annotation and Governance

To orchestrate the various work orders, instead of using a workflow engine, scenarios are organized as a hierarchy of Process Google maps, and state transitions are done by manual annotations. Not just relying on the project manager, any concerned data center personnel can assign responsibility, record status (e.g., green, yellow, red), modify planned duration, report actual duration, and comment on a particular execution. There is no strict sequence that one must follow, as the links are just suggestions on the flow. Therefore, progress will not be held up by a person who was originally assigned to do the work but failed to show up, since any person can take over or reassign the work. Of course, all actions taken against the map will be recorded and communicated to people who subscribe to information about specific work orders. There is extra intelligence behind the process map, such as a mechanism to announce the readiness of a work order to be executed, and email interactions for getting decisions in a process map.

As the process is being executed, results can be reported by annotations to the Deployment Architecture Google map. For example, if a server configuration discovery tool is available, such as IBM TADDM [6], the detailed installation steps performed on the servers can be detected by the discovery tool and reported on the architecture map as machine generated annotations. The architecture map continues to be useful into the steady state, as performance tools can report run-time health check results on servers. The monthly billing which is mostly based on Service Level

Agreement results, such as server availability, can be calculated accordingly and show up on the architecture maps as well. To keep application owner connected, clients are given degrees of access and will be able to make inquiries about the process maps and the architecture maps. As it is mentioned earlier, an enterprise application transition can take months. Clients need to be connected to the data center operations, for the data center to maintain a responsive impression. This open access to clients and delivery persons on the floor has been found key to execution quality improvement.

3.3 Deployment Architecture-Driven Workflow Customization

As was mentioned earlier, an application owner can request a change in the deployment architecture iteratively. Depending on what the change is, only a subset of the transition process is needed. A project manager and/or deployment architect would normally need to have in-depth technical knowledge and discipline to customize the transition process maps. We have thus implemented this intelligence behind the Google maps. The idea is not to construct a custom hierarchy of progress maps from scratch, but to identify irrelevant steps in the super set. Our approach is to compute the differences shown on two successive versions of the architecture map. With a rule-based system, one can determine answers for the decision steps in the process maps and grey out the irrelevant branches.

4   Web Delivered Data Center Governance Services

So far we have given an overview on the enterprise application deployment operations, and established a model for the requirements and the processes. In this section, we will report on the development of a hosting services governance portal.

For different user roles, we have established several personalized tree navigation views, such as *My Clients, My Financials, My Servers,* and *My Actions.* From My Clients, a user can see client accounts and account info, filtered by the personal responsibility info. From a client account, a user can drill down to the client application level and view application information. For an application, one can unfold to find all the iterative client requests toward the application. At the client request level, a user can proceed to view the deployment architecture maps and transition process maps. The map-based views also come with alternative table views, in which the hierarchy is represented by indented rows.

A portal user can find all needed information at various levels inside the My Client tree navigation views. For convenience, relevant client billing cases are also sorted under My Financials tree navigation, for the financial analysts or managers. The navigation design has been given special attention so that a financial analyst doest not miss out any billing. In the same concept, all servers that are to be touched by a portal user can be found in one place under My Servers view. Similarly, all work orders associated with a specialist can be found under My Actions view.

To support these account management, project repositories, and billing functions, we have implemented over one hundred business and operations support system (BSS+OSS) web services in the back office. For the client facing front office functions, we have the client experience begins with requirement definitions and pricing estimates. This is for the purpose of responding to client inquiries in a self-help fashion.

The portal software can also provide a Platform-as-a-Service (PaaS) to another data center, which lacks its own governance system and may be still relying on spreadsheets for account and project management. Moreover, when a client needs to employ multiple federated data centers for the hosting of a single application, having a complete collection of data center offerings at a common portal enables the requirement modeling. A model of the common portal is shown in Fig. 4.

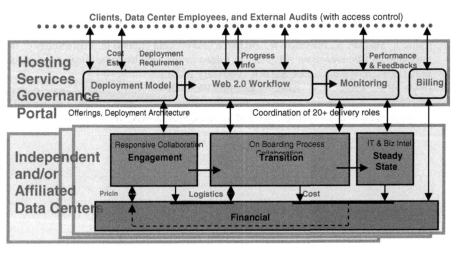

Fig. 4. A Common Hosting Services Governance Portal

5 Concluding Remarks

Data center governance has been found the most significant bottleneck in a hosting services business. The account and project offices in this layer are at the center of the operations, integrating clients, service delivery specialists, tools, and business and operations support system web services. The web 2.0 fashioned open contributions allow best practices by group wisdom to emerge, as timely feedbacks can be recorded during the process execution. The visualized deliverables and execution paths in Google Maps have been found valuable by the users to enhance human discipline without incurring inflexibility. Preliminary analysis shows the implementation of this governance portal has potential to help grow the piloting data center business by more than 50% with rapid deployment. The new centralized accountability database also replaces thousands of isolated spreadsheets. Further improvements are expected as business intelligence data is made available to clients, showing how the client business is supported by IT, and to the data center managers, showing how resources are being utilized and how teaming can be improved.

References

1. Gopisetty, S., Butler, E., Jaquet, S., Korupolu, M., Nayak, T.K., Routray, R., Seaman, M., Singh, A., Tan, C.-H., Uttamchandani, S., Verma, A.: Automated Planners for Storage Provisioning and Disaster Recovery. IBM J. Res. & Dev. 52(4/5), 353–365 (2008)
2. Amazon EC2. Amazon Elastic Compute Cloud
3. Ranjan, S., Rolia, J., Fu, H., Knightly, E.: QoS-Driven Server Migration for Internet Data Centers. In: Proc. IEEE/IFIP Int'l Workshop Quality-of-Service (May 2002)
4. Armbrust, M., et al.: Above the Clouds: A Berkeley View of Cloud Computing, UC Berkeley technical report
5. Varia, J.: Cloud Architectures, white paper by Amazon
6. IBM Tivoli Application Dependency Discovery Manager, IBM Corporation, http://www.ibm.com/software/tivoli/products/taddm/
7. Rolia, J., Singhal, S., Friedrich, R.: Adaptive Internet data centers. In: Proceedings of the International Conference on Advances in Infrastructure for Electronic Business, Science, and Education on the Internet, SSGRR 2000 (July 2000)
8. Doyle, R.P., Chase, J.S., Asad, O.M., Jin, W., Vahdat, A.M.: Model-based resource provisioning in a web service utility. In: Proceedings of the 4th conference on USENIX Symposium on Internet Technologies and Systems, Seattle, WA, March 26-28 (2003)

Focused Search in Digital Archives

Junte Zhang[1] and Jaap Kamps[1,2]

[1] Archives and Information Studies, Faculty of Humanities, University of Amsterdam
[2] ISLA, Faculty of Science, University of Amsterdam

Abstract. We present a system description for an archival information system with three different approaches to gain online access to digital archives created in the metadata standard Encoded Archival Description (EAD). We show that an aggregation-based system can be developed on archival data using XML Information Retrieval (XML IR). We describe the different stages and components, such as the indexing of the digital finding aids in an XML database, the subsequent querying and retrieval of information from that database, and the eventual delivery of that information to the users in a contextual interface.

1 Introduction

Cultural heritage (CH) information from libraries, museums and archives can be increasingly found online. In the past, the physical CH artifacts, like books, paintings or a personal letter, were described and catalogued in paper finding aids by curators. For example, a user who was looking for a personal letter in a collection created by a historical person, had to go to an archive to find that letter by consulting paper finding aids and the archivist. Nowadays, with the advent of digital finding aids to provide online access to these (unique) physical artifacts, that is no longer needed. A major benefit for users is that CH materials are disclosed more effectively and efficiently both in terms of time and effort.

Several metadata schemas are used to create the digital finding aids, such as Dublin Core, MARC, and increasingly, the international standard Encoded Archival Description (EAD). The archives, but also manuscript libraries and museums, are expanding their digital resources by adopting EAD in XML and putting them online as digital archives, which means that structural CH information can be exploited on the Web for web services. The state-of-the-art online archival finding aids in EAD are a nearly one-to-one mapping of paper finding aids. A distinct property of the old paper finding aids and hence also the new ones in EAD, is that these files are long in content and complex in structure with very deep nesting of the elements in the XML tree hierarchy.

This paper outlines a system description for README[1]—an online archival information system that is able to retrieve information within the archives using three approaches that exploit the granularity and structure of archival finding aids in EAD using XML Retrieval in order to provide focused access (see Section 2). Section 3 continues by explaining the different components of the system

---

[1] Acronym for "Retrieving Encoded Archival Descriptions More Effectively."

G. Vossen, D.D.E. Long, and J.X. Yu (Eds.): WISE 2009, LNCS 5802, pp. 463–471, 2009.
© Springer-Verlag Berlin Heidelberg 2009

more in detail. We point to the evaluations of the three system approaches in Section 4, and conclude the paper in Section 5.

2   Related Work

2.1   Encoded Archival Description

An increasing number of archives and manuscript libraries, and also museums, use the international standard Encoded Archival Description (EAD) to encode data that describe unique primary resources in the form of archival materials, such as corporate records and personal (hand-written) papers [5]. These collections may have millions of unique items, which can be in any form or medium.[2]

The archives are organized hierarchically. EAD consists of a set of descriptive elements to describe the archives. The three highest level elements are <EADHEADER>, the optional <FRONTMATTER>, and the archival descriptions in <ARCHDESC>. The components <C_n> of the whole are nested in <ARCHDESC>, where $n \in \{01, ..., 12\}$, see Fig. 4. For example, <C02> is the sub-component of <C01>, and so on. A component can also be unnumbered. The EAD files can be deeply nested and lengthy in content with thousands of pages (or more) [5].

There is no shortage of metadata in archival finding aids [4], but is "just a matter of finding the right hook to make them more accessible." XML Information Retrieval techniques can be employed to deal with this problem and be used to maximally and most effectively exploit these 'hooks.' Using this markup, we can zoom into any of them—at the same time index and retrieve them.

2.2   XML Information Retrieval

The indexing and retrieving of these 'hooks' (elements) is done using XML Information Retrieval (XML IR), which is a branch of Information Retrieval that deals with the retrieval of arbitrary parts of XML files given the XML structure, and attempts to use the XML markup of documents to the fullest for 'focused' information access by not only providing direct access to a whole document, but also to a part of the document. The structure is exploited to expose information.

As illustrated in [8], structured text retrieval supports the representation and retrieval of the individual document components defined by the logical structure as represented in a hierarchical document, such as an EAD file. This structure can be distinguished in two types of units [8]: (a) atomic units (or 'text content elements') that only contain text and no XML elements, and (b) composite units (or 'nested elements') that contain other units and can be further 'decomposed'. The same is true for EAD, see Fig. 4, where atomic units such as <UNITID>, <UNITTITLE> or <UNITDATE> are represented as leafs and composite units like <DID> are non-leaf nodes. However, we extend this representation with *mixed content* nodes, i.e. elements that contain both text and other elements. An instance of a mixed node could be the composite unit <UNITTITLE> that may have been annotated with a semantic tag like <PERSNAME> (which is allowed in EAD).

---

[2] For example, plans, drawings, charts, maps, photographs, audio, and video [5].

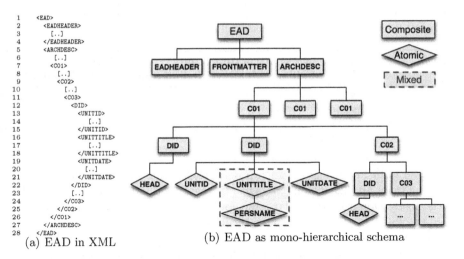

```
1    <EAD>
2      <EADHEADER>
3        [..]
4      </EADHEADER>
5      <ARCHDESC>
6        [..]
7        <C01>
8          [..]
9          <C02>
10          [..]
11          <C03>
12            <DID>
13              <UNITID>
14                [..]
15              </UNITID>
16              <UNITTITLE>
17                [..]
18              </UNITTITLE>
19              <UNITDATE>
20                [..]
21              </UNITDATE>
22            </DID>
23            [..]
24          </C03>
25          </C02>
26        </C01>
27      </ARCHDESC>
28    </EAD>
```
(a) EAD in XML   (b) EAD as mono-hierarchical schema

Fig. 1. Representation of Encoded Archival Description as mono-hierarchical schema using XML elements as nodes for Information Retrieval

3 README System Description

3.1 Digital Finding Aids in XML

We obtained in total 8,159 finding aids from 3 sources: the National Archives of the Netherlands (NA), the International Institute of Social History (IISH), and the Archives Hub (AH). The statistics are shown in Table 1, which shows the number of files from each source, the distribution of the length of content in bytes (without XML markup) and of the structure in terms of XML tags.

We show that there is strong positive and significant correlation on a 95% confidence interval between content length and XML markup (Spearman's ρ and Kendall's τ, $p < 0.01$, 2-tailed). The correlation in the NA data is very strong, likely due to the length which results in more tags. This correlation is less strong for the finding aids from the AH or IISH, because their finding aids were shorter, and sometimes copy-pasted from legacy data, where the conversion to EAD has not been complete, and hence large chunks of text without XML markup occurs.

3.2 Indexing and Storage

Before the indexing and storage, we preprocess the files to make them strictly well-formed and valid XML—which was a prequisite for indexing in an XML database. Many of the files were not well-formed XML (missing closing tags, wrong nesting), and the ones from the Archives Hub were in SGML. In order to map them to well-formed XML, we bootstrap the files using the SGML to XML

Table 1. Statistics of the archival finding aids, where ** is significant at 0.01 level (2-tailed) using Spearman's rho and Kendall's tau

Source	N	Content (bytes)		Structure (count)		Correlation	
		Mean	Median	Mean	Median	Spearman's ρ	Kendall's τ
NA	2,174	53,571.65	12,974	2,891.46	481	0.9596**	0.8280**
IISH	2,866	11,187.19	1,736	481.93	57	0.7678**	0.5916**
AH	3,119	3,886.96	2,054	117.94	65	0.6958**	0.5310**

converter OSX in OpenJade[3], then process them again in XML Lint[4], and then cleaning them up (like making all tags uppercase) in HTML Tidy[5]. Since we deal with mostly Dutch language data, but for example also French and German, we used the ISO/IEC 8859-1 character encoding.

The system is based on MonetDB with the XQuery front-end Pathfinder [1] and the information retrieval module PF/Tijah [3]. All of our 8,159 finding aids in EAD are indexed into a single main memory XML database that completely preserves the XML structure and allows powerful XQuery querying. We indexed the collection without stopword removal, and used the Dutch snowball stemmer.

3.3 Retrieval Model

For the retrieval of individual and any arbitrary elements, we employ statistical language models (LM) [6], i.e. the probability distribution of all possible term sequences is estimated by applying statistical estimation techniques. The probability of each individual term is calculated using the *maximum likelihood estimate* (*mle*), which corresponds to the relative frequency of a term t_i in an element e, $P_{mle}(t_i|e) = \frac{\text{tf}_{i,e}}{\sum_t \text{tf}_{t,e}}$ where $\text{tf}_{i,e}$ is the term frequency t_i normalized by the sum of all frequencies in an element e.

We estimate the probability that the element model can generate the given query q. By applying Bayes' theorem, this can be obtained by

$$P(e|q) = \frac{P(q|e) \cdot P(e)}{P(q)} \propto P(q|e) \cdot P(e) \tag{1}$$

where $P(q)$ can be ignored for ranking, and the prior $P(e)$ is assumed to be uniform. The query likelyhood (or conditional probability) is based on a model that represents an element using a multinomial probability distribution over a vocabulary of terms. For each element, a model on an element is inferred, such that the probability of a term given that model is $p(t|e)$. The model is then used to predict the likelihood that an element could match a particular query q. We make the assumption that each query term can be assumed to be

---

[3] http://openjade.sourceforge.net/
[4] http://www.xmlsoft.org/xmllint.html
[5] http://tidy.sourceforge.net/

```
                              XQuery snippet
1    let $options := <TijahOptions ir-model="LMS" collection-lambda="0.15" returnNumber="M" />
2    let $query_text := tijah:tokenize("query terms")
3    let $query_nexi := concat("//EAD[about(., ", $query_text, ")]")
4    let $qid := tijah:queryall-id($query_nexi, $options)
5    let $nodes := tijah:nodes($qid)
```

Fig. 2. XQuery code that illustrates the initialization of system parameters and the use of NEXI for querying. Here, we search in root nodes only, which corresponds to the full text of the document.

```
                              XQuery snippet
6    let $result := for $node at $relevance in $nodes
7    return
8    <result>
9        <rel>{ $relevance }</rel>
10       <num>{ (count($node/preceding::*) + 1) }</num>
11       <file>{ data($node/ancestor-or-self::EAD/@FILE) }</file>
12       [more xpath selections...]
13   </result>
14   let $total := count($result)
15   return <results total="{$total}"> {
16       for $res in distinct-values($result/file)
17           let $cs-group := $result[file = $res]
18           for $cs-group2 at $rank in $cs-group
19           where $rank <= N
20           order by string($cs-group2/file), number($cs-group2/num), number($cs-group2/rel)
21           return
22           <out id="{$res}">{ $cs-group2 }</out>
23   } </results>
```

Fig. 3. XQuery code that illustrates the retrieval of elements according to relevance, grouping of results by file name, and subsequent re-ordering of the retrieved results given the original document hierarchy

sampled identically and independently from the element model. Applying this assumption, the query likelyhood is obtained by multiplying the likelihoods of the individual terms contained in the query:

$$P(q|e) = \prod_{t \in q} P(t|e)^{n(t,q)} \tag{2}$$

where $n(t,q)$ is the number of times term t is present in query q.

To deal with zero probabilities because of non-existing terms in case there is sparse data, smoothing techniques are applied. The retrieval model uses Jelinek-Mercer smoothing, which is a mixture model between the element model and the collection as background model, so

$$P(t|e) = (1 - \lambda) \cdot P_{mle}(t|e) + \lambda \cdot P_{mle}(t|C) \tag{3}$$

where $P_{mle}(t|C) = \frac{ef_t}{\sum_t ef_t}$, ef_t is the element frequency of query term t in the collection C, and the λ is set to 0.15.

3.4 Querying and User Interfaces

We discuss now the three approaches deployed in the README system, which is written in Perl using XHTML, CSS, and JavaScript. The connection with the

(a) Document retrieval

(b) Element retrieval

(c) Aggregation-based retrieval

Fig. 4. An overview of the three approaches in the README system with the query "koude oorlog spionage" (in English: cold war spying)

database server is made in Perl using a socket and XML RPC. We can search between different sources and within a source—the provenance is made clear by showing an icon in front of a result that corresponds to a source. For each retrieval approach, we also present a user interface (see Fig. 4).

Approach 1: Document Ranking. The XML database is queried using XQuery extended with Narrowed Extended XPath I (NEXI) [7]. For document ranking, we provide the root element (the whole document) as target element. The following piece of XQuery code in Fig. 2 illustrates the procedure in PF/Tijah for document ranking that retrieves M number of documents stored in $nodes. The corresponding interface is depicted in Fig. 4(a).

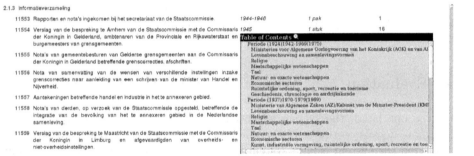

Fig. 5. Deeplinking to the result display with dynamic Table of Contents

Approach 2: Element Relevance Ranking. For element relevance ranking (see Fig. 4(b)), we do not provide a structural hint in the form of a target element, hence any EAD element can be retrieved, including the absolute XPath of an element, such as /EAD[1]/ARCHDESC[1]/DSC[2]/C01[4]/C02[8]/DID[1]. It describes the position of an element in the XML tree hierarchy. The rest of the procedure is the same as the document ranking as described above.

Approach 3: Aggregation-based Ranking. The approach goes a step further than the standard element relevance ranking as Fig. 3 and Fig. 4(c) show. It takes relevance <rel> into account. Any and arbitrary elements can be retrieved. The retrieved elements are returned in original order as in the XML file, by computing the distance of the retrieved element to the root node in <num>. We group the retrieved elements by its creator <file>. Eventually, all retrieved elements are ordered by these variables with the top N number of elements per archive. In our system we set this to 8, but it can be made dynamic by allowing users to move beyond that threshold. As explained in [9], the aggregation-based approach optimally utilizes the context of the archives.

3.5   Result Delivery

The hitlist is connected to the result display with HTTP parameters using CGI: the query, XPath, source, and file name are always stored in the URL for persistency and to facilitate the analysis of the search logs. The system can deep-link (with the element and aggregation approaches) by rendering HTML anchors for each element using its (unique) XPath as anchor identifier. We deliver a result by physically linking a result to its file, and render its result display with the Table of Contents (ToC) using the SAXON XSLT processor[6]—this is faster than retrieving everything again from the index. There is minimal transformation from the original XML file, because EAD is as much document-centric (directly view-able by users in a browser) as it is data-centric. We use the Yahoo! User

---

[6] http://saxon.sourceforge.net/

Interface Library (YUI)[7] to make the ToC dynamic and enable enhanced interaction, see Fig. 5. The ToC can be dragged and collapsed—making it an extra non-obtrusive tool to locate information within the retrieved file.

4 Evaluation

On the one hand, the system has been (preliminary) evaluated with 9 users, and more details on this study can be found in [2]. On the other hand, we have evaluated the system from a system-focused point of view [10]. The user study showed that the element ranking approach was least appreciated out of the 3. The aggregation-based approach was appreciated the most. However, the retrieval experiment showed that the element ranking approach has far better retrieval performance than the aggregation-based approach, though the aggregation-based approach seems to find more relevant results in the beginning due to the organization of the archives—showing support for the aggregation-based approach.

5 Conclusion

We have formally introduced and described the Retrieving Encoded Archival Descriptions More Effectively (README) system that provides enhanced access to cultural heritage information. The system employs the XML IR method as an alternative, more focused means to gain access to online digital archives, effectively exploiting the structure to search and find valuable information.

Acknowledgments. This research is supported by the Netherlands Organisation for Scientific Research (NWO) under project #639.072.601.

References

[1] Boncz, P.A., Grust, T., van Keulen, M., Manegold, S., Rittinger, J., Teubner, J.: MonetDB/XQuery: A Fast XQuery Processor Powered by a Relational Engine. In: SIGMOD 2006, pp. 479–490. ACM, New York (2006)

[2] Fachry, K.N., Kamps, J., Zhang, J.: Access to archival material in context. In: IIiX 2008, pp. 102–109. ACM, New York (2008)

[3] Hiemstra, D., Rode, H., van Os, R., Flokstra, J.: PF/Tijah: text search in an XML database system. In: OSIR 2006, pp. 12–17 (2006)

[4] Kiesling, K.: Metadata, metadata, everywhere - but where is the hook? OCLC Systems & Services 17, 84–88 (2001)

[5] Pitti, D.V.: Encoded Archival Description: An Introduction and Overview. D-Lib Magazine 5(11) (1999)

[6] Ponte, J.M., Croft, W.B.: A language modeling approach to information retrieval. In: SIGIR 1998, pp. 275–281. ACM, New York (1998)

---

[7] http://developer.yahoo.com/yui/

[7] Trotman, A., Sigurbjörnsson, B.: Narrowed Extended XPath I (NEXI). In: Fuhr, N., Lalmas, M., Malik, S., Szlávik, Z. (eds.) INEX 2004. LNCS, vol. 3493, pp. 16–40. Springer, Heidelberg (2005)

[8] Tsikrika, T.: Aggregation-based Semi-Structured Text Retrieval. In: Encyclopedia of Database Systems. Springer, Heidelberg (2009)

[9] Zhang, J., Fachry, K.N., Kamps, J.: Access to Archival Finding Aids: Context Matters. In: Christensen-Dalsgaard, B., Castelli, D., Ammitzbøll Jurik, B., Lippincott, J. (eds.) ECDL 2008. LNCS, vol. 5173, pp. 455–457. Springer, Heidelberg (2008)

[10] Zhang, J., Kamps, J.: Searching Archival Finding Aids: Retrieval in Original Order? In: Agosti, M., Borbinha, J., Kapidakis, S., Papatheodorou, C., Tsakonas, G. (eds.) ECDL 2009. LNCS, vol. 5714, pp. 447–450. Springer, Heidelberg (2009)

Automated Ontology-Driven Metasearch Generation with Metamorph

Wolfgang Holzinger[1], Bernhard Krüpl[1], and Robert Baumgartner[2]

[1] Vienna University of Technology, Institute of Information Systems,
Database and Artificial Intelligence Group (DBAI)
{holzing,kruepl}@dbai.tuwien.ac.at
[2] Lixto Software GmbH, Vienna, Austria
baumgartner@lixto.com

Abstract. We present Metamorph, a system and framework for generating vertical deep Web search engines in a knowledge-based way. The approach enables the separation between the roles of a higher skilled ontology engineer and a less skilled service engineer, which adds new web sources in an intuitive, semi-automatic manner using the proven Lixto suite. One part of the framework is the understanding process for complex web search forms, and the generation of an ontological representation of each form and its intrinsic run-time dependencies. Based on these representations, a unified meta form and matchings from the meta form to the individual search forms and vice versa are created, taking into account different form element types, contents and labels. We discuss several aspects of the Metamorph ontology, which focuses especially on the interaction semantics of web forms, and give a short account of our semi-automatic tagging system.

1 Introduction

Most content on the Web is still in a format that is intended for human beings and is not per se machine readable. The Lixto suite [1] is a commercial product that can be used to extract this content and transform it into a form more suited for automatic processing. Lixto Visual Developer (VD) wrappers are created in an visual and interactive manner by marking relevant content on a web page, and they use Elog and XPath expressions to reference and extract from the relevant pieces.

In this paper, we present the Metamorph system, which extends the hidden web capabilities of Lixto VD for generating vertical deep Web search engines, i.e. engines that search in parallel on a number of web search forms of a particular (vertical) domain. Metamorph provides means to identify, reference, and manipulate web search forms in a knowledge based manner; the knowledge is split into a general web and a domain specific part, is formalized in RDF/OWL plus a set of rules and is capable of covering all kinds of mappings that are necessary to map web forms. Rather than mapping web form elements to those of a central or other remote web forms, Metamorph acknowledges the fact that modern web

G. Vossen, D.D.E. Long, and J.X. Yu (Eds.): WISE 2009, LNCS 5802, pp. 473–480, 2009.

forms can be regarded as mini applications, because they can contain temporal and other dependencies. Consequently, Metamorph goes beyond traditional schema mapping and models web form interactions, i.e. the whole interaction sequence a user of web forms has to perform in order to reach his goal.

1.1   Related Work and Comparison

Unlike many academic and commercial approaches to web scraping, this work focuses primarily on understanding web forms and deep web navigation. In the area of structured data extraction, a number of well-known methodologies have been proposed, eg. Roadrunner [4] for automatic extraction, Dapper [6] in the area of machine learning; interactive approaches have been proposed by mashup enablers such as Intel Mashmaker [13] or Lixto Visual Developer [1]. Our work is orthogonal in many aspects; it is more focused on understanding the flow logic and the interactions of web applications than on extracting from (more or less) static pages.

In [2][3][11][12] tools and methodologies for web data extraction are compared with each other. These tools offer formidable data extraction and integration solutions. However, most such tools lack the support for meta-search specific problems such as form understanding, a workflow-based extraction from multiple sources, techniques for selecting relevant sources, and sometimes even technical issues such as load balancing. On the other hand, in the area of information integration on the Web several mashup assembly platforms have been created including e.g. Yahoo Pipes [17] and IBM Mashup Center [10]. The DeLa system sends queries to HTML forms after having annotated their elements [16]. Embley et al. describe the usage of tokenization techniques for web data extraction [7].

There are also fully automatic approaches: The University of Illinois and SUNY Binghampton develop interesting approaches and prototypes for discovering web data bases, generating search interfaces for particular domains, and data extraction [14]. The WISE-Integrator [8] uses positive matches and predictive matches to build attribute clusters and applies a majority rule to choose global attribute names. The MetaQuerier system [9] automatically extracts and query interfaces from websites by using just form element labels and matches them. Their application follows a generic approach to match any two search interfaces. The DEQUE system [15] models and wraps deep web search forms and result pages.

In contrast to the presented literature, Metamorph firmly relies on a domain ontology that has to be created in advance, but enables higher precision form extraction and mapping because attribute values can be considered as well. A distinguishing point from other systems is that Metamorph considers the integration of web forms as more complex than schema matching. Modern web forms often have dependencies between their controls that are expressed in Javascript code (filling out one field changes the options of another field). Metamorph takes this into account by modelling the interactions a user would need to take to formulate a request, and by constructing an interaction sequence for automatic submission. We also believe that the interpretation of query results is essential to any meta-search framework, and that a feedback loop has to be established, which can improve the domain knowledge quality with every request. The Metamorph framework employs Lixto wrappers for the acquisition and transformation of website query results.

2 Overview of the Metamorph System

Figure 1a shows the main components of the Metamorph system. The central part is the Metamorph generator (shown on the left side) that holds the knowledge base and the inference and planning engine. For every metasearch domain like air travel, hotel search etc. an ontology engineer has to create a domain ontology that is integrated into the knowlege base.

In each domain, there exists a number of search forms on the Web. These forms are tagged and annotated by a service engineer with the help of a semi-automatic tagging tool: Known domain concepts are automatically tagged and can be reviewed and enhanced by the service engineer on a visual level. After that, all annotations are converted into RDF instances and stored in the generator knowledge base.

Whenever the service engineer adds a new form description to the knowledge base, the Inference and Planning Engine compiles a plan that is ready to run inside the Execution Engine, and that is fully independent of the generator. The plan contains information on how to translate any metasearch query that can be posed by a user back into interaction sequences that are compatible with the original web form. Finally, users can pose queries to the execution engine by filling out a metasearch form. The execution engine executes all the plans on all remote websites and aggregates the results and presents them to the user.

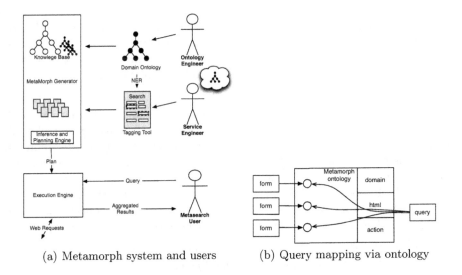

(a) Metamorph system and users   (b) Query mapping via ontology

Fig. 1. Metamorph system overview

In the following sections, we will provide some details about Metamorph's central knowledge base and discuss how web page forms are tagged in a semi-automatic way.

3   The Metamorph Ontology

Our ontology is structured as outlined in figure 1b. Arbitrary web forms are represented in the Metamorph RDF model. A meta-query request posed to the Metamorph system is translated into a query on this model and results in an interaction sequence for all web forms represented in the model. We use RDF/OWL models to formalize the Metamorph ontology, enhanced by rules as provided in the Jena toolkit.

Each search form on a website has its own idiosyncratic way for representing a search request. To capture the specific semantics for such a form, the Metamorph ontology must be able to represent three aspects:

- *html:* The technical details how the local search form is constructed, which HTML input elements were used in which combination and their positions on their source page for further reference.
- *domain:* A domain model rich enough to annotate each semantic reference in the local search form. For our flight–search example, this includes concepts for time and date, geographical locations, passengers and reservations.

Table 1. User interaction primitives

PICK(x)	select option x in a choice field
CLICK(x)	click on element x
ENTER(s,x)	enter string s into textfield x

- *action:* Each HTML form element has an intrinsic action associated with it; a button can be clicked, a string value can be fed into a text field (see table above) Performing the right kind of actions in the correct order will successfully submit a query to the deep web information source.

Interactions are subject to various constraints. Some forms require that the elements in a form are filled in in a certain order; there may be alternatives to fill in certain values (for instance, the user can either use a date picker control or fill in the date in a text field, but not both); the last action to take after filling in all fields is to press the submit button. When constructing the action sequence all these contraints have to be fulfilled.

Example: Suppose there is an select box containing month names. During tagging, the relation from pure text strings to the Month concept has been established. The interaction semantics for each option can be expressed as

```
pick(o1) achieves fillin(monthJanuary)
pick(o2) achieves fillin(monthFebruary)
...
pick(o6) achieves fillin(monthJune)
```

A request posed to the Metamorph system involving the month June will now derive that the corresponding action is to pick the item o6 (a HTML option element). Other fields in the request will yield similar actions. To fully resolve the request we pick from all those generated actions a sequence that is consistent with all constraints that are in effect.

We can take this translation a step further. With the semantic information gathered in our entangled ontologies, we can actually devise a plan for mapping the query *schema*. This plan can then be translated to a scripting language and executed independently of the resource intensive reasoning framework:

```
if (month == january)  pick(o1)
if (month == february) pick(o2)
...
if (month == june)  pick(o6)
```

Note that this script does not any more refer to any internal ontology details. It is purely end-to-end from the global search parameters to the interaction language.

Modeling one-to-many mappings. Sometimes it is necessary to map from an input element to a combination of domain concepts, forming an 1:n relation. Straightforward modeling this with multiple mapping relations is undesirable, because it requires higher-order predicates to reason about these situations. Fortunately, in all cases we studied, the arity of the one-to-many mappings was a constant. Therefore we make this explicit by introducing fixed-arity Tuple concepts. In figure 2a we see the common case where a form element matches a combination of month and year. This combination is made explicit by introducing an individual of class Pair and the relation first-element and second element. In the same manner we can define triples, quadruples and higher order combination concepts.

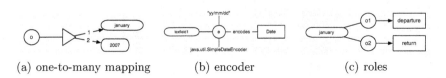

(a) one-to-many mapping   (b) encoder   (c) roles

Fig. 2. Metamorph design patterns

Concept-to-text mapping with encoders. Text fields allow no unambiguous translation of domain concepts to form elements, since it is not clear how to compute an appropriate string representation of a concept. We introduce the notion of *encoders*, external functions that will translate a concept to a fitting string representations. A encoder is a special kind of an external functions whose range is always a string. In figure 2b we see an text field matching an encoder *e*, mapping from the concept Date to a string, using the encoding yy/mm/dd. *e* has a reference to a Java class wrapping up the actual code.

Modeling one-to-many mappings with roles. Sometimes concepts in the request cannot be distinguished by their type alone. To identify them unambiguously, we allow roles to be assign to input concepts. In figure 2c, two form options refer simultaneously to the single individual january. The first option, o1, is used by the form to describe the desired departure date for a flight, o2 is used to describe the date of the return flight. By tagging each option with a role, return and departure respectively, we can capture the different contexts these two individuals stand in. Although both options match an identical concept, they can be distinguished by also taking their roles into account.

4   Tagging Web Forms

The discovery and tagging of relevant forms on a web page takes place in three stages: i) the page is preprocessed with the Mozilla-based Lixto browser component to ensure its consistency and validity; ii) automatic taggers based on named entity recognition, domain grammars and machine learning are deployed on the page to identify forms and their constituents; iii) the tags are revised by a service engineer to ensure the best possible mapping quality. The annotations are currently realized as XPath bound RDF triples; for greater flexibility, we plan to switch to an inline RDFa representation. We adapted the Lixto Visual Developer for the interactive, semi-automatic tagging of web forms. Lixto VD is a Java based wrapper generation tool with a visual user interface that can be used to automatically record a navigation sequence; to parametrize it; and to replay it later by exececuting mouse and key actions and collecting results. The screenshot in Figure 3 shows how a service engineer uses Lixto VD to mark relevant web form elements.

Fig. 3. Screenshot of a tagging session in Metamorph

Automatic tagging. Metamorph follows a knowledge-based approach for automatic tagging. It derives search terms from its ontology and uses gazetteer lists for named entitiy recognition (NER). More complex expressions can be identified by using domain grammars, which are also stored in the central knowledge base. We embedded the GATE natural language processing (NLP) system [5] into Metamorph and make use of its JAPE transducer and gazetteer facilities. Details of the implementation cannot be provided here due to space constraints. Examples for concepts that our GATE application will recognize in the flight search domain are *airport names, iata codes, month names, numbers, person related concepts*, etc. We also allow domain engineers to include a number of domain heuristics in the knowledge base. These are some examples:

- Form element content and tag based heuristics make assumptions on the distribution of content, e.g. that several form elements share some content.
- Form meta data based heuristics recognize that some form elements share the same Javascript validator, or call a function with the name *datepicker()*.
- Cardinality based heuristics exploit the fact that a year has 12 months, and a month 28 to 31 days: If we encounter a select box with 28 to 31 numbers (the actual count may vary in a dynamically created form), it could be a day; a select box with 12 options could be a month selector.

5   Conclusion

Our approach gives the ontology and service engineers a number of possibilities to efficiently create and maintain vertical search scenarios. Since we do not envision a fully automated approach in the spirit of deep Web query probing, it is not meaningful and fair to apply traditional information extraction performance measures. Skilled application designers will fine-tune their applications to reach a robustness and reliability that is far above that of any automatic system. Therefore, we instead point out the main ingredients and "soft measures" why believe our framework to be advantageous to create vertical search scenarios:

- Our main aim is high result precision. The end user only trusts such a service if he trusts each individual result, and believes in the correctness and completeness of the market picture within the scope of the application. Therefore, we provide a visual and interactive system to create and maintain such services.
- The system is easy to learn and it is easy and time-efficient to add new web sources and to maintain existing form matchings, web interactions and data extraction programs.
- The system provides a good robustness to changes. Due to heuristics in the action ontology and a number of alerting conditions and exception handling that can be defined in the web interaction, minor changes pose no problem, and major changes are immediately reported to the service engineer. Further, any changes on the websites regarding data extraction aspects are covered by the robust extraction language used in the Lixto Visual Developer [1].

In the future, we plan to improve our system at the execution side by working on query performance and optimization, to switch to RDFa style annotations to become more tolerant for incorrect HTML code, and to enhance the automatic form detection and tagging component with topological and layout features. Finally, during the course of this project, we realized that many of the employed techniques (in particular the ontology-driven, automatic tagging of relevant concepts) could also be used to provide better accessibility of web pages to blind users. We plan to develop our ideas further into this direction.

References

1. Baumgartner, R., Flesca, S., Gottlob, G.: Visual Web Information Extraction with Lixto. In: Proc. VLDB (2001)
2. Baumgartner, R.: Methoden und Werkzeuge zur Webdatenextraktion. In: Semantic Web: Auf dem Weg zur vernetzten Wissensgesellschaft. Springer, Heidelberg (2006) (in German)
3. Chang, C., Kayed, M., Girgis, M.R., Shaalan, K.F.: A Survey of Web Information Extraction Systems. IEEE Trans. on Knowledge and Data Eng. 18/10 (2006)
4. Crescenzi, V., Mecca, G., Merialdo, P.: Roadrunner: Towards automatic data extraction from large web sites. In: Proc. VLDB (2001)
5. Cunningham, H., Maynard, D., Bontcheva, K., Tablan, V.: GATE: A Framework and Graphical Development Environment for Robust NLP Tools and Applications. In: Proc. ACL (2002)
6. Dapper. Products page (2006), http://www.dapper.net
7. Embley, D.W., Campbell, D.M., Smith, R., Liddle, S.W.: Ontology-based Extraction and Structuring of Information from Data-rich Unstructured Documents. In: Proc. CIKM (1998)
8. He, H., Meng, W., Yu, C., Wu, Z.: WISE-Integrator: An Automatic Integrator of Web Search Interfaces for E-Commerce (2003)
9. He, B., Chang, K.: Automatic complex schema matching across Web query interfaces: A correlation mining approach. ACM Trans. Database Syst. 31/1 (2006)
10. IBM Mashup Center, http://www-306.ibm.com/software/info/mashup-center
11. Kuhlins, S., Tredwell, R.: Toolkits for generating wrappers. Net.Object Days (2002)
12. Laender, A.H.F., Ribeiro-Neto, B.A., Silva, A.S., Teixara, J.S.: A brief survey of web data extraction tools. SIGMOD Rec. 31/2 (2002)
13. Ennals, R., Garofalakis, M.: MashMaker: Mashups for the Masses. In: SIGMOD (2007)
14. Meng, W., Peng, Q.: Clustering e-commerce search engines (2004)
15. Shestakov, D., Bhowmick, S., Lim, E.P.: DEQUE: Querying the Deep Web. Data and Knowledge Engineering 52 (2005)
16. Wang, J., Lochovsky, F.H.: Data Extraction and Label Assignment for Web Databases. In: Proc. WWW (2003)
17. Yahoo Pipes, http://pipes.yahoo.com/pipes

Integrated Environment for Visual Data-Level Mashup Development

Adam Westerski

Universidad Politecnica de Madrid, Madrid, Spain
westerski@dit.upm.es

Abstract. The visual creation tools in the mashup frameworks are supposed to be simple and accessible. Yet at the same time there is a need to extend the capabilities and complexity of mashups. Therefore, in practice, the frameworks become increasingly hard to learn for a casual user. In relation to the emerging mashup creation techniques in Semantic Web area, in our work we propose an idea to split the development of mashups into two stages: data-level and service-level. Each managed by a separate, although well integrated, environments.

Keywords: mashup, web development, integration, tool, semantic web, linked data.

1 Introduction

Inspired by the Yahoo Pipes, the contemporary mashup creation tools, either do not allow much flexibility or are overwhelmingly complex. In the first situation, the mashups are easy to create but also quite simple. On the data level, the generic environments offer basic functionality such as filtering, reorder or aggregation of feeds. In contrast, frameworks that operate on specific types of data, focus only on particular operators valid in a given domain. Therefore they offer little versatility and require some unique knowledge at the same time.

In the context of Semantic Web development, we propose an idea to enrich the construction of data-level mashups with an additional tool for the creation of the service mashups. We would like to present this concept, based on the research conducted, in a European project called Romulus [1], during the integration of the DERI Pipes [2] and the Romulus Mashup Builder (MyCoctail) [3] environments. Additionally with a set of examples (see Sec. 3) we show how the aforementioned tools can be made complementary and extend user possibilities without introducing needless complexity.

2 Methodology

The process of mashup creation is split into two parts: first is the data level, second is the service level (see Fig. 1).

G. Vossen, D.D.E. Long, and J.X. Yu (Eds.): WISE 2009, LNCS 5802, pp. 481–487, 2009.

The first step includes setup of the data sources and performing various data transformations. In our case, we focus on the Semantic Web mashups. Therefore, creating a typical mashup would involve importing metadata from sources encoded as RDF or microformats. Next, all data operations need to be defined. This can limit only to simple merge or aggregation but also selection of subsets or transformation of data available in the repository (for example, in case of RDF, with SPARQL queries). When the entire workflow is constructed one additional step has to be performed in order to ensure compatibility with service- level mashup application. The data has to be serialized into a format that is supported by the upper level. The typical and easy to use input/output format that service mashup platforms tend to use is JSON. Therefore in our solution we propose to set this format as a bridge between the data-level and the service-level environments.

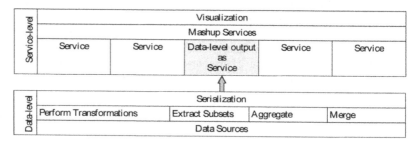

Fig. 1. Integration of service and data level mashup environments

When the semantic metadata information is processed the developer can utilize a service mashup platform to combine the results with other services or just to make a visualization. When properly serialized and exposed, the output of the Semantic Web mashup can be perceived just like a normal service. Therefore, the entire operation becomes straight-forward for users with previous experience with any of the service mashing up platforms. On this stage we also propose to take care of the visualization. The contemporary frameworks (see Sec. 4) have quite extensive support for making the transition from service output to HTML, textual or other kinds of mashup visualization.

In the context of our project, we implemented the described methodology for particular environments: the DERI Pipes(data-level) editor [4] and the Romulus Mashup Builder framework(service-level). The experience gained during the process of integration of both tools is described in the next section.

3 Experiments

In order to test the described methodology in practice, we implemented a simple use case [5]. The goal, for the mashup, is to produce information about the upcoming events extracted from a personal calendar and show friends or acquaintances who also participate in those events. Next, present the information in a web environment (i.e. HTML on a homepage).

The iCalendar instances are used as input data since they can be easily converted into RDF with an external service [6]. After providing DERI Pipes with the data sources (see Fig.2), each is filtered to leave only the required triples (event location, event summary, person name, date information). Next, all data is aggregated and processed: a SPARQL construct extracts subgraphs that contain data about events with more than one participant. Finally when the pipe is saved there is no need to specify any serialization rules, because DERI Pipes engine by default allows to publish the output as JSON.

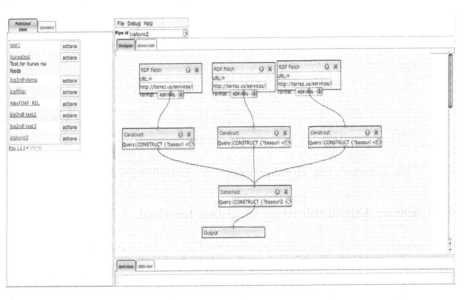

Fig. 2. DERI Pipes development

During the next step, the results from DERI Pipes are utilized in the Romulus Mashup Builder (see Fig.3). The serialized JSON event information is imported into the framework just like an output of an ordinary REST web service. Next, with some simple tools the results are sorted, filtered depending on the date and transformed into simple HTML or a Google Gadget [7].

During the experiment we made a lot of assumptions and set some limitations to simplify the process. The prepared iCalendar files are rather small, we extract events from a fixed period only and from a set number data sources. However, this was enough to notice the basic advantages and disadvantages of the entire process.

Although the final result is rather simple, the data manipulations inside DERI Pipes proved to be enough complex to make the data-level process most time consuming. Even for someone with some basic knowledge about Semantic Web technologies, using such environment is not that easy. The split in tools helps to focus on one task, and allocate human resources better to fully use the knowledge of people with expertise in given area of mashup development.

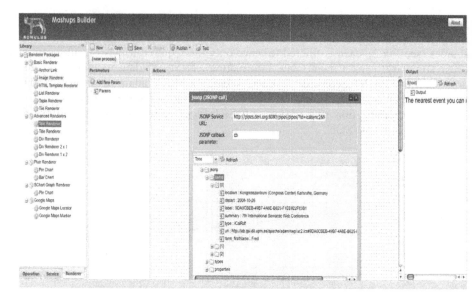

Fig. 3. Romulus Mashup Builder framework with DERI Pipes data imported

4   Problems Encountered and Lessons Learned

During our experiments, we observed that one of the problems of visual mashup tools mentioned earlier in the introduction still remained. On the service level, the visual mashup development in comparison to regular application development with programming languages held many limits. The predefined operators allow to construct only a certain range of applications. In practice, often when we wanted to have some particular features for the mashup uses cases presented for project meetings and reviews, we had to go back to the service mashup tool source code and implement new operators on our own. One might argue that this is due to the simplicity of tool that we have chosen. However it has to be noted that the presented Romulus Mashup Builder has been prepared on the code base of other mature tool called Afrous (for other tools discussion see Sec. 5).

On the other hand, on the data level, the DERI Pipes environment had all the capabilities we needed. However, we encountered a different problem that the Semantic Web community seems to suffer for a long time. There is a number of initiatives that provide millions of RDF triples but in practice hardly anyone has the idea how to put all this information into good use and create some valuable application for the end user. No different in our case, it was not easy to come up with a scenario that could not be achieved without Linked Data and at the same time would prove some value. Therefore, as much as it seems reasonable to put most effort to extending or developing the flaws of the service level, one should remember that we are still unable to truly harness the power of Linked Data and therefore truly evaluate tools such as the DERI Pipes.

5 Related Work

In relation to the discussed methodology and the tools used, there are a lot of existing mashup development environments. Some limit to fulfilling the roles we described in one of levels defined earlier(see Sec. 2), while others try to deliver a complete solution.

Among the service mashup tools the market is quite mature with both free and commercial products available. The Afrous [8] framework or the Yahoo Pipes [9] are good examples of tools for creation of mashups from services and simple data. They offer operators that allow to manipulate data but most of them are rather simple and meant for performing operations on service outputs, popular internet resources such as news feeds (i.e. RSS) or output of well known online services (i.e. Google Spreadsheets can be defined in Afrous as data source).

Regarding tools for development of data mashups and Semantic Web mashups in particular, a lot less has been done. Like most of the Semantic Web tools, the applications are a result of research in progress with some early commercial products just emerging. Apart of the aforementioned DERI Pipes the most notable examples are Banach [10] and recently developed SPARQLMotion [11]. The first has been created as a part of SIMILE project and extends the capabilities of Sesame data store by implementing a transformation pipeline supplied with a number operators. The SPARQLMotion is quite similar regarding capabilities to DERI Pipes, however it is a commercial product. The most notable difference is the model of preparing and publishing the scripts. In contrast to DERI Pipes, the SPARQLMotion is a desktop application that can be integrated with other products of the same company to deliver a much wider range of capabilities like script testing or deployment.

Finally, there is a number of commercial mashup frameworks aimed for enterprises. Most notable examples are JackBe Presto [12] and products developed by Denodo Technologies [13]. Those are far more complex than the ones described previously and allow to compose more sophisticated mashups from selected types of data and mashup services at the same time. Although non of the two directly address Semantic Web aspect they are a good example of an alternative path to the one presented in this paper.

Additionally, with respect to various research projects in the mashup area, a lot of interesting work has been conducted around a framework called the Mixup [14]. The authors present an approach where they model resources (being web applications or services) as components that have their own events and operations [15,16]. For the needs of their model authors present a development process where the components are described with a special language and their composition is defined. Within the same environment it is possible to define the data transformations using XSLT or XQuery.

6 Future Work

In our work, due to the characteristics of our research project, we integrated the service mashup development process only with the Semantic Web data level mashups. Nevertheless, the same concept could be applied to other data centric mashup tools. It is possible to extend our idea further and propose for any data level mashup environment to provide its output for the service level. In practice, this would certainly bring a number of new integration problems. In the idea proposed, we were able to simplify a lot due to selection of particular tools and data formats. In other situations, the data conversion to a uniform format might not be as straight forward as in our case. For individual tools and data formats experiments should be conducted regarding the accuracy of such data mediations.

On the other hand, the entire methodology that we presented assumed information flow only from the data level to the service level. Initially such a bottom-up approach seems good. However, in practice, a situation might occur where the information needs to be pushed back to the data level. Following the presented example (see Sec. 3) we could imagine a mashup were the end user wants to add a new calendar source or even just a single event directly from the HTML form and immediately desire to see the results. In such case, data needs to be passed through the visualization logic (designed on the service level) back to the data level for processing.

Furthermore, we also envision other directions of future research in relation to service level limitations observed in Section 4 and in search of the most convenient way to develop Semantic Web based applications. We would like to conduct more experiments with one or both levels replaced by programming language frameworks instead of visual tools. This takes away the design simplicity but in turn supplies the constructed mashups with more flexibility, reliability and most importantly scalability. Such features should be particularly important and prioritized in mashups constructed for enterprise or commercial applications.

7   Conclusions

In the presented work we proposed an idea to integrate two environments that can be applied on different stages of mashup creation. The conducted experiments have shown that it is feasible to use Semantic Web data mashup engines in conjunction with contemporary, mature, lightweight service mashup frameworks.

The data operations may often require advanced knowledge (like forming SPARQL queries in the presented examples). If we split the process of mashup development in two, it is possible to leave the data-level to experts and still keep service mashup level and visualization accessible for others. Also, if we follow the model of mashup sharing offered by the DERI Pipes, the presented methodology creates an opportunity for average mashup constructors to take advantage of already defined and published sophisticated transformations of various Semantic Web data.

Additionally, our experiments have shown that one should be wary when deciding to forsake mashup development with programming languages for visual tools. The letter seem to provide a number of advantages for rapid mashup construction nevertheless the predefined operators will always be the bottle neck of such solutions.

Acknowledgments

This research project is funded by the European Commission under the R&D project ROMULUS (FP7-ICT-2007-1) and by the Spanish Government under the R&D project Java sobre Ruedas (FIT-350401-2007-8).

References

1. Romulus Project homepage, `http://www.ict-romulus.eu/`
2. Phuoc, D., Polleres, A., Morbidoni, C., Hauswirth, M., Tummarello, G.: Rapid Prototyping of Semantic Mash-Ups through Semantic Web Pipes. In: Proceeedings of the 18th International World Wide Web Conference (WWW 2009), Madrid, Spain. ACM, New York (2009)
3. Romulus Mashup Builder (MyCoctail),
   `http://www.ict-romulus.eu/MashupBuilder`
4. DERI Pipes Editor, `http://pipes.deri.org:8080/pipes/`
5. Mashup environments integration sample,
   `http://lab.gsi.dit.upm.es/apache/adam/swp/mashup_uc1.html`
6. iCal to RDF Service, `http://torrez.us/ics2rdf/`
7. GoogleGadget mashup sample,
   `http://lab.gsi.dit.upm.es/apache/adam/swp/gadgetScreen.jpg`
8. Afrous platform homepage, `http://www.afrous.com`
9. Yahoo! Pipes homepage, `http://pipes.yahoo.com/pipes/`
10. Simile Banach RDF operators, `http://simile.mit.edu/wiki/Banach`
11. SPARQLMotion homepage, `http://www.topquadrant.com/sparqlmotion/`
12. JackBe homepage, `http://jackbe.com/`
13. Denodo Technologies homepage, `http://denodo.com/english/index.html`
14. Yu, J., Benatallah, B., Casati, F., Daniel, F., Matera, M., Saint-Paul, R.: Mixup: a Development and Runtime Environment for Integration at the Presentation Layer. In: Baresi, L., Fraternali, P., Houben, G.-J. (eds.) ICWE 2007. LNCS, vol. 4607, pp. 479–484. Springer, Heidelberg (2007)
15. Daniel, F., Matera, M.: Mashing Up Context-Aware Web Applications: A Component-Based Development Approach. In: Bailey, J., Maier, D., Schewe, K.-D., Thalheim, B., Wang, X.S. (eds.) WISE 2008. LNCS, vol. 5175, pp. 250–263. Springer, Heidelberg (2008)
16. Daniel, F., Matera, M.: Turning Web Applications into Mashup Components: Issues, Models, and Solutions. In: Gaedke, M., Grossniklaus, M., Díaz, O. (eds.) ICWE 2009. LNCS, vol. 5648, pp. 45–60. Springer, Heidelberg (2009)

References

Concept of Competency Examination System in Virtual Laboratory Environment

Przemysław Różewski and Emma Kusztina

West Pomeranian University of Technology in Szczecin, Faculty of Computer Science and
Information Systems, ul. Żołnierska 49, 71-210 Szczecin, Poland
{prozewski,ekushtina}@wi.zut.edu.pl

Abstract. In the article authors consider applying the concept of a virtual
laboratory to creating intelligent systems of competency examination.
Competences make up the base for building qualifications on the basis of
transferring theoretical and procedural knowledge. Three types of virtual
laboratories are distinguished regarding their purpose. Additionally, for a virtual
laboratory working at the level of competences, a procedure for competency
examination was proposed.

Keywords: virtual laboratory, competency model, knowledge management,
distance learning.

1 Introduction

In the recent years, the research problem of knowledge management in education was
enhanced by the aspect of competences [24]. Competences represent knowledge
gained by a student during the learning process [12]. According to ISO standard the
competence is an observable or measurable ability of an actor to perform necessary
action(s) in given context(s) to achieve specific outcome(s) [14]. Presenting
knowledge in the form of competences enables creation of a system describing a
given domain, where the focus point is moved to the side of real competences of a
given person. Competences also allow to describing the given domain in the form of
consecutive levels, which represent the increasing degree of expertise (novice to
expert). Moreover, using competences allows creating a detailed description of the
domain through specifying activities and skills related to the domain in the form of
understandable text descriptions.

The presented advantages were taken under consideration by the European Union
by creating a uniform system of describing knowledge passed to the students called
the European Qualifications Framework for Lifelong Learning (EQF). In the
European Higher Education Area every student can freely shape his/her educational
path basing, among others, on the description of competences provided for academic
courses. The form of describing acquired competences allows recognizing the present
state of the student's knowledge by a different university or an employer. Currently,
this issue is being worked on in the frames of the Bologna Working Group on
Qualification Frameworks [2]. The concept of the Bologna Process assumes creating
an over-European system of competences/qualifications until 2010. Plans are for

G. Vossen, D.D.E. Long, and J.X. Yu (Eds.): WISE 2009, LNCS 5802, pp. 489–496, 2009.
© Springer-Verlag Berlin Heidelberg 2009

creating two complementary systems of competences/qualifications. A general one, called Dublin descriptors (see the work of Joint Quality Initiative [15]), concentrating on such competences as e.g. communicative skills, understanding, creating judgments. The second system, a detailed one (see the work of Tuning Education Structures in Europe [27]) is created for every domain, e.g. mathematics, chemistry.

Traditional methods of transferring competences base on using the natural language. A computer environment, from the point of view of a series of ergonomic and psychological factors greatly limits the use of natural language, especially regarding the scope and quality necessary for the learning process and an appropriate for it process of developing competences. Due to this, a need occurred for developing environments for distance sharing of fundamental and procedural knowledge. Fundamental knowledge reflects conceptual thinking which might result in formulating new paradigms, problems behavior rules, etc. Procedural knowledge is necessary for developing and realizing scenarios, algorithms and performing operations. Individual problems a student comes across usually require using both types of knowledge in different proportions [6].

Unfortunately currently we are missing some effective method for competency examination. On the other hand knowledge examination tools are mainly related to learning-teaching process and based on the learning curve concept [13]. According to this the need for competency examination tool working in e-learning environment is appearing. Authors focused on the problem of developing algorithms and structures of the virtual laboratory, which make up an intelligent system of transferring competences. In the article an algorithm of the virtual laboratory functioning and a corresponding method of competence examination will be presented.

2 Virtual Laboratory

Virtual laboratory is becoming a more and more important element of the knowledge exchange area present in a modern university. Several factors are the reason for this. First of all, training engineers through on-line systems, as shown by [4], is more effective regarding the cost and a facilitated access to resources. The constant development of computer equipment and network infrastructure increases the scope and functioning possibilities of a virtual laboratory, e.g. by enabling virtual access to real machines and equipment [10], [20], [21] or virtual experiments realized in real conditions of working equipment [25]. Individual science domains are using different information technologies and dedicated software to a greater and greater degree, what allows to reduce the distance to the virtual space. Such domains as chemistry (see the work of [9]) or geography (a complex approach was presented in [22]) are being gradually saturated with advanced information systems, what facilitates building corresponding virtual laboratory systems. The last aspect concerns the human factor. Research, lasting for more than a decade now, concerning the human-computer interaction, discussed by [7], allowed adapting the working place of an operator, e.g. a student, to his/her cognitive and psycho-motor requirements. As a result of this, several pre-defined working environments were created, prepared both regarding ergonomics [26] as well as technical solutions (examples in [8]).

The idea of a virtual laboratory is being widely discussed in literature [3], [19]. We can defines virtual laboratory as a heterogeneous, distributed environment, which enables a group of agents (e.g. students or researchers) to work together on a common group of projects. In [19] the concept of a virtual laboratory was extended by defining three mutually-completing each other types of laboratories. The evolution of the virtual laboratory began with simple systems simulating the work of a certain artifact in a restricted manipulation-environment (type 1), e.g. operating an injection moulding machine. The next stage (type 2) are the systems based on using complicated mathematical models, the goal of which was to represent in most realistically the way of working with a given object, e.g. plane simulators. The last generation of virtual laboratories (type 3), which is also the subject of analysis in this article, are the systems dedicated to sharing domain knowledge in a problem-solving environment, concerning the cognitive conditions of the recipient and his/her state of knowledge.

Let us define the third-type laboratory. A virtual laboratory is an information system consisting of the following components: information environment (virtual reality), repository of problems (tasks) and their solutions, scenario of performing laboratory tasks, portioning-knowledge model, mechanism of evaluating the quality of task-performance, mechanism of interactive remote access.

The goal of the laboratory, working at the level of domain knowledge (type 3), is to develop in a student the ability (competency) to formulate a problem and to find means for solving it in the conceptual constraints of a given domain. Such a laboratory allows developing the analysis skill on the basis of theoretical knowledge. The growth of student's knowledge happens during solving tasks of a certain domain that refer to different objects or different processes chosen from the domain. The use of artificial intelligence methods which come from cognitive science, e.g. the structure of a concept or problem solving strategy, is also characteristic [18]. A scenario is what makes up the open space of working in the laboratory [19]. It's aim is to create the best possible conditions for acquiring knowledge, e.g. by using knowledge already acquired by a student for building computer metaphors.

3 Personal Competences Acquisition Procedure

The competence acquisition procedure is presented in fig. 1. The goal of going through the procedure is: (1) students competence acquisition training with the defined: level of theoretical knowledge, type of required competences, duration time of a single training session; (2) collecting statistical data enabling managing the process of education personalization in an education system.

Student is provided, through the mechanisms of virtual laboratory repository, with a set of triples: *domain description fragment – typical task – typical solution* and a corresponding evaluation task. Such set of objects represent different kind of knowledge: theoretical, procedural and project. For describing the domain knowledge an extended ontological model presented in [18] or [28] will be used. The evaluation task should be interpreted in the terminology used in the proposed triple. The presented approach enhances students ability to structuralize their theoretical knowledge and combining it with the results of their own experience.

Let us discuss the procedure.

Input data of the procedure: (1) Domain: subject/topic of study. (2) Model of theoretical domain knowledge (built on the basis of the methodology from [28]). (3) Reference model, enabling the use/development of taxonomy of the problems (tasks) studied during the training. (4) Solved tasks repository: the repository may be based on solutions proposed in [17].

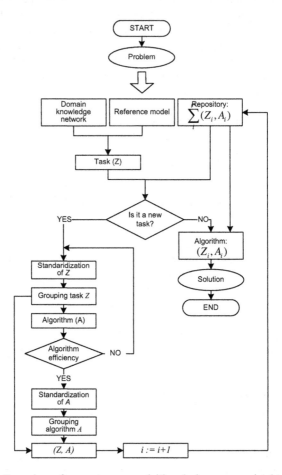

Fig. 1. Procedure of competence acquisition during an organized training

The competence acquisition procedure is performed according to the following steps:

1. Research problem analysis
Deciding if the problem lies in the domain specified in the task. This enables interpreting the problem and presenting it in the terminology of a specified knowledge model with consideration of the existing taxonomy – in other words formulating the input task.

2. Analysis and systematization of experience
Comparing the content of the input task with tasks placed in the repository. As a result, a route is establish, which has to be followed in order to solve the problem: we choose either developing an appropriate algorithm or using an algorithm already existing in the repository.

3. Standardization of the input problem
Preparing the input task token in the repository language (e.g. in the form of an XML document).

4. Accumulating input-task token in the working memory of the current training session

5. Developing an individual algorithm of problem solving
The algorithm may be described with pseudo-code in a standard language or presented as a simulation task.

6. Performing the algorithm
The input data should be chosen directly from the text of the problem being analysed or deducted during its interpretation.

7. Evaluating the effectiveness of the algorithm
At this stage, the algorithm's output results are being interpreted in the context (terminology) of the task being solved.

8. Standardization of the developed algorithm
Preparing the solution algorithm token in the language of the repository (meta information in the form or an XML document).

9. Accumulating the algorithm token in the working memory of the current training session

10. Preparing the knowledge model in the form of a repository update
At this stage, the repository form, containing: a set of keywords – reflecting the content of the stated problem – from the domain knowledge models, task token and algorithm token, has to be filled.

11. Supplementing the existing repository
The required level of complement depends on the subject, goal and stage of training and has to be assigned by the teacher to every student.

4 Competency Examination Method in Virtual Laboratory Environment

Based on the fig. 1 two alterative scenarios can be selected. First one assumes that student is able to choose proper pair task- algorithm in context of selected problem and, based on the virtual laboratory solve the problem. If a student is unable to choose the appropriate pair, he/she should be provided with tools facilitating the process of solving the given task. In our discussion we will focus on first case, because our goal is to recognize the knowledge and competence already obtained by the student.

The examination of competence in virtual learning is based on interaction environment of theoretical knowledge manipulation. Designing of such environment is difficult because it requires building interaction system for abstract concepts and visualization method for theoretical patterns and laws. First step is to recognize the method of theoretical knowledge documentation in traditional didactical materials.

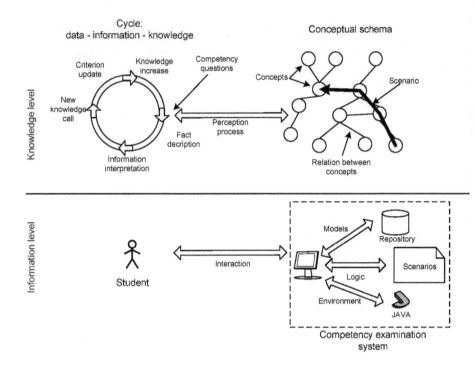

Fig. 2. Levels of competency examination method

Usually following scheme is repeated: some concept in form of theoretical knowledge is related with adequate example or case study. The student's should have ability to relate theoretical knowledge with adequate problem solving method (i.e. selection of proper algorithm). Especially in technical domain the theoretical knowledge is a preface to deal with real problems. In our method we recognize student's problem solving ability by examination of his/her capability to built proper relation of theoretical knowledge with problem demands.

Proposed method (fig. 1) will be discussed on two levels. The knowledge levels is limited by the result of cognitive science [1], [5]. From the cognitive point of view competence examination process is a process of testing student ability to use efficient his/her conceptual schemas. During the cycle of data-information-knowledge the competence are called by the competency questions. The concept of competency questions is rooted in ontology engineering area [11]. The set of the competency questions forms a scenario, which is aimed to discover conceptual relation between concepts in student's personal network of concepts. The structure of competency questions is an expend structure of knowledge repository (task-algorithm) from competences acquisition procedure. The task-algorithm structure has been expended to description-problem-model-solution structure, where description-problem is a detalization of task and what's more model-solution is a detalization of algorithm.

In the framework of discussed problems application for competency examination was developed [23].

5 Summary

In the light of the constant development of distance learning, the issue of a virtual laboratory becomes more and more important. All types of virtual laboratory require analysis and research. However, special attention should be paid to laboratories aimed at sharing domain knowledge on the basis of creating an interactive, virtual working environment allowing interaction with abstract objects. To this issue, the algorithms and procedures of competence transfer presented in this article is dedicated.

Constant development of knowledge systems requires developing methods for controlling knowledge and competences resources. This issue, derived from cognitive science, requires preparing information systems that work at the level of knowledge, on the basis of ontology and artificial intelligence methods. Moreover, knowledge systems operate on new units and structures (e.g. concept, abstraction), the processing of which should be based on new algorithms and procedures.

References

1. Anderson, J.R.: Cognitive Psychology and Its Implications, 5th edn. Worth Publishing, New York (2000)
2. Bologna Working Group on Qualifications Frameworks, A Framework for Qualifications of the European Higher Education Area, report (2005),
   http://www.bologna-bergen2005.no/
3. Benetazzo, L., Bertocco, M., Ferraris, F., Ferrero, A., Offelli, C., Parvis, M., Piuri, V.: A Web-Based Distributed Virtual Education Laboratory. IEEE Transactions on Instrumentation and Measurement 49(2), 349–356 (2000)
4. Bourne, J., Harris, D., Mayadas, F.: Online Engineering Education: Learning Anywhere, Anytime. Journal of Engineering Education 94(1), 131–146 (2005)
5. Chalmers, P.A.: The role of cognitive theory in human–computer interface. Computers in Human Behavior 19(5), 593–607 (2003)
6. Conole, G., Dyke, M., Oliver, M., Seale, J.: Mapping pedagogy and tools for effective learning design. Computers & Education 43(1-2), 17–33 (2004)
7. Danna, K., Griffin, R.W.: Health and Well-Being in the Workplace: A Review and Synthesis of the Literature. Journal of Management 25(3), 357–384 (1999)
8. Duffy, V.G., Wu, F.F., Ng, P.W.P.: Development of an internet virtual layout system for improving workplace safety. Computers in Industry 50(2), 207–230 (2003)
9. García-Luque, E., Ortega, T., Forja, J.M., Gómez-Parra, A.: Using a laboratory simulator in the teaching and study of chemical processes in estuarine systems. Computers & Education 43(1-2), 81–90 (2004)
10. González-Castaño, F.J., Anido-Rifón, L., Valez-Alonso, J., Fernández-Iglesias, M.J., Llamas Nistal, M., Rodríguez-Hernández, P., Pousada-Carballo, J.M.: Internet access to real equipment at computer architecture laboratories using the Java/CORBA paradigm. Computers & Education 36(2), 151–170 (2001)
11. Gruninger, M., Fox, M.S.: Methodology for the Design and Evaluation of Ontologies. In: Proceedings of the Workshop on Basic Ontological Issues in Knowledge Sharing, IJCAI 1995, Montreal (1995)
12. Holmes, G., Hooper, N.: Core competence and education. Higher Education 40(3), 247–258 (2000)

13. Hwang, W.Y., Chang, C.B., Chen, G.J.: The relationship of learning traits, motivation and performance-learning response dynamics. Computers & Education 42(3), 267–287 (2004)
14. ISO 24763/draft: Conceptual Reference Model for Competencies and Related Objects (2009)
15. Joint Quality Initiative: Shared 'Dublin' descriptors for Short Cycle, First Cycle, Second Cycle and Third Cycle Awards, working draft (2004), http://www.jointquality.org/
16. Knudsen, C., Naeve, A.: Presence Production in a Distributed Shared Virtual Environment for Exploring Mathematics. In: Sołdek, J., Pejaś, J. (eds.) Advanced Computer Systems: 8th International Conference, pp. 149–161. Kluwer Academic, Dordrecht (2002)
17. Kushtina, E., Zaikin, O., Różewski, P.: On the knowledge repository design and management in E-Learning. In: Lu, J., Ruan, D., Zhang, G. (eds.) E-Service Intelligence: Methodologies, Technologies and applications. Studies in Computational Intelligence, vol. 37, pp. 497–517. Springer, Heidelberg (2006)
18. Kushtina, E., Zaikin, O., Różewski, P.: Extended ontological model for distance learning purpose. In: Reimer, U., Karagiannis, D. (eds.) PAKM 2006. LNCS (LNAI), vol. 4333, pp. 155–165. Springer, Heidelberg (2006)
19. Kushtina, E.: Concept of open and distance information system. Publisher house of Szczecin University Technology (2006) (in polish)
20. Penarrocha, V.M., Battaler, M.F., Escudero, M.B., Nogueira, A.V.: Virtual Laboratories in Electronic Engineering Education. In: International Conference on Network Universities and e-Learning, Valencia, Spain (2003)
21. Rak, R.J.: Virtual Instrument – the Main Part of Internet Based Distributed System. In: SSGRR 2000, L'Aquila, Italy (2000)
22. Ramasundaram, V., Grunwald, S., Mangeot, A., Comerford, N.B., Bliss, C.M.: Development of an environmental virtual field laboratory. Computers & Education 45(1), 21–34 (2005)
23. Różewski, P., Różewski, J.: Method of competency testing in virtual laboratory. In: Urbańczyk, E., Straszaka, A., Owsiński, J. (eds.) BOS 2006, Akademicka Oficyna Wydawnicza EXIT, Warszawa, pp. 349–360 (2006)
24. Sanchez, R.: Understanding competence-based management: Identifying and managing five modes of competence. Journal of Business Research 57(5), 518–532 (2004)
25. Scanlon, E., Colwell, C., Cooper, M., Di Paolo, T.: Remote experiments, re-versioning and re-thinking science learning. Computers & Education 43(1-2), 153–163 (2004)
26. Shackel, B.: People and computers - some recent highlights. Applied Ergonomics 31(6), 595–608 (2000)
27. Tuning Education Structures in Europe: Final Report Pilot Project - Phase 2 (2005), http://tuning.unideusto.org/tuningeu/
28. Zaikin, O., Kushtina, E., Różewski, P.: Model and algorithm of the conceptual scheme formation for knowledge domain in distance learning. European Journal of Operational Research 175(3), 1379–1399 (2006)

Integrating a Usability Model into Model-Driven Web Development Processes

Adrian Fernandez, Emilio Insfran, and Silvia Abrahão

ISSI Research Group. Department of Information Systems and Computation,
Universidad Politécnica de Valencia, Camino de Vera, s/n, 46022, Valencia, Spain
{afernandez,einsfran,sabrahao}@dsic.upv.es

Abstract. Usability evaluations should start early in the Web development process and occur repeatedly throughout all stages to ensure the quality of the Web application, not just when the product is completed. This paper presents a Web Usability Model, which is aligned with the SQuaRE standard, to evaluate usability at several stages of a Web development process that follows a Model-Driven Development (MDD) approach. The Web Usability Model is generic and must be operationalized into a concrete MDD method by specifying the relationships between the usability attributes of the Usability Model and the modeling primitives of the specific Web development method. To illustrate the feasibility of the approach, we present a case study where the Usability Model has been applied in the evaluation of the models that are produced during the Web application development process.

Keywords: Web Usability Model, Usability Evaluation, Web Metrics, Model-Driven Development, SQuaRE.

1 Introduction

Web applications have become the backbone of business and information exchange and the ease or difficulty that users experience with these systems will determine their success or failure. The challenge of developing more usable Web applications has led to emergence of a variety of techniques, methods, and tools to address Web usability.

Usability evaluations of Web applications can be performed by employing quality models since they define the term *usability* as a quality characteristic that can be decomposed into specific measurable attributes. However, most of the usability evaluation approaches [15], [18], [19] only consider usability evaluation at implementation stages when the product is completed.

As Web applications must be usable to be accepted by users, usability evaluations should start early in the Web development process and occur repeatedly throughout the design cycle, not just when the product is completed to avoid source code maintenance. Usability evaluation at each stage of the Web application development process is a critical part of ensuring that the product will actually be used and be effective for its intended purposes.

In a Model-Driven Web development process, models that specify an entire Web application are used in all steps of the process. This allows usability issues to be considered at early stages by evaluating the models that drive the implementation of a

G. Vossen, D.D.E. Long, and J.X. Yu (Eds.): WISE 2009, LNCS 5802, pp. 497–510, 2009.

final Web application [2]. A Web development process that follows a Model-Driven approach basically transforms models that are independent from implementation details (Platform-Independent Models - PIM) into other models that contain specific aspects from a concrete platform (Platform-Specific Models - PSM). PSM models can be compiled to automatically generate the Web application source code (Code Model - CM). Therefore, a better quality Web application can be obtained by evaluating and correcting models without requiring source code maintenance.

In this paper, we propose a Web Usability Model that is aligned with the ISO/IEC 25000 standard (SQuaRE) [13] in order to evaluate and improve usability at several stages of a Web development process that follows a Model-Driven Development (MDD) approach. The model is generic and must be operationalized into a concrete Web development method based on the MDD approach such as OO-H [8], UWE [14], or WebML [7]. Our strategy assesses intermediate artifacts (PIM and PSM models) as well as the final Web application source code (CM model) in order to take usability into account throughout the entire Web development process.

This paper is organized as follows. Section 2 discusses related work, in particular, previous quality and usability models for Web applications. Section 3 presents the strategy for integrating the Usability Model into a Model-Driven Web development process. Section 4 presents the Web Usability Model. Section 5 shows a case study which describes how the proposed model was applied to evaluate a real Web application that was developed following the OO-H method [8]. Finally, Section 6 presents the conclusions and further work.

2 Related Work

Several quality models for Web usability evaluation have been proposed in the last few years. These models have been defined from scratch or defined based on existing standards such as ISO/IEC 9241-11 [10] and ISO/IEC 9126-1 [9].

Quality models for the Web context that are defined from scratch include the proposals of Becker and Mottay [5], Sutcliffe [19], and Signore [18]. Becker and Mottay [5] present a usability assessment model to identify and measure usability factors. The factors defined are page layout, navigation, design consistency, information content, performance, customer service, reliability, and security. However, all these factors were measured at the final user interface (UI) of a Web application.

Sutcliffe [19] presents a model based on initial attractiveness, navigation and transaction. This work mainly focuses on how attractiveness can be operationalized in terms of design guidance. The attractiveness characteristic was divided into generic aspects of a final UI such as aesthetic design, use of media to direct attention, issues of linking visual styles, etc.

Signore [18] presents a quality model with a set of characteristics relating internal and external quality factors that can be measured by automated tools. The model distinguishes five dimensions related to *correctness* of the source code, *presentation* criteria (page layout, text presentation, etc.), *content* issues (readability, information structure, etc.), *navigation* aspects, and ease of *interaction* (transparency, recovery, help and hints, etc.).

On the other hand, the quality models for the Web context that are defined based on existing standards include the proposals of Olsina and Rossi [16], Calero *et al.* [6],

Seffah *et al.* [17], and Moraga *et al.* [15]. Olsina and Rossi [16] proposed the Web Quality Evaluation Method (WebQEM) to define quality characteristics and attributes based on the ISO/IEC 9126 such as *usability, functionality, reliability,* and *effectiveness*; the Web audience's needs are also incorporated. However, the evaluation of these quality characteristics takes place at the operational phases of the Web application. WebQEM is supported by a tool that relies on a Web-based hyper-document model that supports traceability of evaluation aspects.

Calero *et al.* [6] present the Web Quality Model (WQM), which distinguishes three dimensions: Web features (*content, presentation,* and *navigation*); quality characteristics based on the ISO/IEC 9126 (*functionality, reliability, usability, efficiency, portability,* and *maintainability*); and lifecycle processes from ISO/IEC 12207 [11] (*development, operation* and *maintenance*) including organizational processes such as *project management* and reuse *program management*. WQM incorporates a total of 326 Web metrics (taken from the existing literature) which was classified according to these three dimensions.

Seffah *et al.* [17] present the Quality in Use Integrated Measurement (QUIM) as a consolidated model for usability measurement in Web applications. QUIM combines existing models from ISO/IEC 9126, ISO/IEC 9241-11, and others. It decomposes usability into factors, and then into criteria (a criterion can belong to different factors). Finally, these criteria are decomposed into specific metrics that can quantify the criteria. The QUIM model is supported by an editor tool that manages a repository of usability measurement plans and defines new metrics.

Moraga *et al.* [15] present a usability model oriented to portlets evaluation. Portlets are pluggable UI software components that are managed and displayed in a web portal. The portlet usability model is based on the sub-characteristics from ISO/IEC 9126 (*understandability, learnability,* and *compliance*); nevertheless, the *operability* sub-characteristic was replaced by *customizability*, which is closer to the portlet context. Measures are based on a number ranking with an acceptance threshold.

After reviewing several quality model approaches, we have identified a lack of quality models that can evaluate Web usability not only when the Web application is implemented, but also at earlier stages of development, such as the analysis and design stages. In a previous work, Abrahão and Insfran [3] proposed a usability model for early evaluation in Model-Driven Architecture environments. In this model, usability was decomposed into the same sub-characteristics as the ones in the ISO/IEC 9126 (*learnability, understandability, operability,* and *compliance*), and then decomposed again, into more detailed sub-characteristics and attributes. This last decomposition was performed taking into account a set of ergonomic criteria for UIs [4]. Relationships between the elements from the PIM/CM models of a specific MDD method and the usability attributes of the model were then established. However, the model was not proposed for the Web domain and it did not provide metrics for measuring the model attributes.

3   Integrating a Usability Model into the MDD Process

Recent studies indicate that the adoption of Model-Driven Development (MDD) has increased. Currently, there are several Web development methodologies that follow this approach, such as OO-H [8], WebML [7], or UWE [14]. These methods support the development of a Web application by defining different views (models), including at least one structural model, a navigational model, and an abstract presentation model. Some methods also provide model transformations and automatic code generation.

The usability of a Web application obtained as a result of this transformation process can be assessed at several stages of a MDD process. In this paper, we propose the use of a Web Usability Model that can be applied in the following phases of a MDD process: **i)** in the PIM, to assess different models that specify the Web application independently of platform details (e.g., navigational models, models that represent the abstract UI); **ii)** in the PSM, to assess the concrete interface models related to a specific platform (if they exist); and **iii)** in the CM, to assess the final UI (see Fig. 1).

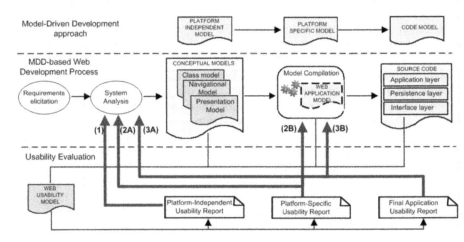

Fig. 1. Integrating a Web Usability Model into the MDD process

It should be noted that the MDD process is driven by the PIM, which is automatically transformed into a PSM, and this PSM into source code. Therefore, the evaluations performed at the PIM produce a *platform-independent usability report* that provides feedback to the system analysis stage (Fig. 1 (1)). Changes in the PIM are reflected in the CM by means of model transformations and explicit traceability between models. This prevents of usability problems to arising in the generated Web application (CM).

There are some usability attributes (e.g., degree of attractiveness) that can only be evaluated on a specific platform and taking into account the specific components of the interface (PSM) or the components that build the final UI (CM). Thus, evaluations performed at the PSM produce a *platform-specific usability report*. If the PSM does not have the required level of usability, this report will suggest changes to correct the following: the PIM models (Fig. 1 (2A)), the transformation rules that transform the PIM models into PSM models, and/or the PSM itself (Fig. 1 (2B)).

Nevertheless, the evaluations at the PIM or PSM level should be done in an iterative way until these models have the required level of usability. This allows usability evaluations at early stages in the Web development process.

Finally, evaluations performed at the CM level produce a *final application usability report*. Rather than suggest changes to improve the final UI (CM), as is usual in other approaches, this report will suggest changes to correct the PIM models (Fig. 1 (3A)), the transformation rules, and/or the PSM models (Fig. 1 (3B)).

4 Web Usability Model

The proposed Web Usability Model is an adaptation and extension of the usability model for model-driven development processes presented in Abrahão and Insfran [3]. The model was adapted to be compliant with the Software Quality Model proposed in the ISO/IEC 25000 (SQuaRE) [13]. Thus, in this section, we first introduce the ISO/IEC SQuaRE followed by a brief description of the main sub-characteristics, attributes, and Web metrics from our Web Usability Model. The entire model including all the sub-characteristics, attributes and their associated Web metrics is available at http://users.dsic.upv.es/~afernandez/WISE09/WebUsabilityModel.

4.1 ISO/IEC 25000 (SQuaRE)

The ISO/IEC 25000, also known as SQuaRE (Software Product Quality Requirements and Evaluation), was created for the purpose of providing a logically organized, enriched, and unified series of standards covering two main processes: software quality requirements specification and software quality evaluation. Both of these processes are supported by a software quality measurement process. This standard replaces the previous ISO/IEC 9126 [9] and ISO/IEC 14598 [12] standards.

In order to define our Web Usability Model, we have paid special attention to the Quality Model Division (ISO/IEC 2501n). SQuaRE proposes three different views for a quality model. These views are related to the context where the model will be applied: *Software Quality Model* to evaluate a concrete software product; *Data Quality Model* to evaluate the quality of the data managed in the product; and *Quality in Use Model* to evaluate how the stakeholders achieve their goals in a specific context of use.

Our Web Usability Model is based in the *Software Quality Model*. The main quality characteristics of the software quality model are: *functionality, security, interoperability, reliability, operability (usability)* and *efficiency*. Although the term *operability* has been proposed in SQuaRE, we use the term *usability* in this work to avoid confusions in terminology. Therefore, the goal of our Web Usability Model is to extend the software quality model proposed in SQuaRE, specifically the usability characteristic, for evaluating Web artifacts that are produced throughout a model-driven development process.

4.2 Specify Sub-characteristics and Attributes

Since SQuaRE [13] only decomposes *usability* into five high-level sub-characteristics: *learnability, understandability, operability, attractiveness* and *compliance*, in our approach these sub-characteristics have been decomposed into other more detailed sub-characteristics or measurable attributes taking into account the ergonomic criteria proposed in Bastien and Scapin [4].

The first three sub-characteristics of the usability are related to user performance and can be quantified using objective measures.

Learnability refers to the attributes of a Web application that facilitate learning. This sub-characteristic includes: *help facilities* such as on-line help and user manual; *predictability*, which refers to the ease with which a user can determine the result of his or her future actions; *informative feedback* in response to user actions; and *memorability* as a measure of how quickly and accurately users can remember how to use a Web application that they have used before. Table 1 shows this decomposition.

Table 1. Decomposition of the *learnability* sub-characteristic

Sub-charac.	Attribute	Meaning
1.1 Help Facilities	1.1.1 Documentation Completeness	Help documents have all information about possible actions that can be performed by the user.
	1.1.2 Multi-user Documentation	All of the kinds of users have been described with their possible actions.
1.2 Predictability	1.2.1 Icon/Link Image Significance	Capability to predict the next action according to the images.
	1.2.2 Icon/Link Title Significance	Capability to predict the next action according to the title of the links or icons.
	1.2.3 Action Determination	Capability to predict the next action according to the user expectations.
1.3 Informative Feedback		Capability to provide information about the state of the transactions (privacy, success tasks, etc.)
1.4 Memorability	1.4.1 Time to Remember	Time needed by users to remember how to use a Web application that they have used before.
	1.4.2 Accuracy	Accuracy with which users can remember how to use a Web application that they have used before.

Understandability refers to the attributes that facilitate understanding. This sub-characteristic includes: optical *legibility* of texts and images (e.g., font size, text contrast, position of the text); *readability*, which involves aspects of information-grouping cohesiveness and density; *familiarity*, the ease with which a user recognizes the UI components and views their interaction as natural; *workload reduction*, which is related to the reduction of user cognitive effort; and finally, *user guidance*, which is related to message quality, immediate feedback, and navigability. Table 2 shows this decomposition.

Operability refers to the attributes that facilitate user control and operation. This sub-characteristic includes: *execution facilities* such as compatible browsers or plug-ins needed; *data validity* of the user inputs; *controllability* of the services execution such as cancel and undo support; *capability of adaptation* which refers to the capacity of the Web application to be adapted to the users' needs and preferences; *consistency* in the execution of services and control behavior; *error management*; and *Web application state monitoring*. Table 3 shows this decomposition.

Table 2. Decomposition of the *understandability* sub-characteristic

Sub-charac.	Attribute	Meaning
2.1 Legibility	2.1.1 Font Size	Adequacy of the font size to the context.
	2.1.2 Contrasting Text	Text always properly visible.
	2.1.3 Disposition	Position of the text in order to be visible in any situation.
2.2 Readability	2.2.1 Information-Grouping Cohesiveness	The degree to which the information is presented in groups with a thematic focus.
	2.2.2 Information Density	Amount of information needed to prevent overloads.
	2.2.3 Information Complexity	Difficulty of understanding the information provided.
2.3 Familiarity	2.3.1 Labeling Significance	Use of labels that are easily recognizable.
	2.3.2 Internationalization	Use of elements that follow standards.
	2.3.3 Metaphor	Use of metaphors to help make the interaction more natural.
2.4 Workload Reduction	2.4.1 Brevity	Reduction of cognitive effort (i.e., actions in a few steps).
	2.4.2 Self-descriptiveness	Elements are shown as concisely as possible.
2.5 User Guidance	2.5.1 Message Quality	The messages are useful for the user to interact correctly.
	2.5.2 Immediate feedback	Guides users to determine what the progress of their actions is.
	2.5.3 Navigability	Ease with which the user moves the content by accessing the Web information that is relevant.

Table 3. Decomposition of the *Operability* sub-characteristic

Sub-charac.	Attribute	Meaning
3.1 Execution facilities	3.1.1. Ease of Installation	The need to install other software components for proper operation.
	3.1.2. Multiplicity	Web application is displayed correctly on different web browsers.
	3.1.3. Updateability	The latest version is always used.
	3.1.4. Update Transparency	The user does not perform manual updates.
3.2 Data Validity		Mechanisms are provided to verify the validity of the user data input.
3.3 Controllability	3.3.1. Edition Deferral	Content inserted can be edited at any time.
	3.3.2. Cancel Support	The actions can be canceled without harmful effects to normal operation.
	3.3.3. Explicit Execution	Information about the actions being carried out is not hidden.
	3.3.4. Interruption Support	The actions can be interrupted without harmful effects to normal operation.
	3.3.5. Undo Support	The actions can be undone without harmful effects to normal operation.

Table 3. (*continued*)

Sub-charac.	Attribute	Meaning
	3.3.6. Redo Support	The actions can be redone for the user to save work.
3.4 Capability of Adaptation	3.4.1. Adaptability	Ability of the Web application to be adapted by users.
	3.4.2. Adaptivity	Ability of the Web application to suit the needs of different users.
3.5 Consistency	3.5.1. Behavior of Controls	Controls always have the same behavior.
	3.5.2. Permanence of Controls	Controls appear if their associated actions can be performed.
	3.5.3. Stability of Controls	Controls perform the actions correctly.
	3.5.4. Order Consistency	Controls are always in the same order so as not to confuse the user.
	3.5.5. Label Consistency	The labels correspond to the actions they represent.
3.6 Error Management	3.6.1. Error Prevention	Capacity to provide mechanisms to prevent common mistakes.
	3.6.2. Error Recovery	Capacity to recover from errors.
3.7 Web application State Monitoring		It is allowed to know information about running processes.

The last two sub-characteristics of the usability are related to the perception of the end-user (**attractiveness**) or evaluator (**compliance**) using the Web Application. This perception is mainly measured using subjective measures. However, some aspects of *attractiveness* that are related to aesthetic design can also be quantified by measuring the *user interface uniformity* in terms of font color, font style, font size, and the position of elements. *Compliance* can be measured by assessing the agreement of the proposed Web Usability Model with respect to the SQuaRE and other Web-design style guides.

4.3 Incorporating Web Metrics to the Usability Model

Once the sub-characteristics and attributes have been identified, Web metrics are associated to the measurable attributes in order to quantify them. The values obtained from the metrics, and the establishment of thresholds for these values, will allow us to determine the degree to which these attributes help to achieve a usable Web application. The metrics included in our model were extracted and adapted from the survey presented in Calero *et al.* [6] and other sources. The metrics selected for this work were mainly the ones that were theoretically and/or empirically validated.

Each metric was analyzed taking into account the criteria proposed in SQuaRE: such as its purpose, its interpretation, its measurement method, the measured artifact, the validity evidence, etc. If the Web metric is applied to the final source code, we also analyzed the possibility of adapting it to be applied at the PIM and/or PSM levels.

Due to space constraints, we illustrate only with some examples how we define and associate the metrics to the attributes of the Web Usability Model:

- *Color Contrast* [20] (attached to attribute 2.1.2 from Table 2): Given two colors (C_1 and C_2) with their RGB codes in decimal notation, the contrast is determined by the formula:

$$\sum | C_1(i) - C_2(i) | \text{ let } i = \{\text{Red Value, Green Value, Blue Value}\} \qquad (1)$$

(Scale type: absolute value greater or equal than 0). Applicable at PIM (if color features are defined in the abstract UI) and applicable at CM (if color features are defined in Cascading Style Sheets files). The interpretation is: the larger the value of the metric, the better color contrast.

- *Breadth of a navigational map* [1] (attached to attribute 2.5.3 from Table 2): Total number of first-level navigational targets[1] in a navigational map. (Scale type: absolute value greater than 0). Applicable at PIM. The interpretation is: the larger the value of the metric (for first-level navigational targets that represent a navigation menu), the harder it is for the user to understand the functionalities of the Web application (several options at once).

- *Depth of a navigational map* [1] (attached to attribute 2.5.3 from Table 2): The longest distance of a root navigational target to a leaf navigational target (Scale type: absolute value greater than 0). Applicable at PIM. It indicates the ease with which a navigational target can be reached (number of steps) and the likely importance of its content. The interpretation is: the larger the distance of a leaf navigational target from the root, the harder it is for the user to reach it.

- *User operation cancellability* [9] (attached to attribute 3.3.2 from Table 3): Ratio between the number of implemented functions that can be cancelled by the user prior to completion and the total number of functions requiring the pre-cancellation capability (Scale type: ratio between 0 and 1). Applicable at PIM, PSM and CM.

5 Applying the Web Usability Model

The Web Usability Model has been operationalized into a concrete Web development method based on the MDD approach. Such an operationalization means specifying the correspondences between the attributes (and their associated metrics) of the Web Usability Model and the elements of the artifacts (PIM, PSM or CM) produced by a specific model-driven Web development method. As an example, we have selected the artifacts produced by the Object-Oriented Hypermedia (OO-H) method to illustrate how the Web Usability Model can be applied for early usability evaluation.

5.1 OO-H Method

The OO-H method [8] provides designers with the semantics and notation for developing Web applications. The method includes: a design process, a pattern catalog, a *Class Diagram*, a navigational map known as *Navigation Access Diagram*

---

[1] The concepts of *navigational map*, *navigational links*, and *navigational targets* refer to the OO-H method modeling primitives that are introduced in Section 5.1. They mainly refer to the fact that the navigation in a Web application corresponds to a directed graph whose nodes correspond to Web pages (represented as *navigational targets* in a Navigation Model) and whose arcs correspond to *navigational links* between these pages.

(NAD), and an *Abstract Presentation Diagram* (APD). The VisualWADE tool (www.visualwade.com) automates the entire OO-H development process.

The OO-H development process starts from the domain information structure that is captured in an UML-compliant class diagram. From there, we can create different NAD instances that represent the navigation dimension. A single NAD is a partial view from the class diagram. It structures the navigational view of the Web application for a specific kind of user. The APD is based on the concept of templates and is directly derived from the NAD. The APD can be refined by applying a pattern catalog. This catalog contains a set of constructs that effectively solve problems identified within Web environments. Once the APD is refined, we can automatically generate a front-end Web application (static or dynamic) for the desired environment, such as HTML, WML, active server pages (ASPs), and JavaServer pages (JSPs).

Several concepts related to the navigational model (NAD) and the abstract UI model (APD) are introduced below to facilitate the explanation about how Web metrics can be applied to them.

Each *navigational map* (or a NAD for a specific user) has a unique *entry point* that indicates the starting point of the navigation process. A *navigational map* is made up of a set of navigational elements that can be specialized as *navigational nodes* and/or *navigational links*. A *navigational node* represents a view over the UML class diagram. A navigational node can be a *navigational target*, a *navigational class*, or a *collection*. A *navigational target* groups elements of the model (i.e., *navigational classes, navigational links and collections*) that collaborate in the coverage of a user navigational requirement. A *navigational class* represents a view over a set of attributes (*navigational attribute*) and operations (*navigational operation*) of a class from the UML class diagram. A *collection* is a hierarchical structure that groups a set of navigational links. *Navigational links* define the navigation paths that the user can follow through the UI. There are two types of links: *source links* when new information is shown at the same view (depicted as an empty arrow); and *target links* when new information is shown at another view (depicted as a bold arrow).

Each *Abstract Presentation Diagram* (APD) represents an *abstract page collection*. An *abstract page* is a set of related information that is shown at the same navigation step. A first version of an APD is automatically generated from NAD, and it can be refined by a pattern catalog.

5.2 A Case Study

As an example, we show how several metrics from the Web Usability Model can be applied to a Web application developed using the OO-H method, which is supported by the VisualWADE tool. The selected Web application is a task management system developed for a Web development company located in Alicante, Spain. The documentation used to apply the model included: the OO-H conceptual model (class, navigational, and abstract presentation diagrams) of the Task Management Web application and the Web Usability Model.

Figure 2 shows a fragment of the navigational model (NAD) that represents the access to the Web application.

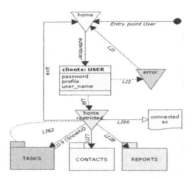

Fig. 2. First-level NAD for the Task Management Web application

Figure 2 shows the navigational access diagram (NAD) at level 0 for the *User* user. The *Entry point User* indicates the entry point to the Web application. The *Clients* navigational class corresponds to a form where the user will log into the system. This process involves a profile, a user name and a password. If the *User* exists, then a menu with a link to each one of the three identified navigational targets (packages Tasks, Contacts and Reports) will be shown (*home restricted* collection). Each navigational target can be further expanded to show detailed internal navigation. If the *User* does not exist, then an error message is shown. As an example, we can apply the following metrics:

- *Breadth of a navigational map* (see Section 4.3): the value of this metric is 4 since there are four navigational targets that the user can access (*Home, Tasks, Contacts* and *Reports*).
- *Depth of a navigational map* (see Section 4.3): the value of this metric is 2 since the longest distance of the *home* root navigational node to a leaf navigational node has 2 navigational links (*LI4* and one of the navigational links: *LI19, LI75* or *LI28*).

The values obtained are relevant to the Web application navigability. If the navigational map is too narrow and too deep, users will have to *click* several times and navigate through several levels to find what they are looking for, if the navigational map is too wide and shallow, users may get lost due to the excessive amount of information that can be accessed. For the type of Web application used in our case study, with a hierarchical structure, values lower than 5 levels of depth and values lower than 9 levels of breadth have been established as thresholds. Since the metrics used in this example obtains values below these thresholds, the navigational map helps to achieve a suitable level of navigability.

Figure 3 shows the PIM models (NAD and APD) that are related to the *Contacts* navigational target (a) and (b), and the final UI (CM model) (c), which is automatically generated from the APD model.

Figure 3 (a) provides detailed information about the *Contacts* navigational target. The *User* can see the information about *allContacts* or s/he can search for a given contact by providing an *initial* or by providing a *string*. These functionalities are represented by the three navigational links that connect the *contact menu* collection and the *Contact* navigational class. In addition, the user can create a new user by executing the *New* method in the *Contact1* navigational class.

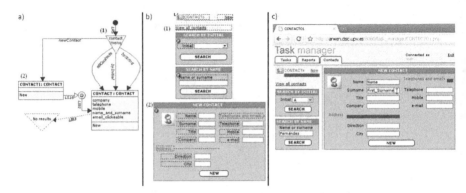

Fig. 3. (a) NAD for the Contact navigational node; (b) the APD generated from the NAD; (c) the final Web UI generated from these models (CM)

Figure 3 (b) shows a fragment of the generated APD. This model includes two abstract pages: a page for the contact menu and searching for a contact (Fig. 3 (b-1)), and a page for the execution of the *New* method from *Contact1* (Fig. 3 (b-2)). Since colors of label texts and background can be specified in this APD model (PIM), we can apply the following metric:

- *Color Contrast* (see Section 4.3): Although it should be noted that the metric must be applied to all the text elements across all the UIs, we only show, as an example, the case of the two labels *Telephones and emails* and *Address,* whose RGB color code of the text is (33, 85, 189) and the RGB color code of the background is (192, 192, 255); by applying the formula (1), the value of this metric results 332. This result is below the proposed threshold in [20] for this metric (greater or equal than 500). This color contrast can affect negatively the legibility of the text. This aspect could be improved, for instance, by changing the text color property of these labels in the APD model in order to get a better color contrast.

Finally, Figure 3 (c) shows the generated final UI. As an example, we can apply the following metric:

- *User operation cancellability* (see Section 4.3): The UI does not provide any explicit control (link or button) to allow users to cancel the insertion of a contact if they decide not to insert the contact; therefore, the value of this metric is 0/1=0. This result is negative because values that are closer to 0 indicate that the user cannot cancel transactions, which negatively affects the *controllability* sub-characteristic. This aspect could be improved, for instance, by including a navigational link in the corresponding NAD that allows to return to the *contact menu*. After correcting the NAD model, a more usable UI can be generated including the corresponding cancel link or button.

Although only an excerpt of the case study is shown, the Web Usability Model can be applied to the entire Web application. In this example, we have selected the OO-H method to operationalize the Web Usability Model; however, it is important to note that the model can be operationalized to other methodologies that follow a Web development process based on a MDD approach (e.g., UWE [14], WebML [7]).

6   Conclusions and Further Work

This paper has presented a Web Usability Model that is aligned with the ISO/IEC 25000 (SQuaRE) for evaluating and improving the usability of Web applications developed using a MDD approach. The aim of this proposed model is to perform usability evaluations not only when the Web application is completed (evaluating a CM), but also at earlier stages of the Web development (evaluating the PIM and PSM models) to provide feedback during the analysis and design stages. In this way, usability is taken into account throughout the entire process, enabling Web applications to be developed with better quality, thereby reducing effort at the maintenance stage.

The Web Usability Model can be very useful not only to evaluate PIMs, but also to discover deficiencies and/or limitations of the PIM expressiveness and the transformation rules to support some usability attributes. For instance, the OO-H method can be extended to support some usability attributes, such as Information-Grouping Cohesiveness (see Table 2, attribute 2.2.1), by incorporating mechanisms to semantically group attributes in the navigational model, thus avoiding the generation of Web forms that have a long list of attributes that are not grouped by any criteria.

We believe that the inherent features of model-driven development processes (e.g., traceability between models by means of model transformations) provide a suitable environment for performing usability evaluations. Specifically, if the usability of an automatically generated UI (e.g., using the VisualWade tool) can be assessed, the usability of any future UI produced by this tool could be predicted. In other words, we are talking about a UI that is *usable by construction* [2], at least to some extent.

Although the model has been operationalized to the OO-H method, it can also be applied to other methods such as UWE or WebML by specifying the relationships between the attributes (and their associated metrics) from the Web Usability Model with the elements of the PIM, PSM, and CM models from other methods.

Further work is intended to define a usability evaluation process including detailed guidelines on how evaluators could apply the Web Usability Model; exploring proper thresholds and aggregation mechanisms for values obtained by individual metrics; and performing analyses of the impact on how the attributes affect (negatively or positively) other attributes of the Usability Model. In addition, we plan to conduct empirical studies to confirm the relationship between the measures obtained at the PIM/PSM levels with the measures obtained when users actually use the Web application. Another aim is to develop a tool to manage the Web Usability Model creating a repository of catalogued metrics following SQuaRE patterns with the capability to support evaluations of the PIM and PSM models, as well as the final Web applications (CM).

Acknowledgments. This work is financed by META project (ref. TIN2006-15175-C05-05), the Quality-driven Model Transformation Project from the *Universidad Politécnica de Valencia*. The authors thank Jaime Gomez from *Universidad de Alicante* for his valuable help in providing the models and the generated Web application used in the case study.

References

1. Abrahão, S., Condori-Fernández, N., Olsina, L., Pastor, O.: Defining and Validating Metrics for Navigational Models. In: Proc. of the 9th Inter. IEEE Software Metrics Symposium, pp. 200–210 (2003)
2. Abrahão, S., Iborra, E., Vanderdonckt, J.: Usability Evaluation of User Interfaces Generated with a Model-Driven Architecture Tool. In: Maturing Usability. Springer HCI series, vol. 10, pp. 3–32 (2007)
3. Abrahão, S., Insfran, E.: Early Usability Evaluation in Model-Driven Architecture Environments. In: Proc. of the 6th IEEE International Conference on Quality Software, pp. 287–294. IEEE Computer Society, Los Alamitos (2006)
4. Bastien, J.M., Scapin, D.L.: Ergonomic Criteria for the Evaluation of Human-Computer Interfaces. Tech. Rep. n.156. INRIA, Rocquencourt, France (1993)
5. Becker, S.A., Mottay, F.E.: A Global Perspective on Web Site Usability. IEEE Software 18(1), 54–61 (2001)
6. Calero, C., Ruiz, J., Piattini, M.: Classifying Web Metrics Using the Web Quality Model 29(3), 227–248 (2005)
7. Ceri, S., Fraternali, P., Bongio, A.: Web Modeling Language (WebML): A Modeling Language for Designing Web Sites. In: Proc. of the 9th WWW Conf., pp. 137–157 (2000)
8. Gomez, J., Cachero, C., Pastor, O.: Conceptual Modeling of Device-Independent Web Applications. IEEE MultiMedia 8(2), 26–39 (2001)
9. ISO/IEC 9126, Software Engineering, Product Quality (2001)
10. ISO/IEC 9241, Ergonomic Requirements for Office Work with Visual Display Terminals (VDTs) (1998)
11. ISO/IEC 12207, Information Technology, Software Life Cycle Processes (1995)
12. ISO/IEC 14598, Information technology, Software Product Evaluation (1999)
13. ISO/IEC 25000, Software Product Quality Requirements and Evaluation (SQuaRE) (2005)
14. Kraus, A., Knapp, A., Koch, N.: Model-Driven Generation of Web Applications in UWE. In: 3rd Inter. Workshop on Model-Driven Web Engineering (2006)
15. Moraga, M.A., Calero, C., Piattini, M., Diaz, O.: Improving a Portlet Usability Model. Software Quality Control 15(2), 155–177 (2007)
16. Olsina, L., Rossi, G.: Measuring Web Application Quality with WebQEM. IEEE Multimedia 9(4), 20–29 (2002)
17. Seffah, A., Donyaee, M., Kline, R.B., Padda, H.K.: Usability Measurement and Metrics: A Consolidated Model. Software Quality Journal 14(2), 159–178 (2006)
18. Signore, O.: A Comprehensive Model for Web Site Quality. In: Proc. of the 7th IEEE Inter. Symposium on Web Site Evolution, pp. 30–36. IEEE Computer Society, Los Alamitos (2005)
19. Sutcliffe, A.: Assessing the Reliability of Heuristic Evaluation for Web Site Attractiveness and Usability. In: Proc. of the 35th Annual Hawaii Inter. Conf. on System Sciences, pp. 1838–1847 (2002)
20. W3C: Techniques For Accessibility Evaluation And Repair Tools. Working Draft (2000)

Entry Pairing in Inverted File

Hoang Thanh Lam[1], Raffaele Perego[2],
Nguyen Thoi Minh Quan[3], and Fabrizio Silvestri[2]

[1] Dip. di Informatica, Università di Pisa, Italy
lam@di.unipi.it
[2] ISTI-CNR, Pisa, Italy
{r.perego,f.silvestri}@isti.cnr.it
[3] Lomonosov Moscow State University, Russia
ntmquan@yahoo.com

Abstract. This paper proposes to exploit content and usage information to rearrange an inverted index for a full-text IR system. The idea
is to merge the entries of two frequently co-occurring terms, either in
the collection or in the answered queries, to form a single, paired, entry.
Since postings common to paired terms are not replicated, the resulting
index is more compact. In addition, queries containing terms that have
been paired are answered faster since we can exploit the pre-computed
posting intersection. In order to choose which terms have to be paired,
we formulate the term pairing problem as a Maximum-Weight Matching
Graph problem, and we evaluate in our scenario efficiency and efficacy
of both an exact and a heuristic solution. We apply our technique: (i) to
compact a compressed inverted file built on an actual Web collection of
documents, and (ii) to increase capacity of an in-memory posting list.
Experiments showed that in the first case our approach can improve the
compression ratio of up to 7.7%, while we measured a saving from 12%
up to 18% in the size of the posting cache.

1 Introduction

Compression plays an important role in modern information retrieval systems,
particularly in large-scale Web Search Engines (WSEs), which crawl and index tens of billions of pages, thus managing an extremely huge inverted index
and document repository. The benefits of effective compression techniques are
twofold. First, they allow cost savings for storage. Second, the memory hierarchy
is better utilized thus resulting in a lower query processing time [1]. It is well
known that fetching compressed data from disk and then decompressing them in
memory, is generally faster than fetching from disk the same data stored uncompressed. Thus, in the case of a disk-resident inverted index, compressing posting
lists decreases the time required to fetch them from secondary storage. On the
other hand, posting list compression remains valuable even for in-memory index settings, since it remarkably increases the portion of the index that can fit
the available memory at the cost of a negligible decompression overhead [2–4].
Previous work has focused on devising effective and efficient coding methods to

G. Vossen, D.D.E. Long, and J.X. Yu (Eds.): WISE 2009, LNCS 5802, pp. 511–522, 2009.

compress the posting lists of inverted indexes [4–7], or to reduce their size by an ad-hoc assignment of document identifiers [8–12]. Differently from previous works on index compression, this paper proposes a new technique for the lossless compression of an inverted index by directly reducing the number of entries stored as well as the number of postings coded. Based on the observation that many terms are highly correlated, i.e. co-occur frequently in the same document, and/or in the same query, we propose an algorithm to code only once the postings that are shared by different, correlated terms. In principle, coding only once the postings of two frequently co-occurring terms results in a reduction of space occupancy proportional to the number of postings saved. In addition, the pairing can be exploited to speed-up query processing time, when these highly related terms occur in the same query. Indeed, choosing the terms to pair is a complex task since the number of terms in the lexicon is huge. In fact, typical candidate terms are likely to be globally frequent and highly correlated in the indexed collection and/or in the queries submitted to the information retrieval system. We formulate the pairing decision problem as an optimization problem in graph theory known as the *Maximum Weight Matching Problem* (MWMP) [13]. MWMP is a classical graph theory problem, which can be exactly solved in time proportional to the cube of the number of vertices. Alternative linear-time approximation algorithms are also known.

Two different series of experiments are conducted on an inverted index built on a large Web Collection. First, we apply our technique to compress the whole inverted file index, obtaining up to 7.7% better compression ratio. Second, we apply the same technique to store in an in-memory posting cache the most frequently accessed posting lists and their intersections [14]. With this sort of static cache, a 12%-18% reduction in size was measured on the given test set.

Note that multi-term indexing is not novel. In particular in [15], an inverted index with multi-term entries was proposed to boost query processing. Beside the traditional, single-term index, the authors built an additional inverted index with frequent multi-keyword entries. The main drawback of their solution is the extra amount of memory needed to store the multi-term entries. On the other hand, our solution actually reduces the memory needed thus leaving free space for other important in-memory structures such as the cache.

In summary, our main contributions are:

- a novel inverted index compression technique based on pairing posting lists of frequently co-occurring terms.
- two types of representations for paired posting lists. The two representations have different pros and cons, which are discussed and evaluated.
- the demonstration on real data of the advantages of using our technique on two different scenarios: (i) inverted file compression, and (ii), static index caching.

The rest of the paper is organized as follows. The related work is presented in the next Section. Preliminaries and background information about inverted index representation and compression techniques are introduced in Section 3.

Section 4 describes the basic idea of terms pairing and the two different representation methods proposed. The problem formulation and the proposed algorithms are discussed in Section 4.1, while the experimental results are reported in Section 5. Finally, Section 6 discusses future work and draws our conclusions.

2   Related Work

As above mentioned, several papers focused on devising effective and efficient methods to encode the document identifiers (DocIDs) contained in the posting lists of Inverted File (IF) indexes, which allows efficient retrieval of documents containing the set of terms specified in a query. Since posting lists are ordered sequences of integer DocID values, and are usually accessed by scanning them from the beginning, these lists are stored as sequences of d-gaps, i.e. differences between successive DocID values. d-gap lists are then compressed by using variable-length encodings, which represent small integers in less space than large ones. Basic d-gaps coding methods are Variable Byte, which does not give the best compression performance, but it has a very short decompression time, and Gamma, which works best for encoding very small values [4]. More complex encoding techniques are Golomb [5], Rice [6], Simple9, Simple16, and PForDelta [7]. By following a radically different approach, Blandford et. al. [8], and Shieh et. al. [9], proposed methods to improve the IF compression performance by globally re-ordering document identifiers. Their approach aimed to reduce the average values of d-gaps by cleverly re-assigning document identifiers. Smaller the d-gaps are, shorter their representation with any variable length encoding method. On the same direction, Silvestri et. al. [10, 11], Blanco et. al. [12] studied efficient approaches to reduce the complexity of re-ordering document identifiers while maintaining a similar compression performance. As previously said, multi-terms indexing is not novel. For example, it was proposed in [15] for supporting efficiently phrase searches. The most frequent phrases mined from query logs were indexed as unique index entries, thus allowing the fast resolution of queries asking for such subset of supported phrases. Such multi-term entries were chosen on the basis of actual frequency of occurrence extracted from query logs. As the distribution of query terms is highly skewed, their experiments showed that the additional multi-terms inverted index could remarkably speed up query processing at the cost of an increase in the size of the whole index. This work is highly related to ours, and their accurate experiments strongly reinforce the validity of our assertion regarding the performance improvement in the query processing process resulting also from our technique. The main difference with respect to the work in [15] is that our proposal does not require extra storage space for storing paired entries, but instead allows the size of the index to be reduced without incurring in any information loss.

3   Preliminaries

Let $\mathcal{D} = \{d_1, d_2, \ldots, d_N\}$ be a collection of N documents, each one identified by a distinct DocID, and $\mathcal{T} = \{t_1, t_2, \ldots, t_T\}$ the set of T distinct terms appearing in the documents of $\mathcal{D}$. Based on $\mathcal{D}$ and $\mathcal{T}$, an IF is constructed by listing, on a term basis, the sequences of documents of $\mathcal{D}$ containing occurrences of terms of $\mathcal{T}$. A DocID list associated with a term of $\mathcal{T}$, is called posting list. Generally, each posting is annotated with additional information regarding the frequency of the term in the document, and the position of each occurrence. This information is however generally stored in different streams of the IF posting list, and the following discussion does not affect such meta-information. Thus, without loss of generality, hereinafter, with the term posting list we will refer to a simple sequence containing the (encoding of) the integer identifiers of the documents in the associated IF entry.

As an example, let us consider two terms $t_1, t_2 \in \mathcal{T}$ such that t_1 and t_2 appear in documents of $\mathcal{D}$ having identifiers 10, 15, 80, 1070, 2000, 2008, and 6, 15, 1070, 1090, 2000, respectively. From the previous assumption, the above ordered sequences of DocIDs constitute the posting lists for terms t_1 and t_2. It is worth noting that each posting list is generally transformed into a sequence of d-gaps before its encoding, i.e., a sequence of differences between consecutive DocIDs appearing in the posting list. Obviously, resulting d-gap values are smaller than original DocIDs, and, they can be more compactly represented by means of variable length encodings. Decoding d-gap values requires extra computation to obtain valid DocIDs. However, this computational load is negligible, as it requires to perform only fast addition operations on data with high spatial locality. In the following, we will briefly recall two of the most commonly used variable length d-gap encoding techniques.

- **Variable Byte (VB) Coding.** According to this scheme, a d-gap x is encoded with a sequence of consecutive bytes, the number of which depends on the value of x. The first bit of each byte indicates wether the byte is the last of the sequence (it is set if that byte is the last one), while the other 7 bits are used to actually encode the d-gap. For example, the codes of the two integer values 2 and 129 are 00000010 and 0000000110000001, respectively.
- **Gamma Coding (GC).** The previous encoding scheme is not particularly efficient to code very small d-gaps, as may happen for very frequent terms of the collection. Gamma uses instead a variable number of bits. A gamma code has two parts: The first, unary part contains a sequence of 1's followed by one 0, where the number of 1's defines the length of the binary representation of the d-gap value that is stored in the second part. With gamma, the codes of the above two integer values 2 and 129 are 110.10 and 111111110.10000001, respectively.

Gamma coding uses single bits to encode integers, while variable byte coding is byte aligned. In the context of very small integral values, gamma code is more effective than variable byte, but decoding is more expensive. In other conditions, variable byte behaves better. As we will see in Section 5, the characteristics of each coding technique affect also the performance of our term-pairing approach.

4 Representing IF Paired Terms

We base our study on the reasonable assumption that: *terms appearing frequently together within the same documents share a lot of common postings.* For example, terms like *FIFA* and *Football*, *Windows* and *Microsoft*, *Linux* and *GNU*, etc, are very likely to co-occur. The union of two posting lists has a number of postings equal to the sum of the postings of the single posting lists, minus the number of common postings appearing in both the paired lists. When the merged posting lists are highly correlated, their union could be remarkably shorter than the sum of the single lists. Let us consider again the above toy example: t_1 and t_2 have the following posting lists associated with: 10, 15, 80, 1070, 2000, 2008, and 6, 15, 1070, 1090, 2000. Pairing $t_1 \cup t_2$ will result in a list made up of 8 postings instead of 11 (the sum of the cardinality of the two single lists). Pairing must preserve the ability of answering queries in which terms are not paired. Therefore, some extra bits are needed to code such information that is necessary for supporting a correct query answering.

We propose two different approaches to encode such paired posting lists. The first representation provides that two extra bits per posting are used to indicate the source of a given posting, e.g., 10 for the first term, 01 for the second, 11 for both. Apart from these extra information, the postings of the merged lists can be coded with any technique. We called this type of representation *Mixed Union* (MU). In the second type of representation the postings of the paired terms are split into 3 partitions. The first partition contains postings common to both terms, the second partition postings for the first term only, and, finally, the last partition belongs to the second term. The DocIDs of each partition can

Before Pairing

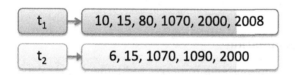

After Pairing

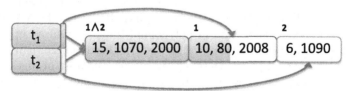

Fig. 1. A simple example of pairing two correlated posting lists: the paired posting list $t_1|t_2$ has 8 postings instead of 11

be ordered and represented with difference coding with the preferred technique. Some extra space is needed also in this case to store the offsets marking the starting points of the second and the third region. Normally, 8 bytes are sufficient for representing the two offsets in each paired list. We called this second kind of representation *Separated Union* (SU). The example in Figure 1 shows two entries paired and encoded with SU. SU has many advantages compared to MU. First, the number of extra space required is fixed (8 bytes) regardless posting list length, while in MU, the number of extra bits required is proportional to posting list length. In the case of a long posting list, MU is not likely to be a good choice. Second, decompression in SU involves each partition separately. In contrast, in MU we have to decompress the whole paired posting lists at a time to filter out the posting list of a single term or of the intersection. On the other hand, the disadvantage of SU is that the d-gap values must be computed locally for each partition, so that their average values are larger than in MU. Choosing which type of representation is the best may depend also on the compression technique adopted for coding the postings.

Paired entries speed-up processing of every kind of query. Conjunctive ones benefit from the intersection portion, to resolve disjunctive we just need to scan the paired posting list, to resolve set-difference (e.g. t_1 and not t_2) we just need to scan the appropriate portion of the paired posting list. Note that lexicon needs not only a slight change. Paired terms will point to two lists the intersection portion and the list of posting for the term not contained within the intersection. Suppose t_1 and t_2 have been paired up. When user requires a query containing both t_1 *and* t_2, the system will retrieve the relative list pointers. They have been paired up, thus, pointers are found to be the same, and the system will read only the intersection portion; otherwise from the lexicon we can obtain what is the relative portion to scan. For instance Figure 1 shows the case for SU. If we want to read the whole posting list for t_1 we have to scan the two lists pointed by the lexicon structure.

4.1   Problem Formulation

The compression benefits deriving from our technique clearly depend from the frequency and correlation degree of the paired terms. The choice of which terms to pair is thus crucial. We formulate the pairing decision problem as an optimization problem, and reduce it to a classical graph theory problem known as the *Maximum Weight Matching Problem* (MWMP) [13]. The MWMP can be solved with an exact algorithm in polynomial time, or with an approximation algorithm in linear time. In this section, we formalize our term-pairing problem.

Let $G(V, E)$ be a graph with a set of vertexes V, and a set of edges E. Suppose that each vertex $v_i \in V$ corresponds to a term t_i of $\mathcal{T}$, and that an edge e_{ij} exists between each couple of vertexes v_i and v_j. Moreover, let us assume that each edge $e_{ij} \in E$ is weighted with the value returned by the following function:

$$w(e_{ij}) = \begin{cases} 0 \ iff \ B_{tech}(t_i, t_j) \leq 0 \\ B_{tech}(t_i, t_j) \ otherwise. \end{cases}$$

The Term-Term Graph

The associated Maximum
Weighted Matching

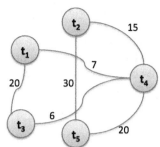
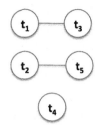

Fig. 2. An example of compression benefit graph. The Maximum Weight Matching for this graph is shown on the right hand side.

where $B_{tech}(t_i, t_j)$ measures (in number of bits) the benefit of pairing terms t_i and t_j according to the technique *tech* adopted, i.e. according to the type of representation for paired entries (MU or SU), and the encoding method used for representing d-gaps (e.g., VB, GC, etc.).

For the above graph G, a set $M \subseteq E$ of edges is a *matching* if no pair of edges of M has a common vertex. Given our benefit weight function $w(e_{ij})$, which assigns weights to the edges of G, a matching M is a *Maximum Weight Matching*, if M is a matching, and $\sum_{e \in M} w(e)$ is maximal. It is straightforward to derive from the Maximum Weight Matching of G the optimal pairing. It suffices to pair together the terms corresponding to nodes at both ends of edges in the matching. Figure 2 shows a simple example of graph with compression benefit weights. The rightmost graph in Figure 2 represents the associated Maximum Weight Matching.

Several exact algorithms for solving the MWMP in polynomial time were proposed such as the Blossom algorithm by J. Edmonds [16], or the one by Gabow [17]. Approximated methods can compute good quality solutions to the MWMP in linear time. In this paper, we use the Preis's linear time half-approximation algorithm [18]. We also experiment the exact algorithm by Gabow [17] with complexity $O(|E|^3)$.

5 Experimental Results

Our terms pairing technique was tested on an IF obtained from WBR99, a real Web collection consisting of 5,939,061 documents, occupying about 22 GB, and containing about 2,700,000 different terms [10, 11]. WBR99 is a snapshot of the Brazilian Web as crawled by TodoBr, a Brazilian search engine (www.todobr.com.br). The lexicon and the uncompressed postings of WBR99 occupy a space of about 3.6 GB. For experimenting the posting cache case we used also a query log of 51 millions queries collected by the same search engine. Two different series of experiments were conducted on the data above. In the first series of tests we evaluate the efficacy of our method in compressing the posting lists. We measure the compression ratio with respect to the size of a traditional, single-term IF adopting the same encoding technique (VB or GC), and containing exactly the same information. The second series of experiments evaluate the applicability of the same idea to the representation of postings within a static posting list cache.

In each experiment conducted, both the exact and approximate algorithms for the MWMP, as well as the Separated and Mixed Union representations for the paired posting lists, were tested. The results of the experiments are reported and discussed in the following subsections.

5.1 Term Pairing for IF Compression

During the analysis of the IF built on the WBR99 collection, we observed that the distribution of term occurrences is highly skewed. Indeed, the posting lists of the $10,000$ most frequent terms account for more than 75% the size of the whole IF! For this reason, in order to prevent our MWMP exact solver from performing exhaustive searching over a very large graph without significant improvement in compression performance, we restricted the size of the problem, and considered the graph of the $k = 10,000$ most frequent terms only. This simple pruning technique makes our problem instance tractable also with the Gabow's exact algorithm with cubic complexity.

To justify our pruning technique, the leftmost plots of Figure 3 reports the compression improvement (in number of bytes) resulting from applying our technique (with VB encoding and SU representation) on the basis of the results of Preis's approximate algorithm for different values of k. As we can see, the improvement increases rapidly when k grows up to 500, but tends to converge for higher values. The rightmost plot of Figure 3 shows instead the ratio between compression improvement and the number of paired terms. As expected, the benefit of our technique is very high when the first most frequent tterms are paired but tends to decrease as the length of posting lists of the paired terms decreases. In the following experiments we thus fixed $k = 10,000$, and considered the MWMP for our benefit graph with $10,000$ most frequent terms.

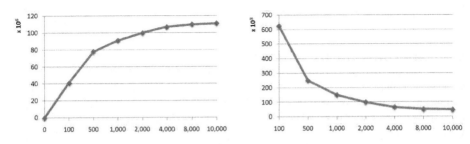

Fig. 3. Compression performance for values of the pruning factor k increasing up to $10,000$. Leftmost plot shows compression improvement, while the plot on the right hand shows the ratio between compression improvement and the number of paired terms.

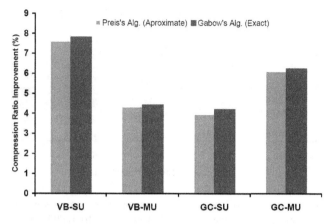

Fig. 4. Compression ratios achieved for VB-SU, VB-MU, GG-SU, and GC-MU, the four possible different combinations of Variable Byte and Gamma Coding, with Separated and Mixed Union representations. The two bars in each case refer to the compression ratios obtained with Gabow and Preis algorithms. The compression improvement is compared with the baseline VB code and Gamma code.

Figure 4 plots the results of the experiment conducted to evaluate the compression improvement resulting from different settings of our term pairing technique. In particular, Variable Byte (VB), and Gamma Code (GC) were combined with either Separated Union or Mixed Union, thus obtaining four different cases denoted with VB-SU, VB-MU, GC-SU, and GC-MU. Moreover, each case corresponds to two bars in the plot: one for the exact Gabow's algorithm, and one for the Preis' approximate one. We can see from the figure that the term pairing approach VB-SU is the most effective with a gain of 7.73% in the compression ratio. SU representation is remarkably better than mixed union with VB encoding. However, with Gamma encoding the opposite holds. This is very likely due to SU increasing the average values of d-gaps. We deserve to a future work to better investigate this fact. We can also observe that the exact algorithm is only slightly better than the approximate algorithm. For example, in the case of VB-SU, the Gabow's exact algorithm gives the a solution resulting in 7.73% better compression ratio, while the Preis's approximate solution reaches an improvement of 7.58%.

5.2 Pairing Cached Posting Lists

In this section, we consider another possible application of our term pairing approach: the representation of posting lists cached in main memory for faster query processing. Previous work [7, 14] has shown that posting list caching in memory is an effective technique to speed up query response time because it save up the cost of expensive disk accesses. Currently, commercial memory devices can be thousands time faster than hard disk, thus, by keeping the most frequently accessed posting lists inside memory, we can reduce the number of expensive

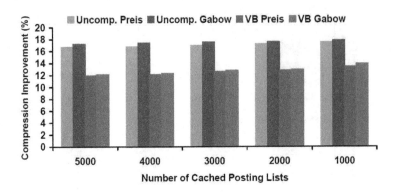

Fig. 5. Term pairing applied to the cache of posting lists: compression ratio improvement for different sizes of the cache (varying from 5,000 to 1,000), and different settings of the term pairing technique. The compression improvement is compared with the baseline VB code.

disk accesses. However, due to limit size of memory devices, cached posting lists must be compressed as much as possible. The more compacted the cached posting lists are the more posting lists can be resident inside memory, thus, reduce the number of disk accesses. In this section, we show empirically that our approach can reduce the cached posting lists size from $12 - 18\%$ compared to the other types of compression techniques. The cache into which the posting lists are kept can be managed with a static or dynamic policy. We will consider here only static posting list caching, since the choice of the best replacement policy to adopt in this case is out of the scope of this paper.

For testing the term pairing technique on cached posting lists we use a query log of 51 millions queries collected in 2003 by the Brazilian search engine TodoBr (the same source of the WBR99 collection). Frequency of terms appearing in the user queries were counted, and these terms then sorted by the ratio of frequency and posting list length [19]. Then, different instances of the associated MWMP were solved by considering the top $1,000, 2,000, 3,000, 4,000, 5,000$ terms sorted by frequency and posting list length. Finally, we compute the space saving in the occupancy of a VB-encoded posting list cache of the same dimension by either applying or not the term pairing technique. We consider only SU since it better pairs up with the VB encoding. Moreover, we test also the behavior of our term pairing technique in the case uncompressed DocID-based postings. Recently, Baeza-Yates et. al. [19] showed that compression is advantageous also applied to cached posting lists. In fact, fixed the amount of available memory, compression allows a larger number of posting lists to be cached, and thus the cache hit ratio to be improved. However, our term pairing technique is itself a compression method, and it is interesting to evaluate its efficacy alone on uncompressed list of DocIDs.

Figure 5 reports the results of our tests. On the horizontal axis we report the size of cache in terms of number of cached posting lists, while on the vertical axis we plot the improvement in the actual size of the cache obtained applying our term pairing approach. We can see from the figure that term pairing is very effective in this case, allowing improvements ranging from 12% to 18%. We thus obtained better results from our technique when applied to posting list caching than to the whole IF. The reason for this behavior is that the cache is much smaller than the whole IF, and that it is filled with terms which frequently occur in queries. Even if the distribution of terms in queries and collections is not the same, these terms resulted to be frequent also in the collection, and as shown in the plot on the right of Figure 3, the larger the length of to-be-paired posting lists, the more the compression improvement obtained by pairing them.

6   Conclusions and Future Work

In this paper, we proposed a novel inverted index compression technique based on pairing the posting lists of highly correlated terms. We formulated term pairing as an optimization problem, and reduced it to the *Maximum Weight Matching Problem* that can be solved with exact polynomial algorithms, or approximated in linear time.

We demonstrated on real data the validity of our proposal by applying it to two different scenarios: the compression of the whole inverted file index, and of the posting lists cached in memory to fasten query processing. In both cases, the experiments conducted obtained very good results. In the case of IF compression we measured an improvement in terms of compression ratio up to 7.7 %. An impressive improvement (up to 18%) was measured for the case of static caching of index entries. Moreover, our technique is very efficient and can be applied even to huge IFs such as those managed by large-scale Web search engines. In fact, we showed that the size of the optimization problem can be strongly reduced to consider a few thousands of most frequent terms only, since the distribution of posting list length is highly skewed and our pairing technique works effectively for long, correlated posting lists. Moreover, results obtained by exploiting the (linear-time) approximated solution for the (reduced) Maximum Weight Matching Problem, were very similar to the one derived from the optimal solution obtained with a solver having cubic complexity. We plan to investigate in the future several important issue. First of all we will verify in which measure, our term pairing approach can speed up query processing. We based our assumptions on query processing speed-up on the results reported in [15]. We are confident our method will allow to obtain, at least, the same speed-up figures as their. Moreover, we will investigate the combination of pairing and index pruning techniques [20] for both cached posting lists and IF compression.

References

1. Roy, S., Kumar, R., Prvulovic, M.: Improving system performance with compressed memory. In: IPDPS 2001: Proceedings of the 15th International Parallel & Distributed Processing Symposium, p. 66. IEEE Computer Society, Washington (2001)
2. Turpin, A., Tsegay, Y., Hawking, D., Williams, H.E.: Fast generation of result snippets in web search. In: Kraaij, W., de Vries, A.P., Clarke, C.L.A., Fuhr, N., Kando, N. (eds.) SIGIR, pp. 127–134. ACM, New York (2007)

3. Zobel, J., Moffat, A.: Inverted files for text search engines. ACM Comput. Surv. 38(2), 6 (2006)
4. Witten, I.H., Moffat, A., Bell, T.C.: Managing Gigabytes – Compressing and Indexing Documents and Images, 2nd edn. Morgan Kaufmann Publishing, San Francisco (1999)
5. Golomb, S.: Run-length encodings. IEEE Transactions on Information Theory 12(3), 399–401 (1966)
6. Rice, R.F., Plaunt, J.R.: Adaptive variable-length coding for efficient compression of spacecraft television data. IEEE Trans. Commun. COM-19, 889–897 (1971)
7. Zhang, J., Long, X., Suel, T.: Performance of compressed inverted list caching in search engines. In: WWW 2008: Proceeding of the 17th international conference on World Wide Web, pp. 387–396. ACM, New York (2008)
8. Blandford, D., Blelloch, G.: Index compression through document reordering. In: DCC 2002: Proceedings of the Data Compression Conference (DCC 2002), p. 342. IEEE Computer Society, Washington (2002)
9. Shieh, W.Y., Chen, T.F., Shann, J.J.J., Chung, C.P.: Inverted file compression through document identifier reassignment. Inf. Process. Manage. 39(1), 117–131 (2003)
10. Silvestri, F., Orlando, S., Perego, R.: Assigning identifiers to documents to enhance the clustering property of fulltext indexes. In: SIGIR 2004: Proceedings of the 27th annual international ACM SIGIR conference on Research and development in information retrieval, pp. 305–312. ACM, New York (2004)
11. Silvestri, F.: Sorting out the document identifier assignment problem. In: Amati, G., Carpineto, C., Romano, G. (eds.) ECiR 2007. LNCS, vol. 4425, pp. 101–112. Springer, Heidelberg (2007)
12. Blanco, R., Barreiro, A.: Tsp and cluster-based solutions to the reassignment of document identifiers. Inf. Retr. 9(4), 499–517 (2006)
13. Garey, M.R., Johnson, D.S.: Computers and Intractability: A Guide to the Theory of NP-Completeness. W. H. Freeman & Co., New York (1979)
14. Long, X., Suel, T.: Three-level caching for efficient query processing in large web search engines. In: WWW 2005: Proceedings of the 14th international conference on World Wide Web, pp. 257–266. ACM, New York (2005)
15. Chaudhuri, S., Church, K.W., Knig, A.C., Sui, L.: Heavy-tailed distributions and multi-keyword queries. In: Kraaij, W., de Vries, A.P., Clarke, C.L.A., Fuhr, N., Kando, N. (eds.) SIGIR, pp. 663–670. ACM, New York (2007)
16. Edmonds, J., Johnson, E.L., Lockhart, S.C.: Blossom i: a computer code for the matching problem. Unpublished report, IBM T. J. Watson Research Center (1969)
17. Gabow, H.N.: An efficient implementation of edmonds' algorithm for maximum matching on graphs. J. ACM 23(2), 221–234 (1976)
18. Preis, R.: Linear time 1/2-approximation algorithm for maximum weighted matching in general graphs. In: Meinel, C., Tison, S. (eds.) STACS 1999. LNCS, vol. 1563, pp. 259–269. Springer, Heidelberg (1999)
19. Baeza-Yates, R., Gionis, A., Junqueira, F., Murdock, V., Plachouras, V., Silvestri, F.: The impact of caching on search engines. In: SIGIR 2007: Proceedings of the 30th annual international ACM SIGIR conference on Research and development in information retrieval, pp. 183–190. ACM, New York (2007)
20. Blanco, R., Barreiro, A.: Static pruning of terms in inverted files. In: Amati, G., Carpineto, C., Romano, G. (eds.) ECiR 2007. LNCS, vol. 4425, pp. 64–75. Springer, Heidelberg (2007)

STC+ and NM-STC: Two Novel Online Results Clustering Methods for Web Searching

Stella Kopidaki, Panagiotis Papadakos, and Yannis Tzitzikas

Institute of Computer Science, FORTH-ICS, Greece,
Computer Science Department, University of Crete, Greece
{skopidak,papadako,tzitzik}@ics.forth.gr

Abstract. Results clustering in Web Searching is useful for providing users with overviews of the results and thus allowing them to restrict their focus to the desired parts. However, the task of deriving single-word or multiple-word names for the clusters (usually referred as *cluster labeling*) is difficult, because they have to be syntactically correct and predictive. Moreover efficiency is an important requirement since results clustering is an online task. *Suffix Tree Clustering (STC)* is a clustering technique where search results (mainly snippets) can be clustered fast (in linear time), incrementally, and each cluster is labeled with a phrase. In this paper we introduce: (a) a variation of the STC, called STC+, with a scoring formula that favors phrases that occur in document titles and differs in the way base clusters are merged, and (b) a novel non merging algorithm called NM-STC that results in hierarchically organized clusters. The comparative user evaluation showed that both STC+ and NM-STC are significantly more preferred than STC, and that NM-STC is about two times faster than STC and STC+.

1 Introduction

Web Search Engines (WSEs) typically return a ranked list of documents that are relevant to the query submitted by the user. For each document, its title, URL and *snippet* (fragment of the text that contains keywords of the query) are usually presented. It is observed that most users are impatient and look only at the first results. Consequently, when either the documents with the intended (by the user) meaning of the query words are not in the first pages, or there are a few dotted in various ranks (and probably different result pages), it is difficult for the user to find the information he really wants. The problem becomes harder if the user cannot guess additional words for restricting his query, or the additional words he chooses are not the right ones for restricting the result set.

A solution to these problems is *results clustering* which provides a quick overview of the search results. It aims at grouping the results into topics, called *clusters*, with predictive names (labels), aiding the user to locate quickly one or more documents that otherwise he wouldn't practically find especially if they are low ranked (and thus not in first result pages). Results clustering algorithms should satisfy several requirements. First of all, the generated clusters should be characterized from high intra-cluster similarity. Moreover, results clustering

G. Vossen, D.D.E. Long, and J.X. Yu (Eds.): WISE 2009, LNCS 5802, pp. 523–537, 2009.

algorithms should be efficient and scalable since clustering is an online task and the size of the answer set can vary. Usually, only the $top - L$ documents are clustered in order to increase performance. In addition, the presentation of each cluster should be concise and accurate, allowing users to detect what they need quickly. *Cluster labeling* is the task of deriving readable and meaningful, single-word or multiple-word names for clusters, in order to help the user to recognize the clusters/topics he is interested in. Such labels must be predictive, allowing users to guess the contents of each cluster, descriptive, concise and syntactically correct. Finally, it should be possible to provide high quality clusters based on small snippets rather than the whole documents.

Clustering can be applied either to the original documents (like in [3,10,7]), or to their (query-dependent) snippets (as in [25,23,17,6,27,8,20]). For instance, clustering meta-search engines (MWSEs) (e.g. clusty.com) use the results of one or more search engines (e.g. Google, Yahoo!), in order to increase coverage/relevance. Therefore, meta-search engines have direct access only to the snippets returned by the queried search engines. Clustering the snippets rather than the whole documents makes clustering algorithms faster. Some clustering algorithms [6,4,24] use internal or external sources of knowledge like Web directories (e.g. DMoz[1], Yahoo! Directory), dictionaries (e.g. WordNet) and thesauri, online encyclopedias (e.g. Wikipedia[2]) and other online knowledge bases. These external sources are exploited to identify key phrases that represent the contents of the retrieved documents or to enrich the extracted words/phrases in order to optimize the clustering and improve the quality of cluster labels.

Suffix Tree Clustering (STC) [25] is a clustering technique where search results (mainly snippets) are clustered fast (in linear time), incrementally, and each cluster is labeled with a common phrase. Another advantage of STC is that it allows clusters to overlap. In this work we introduce: (a) a variation of the STC, called STC+, with a scoring formula that favors phrases that occur in document titles and differs in the way base clusters are merged, and (b) a novel algorithm called NM-STC (Non Merging - STC) that adopts a different scoring formula, it does not merge clusters and results in hierarchically organized labels. The advantages of NM-STC are: (a) the user never gets unexpected results, as opposed to the existing STC-based algorithms which adopt overlap-based cluster merging, (b) it is more configurable w.r.t. desired cluster label lengths (STC favors specific lengths), (c) it derives hierarchically organized labels, and (d) it favors occurrences in titles (as STC+) and takes into account IDFs, if available. The empirical evaluation showed that users prefer the STC+ and NM-STC than the original STC. NM-STC is currently in use by Mitos WSE [13][3].

The rest of this paper is organized as follows. Section 2 discusses related work. Section 3 formulates the problem and introduces notations. Section 4 describes the clustering algorithms and Section 5 reports experimental results. Finally Section 6 concludes and identifies issues that are worth further research.

---

[1] www.dmoz.org

[2] www.wikipedia.org

[3] http://groogle.csd.uoc.gr:8080/mitos/

2   Related Work

At first we discuss clustering approaches based on document vectors and then approaches based on snippets (focusing on STC). Finally, we discuss cluster presentation and user interaction.

Document Vector-Based Approaches. Traditional clustering algorithms either flat (like K-means) or hierarchical (agglomerative or divisive) are not based on snippets but on the original document vectors and on a similarity measure. For instance, a relatively recent approach is Frequent Itemset Hierarchical Clustering (FIHC) [7] which exploits the notion of frequent itemsets used in data mining. In brief, such approaches can be applied only on a stand alone engine (since they require accessing the entire vectors of the documents) and they are computationally expensive.

Snippet-Based Approaches. Snippet-based approaches rely on snippets and there are already a few engines that provide such clustering services (Clusty[4] is probably the most famous one). Suffix Tree Clustering (STC) [25] is a key algorithm in this domain and is used by Grouper [26] and $Carrot^2$ [23,17] MWSEs. It treats each snippet as an ordered sequence of words, identifies the phrases (ordered sequences of one or more words) that are common to groups of documents by building a suffix tree structure, and returns a flat set of clusters that are naturally overlapping. Several variations of STC have been proposed. For instance, the trie can be constructed with the N-grams instead of the original suffixes. The resulting trie has lower memory requirements (since suffixes are no longer than N words) and its building time is reduced, but less common phrases are discovered and this may hurt the quality of the final clusters. Specifically, when N is smaller than the length of true common phrases the cluster labels can be unreadable. To overcome this shortcoming [11] proposed a join operation. A variant of STC with N-gram is STC with X-gram [20] where X is an adaptive variable. It has lower memory requirements and is faster than both STC with N-gram and the original STC since it maintains fewer words. It is claimed that it generates more readable labels than STC with N-gram as it inserts in the suffix tree more true common phrases and joins partial phrases to construct true common phrases, but no user study results have been reported in the literature. The performance improvements reported are small and from our experiments the most time consuming task is the generation of the snippets (not the construction of the suffix tree). Another approach based on STC is ESTC (Extended STC) [2], an extension of STC appropriate for application over the full texts (not snippets). To reduce the (roughly two orders of magnitude) increased number of clusters, a different scoring function and cluster selection algorithm is adopted. The cluster selection algorithm is based on a greedy search algorithm aiming at reducing the overlap and at increasing the coverage of the final clusters. We do not share the objective of reducing overlap as in practice documents concern more than one topic. The comparison of ESTC with the original STC was done

---

[4] www.clusty.com

using a very small cluster set (consisting of only two queries) and no user study has been performed. Moreover, the major part of the evaluation was done assuming the entire textual contents of the pages (not snippets), or on snippets without title information. Summarizing, clustering over full text is not appropriate for a (Meta) WSE since full text may not be available or too expensive to process. Other extensions of STC for oriental languages and for cases where external resources are available are described in [28,21].

Another snippet-based clustering approach is *TermRank* [8]. TermRank succeeds in ranking discriminative terms higher than ambiguous terms, and ambiguous terms higher than common terms. The $top - T$ terms, can then be used as feature vectors in K-means or any other Document Vector-based clustering algorithm. This approach requires knowing TF, it does not work on phrases (but on single words) and no evaluation results over snippets have been reported in the literature.

Another approach is Findex [12], a statistical algorithm that extracts candidate phrases by moving a window with a length of $1..|P|$ words across the sentences (P), and fKWIC which extracts the most frequent keyword contexts which must be phrases that contain at least one of the query words. In contrast to STC, Findex does not merge clusters on the basis of the common documents but on the similarity of the extracted phrases. However, no comparative results regarding cluster label quality have been reported in the literature.

Finally, there are snippet-based approaches that use *external resources (lexical or training data)*. For instance, SNAKET [6] (a MWSE) uses DMoz web directory for ranking the *gapped sentences* which are extracted from the snippets. *Deep Classifier* [24] trims the large hierarchy, returned by an online Web directory, into a narrow one and combines it with the results of a search engine using a discriminative naive Bayesian Classifier. Another (supervised) machine learning technique is the *Salient Phrases Extraction* [27]. It extracts *salient phrases* as candidate cluster names from the list of titles and snippets of the answer, and ranks them using a regression model over five different properties, learned from human training data. Another approach that uses several external resources, such as WordNet and Wikipedia, in order to identify useful terms and to organize them hierarchically is described in [4].

Cluster Presentation & User Interaction. Although cluster presentation and user interaction approaches are somehow orthogonal to the clustering algorithms employed, they are crucial for providing flexible and effective access services to the end users. In most cases, clusters are presented using lists or trees. Some variations are described next. A well known interaction paradigm that involves clustering is Scatter/Gather [3,10] which provides an interactive interface allowing the users to select clusters, then the documents of the selected clusters are clustered again, the new clusters are presented, and so on. In our case we adopt the interaction paradigm of *dynamic taxonomies* [16] as it is the de facto standard in e-commerce (and users are already familiar with), and it can enable guided browsing over *explicit* and *mined* metadata. The automatically derived cluster labels fall into the latter category.

3   Problem Statement and Notations

We consider important the requirements of *relevance, browsable summaries, overlap, snippet-tolerance, speed* and *incrementality* as described in [25]. Regarding the problem of cluster labeling we have observed that: (a) *long labels are not very good* (e.g. not convenient for the left frame of a WSE, or for accessing the WSE through a mobile phone) (b) *very short labels (e.g. single words) are not necessarily good* (e.g. longer labels could be acceptable, or even desired, in a system that shows the cluster labels in a horizontal frame) (c) *an hierarchical organization of labels can alleviate the problem of long labels*, and (d) *the words/phrases appearing in titles are usually better (for cluster labeling) than those appearing only in snippets*. Observations (a) and (b) motivate the need for configuration parameters. Observations (c) and (d) motivate the algorithms STC+ and NM-STC that we will introduce.

Configuration Parameters. We have realized that several configuration parameters are needed for facing the needs of a modern WSE. We decided to adopt the following: K : number of top elements of the answer to cluster, LL_{max} : max cluster Label Length, LL_{min} : min cluster Label Length, and NC_{max} : max Number of Clusters. Obviously it should be $NC_{max} < K$. However the size of the current answer should also be taken into account. Specifically if $ans(q)$ is the answer of the submitted query, then we shall use A to denote the first K elements of $ans(q)$. However, if $|A| < K$ then we assume that $K = |A|$.

Notations. We use Obj to denote the set of all documents, hereafter objects, indexed by a WSE, and A to denote the top-K elements of the current answer as defined earlier (i.e. $A \subseteq Obj$ and $|A| = K$).

We use W to denote the set of words of the entire collection, and $W(A)$ to denote the set of the words that appear in a set of documents A (this means that W is a shortcut for $W(Obj)$).

Let $A = \{a_1, \ldots, a_K\}$. For each element a_i of A we shall use $a_i.t$ to denote the title of a_i, and $a_i.s$ to denote the snippet of a_i. Note that the elements of $W(A)$ are based on both titles and snippets of the elements of A.

If a is a text, then we shall use $P(a)$ to denote all phrases of a that are *sentence suffixes*, i.e. start from a word beginning and stop at the end of a sentence of a. For example $P("this is a test") = \{"this is a test", "is a test", "a test", "test"\}$, while $P("this is. A test") = \{"this is", "is", "A test", "test"\}$.

We shall use $P(A)$ to denote all phrases of the elements of A, i.e. $P(A) = \bigcup_{a \in A}(P(a.t) \cup P(a.s))$.

If p is a phrase we shall use $Ext(p)$ to denote the objects (of A) to which p appears, i.e. $Ext(p) = \{a \in A \mid p \in a\}$. Also, we shall use $w(p)$ to denote the set of words that phrase p contains.

4   STC, STC+ and NM-STC

Our goal is to improve STC, specifically: (a) to improve the quality of cluster labels by exploiting more the titles (document titles can give more concise labels),

(b) to define a more parametric algorithm for facing the requirements of modern WSEs, and (c) to derive hierarchically organized labels. Specifically below we describe the original STC, a variation that we have devised called STC+, and a new algorithm called NM-STC.

Original STC. In brief, Suffix Tree Clustering (STC) uses the titles and snippets of the search results in order to create groups of documents that share a common phrase. Specifically, titles and snippets, after a preprocessing phase, are inserted in a generalized suffix tree structure which allows us to identify the common phrases and the documents they appear. The suffix tree [22,9] is a data structure that can be constructed in linear time with the size of the collection, and can be constructed incrementally as the documents are being read [19]. A set of documents that share a common phrase is called *base cluster*. Finally, a merging step of base clusters (based on the overlap of their documents) leads to the final clusters which are scored and presented to the user.

In more detail, the algorithm starts with the suffix tree construction. For each sentence of the input data all suffixes are generated and are inserted into the suffix tree. Each node of the tree that contains two or more documents is a base cluster. Each base cluster that corresponds to a phrase p is assigned a score which is calculated with the following formula:

$$score(p) = |\{a \in A \mid p \in a.t \text{ or } p \in a.s\}| * f(effLen(p))$$

where $effLen(p)$ is the effective length of label p defined as:

$$effLen(p) = |w(p)| - |common(p)| \text{ where}$$
$$common(p) = \{w_i \in p \mid df(w_i, A) \le 3 \text{ or } \frac{df(w_i, A)}{|A|} > 0.4\}$$

where $df(w_i, A) = |\{d \in A \mid w_i \in d\}|$.

The function f (that takes as input the effective length), penalizes single words, is linear for phrases with effective length from two to six words, and is constant for bigger phrases, specifically:

$$f(effLen(p)) = \begin{cases} 0.5 & \text{if } effLen(p) \le 1 \\ effLen(p) & \text{if } 2 \le effLen(p) \le 6 \\ 7.0 & \text{if } effLen(p) > 6 \end{cases}$$

Afterwards, the overlap is calculated for all pairs of base clusters. Overlap is defined with a binary similarity measure. The similarity between two base clusters C_i and C_j is defined as $sim(C_i, C_j, 0.5)$ where:

$$sim(C_i, C_j, thres) = \begin{cases} 1 & \text{if } \frac{|C_i \cap C_j|}{|C_i|} > thres \text{ and } \frac{|C_i \cap C_j|}{|C_j|} > thres \\ 0 & \text{otherwise} \end{cases}$$

The next step is the merging of the base clusters. In brief, each final cluster contains all base clusters that can be merged (two base clusters can be merged if their similarity equals 1). As a result the document set of a final cluster is the union of its base clusters' document sets and its cluster label is the label of the base cluster with the highest score. Due to cluster merging there can be documents that do not contain the label p. Let $C(p)$ be the document set of a cluster label p. The exact scoring formula for a final cluster is $score(p) = |C(p)| * f(effLen(p))$. Finally, clusters are sorted according to their score and are presented to the user.

STC+: A Variation of STC. Here we describe a variation of STC which differs in the way that clusters are scored and in the way base clusters are merged. Specifically, we adopt the following scoring formula:

$$score(p) = (|\{a \in A \mid p \in a.t\}| + |\{a \in A \mid p \in a.t \text{ or } p \in a.s\}|) * f(effLen(p))$$

This formula favors phrases that occur in titles. In addition, we have modified the function f. Our variation penalizes single words and phrases that their effective length is bigger that 4 words, and is linear for phrases with effective length two to four words. These values are a good compromise between the reported results of the user study at Section 5, favoring small phrases, and the avoidance of single-word labels. Specifically our function f is defined as:

$$f(effLen(p)) = \begin{cases} 0.5 & \text{if } effLen(p) \leq 1 \text{ or } effLen(p) > 4 \\ effLen(p) & \text{if } 2 \leq effLen(p) \leq 4 \end{cases}$$

Regarding the computation of the similarity measure (that determines cluster merging) we consider as threshold the value 0.4 instead of 0.5. From our experience, this value creates fewer and bigger clusters and solves some problematic cases of the original STC. For example, a base cluster with 2 documents that is compared with a base cluster with 4 documents cannot be merged even if they have 2 common documents, because $2/4 = 0.5$. Therefore we used $sim(C_i, C_j, 0.4)$. A lower than 0.4 threshold would decrease the *label precision* as it will be explained in Section 5. Note that the title set of a final cluster is the union of its base clusters' title sets. Let $T(p)$ be the set of titles of a cluster label p. The exact scoring formula for a final cluster is $score(p) = (|T(p)| + |C(p)|) * f(effLen(p))$.

NM-STC: A New Clustering Algorithm. Here we introduce an algorithm called NM-STC (Non Merging - Suffix Tree Clustering). As in STC, we begin by constructing the suffix tree of the titles and snippets. Then we score each node p of that tree. Let p be a phrase (corresponding to a node of the suffix tree). Below we define four scoring functions:

$$score_t(p) = |\{a \in A \mid p \in a.t\}|$$
$$score_s(p) = |\{a \in A \mid p \in a.s\}|$$
$$score_{ts}(p) = score_t(p) * |A| + score_s(p)$$
$$score_{tsi}(p) = score_t(p) * |A| * N + score_s(p) * N + PIDF(p)$$

PIDF stands for Phrase IDF and N is the total number of indexed documents ($N = |Obj|$). If p is a single word (w), then $PIDF(p)$ is the IDF of w (i.e. $IDF(w) = \frac{N}{|\{d \in Obj \mid w \in d\}|}$). If p is a phrase consisting of the words $\{w_1, \ldots, w_m\}$, then PIDF is the average IDF of its words, i.e.

$$PIDF(p) = \frac{1}{m} \sum_{i=1}^{m} IDF(w_i)$$

or alternatively $PIDF(p) = \max_{w \in p}(IDF(w))$. In our experiments we used the average IDF. The IDF can be computed based on the entire collection if we are in the context of a single WSE. In our case, the index of Mitos stores only the stems of the words, so $IDF(w)$ is estimated over the stemmed words. If we are in the context of a MWSE, then IDF could be based on external sources, or on the current answer[5].

NM-STC uses the $score_{tsi}(\cdot)$ scoring formula. This scoring function actually quantifies a qualitative preference of the form $title \triangleright snippet \triangleright PIDF$, where $\triangleright$ denotes the priority operator [1]. Notice that PIDF has the lowest priority. It is used just for breaking some ties. From our experiments, the number of broken ties is low, so it does not affect significantly the results. Also, $score_{tsi}(\cdot)$ can be applied on STC+ instead of its scoring formula.

NM-STC at first scores all labels of the suffix tree using the function $score_{tsi}(\cdot)$. Subsequently it selects and returns the top-NC_{max} scored phrases. Let B be the set of top-NC_{max} scored phrases. Note that it is possible for B to contain phrases that point to the same objects, meaning that the extensions of the labels in B could have big overlaps. In such cases we will have low "coverage" of the resulting clustering (i.e. the set $\cup_{p \in B} Ext(p)$ could be much smaller than A).

Recall that STC merges base clusters having a substantial overlap in order to tackle this problem. However that approach leads to labels whose extension may contain documents that do not contain the cluster label (in this way users get unexpected results). Instead NM-STC follows a different approach that is described in the sequel, after first introducing an auxiliary notation. If $n(p)$ and $n(p')$ denote the nodes in the suffix tree that correspond to phrases p and p' respectively, we shall say that p is narrower than p', and we will write $p < p'$, iff $n(p)$ is a descendent of $n(p')$, which means that p' is a prefix of p. For instance, in our running example of Figure 1 we have $n("a\ b") < n("a")$.

Returning to the issue at hand, our approach is the following: We fetch the top-NC_{max} labels and we compute the *maximal* elements of this set according to $<$. In this way we get the more broad labels (among those that are highly scored). If their number is less than NC_{max} then we fetch more labels until reaching to a set of labels whose maximal set has cardinality NC_{max}. So the algorithm returns the smaller set of top-scored phrases B that satisfies the equation $|maximal_<(B)| = NC_{max}$ if this is possible (even if B is the set of all nodes of the suffix tree, it may be $|maximal_<(B)| < NC_{max}$).

---

[5] $IDF(w) = \frac{|A|}{|\{d \in A \mid w \in d\}|}$.

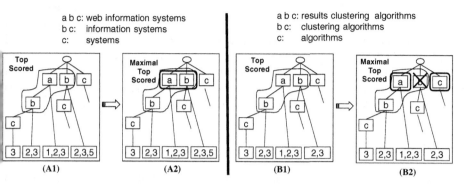

Fig. 1. Two examples of NM-STC

The extra labels fetched (i.e. those in $B \setminus maximal_<(B)$) are exploited by the GUI for providing an *hierarchical organization* of the labels (where the user can expand the desired nodes to see their immediate children and so on). Consider the example in Figure 1.(A1), and assume that $NC_{max} = 2$. The set of top-3 scored labels whose maximal elements are two are marked (as shown in Figure 1.(A2)). At the GUI level, the user can expand a and see the label b.

The algorithm is sketched bellow. It takes as input a tree (the suffix tree) and returns another tree (the cluster label tree). Of course it also takes as input the configuration parameters, as well as the current query q.

Alg. $NM - STC$
Input: sf:SuffixTree, NC_{max}, LL_{min}, LL_{max}, q
Output: cluster label tree
(1) ScoreLabelsOf(sf)
(2) ZeroScoreLabelsEqualTo(sf,q)
(3) ZeroScoreLabelsLabelSize(sf,LL_{min}, LL_{max})
(4) toplabs = getTopScored(sf, NC_{max})
(5) Done=False
(6) while Done=False
(7)   maxTopLabs = maximal$_<$(toplabs)
(8)   maxTopLabls = ElimSubPhrasesSameExt(maxTopLabs)
(9)   missing = NC_{max} - |maxTopLabs|
(10)   if (missing>0)
(11)   toplabs = toplabs $\cup$ getNextTopScored(sf,missing)
(12)   else Done=True
(13)end while
(14)return toplabs, $<_{|toplabs}$

If a cluster label p contains only query words (i.e. $w(p) = w(q)$), then we exclude it from consideration, as such labels would be useless for the users. This is done by zeroing the scores of such labels (step (2)). At step (3) we zero the scores of the labels that do not satisfy the LL_{min} and LL_{max} constraints. The function getTopScored(sf, NC_{max}) returns the NC_{max} most highly scored nodes. At step (8) we remove from the list of maximal labels those that are subphrases of other labels and contain the same documents. Specifically, if $w(p) \subseteq w(p')$ and $Ext(p) = Ext(p')$ then we exclude p. This is shown in the example illustrated in Figure 1.(B1 and B2): the node b is discarded because it has the same extension with the node b that is child of a. The function getNextTopScored(sf, M) returns the next M labels in the ranked list of labels (that are not already consumed).

5   Experimental Evaluation

Implementation. The algorithms have been implemented over Mitos [15,14,13][6]. The snippets in our experiments were quite small: up to two sentences, each one consisting of 11 words maximum. The results of clustering are presented to the user using the FleXplorer API [18], that supports the interaction paradigm of *dynamic taxonomies*. The hierarchy of cluster labels (by NM-STC) can be considered as a subsumption relation since it satisfies $p < p' \implies Ext(p) \subseteq Ext(p')$, i.e. if p is child of p' then the objects associated with p are subset of those associated with p', and this allows exploiting the interaction paradigm of dynamic taxonomies. At the presentation layer the user initially views the maximal elements of the cluster label tree along with the number of $|Ext(p)|$ and a symbol indicating whether that node has children. By clicking on one of these nodes the direct children of that node appears too. The process of unfolding (expanding) labels resembles the process of extending a natural language phrase. By construction all these phrases are syntactically correct.

Evaluation by Users. We conducted a comparative evaluation over Mitos. We defined 16 queries of different sizes consisting of small (single words), medium (2 to 3 words), and big (4 or more words) queries[7]. The queries were randomly chosen and their results sizes range from 14 to 5029 hits. The queries were given to 11 persons (from 22 to 30 years old, familiar with computers and Web searching). Every participant had to submit each of these queries to a special evaluation system[8] that we developed which visualizes the results of the three clustering algorithms (STC, STC+, NM-STC) in parallel (we used the parameters $K = 100$, $LL_{min} = 1$, $LL_{max} = 4$, $NC_{max} = 15$). The users did not know which algorithms were used, and they were free to submit whatever query they liked. After inspecting the results, each participant had to rank the three methods according to (a) label readability, (b) cluster ordering, (c) number of clusters and (d) overall quality. In this way we collected 16 * 11 * 4 = 704 user assessments in total. The users expressed their preference by providing numbers from {1, 2,

---

[6] Developed by the Dep. of Computer Science (U. of Crete) and FORTH-ICS.

[7] For more see: http://groogle.csd.uoc.gr:8080/mitos/files/clusteringEvaluation/UserEval.xls

[8] http://groogle.csd.uoc.gr:8080/clusteringEvaluation/, select Advanced Search, Results options: Clustering

3}: 1 to the best, and 3 to the worst. Ties were allowed, e.g. STC:1, STC+:1, NM-STC:2 means that the first two are equally good, and NM-STC is the worst. In case all three were indifferent (they liked/disliked them equally), they were giving the value 0. We aggregated the rankings using Plurality Ranking (PR) (i.e. by considering only the winners) and Borda Ranking (BR) [5]. The middle part of Table 1 reports the average results[9]. In the PR column, the higher a value is, the better, while in the BR column the less a value is, the better. The rightmost part of Table 1 shows the relative ranking of the algorithms: 1 for the best, 2 for the second, and 3 for the third in preference algorithm (according to PR and BR). Notice that the relative ordering is the same for both PR and BR. The results show STC+ and NM-STC are clearly the most preferred algorithms according to each of the three criteria, and according to the overall assessment. In particular, NM-STC yields the more readable labels, STC+ yields the best cluster label ordering and NM-STC yields the best number of clusters. Regarding criterion (d) (overall quality), STC+ obtained the best result (PR: 7.08), NM-STC a slightly lower (PR: 6.91), while STC a much lower value (PR: 3.41).

Table 1. Comparative Evaluation by Users

Criterion	STC		STC+		NM-STC		STC		STC+		NM-STC	
	PR	BR	PR	BR	PR	BR	PR	BR	PR	BR	PR	BR
(a) Label Readability	2.41	33.5	6.25	23.16	9.41	20.83	3	3	2	2	1	1
(b) Cluster Ordering	4.75	28.33	7.33	21.75	6.41	24.9	3	3	1	1	2	2
(c) Number of clusters	2.33	33.5	5.83	23.33	10.41	19.91	3	3	2	2	1	1
(d) Best method (overall)	3.41	31.08	7.08	21.75	6.91	23.5	3	3	1	1	2	2

In addition, we asked the participants to answer a small questionnaire. Table 2 shows the questions and the answers received. The results show that the majority prefers (a) hierarchically organized labels, (b) labels comprising one to three words, and (c) 10-15 clusters.

Table 2. Questionnaire

Question	Results
Do you prefer Flat or Hierarchical cluster labels?	Flat (24%), Hierarchical (58%), Both are fine (18%)
Preferred cluster label length	$1 - 3(75\%)$ $3 - 6(25\%)$
Preferred number of clusters	< 10 (25%) $10 - 15$ (62.5%) $15 - 20$ (12.5%)

Clustering Evaluation Metrics. We conducted an additional comparative evaluation between STC, STC+, and NM-STC. We used the metrics defined in Table 3. B denotes the set of the labels returned by a clustering algorithm, and

---

[9] The PR value was computed by summing all ones (i.e. first positions) and then dividing by 11*16 (i.e. $|users| \times |queries|$).

for a $p \in B$ we use $C(p)$ to denote the set of objects that are assigned to cluster label p by the clustering algorithm.

Coverage measures the degree that clusters' extensions cover the answer A (the closer to 1, the better the clusters "cover" the answer A). Its value is low if the clusters cover a small portion of A and this implies that the clusters do not summarize the entire contents of A. The *label precision* of a label p is the percentage of objects in the extension of p that contain all words of p. It is clear that the label precision of NM-STC is (by construction) always 1, but this is not true for the other STC-based algorithms (due to the base cluster merging).

Table 3 reports the average values for the queries used in the empirical evaluation. The overlap for NM-STC is computed over the maximal elements of B (i.e. those in $maximal_<(B)$). The results show that STC and STC+ have exactly the same coverage while NM-STC has slightly lower[10]. STC+ and NM-STC give smaller names than STC. STC+ and NM-STC have higher overlap (which is not bad). The label precision of STC+ is smaller than that of STC due to the threshold 0.4 vs 0.5 in base cluster merging. For threshold=0.3 the label precision of STC+ drops to 0.60 while for threshold=0.2 it further drops to 0.47. These results motivate the reason for not further decreasing this threshold.

Table 3. Evaluation Metrics and Results

Name	Definition		STC	STC+	NM-STC
coverage	$coverage = \frac{|\cup_{p \in B} C(p)|}{|A|}$		0.994	0.994	0.869
average label length	$LL_{avg} = avg_{p \in B} |w(p)|$		3.185	2.906	2.249
overlap	$AvO = \frac{2}{|B|(|B|-1)} \sum_{i=1}^{|B|} \sum_{j=i+1}^{|B|} JO(p_i, p_j)$ where $JO(p_i, p_j) = \frac{|C(p_i) \cap C(p_j)|}{|C(p_i) \cup C(p_j)|}$		0.038	0.048	0.099
label precision	$AvLP = \frac{1}{|B|} \sum_{p \in B} LabelPrec(p)$ where $LabelPrec(p) = \frac{|\{o \in C(p) \ | \ w(p) \subseteq w(o)\}|}{|C(p)|}$		0.893	0.756	1.0

Time Performance. For the evaluation queries we counted the average time to cluster the top-100, the top-200 and the top-300 snippets. In NM-STC the IDF of the terms are in main memory from the beginning. Also recall that PIDF could be omitted from the scoring formula as it does not seem to influence the results (except in cases of very small result sets). The measured times (in seconds) are shown next (using a Pentium IV 4 GHz, 2 GB RAM, Linux Debian).

Alg	Top-100	Top-200	Top-300
STC	0.208	0.698	1.450
STC+	0.228	0.761	1.602
NM-STC	0.128	0.269	0.426

Notice that NM-STC is (two to three times) faster than STC and STC+. This is because NM-STC does not have to intersect and merge base clusters.

---

[10] In general all coverage values are acceptably high, e.g. higher than those in [12], and by adding an artificial "rest" cluster label we could achieve 100% coverage.

6   Conclusion and Future Work

In this work we focused on suffix tree clustering algorithms because they are fast, they do not rely on external resources or training data, and thus they have broad applicability (e.g. different natural languages). We presented a variation of the STC, called STC+, with a scoring formula that favors phrases that occur in document titles, and a novel suffix tree based algorithm called NM-STC that results in hierarchically organized clusters. The advantages of NM-STC are that: (a) the user never gets unexpected results, as opposed to the existing STC-based algorithms which adopt overlap-based cluster merging, (b) it is more configurable w.r.t. desired cluster label lengths (STC favors specific lengths), (c) it derives hierarchically organized labels, and (d) it favors occurrences in titles (as STC+) and takes into account IDFs, if available. The user evaluation showed that both STC+ and NM-STC are significantly more preferred than STC (STC+ is slightly more preferred than NM-STC). In addition NM-STC is about two times faster than STC and STC+. In future we plan to work towards further improving the quality of cluster labels and the interaction with the user.

References

1. Andreka, H., Ryan, M., Schobbens, P.-Y.: Operators and Laws for Combining Preference Relations. Journal of Logic and Computation 12(1), 13–53 (2002)
2. Crabtree, D., Gao, X., Andreae, P.: Improving web clustering by cluster selection. In: Procs of the IEEE/WIC/ACM Intern. Conf. on Web Intelligence (WI 2005), Compiegne, France, September 2005, pp. 172–178 (2005)
3. Cutting, D.R., Karger, D., Pedersen, J.O., Tukey, J.W.: Scatter/Gather: A cluster-based approach to browsing large document collections. In: Procs. of the 15th Annual Intern. ACM Conf. on Research and Development in Information Retrieval (SIGIR 1992), Copenhagen, Denmark, June 1992, pp. 318–329 (1992)
4. Dakka, W., Ipeirotis, P.G.: Automatic extraction of useful facet hierarchies from text databases. In: Procs. of the 24th Intern. Conf. on Data Engineering (ICDE 2008), Cancún, México, April 2008, pp. 466–475 (2008)
5. de Borda, J.C.: Memoire sur les Elections au Scrutin. Histoire de l'Academie Royale des Sciences, Paris (1781)
6. Ferragina, P., Gulli, A.: A personalized search engine based on web-snippet hierarchical clustering. In: Procs. of the 14th Intern. Conf. on World Wide Web (WWW 2005), Chiba, Japan, May 2005, vol. 5, pp. 801–810 (2005)
7. Fung, B.C.M., Wang, K., Ester, M.: Hierarchical Document Clustering Using Frequent Itemsets. In: Procs. of the SIAM Intern. Conf. on Data Mining, San Francisco, CA, USA, May 2003, vol. 30 (2003)
8. Gelgi, F., Davulcu, H., Vadrevu, S.: Term ranking for clustering web search results. In: 10th Intern. Workshop on the Web and Databases (WebDB 2007), Beijing, China (June 2007)
9. Gusfield, D.: Algorithms on Strings, Trees, and Sequences: Computer Science and Computational Biology. ACM SIGACT News 28(4), 41–60 (1997)
10. Hearst, M.A., Pedersen, J.O.: Reexamining the cluster hypothesis: Scatter/Gather on retrieval results. In: Procs. of the 19th Annual Intern. ACM Conf. on Research and Development in Information Retrieval (SIGIR 1996), Zurich, Switzerland, August 1996, pp. 76–84 (1996)

11. Janruang, J., Kreesuradej, W.: A new web search result clustering based on true common phrase label discovery. In: Procs. of the Intern. Conf. on Computational Intelligence for Modelling Control and Automation and Intern. Conf. on Intelligent Agents Web Technologies and International Commerce (CIMCA/IAWTIC 2006), Washington, DC, USA, November 2006, p. 242 (2006)

12. Käki, M.: Findex: properties of two web search result categorizing algorithms. In: Procs. of the IADIS Intern. Conf. on World Wide Web/Internet (IADIS 2005), Lisbon, Portugal (October 2005)

13. Papadakos, P., Kopidaki, S., Armenatzoglou, N., Tzitzikas, Y.: Exploratory web searching with dynamic taxonomies and results clustering. In: Procs. of the 13th European Conf. on Digital Libraries (ECDL 2009), Corfu, Greece (September 2009)

14. Papadakos, P., Theoharis, Y., Marketakis, Y., Armenatzoglou, N., Tzitzikas, Y.: Mitos: Design and evaluation of a dbms-based web search engine. In: Procs. of the 12th Pan-Hellenic Conf. on Informatics (PCI 2008), Greece (August 2008)

15. Papadakos, P., Vasiliadis, G., Theoharis, Y., Armenatzoglou, N., Kopidaki, S., Marketakis, Y., Daskalakis, M., Karamaroudis, K., Linardakis, G., Makrydakis, G., Papathanasiou, V., Sardis, L., Tsialiamanis, P., Troullinou, G., Vandikas, K., Velegrakis, D., Tzitzikas, Y.: The Anatomy of Mitos Web Search Engine. CoRR, Information Retrieval, abs/0803.2220 (2008), http://arxiv.org/abs/0803.2220

16. Sacco, G.M., Tzitzikas, Y. (eds.): Dynamic Taxonomies and Faceted Search: Theory, Practise and Experience. Springer, Heidelberg (2009)

17. Stefanowski, J., Weiss, D.: Carrot2 and language properties in web search results clustering. In: Menasalvas, E., Segovia, J., Szczepaniak, P.S. (eds.) AWIC 2003. LNCS (LNAI), vol. 2663. Springer, Heidelberg (2003)

18. Tzitzikas, Y., Armenatzoglou, N., Papadakos, P.: FleXplorer: A Framework for Providing Faceted and Dynamic Taxonomy-Based Information Exploration. In: 19th Intern. Workshop on Database and Expert Systems Applications (FIND 2008 at DEXA 2008), Torino, Italy, September 2008, pp. 392–396 (2008)

19. Ukkonen, E.: On-line construction of suffix trees. Algorithmica 14(3), 249–260 (1995)

20. Wang, J., Mo, Y., Huang, B., Wen, J., He, L.: Web Search Results Clustering Based on a Novel Suffix Tree Structure. In: Rong, C., Jaatun, M.G., Sandnes, F.E., Yang, L.T., Ma, J. (eds.) ATC 2008. LNCS, vol. 5060, pp. 540–554. Springer, Heidelberg (2008)

21. Wang, Y., Kitsuregawa, M.: Use link-based clustering to improve Web search results. In: Procs. of the Second Intern. Conf. on Web Information System Engineering (WISE 2001), Kyoto, Japan (December 2001)

22. Weiner, P.: Linear pattern matching algorithms. In: 14th Annual Symposium on Foundations of Computer Science, USA, October 1973, pp. 1–11 (1973)

23. Weiss, D., Stefanowski, J.: Web search results clustering in Polish: Experimental evaluation of Carrot. In: Procs. of the International IIS: Intelligent Information Processing and Web Mining (IIPWM 2003), Zakopane, Poland (June 2003)

24. Xing, D., Xue, G.R., Yang, Q., Yu, Y.: Deep classifier: Automatically categorizing search results into large-scale hierarchies. In: Procs. of the Intern. Conf. on Web Search and Web Data Mining (WSDM 2008), Palo Alto, California, USA, February 2008, pp. 139–148 (2008)

25. Zamir, O., Etzioni, O.: Web document clustering: A feasibility demonstration. In: Procs. of the 21th Annual Intern. ACM Conf. on Research and Development in Information Retrieval (SIGIR 1998), Melbourne, Australia, August 1998, pp. 46–54 (1998)

26. Zamir, O., Etzioni, O.: Grouper: A dynamic clustering interface to web search results. Computer Networks 31(11-16), 1361–1374 (1999)
27. Zeng, H.J., He, Q.C., Chen, Z., Ma, W.Y., Ma, J.: Learning to cluster web search results. In: Procs. of the 27th Annual Intern. Conf. on Research and Development in Information Retrieval (SIGIR 2004), Sheffield, UK, July 2004, pp. 210–217 (2004)
28. Zhang, D., Dong, Y.: Semantic, Hierarchical, Online Clustering of Web Search Results. In: Yu, J.X., Lin, X., Lu, H., Zhang, Y. (eds.) APWeb 2004. LNCS, vol. 3007, pp. 69–78. Springer, Heidelberg (2004)

Spatio-Temporal-Thematic Analysis of Citizen Sensor Data: Challenges and Experiences

Meenakshi Nagarajan, Karthik Gomadam, Amit P. Sheth, Ajith Ranabahu, Raghava Mutharaju, and Ashutosh Jadhav

Knoesis Center, Wright State University, Dayton, OH, USA
{meena,karthik,amit,ajith,raghava,ashutosh}@knoesis.org

Abstract. We present work in the **spatio-temporal-thematic** analysis of citizen-sensor observations pertaining to real-world events. Using Twitter as a platform for obtaining crowd-sourced observations, we explore the interplay between the 3 dimensions in extracting insightful summaries of observations. We present our experiences in building a web mashup application, *Twitris*[1] that also facilitates the spatio-temporal-thematic exploration of **social signals** underlying events.

1 Introduction

The emergence of mircoblogging platforms like Twitter, friendfeed etc. have revolutionized how unfiltered, real-time information is disseminated and consumed by citizens. A side effect of this has been the rise of citizen journalism, where humans as sensors are "playing an active role in the process of collecting, reporting, analyzing and disseminating news and information"[1]. A significant portion of information generated and consumed by this interconnected network of participatory citizens is *experiential* in nature [2], i.e., contains first-hand observations, experiences, opinions made in the form of texts, images, audio or video about *real-world events*. In the recent past, such experiential attributes of an event have proved valuable for crowdsourced situational awareness applications. An example of this are observations that originated from Mumbai during the 2008 terrorist attacks. The relayed multimodal observations (texts, images and videos) formed a rich backdrop against traditional reports from the news media.

Perhaps, the most interesting phenomenon about such citizen generated data is that it acts as a lens into the social perception of an event in any region, at any point in time. Citizen observations about the same event relayed from the same or different location offer multiple, and often complementary viewpoints or storylines about an event. What is more, these viewpoints evolve over time and with the occurence of other events, with some perceptions gaining momentum in certain regions after being popular in some others.

Consequently, in addition to what is being said about an event (theme), where (spatial) and when (temporal) it is being said are integral components to the

---

[1] http://en.wikipedia.org/wiki/Citizen_journalism

G. Vossen, D.D.E. Long, and J.X. Yu (Eds.): WISE 2009, LNCS 5802, pp. 539–553, 2009.

analysis of such data. The central thesis behind this work is that citizen sensor observations are inherently multi-dimensional in nature and taking these dimensions into account while processing, aggregating, connecting and visualizing data will provide useful organization and consumption principles.

Such an n-dimensional analysis is analogous to past efforts in processing of social stream, newswire or blog data where thematic, temporal, spatial and social aspects of the data have been taken into account. In [3], the goal was to extract events from social text streams taking content, social, and temporal aspects into account. An event in their work is a set of text pieces (topically clustered) conditioned by social actors that talk about the same topic over a certain time interval with similar information flow patterns. Work in [4] attempts to identify spatiotemporal thematic patterns in blog data. They extract common themes (semantically coherent topics defined over a text collection) from weblogs and subsequently generate theme life cycles for a given location and theme snapshots for a given time period. [5] used a graph-theoretic approach to discover storylines or latent themes among the top search results for a query.

In our work, we do not attempt to identify available latent themes, storylines or events in a given corpus of text. We start with a corpus of observations pertinent to an event and attempt to extract meaningful units that are good descriptors of the underlying event. We also take an *entity-driven approach* to summarize social perceptions in citizen observations, as opposed to a document collection approach in past efforts. We also do not concern ourselves with the social aspect or attributes of the poster. Since our goal is to facilitate summaries for situation awareness applications we care more about "knowing what is going on so you can figure out what to do" [6].

1.1   Contributions

Our work is motivated by the need to easily assess local and global social perceptions or **social signals** underlying events over time. Data pertaining to real-world events have unique characteristics because of the event they represent. Certain real-world events naturally have a spatial and temporal bias while some others do not. For example, when observing what India is saying about the Mumbai attack, one might wish not to be biased by global and possibily contrasting perceptions from Pakistan. The larger goal of our ongoing work is to perform a spatial, temporal and thematic integration of citizen sensor observations. In this paper, we present the first step in this direction - analyzing data in these three dimensions to study what constitutes good **spatial, temporal and thematic slices** of observations underlying events.

Using Twitter as our platform for observations, we find that the confluence of space, time and theme in analyzing tweets allows us to extract insightful summaries of citizen perceptions behind events. Of the many analysis that are possible over Twitter data and available metadata for extracting social perceptions, we conduct the following investigations in our work:

1. What is a region paying attention to today? Our first goal is to extract meaningful descriptors or entities, i.e. *key words and phrases*, from mass citizen observations pertaining to an event for any spatial and temporal setting. Selecting discriminatory keywords has been a problem of historical importance with probability distribution methods like TFIDF being the most popular [7]. In our work, cues for a descriptor's importance are found in a corpus, in space and time. Consider this scenario where two descriptors 'mumbai attacks' and 'hawala funding' pertaining to the Mumbai Terror Attack occurred in the Tweets[2] originating from the US on the same day. The phrase 'Mumbai attacks' occurred every day the last week while 'hawala funding' is a new descriptor for today. Users are more likely to be interested in novel perspectives and experiences. Looking at spatial contexts, we also find that 'hawala funding' did not appear in any other country on the same day, while 'mumbai attacks' occured in almost all countries that day. This suggests that the discussion around 'hawala funding' is a perspective shared by citizens local to this spatial setting while 'mumbai attacks' is a weaker descriptor in terms of uniqueness to the local region. Our algorithm exploits this *interplay between space, theme and time* in order to cull out words and phrases that best summarize citizen observations.

2. What are they saying about the entity or descriptor? Since the social perception of an event may vary within and between spatial regions and temporal settings, there is a need to group and understand the context of discussion or storylines surrounding a descriptor. Using well understood principles of information theory, we extract an entity's strong thematic context i.e. strongly associated descriptors, while taking into account its spatial and temporal settings. Figure 4(a) shows an example of discussions surrounding two event descriptors, in different countries on the same day that we were able to extract.

Our approach to presenting extracted descriptors and surrounding adopts the interface design paradigm of *experience design*[3]. One of the goals of experience design is to consider the multiple contexts surrounding the use of an application and create unified user interaction models across all contexts. Our challenge was to create a visualization model that allows users to browse thematic descriptors of events in their spatio-temporal contexts.

We present our approach for extracting and visualizing event descriptors as an implemented system, Twitris [1] (a portmanteau of Twitter and Tetris, for aranging activity in space, time and theme) that allows users to browse extracted summaries of citizen-sensor activity. Ideally, evaluating our system would involve measuring the efficacy of our algorithms in extracting event descriptors and the effectiveness of our interface in summarizing user activity. Owing to space restrictions, we limit our discussion in this paper to only the description of the Twitris system. Evaluations will be made available in an extended version of this paper at [1].

In the rest of this paper, we present our challenges and experiences in obtaining close to real-time citizen observations from Twitter (section 2), processing

---

[2] 140 character long messages posted by users on Twitter.
[3] http://en.wikipedia.org/wiki/Experience_design

them in space, theme and time (section 3) and presenting the extracted summaries within their multi-dimensional contexts (section 4).

2   System Overview

Twitris is currently designed to
- Collect user posted tweets pertaining to an event from Twitter
- Process obtained tweets to extract key descriptors and surrounding discussions
- Present extracted summaries to users
The duration and intervals of data collection and processing are configured based on the event being analyzed. Figure 1 illustrates the various steps and services involved in data collection, analysis and visualization.

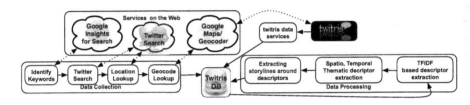

Fig. 1. Data Collection, analysis and visualizing in Twitris

Gathering Topically Relevant Data

The process of obtaining citizen observations from Twitter deserves some explanation since Twitter does not explicitly categorize user messages into topics. However, there is a search API[4] to extract tweets. A recent trend in Twitter has been the community-driven convention of adding additional context and metadata to tweets via *hashtags*, that can also be used to retrieve relevant tweets. Hashtags are similar to tags on Flickr, except they are added inline to a tweet. They are created simply by prefixing a word with a hash symbol, for example, users would tag a tweet about Madonna using the hashtag #madonna.

Our strategy for obtaining posts relevant to an event uses a set of seed keywords, their corresponding hashtags and the Twitter search API. Seed keywords are obtained via a semi-automatic process using Google Insights for Search[5], a free service from Google that provides top searched and trending keywords across specific regions, categories, time frames and properties. The intuition is that keywords with high search volumes indicate a greater level of social interest and therefore more likely to be used by posters on Twitter.

We start with a search term that is highly pertinent to an event and get top X keywords during a time period from Google Insights. For the g20 summit event for example, one could use the keyword g20 to obtain seed keywords. These keywords are manually verified for sufficient coverage for posts using the Twitter

---

[4] http://search.twitter.com/search.json
[5] http://www.google.com/insights/search/

Search API, placed in set $\hat{K}$, and used to kick-start the data collection process. Past this step, the system automatically collects data every few hours. The list of keywords $\hat{K}$ is also continually updated using two heuristics:

1. The first uses Google Insights to periodically obtain new keywords using keywords in $\hat{K}$ as the starting query.
2. The second uses the corpus of tweets collected so far to detect popular keywords that were not previously used for crawling. A keyword is considered to be a good data extractor if it has a high TFIDF score [7] and high collocation scores with the keywords in $\hat{K}$. The keyword with the highest score is periodically added to the set $\hat{K}$.

In this work, we collected data for three events - one long-running global financial crisis event and two short-lived events, the g20 summit and the Mumbai terror attack event. The nature of an event determines the strategy for data collection. For long-running events, data is collected on a regular basis but in longer intervals. Shorter events demand more frequent data collection and continuous update of keywords.

Spatial, Temporal and Thematic Attributes of Twitter Posts. The content of a Twitter post is the thematic component of a citizen observation. In this work, we ignore urls and links posted by users in a tweet and only use the textual component.

Spatial attributes for Twitter data can be of two types - location where the data originated from, and the location mentioned *in* the content. We do not concern ourselves with the latter since our goal is to study the social signals *originating* from a location in response to an event. There are two ways to obtain the spatial information associated with a tweet. The first method is to provide a location as a parameter to the search API. The other is to use the poster's location as an approximation for the origination of the tweet. We adopt the second alternative, as our crawl needs to be location independent.

The location information for an author either has geocoordinates (in cases where GPS enabled devices were used in accessing Twitter) or has a location descriptor (city, state or country) free-text information provided by posters in their profiles. In case of the former, we use the coordinate information as is, while in the latter, we make use of Google GeoCoding API [6] to identify the coordinates. We realize the limitations of this approach (for example, an author might have posted a tweet from Boston, but updated his location later), but given the lack of geocoding information in the tweets, we consider this approach as a sufficient approximation.

For this work, we collected nearly 310,000 tweets for the financial crisis event starting from Nov 22 2008, out of which we could get location information for nearly 160,000 tweets. Nearly 76% of this data was contributed by users in the US. We collected approximately 75,000 tweets for the g20 event between March 9, 2009 and April 10, 2009; 50,000 of which had location information. Majority

---

[6] http://code.google.com/apis/maps/documentation/geocoding/index.html

of these tweets originated from the US or the UK (57% and 21% respectively). For the Mumbai terror attack, data was collected between November 29, 2008 and February 28th, 2009. We collected around 10,000 tweets, 6000 of which had location information. Over 70% of these tweets originated from the US and India (38% and 34% respectively).

The temporal information for each tweet is obtained from the time the tweet was posted (available via the API). Since we are interested in social signals over time, we do not concern ourselves with identifying temporal information that might be available *in* the content of a tweet.

We model a tweet t as a 4-tuple; $t = \{t_{id}, t_c, t_t, t_g\}$ where t_{id} is a unique alpha-numeric identifier, t_c is the textual content, t_t and t_g are the time and geographical coordinates obtained for the tweet. $t_g = \{lat, lng\}$ where lat is the latitude and lng is the longitude of the geographical coordinates of t_g.

3   Processing Citizen Observations

Fundamental to the processing of citizen observations is a simple intuition - "depending on what the event is, social perceptions and experiences reported by citizen sensors might not be the same across spatial and temporal boundaries". One of the goals in the formulation of our algorithm was to preserve these different story-lines that naturally occur in data. The two questions we wish to answer via our work are:

a. For any given spatial location and temporal condition, can we get an idea of what entities or event descriptors are dominating the discussion in citizen observations?

b. If we know dominant descriptors, can we tell what people are saying about them in different parts of the world and over time?

Broadly, our entity-centric approach to summarizing observations in its three-dimensional space consists of the following steps – partitioning available observations into processable sets based on spatial and temporal biases induced by an event, extracting key descriptors and their contexts.

3.1   Defining Spatio-Temporal Sets

Different events have different spatial and temporal biases that need to be considered while processing observations pertaining to the event. We first partition the volume of tweets into spatio-temporal sets based on two tuneable parameters - the spatial parameter δ_s and the temporal parameter δ_t. Together these two define the granularity at which we are interested in analyzing observations. δ_s for example is defined to cover a spatial region - a continent, a country, city etc. Similarly, δ_t is defined along the time axis of hours, days or weeks.

Depending on the spatial and temporal bias that an event has, the user picks values for δ_s and δ_t. In the Mumbai event for example, there might be interest in looking at *country level* activity on a *daily* basis. For longer running events like the financial crisis, we might be interested in looking at *country level* activity on a *weekly* basis. For events local to a country, a possible split could be by cities.

Using these two parameters, we slice our data into *Spatio-Temporal Sets* $S=\{S_1,S_2...S_n\}$ where n is the number of sets generated by first partitioning using δ_s and next using δ_t. If δ_s = 'country' and δ_t = '24 hour', observations are grouped into separate spatial (country) clusters. Every spatial set is then divided further into sets that group observations per day, generating n spatio-temporal sets.

Observations are grouped in a spatio-temporal set depending on the values they have for their timestamps and geocode attributes (see Section 2). A spatio-temporal set can be represented as $S_i=\{T_i,\delta_{si},\delta_{ti}\}$ where $T_i=\{t_1,t_2,..\}$ is a set of tuples where $t_i=\{t_{id},t_c,t_t,t_g\}$ such that $\forall t_i \in T_i$; $t_g \in \delta_{si}$ and $t_t \in \delta_{ti}$. By processing sets in isolation for key descriptors, we ensure that the social signals present in one do not amplify or discount the effect of signals in the other sets.

3.2   Extracting Strong Event Descriptors

Given a spatio-temporal set definition, we proceed to extract strong descriptors that are local to this set. In other words, extracted descriptors need to preserve the social signals local to a spatio-temporal set. This can trivially be a function of the probability distribution of the descriptors in the corpus T_i defined by the spatio-temporal set. There has been a plethora of work in the area of extracting important keywords in a corpus [8]. In our case, there are additional strong cues in the entity's temporal and spatial contexts that could be exploited. Here, we formalize the interplay between the three dimensions and define functions that extract strong local event descriptors.

Considering each tweet t_i as a sequence of words, we define a descriptor in our work as a vector of n-grams [7]. Each t_i can then be represented as a vector of word tokens $ngrams_i=\{w_1,w_2,...\}$ where w_i is the weight of the ith n-gram. w_i is quantified as a function of the n-gram's thematic, spatial and temporal scores computed as follows. Note that the vector representation of each tweet is constructed after removing stop word unigrams, removing all url segments and domain specific stop words like retweet, rt@ etc. Lucene is used as the indexing mechanism. We also discard all hyperlinks and use only the text portion of tweets.

A. Thematic Importance of an event descriptor: We start by calculating the thematic score of an n-gram descriptor, $ngram_i(tfidf)$, as a function of its TFIDF score in addition to using the following heuristics. These are necessary in order to extract meaningful descriptors from volumes of tweets.

1. The descriptor's TFIDF score is calculated from the Lucene index. This score reflects how important a word is to an observation in a collection of observations in the spatio-temporal set.
2. Supporting the intuition that descriptors with nouns in them are stronger indicators of meaningful entities, we parse a tweet using the Stanford natural

---

[7] We set $n=3$ in all our experiments.

language parser and amplify (add to) its TFIDF score by the fraction of words that are tagged as nouns.

3. The TFIDF score is also amplified based on the fraction of words that are not stop words.

4. Lower and higher-order n-grams that have overlapping segments ('general' and 'general motors') and the same TFIDF scores are filtered by picking the higher-order n-gram. The n-grams in each observation are sorted by their $ngram_i(tfidf)$ score and the top 5 are picked for further analysis. Picking top 5 is a satisfactory filter given that the length of our observations is at most 140 characters.

Owing to the varied vocabulary used by posters to refer to the same descriptor, region specific dictions and evolving popularity of words, we found that the above thematic score was not representative of a descriptor's importance. Consider this scenario where the phrase 'Big 3' meant to refer to the three car giants 'GM', 'Ford' and 'Chrysler' was not used as frequently as the three words together or vice versa. The presence of contextually relevant words should ideally strengthen the score of the descriptor. However, we also need to pay attention to changing viewpoints in citizen observations that may result in descriptors occuring in completely different contexts. If the usage of 'Ford' is not in the context of the 'Big Three', i.e. discussions around Ford surround its new 'Ford Focus' model, its presence should not affect 'Big Three's' importance.

Contextually Enhanced Thematic Score: Here, we describe how the thematic score of an extracted descriptor, 'Big 3' in the above example, is amplified as a function of the importance of its strong associations - 'General Motors', 'Ford' and 'Chrysler' and the association strengths between the descriptor and the associations. For sake of brevity, let us call the $ngram_i$ descriptor whose thematic score we are interested in affecting as the focus word fw and its strong associations as $C_{fw}=\{aw_i,aw_2...\}$. The thematic score of the focus word is then enhanced as:

$$fw(th)=fw(tfidf)+\sum assoc_{str}(fw,aw_i)*aw_i(tfidf) \qquad (1)$$

where $fw(tfidf)$ and $aw_i(tfidf)$ are the TFIDF scores of the focus and associated word as per Step 3 in the previous section; $assoc_{str}(fw,aw_i)$ is the association strength between the focus word and the associated word. Here we describe how we find strong associations for a focus word and compute $assoc_{str}$ scores.

Our algorithm begins by first gathering all possible associations for fw and places it in C_{fw}. We define *associations* or the *context of a word* as thematically strong descriptors (in the top 5 n-grams of an observation) that co-occur with the focus word in the given spatio-temporal corpus. The goal is to amplify the score of the focus word only with the strongly associated words in C_{fw}. One way to measure strength of associations is to use word co-occurence frequencies in language [9]. Borrowing from past success in this area, we measure the association strength between the focus word and the associated words $assoc_{str}(fw,aw_i)$ using the notion of point-wise mutual information in terms of co-occurrence statistics. We measure $assoc_{str}$ scores as a function of the point-wise mutual information between the focus word and the *context of* aw_i. This is done to ensure that the association strengths are determined *in the contexts* that the descriptors occur in. Let us call the contexts for aw_i as $Caw_i = \{caw_1, caw_2 ..\}$, where caw_k's are thematically strong descriptors that collocate with aw_i. $assoc_{str}(fw, aw_i)$ is computed as:

$$assoc_{str}(fw, aw_i) = \frac{\sum_k (pmi(fw, caw_k))}{|Caw_i|}, \forall caw_k \in Caw_i$$

where the point-wise mutual information between fw and caw_k (the context of aw_i), is calculated as:

$$pmi(fw, caw_k) = log \frac{p(fw, caw_k)}{p(fw)p(caw_k)} = log \frac{p(caw_k|fw)}{p(caw_k)} \tag{2}$$

where $p(fw) = \frac{n(fw)}{N}$; $p(caw_k|fw) = \frac{n(caw_k, fw)}{n(fw)}$; $n(fw)$ is the frequency of the focus word; $n(caw_k, fw)$ is the co-occurrence count of words caw_k and fw; and N is the number of tokens. All statistics are computed with respect to the corpus defined by the spatio-temporal setting. As we can see, this score is not symmetric and if the context of aw_i is poorly associated with fw, $assoc_{str}(fw, aw_i)$ is a low score.

At the end of evaluating all associations in C_{fw}, we pick those descriptors whose association scores are greater than the average association scores of the focus word and all associations in C_{fw}. The thematic weights of these associations along with their strengths are plugged into Eqn 1 to compute the enhanced thematic score $ngram_i(th)$, of the n-gram descriptor.

B. Temporal Importance of an event descriptor: While the thematic scores are good indicators of what is important in a spatio-temporal setting, certain descriptors tend to dominate discussions. In order to allow for less popular, possibly interesting descriptors to surface, we discount the thematic score of a descriptor depending on how popular it has been in the recent past. The temporal discount score for a n-gram, a tuneable factor depending on the nature of the event, is calculated over a period of time as:

$$ngram_i(te) = temporal_{bias} * \sum_{d=1}^{D} \frac{ngram_i(th)^d}{d}$$

where $ngram_i(th)^d$ is the enhanced thematic score of the descriptor on day d, D is the duration for which we wish to apply the dampening factor, for example, the recent week. However, this temporal discount might not be relevant for all applications. For this reason, we also apply a $temporal_{bias}$ weight ranging from 0 to 1 - a weight closer to 1 gives more importance, while a weight closer to 0 gives lesser importance to past activity.

C. Spatial Importance of an event descriptor: We also discount the importance of a descriptor based on its occurence in other spatio-temporal sets. The intuition is that descriptors that occur all over the world on a given day are not as interesting compared to those that occur only in the spatio-temporal set of interest. We define the spatial discount score for an n-gram as a fraction of spatial sets or partitions (e.g. countries) that had activity surrounding this descriptor.

$$ngram_i(sp) = \frac{k}{|spatio-temporalsets|} * (1 - spatial_{bias})$$

Event descriptors sorted by their TFIDF scores				Event descriptors sorted by their enhanced spatio-temporal-thematic scores			
mumbai	1.4553	pakistan pres promised	1.0065	foreign relations perspective	1.7185	photographers capture images	1.3028
photographers capture images	1.3998	mumbai attacks	0.9594	india prime minister	1.5853	rejected evidence provided	1.2933
images of mumbai	1.2792	foreign relations	0.9490	country of india	1.5295	mumbai attacks	1.2048
foreign relations perspective	1.2165	rejected evidence	0.8741	pakistan pres promised	1.5080	images of mumbai	1.1822
attacks in mumbai	1.1261	evidence provided	0.8741	foreign relations	1.4510	mumbai	1.1083
photographers capture	1.0986	uk indicating	0.8741	rejected evidence	1.3758	mumbai attacks in	1.0797
capture images	1.0986	mumbai attacks in	0.7927	evidence provided	1.3758	photographers capture	1.0017
india prime minister	1.0839	rejected evidence provided	0.7916	uk indicating	1.3758	capture images	1.0017
country of india	1.0280			attacks in mumbai	1.3293		

(a)

Day1	Day2	Day3	Day4	Day5
world india blasts	november 2008 donation	liking	mumbai outfit bjp	foreign relations perspective
blasts pakistani denial	manmohan singh	terror outfit	terror backlash	india prime minister
india blasts pakistani	solution india	work	india network	country of india
world india	2008 donation page	teachings	paki gov	pakistan pres promised
attack mahal	donation page provided	assisting terror outfits	punjabi taliban	foreign relations
denial on terrorism	newspakistan seeks	mafia assisting terror	obama aide	rejected evidence
hotels scarred	closure	statesman terror mafia	backlash	uk indicating
month attack mahal	rtt news voice	india expert	cripple	photographers capture images
terror hotels	long term damage	terrorist attacks awaken	earthquake dia plane	rejected evidence provided
nri family	economy manmohan singh	teachings exposed	strife china earthquake	mumbai attacks
alleged terror attacker	attacks in mumbai	attacks awaken bollywood	terrorism pakistan	images of mumbai
a month attack	quickfix solution india	film stars dictate	thing terrorism	mumbai
defiant terror inches	seeks closure	terror mafia assisting	war on terror	mumbai attacks in
terror attacker seeks	terror attack	revision of history	a mumbai outfit	
newsnri family drawn	manmohan singh rtt	efforts asks china	attack punjabi taliban	

(b)

Fig. 2. (a) Extracted descriptors sorted by TFIDF vs. spatio-temporal-thematic scores (b) Top 15 extracted descriptors in the US for Mumbai attack event across 5 days

where k = number of spatio-temporal sets the n-gram occured in. Similar to the temporal bias, we also introduce a $spatial_{bias}$ that gives importance to local vs. global activity for the descriptor on a scale of 0 to 1. A weight closer to 1 does not give importance to the global spatial discount while a weight closer to 0 gives a lot of importance to the global presence of the descriptor.

Depending on the event of interest, both these discounting factors can also vary for different spatio-temporal sets. For example, when processing tweets from India for the Mumbai attack setting the $spatial_{bias}$ to 1 eliminates the influence of global social signals. While processing tweets from the US, one might want a stronger global bias given that the event did not originate there. Both these parameters are set before we begin the processing of observations.

Finally, the spatial and temporal effects are discounted from the final score, making the final spatio-temporal-thematic (STT) weight of the n-gram as

$$w_i = ngram_i(th) - ngram_i(te) - ngram_i(sp) \tag{3}$$

Figure 2(a) illustrates the effect of our enhanced STT weights for extracted event descriptors pertaining to the Mumbai terror attack event, in the US on a particular day. We used a temporal bias of 1 suggesting that past activity was important and a spatial bias of 0 giving importance to the global presence of the descriptor. As we see, descriptors generic to other spatial and temporal settings (e.g., mumbai and mumbai attacks) get weighted lower, allowing the more interesting ones to surface higher.

Figure 2(b) shows top 15 extracted descriptors in the US across five days (days that had atleast three citizen observations). As we see, the descriptors extracted

)y our system offer a good indication of what is being talked about on those
lays. In an ongoing user study, we are showing users tweets on any given day
.nd investigating how useful descriptors extracted by our system are compared
o those generated using the TFIDF baseline. Results of the same will be made
.vailable at [1].

₿.3 Discussions around Event Descriptors

Vhile it is useful to know what entities people are talking about, there might be
lifferent storylines surrounding these entities that could offer an insight into the
ocial perceptions of an event. The goal here is to thematically group discussions
urrounding event descriptors, while also allowing users to observe how these
liscussions change over time and space. We take a simple clustering approach
o this problem, forming k clusters, each representing a viewpoint or storyline
vithin a spatio-temporal setting. While this is similar in spirit to clustering of
locuments to reveal storylines as presented in [5], we use a mutual information
based approach.

Let us call the n-gram of interest as the *focus word* fw. The steps involved in
dentifying storylines surrounding fw are the following (see Figure 3):

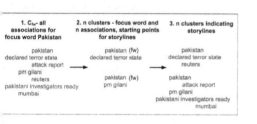

1. As in our previous algorithm, we find all associations
for a focus word; $C_{fw}=\{aw_i, aw_2...\}$,
i.e. thematically strong descriptors that collocate with the fw
in the given spatio-temporal
corpus.

2. In order to pick cues for complementary viewpoints, we pick n
associations from C_{fw} such that
$n<|C_{fw}|$ and all n associations
are weakly associated with each

Fig. 3. Extracting discussions around descrip-
ors

other (lending support for separate threads of discussions). Weak associations
.re indicated by negative pmi scores (see computed association strengths in the
.arlier section). As before, association strengths are computed only from the
underlying corpus of tweets in a spatio-temporal setting in order to preserve
ibserved signals. Figure 3 shows an example where 'Pakistan' is the focus word
.nd the 2 associations offering cues for separate storylines are 'declared terror
tate' and 'pm gilani'.

₿. For each of the n associations, we create a cluster populated with a pair
if words - the focus word and the association (see bullet 2 in Figure 3). The
.ssociation is further removed from C_{fw}. The idea is to expand each cluster pro-
ressively by adding strongly associated descriptors from C_{fw}. Descriptors are
.dded to a cluster if they result in a positive change in the *Information Content*
if the cluster [9], i.e. increase the amount of information that was present in the
luster.

Creating word clusters using association strengths have been used in the past for assigning words to syntactic and semantic categories, learning language models and so on.

The next step is to expand each of the n clusters. Let us refer to the cluster n_i with the focus word fw and one association word as $C1$ and the associations for fw, C_{fw} as $C2$. The idea is to gradually expand $C1$ by adding keywords from $C2$ that are strongly associated with $C1$. At every iteration, the algorithm measures the change in Information Content (IC) of $C1$, $IC(C1,k_i)_\delta$, before and after adding every descriptor k_i from $C2$ to $C1$ as:

$$IC(C1,k_i)_\delta = IC(C1,k_i) - IC(C1) \tag{4}$$

where $IC(C1,k_i)$ is the information content of $C1$ after adding keyword k_i from $C2$. $IC(C1,k_i)_\delta$ is *positive* when k_i is *strongly associated* with words in $C1$ and *negative* when k_i is *unrelated* to words in $C1$. $IC(C1)$ is the strength of the semantic associations between words in the cluster and is defined as the average pairwise Mutual Information (MI) of the words.

$$IC(C1) = MI(C1) \binom{|C1|}{2} \tag{5}$$

where $|C1|$ denotes the cardinality of the cluster $C1$ and $\binom{|C1|}{2}$ is the number of word pairs in the cluster $C1$, normalizing for clusters of different sizes. $MI(C1)$ is the Mutual Information of cluster $C1$, defined as the sum of pairwise mutual information of words within the cluster.

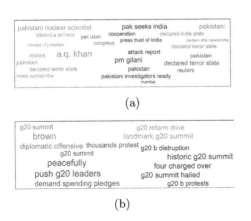

(a)

(b)

Fig. 4. (a) Discussions surrounding focus word "Pakistan" in the US (shades of blue), India (orange) and Pakistan (shades of red) on a particular day (b) Discussions surrounding focus word "g20" in Denmark across 4 days shown in different colors

$$MI(C1) = \sum_{w_i,w_j \in C1, i \neq j} PMI(w_i,w_j) \tag{6}$$

where $PMI(w_i,w_j)$ is reused from 2. The descriptor k_i from $C2$ that results in a positive and minimum $IC(C1,k_i)_\delta$ score is added to $C1$ and removed from $C2$. Additionally, keywords resulting in negative $IC(C1,k_i)_\delta$ scores are discarded as weak associations. The algorithm terminates when all keywords in $C2$ have been evaluated or when no more keywords in $C2$ have positive $IC(C1,k_i)_\delta$ scores (no strong associations with $C1$). All co-occurence statistics are obtained only from the underlying corpus of tweets in a spatio-temporal setting in order to preserve observed signals.

The reasoning behind picking the descriptor that offers a minimum delta as opposed to the maximum delta in Information Content is as follows. A keyword c_i occuring in specific contexts with words in $C1$ will increase the Information Content of the $C1$ relatively less than a keyword that occurs in generic contexts. This strategy has the tendency of adding specific to general keywords from $C2$ to $C1$. At the end of this process n clusters are populated with strongly associated descriptors from C_{fw}, with each cluster representing a viewpoint in terms of cohesive descriptors (see Figure 3). We note here that a descriptor can belong to more than one cluster. Figures 4(a) and 4(b) also provide examples showing viewpoints varying over space and time for two focus words, "Pakistan" and "g20". This view is different from what is available on Twitris and has been altered for presentation purposes.

Thematic Integration - Discussion: In this work, we do not attempt to reconcile descriptors that refer to the same real-world entity of interest i.e. we do not reconcile that 'pak istan' and 'pakistan' in Figure 4(a) are the same or that entity 'general motors' and 'gm' are the same. In our ongoing efforts we are using domain models culled from DBPedia [10] in addition to word-sense disambiguation techniques to disambiguate and annotate entity references. This will also allow us to thematically integrate citizen sensor observations.

4   User Interface and Visualization

The primary objective of the Twitris user interface is to integrate the results of the data analysis (extracted descriptors and surrounding discussions) with emerging visualization paradigms to facilitate *sensemaking*. Sensemaking, defined in [11], is the understanding of connections between people, places and events. Awareness of *who, what, when and where* is a critical component in sensemaking. Attributes of *who* posted a tweet does not play a role in this work. The Twitris user interface facilitates effective browsing of the *when, where*, and *what* slices of social perceptions behind an event. Figure 5(a) illustrates the theme, time and space components of the interface. To start browsing, users are required to select an event from the start screen (not shown due to space considerations). Once a theme is chosen by the user, the date is set to the earliest date of recorded observations for an event and the map is overlaid with markers indicating the spatial locations from which observations were made on that date. We call this the spatio-temporal slice. Users can further explore activity in a particular space by clicking on the overlay marker. The event descriptors extracted from observations in this spatio-temporal setting are displayed as a tag cloud. The current version of Twitris displays the top 15 descriptors weighted by their spatio-temporal-thematic (STT) scores. The STT scores determine the size of the descriptor in the tag cloud, illustrated in Figure 5(b).

At this stage, the descriptors serve as the focal point for further browsing and exploring of discussions or storylines. On clicking a descriptor of interest, the user is shown discussions surrounding the descriptor on that day from all spatial

Fig. 5. (a) Visualization components (b) Extracted *tag cloud* of descriptors for USA

regions (see sample in Figure 4(a)). We show all storylines on the same screen to allow users to contrast and compare complimentary discussions. The descriptors for these storylines are weighted by their STT scores. Subsequent interaction with any keyword leads the user to discussions surrounding the selected keyword. At any point in time, the user has the option of exiting this view and going back to the current spatio-temporal slice. The alpha version of Twitris can be accessed at http://twitris.dooduh.com.

5   Discussion and Conclusion

This work is a first step in the spatio-temporal-thematic integration of citizen-sensor observations. We presented our system Twitris, one possible approach for processing and presenting crowd-sourced, event related data in its naturally occuring spatio-temporal-thematic contexts. Our entity-driven approach allowed us to cull meaningful units of social perceptions and explore how their discussions varied across space and time. We posit that such crowd-sourced summaries can supplement situation awareness and decision-making applications.

Few other prototypes similar to ours are available today. VoteIndiaReport[8] is one such example of a collaborative citizen-driven election monitoring platform for the 2009 Indian general elections. Besides situation awareness applications where people can track what a crowd is saying, other possible applications of our work include, search over real-time event related data; monitoring of citizen opinions and sentiments across spatial distributions; studying patterns in evolution of citizen perceptions behind events etc. There are several other exciting avenues for future work. Some of immediate interest to us include the semantic annotation of extracted descriptors in order to facilitate integration of citizen-sensor observations.

References

1. Twitris: Twitter through space, time and theme, http://twitris.dooduh.com
2. Jain, R.: Experiential computing. Commun. ACM 46(7), 48–55 (2003)

---

[8] http://votereport.in/

3. Zhao, Q., Mitra, P., Chen, B.: Temporal and information flow based event detection from social text streams. In: AAAI, pp. 1501–1506 (2007)
4. Yang, Y., Pierce, T., Carbonell, J.: A study of retrospective and on-line event detection. In: SIGIR 1998, pp. 28–36. ACM, New York (1998)
5. Kumar, R., Mahadevan, U., Sivakumar, D.: A graph-theoretic approach to extract storylines from search results. In: KDD, pp. 216–225 (2004)
6. Adam, E.: Fighter cockpits of the future, October 1993, pp. 318–323 (1993)
7. Salton, G., Buckley, C.: Term-weighting approaches in automatic text retrieval. Information Processing and Management 24(5), 513–523 (1988)
8. Turney, P.: Extraction of keyphrases from text: Evaluation of four algorithms. Technical report, National Research Council, Institute for Information Technology (1997)
9. Church, K.W., Hanks, P.: Word association norms, mutual information, and lexicography. In: Proceedings of the 27th annual meeting on ACL (1989)
10. Thomas, C., Mehra, P., Brooks, R., Sheth, A.P.: Growing fields of interest - using an expand and reduce strategy for domain model extraction. In: Web Intelligence, pp. 496–502 (2008)
11. Klein, G., Moon, B., Hoffman, R.: Making sense of sensemaking 1: alternative perspectives. IEEE Intelligent Systems 21(4), 70–73 (2006)

Visual Mining of Web Logs with DataTube2

Florian Sureau[1], Frederic Plantard[1], Fatma Bouali[2,1], and Gilles Venturini[1]

[1] Université François Rabelais de Tours, Laboratoire d'Informatique,
64 Av. Jean portalis,
37200 Tours, France
`venturini@univ-tours.fr`
[2] Université de Lille2, IUT, Dpt STID,
2527, Rue du Maréchal Foch
59100 Roubaix, France
`Fatma.Bouali@univ-lille2.fr`

Abstract. We present in this paper a new method for the visual and interactive exploration of Web sites logs. Web usage data is mapped onto a 3D tube which axis represents time and where each facet corresponds to the hits of a given page and for a given time interval. A rearrangement clustering algorithm is used to create groups among pages. Several interactions have been implemented within this visualization such as the possibility to add annotations or the use of a virtual reality equipment. We present results for two Web sites (1148 pages over 491 days, and 107 pages over 625 days). We highlight the actual limits of our system (9463 pages over 153 days) and show that it outperforms similar existing approaches.

1 Introduction

Web usage mining (WUM) [1] is a challenging problem for data mining methods because it consists of analyzing large amount of complex and time-dependent data, and often with the constraint of presenting the results to non-expert in data mining. Among the WUM methods [2], we have concentrated our attention on those that involve the so-called Visual Data Mining (VDM) domain: these methods use data visualizations and interactions to let the user discover useful knowledge in an intuitive and interactive way [3] [4] [5]. They also facilitate the presentation of results to other people.

The remaining of this paper is organized as follows: section 2 describes existing VDM approaches for WUM and positions our work with respect to these approaches. Section 3 presents our approach, called DataTube2, and more precisely the organization of the visualization and the visual encoding of the data, the use of a rearrangement clustering algorithm, and finally, the graphical interactions (selection, annotations, etc) and their implementation in a virtual reality environment. Section 4 presents the results obtained on real Web logs. Section 5 concludes and proposes several perspectives on this work .

G. Vossen, D.D.E. Long, and J.X. Yu (Eds.): WISE 2009, LNCS 5802, pp. 555–562, 2009.

2   Existing Approaches: Visual Mining of Log Data

VDM methods applied to WUM should deal with a large amount of data and should take into account the complexity of the data and their temporal aspects. They should provide the user with easy to use and understand visualizations and interactions. Reaching these objectives is a challenging research task for VDM. One of the pioneers is probably Webviz [6] which displays a graph of web pages where links can be colored according to the visits to these pages. VisVIP [7] uses the same pages display principle but represents the web navigation as a curve, and the time spent on each page with a column. MIR [8] is one of the unique use of a metaphor to represent web logs: the web site is a city where each building represents a web page, and the users' navigation is represented by the moves of an avatar. Among the methods which can deal with the largest amounts of data, one must mention TimeTube [9] where the logs of a 7588 pages Web site have been represented (tree representation). This system has the advantage of representing the Web site structure, but its main drawback is that it gives time a minor role: only a few time instants are visualized. DataJewel [10] is another example which uses a calendar representation in conjunction with a pixel-based visualization (each day of the calendar is filled with pixels that represent access to pages for instance). Calendar representation is easy to understand for the user. However, the filling of the calendar does not help the user to perceive the absence of hits or pages with similar behavior. One must also mention the use of Kohonen's Self-Organizing Maps [11]) where pages are clustered together according to their co-occurrence in users navigation. Our method belongs to this last kind of methods where a priority is given to the amount of data and to knowledge discovery using a clustering algorithm.

Finally, one must mention basic plots and graphs of Web usage data as provided by commercial or industrial tools, like for example Google Analytics. Those tools are very useful for many web sites: they may trace the activity of a page, the global activity of a site, the origin of users, etc. When many pages are considered, such standard tools cannot provide for instance a graph that include the activity of all pages (such as TimeTube for instance). In addition, if one wishes to highlight additional information (pages with similar activities), then such functionalities are not provided by standard tools because the use of a clustering algorithm would be time-consuming.

3   DataTube2

3.1   Definition of the Visualization

From a general point of view, we consider that the temporal data to analyze is described with n attributes over k time steps (or intervals). These n attributes (denoted by $A_1, .., A_n$) are supposed to be numeric. Several scales can be used for the $t_1, ..., t_k$ time steps (e.g. hours, days, months, etc). The input data of our method can thus be represented as a $n \times k$ matrix where $A_i(t_j)$ denotes the value of the i-th attribute at time-step (or interval) t_j. As far as WUM is concerned,

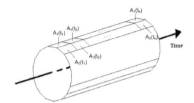

Fig. 1. Definition of the temporal tube

each attribute A_i represents for instance the number of hits of a page P_i of the considered Web site.

DataTube2 is initially based on Mihael Ankerst's DataTube visualization [12] that we have significantly extended in order to fit WUM requirements. This includes the addition of new visual elements and new interactions, the integration of a clustering algorithm, and the ability to deal with much larger amount of data (the initial version was apparently limited to $n = 50$ and $k < 100$). The visualization in DataTube2 uses a 3D temporal tube as shown in figure 1 where the tube axis represents the time flow and where each attribute value $A_i(t_j)$ is represented by a rectangular facet. A time-step t_j is thus represented as a ring in the tube, while the evolution of a given attribute over time is represented as a line which is parallel to the tube axis. We have defined several ways to visually encode the Web usage data: with colors (three values are defined by the user: minimum, intermediate, maximum), with the width of the facets, or with the height of the facets (w.r.t. the tube axis). These different modes can be combined together. Missing values (which may reflect the lack of event in the considered time interval) are represented in a default color (black, for example, in all of our visualizations).

We have added in DataTube2 an explicit time axis in order to give a scale for the time flow and to help the user in locating events over time. This axis takes the form of a "path" consisting of slabs, where each slab corresponds to a time-step t_i. This path is placed inside the tube, below the tube axis. The slabs are transparent in order to enable the perception of data located below them. In addition, a text label periodically indicates to which time-step a slab corresponds to. To highlight a given time-step, one can select it by clicking on the corresponding slab. Finally, the user can add annotations on the time axis.

3.2   Clustering Algorithm

Since many pages may have a similar activity, it is very important to help the user to visually detect those groups of pages, as well as other information about them like their size or the reason why they form a group. This greatly improves the clarity and the usefulness of the visualization. For this purpose, we have used a simple rearrangement clustering algorithm where similar attributes (i.e. with similar temporal behavior) are displayed next to each other in the tube. Many methods of such reorganization exist, including recent work like [13]. Here we use a classical and popular method for matrices reorganization, the Bond Energy Algorithm [14]. Its complexity is polynomial and we show in section 4 that it performs well.

3.3 Interactions

Regarding the navigation in the visualization, the user is initially placed at the tip of the tube axis and he faces the inside of the tube (see figure 2 for instance): he obtains a global view of all data, exhibiting for example, major trends, groups of similar pages (see previous section) and missing data (pages which did not exist yet, or pages which disappeared). Obtaining a zoom is achieved by "perspective effects" (data located far away from the user appears smaller and with less details than data close to the user) and by the user's moves: the sides of the tube are close to the central axis, which allows the user to quickly reach them and to locally observe attributes with more details.

Regarding the interactive selection of data, each facet is clickable. A left click triggers the display of the attribute name (page name for instance), the considered time-step and the value $A_i(t_j)$, in the upper right corner of the screen. A right click also enables to dynamically add annotations on a facet. Thus the user can store notes or "landmarks" related to the discovered knowledge and mark a special event in order to better observe its causes or consequences (for instance, an "advertising campaign" and its successive effects on the pages activities). The user can also use these annotations for the interactive presentations of data and extracted knowledge. These annotations can be either a graphical element such as an image chosen by the user or a visual marker (sphere). One can associate with these annotations a link (URL), a sound or a text displayed in a separate window.

DataTube2 can be run on a standard computer with a 2D screen. However, the perception of the third dimension is important in this tubular representation because it greatly helps the user to perceive the time flow (tube axis). So we have therefore develop the possibility to run DataTube2 in a virtual reality environment called VRMiner [15].

4 Results

We have applied DataTube2 to several logs obtained from real Web sites as shown in table 1. Our tests were performed on a MacBook Pro (2.4GHz Intel Core Duo, 4GB of RAM).

Table 1. Logs from real Web sites used for our experimental tests

Web site	# values	n	k	Vis. time	Clust. time	Clust. efficiency
Polytech	563 668	1148	491 days	1.4s	22.5s	1.19
Polytech-Init	1 447 839	9 463	153 days	34s	8 min.	1.03
Antsearch	66 875	107	625 days	407ms	234ms	1.39

In table 1, we have evaluated the execution times of both the visualization and clustering algorithms. In this table, "Vis. time" represents the time needed to build the visualization and "Clust. time" represents the time needed to reorganize the visualization with BEA. The construction of the visualization is linear and thus fast compared to BEA which requires more time especially when the number of pages increases (quadratic complexity). However the global execution time is quite acceptable for the user. In this table we have also measured the efficiency of the clustering algorithm both in a quantitative and visual way. "Clust. efficiency" is thus the ratio between the sum of similarities of adjacent attributes in the final reorganized visualization and the same sum but for the initial visualization. Obviously the clustering step reorganizes the visualization by placing pages with similar behavior next to each others.

We present now typical results and knowledge which can be visually extracted with our tool. In all visualizations, we have visually encoded the number of hits per day with a color ranging from green (low number of hits) to red (high number). First, the user initially has a global view of all log data, such as those represented in figure 2. On top of this figure, pages are ordered around the tube according to their date of creation, which results in a spiral-like shape. One immediately perceives the pages which, after their creation, do not receive much attention like the pages labeled "1" in the figure. It is also possible to detect the periods where no pages have been added to the site (see the area labeled "2" in the figure) or where many pages have been added (see area "3"). The area "4" corresponds to pages which, during a given time interval, received more attention than the others.

In the bottom of figure 2, the clustering algorithm has been used to group together pages with similar activities. One notices the many differences between the top (sorted by date of creation) and bottom pictures. The clustering algorithm groups together pages which were 1) created at the same time (period with no activity) and 2) which, once created, behave similarly. Many such groups can be detected (see for instance the groups labeled "A"). Then, more specific groups can be found. Group "B" corresponds to pages which, after a period of high activity, where not viewed anymore, and then viewed again. The webmaster may detect in such a way pages which are not accessible for some time. Finally, we highlight another group "C": this group can be divided into two subgroups which share important similarities and which were placed next to each others in the visualization.

We have let the Webmasters test DataTube2 and we report here the obtained comments. They were not aware of such a visualization tool before and they quickly learn its use. The time needed to explain the characteristics of the visualization and the interactions was short thanks to the tubular shape which can be easily explained and understood. These people were easily able to highlight the above-mentioned information and they especially appreciated being able to have a global view of the data. They were able to give name to groups of pages (i.e. "News", "Press", "Gallery", "Courses", etc) by recognizing specific clusters of pages with similar behavior, and were able to understand the shown behavior

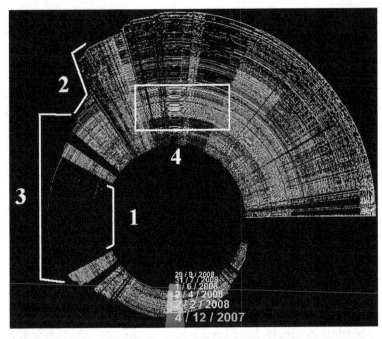

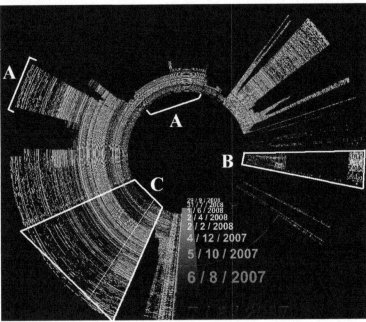

Fig. 2. DataTube2 typical visualizations: the first visualization (top) corresponds to the ordering of pages by date of creation, while the second one (bottom) is obtained after running the clustering algorithm (see text for explanation)

(like for instance pages dealing with "Courses" which often change). For the Polytech logs, the Webmaster has studied the influence of the end of the school period, the holidays and the beginning of the school on the site visits.

Finally, we have tested the actual maximum capacity of DataTube2 with a large amount of pages. In this case, pages have been ordered according to their date of creation, which results in a spiral that represents the history of the Web site since its creation. The activity of all pages is globally represented. We have a total amount of 9463 pages over 153 days. However, the interactions are limited because the frame rate of the display is too slow (about one per second). So this visualization should be considered as static, i.e. the user cannot easily move around. As mentioned in the next section, DataTube2 outperforms previous visualization of Web logs, both in terms of number of pages or time steps.

5 Discussion and Conclusion

We have presented here a new VDM method and its application to WUM. We have tested it on different web sites with hundreds of pages. Webmasters easily understood its functionalities. The clustering algorithm improves the visualization by showing similarities on pages access. So webmaster have a complete vision of the activity over time and are able to perceive at least the following information: the number of visits to web pages, the areas of a site which are difficult to reach and which receive a small number of hits, important times of the year, the week or the day (when an hour scale is selected). The user is also informed on groups of pages with similar activities. He may obtain a global view but also details on any part of the data. Moreover, we have implemented DataTube2 in a virtual reality in order to allow the user to efficiently explore and analyze the temporal aspect of the data.

Compared to industrial tools such as AWStats or Google Analytics, our visualization allows the user to perceive at once the activities of many more pages, as well as groups of pages with similar activities. We have shown that our implementation of DataTube may visualize about 1.500.000 values with a log of 9463 pages over 153 days (these numbers are higher than the values mentioned in the state of art of visual methods, but also for other non visual approaches [16]). If ones compares our results to those obtained in the VDM literature (see section 2) which, as far as we know, are the only one to visually handle large volumes of log data, one must notice that Datatube2 visualizes at least as many pages and many more time-steps than TimeTube [9] (limited to a few time steps), and many more pages than DataJewel [10] (limited to a few pages).

We are currently adding more interactions and graphical requests in the visualization, and we are preparing the visualization of other information such as users' sessions. In this case attributes would be the users and "time" steps would be the pages or groups of pages. We are also studying how to represent the structure of the Web site within the tubular representation.

References

1. Srivastava, J., Cooley, R., Deshpande, M., Tan, P.N.: Web usage mining: Discovery and applications of usage patterns from web data. SIGKDD Explorations 1(2), 12–23 (2000)
2. Facca, F.M., Lanzi, P.L.: Mining interesting knowledge from weblogs: a survey. Data Knowl. Eng. 53(3), 225–241 (2005)
3. Cleveland, W.S.: Visualizing Data. Hobart Press, New Jersey (1993)
4. Shneiderman, B.: The eyes have it: A task by data type taxonomy for information visualizations. In: IEEE Visual Languages. Number UMCP-CSD CS-TR-3665, College Park, Maryland 20742, U.S.A., pp. 336–343 (1996)
5. Wong, P.C., Bergeron, R.D.: 30 years of multidimensional multivariate visualization. In: Scientific Visualization — Overviews, Methodologies and Techniques, pp. 3–33. IEEE Computer Society Press, Los Alamitos (1997)
6. Pitkow, J., Bharat, K.: WEBVIZ: A Tool for World-Wide Web Access Log Visualization. In: Proceedings of the First International World Wide Web Conference, May 1994, pp. 271–277 (1994)
7. Cugini, J., Scholtz, J.: VISVIP: 3D visualization of paths through web sites. In: Proceedings of the Tenth International Workshop on Database and Expert Systems Applications, pp. 259–263 (1999)
8. Kizhakke, V.: MIR: A tool for visual presentation of web access behavior. Master's thesis. University of Florida (2000)
9. Chi, E., Pitkow, J., Mackinlay, J., Pirolli, P., Gossweiler, R., Card, S.: Visualizing the evolution of web ecologies. In: Proceedings of the Human Factors in Computing Systems, pp. 400–407 (1998)
10. Ankerst, M., Jones, D., Kao, A., Wang, C.: Datajewel: Tightly integrating visualization with temporal data mining. In: ICDM Workshop on Visual Data Mining (1996)
11. Benabdeslem, K., Bennani, Y., Janvier, E.: Visualization and analysis of web navigation data. In: Dorronsoro, J.R. (ed.) ICANN 2002. LNCS, vol. 2415, pp. 486–491. Springer, Heidelberg (2002)
12. Ankerst, M.: Visual Data Mining. PhD thesis, Faculty of Mathematics and Computer Science. University of Munich (2000) ISBN 3-89825-201-9
13. Climer, S., Zhang, W.: Rearrangement Clustering: Pitfalls, Remedies, and Applications. The Journal of Machine Learning Research 7, 919–943 (2006)
14. McCormick, W., Schweitzer, P., White, T.: Problem decomposition and data reorganization by a clustering technique. Operations Research 20(5), 993–1009 (1972)
15. Azzag, H., Picarougne, F., Guinot, C., Venturini, G.: Vrminer: A tool for multimedia database mining with virtual reality. In: Processing and Managing Complex Data for Decision Support, pp. 318–339 (2005)
16. Jin, X., Zhou, Y., Mobasher, B.: Web Usage Mining Based on Probabilistic Latent Semantic Analysis. In: Proceedings of the ACM SIGKDD Conference on Knowledge Discovery and Data Mining (KDD 2004), pp. 197–205 (2004)

Keys in XML:
Capturing Identification and Uniqueness

Michael Karlinger[1], Millist Vincent[2], and Michael Schrefl[1]

[1] Johannes Kepler University, Linz, Austria
{karlinger,schrefl}@dke.uni-linz.ac.at
[2] University of South Australia, Adelaide, Australia
millist.vincent@unisa.edu.au

Abstract. In this article a new type of key constraint in XML, called an *XKey*, is proposed. The motivation for an XKey is based on the observation that existing approaches do not always capture the fundamental properties of a key, namely identification and uniqueness, and it is shown that an XKey always has these properties. It is also shown that an XKey has the desirable property of extending the notion of a relational key.

Keywords: XML, Integrity Constraints, Keys.

1 Introduction

Integrity constraints are one of the oldest and most important topics in database research, and they find application in a variety of areas such as database design, data translation and data storage [1]. With the adoption of XML [2] as the industry standard for data interchange over the internet, and the increasing usage of XML as a format for the permanent storage of data in database systems [3], the study of integrity constraints in XML has increased in importance in recent years (cf. [4] for a recent survey of the topic).

While many different types of integrity constraints have been proposed and studied, the most important type of integrity constraint is probably a key constraint, irrespective of the data model used, since it is the fundamental means by which entities in a database can be identified. A very simple type of a key constraint for XML is offered by DTDs [2] in the form of an Id constraint. More sophisticated key frameworks have recently been proposed in [5], and in the **key** and the **uniqueness** constraints of XML Schema [2]. In these approaches, a key is syntactically defined by a statement of the form $(T, (P_1, \ldots, P_n))$, where T is a path referred to as the *selector* and $P_1, \ldots, P_n$ are paths called *fields*, and the semantics of a key then requires that T nodes in the XML tree (document) are identified by the combination of $P_1, \ldots, P_n$ nodes.

While these approaches have made an important contribution to the specification and study of XML keys, they have several important limitations that we now highlight in the following example. Suppose that we wish to store information about customers of a phone company. Two sample XML documents are shown in Fig. 1. Suppose also that the application specifies the constraint that customers are identified by the **code** and **number** of their phones,

G. Vossen, D.D.E. Long, and J.X. Yu (Eds.): WISE 2009, LNCS 5802, pp. 563–571, 2009.

(a)

```
<Customers>
<Customer name="Jones">
<Phone code="0660" number="44444"/>
</Customer>
<Customer name="Smith">
<Phone code="0660" number="11111"/>
<Phone code="0990" number="44444"/>
</Customer>
</Customers>
```

(b)

```
<Customers>
<Customer name="Miller">
<Phone code="0880" number="33333"/>
<Phone code="0880" number="33333"/>
</Customer>
</Customers>
```

Fig. 1. Example XML Documents Representing Customers and their Phones

i.e. the key is $\kappa = $ (Customers.Customer, (Phone.code, Phone.number)), where Customers.Customer is the selector and Phone.code and Phone.number are the fields.

In reference to the approach of [5], its first limitation is that while it is intended to capture the *identification property* of a key, it does not always do this, as we now explain. From an intuitive view point, the XML document in Fig. 1a satisfies κ since the combination of code plus number of each phone is unique for the two customers. However, according to the semantics of [5], when there are multiple fields and there is more than one field node per field then all possible combinations of field nodes are required to identify the selector node. Hence κ is violated in Fig. 1a according to the semantics in [5], since both customer nodes have the field node combination of 0660 and 44444.

The second limitation of the approach in [5] is that it does not capture, nor was intended to capture, the *uniqueness property* of a key, which we now illustrate. In the XML document in Fig. 1b, key κ is satisfied according to the semantics in [5], which is however not desirable since the phone 0880/33333 is stored twice. This is a disadvantage, since having a key that is not unique results in redundancy and update problems similar to what occurs in relational databases. For example, if the code or number of one of the phones of Miller is modified but not the other, then the document becomes inconsistent.

XML Schema provides two types of identification constraints, a key constraint and a unique constraint, with the intention that a key constraint correspond to a primary key and a unique constraint correspond to a candidate key. The two constraints are both specified using the same syntax (given earlier), but have slightly different semantics. While a key constraint specifies that there must be at least one field node per field, a unique constraint allows the field nodes to be empty. Both constraints however require that, for each selector node and each field, there is at most one field node. So, for example, in Fig. 1a this would require that a customer can only have at most one phone, and so κ would be violated even though the combination of code plus number of each phone is unique and effectively identifies the customer it belongs to. We regard this approach as being too strict and not essential for capturing the identification

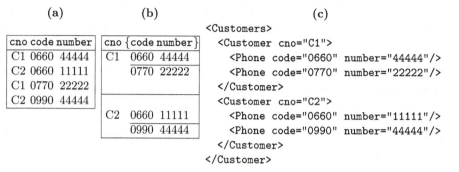

(a)   (b)   (c)

cno	code	number
C1	0660	44444
C2	0660	11111
C1	0770	22222
C2	0990	44444

cno	{code	number}
C1	0660	44444
	0770	22222
C2	0660	11111
	0990	44444

```
<Customers>
  <Customer cno="C1">
    <Phone code="0660" number="44444"/>
    <Phone code="0770" number="22222"/>
  </Customer>
  <Customer cno="C2">
    <Phone code="0660" number="11111"/>
    <Phone code="0990" number="44444"/>
  </Customer>
</Customer>
```

Fig. 2. Relation Phones **(a)** flat, **(b)** nested, and **(c)** mapped to XML

and uniqueness property of a key, and so we will later define a key constraint differently so that κ is satisfied in Fig. 1a (but not in Fig. 1b).

The second limitation of the work in [5], and the XML Schema constraints is that they do not extend the semantics of a relational key. To illustrate this, consider the following example, closely related to the one given earlier.

The relation shown in Fig. 2a stores details of phones and the customers that they belong to. The key for relation Phones is (code, number), and so code plus number identifies the number of a customer (cno), but cno does not identify code and number since a customer may have more than one phone.

We now map relation Phones to an XML document by first nesting on {code, number}, and then directly to an XML document as shown in Fig. 2. This mapping is an instance of a general method of mapping a relation to an XML document, which was originally presented in [6]. We also name the XML document as Customers, rather than Phones, to reflect the fact that the details of phones are now nested under cno as a result of the mapping. As a result of the nesting, cno is now unique in Customers and so, as one would expect, the key (Customers.Customer, (cno)) holds in Customers. However, since (code, number) is a key in Phones one would also expect that (code, number) identifies customers in Customers, and hence that the key (Customers.Customer, (Phone.code, Phone.number)) would hold. However, this is not the case under either the semantics of [5] or XML Schema, for the same reasons that the XML document in Fig. 1a violates κ.

Having an XML key constraint that extends the semantics of a relational key is important in several areas. Firstly, in the area of XML publishing [7], where a source relational database has to be mapped to a single predefined XML schema, knowing how relational integrity constraints map to XML integrity constraints allows the XML document to preserve more of the original semantics. This argument also applies to 'data-centric' XML [8], where XML databases (not necessarily with predefined schemas) are generated from relational databases.

The first contribution of our paper is to propose a new key constraint for XML, called an *XKey*. An XKey specifies that field nodes related by a semantic property called *closest* are required to be unique, thus obviously capturing the uniqueness property and eliminating the redundancy problems discussed earlier. However, we also show that a consequence of the uniqueness property of an XKey is that selector nodes are identified by field nodes, and so an XKey simultaneously captures both the uniqueness and identification properties of a key.

Our second contribution is to show that an XKey extends the semantics of a relational key, thus eliminating the third limitation of the existing approaches discussed earlier. We do this by showing that in the special case where the XML tree is derived from a flat relation by first mapping it to a nested relation by an arbitrary sequence of nest operations, then the XML tree satisfies an XKey if the flat relation satisfies the corresponding relational key.

The rest of the paper is organized as follows. Section 2 contains preliminary definitions, and Sect. 3 contains the definition of our XKey. Finally, Sect. 4 gives an overview over related work.

2 XML Trees, Paths and Reachable Nodes

In this section we present some preliminary definitions. First, following the model adopted by XPath and DOM [2], we model an XML document as a tree as follows. We assume countably infinite, disjoint sets **E** and **A** of element and attribute labels respectively, and the symbol $\mathcal{S}$ indicating text. Thereby, the set of labels that can occur in the XML tree, **L**, is defined by $\mathbf{L} = \mathbf{E} \cup \mathbf{A} \cup \{\mathcal{S}\}$.

Definition 1. *An XML tree* $\mathbb{T}$ *is defined by* $\mathbb{T} = (\mathbf{L}, \mathbf{V}, E, \mathrm{lab}, \mathrm{val}, v_\rho)$, *where*

– **V** *is a finite, non-empty set of nodes;*
– *the function* lab : $\mathbf{V} \to \mathbf{L}$ *assigns a label to every node in* **V**. *A node* v *is called an* element node *if* $\mathrm{lab}(v) \in \mathbf{E}$, *an* attribute node *if* $\mathrm{lab}(v) \in \mathbf{A}$, *and a* text node *if* $\mathrm{lab}(v) = \mathcal{S}$;
– $v_\rho \in \mathbf{V}$ *is a distinguished element node, called the* root node, *and* $\mathrm{lab}(v_\rho) = \rho$;
– *the parent-child relation* $E \subset V \times V$ *defines the directed edges connecting the nodes in* **V** *and is required to form a tree structure rooted at node* v_ρ. *Thereby, for every edge* $(v, \bar{v}) \in E$,
  1. v *is an element node and is said to be the* parent of $\bar{v}$. *Conversely,* $\bar{v}$ *is said to be a* child of v;
  2. *if* $\bar{v}$ *is an attribute node, then there does not exist a node* $\tilde{v} \in \mathbf{V}$ *and an edge* $(v, \tilde{v}) \in E$ *such that* $\mathrm{lab}(\tilde{v}) = \mathrm{lab}(\bar{v})$ *and* $\tilde{v} \neq \bar{v}$;
– *the partial function* val : $\mathbf{V} \to$ *string assigns a string value to every attribute and text node in* **V**.

We also denote the parent of node v in a tree by parent(v), and the set of ancestor nodes of v by ancestor(v). An example of an XML tree is presented in Fig. 3, which is the tree representation of the XML document in Fig. 2, where $\mathbf{E} = \{\rho, \mathtt{Customer}, \mathtt{Phone}\}$ and $\mathbf{A} = \{\mathtt{cno}, \mathtt{code}, \mathtt{number}\}$.

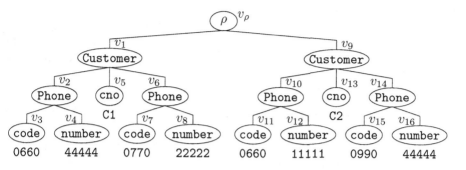

Fig. 3. Tree Representation of the XML Document in Fig. 1c

The notion of a path, which we now present together with some frequently required operators on paths, is central to all work on XML integrity constraints.

Definition 2. *A path $P = l_1. \cdots .l_n$ is a non-empty sequence of labels (possibly with duplicates) from* **L**. *Given paths $P = l_1. \cdots .l_n$ and $\bar{P} = \bar{l}_1. \cdots .\bar{l}_m$ we define*

- *P to be a* legal *path, if $l_1 = \rho$ and $l_i \in$ **E** $\forall i \in [1, n-1]$.[1]*
- *P to be a* prefix *of $\bar{P}$, denoted by $P \subseteq \bar{P}$, if $n \leq m$ and $l_i = \bar{l}_i \ \forall i \in [1, n]$.*
- *the* concatenation *of P and $\bar{P}$, denoted by $P.\bar{P}$, to be $l_1. \cdots .l_n.\bar{l}_1. \cdots .\bar{l}_m$.*
- *the* intersection *of P and $\bar{P}$ if both are legal paths, denoted by $P \cap \bar{P}$, to be the longest path that is a prefix of both P and $\bar{P}$.*
- *$\text{parent}(P) = l_1. \cdots .l_{n-1}$, if $n > 1$, to denote the parent path of P.*
- *$\text{last}(P) = l_n$ to denote the final label in P.*

For example, if **E** $= \{\rho, \text{Phone}\}$ and **A** $= \{\text{code}, \text{number}\}$ then code.Phone is a path but not a legal one, whereas ρ.Phone.code is a legal path. Also, ρ.Phone $\subseteq$ ρ.Phone.code and if $P = \rho$.Phone.code and $P' = \rho$.Phone.number, then $P \cap P' = \rho$.Phone.

We now define a path instance, which is essentially a downward sequence of nodes in an XML tree emanating from the root node.

Definition 3. *A path instance $p = v_1. \cdots .v_n$ is a non-empty sequence of nodes such that $v_1 = v_\rho$ and $\forall i \in [2, n], v_{i-1} = \text{parent}(v_i)$. The path instance p is said to be* defined over *a path $P = l_1. \cdots .l_n$, if $\text{lab}(v_i) = l_i \ \forall i \in [1, n]$.*

For example, referring to Fig. 3, $v_\rho.v_1.v_2$ is a path instance and it is defined over the path ρ.Customer.Phone.

The next definition specifies the set of nodes reachable in a tree from the root node by following a path.

Definition 4. *Given a tree $\mathbb{T} = (\mathbf{L}, \mathbf{V}, E, \text{lab}, \text{val}, v_\rho)$ and a path P, the function $N(P)$ returns the set of nodes defined by $N(P) = \{v \in \mathbf{V} \mid v$ is the final node in path instance p and p is defined over $P\}$.*

---

[1] $[1, n]$ denotes the set $\{1, \ldots, n\}$.

For instance, referring to Fig. 3, if $P = \rho.\texttt{Customer.cno}$, then $\mathrm{N}(P) = \{v_5, v_{13}\}$. We note that it follows from our tree model that for every node v in a tree $\mathbb{T}$ there is exactly one path instance p such that v is the final node in p and therefore $\mathrm{N}(P) \cap \mathrm{N}(\bar{P}) = \emptyset$ if $P \neq \bar{P}$. We therefore say that P is *the* path such that $v \in \mathrm{N}(P)$.

3 Defining an XML Key

In this section we present the syntax and semantics of our definition of an XKey, starting with the syntax. As noted previously, our syntactic framework is the same as that used in specifying **key** and **unique** constraints in XML Schema, and the framework used in [5] for specifying XML keys.

Definition 5. *An XKey is a statement of the form* $(T, (P_1, \ldots, P_n))$, *where* T *is a path called the* selector, *and* $P_1, \ldots, P_n$ *are paths called* fields, *such that for all* $i \in [1, n]$, $T.P_i$ *is a legal path that ends in an attribute or text label.*

We now compare this definition to the key constraint in XML Schema, which is the basis for the syntax of an XKey. (i) We only consider simple paths in the selectors and fields, whereas XML Schema allows for a restricted form of XPath expressions. (ii) In contrast to an XKey, an XML Schema key also allows for relative constraints, whereby the key constraint is only evaluated in part of the XML tree. (iii) The restrictions on fields means that we only consider the identification of selector nodes by text/attribute nodes, whereas the key constraint in XML Schema also allows for field nodes being element nodes.

We should mention that restrictions (i) - (iii) are not intrinsic to our approach, and Definition 5 can easily be extended to handle these extension. Our reason for not considering these extensions here is so that we can concentrate on the main contribution of our paper, which is to apply different semantics to an XKey so as to capture the identification and uniqueness property of a key.

To define the semantics of an XKey, we present first a definition, originally presented in [6], which is central to our approach and is what distinguishes it from other approaches. The intuition behind it is as follows. In defining relational integrity constraints, it is implicit that the relevant data values belong to the same tuple. The following *closest* definition extends this property of two data values belonging to the same tuple to XML, that is if two nodes in the tree satisfy the *closest* property, then 'they belong to the same tuple'.

Definition 6. *Given nodes* v_1 *and* v_2 *in an XML tree* $\mathbb{T}$, *the boolean function* closest(v_1, v_2) *is defined to return* true, *iff there exists a node* v_2^1 *such that (i)* $v_2^1 \in$ aancestor(v_1), *and (ii)* $v_2^1 \in$ aancestor(v_2), *and (iii)* $v_2^1 \in \mathrm{N}(P_1 \cap P_2)$, *where* P_1 *and* P_2 *are the paths such that* $v_1 \in \mathrm{N}(P_1)$ *and* $v_2 \in \mathrm{N}(P_2)$ *and the* aancestor *function is defined by* aancestor$(v) =$ ancestor$(v) \cup \{v\}$.

For instance in the tree in Fig. 3, closest(v_2, v_5) is true since $v_2 \in \mathrm{N}(\rho.\texttt{Customer.} \texttt{Phone})$, $v_5 \in \mathrm{N}(\rho.\texttt{Customer.cno})$ and $v_1 \in \mathrm{N}(\rho.\texttt{Customer})$ is an *aancestor* of both v_2 and v_5, where ρ.Customer $= \rho$.Customer.Phone $\cap \rho$.Customer.cno. Also, closest(v_1, v_5) is true since v_1 is an *aancestor* of both v_1 and v_5 and ρ.Customer $= \rho$.Customer $\cap \rho$.Customer.cno. However, closest(v_1, v_{13}) is false since $v_{13} \in \mathrm{N}(\rho$.Customer.cno$)$, but v_1 and v_{13} have no common *aancestor* node in $\mathrm{N}(\rho$.Customer$)$.

This leads to the definition of the semantics of an XKey.

Definition 7. *An XML tree* $\mathbb{T}$ *satisfies an XKey* $\sigma = (T, (P_1, \ldots, P_n))$, *denoted by* $\mathbb{T} \vDash \sigma$, *iff whenever there exist selector nodes* $\{v, v'\} \subseteq \mathrm{N}(T)$ *and sets of field nodes* $v_1, \ldots, v_n$ *and* $v'_1, \ldots, v'_n$ *such that*

i) $\forall i \in [1, n]$, $\{v_i, v'_i\} \subseteq \mathrm{N}(T.P_i)$ *and* $v_i \in \mathrm{ancestor}(v)$ *and* $v'_i \in \mathrm{ancestor}(v')$;
ii) $\forall i, j \in [1, n]$, $\mathrm{closest}(v_i, v_j) = \mathrm{closest}(v'_i, v'_j) = \mathrm{true}$;
iii) $\forall i \in [1, n]$, $\mathrm{val}(v_i) = \mathrm{val}(v'_i)$,
then $\forall i \in [1, n], v_i = v'_i$.

Clearly, our definition of an XKey captures the uniqueness property of the sets of field nodes in a key σ, since if $\mathbb{T} \vDash \sigma$ then there cannot exist two distinct sets of field nodes for σ that are value equal. Also, our definition captures the identification of selector nodes by the combination of field nodes. That is, if $\mathbb{T} \vDash \sigma$ and v, v' are selector nodes for σ, then $v = v'$ if there exist field nodes $v_1, \ldots, v_n$ for v and $v'_1, \ldots, v'_n$ for v' such that $\mathrm{val}(v_i) = \mathrm{val}(v'_i)$ for all $i \in [1, n]$. This is because if $v \neq v'$, then since $\mathbb{T}$ is a tree a field node cannot be a descendant of both v and v' and hence the sets of field nodes $v_1, \ldots, v_n$ and $v'_1, \ldots, v'_n$ must be distinct, which is a contradiction and so $v = v'$.

For instance, if $\bar{\mathbb{T}}$ is the tree in Fig. 3, then nodes v_1 and v_9 are the selector nodes for the XKey $\kappa' = (\rho$.Customer$, ($Phone.code, Phone.number$))$ in tree $\bar{\mathbb{T}}$, and the only sets of field nodes that pairwise satisfy the *closest* property are $\{\{v_3, v_4\}, \{v_7, v_8\}\}$ for v_1 and $\{\{v_{11}, v_{12}\}, \{v_{15}, v_{16}\}\}$ for v_9. These sets of field nodes are obviously unique, since none of them are value equal, and therefore tree $\bar{\mathbb{T}}$ satisfies κ'. Note that the selector nodes v_1 and v_9 are indeed identified by each of the sets of field nodes $\{v_3, v_4\}, \{v_7, v_8\}$ and $\{v_{11}, v_{12}\}, \{v_{15}, v_{16}\}$, respectively.

Now, recall from the introductory example that $\mathbb{T}$ is the tree obtained from relation **Phones** (cf. Fig. 2a) according to the general mapping procedure originally presented in [6], whereby flat relation **Phones** is first nested on $\{$code, number$\}$ and then mapped directly to XML. In this example $($code, number$)$ is the key for **Phones**, and its semantics is preserved by the XKey κ' in the obtained tree $\mathbb{T}$ since $\mathbb{T} \vDash \kappa'$ as shown above. Hence κ' exemplifies the property of an XKey to preserve the semantics of a relational key in case that the XML document is obtained from a complete relation by the mapping procedure in [6]. We omit a formal analysis of this property of an XKey here for reasons of space requirements and refer the reader to [9] instead.

We note finally that κ' is violated in tree $\bar{\mathbb{T}}$ according to both the semantics of [5] and XML Schema, which shows that these approaches do not have the desirable property of preserving the semantics of a relational key.

4 Related Work and Discussion

In recent years, several types of XML Integrity Constraints (XICs) have been studied. We focus here on key and related types of constraints and refer the reader to [4] for a survey of other types of XICs.

Related to keys in XML are functional dependencies in XML (XFDs), which have been proposed using a 'tree tuple' approach [10] and a 'closest node' approach [6][2]. Tailored to the selector/field framework, an XFD achieves the identification of selector nodes in the same, sophisticated way an XKey does. It however does not account for the uniqueness of field nodes. This together with the limitations of the well recognized proposals towards XML keys in [5] and the XML Schema specification, which we have illustrated throughout the paper, in fact motivated the definition and study of an XKey.

The XML key presented in [11] does not use the selector/field framework, but instead identifies element nodes by a subset of their attributes. The targeted element nodes are thereby designated by either a type in a DTD or by a path expression. This approach is less expressive than an XKey since it does not allow for the identification of element nodes by descending field nodes.

In future work we will investigate the consistency and implication problems for XKeys, which are fundamental to any type of integrity constraint. These problems are formulated as the questions of whether there exists at least one XML document that satisfies a given set of XKeys, and whether a single XKey must hold in an XML document given that a set of XKeys holds, respectively.

References

1. Abiteboul, S., Hull, R., Vianu, V.: Foundations of Databases. Addison-Wesley, Reading (1995)
2. Möller, A., Schwartzbach, M.: An Introduction to XML and Web Technologies. Addison Wesley, Reading (2006)
3. Beyer, K.S., Cochrane, R., Josifovski, V., Kleewein, J., Lapis, G., Lohman, G.M., Lyle, R., Özcan, F., Pirahesh, H., Seemann, N., Truong, T.C., der Linden, B.V., Vickery, B., Zhang, C.: System RX: One Part Relational, One Part XML. In: SIGMOD, pp. 347–358. ACM, New York (2005)
4. Fan, W.: XML Constraints: Specification, Analysis, and Applications. In: DEXA Workshops, pp. 805–809. IEEE Computer Society Press, Los Alamitos (2005)
5. Buneman, P., Davidson, S.B., Fan, W., Hara, C.S., Tan, W.C.: Reasoning about keys for XML. Information Systems 28(8), 1037–1063 (2003)
6. Vincent, M.W., Liu, J., Mohania, M.: On the Equivalence between FDs in XML and FDs in Relations. Acta Informatica 44(3-4), 207–247 (2007)
7. Fan, W.: XML Publishing: Bridging Theory and Practice. In: Arenas, M., Schwartzbach, M.I. (eds.) DBPL 2007. LNCS, vol. 4797, pp. 1–16. Springer, Heidelberg (2007)
8. Vakali, A., Catania, B., Maddalena, A.: XML Data Stores: Emerging Practices. IEEE Internet Computing 9(2), 62–69 (2005)

---

[2] These two approaches have been shown to be equivalent in complete XML trees [6].

9. Karlinger, M., Vincent, M., Schrefl, M.: Keys for XML. Technical Report 09.03, Dept. of Business Informatics - DKE, JKU Linz (2009)
10. Arenas, M., Libkin, L.: An information-theoretic approach to normal forms for relational and XML data. J. ACM 52(2), 246–283 (2005)
11. Arenas, M., Fan, W., Libkin, L.: On the Complexity of Verifying Consistency of XML Specifications. SIAM J. Comput. 38(3), 841–880 (2008)

Query Expansion Based on Query Log and Small World Characteristic

Yujuan Cao[1,2], Xueping Peng[1], Zhao Kun[1], Zhendong Niu[1,3], Gx Xu[1],
and Weiqiang Wang

[1] The School of Computer Science and Technology, Beijing Institute of Technology, Beijing,
100081, China
[2] Beijing Command & Control Center, Beijing, 100094, China
{qiushuichangtian,pengxp,kzhao,zdniu,xuguixian2000,
princeWang}@bit.edu.cn

Abstract. Automatic query expansion is an effective way to solve the word mismatching and short query problems. This paper presents a novel approach to Expand Queries Based on User log and Small world characteristic of the document (QEBUS). When the query is submitted, the synonymic concept of the query is gotten by searching a synonymic concept dictionary. Then the query log is explored and the key words are extracted from the user clicked documents based on small world network (SWN) characteristic. By analyzing the semantic network of the document based on SWN and exploring the correlations between the key words and the queries based on mutual information, high-quality expansion terms can be gotten. The experiment results show that our technique outperforms some traditional query expansion methods significantly.

Keywords: Query expansion, query log analysis, small world characteristic, mutual information.

1 Introduction

Search engines have become the main tool for information retrieval. Most of search engines still rely on the key words in the query to search and rank Web Pages. However it is general consensus that the authors and the users always use different terms to describe the same concept, and web users always submit short term queries. These are the key reasons that affect the precision of the search engine. Query expansion is an efficient approach to solve the problem by automatically adding additional terms to the query.

Although web users usually input short queries with little or no context information associated with them, they click the URL which they consider relevant. These clicks associate a set of query terms with a set of WebPages and can provide high level suggestions for expanding the original user query with additional context.

This paper investigate a new approach (QEBUS) Expand Queries Based on User log and Small world characteristic of the document. Our work is different from the traditional approach in three aspects.

G. Vossen, D.D.E. Long, and J.X. Yu (Eds.): WISE 2009, LNCS 5802, pp. 573–580, 2009.

(1) For the queries not in the user logs, we maintain a synonymic concept dictionary. By searching the dictionary, both the query and the synonymic concept are submitted to the search engine. As the user log becomes larger, the dependence on the concept dictionary will get weaker.

(2)For the queries in the user logs, the WebPages clicked by the users with same preference are selected. The keywords are extracted based on small world characteristic of the document. This step can improve the quality of extracted terms dramatically.

(3) Correlations between the key words and the queries are explored not only based on mutual information but also on key words distribution in related documents.

Our experiments show that our query expansion approach can improve the precision of the search result significantly.

The remainder of this paper is organized as follows. In Section 2, we discuss the related work. QEBUS are described in Section 3. Experiment results and evaluations are presented in Section 4. Conclusion and future work are introduced in Section 5.

2   Related Work

Traditional works on query expansion can be divided into three categories: global analysis, local analysis (pseudo-relevant) and local context-sensitive analysis.

Global analysis examines the relationship of words in the whole collection, includeing Deerwester's Latent Semantic Index (LSI)[4], Y. Jing's PhraseFinder[15] and the approach presented by Fabienne[6]. The disadvantage of these approaches is that corpus-wide statistic is required, so it is expensive in terms of space and time.

Local analysis is the approach extracting terms from top-N documents retrieved by the initial queries instead of global concept database. The most frequent non-stop words among the top ranked passages are counted and added to the original queries [14,2,10]. Local analysis highly depends on the quality of the documents retrieved in the initial retrieval.

One of the best ways to determine search needs is through user's observation. Cui [8],Fonseca and Golgher [1] utilize user click through data to extract semantic similarity. Radlinski[5], Rosie[12] use query sessions as the source information for query expansion. By studying the web search behavior, White[13] found that experts are more successful in finding what they are looking for than non-experts. Instead of teaching a non-expert to be an expert, our QEBUS helps users with query expansion.

3   Key Words Extraction and Query Expansion Model

3.1   Small World Phenomenon

The small-world experiment was conducted by Milgram who examined the average path length for social networks of people in the United States. The research was groundbreaking in that it suggested that human society is a small world type network characterized by short path lengths and high cluster, which are often associated with the phrase "six degrees of separation".

Recent research on networks that occur in a number of biological, social and man-made systems showed that they share a common feature. To formalize the notion of a small world, Watts and Strogatz [3] define the clustering coefficient C and the characteristic path length d of the graph.

The clustering coefficient C is a measure of the clique of the local neighborhoods. The characteristic path length d is the average path length over all pairs of nodes. The graphs that have SW property are often neither completely regular nor completely random. Graphs with SW structure are highly clustered, but the path length between nodes is small (It can be seen that $C \gg C_{random}$ and $d \approx d_{random}$).

Yutaka Matsu [16] showed that the graph derived from a document also has the small world characteristics. It has been proved by Ramon Ferrer [11] that the small world phenomenon also exists in human language.

3.2 Building Term Co-occurrence Graph

A term co-occurrence graph can be constructed from a document as follows.

(1) After word segmentation (for Chinese document) and stop words removing, we select frequent terms $\{t_i\}$ which appear frequency $f > f_{thr}$. With this method, the nodes of the Term Co-occurrence Graph were selected.

(2) For a given term (node), which nodes should be selected as its neighbors? Jaccard coefficient is appropriate for our feature extraction task and has previously shown excellent empirical performance in natural language processing. For every pair of $\{t_i, t_j\}$, Jaccard coefficient $J_{ti,tj} = \dfrac{n_{ti,tj}}{n_{ti} + n_{tj} - n_{ti,tj}}$ is calculated. Where $n_{ti,tj}$ is the number of sentences that contain both t_i and t_j, $n_{ti} + n_{tj} - n_{ti,tj}$ is the number of sentences that contain either of t_i or t_j. If $J_{t_i,t_j} > J_{thr}$ (J_{thr} is the user-given threshold), an edge is added between t_i and t_j.

(3) The term co-occurrence graph of the document can be defined as $G_L = (T_L, E_L)$, where $T_L = \{t_i\}$, t_i is the terms selected after step (1), $E_L = \{\{t_i, t_j\}\}$ is the set of edges or connections between terms t_i and t_j, L is the number of nodes in the graph.

3.3 SW Properties of Term Co-occurrence Graph

After constructing the term co-occurrence graph, we will calculate its two basic statistical properties: the clustering coefficient C and the path length d. For a term $t_i \in T_L$ with k neighbors, we use $\Gamma_i = \{j | \xi_{i,j} = 1\}$ to indicate the set of nearest neighbors. $\xi_{i,j} = 1$ indicates there is an edge between t_j and t_i otherwise $\xi_{i,j} = 0$. The clustering coefficient of the graph can be defined as $C = \frac{1}{L}\sum_{i=1}^{L} C_i$, where C_i is the node $t_i's$ clustering coefficient. $C_i = \dfrac{\varphi_i}{k \times (k-1) \div 2}$, k is the number of t_i's neighbors; φ_i is the number of edges which actually exist between the neighbors of t_i, $\varphi_i = \sum_{m,n=1}^{k} \xi_{m,n} | t_m, t_n \in \Gamma_i, m \neq n$. The second property is the path length. For given two terms $t_i, t_j, \in T_L$, let $d_{min}(i,j)$ represent the minimum path length between them. For term t_i, the path length can be calculated by $d_i = \frac{1}{L-1}(\sum_{j=1,j\neq i}^{L} d_{min}(i,j))$. The average path length of the term co-occurrence graph is $d = \frac{1}{L}(\sum_{i=1}^{L} d_i)$.

3.4 User Log Description

User access log are derived from the database in one of our laboratory research project IICSS (Internet Information Crawl and Services System), including user id, query terms, user clicked URL, user category and the visiting time. Table1 describes the log information. Where userCatagory is the Category ID of the user (User selected the second level categories he interested in from the Open Directory Project manually).

Table1. Information included in web access log

#	Query terms	visitTime	userID	userCata	User clicked URL
1	Topol (Bai Yang)	08-09-18 10:33:48	Adm 001	A13,A15	http://news.xinhuanet.com/mil/2008-02/2 8/content_7685125.htm
2	Topol (Bai Yang)	08-09-18 10:34:40	Adm 001	A13,A15	http://www.space.cetin.net.cn/docs/ht990 3/ht990316.htm
	...	...	...	...	

3.5 Key-Words Extracting

The small world property of the document gives us some inspiration. The distribution of terms in the document is not equal. Each term has different contribution to the content and structure of the document. When expressing his idea, the author may repeat some concepts and then extend document basing on them. The key words represent the main topic and the fundamental concepts of the document.

Key words are the key nodes in the term co-occurrence graph. For the convenience of description, we cite the definitions adopted by Zhu [9]:

Definition 1: CN is the original terms co-occurrence graph which was constructed after word segmentation and stop word removing, and d is the average path length of the CN.

Definition 2: CN_i is the terms co-occurrence graph where the ith node is absent, and d_i is the average path length of the CN_i.

Definition 3: $CB_i=d_i-d$ is the contribution of the ith node. The nodes with larger CB_i are more important to keep the graph well connected.

In the case of term co-occurrence graph, the terms with high CB_i are the 'short cuts' connect vertices. If the node with large CB_i is absent in the graph, the average length of the graph will get very large. In the context of documents, if the terms with large CB_i is absent, the topics are divided and the basic concepts are lost connections. So by finding the terms with high CB_i, the key-words can be extracted accordingly.

3.6 Query Expansion

Our statistic shows that more than 90% query terms are extracted as the key words from the user clicked document. By exploring the relationship between the query terms and the key words in users' access documents, terms which have close relationships to the original query can be gotten.

Users in the same category have same preference. But the users in different category have different interests. For a certain query, the WebPages clicked by users in category 1 may far from the WebPages clicked by users in category 2. For example, when a user inputs a Chinese query 'Chang'E', many WebPages related to 'Chang'E' will present to him. Some of the WebPages are the classical stories about a Chinese goddess live in the moon; others are news about the 'Chang'E' moon satellite of China. The literary lovers will click the classical stories with high property but an astronomic enthusiast will look through the news about 'Chang'E' satellite instead.

For a certain query, from the documents clicked by users in same category, we extract 20 key words using previous method. $t_{1,1}, t_{1,2}, t_{1,3}...t_{1,20}$ are the key words extracted from the document1, $t_{2,1}, t_{2,2}, t_{2,3}...t_{2,10}$ are the key words extracted from document2, After removing overlap terms, A new list $Vec=(T_1, T_2, T_3...T_k)$ is gotten.

The relativity between query terms and key words can be evaluated on the basis of mutual information and key words distribution in related documents. The correlation between query terms and key words can be expressed as:

$$Rel(q, T_i) = \frac{N_{userclick\_T_i}}{N_{userclick}} \times \frac{N_{q,T_i}}{N} \times log \frac{N_{q,T_i}}{N_q N_{T_i}} \tag{1}$$

Let's define $D_{userclick}$ as the users with similar interest clicked documents when submit query q. $N_{userclick}$ is the total number of $D_{userclick}$, $N_{userclick}$ is the number of documents which contain T_i in the $D_{userclick}$, $N_{q,Ti}$ is the number of documents where query q and term T_i are co-occurrence in the corpus, N_q is the number of documents which contain q in the corpus, N_{Ti} is the number of documents which contain the term T_i in the corpus, and N is the total number of documents in the corpus. By search $\{q,T_i\},\{q\}$ and $\{ T_i \}$ in our BIT-Search-Engine system (one of our laboratory research project), $N_{q,Ti}$, N_q and N_{Ti} are easy to be gotten.

4 Experiment

4.1 Experiment Data Set

Experiment data set comes from one of our laboratory research project CICS (Internet Information Crawl and Services System), which contains about 2,768,763 WebPages and more than 10 thousand query requests are recorded in the user log. There are 19 undergraduate students as volunteers who give their feedbacks to this experiment. The length of queries in our experiments is very close to those employed by the real web users and the average length of all queries is 2.1 words. 16 queries used in the experiments are listed in Table 2.

Relevant documents are judged according to the volunteers' manual selections and standard relevant document sets are prepared for all of the 16 queries.

Table 2. 16 queries used in the experiment

Topol(Bai Yang)	Nuclear submarine
unmanned aerial vehicle	Space Shuttle Endeavor
Chang'E	Chandrayaan-1 spacecraft
Shenzhou VII	Bulava
F-35	ARJ21-700
Somali pirate	Phoenix Mars probe
Large Aircraft Company	Airshow
Apollo program	BeiDou Satellite

4.2 Quality of Expansion Terms

In Chinese, Topol (Bai Yang) is a word has multi-meanings. It can be the Topol-M missile; the name of a table tennis player; or a famous prose written by Mao Dun. For the users who are interested in military topics, query "**TOPOL**" is mainly related with a missile of Russia. Some very good terms, such as "**TOPOL-M**", "**Russia**", "**missile silo**", "**intercontinental ballistic missile**", even "**GLONASS**", "**DF-31**" can be obtained by our techniques.

We chose TF/IDF as the base line extracting key words from the document. Relevant terms are judged according to the volunteers' manual selections. Table 3 shows the percentage of the relevant terms in the top 36 suggested by Local Context Analysis and our method based on small world network and user logs. As we can see, the terms expanded by our method have better quality.

Table 3. Percentage of relevant terms

Query	TF/IDF (base line)	QEBUS	Query	TF/IDF (base line)	QEBUS
Topol(Bai Yang)	47.2%	69.4%	Nuclear submarine	55.6%	72.2%
unmanned aerial vehicle	63.9%	75.0%	Space Shuttle	52.8%	61.1%
Chang'e	50.0%	66.7%	Chandrayaan-1	55.6%	69.4%
Shenzhou VII	52.8%	72.2%	Bulava	63.9%	80.6%
F-35	52.8%	58.3%	ARJ21-700	66.7%	83.3%
somali pirate	50.0%	63.9%	Phoenix Mars	52.8%	75.0%
Large Aircraft Company	52.8%	61.1%	Airshow	55.6%	72.2%
Apollo	47.2%	77.8%	BeiDou	50.0%	66.7%

4.3 The Effectiveness of Query Expansion

We use the popular precision score in IR and authority score following Xue[7] to evaluate the results before and after query expanding. For a given query Q, let $|D|$ be the size of relevant WebPages to the query. Let TOP be the top N documents retrieved by our system. *Precision* can be defined as:

$$precision = \frac{|D \cap TOP|}{|TOP|} \qquad (2)$$

For a given query Q, we ask our volunteers to identify top 10 authoritative pages according to their own judgments. Let A be the set of 10 authority WebPages to the query Q, and N be the set of top 10 documents retrieved by our system. *Authority* can be defined as:

$$authority = \frac{|A \cap N|}{|A|} \qquad (3)$$

Precision measures the degree of accuracy of the algorithm, while *authority* measurement is more relevant to users' degree of satisfactory on the performance of the search engine.

We chose no query expansion as the base lines, compare the local context analysis extracting keywords by TF/IDF (LTF/IDF); the local context analysis extracting keywords by SWM (LSWM); Query Expansion Based on User Log extracting keywords by TF/IDF(QETF/IDF) and QEBUS, Overall *precision* and *authority* is presented in Fig.1 and Fig.2.

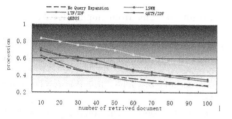
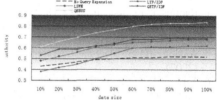

Fig. 1. Precision for no query expansion, LTF/IDF, LSWM, QETF/IDF and QEBUS

Fig. 2. Authority for no query expansion, LTF/IDF, LSWM, QETF/IDF and QEBUS

QEBUS shows best precision and authority scores over other approaches. One reason is local context analysis searches expansion terms in the top-ranked retrieved documents and is more likely to add some irrelevant terms into the original query, but QEBUS selects expansion terms in a relatively narrower but more concentrated area based on user log. The other reason that expansion terms extracted based on SWN are more relevant to the original queries. But for the TF/IDF method, the noise metadata is introduced with high probability.

The experiment results show that our query expansion approach based on user log and small world characteristic of the document achieves best performance. It brings 69.6% and 54.1% improvement in both precision and authority over the base line.

5   Conclusion and Future Work

In this paper, we presented a query expansion method (QEBUS) based on user log and small world characteristic of the document.. Experiments show that QEBUS can achieve substantial performance improvements.

Here we expand queries in the document which the users in same category clicked, that is simple but somewhat coarseness. Future work includes personalized query expansion by accurately finding the document match the user's interest in the user log when he input a query.

Small World Characteristic of document is not only helpful to query expansion but also significant to text category, topic analysis, texts digest etc. We believe this is a very promising research direction.

References

1. Fonseca, B.M., Golghe, P.: Concept Based Interactive Query Expansion. In: Proceedings of CIKM 2005, pp. 696–703 (2005)
2. Buckley, C., Singhal, A., Mitra, M., Salton, G.: New Retrieval Approaches Using SMART. In: Proceedings of the TREC 4 Conference, pp. 25–48 (1995)
3. Watts, D., Strogatz, S.: Collective dynamics of small-world networks. Nature, 440–442 (1998)
4. Deerwester, S., Dumais, S.T., Landauer, T.K., Furnas, G.W., Harshman, R.A.: Indexing by latent semantic analysis. Journal of the Society for Information Science 41(6), 391–407 (1990)
5. Radlinski, F., Joachims, T.: Query chains: learning to rank from implict feedback. In: Proceedings of the Eleventh ACM SIGKDD, pp. 239–248 (2005)
6. Moreau, F., Claveau, V., Seillot, P.: Automatic Morphological Query Expansion Using Analogy-Based Machine Learning. In: Advances in information Retrieval, pp. 222–233 (2007)
7. Xue, G.-R., Zeng, H.-J., et al.: Optimizing Web Search Using Web Click-through Data. In: Proceeding of CIKM 2004, pp. 118–126 (2004)
8. Cui, H., Wen, J.-R., Nie, J.-Y., Ma, W.-Y.: Probabilistic query expansion using query logs. In: Proceedings of the Eleventh International Conference on WWW, pp. 325–332 (2002)
9. Zhu, M.X., Cai, Z., Cai, Q.S.: Automatic Keywords Extraction of Chinese Document Using Small World Structure. In: Proceeding of Natural Language Processing and Knowledge International Conference, pp. 26–29 (2003)
10. Theobald, M.: Efficient and Self-tuning. Incremental Query Expansion for Top-k Query Processing. In: Proceeding of the SIGIR 2005, pp. 242–249 (2005)
11. Cancho, R.F., Sole, R.V.: The small world of human language. In: Proceedings of the Royal Society of London, pp. 2261–2265 (2001)
12. Jone, R., Rey, B.: Generating Query Substitutions. In: Proceedings of International Conference on WWW, pp. 387–396 (2006)
13. White, R.W., Dumais, S.T., et al.: Characterizing the Influence of Domain Expertise on Web Search Behavior. In: Proceeding of WSDM 2009, pp. 132–141 (2009)
14. Xu, J.X., Croft, W.B.: Improving the effectiveness of information retrieval with local context analysis. ACM Transactions on Information Systems 18(1), 79–112 (2000)
15. Jing, Y., Croft, W.B.: An association thesaurus for information retrieval. Proceedings of RIAO 1994, 146–160 (1994)
16. suo, Y.M., Ohsawa, Y.: KeyWorld: Extracting Keywords in a Documents as a Small World. In: Proceedings of DS-2001, pp. 271–281 (2001)

E-Biology Workflows with CALVIN

Markus Held[1], Wolfgang Blochinger[2], and Moritz Werning[3]

[1] Symbolic Computation Group, Eberhard Karls University
Sand 14, 72076 Tübingen, Germany
mheld@informatik.uni-tuebingen.de
[2] Institute of Parallel and Distributed Systems, University of Stuttgart
Universitätsstr. 38, 70569 Stuttgart, Germany
wolfgang.blochinger@ipvs.uni-stuttgart.de
[3] SUM IT AG
Täfernstr. 28, 5405 Baden-Dättwil, Switzerland
moritz.werning@sumit.ch

Abstract. Web portals enable sharing, execution and monitoring of scientific workflows, but usually depend on external development systems, with notations, which strive to support general workflows, but are still too complex for every-day use by biologists. The distinction between web-based and non-web based tools is likely to further irritate users. We extend our work on collaborative workflow design, by introducing a web-based scientific workflow system, that enables easy-to-use semantic service composition with a domain specific workflow notation.

1 Introduction

Biologists usually "connect" web applications or services by cutting and pasting data. As this is error-prone and hard to retrace, many different bioinformatics workflow systems have emerged [1]. Increasingly web portals are used to access and to share scientific workflows. Some provide workflow construction facilities via Java Web Start, while true web-based workflow tools lack sophisticated user experience. Often, desktop-based scientific workflow systems with complex user interfaces are used.

Supporting a large set of different workflows and different types of services increases the complexity of a notation, thus reducing usability by domain experts. In contrast, high user-friendliness limits the possible set of workflow patterns and access to arbitrary services. Domain experts should be able to compose and execute workflows in a domain specific modeling system, and fall back to a collaboration with software engineers if a more complex workflow model is needed. We propose a hybrid approach of augmenting a collaborative workflow design tool with a biology-specific workflow system, where a reduced workflow notation is compiled to the Business Process Execution Language (BPEL) [2]. In this paper, we formalize e-biology processes, deriving requirements for workflow systems, and show, how low-level workflow languages can be combined with domain-specific workflow notations to provide maximum ease-of-use and flexibility. We present the workflow system CALVIN[1], which abstracts from many of the intricacies of workflow design, builds on similar technology as and augments our collaborative workflow design system HOBBES [3].

---

[1] See http://www-sr.informatik.uni-tuebingen.de/workflows for demos.

G. Vossen, D.D.E. Long, and J.X. Yu (Eds.): WISE 2009, LNCS 5802, pp. 581–588, 2009.
© Springer-Verlag Berlin Heidelberg 2009

2   Requirements Analysis

We have held meetings and interviews with research staff from the Tübingen Center for Plant Molecular Biology (ZMBP[2]) to evaluate their requirements on a workflow system, and have given demonstrations of our evolving workflow system. At the ZMBP, "in silico experiments" are frequently used to prepare "wet" experiments in the laboratory. Existing workflow solutions have been evaluated but failed to satisfy the users, due to intricate user interfaces and lack of user interaction.

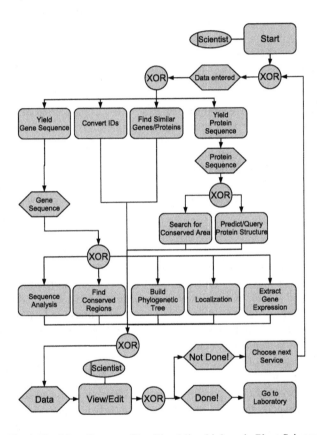

Fig. 1. The Meta-Process of in silico Microbiology in Plant Science

Figure 1 represents a *Meta*-Process of computational plant science, given in the Event-Driven Process Chain notation. We have derived the Meta-Process from our interviews at the ZMBP, and informal drawings[3] from ZMBP staff members. The Figure does not represent a specific bioinformatics workflow, but outlines the daily usage of web applications by biologists. Every path between the events "Data entered" and

---

[2] http://www.zmbp.uni-tuebingen.de, last accessed: 22/09/2008.

[3] http://www-sr.informatik.uni-tuebingen.de/workflows/draw.htm

"Data" represents a pipeline of data processing. The "view/edit" activity triggers either the execution of a new pipeline or the end of the in silico experimenting phase. In many cycles, the "view/edit" activity can effectively be left out, and is only enforced by the "copy & paste" mode of operation. In some cycles it is necessary to enable a biologist to edit the data or decide, whether to go on with the workflow. All input/output data has to be recorded for tracing the experiment. Effectively, the set of cycles performed by a biologist before going on to a "wet" experiment, forms a tree, where the result of one in silico experiment is the input to a set of other in silico experiments.

2.1 Requirements

Collaboration [R1]. *Gil* et al. see a need to "orchestrate the steps of scientific discovery and bridge the differing expertise of collaboration members" [4]. E-biology collaborations consist of biologists, bioinformaticians, and software engineers. Biologists will prefer "stripped down" workflow notations, that enable them to easily sketch *runnable* workflows, while software engineers need a complete workflow language.

Reproducibility [R2]. Reproducibility of scientific analyses is needed as well [4]. In "copy & paste" processes biologists see all results of all service invocations. There is no guarantee, that a service will always give the correct answers, as databases can be corrupted or services be subject to software errors. Hence, each workflow result will have to document the actual control-flow and data-flow of the workflow instance, i.e. the results of every activity in the workflow. Thus, biologists need an interface to easily navigate through intermediary and final results.

Intuitive Composition [R3]. Biology curricula do not encompass programming, so biologists strongly differ in their computing skills. Workflow notations for biologists have to be kept very simple and may only provide necessary features, leaving out control structures where possible. [5] point outs, that "wet laboratory biologists are uncomfortable using even the most abstract workflow tools currently available".

Service Invocations at Build Time [R4]. Users may want to invoke services at build time. First, this enables an exploratory way of workflow construction. As [6] points out, users sometimes will start composing a workflow with a given piece of information without knowing the goal. Second, biology web services are provided by research institutions, that cannot guarantee the correctness or the availability of a service. Thus, testing a service enhances the chance of yielding a correct workflow for a given task.

Semantic Service Discovery [R5]. When constructing a workflow, a typical task is to find a service, that can serve as a successor for a given activity. The opposite scenario can also be the case, where a predecessor for an activity is needed, e.g. if a user is searching for a way to get to a specific result type.

User Interaction [R6]. It can be necessary to interact with a workflow at predefined events in the workflow. This matches the "view/edit" activity from the meta-process. In data-flow oriented models, these events can be identified as the invocation or return of activities. After viewing the input/output of an activity, the user may decide either to resume the workflow, to alter the data and resume or to quit the workflow execution.

Web Integration [R7]. The web browser is the standard e-science tool for biologists. Users are most likely to accept a new system if it is integrated into the environment they are used to. Even if department policies allow installing new software, many biologists prefer using pre-configured and centrally managed systems.

Standards Conformance [R8]. Scientific workflows lack a common standard. To ensure that a workflow can be understood and used by future users, it has to conform to a standard language, e.g. BPEL, as [5] recommends.

3   The CALVIN Life Science Workflow System

We now introduce the CALVIN System, which enables biologists to easily define workflows for common tasks in a simplified workflow notation. If more sophisticated workflows are needed, biologists can request the help of software engineers or bioinformaticians [R1], to refine the workflow via a BPEL editor, e.g. HOBBES [3].

CALVIN can be accessed on the web [R7]. The main screen consists of an editor canvas, showing the activities and data-flow connections of the workflow. The workflow notation is kept very simple and effectively represents a tree of exploration steps so users do not have to deal with control structures [R3]. Services that process the output type or produce the input type of an activity can be found using a semantic search facility. By clicking on an activity, a query window is opened, that can be used to search the BioMOBY database for a list of adequate services [R5] [7][8]. Users can open a description of the service represented by an activity, or invoke the service directly from the activity properties menu. This enables testing the behavior of a service prior to running the workflow, thus enabling an explorative and data-oriented way of workflow composition [R4]. Activities can be marked as requiring user interaction, before or after their execution [R6]. Workflows are compiled to BPEL and deployed to an execution engine. We have chosen BPEL, as it represents a commonly accepted standard [R8]. Deployed CALVIN workflows can be re-used as new services. Outputs of a CALVIN service can serve as input of other activities.

The CALVIN Workflow Management Console presents a list of the workflows that are available on the server and can be loaded into the editor. The workflows are already deployed in the BPEL execution engine and can be executed from the console. Before beginning the actual execution, a window will show a graphical editor for workflow inputs. The input variables are sorted by the activities that they are provided to. Two different kinds of input parameters are available, primary inputs, which consist of biological data, and secondary parameters that influence the behavior of a service (e.g. its output format). Standard parameters are provided, that can be overwritten by the user. Every input variable is presented with a description provided by the BioMOBY database. During workflow interaction, the user can be prompted to verify if the workflow should go on, or to view and edit result data [R6]. External clients can be developed using the WSDL file provided by a workflow. Those WSDL-files are annotated with documentation data from the BioMoby database, that yield a complete description of the semantics of each service invocation.

Every workflow execution yields a result file containing the time of invocation, the inputs and service parameters, and all final and intermediate results. Together with the serialized workflow model, this enables retracing every event in the workflow and the origin of its results [R2]. The result files can either be downloaded from the server or be explored using an AJAX based provenance browser.

Compilation to BPEL enables the development of arbitrary workflows beyond the limits of any domain-specific workflow language. Leaving the WSDL interface of a BPEL document unchanged is a sufficient condition for the invocation of the workflow from CALVIN. A mapping from BPEL to the CALVIN notation is impossible, since BPEL is Turing-complete. It is not *necessecary*, on the other hand, since modified CALVIN workflows can be embedded in new CALVIN workflows. As sophisticated workflow development demands a close cooperation of domain experts and software engineers, HOBBES enables teams to collaboratively edit a BPEL model [R1].

3.1   Example: Searching for Orthologous Gene Sequences

Figure 2 shows a workflow for searching for orthologous gene sequences, a common case in genomics. Genes from two species are called orthologous, if they are divergent copies of a single gene in a common ancestor species. The input is a list of sequence identifiers, which first are converted to the needed ID format in step ❶ and then yield the according sequences in step ❷. The sequences are subject to three different BLAST searches (❸, ❹, ❺) to query different databases with different parameters at the same time. Before that, two sequence conversions are necessary (❻, ❼). Afterward, sequence identifiers are extracted from the results, which can be used for further processing.

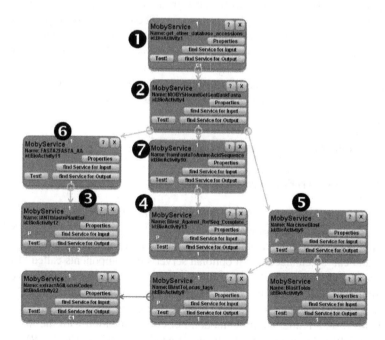

Fig. 2. Search for Orthologous Gene Sequences

3.2   Representation of Biology Specific Workflow Models

The CALVIN workflow notation represents a tree of exploration steps, which has to be transformed to a complete workflow. This implies, that not all workflows can be expressed via CALVIN, and that workflows have to be automatically augmented by the system. During the transformation process, the data-flow links are compiled to control-flow links and variable assignments. Additional data-flows augment the tree to a directed acyclic graph, that collects all produced data elements. Workflow models as viewed by biologists are represented by a tree $T = (N, E), E \subset N \times N$ with root n_1, where N is a set of BioMoby activities. CALVIN compiles the tree model T to a complete workflow model W, by adding a start activity α and a final activity ω, a set of control flow edges C, a set of data flow edges D which connect activity inputs and outputs, and a set of parameter edges P:

$$W = (N \cup \{\alpha, \omega\}, C, D, P), \ \alpha \notin N \wedge \omega \notin N$$
$$C = E \cup \{(n, \omega) | \forall k \in N : (n, k) \notin E\} \cup \{(\alpha, n_1)\}$$
$$D = E \cup \{(\alpha, n_1)\} \cup N \times \{\omega\}$$
$$P = \{(\alpha, n) \in \{\alpha\} \times N, \ where \ n \ has \ parameters\}$$

W consists of three graphs defined on the same node set $N \cup \{\alpha, \omega\}$. α takes the client's input and serves parameters to those activities, which have parameters. ω takes the output of all activities and sends the answer message. The interface of a workflow is given as a Tuple $\tau = (\iota, o(n_1), \ldots, o(n_{|N|}))$, where ι is the BioMoby type of its input message, and the $o(n_i)$ denote those message parts of its output message, which accord to the output of an activity. An $o(n_i)$ is a tuple of a message part name and a description of its BioMoby type. If n_j represents a CALVIN service, it yields a tuple $(o(n_{j,1}), \ldots o(n_{j,k}))$, which is added to τ instead of a single $o(n_j)$ Outputs of CALVIN services are treated as virtual nodes and can be used as input sources for other activities.

4   Architecture and Implementation

4.1   The CALVIN Architecture

The HOBBES and CALVIN clients have been implemented in Adobe Flex[4], which is based on Flash. Flex supports declarative GUI design in an XML language (MXML) with mapping to the Actionscript language. Its communication facilities support HTTP requests and can be enhanced with optional server side components called "Lifecycle Data Services" (LCDS), which enable server-to-client notification. Client/server Communication in CALVIN is facilitated via LCDS *Remote Objects*, which map client-side Actionscript objects to server side Java objects. For every session, one *BioController* object holds a server-side workflow model. For communication with the *ActiveBPEL* engine, one *BPEL Engine Controller* is instantiated per session. The *MOBY Manager* remote object enables service queries via BioMOBY [7].

---

[4] http://www.adobe.com/devnet/flex/, last accessed: 24/10/2007.

4.2 Transformation of CALVIN Workflows to BPEL Object Models

For each session, CALVIN holds a server-side and a more light-weight client-side object model, which communicate via transfer objects. When compiling and deploying a CALVIN workflow, it is transformed to a HOBBES BPEL Object Model (BOM), which is afterward compiled to a BPEL document. Before compiling the BPEL model, the BioMoby WSDL definitions have to be adapted by adding Partner Link Type definitions. CALVIN generates a WSDL definition for the process, including input and output messages whose message parts are annotated with BioMoby activity descriptions. The BOM is then generated by first importing all WSDL definitions and adding a global Flow activity with a Receive and a Reply activity. For every CALVIN activity, a Sequence activity is added, with an input and an output assignment, and a service invocation. Control flow edges are mapped to BPEL Flow Links, and data flow edges to Assign activities. If user interaction is required before or after the execution of an activity, CALVIN inserts code which polls a messaging singleton via XPath custom functions. The BOM is compiled to a BPEL file, which is saved to a temporary directory with WSDL files and other necessary files. A deployment script compresses the directory to an ActiveBPEL archive, which is then copied to the workflow deployment directory. After a CALVIN workflow has been deployed, it can be reused as an activity within other CALVIN workflows. Workflows can be reused as long as their WSDL definition is compatible with the CALVIN system.

5 Related Work

REMORA is a web-based DAG editor with BioMOBY access, where workflows are saved and executed on the server [9]. BioWMS contains a web-based workflow editor [10], presenting workflows as static HTML pages with embedded graphics, where changes lead to reloading the page. *Taverna* is a desktop-based workflow system for bioinformaticians [11], for composing and executing workflows, given in the Scufl language. No standardized Scufl specification exists and "the language itself should be considered volatile"[5]. Lanzen and Oinn point out that "in the standard version of the Taverna Workbench, a user cannot control the behaviour of a workflow once it is running" and have introduced an interaction extension with email notification [12].

6 Conclusion

We have presented the scientific workflow system CALVIN, which enables life scientists to easily compose workflows. It has been implemented as a Rich Internet Application and supports semantic service composition. Workflows are compiled to the standard language BPELand can be managed and executed on the server. In contrast to other systems, CALVIN targets biologists instead of bioinformaticians, and provides a user-friendly interface, where user interaction with workflows has been incorporated.

---

[5] http://www.ebi.ac.uk/~tmo/mygrid/XScuflSpecification.html, last accessed 30/09/2008.

Acknowledgements. We would like to thank Dierk Wanke, Kenneth Berendzen, and Klaus Harter from the ZMBP for their helpful advice on processes in modern biology.

References

1. Taylor, I.J., Deelman, E., Gannon, D.B., Shields, M.: Workflows for e-Science: Scientific Workflows for Grids. Springer, New York (2006)
2. OASIS: Web Services Business Process Execution Language Version 2.0 (April 2007), http://docs.oasis-open.org/wsbpel/2.0/wsbpel-v2.0.pdf (last accessed October 24, 2007)
3. Held, M., Blochinger, W.: Structured collaborative workflow design. Future Generation Computer Systems 25(6), 638–653 (2009)
4. Gil, Y., Deelman, E., Ellisman, M., Fahringer, T., Fox, G., Gannon, D., Goble, C., Livny, M., Moreau, L., Myers, J.: Examining the Challenges of Scientific Workflows. IEEE Computer 40(12), 24–32 (2007)
5. Barker, A., van Hemert, J.: Scientific Workflow: A Survey and Research Directions. In: Wyrzykowski, R., Dongarra, J., Karczewski, K., Wasniewski, J. (eds.) PPAM 2007. LNCS, vol. 4967, pp. 746–753. Springer, Heidelberg (2008)
6. Gibson, A., Gamble, M., Wolstencroft, K., Oinn, T., Goble, C.: The data playground: An intuitive workflow specification environment. In: E-SCIENCE 2007: Proceedings of the Third IEEE International Conference on e-Science and Grid Computing, pp. 59–68. IEEE Computer Society, Washington (2007)
7. Wilkinson, M.D., Links, M.: BioMOBY: an open-source biological web services proposal. Briefings In Bioinformatics 3(4), 331–341 (2002)
8. The BioMoby Consortium: Interoperability with Moby 1.0 It's better than sharing your toothbrush! Briefings In Bioinformatics 9(3) (2008)
9. Carrere, S., Gouzy, J.: REMORA: a pilot in the ocean of BioMoby web-services. Bioinformatics 22(7), 900–901 (2006)
10. Bartocci, E., Corradini, F., Merelli, E., Scortichini, L.: BioWMS: a web-based Workflow Management System for bioinformatics. BMC Bioinformatics 8(1) (2007)
11. Oinn, T., Addis, M., Ferris, J., Marvin, D., Senger, M., Greenwood, M., Carver, T., Glover, K., Pocock, M.R., Wipat, A., Li, P.: Taverna: a tool for the composition and enactment of bioinformatics workflows. Bioinformatics 20(17), 3045–3054 (2004)
12. Lanzén, A., Oinn, T.: The Taverna Interaction Service. Bioinformatics 24(8), 1118–1120 (2008)

Security Policy Definition Framework for SOA-Based Systems

Bartosz Brodecki, Piotr Sasak, and Michał Szychowiak

Poznań University of Technology
Piotrowo 2, 60-965 Poznań, Poland
{bbrodecki,psasak,mszychowiak}@cs.put.poznan.pl

Abstract. This paper presents an extended architecture of a policy definition framework fine-tuned for service-oriented environments conforming to the SOA distributed processing paradigm. We establish key requirements for such a framework, and use these to confront existing distributed policy frameworks. We also define a policy language destined to fulfill all recognized requirements and give a brief overview of its syntax.

1 Introduction

Service Oriented Architecture (SOA [1]) is today a well-known paradigm for developing services distributed through a loosely-coupled environment encompassing different control domains. Services are made accessible typically by providing descriptions for functions, related constraints and requirements for interactions. SOA implicitly decouples interaction entities into two distinct roles of service consumer and service provider. A *policy* represents some constraints or conditions of the access to and use of a service or any other entity managed by any participant. Each of those constraints or conditions is expressed in the form of a policy assertion which may be evaluated and is ensured by policy enforcement mechanisms. Probably the most important attribute of SOA systems is high interoperability in spite of multiple development technologies and technical constraints of a service implementation. A security policy adopted for such a diverse and heterogeneous environment is required to manage security related problems of SOA interactions. In this paper we review the prerequisites for SOA-compliant security policy management framework and confront them with existing solutions. In response to several deficiencies, we propose a new language to fully support the SOA paradigm.

This paper is organized as follows. Firstly, in section 2, we define key requirements for an adequate SOA-compliant security policy framework and review a representative excerpt of currently available solutions. Secondly in section 3, we describe our proposal. Concluding remarks are given in section 4.

2 Security Policy Framework for SOA

In this section we attempt to define key requirements for a SOA-compliant security policy framework and language. In fact, a considerable number of separate issues must

G. Vossen, D.D.E. Long, and J.X. Yu (Eds.): WISE 2009, LNCS 5802, pp. 589–596, 2009.

be taken into account. Until now, a remarkable effort has been made to find a comprehensive solution, yet there is still no ready to use result which is able to cover all security requirements. Further, in subsection 2.1 we review some policy frameworks and emphasize their advantages and deficiencies.

First we extract key features of an ideal security policy framework for SOA-based systems. In order for such a framework to fully support the SOA paradigm we recognize the following requirements:

1. Support for a distributed and loosely coupled system. A SOA policy is required to express not only authorization (access) restrictions (authorizing policy subjects to access policy targets), what is currently typical, but also security obligations (by which a policy target expresses requirements that any interaction is expected to fulfill) and capabilities (by which a subject specifies mechanisms it can provide to fulfill target-side requirements) that must be satisfied by all participants of the service interaction (e.g. the communication protection will be set up most likely with negotiation of obligations and capabilities). Ability to express obligations and capabilities is imperative for true SOA environments, where interactions (possibly nested) can be established automatically and dynamically without any human intervention or coordination.

2. Distributed decision support. Large scale systems, especially-SOA based, can be composed into a federation. In this context we need ability to express security policies for other autonomic systems, acquire and incorporate security policies from other federated systems, define distributed trust relationships and rights delegation from one subject to another.

3. Multilayer design. An ideal security policy language should have hierarchical design, in which the bottom layer provides connection to platform specific security components and provides security functionalities for the next higher level, and each higher level allows to aggregate policy items in more abstract concepts. At the top, we should have a general human readable policy.

4. Modular and extensible language. An ideal security policy language should be modular in order to allow easy extensions for custom needs.

5. Low overhead for policy evaluation. Large number of policy statements and complicated decision chains will cause noticeable operating const. Therefore, policy statements should have a maximum simplified form.

We believe that those principles constitute the foundation of security policy frameworks for any forthcoming SOA-compliant systems.

2.1 Related Work

Many policy frameworks and languages have been proposed until now in literature. Some of them have reached a maturity and received real-world implementations. Here we review the most representative examples currently available in distributed systems.

XACML (eXtensible Access Control Markup Language [2]) is a broadly used standard supported by OASIS and W3C. It offers an XML-based declarative language for defining access control policy for WS services. It is the policy language recommended in the scope of WS-Policy [3] and WS-SecurityPolicy [4] frameworks. XACML's main problem is its very verbose XML notation, which slows down the processing and requires software assisted policy authoring, making assertion analysis difficult. From a SOA point of view, limitations include the lack of possibility to specify obligation and capabilities for service interactions, as well as no delegation support or conflict avoidance procedures. Also, XACML operates on a centralized architecture inadequate for SOA-based systems.

In addition to XACML which specifies an access control policy, **SAML** (Security Assertion Markup Language [5]) is often used to transport security assertions on service interactions. Typically, assertions contain information that service providers use to make access control decisions.

SecPAL (Security Policy Assertion Language [6]) is a logic-based authorization language from Microsoft. It is a research project intended to balance syntactic simplicity with policy expressiveness. SecPAL has a flat architecture, but it offers some features which are interesting from the SOA viewpoint, such as delegation of rights, separation of duties, expiration constrains, among others. Its clear, readable syntax emerges from its very simple structure and statements which are very close to natural language. Effective decision procedures are formally confirmed by translation into Datalog with Constraints [7]. SecPAL also offers an option of automatic translation of rules into XML syntax, widely accepted in SOA systems.

SecPAL is remarkably very friendly to read. Moreover, it is formally verifiable, has an important feature of flexibly expressing delegation of authority and offers automatic transformation to XML. Its ability to express a large set of domain-specific constrains makes it a very complete but complex solution. Limitations mainly include lack of obligations and capabilities.

Ponder [8] and Ponder2 [9] are language frameworks developed at Imperial College. They offer a declarative, object-oriented and platform-independent language, that maps its records to low level functions in an existing underlying platform. Ponder has a very compact notation, although it is hardly readable because of its highly specialized grammar and syntax. The formal syntax allows, at least potentially to perform some automatic correctness evaluation of policy rules. The main advantage in the SOA-based environments is the support of distributed policy relationship. Ponder2 has adopted a multilayered architecture [10], but the quantity of distinct transformations required, makes this solution too complex for SOA systems. Yet, Ponder and Ponder2 are deficient in expressing distributed trust, interaction obligations and capabilities.

As we have seen, none of the presented solutions fulfill all the requirements recognized at the beginning of this section, what limits their applicability for SOA-based systems.

3 ORCA Framework

In this section we outline our proposal for a policy framework for SOA-based systems, which aims at addressing requirements defined in section 2. Further, we present a brief overview of the syntax of our ORCA language.

Since it is extremely difficult to fulfill multiple requirements that we have recognized in section 2, we adopt a layered approach to build a policy language model. Each layer focuses on a particular subset of the requirements, and provides fine-tuned building blocks for a global policy of a SOA-based system.

3.1   Framework Architecture

The proposed framework architecture conforms to and extends the basic security model proposed by ISO [14] and IETF [15]. Figure 1 presents key components of our framework architecture.

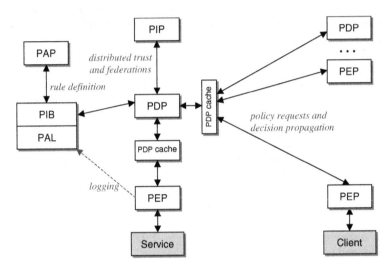

Fig. 1. Policy data-flow model

This figure gives an overview of how key elements are organized in a distributed services infrastructure. Separation of components allows for more flexibility in managing entire policy and provides a clear overview on policy decision evaluation and enforcement. PAP (Policy Administration Point) is a policy manager's interface for definition and management of policy rules. PIB (Policy Information Base) is a kind of storage for policy rules. PAL (Policy Audit Log) is a place for keeping log trails about policy enforcement events. PDP (Policy Decision Point) is the heart of the framework, where policy rule calculations take place. PDP cache is responsible for caching PDP decisions, thus plays an important role in improving overall performance of the framework. It is important to note that PDP cache must address cache coherency issues. This can be accomplished using session guarantees [16] or similar consistency management approaches. PEP (Policy Enforcement Point) is responsible for enforcing policy decisions made by the PDP. PIP (Policy Information Point) is used for acquiring additional information, not available locally (in a local PIB) for the PDP, required to resolve proper decisions. Typically, PIP obtains information from other administration domains. This can be useful in federated systems where some part of knowledge needed to take proper local decisions can be distributed across entire federated system. We implement PIP, PDP, PDP cache, PIB and PAL as distinct SOA-compliant services. Moreover, we allow for a hierarchical relationship of several PDP services, governing fine-grained system sub-domains and composing a larger SOA environment. Interaction between distinct administration (top-level) domains is supported with use of PIP entities.

3.2 Language Architecture

Since SOA environment spreads across multiple administration domains, it usually requires simple solutions for interoperability reasons. Therefore, our framework consists of only four layers (which gives a much simplified architecture compared to the proposition based on Ponder2 [10], for instance).

Our policy language model is decomposed throughout only four most important layers of abstraction (Figure 2). At the top of our model, the System Model Layer is intended to specify only basic security prerequisites for system model items (i.e. metapolicy). This layer can benefit from UML-based languages which are helpful for system model designers. As this issue has been addressed in literature (e.g. [11], [12]) we are not concerned with this layer in this paper. The opposite bottom Physical Layer is device and service implementation-specific, and provides only low level access to different functionalities managed by higher layers (examples of such functionalities are file system access control mechanisms or firewall configurations). Higher level policy rules will be mapped here onto corresponding configuration parameters of a given "physical" technology (e.g. JAAS permissions in an EJB application). This layer is also out of the scope of our interest in this paper.

The System Layer is the best place for policy language suited for specifing SOA policy. Compared to [10] it combines the functionalities acquiring policy rules and analyzes them. This approach can be seen as a one step process whereas the approach presented in [10] as a two step process. We believe that the most adequate solution for the System Layer is a high-level human-readable language, well suited for specifying general policy rules as well as being easy to manage by people who do not necessarily have and extensive computer engineering background. Unlike suggestions in [11] where policy rules can become quite complex and require complicated parsing, we use for that purpose a constraint natural language with a very closed syntax and restricted keywords. Thus, we omit the heavily complex problem of parsing natural language. The keywords list is not hardcoded into our language framework. It may be easily extended by a system administrator. These keywords should be understandable for all kind of policy managers.

Policy rules specified in structured natural language can be incomplete or conflicting with each other. A tool is needed to transform policy rules to an abstract logical model for correctness evaluation. This problem has already been well recognized and addressed by some languages, in the usual case by directly using (or transforming policy rules into) a logic-based programming language as Prolog or Datalog (e.g. in SecPAL, Cassandra, Binder, Lithium, DL or RT/RT^C languages). Due to space limitations we do not address this problem here.

The Interaction Layer specifies rules related to particular system components (services) by instantiating general rules inherited from the System Layer into detailed policy assertions for each component. This layer perceives the entire system as a collection of concrete single services, and gathers knowledge about service interactions. In our framework we have decided to incorporate at this layer an automatic translation to XACML/SAML, being both broadly understood in most Web services implementations.

Hence, for the rest of this paper, we focus only on the System Layer and its language.

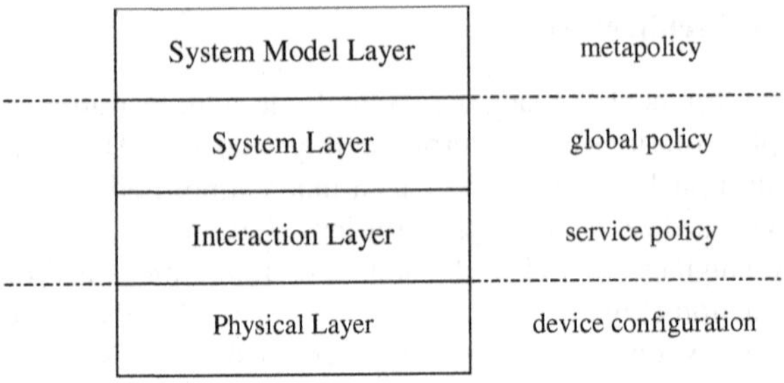

System Model Layer	metapolicy
System Layer	global policy
Interaction Layer	service policy
Physical Layer	device configuration

Fig. 2. Layered policy language architecture of ORCA

3.3 System Layer Policy Rules

We consider the following fundamental entities related to security policy: a target that is to be protected (e.g. resource or service); a policy subject performing *actions* on targets (e.g. principal or client issuing access requests); and mechanisms by means of which the target is protected.

In spite of access control, obligations and capabilities are truly necessary in SOA-based communication to allow both participants to agree on one of possible alternative security requirements. Moreover, policy rules should be expressed in a maximum simplified syntax, to facilitate full interoperability. Unfortunately, according to our knowledge, there is no language currently providing all these features. This makes it necessary to construct a new, simple policy language, allowing to define all required types of policy rules.

We propose ORCA (Obligations-Requirements-CApabilities) policy language, based on a natural language (similarly to SecPAL), simple and easy to understand and manage in a SOA environment. It is a constrained natural-like language, with only few syntactical constructions allowed. Due to space restrictions, we cannot provide here a full description of the language. We give only some examples of policy rules.

A generic form of a restriction rule syntax in ORCA is the following:

```
<Subject> X can access <Target> Y for {<action>}, <condition>.
```

where <Subject> is principal (user, role) or service; <Target> is resource or service; X and Y are constants or variables representing names, aliases or identities (local or global, including IP address, URL, UDDI, federated IDs, etc.); allowed actions are related to the target (ORCA defines the following keywords: invoke, read, modify, append, create, delete, full access or any access); finally, optional condition restricts the allowed action to a specific time, source, delegation, or with any self-defined predicate (the latter allows for simple policy extensions). As we may see, the syntax is pretty clear and easy to follow. For instance, a simple restriction rule might be:

```
Role manager can access https://secret/ for {full access}.
```

A sample predicate condition might be the following:

```
User X can access file://Y for {full_access},
    if owner(file://Y)=X.
```

As settled earlier, a very important condition for SOA-based systems is delegation. The generic syntax of a delegation definition rule is the following:

`<Subject>` *X* **can delegate** `<Subject>` *Y* **for** `<Target>` *Z*, `<condition>`.

The delegation assertion will be included in a request message, e.g. as a SAML assertion or an instance of WSS security token [13]. Then, the allowed delegations may be used to express access restriction:

Service *http://secret/x-srv* **can access** *https://secret/x-file* **for** {read, append}, **on behalf of** user *j_bond*.

Two generic forms of an obligation rule syntax are:

`<Subject>` *X* **must** `<action>` **with** {`<attribute>`}, `<condition>`.

`<Target>` *X* **requires to** `<action>` **with** {`<attribute>`}, `<condition>`.

where `<action>` is authenticate, sign or encrypt; and {`<attribute>`} is an ordered set of attribute IDs (e.g. WSS-compliant names of accepted digital signature algorithms). Generic forms of a capability rule syntax are also two:

`<Subject>` *X* **can** `<action>` **with** {`<attribute>`}, `<condition>`.

`<Target>` *X* **can** `<action>` **with** {`<attribute>`}, `<condition>`.

Finally, a generic form of a distributed trust rule syntax is the following:

`<Target>` *X* **can trust** `<Subject>` *Y* **for** {`<action>`}, `<condition>`.

where `<Subject>` is a principal or an authority.

4 Conclusions

In this paper we proposed a novel security policy definition framework for SOA-compliant environments. The proposal aims at addressing important requirements neglected by currently available solutions. The presented framework differs from most existing policy frameworks in focusing on aspects crucial for SOA-based systems, such as high modularity and extensibility, multilayered language design and support for interaction obligations and capabilities, among others.

There are still some additional issues that may be valuable for SOA security policy. Good examples of such issues are information flow control (e.g. covered by DRM languages as XrML), automatic correctness evaluation and reliability requirements definition. These however remain as further work for our framework.

Acknowledgment. The research presented in this paper was partially supported by the European Union in the scope of the European Regional Development Fund program no. POIG.01.03.01-00-008/08.

References

1. MacKenzie, C.M., Laskey, K., McCabe, F., Brown, P., Metz, R.: Reference Model for Service Oriented Architecture. OASIS Committee Draft 1.0, OASIS Open (2006)
2. Moses, T.: eXtensible Access Control Markup Language (XACML) version 2.0. OASIS Open (2005)

3. Bajaj, S., et al.: Web Services Policy 1.2 – Framework (WS-Policy). W3C Member Submission (2006)
4. Della-Libera, G., et al.: WS-SecurityPolicy. Public Consultation Draft Release, Version 1.1 (2005)
5. Cantor, S., Kemp, J., Philpott, R., Maler, E.: Assertions and Protocols for the OASIS Security Assertion Markup Language (SAML) V2.0. OASIS Open (2005)
6. Becker, M.Y., Fournet, C., Gordon, A.D.: SecPAL: Design and Semantics of a Decentralized Authorization Language. Technical Report MSR-TR-2006-120, Microsoft Research, Cambridge (2006)
7. Li, N., Mitchell, J.C.: Datalog with constraints: A foundation for trust management languages. In: Dahl, V., Wadler, P. (eds.) PADL 2003. LNCS, vol. 2562, pp. 58–73. Springer, Heidelberg (2003)
8. Damianou, N., Dulay, N., Lupu, E., Sloman, M.: Ponder: A language for specifying security and management policies for distributed systems. Technical Report, Imperial College, London (2000)
9. Twidle, K., Dulay, N., Lupu, E., Sloman, M.: Ponder2: A Policy System for Autonomous Pervasive Environments. In: Proc. 5th Int'l Conf. Autonomic and Autonomous Systems ICAS, Valencia, Spain (2009)
10. Schloegel, K., et al.: Security Policy Automation – from Specification to Device Configuration. In: 26th Army Science Conference (2008)
11. Jurjens, J.: UMLsec: Extending UML for Secure Systems Development. In: Jézéquel, J.-M., Hussmann, H., Cook, S. (eds.) UML 2002. LNCS, vol. 2460, p. 412. Springer, Heidelberg (2002)
12. Lodderstedt, T., Basin, A.D., Doser, J.: SecureUML: A UML-Based Modeling Language for Model-Driven Security. In: Jézéquel, J.-M., Hussmann, H., Cook, S. (eds.) UML 2002. LNCS, vol. 2460, p. 426. Springer, Heidelberg (2002)
13. Nadalin, A., Kaler, C., Monzillo, R., Hallam-Baker, P.: Web Services-Security: SOAP Message Security 1.1 (WS-Security 2004). OASIS Open (2006)
14. ISO/IEC 10181-3:1966 Information technology – Open Systems Interconnection – Security frameworks for open systems: Access control framework (1966)
15. Westerinen, A., et al.: Terminology for Policy-Based Management, IETF RFC 3198 (2001)
16. Terry, D.B., Demers, A.J., Petersen, K., Spreitzer, M., Theimer, M., Welch, B.W.: Session guarantees for weakly consistent replicated data. In: 3rd Int'l Conf. Parallel and Distributed Information Systems, Austin (1994)

Engineering Accessibility in Web Content Management System Environments

Juan Miguel López, Afra Pascual, and Antoni Granollers

Griho Research Group, University of Lleida, Jaume II St. 69, 25001 Lleida, Spain
{juanmi,apascual,tonig}@diei.udl.cat

Abstract. Law in most countries around the world enforces accessibility requirements in websites, mainly the ones related with public administration. Evaluating accessibility is a long and laborious process that requires manual evaluation. In Web 2.0 environments, the great amount of data generated by users makes necessary further effort in order to validate web content accessibility. This paper introduces an accessibility evaluation methodology based on web content accessibility analysis and the study of web content management by users in Web Content Management System (CMS) environments. The main aim of proposed approach is to optimize the accessibility evaluation process by minimizing the effort it takes to achieve a certain accessibility level. Proposed methodological approach is used as the basis for a generic framework, which is intended to engineer accessibility in all kind of CMS environments. Proposed framework also suggests corrective accessibility maintenance activities for webmasters who are interested in the improvement of the accessibility. The paper how a prototype developed following the framework works in a concrete CMS environment.

Keywords: Web Content Management Systems, Web accessibility evaluation, monitoring, user logs.

1 Introduction

Demographic importance of accessibility is remarkable. For instance, according to the Eurostat [5], from a total population of 362 million people in Europe in year 1996, a 14,8% of the population between 6 and 64 years old had physical, psychological or sensorial disabilities. There are also powerful legal reasons in order to develop accessible web user interfaces. For instance, Section 508 [12] requires Federal agencies in the United States to make their electronic and information technology accessible to people with disabilities. This kind of legislative changes have also been performed in more other countries around the world, such as European Union countries.

Even though software engineering has been a productive research area in the last decades, web engineering is a relatively new one. It refers to specific methods, technologies and models for web application development since these applications have special characteristics. In fact, web applications differ from other traditional software applications in a wide range of aspects, such as the timeframe assigned for

G. Vossen, D.D.E. Long, and J.X. Yu (Eds.): WISE 2009, LNCS 5802, pp. 597–604, 2009.

their development, differences in the characteristics of end-users in terms of age, education and web navigational experience [9]. Because of these special characteristics of web applications, it has been necessary to define specific methods, technologies and models for their development.

In this context, Web 2.0 environments (more participative and with constant changes) enhance the importance for supplying methodologies, mechanisms and tools able to verify accessibility compliance. In this context, Web Content Management Systems (CMS) provide a way for users to manage web content. Aspects such as providing betterment proposals in web content management by users with no technical skills and optimizing the accessibility evaluation process by reusing results from previous accessibility evaluations are main points to be taken into account. This last aspect is especially important given the great increase on the amount of user managed web content that introducing the Web 2.0 paradigm implies.

This paper is as structured as follows. Section 2 describes the background of presented work. Section 3 introduces a methodology to verify accessibility in CMS environments, emphasizing its approach towards solving accessibility problems. In order to provide support for proposed methodology, a framework for monitoring accessibility is proposed. A prototype developed to implement the proposed methodology and tested in a concrete CMS that manages a real website is described in Section 4. Finally, Section 5 shows conclusions and future work.

2 Related Work

Traditionally, accessibility evaluation has been performed revising the fulfilment of WCAG 1.0 guidelines proposed by the Web Accessibility Initiative (WAI) in the World Wide Web Consortium (W3C). In order to fulfil an accessibility evaluation for a website, (X)HTML content and CSS style sheet linked to each web page are reviewed as a first step. Then, automatic accessibility evaluation tools are used [4], which show a revision of automatically detected problems. These tools also point out several possible problems that cannot be automatically revised and require manual revision by accessibility evaluators. Use of assistive technology such as screen readers or text browsers, together with visualization of web pages in different browsers, provide support for manual revisions. All mentioned steps form part of the accessibility evaluation methodology provided by the W3C [6].

Web 2.0 paradigm has changed the way the Web is used and perceived. Rather than a mechanism to provide information, the web is now interactive and harnessing the wisdom of many through wikis, blogs, and e-communities [7]. New terms such as social networking and collective intelligence have been coined to explain the new phenomenon. As for web 2.0 technologies, beyond basic HTML the most widely used technologies for implementing web 2.0 are scripting and Cascading Style Sheets (CSS). Scripting can make use of XmlHttpRequest for optimize data transfer over then standard HTTP web protocol. Rich Internet Application (RIA) technology provides more efficient and collaborative web applications. Accessibility is a major concern in web 2.0 [7]. Since most existing accessibility evaluation tools evaluate the resulting HTML pages, as more dynamic server side web development technologies are used, it is difficult for a tool to determine the exact source of the error. Adding

Web 2.0 dynamic updates into the mix and the testing strategy gets much more difficult. In this context, new tools are needed to address Web 2.0 applications. These new interaction models are pushing the limits of web technologies and the ability of assistive technologies to interpret the changing face of the Web [7].

CMS systems do not enforce users in aspects that should be taken into account in order to generate accessible web content. In a website managed by users using a CMS, the templates used to sketch and generate new web pages should be verified in order to eliminate the risk of introducing accessibility faults in web content. In addition, all content introduced by users should be verified for ensuring the fulfilment of accessibility guidelines. In this sense, CMS systems usually do not generate standard accessible code and allow few user modifications towards improving website accessibility. These modifications are often insufficient to provide entirely accessible websites to people with disabilities [10].

Accessibility monitoring tools are systems that constantly monitor accessibility compliance in given websites. They usually notify the website administrator whether accessibility errors are detected or manual evaluations must be performed. Furthermore, existing accessibility monitoring tools provide a constant website analysis that allows knowing the state of the website accessibility on every moment [8]. Nevertheless, for CMS environments they do not analyze causes for not accessible contents, they simply evaluate the evolution of web content accessibility.

3 Methodological Approach and Description of the Framework for Engineering Accessibility in CMS Environments

In order to support accessibility, it must be taken into account in all stages of software to be developed. Several existing methodological approaches include it as a main factor to be taken into account from the beginning of a software lifecycle to the end [3]. Keeping the evolutionary nature of web applications in mind, following the classic Boehm's spiral model [2], and taking modern methods for web and software engineering into account, the development phases should be applied in an iterative and incremental manner, in which the various tasks are repeated and refined until results meet the requirements. At each iteration, current versions of the system should be tested and evaluated, and then extended or modified to meet requirements in a better manner. In this context, accessibility requirements are aimed to be fulfilled. In most countries, accessibility is a legal requirement that developed web applications and systems must fulfil. Besides, evolutionary nature of web applications makes accessibility a key aspect to be considered for maintenance, as modifications on web content have a risk factor related to accessibility compliance. This is especially important in web 2.0 environments, where web content can be managed by a wide range of users.

In order to define proposed methodology, it is departed from classical software engineering phases taking specific features related to web environments into account, but having in mind that CMS environments suppose a major challenge as the involvement of users as web content editors and managers make maintenance phase be even more important than in typical web environments. In this sense, the methodology is rooted on web engineering principles and web application's lifecycle.

On the other hand, existing accessibility guidelines for web content and authoring tools must be followed, in order to check whether the proposed web content management system and generated web content are accessible. Proposed methodology for considering accessibility in CMS environments is organized based on these assumptions. Phases of the methodology are depicted in Figure 1.

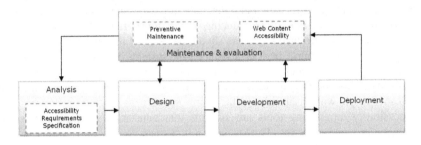

Fig. 1. Schematic approach for Web applications' lifecycle in CMS environments

Accessibility requirements specification is the activity in which the application analyst collects and formalizes the essential information about the application domain and expected functions [9] . This aspect does not significantly differ from requirement collection for traditional applications. Anyway, specification of accessibility requirements is necessary to demonstrate what accessibility issues have to be taken into account and to describe the decisions to be made within each lifecycle phase in order to fulfil them [1] .

According to [3] four types of maintenance exist related to website engineering: corrective maintenance (i.e. fixing problems with the website behaviour or inserting missing contents), adaptive maintenance (i.e. upgrading the site with respect to new technologies, like new browsers' capabilities), perfective maintenance (i.e. improving the site behaviour or content), and preventive maintenance (i.e. fixing problems in behaviour or content before they affect users). In this context, CMS accessibility compliance heavily lays on preventive maintenance, as a big amount of accessibility errors can be solved by providing proper web content management environments. Monitoring web content changes performed by users can be a good indicator for finding potential web content management user interface issues related with accessibility problems. In the context of CMS environments, web content accessibility evaluation must be carried out after maintenance activities. This aspect is due to the fact that evaluating web content accessibility provides little value if corrective measures are not taken in the maintenance phase in order to correct detected CMS environment related accessibility issues. Otherwise, same accessibility errors would be repeated again and again, as the causes related to their appearance would not be solved.

To put proposed methodological approach into practice in a trustworthy way, a generic framework has been designed with the aim of engineering the accessibility in all kind of CMS environments. In order to support preventive maintenance, data from all the different sources available was examined in order to infer possible causes for lack of accessibility. Available data sources in CMS environments include system change logs, system user logs, historic data about previous accessibility evaluations, data about the examined CMS environment and how it manages web content. Figure 2 shows the architecture for the proposed framework.

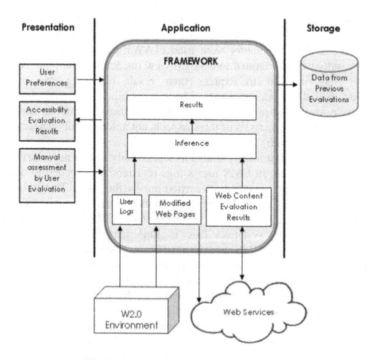

Fig. 2. Architecture for proposed framework

User log data for analysis is received from the CMS environment analyzed. Accessibility related changes from previous evaluation are obtained from the administration area of the framework, where changes among the different versions of modified web pages are stored. HTML code of web pages to be analyzed is obtained from the CMS environment. Selected ones are only the ones which have been modified from the last accessibility evaluation. This is made with the aim of optimizing time and resources. It eliminates a great amount of redundancy from the accessibility evaluation.

4   Case Studio: Web Site Managed by a CMS

A prototype implementing proposed framework was performed and integrated in a CMS. Concretely, it was integrated in the OpenCMS environment that manages the http://griho.udl.cat website. The prototype had to provide feedback about the accessibility compliance on the workflow of the CMS. It also had to be flexible enough to be integrated in the normal workflow of the system, and be able to support different roles. Under these circumstances, it would be able to focus on analyzing concrete problems related to accessibility in CMS environments. Accessibility requirements specification was performed by taking the legal framework into account. In this case, the fulfilment of Spanish law regarding accessibility [11] made necessary some adjustments from WCAG, as there are four priority level changes among the guidelines. In this sense, maintenance regarding accessibility evaluation also had to be adapted. To follow the W3C methodology [6] for evaluation accessibility, two automatic accessibility evaluators were used (TAW1 and EvalAccess2). Analysed web pages results were integrated in a single view inside the prototype. At the same time, they were adapted to express their result regarding the accessibility requirements for the concrete case. The accessibility of web contents was automatically re-evaluated in a daily basis. The evaluation requires an expert human evaluator to complete the analysis of those aspects not automatically detectable, as the W3C methodology states [6].

To detect the potential problems related to accessibility, it was necessary to acquire information only available in CMS user's logs registers. We needed to analyze the information related to the management carried out by the users. This information is automatically managed by the CMS and stored in its internal logs registers. Related to this aspect, it is necessary to have in mind that each CMS has its own particular presentation and storage systems. This is important because to enable data examination, corresponding CMS module must be installed and its data available for evaluators. In this sense, it must also be taken into account that information providers, in this case the CMS users, usually are not aware of the need for creating accessible content, and the tools do not do provide support to enable them in this feature.

Accessibility improvement recommendations were determined by analysing the data obtained in user logs, previously performed accessibility evaluations and the result of web content accessibility evaluations performed automatically and manually on current web pages. Results were statistically treated to detect high accessibility errors percentages related to concrete HTML elements. This way, it can be determined which errors are persistent in the system. Changes record and user log analysis allowed determining the origin of the error, which can be on the content or on the template. The system analysed the possible causes for the error and the factors that may have influence on them. This way, the system proposed recommendations to solve the persistent accessibility problem.

System's user interface is divided in three parts. The main menu, placed on the top, includes navigational actions to accede to the evaluation results, whether incremental, current or last evaluation results. Every evaluation displayed evaluation results for each evaluated page show all the information about the guidelines that have been evaluated as accessibility errors. The page related to the CMS evaluation displayed the problems found that would have influence in all web pages stored in the CMS.

In this sense, Figure 3 depicts how the system found a problem regarding the alternative text of images in the website. As most images had no alternative text, the system performed an analysis to infer possible causes for this situation. As a result, the system provided a recommended action for the webmaster of the web site, which

---

[1] http://www.tawdis.net/taw3/cms/es
[2] http://sipt07.si.ehu.es/evalaccess2/index.html

was to edit the template of the CMS so the images appeared with alternative text. This action could also suppose the necessity of changing the way users include images in the web site, but it required further analysis regarding the web editor used in the system, which is not currently developed in the prototype.

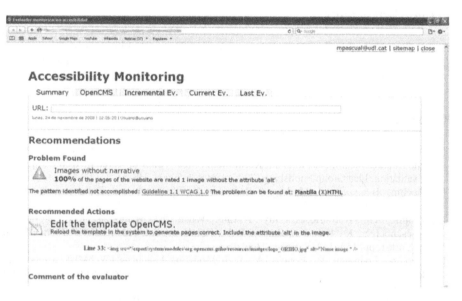

Fig. 3. Screenshot of the developed prototype

5   Conclusions and Future Work

This paper introduces a methodological approach and a framework for implementing accessibility evaluations for Web 2.0 contexts. It is based on Web content accessibility analysis and the study of web content management by users in CMS environments. The framework here presented can be used to achieve four main objectives. First, to improve the accuracy of accessibility evaluation including results up to three different automatic accessibility evaluators, thus fulfilling the methodological background for accessibility evaluations provided by the W3C [6]. Second, to optimize manual accessibility evaluation process. It is performed by taking into account accessibility guidelines checked in previous manual evaluations and that still have validity when the web elements analyzed do not change from one evaluation to the next. Third, the result of the accessibility evaluation is not focused only on checking web content, it also addresses aspects related to web content management in evaluated systems. In this sense, the framework provides information about possible corrective accessibility maintenance activities for webmasters based on logs from the CMS environment. Finally, to minimize the amount of time and resources involved in evaluating accessibility. Provided benefits are expected to be useful for webmasters and human accessibility evaluators.

   Presented prototype is built on a concrete CMS scenario, in this case OpenCMS. As future work it is foreseen to complete it by including more inference rules and aspects to be taken into account for inferring possible causes for accessibility errors, like the use of external components such as web editors. It is also expected to provide support for more CMS environments.

Acknowledgements

The work described in this paper has been partially supported by Spanish Ministry of Science and Innovation through the Open Platform for Multichannel Content Distribution Management (OMediaDis) research project (TIN2008-06228).

References

[1] Abascal, J., Arrue, M., Vigo, M.: A Methodology for Web Accessibility Development and Maintenance. In: Zaphiris, P., Kurniawan, S. (eds.) HCI Research in Web Design and Evaluation. Idea Group Publishing (2006) ISBN. 1-59904-248-7

[2] Boehm, B.A.: Spiral Model of Software Development and Enhancement. IEEE Computer 21(5), 61–72 (1988)

[3] Brajnik, G.: Web Accessibility Testing: When the Method is the Culprit. In: Miesenberger, K., Klaus, J., Zagler, W.L., Karshmer, A.I. (eds.) ICCHP 2006. LNCS, vol. 4061, pp. 156–163. Springer, Heidelberg (2006)

[4] Ceri, S., Fraternali, P., Bongio, A.: Web Modeling Language (WebML): a modeling language for designing Web sites. In: Proceedings of the World Wide Web WWW9 Conference, Amsterdam (May 2000)

[5] Eurostat. Health Stadistics. Luxembourg: Office for Oficial Publications of the European Communities (2002), http://ec.europa.eu/health/ph_information/dissemination/reporting/eurostat_health2002_3_en.pdf (retrieved on June 2009) ISBN 92-894-3730-8

[6] Evaluating Web Sites for Accessibility, http://www.w3.org/WAI/eval/Overview.html (retrieved on June 2009)

[7] Gibson, B.: Enabling an Accessible Web 2.0.W4A2007 - Keynote. In: Co-located with the 16th International World Wide Web Conference, Banff, Canada, May 7-8 (2007)

[8] IBM Rational Policy Tester Accessibility (2009), http://www-01.ibm.com/software/awdtools/tester/policy/accessibility/ (retrieved on June 2009)

[9] Mendes, E., Mosley, N., Counsell, S.: The need for Web Engineer: an introduction. In: Web Engineering, pp. 1–27. Springer, Heidelberg (2006)

[10] Rainville-pitt, S., D'Amour, J.M.: Using a CMS to create fully accessible websites. In: W4A 2007- ACM International Conference Proceeding Series (2007)

[11] Royal decree number 1494/2007, by the one the regulation about basic terms for the access to technologies, products and services related with information society and social media networks by users with disabilities are approved. In: Presidency Ministry. Spanish Official State Bulletin, vol. 279, pp. 47567–47572 (2007) (in spanish)

[12] Section 508, http://www.section508.gov/ (retrieved on June 2009)

Author Index